Commingled Human Remains

Commingled Human Remains

Methods in Recovery, Analysis, and Identification

Edited by

Bradley J. Adams

John E. Byrd

ELSEVIER

Amsterdam • Boston • Heidelberg • London
New York • Oxford • Paris • San Diego
San Francisco • Singapore • Sydney • Tokyo

Academic Press is an imprint of Elsevier

Academic Press is an imprint of Elsevier
The Boulevard, Langford Lane, Kidlington, Oxford, OX5 1GB, UK
525 B Street, Suite 1800, San Diego, CA 92101-4495, USA

First published 2014

British Library Cataloguing in Publication Data
A catalogue record for this book is available from the British Library

Library of Congress Cataloguing in Publication Data
A catalog record for this book is available from the Library of Congress

ISBN: 978-0-12-405889-7

For information on all Academic Press publications
visit our website at store.elsevier.com

14 15 16 17   10 9 8 7 6 5 4 3 2 1

Contents

Preface

Public fascination with the rapid developments of forensic science in recent years has led to greater expectations of success in the field of human identification. This relates to field recovery, laboratory analysis, and analytical findings. These high expectations may translate into pressure on human identification operations to succeed in the face of sometimes daunting challenges created by the circumstances of the incident.

Complex mass fatality events can result in the intermixing, or commingling, of human remains from numerous individuals. As the number of individuals increases, so do the challenges associated with the forensic investigation and the level of skill needed for case resolution. Body fragmentation adds an even further level of difficulty since each separate fragment has to be initially treated independently until it can be proven to link to another. With forensic investigations, commingling must be resolved to the greatest extent possible since it impairs personal identification of the decedents and prevents the return of remains to next of kin. Even in the archaeological context when personal identification is not an issue, accurate sorting and reliable estimates of the number of individuals are critical to an understanding of the population demographics and cultural practices.

The treatment of these complex scenarios, and more generally the science of identification, have tremendously benefited from advancements in basic research, improvements in crime scene procedures, development of reference databases, improvements in computer technology, the addition of molecular biology, and more. This volume is a collection of essays dedicated to the description of many of these tools, as well as more general discussions of ethics, policy, logistics, documentation, and other more administrative issues that relate to the challenges associated with the recovery, analysis, and identification of commingled human remains. The authors share their experiences in grappling with these problems over many years. The authors and the reader share in a commitment to develop best practices to overcome the challenges associated with complex commingling.

Portions of this book were originally published in 2008 (Adams and Byrd) but have now been updated and expanded. Several new chapters have also been added which address contemporary issues associated with commingled remains. The primary focus of this book is the recovery, analysis, and identification of human remains in the forensic context. Although much of the focus of the book is derived from anthropologists, the goal is to present methodological recommendations that will be useful to practitioners in various forensic disciplines. Experts with a diverse range of experience and backgrounds have been brought together in order to present their research, recommendations, and lessons learned. The close working relationship between experts in forensic biology and anthropology is emphasized. Throughout the chapters, the reader will gain valuable information which can be used when complex challenges associated with commingled human remains are encountered.

In Chapter 1, Ubelaker provides an historical overview of the anthropological attention given to commingled human remains. As he points out, until recently the issue of commingling has only been glossed over in forensic anthropology textbooks. Greater attention to this topic has been recognized as the discipline experiences an increasing emphasis on mass fatality events such as aircraft crashes, terrorist attacks, natural disasters, human rights violations, and other contexts where human remains are apt to be commingled. This chapter sets the stage for the diverse topics covered throughout the rest of the volume.

The next three chapters discuss the challenges associated with the recovery of commingled remains. The chapter by Tuller and Hofmeister (Chapter 2) presents recommendations for mapping and spatial interpretation of commingled bodies in mass graves. They explore spatial analysis and the use of a computer program to assess the potential reassociation of disarticulated body parts. The chapter by Naji et al. (Chapter 3) focuses on the recovery, documentation, and analysis of fragmentary and burned remains. They present recommendations for bone identification, recovery of cremated remains, and the documentation of these small fragments in their field context for subsequent interpretation. The chapter by Marx et al. (Chapter 4) presents the Federal Bureau of Investigation Evidence Response Team's guidelines for scene documentation and evidence recovery. They discuss how three-dimensional mapping of human remains and associated evidence can aid in the interpretation, reconstruction, and presentation of a crime or disaster scene. All three of these chapters include case examples to show the importance of thorough field recovery and documentation. Though field context has always played an informal role in the process of sorting remains, these chapters provide convincing arguments that field context is a significant line of evidence that must be captured by appropriate field recovery procedures. Proper training and experience with archaeological techniques are essential for personnel tasked with the recovery of commingled human remains. Field data and spatial relationships can potentially indicate associations of fragmentary remains with each other, as well as other evidence critical to case resolution. Failure to adequately document field context can jeopardize all phases of the investigation.

The next seven chapters focus on various analytical methods for dealing with commingled remains. The chapter by Viner (Chapter 5) presents an overview of the role of radiology in mass fatality events. He presents the various technological options currently available and provides recommendations and procedures for the most appropriate types of radiographic evaluation for victim identification and resolution of commingling. Schaefer (Chapter 6) presents a method to compare stages of epiphyseal union in the recognition and sorting of commingled remains. Through a systematic analysis it is possible to identify relationships that are incongruous and indicative of commingling; this chapter also identifies typical fusion patterns and presents methods to statistically evaluate fusion stages between various elements. Perrone et al. (Chapter 7) test a novel approach of using X-ray fluorescence spectrometry to sort commingled remains. While more research is needed, their results indicate that this technique shows promise for segregating individuals in small-scale scenarios. The chapter by Byrd and LeGarde (Chapter 8) explores laboratory methods for objectively sorting remains, in essence "rebuilding" individuals, via segregation based on osteometrics. Numerous statistical models and recommendations are presented for use by the reader. Konigsberg and Adams (Chapter 9) discuss various options available for determination of the number of individuals represented by a commingled assemblage and provide a critical comparison of different methods. The methods presented in this chapter are most useful for well-preserved remains. Herrmann et al. (Chapter 10) also discuss quantification, but they focus on situations where bone preservation is poor. They present two different methods, one based on bone landmarks and another which employs the analysis of fragment shapes within a geographic information system. The chapter by Warren and Van Deest (Chapter 11) concerns commercially cremated remains and the fact that some degree of commingling is often inevitable. They detail the factors that lead to commingling, the types of analyses that can be completed, and the situations in which commingling in commercial cremation becomes a potential legal issue when families suspect the mishandling of bodies by funeral homes. All seven of these chapters provide informative examples of the various techniques that are available to assist in the analysis of commingled remains. These chapters cover a diverse range of topics, most of which focus on laboratory analysis, which can be applied to challenging scenarios.

The next three chapters focus on the role of DNA analysis in the analysis of commingled remains. The introduction of DNA technology into forensic science has revolutionized the process of identification. It has also proven essential to the process of sorting commingled remains, especially those that are too fragmentary to be suitable for gross techniques. However, excitement over the boost we have enjoyed as a result of the introduction of DNA testing can promote naiveté on the part of administrators and the general public as to the reality of these capabilities. It is easy to presume that use of DNA testing renders other methods superfluous, but this is certainly not the case. Mundorff et al. (Chapter 12) discuss how the results of anthropological and DNA analyses complement each other and they present candid examples from the World Trade Center disaster of lessons learned. This interdisciplinary collaboration proved vital in the process of identifying victims' remains by improving the identification efforts and revealing errors that would have been otherwise missed. The chapter by Hines et al. (Chapter 13) provides recommendations for DNA sampling (element and location) based on the vast experience of the International Commission on Missing Persons and their work in the former Yugoslavia. They present an empirical evaluation of the relative preservation of DNA in different skeletal elements and provide recommendations for efficient DNA-based sampling and reassociations. Puerto et al. (Chapter 14) present broad recommendations for dealing with commingled remains from the field to the laboratory based on the experiences gleaned by the Equipo Argentino de Antropología Forense from human rights cases. In particular, they focus on the roles of anthropology and DNA and present useful findings and recommendations based on thousands of DNA test results. All three of these chapters show that a well-considered sampling strategy is necessary when attempting to reassociate remains and identify individuals. The state of the art for resolving commingling incorporates a mixture of traditional methods (e.g., gross techniques) and cutting-edge technology (e.g., DNA testing).

The next five chapters present interesting case examples stemming from specific incidents or contexts. Regan and Tremaine (Chapter 15) provide an overview of how the U.S. military deals with complex commingling from wartime fatalities resulting from blast and crash incidents. Case examples from the Armed Forces Medical Examiner System are presented. Kahana (Chapter 16) describes the types of commingling scenarios encountered from suicide bombings in Israel. She presents the challenges of balancing the religious requirements of the diverse societies living in Israel, while at the same time maintaining the required standards of forensic investigation. Mundorff (Chapter 17) compares and contrasts three different mass fatality events that occurred in New York City with specific attention on the role of triage at the morgue and the role of anthropology in this facet of the identification process. The incidents include: the WTC disaster, the crash of American Airlines Flight 587, and the crash of the Staten Island Ferry. The chapter by Steadman et al. (Chapter 18) discusses the crash of Colgan Air Flight 3407 and the various components from field recovery to victim identification that lead to its successful resolution. They show how early decisions regarding recovery and triage protocols can significantly reduce commingling issues in a mass fatality incident. Jin et al. (Chapter 19) describe the protocols utilized by the Joint POW/MIA Accounting Command in the analysis of commingled remains from past U.S. conflicts. They present the challenges associated with a large assemblage of commingled remains representing casualties from the Korean War. Overall, the case examples presented in these five chapters provide the reader with diverse scenarios. The chapters not only highlight the challenges associated with recovery, analysis, and identification of commingled remains, but they also provide suggestions and recommendations for successfully overcoming obstacles.

The final four chapters cover more general issues including the nexus between policy and method and between condition of remains and administrative procedures. These "big picture" topics should be considered in any mass fatality event. Hennessey (Chapter 20) discusses an often overlooked facet of large mass fatality incidents: the possibility of data commingling and the importance of administrative review. He clearly illustrates the pitfalls associated with the collection of large amounts of data and the likelihood of confusion and errors. Even if great care is exercised in the recovery and analysis of remains, the identification process may be compromised if the data are not managed properly. The chapter by Kontanis and Sledzik (Chapter 21) presents a wide range of topics, including data that show how the timeliness of identifications is correlated with the level of fragmentation and type of incident. They also discuss important ethical considerations associated with the identification process. Conlon (Chapter 22) presents a high level overview of mass fatality management and the expectations that leadership should have when confronted with a mass fatality incident. She discusses the components that will drive a successful operation and presents recommendations for mass fatality planning and preparedness based on data compiled from mass fatality events in the U.S. between 2000 and 2013. The final chapter by Wagner (Chapter 23) takes a cultural anthropological look at the issue of commingling. She examines social and ethical dilemmas raised by commingled remains as they are understood and experienced by surviving families. While this chapter is framed around victims' families and community leaders associated with the mass graves of Srebrenica, her discussion broaches topics that have arisen in most all mass fatality events.

The chapters in this updated volume reveal that the public's heightened expectations for quality in forensic recovery and identification of the dead have a legitimate basis. Novel methods and increased rigor in analysis and data management have lead to significant gains in our ability to deal with commingled remains. We are confident that the reader will find many useful tools in the pages that follow which can be utilized for the successful recovery, analysis, and identification of commingled remains.

Bradley J. Adams

John E. Byrd

Reference

Adams, B.J., Byrd, J.E. (Eds.), 2008. Recovery, Analysis, and Identification of Commingled Human Remains. Humana Press, Totowa, NJ.

About the Editors

Bradley J. Adams, Ph.D., D-ABFA is Director of the Forensic Anthropology Department for the Office of Chief Medical Examiner in New York City. Dr. Adams and his team are responsible for all forensic anthropology casework in the five boroughs of New York City (Manhattan, Brooklyn, Queens, the Bronx, and Staten Island). Dr. Adams and his team are also integral players in the ongoing work related to identification efforts of 9/11 victims of the World Trade Center attacks. From 1997–2004, Dr. Adams was a Forensic Anthropologist and Laboratory Manager at the Central Identification Laboratory (CIL) in Hawaii. While with the CIL, he directed large-scale operations in remote locations across the globe in an effort to recover and identify the remains of missing U.S. military personnel. He is a Diplomate (#78) of the American Board of Forensic Anthropology and a Fellow with the American Academy of Forensic Sciences.

John E. Byrd received his Ph.D. from the University of Tennessee, Knoxville in 1994 and is a Diplomate of the American Board of Forensic Anthropology. He joined the Joint POW/MIA Accounting Command's Central Identification Laboratory in August 1998 as a Forensic Anthropologist. Dr. Byrd became a Laboratory Manager in 1999 and the Laboratory Director in 2009. He currently serves on the Editorial Board of the Journal of Forensic Sciences, as the Treasurer for the American Board of Forensic Anthropology, and on the Forensic Advisory Committee of the International Committee of the Red Cross. Dr. Byrd has published on Tuscarora subsistence practices through the North Carolina Archaeological Council, co-edited the book *Recovery, Analysis, and Identification of Commingled Human Remains*, and written articles for the Journal of Field Archaeology, Journal of Anthropological Archaeology, Forensic Sciences International, Journal of Forensic Sciences, as well as others.

About the Contributors

Sylvain Amory completed a Ph.D. focused on ancient DNA analysis of Siberian mummies using forensic DNA typing techniques at the Institute of Legal Medicine in Strasbourg (France). Later he served as a post-doctoral fellow at the Institute of Legal Medicine in Innsbruck (Austria) working on the development of a method for the characterization of Asian mtDNA haplogroups. In August 2008 he joined the ICMP as DNA development and validation coordinator. Within ICMP's DNA laboratory he is responsible for the optimization and implementation of methods used for high-throughput DNA based identifications of degraded human remains.

Aurélié André is an anthropologist specialized in cremation burials working for the archaeology department for the city of Lyon (France).

Eric J. Bartelink is an Associate Professor in the Department of Anthropology and Director of the Human Identification Laboratory at California State University, Chico. He received his B.S. in Anthropology at Central Michigan University (1995), his M.A. in Anthropology at California State University, Chico (2001), and his Ph.D. in Anthropology at Texas A&M University (2006). He became the 89th Diplomate of the American Board of Forensic Anthropology in 2012. Eric's interests are in forensic anthropology and bioarchaeology, and he has conducted research focused on skeletal trauma, taphonomy, paleopathology, and stable isotope analysis. He has conducted an extensive research program focused on central California bioarchaeology, and also conducted work on ancient American Samoan populations. In 2000, he assisted with the excavation of mass graves in Bosnia-Herzegovina through the United Nations International Criminal Tribunal for the Former Yugoslavia, and also assisted in the identification of victims from the World Trade Center 9/11 disaster in 2002 and 2003. He has published articles in the Journal of Forensic Sciences, American Journal of Physical Anthropology, Journal of Archaeological Sciences, International Journal of Osteoarchaeology, Journal of Archaeological Method and Theory, Archaeometry, International Journal of Paleopathology, Pacific Coast Archaeological Society Quarterly, and California Archaeology.

Camille de Becdelièvre is a French Ph.D. candidate in the Laboratory for Bioarchaeology, University of Belgrade (Belgrade, Serbia). He received his master's degree in biological anthropology and prehistory at the University of Bordeaux (France). His graduate research focused on the analyses of cremated remains from the Neolithic collective grave of La Truie

Pendue (Yonne, France) and on the application of GIS-based methods to the analysis of commingled and fragmented assemblages. He is currently involved in the European BEAN project – Bridging the European and Anatolian Neolithic: demography, migration, and lifestyle at the advent of civilization – where he is studying Balkan's Early Holocene populations and their reaction to the process of Neolithisation in demography, mobility, and diet. His work integrates both macroscopic analyses of skeletal remains as well as state of the art techniques in paleo-imaging and isotopic analyses from bioarchaeological markers.

Erik T. Bieschke, M.S. has been a Criminalist for the San Diego Police Department since 2008. Prior to that, he spent nine years in the Department of Forensic Biology for the Office of Chief Medical Examiner, City of New York, three of which he was assigned to the World Trade Center DNA Identification Unit. His primary role in that effort was to identify, investigate, and resolve conflicts in the DNA data.

Ashley L. Burch, M.A. is currently an ORISE post-graduate fellow (forensic anthropologist) at the Joint POW/MIA Accounting Command's Central Identification Laboratory. Her fellowship research has focused on establishing methods and standards for the resolution of large-scale commingled assemblages of human remains for the purpose of identifying missing armed-service members. She received her bachelor's degree in anthropology from Michigan State University in 2007 and her M.A. in Anthropology (forensic option) from the University of Montana in 2010. Her research interests include human identification and anthropological genetics, disease, and adaptation.

Elissia Conlon has served New York's Medical Examiner community for twelve years. During her career she served as a contract anthropologist on World Trade Center Recovery Operations before formally joining the City of New York Office of Chief Medical Examiner (OCME) in 2008. While employed at OCME, Elissia has been assigned to the Special Operations Division where she has focused her experience in mass fatality management operations and maintains her hazardous materials technician certification. While with the OCME she has been instrumental in developing the agency's mass fatality management planning, preparedness, and response capabilities. Since 2009 she has served as the agency's Operations Center Manager coordinating information and resources in support of mass fatality operations. Elissia has served as the agency's State Homeland Security and Urban Area Security Initiative (UASI) grant manager which is necessary to sustain and augment the agency's development and implementation of preparedness initiatives. She has participated in several federal mass fatality management working groups, such as the Mortuary Affairs Science and Technology Working Group. She is currently a committee member of the Scientific Working Group for Disaster Victim Identification.

Kevin Dennis Dalton is a Lecturer in the Department of Anthropology and a Senior Scientist for the Archaeological Research Program at California State, Chico. He received his B.A. (2002) and M.A. (2011 with distinction) at California State University, Chico. Kevin is a

Registered Professional Archaeologist and has extensive experience in forensic archaeology. His interests are in the archaeology prehistoric foragers and landscapes, zooarchaeology, XRF, and GIS. Kevin has conducted work in East Africa, the Pacific Islands, California, and the North American Great Basin. He has published articles in the Journal of Taphonomy and the Western North American Naturalist.

Joanne Bennett Devlin, Ph.D. received her B.A. in Anthropology with a specialization in archaeology from Hamilton College in New York. She earned her M.A. and Ph.D. from the University of Tennessee, where she is currently a faculty member. She is assistant director of the Forensic Anthropology Center and oversees casework and training. Her current research foci include taphonomic signatures of fire, geophysical recognition of graves, and skeletal excavation. She is a member of the biometrics team with the National Center for Missing and Exploited Children.

Dennis C. Dirkmaat, Ph.D., D-ABFA is the Chair of the Applied Forensic Sciences Department at Mercyhurst University, Erie, Pennsylvania. He has conducted over 400 forensic anthropology cases for 40 coroner and police agencies throughout Pennsylvania, New York, and Ohio. He has published numerous articles on the role of archaeology in forensic investigations. He recently published *A Companion to Forensic Anthropology* (2012). Dr. Dirkmaat has participated as a forensic anthropologist during mass fatalities in Pittsburgh (USAir 427), the island of Guam (KAL 801), and Rhode Island (Egypt Air 990). In September 2001, he served as the primary scientific advisor to the Somerset County Coroner during the recovery and identification of victims of United Flight 93 in Pennsylvania. Dr. Dirkmaat, consulting for the Erie County Medical Examiner's Office, directed the recovery of victims of Colgan Air 3407 in February 2009. Dr. Dirkmaat has completed two major grant projects for NIJ involving the design of scene processing protocols for mass disasters and fatal fire scenes. He is involved with the Scientific Working Group for Forensic Anthropology (SWGANTH) and the Scientific Working Group-Disaster Victim Identification (SWG-DVI).

Sélim Djouab is a French biological anthropologist who graduated in archaeology at the University of Lille with a minor in medical sciences. He received his master's degree in biological anthropology and prehistory at the University of Bordeaux (France). His master's thesis dealt with methodological aspects of cremation burials from the protohistoric site of Glomel (Côtes-d'Armor, France). He is currently a field director for anthropology at the Hadès contract archaeology company, in addition to field work at the protohistoric megalithic collective burial, UNESCO-listed, site of Wanar (Senegal).

Mercedes Doretti graduated from the National University of Buenos Aires with a licentiate in Anthropology in 1987. She also received a fellowship from the American Association for the Advancement of Sciences for training in forensic anthropology in 1986, and completed courses in human osteology and biomechanics as part of the Master's Program in Anthropology at Hunter College, City University of New York. She began applying forensic anthropology and archaeology to cases of "disappearances" in Argentina in 1984. She co-founded the Argentine Forensic Anthropology Team (Equipo Argentino de Antropologia Forense) in 1986 and has since worked with the team full-time. In 2003, she also co-founded and was the first president of the Latin American Forensic Anthropology Association. She has worked as an expert witness and consultant for local and international tribunals, truth commissions, and local and international human rights organizations in more than 25 countries in Latin America, Africa, Asia, and Eastern Europe. She has published several technical articles on forensic sciences as well as on the application of forensic anthropology and archaeology to the investigation of human rights violations. Doretti was awarded a MacArthur Fellowship in 2007 in recognition of her experience, accomplishments, and her potential to do creative work in the fields of human rights and forensics. Since 1992, she has coordinated EAAF's New York office.

Henri Duday is an emeritus research director at the CNRS in France. He has dedicated most of his research to developing and refining methods to analyze and interpret funerary practices by placing the deceased remains at the center of the discourse on the archaeology of Death. The study of cremation burials has always been a significant part of his work, especially through the analysis of several funerary complexes from the Early Iron Age period in southern France. For the past ten years, this theme became prominent among his research interests in Bordeaux and field work on major Roman sites such as the necropolises of Cuma, Via Triumphalis in the Vatican, or Classe in Ravenna. The excavation of the Porta Nocera necropolis in Pompeii, for which the monograph has just been released from the "Ecole française de Rome" editions, marks a new stage in our knowledge of cremation practices during Antiquity.

Sofía Egaña received a licentiate in Anthropology from the National University of Rosario, Argentina and is a full-time researcher for the Argentine Forensic Anthropology Team (EAAF), where she currently works in the department of anthropological analysis of skeletal human remains. Since she joined the staff of EAAF she has acted as an expert witness for the judiciary, special commissions of inquiry, and international tribunals. She has worked for EAAF in Argentina, Timor-Leste, El Salvador, Brazil, Mexico, and South Africa on the application of forensic anthropology and archaeology to the investigation of human rights cases. She has conducted training seminars, presentations, and lectures on the application of forensic sciences in both academic and legal contexts. She is member of the Latin American Association of Forensic Anthropology.

Ann D. Fasano received her B.A. in Biology from Boston University and her M.S. in Forensic Anthropology from Boston University School of Medicine. Since 1995 she has been a Special Agent with the FBI and was assigned to the Phoenix Division where she became the senior team leader over the FBI Evidence Response Team. In 2006 she became a Supervisory

Special Agent in the FBI Laboratory's Evidence Response Team Unit. She has been responsible for the crime scene training of new agents at the FBI academy as well as the field ERT members. She is currently managing operational matters. Her crime scene experience expands from processing homicides, mass shootings, and the recovery of human remains from landfill and well recovery operations. She has been deployed to NewYork 9/11, Iraq, Uganda, Pakistan, Mexico, the mass shooting in Arizona, the Wisconsin Sikh Temple shooting, the Boston Marathon bombings, the Washington Navy Yard shooting, and other domestic complex crime scenes. She manages an annual FBI ERT class in the recovery of human remains in conjunction with the University of Tennessee. She has conducted crime scene training in the U.S., Pakistan, Africa, and Asia.

Janet E. Finlayson is a M.A. student in physical anthropology in the Department of Anthropology at California State University, Chico. She earned her B.S. in Anthropology at Michigan State University in 2011, where she participated in archaeological field work and bioarchaeological skeletal analysis. Janet served as an intern at the Harris County Institute of Forensic Sciences in the summer of 2013. Her research interests include forensic anthropology and bioarchaeology. She has participated in research involving X-ray fluorescence analysis, validation studies, and observing skeletal indicators of stress in prehistoric California populations.

Ian Hanson, MSc, MIfA is the Deputy Director of Forensic Science for Archaeology and Anthropology at the International Commission on Missing Persons (ICMP), responsible for managing operations and the scientific process of search, location, recovery, and examination. Previously he was Senior Lecturer in Forensic Archaeology at Bournemouth University, UK. He has 26 years of excavation experience, with more than 16,000 hours spent working on field investigations. Since 1997 he has undertaken human rights and forensic investigations for the UNICTY, UNDPKO, FCO, ICMP, and other agencies in the Balkans, Middle East, Central America, and Africa. An expert witness and report writer, he has advised non-governmental organizations on forensic science, operational, and field management matters since 2000. He is an expert advisor for the Serious Organized Crime Agency, UK (SOCA) and a Fellow of the American Academy of Forensic Sciences (AAFS).

Michael Hennessey is the Director of Disaster Response at Gene Codes Forensics. He was the onsite project manager for Gene Codes Forensics during the 2001 World Trade Center identification effort at the New York City Office of Chief Medical Examiner. Mr. Hennessey served on the DNA Subcommittee of the Thailand Tsunami Victim Identification Project (Phuket, Thailand) and has conducted trainings in Mexico, Guatemala, El Salvador, and Kenya. He serves on the Scientific Advisory Board of the Forensic Anthropology Foundation of Guatemala and has an MBA from the University of Michigan.

Nicholas P. Herrmann, Ph.D. is an Associate Professor of Anthropology specializing in forensic anthropology and bioarchaeology at the Mississippi State University in the Department of Anthropology and Middle Eastern Cultures. He has an M.A. in Anthropology from Washington University in St. Louis and a Ph.D. in Biological Anthropology from the University of Tennessee, Knoxville. He consults on forensic casework within the state of Mississippi and has bioarchaeological field work experience in Honduras, El Salvador, the U.S. (Southwest, Southeast, and Midwest), and Greece. His research in forensic anthropology and bioarchaeology focuses on stature estimation, stable isotopes and trace elements, GIS applications, burned bone trauma, and commingled human remains.

David Z.C. Hines is a doctoral candidate at the University of Florida. He has worked extensively on mass graves and related issues in Iraq from 2005 through 2007 as an osteoarchaeologist for the Regime Crimes Liaison Office Mass Graves Investigation Team (RCLO/MGIT), and since 2010 as forensic anthropology trainer for the Iraq offices of the International Commission on Missing Persons. In the U.S., he has worked as a graduate assistant at the University of Florida's C.A. Pound Human Identification Laboratory, as a medicolegal death investigator for the Medical Examiner's Office in Jacksonville, Florida, and as owner-operator of OsCoxa, LLC.

Michael J. Hochrein has been a Special Agent with the Federal Bureau of Investigation for more than twenty-five years. He is currently assigned to the Laurel Highlands Resident Agency within the FBI's Pittsburgh Division. There, he investigates a variety of federal violations including violent crimes, computer crimes, public corruption, and financial crimes. Prior to joining the FBI, Agent Hochrein was a field archaeologist and analyst on salvage and research projects. Specializing in historical archaeology, he worked for the Carnegie Museum of Natural History and University of Pittsburgh Cultural Resources Management Program. He maintains memberships in the Society of American Archaeology, American Academy of Forensic Sciences, International Association of Identification, and International Association of Homicide Investigators. As an FBI Evidence Response Team member, Agent Hochrein develops and conducts research, teaches, publishes articles, and testifies in areas of geotaphonomy and forensic archaeology, as well as crime scene mapping and general evidence collection. As an FBI certified police instructor and adjunct instructor of the FBI Academy, Agent Hochrein has traveled to the Middle East, Africa, Europe, and Southeast Asia to assist in crime scene investigation training for national police organizations.

Ute Hofmeister, M.A. is presently Regional Forensic Coordinator for the Americas for the International Committee of the Red Cross (ICRC), based in Bogotá, Colombia. She is a specialist in forensic archaeology and anthropology with particular focus on documentation and management of forensic data and on issues of psycho-social attention of families of missing persons applied to human rights and humanitarian investigations. Since 1995 she has worked for both international organizations and local NGOs (UN, ICTY, ICMP, EAAF, FAFG) as a forensic expert in exhumations - mainly in the Balkans and Latin America - until joining the ICRC in 2005. Since then she has been advising and training governments, forensic experts, and civil society organizations of over 40 countries on issues concerning the search for and forensic identification of missing persons. She has helped develop national and international standardized protocols and guidelines on these topics. Furthermore, she lead the development of various electronic forensic data management tools, including the ICRC's AMPM database which is now used in over 20 countries.

René L.M. Huel first joined the International Commission on Missing Persons (ICMP) in August 2004 as a DNA Scientist. In 2006 he was appointed Head of Laboratories for ICMP where he currently supervises 25 people in two facilities in Bosnia. As a member of ICMP's DNA laboratories Mr. Huel has been involved in developing and validating new technologies in the lab and helped oversee the initial ISO accreditation (ISO 17025) of the labs in 2007. The labs continue to process samples from a variety of contexts and countries from around the world including from DVI, post conflict, and individual missing person's cases.

Jennie Jin is an ORISE post-doctoral fellow at the Joint POW/MIA Accounting Command's Central Identification Laboratory (JPAC-CIL). She is the project manager for "the Korea 208" assemblage at the CIL. Dr. Jin earned a B.A. in Archaeology from Seoul National University in Korea in 2002. She started her graduate program at Stanford University, where she earned an M.A. in Anthropology in 2005 with a specialization in human skeletal biology and paleo-anthropology. In 2010, she earned a Ph.D. from the Pennsylvania State University with a dissertation that focused on the analysis of animal bones from a 9000-year-old site in Yunnan Province, southwest China. Her research has received support from the Henry Luce Foundation/American Council of Learned Societies, the Korea Foundation for Advanced Studies, Pennsylvania State University, and Stanford University. She has field and laboratory experience in China, Korea, Russia, South Africa, Tanzania, and Honduras and is actively involved with ongoing archaeological field work in China through the Research in Asian Paleoanthropology Program. Her work has been published in several international peer-reviewed journals, such as Journal of Archaeological Science, Evolutionary Anthropology, and Quaternary International.

Tzipi Kahana is a forensic anthropologist in the Division of Identification and Forensic Sciences of The Israel National Police where she is responsible for dental, anthropologic, and radiographic identification of human remains. She specializes in identification of victims from mass casualties. She has been part of the interdisciplinary team from the Israel National Police and the National Centre of Forensic Medicine in charge of preparing the forensic emergency response planning and training in mass casualty incidents in Israel. Her professional experience has been instrumental in the identification of victims from mass casualty incidents in Israel, Argentina, Korea, Ukraine, Kenya, Congo, Comoro, Thailand, Namibia, and New Zealand. Dr. Kahana earned a Ph.D. in basic medical sciences from the Hebrew

University in Hadassah Medical School in 1997 with a specialization in forensic anthropology from the Laboratory of Human Identification of the University of Arizona, Department of Anthropology. In 2009 she earned a second Ph.D. in Forensic Anthropology from the University of Granada, Spain.

Cheryl Katzmarzyk joined the ICMP in 2005 to establish the Lukavac Re-Association Center, a facility utilizing DNA, anthropology, bioinformatics, and associated evidence to re-associate highly commingled human remains recovered from secondary mass graves of the Srebrenica massacre. She remained its manager and became Head of Anthropological Examinations until 2010, at which time she left to join Leiden University. Prior to joining the ICMP, Cheryl worked for the UN-ICTY in Bosnia and Kosovo and conducted research in Sri Lanka. She is currently a Regional Forensic Advisor within the Forensic Services of the International Committee of the Red Cross.

Lyle W. Konigsberg is a Professor of Anthropology at the University of Illinois at Urbana-Champaign, where he teaches anatomy in the Medical School and anthropology in the Anthropology Department. He received his Ph.D. from Northwestern University and was a post-doctoral scientist in the Department of Genetics at the Texas Biomedical Research Institute in San Antonio, Texas. Following his post-doc he was Assistant, Associate, and then Full Professor of Anthropology at the University of Tennessee, Knoxville. He was Vice President and Secretary-Treasurer of the American Association of Physical Anthropologists. His research focuses on human biological variation, population and quantitative genetics, human skeletal biology, and paleodemography.

Elias J. Kontanis serves as the Coordinator – Medicolegal Operations for the National Transportation Safety Board (NTSB). In this capacity he is responsible for facilitating the victim recovery and identification process following transportation mass fatality incidents. Prior to his current position with the NTSB, he served as a forensic anthropologist with the Joint POW/MIA Accounting Command – Central Identification Laboratory. Elias served as a member of the Department of Health and Human Services Disaster Mortuary Operational Response Team, where he participated in the victim identification efforts following the crash of EgyptAir flight 990 and the September 11, 2001 attacks on the World Trade Center. He has also worked as a forensic anthropologist in the Republic of Cyprus with Physicians for Human Rights and has consulted for various city and county medical examiner jurisdictions. Elias earned a Ph.D. in Biology from Cornell University in 2005 and is a Registered Medicolegal Death Investigator. He is also an active FAA Certificated Flight Instructor and Advanced Ground Instructor and serves as an FAA Safety Team Representative.

Carrie LeGarde obtained a B.A. in Anthropology and a B.A. in Human Biology from the University of Montana in 2009. During this time, Carrie worked as a Forensic Firearm Technician and Evidence Technician at the Montana State Crime Lab. In 2010, she enrolled in the University of Montana's Forensic Anthropology M.A. program, studying asymmetry of the humerus and the possible relationship to handedness. In 2012, she received her M.A. in Forensic Anthropology and joined the JPAC-CIL as an Oak Ridge Institute for Science and Education (ORISE) fellow.

Mark M. LeVaughn, MD is the Chief Medical Examiner for the State of Mississippi and Affiliate Professor of Pathology at the University of Mississippi, School of Medicine. He received his MD degree from the University of Tennessee, College of Medicine. He did his Pathology training at West Virginia University and University of Tennessee. He is certified by the American Board of Pathology in Anatomic Pathology and Forensic Pathology and is a member of NAME and AAFS. He has performed over 7000 autopsy examinations and has assisted numerous Coroner and Law Enforcement Offices with training and crime scene investigations in Kentucky, Indiana, Illinois, New York, and Mississippi. He has authored and co-authored several publications and presented at national meetings in the field of Forensic Pathology. His forensic interests are Odontology and Anthropology. He served as Deputy Chief Medical Examiner for Erie County in Buffalo at the time of the crash of Flight 3407. His primary role was Victim Family Liaison for Erie County.

Elaine Mar-Cash, M.S.F.S. is a Senior Subject Matter Expert at Gene Codes Forensics and serves on the Scientific Advisory Board of the Forensic Anthropology Foundation of Guatemala. Previously she worked in the Forensic Biology Department of the Office of Chief Medical Examiner, City of New York, where she was the lead supervisor of the World Trade Center DNA Identification Unit, the crash of American Airlines Flight 587, and the Missing Persons Group. As a Criminalist, she has worked on hundreds of homicide, sexual assault, and burglary cases. Following the Boxing Day Tsunami of 2004, she served on the Scientific Advisory Board to the Thai Tsunami Victim Identification Command in Phuket, Thailand. She has a M.S. in Forensic Science from John Jay College of Criminal Justice, City University New York.

Richard B. Marx worked at the Alabama Department of Forensic Sciences from 1985-1997 and earned a B.S. in Chemistry from the University of Alabama Huntsville. Special Agent (SA) Marx entered the FBI in 1997 and worked on the Philadelphia Division's bank robbery squad. He processed the 1998 U.S. Embassy bombing in Nairobi, Kenya and worked morgue operations at the 1999 EgyptAir Flight 990 crash. In 2001, SA Marx responded to the 9/11 attacks in New York City and was in charge of the forensic recovery operation that sifted 1.8 million tons of World Trade Center debris and recovered over 4500 human remains. In 2005, SA Marx was the Scientific Chairperson for Thailand Tsunami Victim Identification Group for victim remains. SA Marx became a Supervisory Special Agent (SSA) in the FBI Laboratory's Evidence Response Team Unit in 2006 and has since been deployed to Iraq, Afghanistan, Saudi Arabia, and Mexico City. SSA Marx has led FBI teams at the 2012 Aurora Century

Cinema 16 mass shooting in Colorado, the 2013 Algerian U.S. hostage killings, the 2013 Boston Marathon Bombing, the 2013 Asiana Flight 214 crash in San Francisco, and the 2013 Navy Yard shooting in Washington, D.C. He earned a M.S. in Forensic Anthropology from the Boston University School of Medicine in 2013.

Raymond G. Miller, DDS, FAAFS is a private practitioner of general dentistry in Lancaster, New York. He is the Forensic Dental Consultant to the Medical Examiner's Office in Erie County, New York, a Clinical Associate Professor at the University at Buffalo School of Dental Medicine, Department of Oral Diagnostic Sciences, and a Fellow in the Odontology Section of the American Academy of Forensic Sciences. He is co-founder of the Laboratory for Forensic Odontological Research at the University at Buffalo School of Dental Medicine. He is a member of the federal Disaster Mortuary Operational Response Team through the National Disaster Medical System and deployed to the World Trade Center after September 11, 2001, Hurricane Katrina 2005, and served as Dental Section Chief during the crash of Flight 3407 in Clarence, New York in 2009. He is also a Lieutenant Colonel with the 107th Airlift Wing of the New York Air National Guard and deployed to Iraq as a dental officer in 2008 in support of Operation Iraqi Freedom.

Amy Z. Mundorff, Ph.D. is currently an Assistant Professor in the Department of Anthropology at the University of Tennessee. Much of her research focuses on managerial aspects of Disaster Victim Identification (DVI) and developing new techniques to locate clandestine burials. From 1999–2004, Amy was the Forensic Anthropologist for the Office of Chief Medical Examiner, the City of New York. She helped direct mortuary operations for several disasters, including the World Trade Center attacks, the crash of American Airlines Flight 587, and the Staten Island Ferry crash.

Stephan Naji is a research associate at the University of Bordeaux (France). His training, both in archaeology (University of Paris La Sorbonne, France) and in biological anthropology (University of New Mexico, U.S.) lead to a Ph.D. at the École Pratique des Hautes Études (Paris, France) focused on a bioarchaeological analysis of a French medieval cemetery. His current research interests focus on field methods in human remains excavation, also known as archaeothanatology, in various geo-chronological contexts in France, Italy, and Peru, and on a dental histology technique for estimating age-at-death known as cementochronology.

Elizabeth Okrutny graduated (with high distinction) in 2010 with a B.S. in Forensic Biology and minors in Chemistry and Biochemistry from Ohio Northern University. Shortly after, she moved to Orlando to start graduate school at the University of Central Florida. For her thesis, she compared post-cranial osteometric measurements from a South Korean skeletal collection to several U.S. collections to determine which post-cranial osteological landmarks most reliably predict ancestry. She graduated with her M.A. in Anthropology in May 2012, and in June began working on the K208 project at the JPAC-CIL as an ORISE post-graduate fellow.

Thomas J. Parsons has been the Director of Forensic Science at the International Commission on Missing Persons (ICMP) in Sarajevo, Bosnia and Herzegovina since 2006. He supervises a large team of forensic science staff in a multidisciplinary approach to identification of missing individuals involving forensic archaeology, anthropology, pathology, and high throughput DNA analysis. These sciences have been applied to the investigation and/or human identification of mass graves, missing persons cases, and mass disasters worldwide, often on a very large scale. The ICMP has made DNA identification matches to over 18,000 individuals. ICMP training and capacity building are also large parts of ICMP forensic activity, currently with large programs in Libya and Iraq. Dr. Parsons is on the editorial board of Forensic Science International Genetics, a Board Member of the U.S. Scientific Working Group on DVI, and a Board Member of the AAAS Committee for Scientific Responsibility and Freedom. Prior to joining the ICMP, he was Chief Scientist at the U.S. Armed Forces DNA Identification Laboratory.

Alexandra Perrone is a Lecturer in the Department of Anthropology and the Human Identification Laboratory supervisor at California State, Chico. She earned her B.A. in Anthropology from University of California, Santa Barbara (2008) and a M.A., with distinction, at California State University, Chico (2013). Her research interests include forensic anthropology, bioarchaeology, and paleopathology. Alexandra has conducted work in Hawaii, Greece, England, and California.

Mercedes Salado Puerto initially received a licentiate as a biologist and completed her doctorate in the Department of Biological Anthropology, Universidad Autónoma de Madrid (Spain). As a forensic anthropologist she was a member of the Guatemalan Forensic Anthropology Team from 1998 to 2003. She is a member of the Argentine Forensic Anthropology Team (EAAF), where she currently works as identification coordinator. She specializes in the historical investigation of cases of political violence (analysis of written and oral sources, collecting antemortem data from relatives of the missing, interviews with witnesses, organization of information), archaeological exhumation of individuals and mass graves, and analysis of skeletal remains. She has been involved in forensic investigations and training in Argentina, Bosnia-Herzegovina, Burundi, Colombia, Cyprus, Chile, Guatemala, Iran, Iraq, Morocco, Mexico, Nepal, Panama, Peru, South Africa, Sudan, Thailand, Timor-Leste, Togo, Uruguay, and Vietnam. She has been Lecturer in the Post-graduate Diploma in Forensic Anthropology and Human Rights (Universidad Nacional Mayor de San Marcos, Perú); the Master's Program in Forensic Anthropology and Bioarchaeology (Graduate School of the Pontificia Universidad Católica del Perú); and the Doctoral Program in Anthropology at the Universidad Nacional de Córdoba (Argentina). She is a member of the Latin American Association of Forensic Anthropology and the International Committee of the Red Cross Forensic Advisory Group.

Laura A. Regan is a Lieutenant Colonel (Dr.) and has served on active duty in the U.S. Air Force for nearly 20 years. She is currently assigned as Director of Operations and Assistant

Professor of Biology, Department of Biology, United States Air Force Academy, Colorado. A forensic anthropologist by training, her specialties include mass fatality management, air mishaps, body fragmentation, thermally degraded remains, and stable isotope geochemistry. For seven years, she served in a variety of capacities with the Armed Forces Medical Examiner System and has performed casework around the globe, consulting for various federal and state entities, to include local and federal law enforcement and intelligence agencies. Her casework includes a multitude of military blast events, over 40 military air mishaps, the crash of Colgan Air Flight 3407, the mass shooting at Ft. Hood Texas, the search and recovery of American citizens in the aftermath of the Haiti earthquake, and, as a member of an international tripartite commission, the search, recovery, and repatriation of Kuwaiti and Iraqi fatalities from the First Gulf War. She is the co-chair of the Anthropology Sub Committee of the Scientific Working Group on Disaster Victim Identification.

Stéphane Rottier is a French Assistant Professor in Funerary Anthropology and Palaeobiology of Holocene populations at the University of Bordeaux, UMR PACEA (France) since 2007. He graduated in scientific methods applied in archaeology with a minor in biology and geology and received his Ph.D. in Archaeology in 2003. His current research interests include biocultural and funerary practices in late European prehistory (Neolithic, Bronze Age, and Iron Age) and grave excavation methods.

Maureen Schaefer is an Assistant Professor of Anatomy and Adjunct Professor of Anthropology at Michigan State University. She received her doctoral degree from the University of Dundee, Scotland (2007) analyzing epiphyseal union times in Bosnian males. Her main interests involve growth and development of the skeleton for purposes of age estimation in both the living and deceased.

Robert Shaler received his doctoral degree from the Pennsylvania State University in 1968. He joined the scientific staff of the Pittsburgh and Allegheny County Crime Laboratory in 1970 and in 1977 he joined the Aerospace Corporation. From 1978-1987 he joined the staff of the New York City Medical Examiner's Office as the head of its serology laboratory. He then moved to the Lifecodes Corporation, the nation's first forensic DNA typing laboratory. Dr. Shaler returned to the Medical Examiner's Office in 1990 where he created a modern Department of Forensic Biology. In the wake of the terrorist attacks on the World Trade Center, he assumed overall responsibility for the DNA identification efforts. In July 2005, he retired from the Medical Examiner's office and authored *Who They Were*, an account of the WTC DNA identification effort. He accepted a professorship at The Pennsylvania State University in 2005 and founded and was the first director of its forensic science program. He retired from full-time teaching in 2010, authored a textbook, *Crime Scene Forensics – A Scientific Method Approach*, and taught crime scene investigation to non-forensic science majors for Penn State's World Campus until 2012. He currently does forensic consulting for law enforcement and private attorneys.

Paul S. Sledzik is Director of the NTSB's Transportation Disaster Assistance Division (TDA), a position he has held since October 2010. Paul and his staff coordinate family assistance in all modes of transportation in conjunction with local, state, and federal agencies, non-governmental agencies, and transportation operators. Since the office was established in 1996, TDA has responded to over 150 transportation accidents. Prior to this position, Paul served as the manager of medicolegal operations for the TDA Division for six years. Before joining the NTSB, he served for six years as the team leader for the Region 3 Disaster Mortuary Operational Response Team, a division of the U.S. Department of Health and Human Services, where he managed a team of 100 in mass fatality response. During his career, he participated in the response to over 30 mass fatality events and transportation accidents. Trained as a forensic anthropologist, Paul has served as a consultant and advisor to several federal and non-governmental agencies on issues of human identification and disaster response. He is a Fellow of the American Academy of Forensic Sciences and his scientific articles have appeared in professional journals and textbooks.

Jessica C. Stanton received her bachelor's degree in anthropology/archaeology from the University of West Florida and master's degree from Mississippi State University, focusing on archaeology and biological anthropology. Her thesis research addressed quantification and analysis of mortuary practices with fragmented, commingled human remains. Ms. Stanton is currently working as an archaeologist and osteologist for Tennessee Valley Archaeological Research.

Dawnie Wolfe Steadman, Ph.D., D-ABFA is a Professor of Anthropology at the University of Tennessee and the Director of the Forensic Anthropology Center. Her teaching and research interests include bioarchaeology, paleopathology, and forensic anthropology. She is a Board Certified forensic anthropologist and currently serves on the Board of the American Board of Forensic Anthropology. She serves as a consultant for a number of medico-legal agencies in the U.S. She is a member of the Disaster Mortuary Operational Response Team (DMORT) and has assisted with the identification of victims from the World Trade Center disaster on September 11, 2001, the Tri-State Crematorium incident in 2002, and the crash of Colgan Air Flight 3407. Dr. Steadman is also involved in forensic human rights investigations and has worked in South America, Europe, and Africa.

Ladd A. Tremaine is currently appointed as the Armed Forces Medical Examiner, and Director of the Armed Forces Medical Examiner System. He is a graduate of the University of Washington and the Uniformed Services University of Health Sciences School of Medicine. He has served as a General Pediatrician, Anatomic Pathologist, Clinical Pathologist, and Deputy Medical Examiner for the U.S. Army prior to his current position.

Hugh Tuller, M.A. currently works as a forensic anthropologist for the Joint POW/MIA Accounting Command (JPAC), the U.S. government's effort at locating and identifying military service members and civilian employees who have gone missing during past conflicts. In addition to laboratory work at JPAC, he has led dozens of Search and Recovery Missions in Southeast Asia, The Pacific Islands, and Europe. In the past, he has worked for the United Nation's International Criminal Tribunal for the Former Yugoslavia (ICTY); the International Commission on Missing Persons (ICMP), based in Sarajevo; and the Committee on Missing Persons (CMP) in Cyprus, under the auspices of the Argentine Forensic Anthropology Team.

Douglas H. Ubelaker is a curator and senior scientist at the Smithsonian Institution's National Museum of Natural History in Washington, D.C. where he has been employed for nearly four decades. Since 1978, he has served as a consultant in forensic anthropology. In this capacity he has served as an expert witness, reporting on more than 900 cases and has testified in numerous legal proceedings. He is a Professorial Lecturer with the Departments of Anatomy and Anthropology at The George Washington University and is an Adjunct Professor with the Department of Anthropology, Michigan State University. Dr. Ubelaker has published extensively and has served on the editorial boards of numerous leading scientific publications. Dr. Ubelaker received a B.A. and a Doctor of Philosophy from the University of Kansas. He has been a member of the American Academy of Forensic Sciences since 1974 and achieved the status of Fellow in 1987 in the Physical Anthropology Section. He served as the 2011–2012 President of the AAFS. He is a member and Fellow of the American Association for the Advancement of Science and a member and Fellow of the Washington Academy of Sciences, serves on the Forensic Sciences Foundation Board of Directors, is a Diplomate of the American Board of Forensic Anthropology, and a recipient of numerous awards.

Traci L. Van Deest completed her doctorate in the Department of Anthropology at the University of Florida in 2014. Her dissertation research investigates physical and biochemical alterations in experimentally heated bone and the relationship to fluorescence under ultraviolet light. She also serves as a graduate analyst conducting casework for the C.A. Pound Human Identification Laboratory. She earned her M.A. in Anthropology from California State University, Chico in 2007, where she researched the relationship of the weight of cremated remains to aspects of the biological profile. Her research interests include heat alteration of skeletal tissue, cremated remains, human variation and anatomy, trauma analysis, and skeletal biology. Ms. Van Deest is an active student member of the Anthropology section of the American Academy of Forensic Sciences and has participated in the Scientific Working Group for Forensic Anthropology. Throughout her graduate career, Ms. Van Deest has served as a teaching assistant and instructor in courses on human osteology, biological anthropology, forensic anthropology, and gross anatomy.

Matthew Vennemeyer has a background primarily in the areas of forensic anthropology, forensic archaeology, and medicolegal death investigation. Much of his profession has been in both forensic excavations and mortuary/laboratory examinations, with applications involving mass grave investigations and other large-scale operations for the purpose of documentation of evidence and identification of human remains, usually in regions of conflict and suspected genocide. For a period of years, he was employed as a physical anthropologist and medicolegal death investigator for several government agencies in Missouri, U.S. In 2000, he worked in Kosovo for the International Criminal Tribunal for the former Yugoslavia. From 2005 to 2007, he continued mass grave operations in Iraq for the Regime Crimes Liaison Office before returning to the Western Balkans and assisting in forensic excavations and DNA identifications for the International Commission on Missing Persons from 2008 to 2013. He is currently a Forensic Advisor with the International Committee of the Red Cross in Libya, where many thousands remain missing and unidentified.

Dianne Vertes, Ph.D., MD has recently retired from her position as Chief Medical Examiner at the Erie County Medical Examiner's Office in Buffalo, New York. Dr. Vertes is board certified in Anatomic, Clinical, and Forensic Pathology, is licensed to practice in New York, Michigan, California, and Arizona, and is a member of NAME and AAFS. She is now continuing her forensic practice on a locum tenens basis primarily in New York, having consulted and/or joined the staff in Chautauqua, Cattaraugus, Dutchess and Broome Counties. Her major interest remains the practice of forensic pathology, enjoying the interplay of various professions such as jurisprudence, criminology, anthropology, and forensic dentistry. She enjoys the challenge of teaching, both formally and informally (at the table). She considers the role she played in the aftermath of the Colgan Air Flight 3407 crash as one of her major accomplishments.

Mark D. Viner has over 30 years of experience as radiographer and radiology manager and is currently a senior manager at Barts and The Royal London Hospitals. His expertise is in forensic imaging and emergency planning. He is a Fellow of Cranfield University Forensic Institute where he is module leader for forensic radiography. He is also the CEO of the Inforce Foundation, a charity dedicated to the education and training of forensic professionals involved in the forensic investigation of mass fatality incidents. He is a founder member and first chair of the International Association of Forensic Radiographers and currently holds the office of External Liaison Officer. He is also a founder board member and first Vice-Chair of the International Society of Forensic Radiology and Imaging and a member of the editorial board of the Journal of Forensic Radiology and Imaging. He has acted as an advisor to The Government Office for London, The Home Office and to the International Criminal Court in The Hague. He coordinated the forensic radiography team for the ICTY in Bosnia, Croatia, and Kosovo from 1996-2001. He has worked as a forensic radiography consultant in the Balkans, Sierra Leone, and the Irish Republic and for several high profile cases in the UK, including several terrorist incidents such as the response to the 7th July London Bombings.

Carlos María Vullo is a biochemist, graduating with his licentiate from the National University of Córdoba, Argentina and then obtaining his Ph.D. in Chemical Sciences, also from the National University of Córdoba. He founded the Histocompatibility and Immunogenetics

Laboratory at the University Clinic Hospital in Córdoba, Argentina, where he was Director from 1982 to 2003. He has been the Director of the Forensic DNA Laboratory for the Argentine Forensic Anthropology Team (EAAF) since 2005. He has utilized forensic genetics for human identification of victims of human rights violations in different Latin American countries such as Argentina, Uruguay, Bolivia, El Salvador, and Panama. In addition, he has worked on similar cases from South Africa, East Timor, and Vietnam, among others. He has conducted training sessions in forensic genetics for scientists from El Salvador, Bolivia, Thailand, and Nigeria. He is also Director of the Immunogenetics Laboratory (LIDMO, Córdoba, Argentina), working on immunogenetics for organ transplantations. He has published more than 50 scientific papers concerning immunogenetics and forensic genetics.

Sarah Wagner is an Assistant Professor of Anthropology at George Washington University and author of *To Know Where He Lies: DNA Technology and the Search for Srebrenica's Missing* (University of California Press, 2008), and co-author with Lara Nettelfield of *Srebrenica in the Aftermath of Genocide* (Cambridge University Press, 2014). Her research focuses on forensic science, post-conflict intervention, and memory. Other publications include: "The Making and Unmaking of an Unknown Soldier," Social Studies of Science 43(5): 631–656, and "A Curious Trade: The Recovery and Repatriation of US Missing In Action from the Vietnam War," Comparative Studies in Society and History (forthcoming).

Michael W. Warren is an Associate Professor of Anthropology at the University of Florida, with research interests in forensic identification, human variation, and trauma analysis. He is a Fellow of the American Academy of Forensic Sciences and a Diplomate of the American Board of Forensic Anthropology. Dr. Warren serves as a consultant for several Medical Examiners in the state of Florida.

CHAPTER 1

Commingling Analysis: Historical and Methodological Perspectives

Douglas H. Ubelaker

Department of Anthropology, Smithsonian Institution, Washington, D.C.

In 1962, Wilton Krogman published the first major text focused specifically on forensic anthropology. Although *The Human Skeleton in Forensic Medicine* (Krogman 1962) is widely recognized as a classic historical text, it presents little discussion of issues of commingling in the analysis of human remains. *Essentials of Forensic Anthropology*, the more focused 1979 follow-up text by T. Dale Stewart (Stewart 1979) devoted only two of its 300 pages to commingling topics despite existing publications that focused on bone weight analysis (Baker and Newman 1957), ultraviolet fluorescence (Eyman 1965; McKern 1958), forensic neutron activation (Guinn 1970), statistical approaches to commingling issues (Snow and Folk 1965), and other considerations (Kerley 1972). Stewart noted (1979:38) that most remains studied by forensic anthropologists at that time had been found as primary skeletons. For such cases, context and field documentation indicated that commingling was likely not a major issue.

In 2013, many skeletons studied by forensic anthropologists are also found as primary interments. Increasingly, however, cases are presented involving commingling issues. Mass disasters (Blau and Briggs 2011; Stewart 1970), cremation litigation (Murray and Rose 1993), human rights investigations (Garrido Varas and Intriago Leiva 2012), separation of recent from ancient remains, and many other types of modern cases (Ritter 2007) raise questions such as, "How many individuals are represented in a group of remains?" and "How can remains of single individuals be identified within collections of remains from multiple individuals?" These problems are exacerbated by events of terrorism leading to extensive fragmentation. Cases and questions involving commingling issues are highly variable and problem specific in modern forensic anthropology (Adams and Byrd 2006; Ubelaker 2002).

The methodology employed in answering these questions can also be highly variable (Rösing and Pischtschan 1995). As with most analysis in forensic anthropology, there is no "cookbook" approach to commingling issues. Practitioners must be aware of the myriad of techniques available and craft a case-specific protocol to address the particular problems at hand.

The chapters assembled in this volume represent a testimony to the growing need for commingling analysis within forensic anthropology and to the vast array of approaches available

Commingled Human Remains. http://dx.doi.org/10.1016/B978-0-12-405889-7.00001-0

now to meet that need. Although basic inventory and documentation techniques are desirable in all cases, specific problems call for the selection of particular methods. This volume provides the reader with an overview of both the problems and the solutions.

Separation of Bone and Tooth from Other Materials

Some problem applications call for identification of bone and tooth materials and their separation from other, similarly appearing items. These issues emerge particularly in small particle analysis of fragmentary and/or burned materials. Since DNA analysis can be employed even with small, fragmentary evidence to contribute to identification, many submitted cases involve such evidence. Particles of drywall, plastic, geological materials, and many other items can resemble bone and tooth, especially after exposure to intense heat or other taphonomic factors. Likewise, bone and tooth can be difficult to recognize as such after taphonomic alteration.

When gross morphology is inadequate to distinguish materials in such cases, microscopy can be useful. A high-quality dissecting microscope may allow detection of structure unique to bone and tooth (Ubelaker 1998). However, lack of such detail may be problematic because some bone and tooth fragments can be altered to the extent that surface diagnostic features may be lacking. Thin sections may be useful in such cases, but preparation techniques are destructive and may preclude molecular analysis with very small fragments.

Scanning electron microscopy/energy dispersive spectroscopy (SEM/EDS) provides a useful new tool in separating nonbone and tooth material (Ubelaker et al. 2002). Analysis presents not only a highly magnified surface image, which may in itself be useful, but also compositional spectra that can identify elemental structure. The presence and relative proportions of the constituent elements can be useful to distinguish bone and tooth from other materials. A comparative database of analyses of many known materials, including bones and teeth representing a variety of conditions, is now available to provide the probabilities of association. This system is especially useful to exclude materials from being bone or tooth but also can be helpful in the diagnosis of their presence (Ubelaker et al. 2002).

Recognition of Nonhuman Animal

In some commingling cases, it may be necessary to document the presence of nonhuman animals or even determine species. Again, morphological assessment is the initial method of choice if the materials present diagnostic information. If bone and tooth fragments lack the necessary morphological features due to fragmentation or taphonomic alteration (Haglund and Sorg 1997), then microscopy may prove helpful. If sufficient material is present to support preparation of ground thin sections, the occurrence of plexiform bone or a characteristic osteon banding pattern may rule out a human origin (Mulhern and Ubelaker 2001, 2012). However, the presence of a typical human microscopic pattern is not necessarily diagnostic for human because that general pattern can be shared with some other animals (Mulhern and Ubelaker 2003).

In such cases, the technique of choice likely would be protein radio-immunoassay (pRIA). Very small samples (200 mg or less) can be utilized not only to conclusively and quantitatively separate human from nonhuman but also to identify nonhuman species (usually at the family level) if necessary (Ubelaker et al. 2004). The technique involves protein extraction followed by a solid-phase double-antibody radio-immunoassay utilizing controls of antisera (raised in rabbits) and radioactive (iodine-125) marked antibody of rabbit gamma globulin developed in donkeys.

Separation of Ancient and Modern Remains

Case analysis may call for the separation of remains of recently deceased individuals from those who died long ago. Scenarios calling for such analysis might include a collection of remains found in the possession of an individual suspected of both grave robbing and homicide, remains of a potential homicide victim found in an old cemetery with evidence of looting, or a mass disaster with modern victims at the site of a cemetery or other such collection of older remains.

Presented with such problems, authorities might consider radiocarbon analysis, focusing particularly on artificial radiocarbon. Atmospheric testing of thermonuclear devices beginning in the early 1950s produced abnormally high levels of artificial radiocarbon that, through the food chain, were incorporated into the tissues of all living things, including humans (Taylor 1987). Levels increased steadily until about 1963 when international test ban agreements ceased the practice. Atmospheric levels of artificial radiocarbon have subsequently declined but still remain above pre-1950 levels. If analysis detects elevated levels of radiocarbon, the investigator knows that the individual was alive after 1950. Analysis of different tissues and consideration of the age at death of the individual may help pinpoint the birth dates and the death dates of the individual within the bomb-curve period (Ubelaker 2001; Ubelaker and Houck 2002; Ubelaker et al. 2006).

Sorting Procedures

Once nonhuman materials have been separated out, analysis of the human remains usually begins with careful inventory (Buikstra and Ubelaker 1994). The extent and nature of the inventory are typically problem driven but should document in appropriate detail what bones or parts of bone are present, approximate ages at death, and bone side (left or right). Other observations that may prove relevant include bone morphology, bone size, and articulation patterns (Buikstra and Gordon 1980; Buikstra et al. 1984; Kerley 1972; London and Curran 1986; London and Hunt 1998). Inventory and morphological assessment may be supplemented with such techniques as ultraviolet fluorescence (Eyman 1965; McKern 1958), radiography, serological testing, neutron activation, trace element analysis (Finnegan 1988;

Finnegan and Chaudhuri 1990; Fulton et al. 1986; Guinn 1970), and bone weight (Baker and Newman 1957) and density studies (Galloway et al. 1997; Lyman 1993; Willey et al. 1997).

Modern DNA techniques are increasingly employed in commingling cases, especially to identify fragmentary evidence and assemble separated remains of single individuals following mass disasters (Jakovski et al. 2010). As noted in this volume, DNA technology and other complex approaches are best used in consideration of context and the prudent use of resources, as well as the nature of evidence preservation (Misner et al. 2009). Selection of remains to be analyzed for DNA should be driven by context, morphological analysis, and available resources. It would not be logical to obtain DNA profiles from more than one bone in an assemblage, if they were all found in articulation. Similarly, it would not be necessary to have DNA data from more than one bone fragment of several found in separate locations if morphological study found that they fit together and originated from a single bone.

Approaches to documenting the minimum number of individuals (MNI) present have evolved beyond simple counts of elements present and their duplication (Allen and Guy 1984; Casteel 1972, 1977; Chase and Hagaman 1987; Steele and Parama 1981; Wild and Nichol 1983). Methodological and statistical approaches available include computer procedures for matching bones by size (Gilbert et al. 1981), a modified mark-capture procedure (LeCren 1965), the Lincoln Index based on matching pairs of bones (Winder 1992), and the more complex Lincoln/Peterson Index (Adams 1996; Adams and Konigsberg 2004). These approaches not only refine the estimation of the MNI but seek to establish the most likely number of individuals (MLNI) present (Nikita and Lahr 2011).

The chapters in this volume explore the issues just discussed in great depth. They present the range of problems encountered in modern forensic anthropology that call for commingling analysis. They also present the growing methodology to address these problems. Anthropologists continue to study remains brought to them by law enforcement officials in their laboratories, similar to the way it was done when Wilton Krogman and T. Dale Stewart were publishing their volumes more than two decades ago. However, today, anthropologists deal with commingling issues at crash sites, makeshift morgues, and medical examiners' offices, frequently working alongside other professionals as part of analysis teams. The nature of the cases and the format and methodology for their analysis continue to evolve. This volume documents important aspects of that evolution and provides the reader with the information needed for successful resolution of commingling issues.

References

Adams, B.J., 1996. The Use of the Lincoln/Peterson Index for Quantification and Interpretation of Commingled Human Remains. Department of Anthropology, University of Tennessee, Knoxville.

Adams, B.J., Byrd, J.E., 2006. Resolution of small-scale commingling: A case report from the Vietnam War. Forensic Sci. Int. 156, 63–69.

Adams, B.J., Konigsberg, L.W., 2004. Estimation of the most likely number of individuals from commingled human skeletal remains. Am. J. Phys. Anthropol. 125 (2), 138–151.

Allen, J., Guy, J.B.M., 1984. Optimal estimations of individuals in archaeological faunal assemblages: How minimal is the MNI? Archaeol. Oceania. 19, 41–47.

Baker, P.T., Newman, R.W., 1957. The use of bone weight for human identification. Am. J. Phys. Anthropol. 15 (4), 601–618.

Blau, S., Briggs, C.A., 2011. The role of forensic anthropology in Disaster Victim Identification (DVI). Forensic Sci. Int. (205), 29–35.

Buikstra, J.E., Gordon, C.C., 1980. Individuation in forensic science study: Decapitation. J. For. Sci. 25 (1), 246–259.

Buikstra, J.E., Gordon, C.C., St. Hoyme, L., 1984. The case of the severed skull: Individuation in forensic anthropology. In: Rathburn, T.A., Buikstra, J.E. (Eds.), Human Identification: Case Studies in Forensic Anthropology. Charles C. Thomas, Springfield, IL, pp. 121–135.

Buikstra, J.E., Ubelaker, D.H. (Eds.), 1994. Standards for Data Collection from Human Skeletal Remains, Proceedings of a Seminar at The Field Museum of Natural History (Arkansas Archeological Survey Research Series No. 44). Spiral ed. Arkansas Archeological Survey, Fayetteville.

Casteel, R.W., 1972. Some biases in the recovery of archaeological faunal remains. Proc. Prehistoric. Soc. (38), 382–388.

Casteel, R.W., 1977. Characterization of faunal assemblages and the minimum number of individuals determined from paired elements: Continuing problems in archaeology. J. Archaeol. Sci. (4), 125–134.

Chase, P.G., Hagaman, R.M., 1987. Minimum number of individuals and its alternatives: A probability theory perspective. OSSA 13, 75–86.

Eyman, C.E., 1965. Ultraviolet fluorescence as a means of skeletal identification. Am. Antiq. 31 (1), 109–112.

Finnegan, M., 1988. Variation of Trace Elements Within and Between Skeletons Using Multiple Sample Sites. Paper presented at the 15th Annual Meeting of the Paleopathology Association, Kansas City, MO.

Finnegan, M., Chaudhuri, S., 1990. Identification of Commingled Skeletal Remains Using Isotopic Strontium. Paper presented at the 42nd Annual Meeting of the American Academy of Forensic Sciences, Cincinnati, OH.

Fulton, B.A., Meloan, C.E., Finnegan, M., 1986. Reassembling scattered and mixed human bones by trace element ratios. J. Forensic Sci. 31 (4), 1455–1462.

Galloway, A.P., Willey, P., Snyder, L., 1997. Human bone mineral densities and survival of bone elements: A contemporary sample. In: Haglund, W.D., Sorg, M.H. (Eds.), Forensic Taphonomy: The Postmortem Fate of Human Remains. CRC Press, Boca Raton, FL, pp. 295–317.

Garrido Varas, C., Intriago Leiva, M., 2012. Managing commingled remains from mass graves: Considerations, implications and recommendations from a human rights case in Chile. Forensic Sci. Int. 219, e19–e24.

Gilbert, A.S., Singer, B.H., Perkins, D.J., 1981. Quantification experiments on computer-simulated faunal collections. OSSA 8, 79–94.

Guinn, V.P., 1970. Forensic neutron activation analysis. In: Stewart, T.D. (Ed.), Personal Identification in Mass Disasters. Smithsonian Institution, Washington, D.C., pp. 25–35.

Haglund, W.D., Sorg, M.H. (Eds.), 1997. Forensic Taphonomy: The Postmortem Fate of Human Remains. CRC Press, Boca Raton, FL.

Jakovski, Z., Nikolova, K., Janeska, B., Cakar, Z., Stankov, A., Poposka, V., Palvovski, G., Duma, A., 2010. Forensic DNA analysis in the identification of human remains in mass graves. J. Clin. Pathol. Forensic Med. 1 (1), 001–004.

Kerley, E.R., 1972. Special observations in skeletal identification. J. Forensic Sci. 17 (3), 349–357.

Krogman, W.M., 1962. The Human Skeleton in Forensic Medicine. Charles C. Thomas, Springfield, IL.

LeCren, E.D., 1965. A note on the history of mark-recapture population estimates. J. Anim. Ecol. 34, 453–454.

London, M.R., Curran, B.K., 1986. The use of the hip joint in the separation of commingled remains (abstract). Am. J. Phys. Anthropol. 69, 231.

London, M.R., Hunt, D.R., 1998. Morphometric segregation of commingled remains using the femoral head and acetabulum (abstract). Am. J. Phys. Anthropol. 26 (Suppl.), 152.

Lyman, R.L., 1993. Density-mediated attrition of bone assemblages: New insights. In: Hudson, J. (Ed.), From Bones to Behavior. Center for Archaeological Investigations, Carbondale, IL, pp. 324–341.

McKern, T.W., 1958. The Use of Shortwave Ultraviolet Rays for the Segregation of Commingled Skeletal Remains. Environmental Protection Research and Developments Command, Quartermaster Research and Development Center Environmental Protection Research Division, Natick, MA.

Misner, L.M., Halvorson, A.C., Drier, J.L., Ubelaker, D.H., Foran, D.R., 2009. The correlation between skeletal weathering and DNA quality and quantity. J. Forensic Sci. 54 (4), 822–828.

Mulhern, D.M., Ubelaker, D.H., 2001. Differences in osteon banding between human and nonhuman bone. J. Forensic Sci. 46 (2), 220–222.

Mulhern, D.M., Ubelaker, D.H., 2003. Histologic examination of bone development in juvenile chimpanzees. Am. J. Phys. Anthropol. 122 (2), 127–133.

Mulhern, D.M., Ubelaker, D.H., 2012. Differentiating human from nonhuman bone microstructure. In: Crowder, C., Stout, S. (Eds.), Bone Histology: An Anthropological Perspective. CRC Press, Boca Raton, FL, pp 109–134.

Murray, K.A., Rose, J.C., 1993. The analysis of cremains: A case study involving the inappropriate disposal of mortuary remains. J. Forensic Sci. 38 (1), 98–103.

Nikita, E., Lahr, M.M., 2011. Simple algorithms for the estimation of the initial number of individuals in commingled skeletal remains. Am. J. Phys. Anthropol. 146, 629–636.

Ritter, N., 2007. Identifying remains: Lessons learned from 9/11. Natl. Inst. Justice J. 256, 20–26.

Rösing, F.W., Pischtschan, E., 1995. Re-individualisation of commingled skeletal remains. In: Jacob, B., Bonte, W. (Eds.), Advances in Forensic Sciences. Verlag, Berlin, pp 38–41.

Snow, C.C., Folk, E.D., 1965. Statistical assessment of commingled skeletal remains. Am. J. Phys. Anthropol. 32, 423–427.

Steele, D.G., Parama, W.D., 1981. Frequencies of dental anomalies and their potential effect on determining MNI counts. Plains Anthropologist 26 (91), 51–54.

Stewart, T.D. (Ed.), 1970. Personal Identification in Mass Disasters. Smithsonian Institution, Washington, D.C.

Stewart, T.D., 1979. Essentials of Forensic Anthropology. Charles C. Thomas, Springfield, IL.

Taylor, R.E., 1987. Radiocarbon Dating: An Archaeological Perspective. Academic Press, Orlando, FL.

Ubelaker, D.H., 1998. The evolving role of the microscope in forensic anthropology. In: Reichs, K.J. (Ed.), Forensic Osteology, Advances in the Identification of Human Remains. Charles C. Thomas, Springfield, IL, pp. 514–532.

Ubelaker, D.H., 2001. Artificial radiocarbon as an indicator of recent origin of organic remains in forensic cases. J. Forensic Sci. 46 (6), 1285–1287.

Ubelaker, D.H., 2002. Approaches to the study of commingling in human skeletal biology. In: Haglund, W.D., Sorg, M.H. (Eds.), Advances in Forensic Taphonomy, Method, Theory, and Archaeological Perspectives. CRC Press, Boca Raton, FL, pp. 331–351.

Ubelaker, D.H., Buchholz, B.A., Stewart, J., 2006. Analysis of artificial radiocarbon in different skeletal and dental tissue types to evaluate date of death. J. Forensic Sci. 51 (3), 484–488.

Ubelaker, D.H., Houck, M.M., 2002. Using radiocarbon dating and paleontological extraction techniques in the analysis of a human skull in an unusual context. Forensic Sci. Comm. (4), 4.

Ubelaker, D.H., Lowenstein, J.M., Hood, D.G., 2004. Use of solid-phase double-antibody radioimmunoassay to identify species from small skeletal fragments. J. Forensic Sci. 49 (5), 924–929.

Ubelaker, D.H., Ward, D.C., Braz, V.S., Stewart, J., 2002. The use of SEM/EDS analysis to distinguish dental and osseous tissue from other materials. J. Forensic Sci. 47 (5), 940–943.

Wild, L., Nichol, R., 1983. Estimation of the original number of individuals using estimators of the Krantz type. J. Field Archeol. (10), 337–344.

Willey, P., Galloway, A.P., Snyder, L., 1997. Bone mineral density and survival of elements and element portions in the bones of the Crow Creek Massacre victims. Am. J. Phys. Anthropol. 104, 513–528.

Winder, N.P., 1992. The removal estimator: A "probable numbers" statistic that requires no matching. Int. J. Osteoarcheol. (2), 15–18.

CHAPTER 2

Spatial Analysis of Mass Grave Mapping Data to Assist in the Reassociation of Disarticulated and Commingled Human Remains

Hugh Tuller[1], Ute Hofmeister[2]

[1]*Joint POW/MIA Accounting Command, Central Identification Laboratory, Hickam AFB, Hawaii, USA,* [2]*International Committee of the Red Cross, Geneva, Switzerland*

Introduction

When considering possible solutions to the problem of sorting commingled human remains from a mass grave context, one is inclined to think of methods conducted within a laboratory setting (Dirkmaat et al. 2008; Ubelaker 2002), such as physical pair matching of skeletal elements, evaluation of skeletal joint articulation, statistical analysis of skeletal measurements, or other such techniques that use information generated during mortuary analysis (Buikstra et al. 1984; Byrd and Adams 2003; Rodriguez 2005); in short, these techniques focus on the remains well after they have been recovered from the grave. When attempting to tackle problems of commingling, mortuary practitioners unfortunately often do not consult data generated during the excavation of a mass grave. Nevertheless, observations and recordings taken during proper excavation can directly assist in the reassociation of disarticulated and commingled remains. This chapter presents a study using spatial relationship and grave depositional event data to categorize the likely affiliation between disarticulated remains within a mass grave.

The potential of disarticulation and commingling of bodies and body parts is an issue in every mass grave. Not only are bodies initially commingled as they are deposited in the grave, but the condition of the bodies prior to burial, decomposition processes, the intentional destruction and/or tampering of the bodies by those who buried them, and other taphonomic processes contribute to the eventual disarticulation and mixing of elements. This can be compounded when a mass grave is disturbed and remains are removed to a secondary burial location(s) (what Jessee and Skinner 2005 refer to as "secondary inhumation sites"). Care in exposing and removing remains from a grave by an observant excavator, knowledgeable in human skeletal

Commingled Human Remains. http://dx.doi.org/10.1016/B978-0-12-405889-7.00002-2

anatomy, is the single most important step in limiting (and, one hopes, eliminating) further disarticulation during the recovery. Without a controlled excavation, disarticulation will be compounded, further adding to the already confused mix within the grave. Yet careful exposure and removal of remains do not have to be the only contributions a proper excavation makes. A well-documented archaeologically led excavation generates data that may be used not only for prevention of further commingling, but for resolving commingled remains.

Recognition of archaeological techniques and observations as potential key elements in assisting forensic casework has been acknowledged in the past (Bass and Birkby 1978; Dirkmaat and Adovasio 1997; Dirkmaat and Cabo 2012; Morse et al. 1976; Owsley 2001; Skinner 1987; Tuller and Đurić 2006). Nevertheless, no suggestion has been proposed as to how archaeological observations can be logically and consistently utilized within mortuaries, especially those processing hundreds of remains from mass graves. Unfortunately, mass grave investigation is often sharply divided between two activities—recovery operations (grave excavation) and mortuary examination (autopsy)—with neither activity having much contact with the other. Although the forensic anthropologist or pathologist in charge of the mortuary may fully respect the contributions that archaeology makes during the recovery operations, he or she may be unaware of the potential role archaeology can play in sorting commingled remains *after* the excavation. Archaeology, for the most part, is still very much viewed by mission planners as an outdoor (or at least out of mortuary) activity with no further connection to the mortuary other than delivering remains and associated evidence to the mortuary as intact as possible. Only under unusual circumstances does archaeology seem to be consulted during mortuary examination.

For example, Haglund (2001) describes such a circumstance in which excavation maps displaying the position of remains within a mass grave were used to help sort out fragmented crania superimposed on each other. Although Haglund uses this example as one of several positive contributions archaeology can bring to the investigation of mass graves, he unfortunately does not detail how the maps were used. It is assumed that the physical maps, not the recorded electronic spatial data used to create the maps, were consulted to help rectify the commingling issue. Furthermore, it seems that this use of excavation maps may have been an isolated example, that the maps were consulted only after the commingling issue with this particular case was recognized in the mortuary, and the use of maps was not a standard aspect of their mortuary operation. No further reference of map use within their mortuary was mentioned.

In our study, a computer algorithm is used to analyze spatial relationships between disarticulated and commingled remains within a mass grave. Similar to Haglund's example using maps to assist in sorting commingled crania to adjacent bodies, the algorithm examines the spatial data generated during the electronic survey of bodies and body parts within a grave and compares the locations of disarticulated elements to all possible matching points. The hypothesis is that a disarticulated body part closest to the point on the body missing that part is the more likely correct match out of all other possible matching body parts within the grave. Such an algorithm can be run prior to or during mortuary examination, providing mortuary personnel with immediate suggestions as to which disarticulated body part(s) may belong to a particular body. When one is confronted with hundreds of bodies and body parts from a mass grave to sort through, prior knowledge of potential matching elements can be an effective starting point for rectifying commingling issues. Although not a definitive method or technique for reassociation, spatial analysis provides an objective and systematic approach based on the nature of the grave that may aid in reassociations.

In addition to generating data that can be analyzed spatially, an archaeological approach to mass grave excavation can identify events in the creation of the grave, which, in turn, has potential to assist in resolving commingling issues. Specifically, the identification of depositional events of human remains within a grave, when combined with spatial analysis, can narrow the search parameters of possible matching disarticulated body parts within a group of recovered remains (Tuller et al. 2005).

Materials and Methods

The focus of this study is on the largest of a series of mass graves excavated during 2002 on the Special Police Training Grounds in Batajnica, a suburb of Belgrade, in Serbia. Victims in the grave were shown to be Kosovar Albanians killed in the spring of 1999 and transported up to Belgrade for disposal. Although overall control of the site and the associated evidence belonged to the Belgrade District Court, the actual excavation of the grave was conducted by forensic archaeologists from the International Commission for Missing Persons (ICMP) assisted by a crew of archaeologists from the University of Belgrade. Both authors of this chapter were employed by ICMP at the time of this excavation.

The grave in discussion, designated BA05 (Batajnica 05), was approximately 25 m long, 3 m wide, and 2 m in depth. We can deduce from the archaeological findings that a front-end loader type construction machine dug the grave, creating a ramp down into the earth at one end as it removed soil (Figure 2-1). BA05 was a complex mass grave in that it consisted of elements of both primary and secondary depositions, as well as having areas within the grave where attempts were made at cremating the grave contents. Furthermore, we can infer that although many of the bodies transported to Belgrade from areas in Kosovo were gathered off the surface of the ground and loaded onto trucks, some were wrapped in blankets or plastic sheeting, whereas others were dug up from graves where they were originally buried. A situation occurred in which, on one extreme, a number of trucks likely carried neatly packaged bodies, whereas others contained jumbled mixes of soil, bodies, pieces of coffin, and other burial artifacts. Before the trucks deposited their loads into the grave, the base of the grave was lined with old vehicle tires and pieces of lumber. The first trucks backed into the grave, where they dumped their loads. Later trucks dumped their contents on the surface of the ground next to the grave, where the remains were then either pushed directly into the

Figure 2-1
Completed excavation of BA05 mass grave. Ramp into the grave begins near the bottom of the photograph. Note vehicle tires on the base of the grave.

grave from the side or were first set afire and allowed to burn for a time before being pushed in. As remains and backfill were deposited into the grave, gasoline and additional tires were added to the mix in an apparent attempt to keep the fires going.

The perpetrators, however, were not as methodological in the destruction of the bodies as they had planned. Perhaps because of fear of ongoing NATO bombing strikes in the area at the time, or simply because those carrying out the orders to make the graves were not enthusiastic about their assigned task, the separate body deposits appeared to have been buried shortly after they were deposited in the grave, putting out many of the fires almost as quickly as they were started. As bodies mounded up over the edge of the grave, a construction machine repeatedly drove over the top of the remains, crushing them down into the grave as it deposited more soil. The combined activities of different body collection strategies in Kosovo, the act of transporting them to Belgrade by truck, attempts at destroying them by fire, and machine activities made the excavation, recording, and recovery of the human remains within this grave extremely challenging.

To accurately map spatial relations within and around the grave, the ICMP archaeologists employed an electronic Sokkia set 600 total station equipped with a Sokkia SDR 31 data logger. Total stations, which are being increasingly used at archaeological sites and outdoor crime scenes, are becoming familiar equipment at mass grave excavation sites. Capable of recording position points in three dimensions in a fraction of the time traditional tape measure and transits take, a total station's data can be downloaded by computer programs and rendered into three-dimensional maps, illustrating the exposed human remains, artifacts, and grave features in any imaginable combination (Wright et al. 2005).

While a single point recorded from a complete body or disarticulated body part in a grave can be used to represent those remains on a map, excavators of mass graves using total stations typically record a series of points to represent a set of remains. This series of points can then be connected in a stick-figure manner in a geographic information system (GIS) program to represent a body for map purposes. Points recorded on a complete body are typically the head and all major limb joints. During the excavation of mass grave BA05, a total of 15 points for a complete body were recorded. In addition to the head and joint points mentioned, a central pelvis, central body mass, and when found in isolation, the mandible, had points taken on them. Although the number of points recorded may seem excessive, we have found that it takes only 3–4 minutes to survey a complete body and does not interfere with the flow of work. Indeed, recording the series of points forces the person recovering the body to check that all the major elements are present, helps to eliminate possible commingling mistakes during the recovery, and ensures an accurate field inventory of the remains.

Many total stations and data loggers have limited capacity for recording text to describe the points recorded. The Sokkia data loggers used by ICMP could accommodate only up to 16 characters and spaces in their description field. Although this small field limits the amount of text that may be attached to a particular record, one would not necessarily want to be slowed down inputting long descriptive text during the excavation. It may be possible to preprogram newer data loggers or alternatives such as a tablet, PCs, or laptops with these codes to operate in a quicker usable format.

At Batajnica, to bypass the lack of available space and ensure speedy input of text, team members used short descriptive codes adopted from the International Criminal Tribunal for the former Yugoslavia's (ICTY) mass grave survey procedures (Hanson et al. 2000) to identify the points taken. Points recorded on a body received a four-letter code beginning with the side from where the point was being taken, followed by the first three letters of the body element. A left shoulder would be recorded as LSHO. Elements such as the cranium (CRAN) that do not have a side used the first four letters of the name of element. Table 2-1 lists the codes and elements they represent used during the excavation of BA05. Figure 2-2 displays the codes on a skeletal homunculus.

A total station records the location of a given point in X, Y, and Z (e.g., north, east, and elevation) numeric coordinate format. Each body or body part uncovered in the grave received a unique evidence number. This evidence number was added to the mass grave identifier (BA05) along with the four-letter body location code. A string of recorded total station codes for a single point taken on a body may read BA05 123B RELB followed by the X, Y, and Z numerical coordinates. In this example, BA05 represents the grave number at Batajnica, 123B

Table 2-1: Body Points Recorded and their Associated Total Station Codes

Code Entry	Description
CRAN	Cranium
RSHO	Right Shoulder
RELB	Right Elbow
RWRI	Right Wrist
LSHO	Left Shoulder
LELB	Left Elbow
LWRI	Left Wrist
CPEL	Central Pelvis Point
RPEL	Right Pelvis Point
LPEL	Left Pelvis Point
RKNE	Right Knee
RANK	Right Ankle
LKNE	Left Knee
LANK	Left Ankle
CPOI	Central Point—Body
MAND	Mandible (if disarticulated)

is the individual body evidence number (B = Body), and RELB indicates that the point recorded was the right elbow. A complete body would be represented by 15 sets of these codes, whereas an individual body part (BP = Body Part), for example, an unassociated disarticulated left arm, would have only three points recorded: the shoulder (LSHO), elbow (LELB), and wrist (LWRI). Figure 2-3 shows an example of what a complete body may look like after exposure in a grave and then rendered in a map as a stick figure, each position point taken labeled with the appropriate code. It should be noted here that although 15 points were taken on a complete body, the central point (CPOI) taken on the body was not used in our spatial analysis for reasons explained in the "Discussion" section.

A few words regarding body (B) versus body parts (BP) classifications: there is currently no standard used in the international community of mass grave investigators regarding the definition of what constitutes a body or body part. Indeed, this is a constant source of debate among practitioners—debates that unfortunately too often take place at the graveside as the first disarticulated remains are about to be removed. Although it may seem obvious that a complete articulated body can be defined as a body (B), it becomes less clear how to classify a body in progressively disarticulated condition. At what point does a body become categorized as a body part? It is easy to imagine that an unassociated disarticulated limb or skull will be categorized as a body part (BP), but should remains consisting of a torso missing its head and a leg be

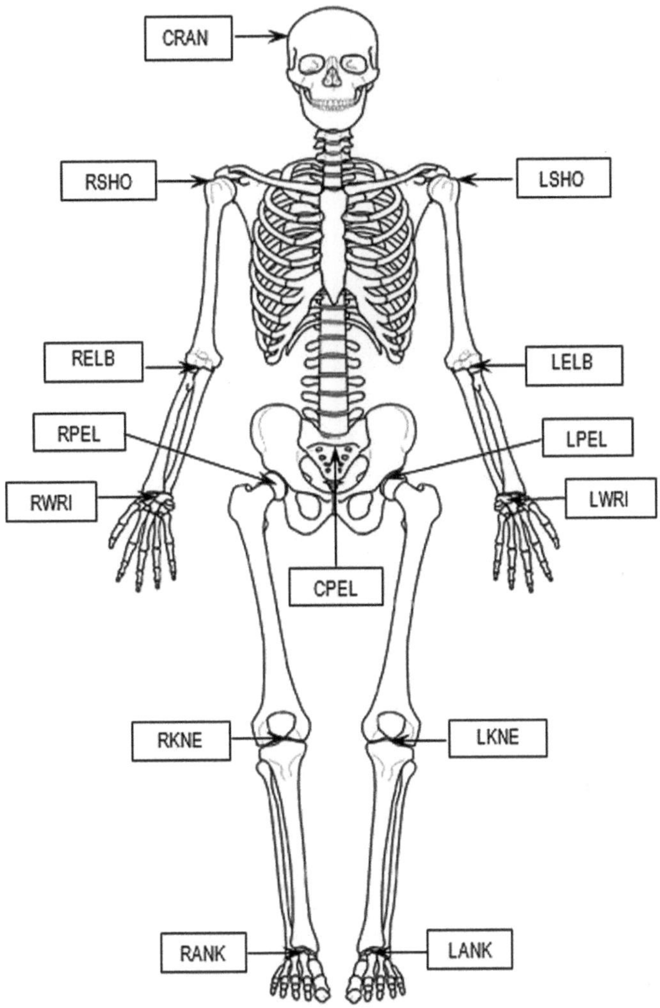

Figure 2-2
ICTY survey points used for this analysis as depicted on skeletal homunculus.

considered a body part or body? What if it is also missing the other leg and an arm? Or if, as regularly happens, the remains become disarticulated at the lumbar vertebrae and the upper half is missing a limb or two? There are proposals, such as if 75% of the remains are present, it can be categorized as a B, and less than 75%, a BP (Wagner 2008). However, they promote disagreements in the grave between recovery team members over how much of the body is present. Currently, the categorization of remains is usually left up to the lead archaeologist or the individual team member removing the remains from the grave. This decision may be made without thought as to how the categorization may affect mortuary operations. With greater worldwide interest in the forensic investigation of atrocities and their associated mass graves, standardization of these categorizations in a comprehensive manner should be considered, particularly in light of the ever-increasing use of electronic spatial recording devices.

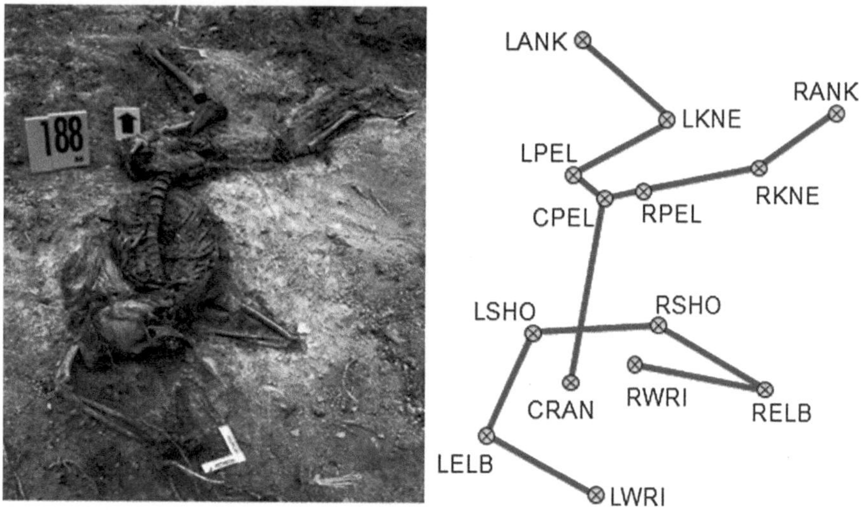

Figure 2-3
Body 188B *in situ* and represented in map form.

In mass grave BA05, as with many excavated graves, the categorization occurred in an *ad hoc* fashion. Although most of the remains were intact enough to be classified as Bs, on occasion disarticulation made this distinction unclear, and the lead archaeologist had to decide its categorization. In general, if 50% or more of a body was present, then it was categorized as a B. Most BPs tended to be disarticulated limbs consisting of at least two articulating bones. Single disarticulated bones without apparent association were categorized as "general bones" (GB) and their provenience not recorded by the total station (as a result of this study, the authors now advocate the recording of all long bones as well as a carefully planned classification system for potential spatial analysis). The exceptions to these general rules were hands and feet. Complete hands and feet were recorded as BPs. Partial hands and feet were collected as GBs because these bones are relatively small. It should be recognized that although it is desirable to reassociate as many disarticulated elements back to their bodies as possible, a number of elements such as unassociated ribs and the bones of the hands and feet are often beyond the capacity of anthropology to reassociate given the number of remains within large mass graves. Until DNA technology becomes easier and cheaper, the possibility of reassociating such elements with limited funding and time constraints is economically out of reach. Numerous GBs, as well as hands, feet, and sections of torso (ribs and vertebrae), will not be reassociated because of these reasons, so mission planners from relevant governmental organizations and family associations will have to decide what to do with these "extra" elements.

In addition to recording points on a body/body part for spatial analysis, surveying the remains also renders a basic skeletal inventory of that case, and the data can act as a backup to any evidence/photographic log or other documentation source. In addition, all the individual bodies or body part points can be downloaded to provide an instant inventory for mortuary use. A quick glance at a case's code will indicate not only if it is a body (B) or body part (BP), but what elements that case consists of. Elements absent from the inventory represent disarticulated elements—an important heads-up for an anthropologist or pathologist getting ready to begin an autopsy.

According to records, within the BA05 mass grave, 378 cases comprising 289 Bs and 89 BPs, and 594 single disarticulated bones and bone fragments (GBs) were recovered from 12 separate deposits of human remains. Each deposit, identified through archaeological techniques, represents a truck load dumped into the grave, or a collection of bodies dumped on the surface beside the grave and then pushed into the grave by a construction machine. The excavation team recorded location points on all bodies and body parts, as described. In addition, the individual deposit within the grave from which the remains were recovered was noted. As mentioned, the single disarticulated bone and bone fragments (GBs) were not recorded by the total station, but were instead gathered in separate bags according to the deposit from which they were recovered. Because no points were recorded from these elements, the GBs are not included in this study. Again, as a result of this analysis, we would suggest that single, disarticulated long bones receive the same attention as Bs and BPs if spatial analysis is to be conducted.

All Bs, BPs, and artifacts were assigned an individual, sequentially assigned evidence number. The remains and artifacts were placed in separate body bags or smaller sealed plastic bags depending on their size. The unique evidence number was recorded in an evidence log book and written on the outside of the body/evidence bag. A separate slip of paper with the evidence number was sealed in a Ziploc-type bag and placed inside the body bag with the remains. The remains were then transferred to a storage area to await autopsy. The mortuary/evidence personnel were provided a copy of the evidence log.

Autopsies were conducted on site while the excavation of the Batajnica mass graves was ongoing. This manner of operation precluded most reassociation efforts. Reassociation can be attempted only after a grave is completely excavated and a remains inventory established; otherwise, one risks the chance of missing a matching element still buried within the grave. Due to both legal and political considerations between the Belgrade authorities and ICMP, DNA took the lead in identification and reassociation of recovered remains. During autopsy, hard tissue samples were taken from all bodies and body parts and later processed through ICMP DNA laboratories. It was through DNA results that reassociations were eventually established. Not only did positive results assist in identification, but identical sequences between disarticulated body parts and bodies allowed for reassociation of 41 disarticulated elements from the BA05 mass grave.

Because there was little opportunity for reassociation methodologies to be applied at Batajnica, analysis of the spatial relationship of remains within BA05 presented here was conducted at a much later time and was not part of the original mortuary effort. The spatial analysis was performed without prior knowledge of ICMP DNA reassociation results, which serve as a control.

A spatial analysis program, derived from Microsoft Access, was used on the BA05 survey data to calculate the distance between bodies missing elements and potential matching body parts in the mass grave. The formula used for this analysis calculates the distance between two points recorded in three-dimensional space and then produces a list of potential matches in order from nearest to farthest. It is important to use three-dimensional distances, and not, as is sometimes done, two-dimensional maps (Haglund 2001), which will distort the real relationships between elements. The idea of using mass grave mapping data to search for nearest probable matches has likely occurred to many people in the past; however, few seem to have actually gone as far as to develop the idea. One person who has attempted to use mass grave map data in this manner is Richard Wright.

Wright kindly provided ICMP with a Microsoft Excel–based program for spatial analysis (Wright 2003) that he adapted from his earlier cranial morphometric research (Wright 1992). Unfortunately, Wright's spatial analysis program lacked the option to narrow the search to only those elements that could potentially match the remains being examined. Instead, it computed the distance from the point one wished to search from, say an RELB for a missing lower right arm, to *all* other points recorded within the grave, regardless of whether or not those points were lower right arm points. Instead of a list of potential disarticulated right lower arms, the program provided a list organized by distance, which included crania, shoulders, knees, wrists, and all the other points recorded within the grave. Although Wright's program did allow the number of points displayed to be limited, this did not diminish the fact that numerous points with no relationship to the remains being examined had to be manually filtered to reveal those that did represent the potential matches one was searching for.

The spatial analysis program designed for this study was based on a number of SQL Queries in Microsoft Access and allowed data gathered from the total station or GIS software to be imported in various formats. Unlike Wright's program, this program lists only potential matches in the results of a query. All other points are ignored, and thus, filtering is automatic.

The spatial analysis program was specifically created for this study and was never intended for public distribution. At the time of this study, the ICMP was not analyzing spatial data to help solve commingling problems, nor has it necessarily embraced the possibilities since. The intention of this study was to demonstrate the potential use of such mapping data, not to provide step-by-step guidance on how to create a Microsoft Access (or other program) database. Such guidance could not keep up with evolving computer program technology, and it is certain that anyone wishing to use such a program would want to tailor it to his or her specific needs. If an organization or individual wishes to analyze mapping data, the authors encourage the exploration of a number of commercially available database programs that are capable of performing the analysis. As mentioned, we used Microsoft Access, already available on most PCs. Anyone experienced in creating SQL Queries in MS Access or a similar program should be able to make a program capable of spatially analyzing total station data given the parameters described in the following text. If no current team member is experienced in database management, we suggest that an information technology (IT) specialist be employed to create queries and train staff on the program's operation. Database management is one of many aspects of mass grave investigation that must be planned for in advance. A spatial analysis program to be used in the mortuary can be created at the same time and incorporated into overall operating procedures.

For this study, the steps for running searches in our spatial analysis program were as follows:

From a given case, the code of the specific point where disarticulation occurs is entered. For a body (e.g. case 030B) missing a right lower leg, this would be "030B RKNE." Next, possible codes of matching elements are entered. With the data from mass grave BA05, the code would have been another "RKNE." As a result of this study, the point codes have been modified to perform more detailed queries as later detailed in the "Discussion" section. In addition to searching for elements with matching codes, one can use a wildcard in the search (e.g., to find both left and right lower legs) in case they were sided incorrectly during excavation. If desired, the search may further be limited to a certain deposit of human remains within the grave, thus narrowing the possibilities even more. Tables 2-2 and 2-3 display results of a spatial analysis query for the sample case.

The result of this query is a list of potential matching elements, ranked by three-dimensional distance from nearest to farthest (Table 2-2). Displayed in the table is the target point (the right knee of case 030B, in this example), the deposit from which the remains were recovered (if applicable), the case number of the possible matching body part, the distance in meters from the targeted point, the element of the body part queried for (right knee in this example), and the ranking of the possible matching body part. The ranks are listed according to distance with rank 1 being the closest, rank 2, the second closest, and so on.

It is also possible to include the inventory on all the points surveyed on each body or body part, so as to give an idea what elements are present in each case. In this manner, when the

Table 2-2: Sample Results of Spatial Query Showing Possible Matches, Listed in Order of Distance from the Targeted Point (030B RKNE), When Searching for a Right Lower Leg

Body Survey Code	Deposit Number	Case Number	Distance in Meters	Element	Rank
030B RKNE	1	058BP	0.24866	RKNE	1
	1	067BP	0.89834	RKNE	2
	8	225BP	3.62864	RKNE	3
	9	300BP	5.525004	RKNE	4
	9	425BP	5.646783	RKNE	5
	11	347BP	10.35154	RKNE	6

Table 2-3: Detailed Query Result Showing Four Possible Lower Leg Matches, by Distance, to Case 030B with all Recorded Points Displayed

Case Number	Distance in Meters	Deposit Number	Recorded Code Present
058BP	0.24866	1	**058BP RKNE**
			058BP LKNE
			058BP RANK
			058BP LANK
067BP	0.89834	1	**067BP RKNE**
			067BP LKNE
			067BP RANK
			067BP LANK
225BP	3.62864	8	**225BP RKNE**
			225BP RANK
300BP	5.525004	9	**300BP RKNE**
			300BP LKNE
			300BP RANK
			300BP LANK

potential matching part inventory shows the body part to have repeated elements with the case body, the potential matching part may be removed from initial consideration. This could eliminate the need to physically retrieve the possible matching body part from the collective remains in storage (no small task when there are hundreds of remains to sort through) while those body parts that better match with the body are examined.

For example, in Table 2-3 the first (and thus closest) body part to the targeted 030B RKNE is case number 058BP at just under 0.25 m distance. Examination of all the points recorded on 058BP reveals that it consists of both left and right lower legs. Both knee and ankle points are present (RKNE, LKNE, RANK, and LANK), but no pelvic points that would indicate the presence of a femur were recorded. If case 030B has a left lower leg, 058BP can be excluded as a potential match. On the other hand, if the body is missing both lower legs, 058BP should be considered as the best possible match according to distance and elements present.

For the 378 cases (289 Bs and 89 BPs) recovered from the BA05 mass grave at the time of the study, 41 reassociations had been completed on the basis of matching DNA. Nine of these matches were excluded because of lack of sufficient data for the queries. The lacking data were, in part, information on what body elements the matching parts consisted of (due to lack of clarity in the field and the inaccessibility of certain anthropological data at the time of this study) and, in part, missing spatial data (coordinates). For each of the remaining 32 cases, a query was run, producing a list of possible matches. On each list, the ranks were numbered, and the match that was actually corroborated by DNA was marked.

Again, the hypothesis is that the nearest ordered disarticulated body part is more likely to be the matching element than all other possible matching body parts within the grave. This hypothesis should certainly be expected to be valid in a simple primary mass grave. On the other hand, it is likely that the stronger the commingling, as we find in complex secondary mass graves or cases of intentional commingling of remains, the less likely the hypothesis is to be true. However, running the analysis against disarticulated remains from the *same deposit* should help alleviate this problem, even in a secondary mass grave, especially if it consists of clearly defined deposits from different primary sites.

As explained, spatial analysis will produce a list, ordered by distance, of every possible match within the grave. Yet, as noted, mass graves may be made of separate deposits of bodies gathered from different geographic locations. Remains recovered from BA05, for example, came primarily from three different municipalities in Kosovo (Tuller et al. 2005). Analysis of the spatial relationships between all remains within BA05 would produce a list that contains possible matches of body parts originating from different municipalities. If one narrows down the search to the separate deposits within the grave, particularly complex graves such as secondary burials, the accuracy of the list produced by the spatial analysis program should increase.

Results

From the 32 DNA reassociated body parts, 88% (28 reassociations) of the total were first in rank. That is, the actual matching body part was closer to the body it belonged to than all other potential matching parts. Six percent (two reassociations) were second in rank; 3% (one reassociation), third; and 3% (one reassociation), fourth in rank (Figure 2-4).

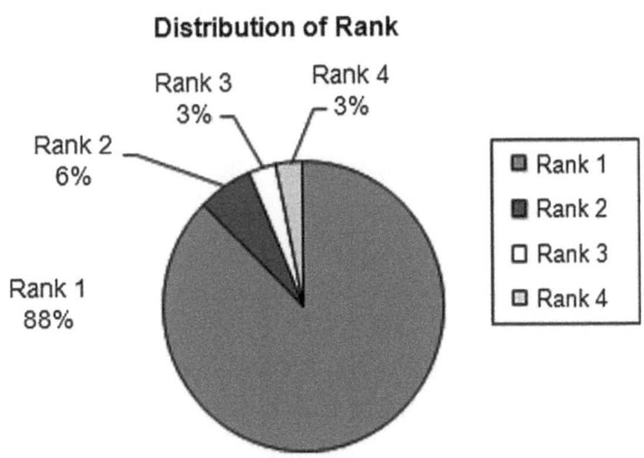

Figure 2-4
Distribution of confirmed matching elements by their rank in the list of possible matching elements.

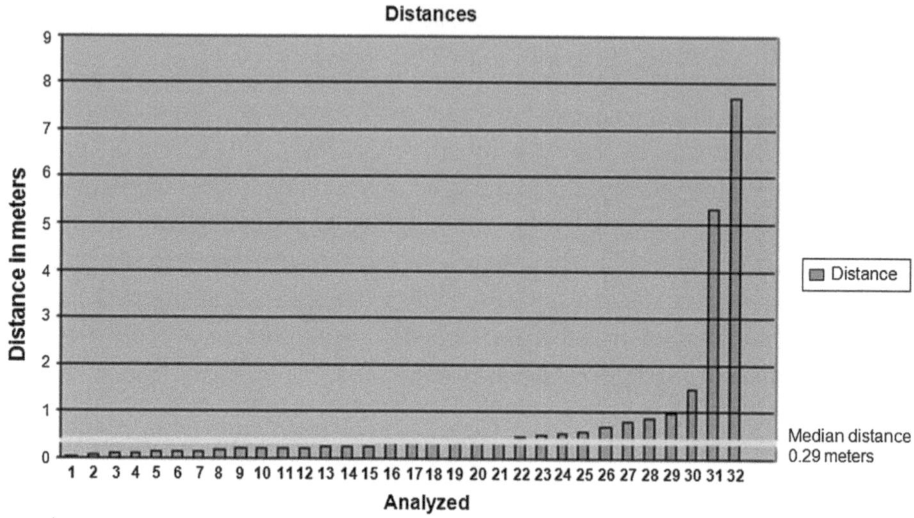

Figure 2-5
Distances between reassociated body parts, listed by case (median 0.29 m, mean 0.75 m).

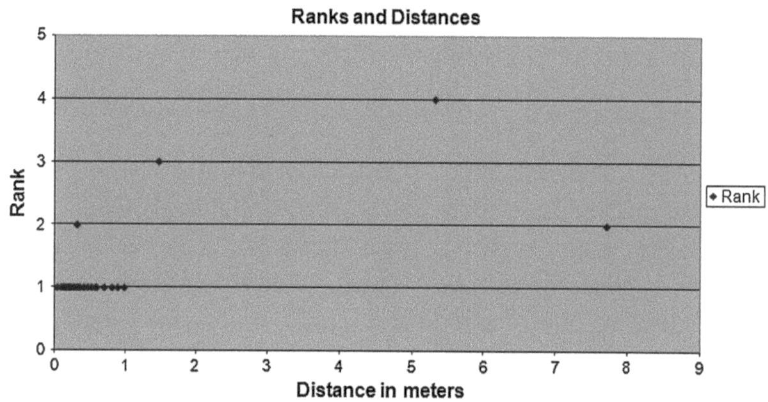

Figure 2-6
Correlation between ranks and distances.

The resulting lists of potential matches produced by the spatial analysis were usually 10 or more long and often over 20 in length. These large lists of possible matches indicate that the results are not simply due to a lack of alternative matches in the grave.

As would be expected in a predominantly primary grave, the distance between most matching body parts was considerably less than 1 m. The median distance between the matching elements, from one mapped articulation point to the other, was 0.29 m (Figure 2-5). In two cases, the matching elements were over five and seven meters away. These outliers may be explained by machine action within the grave which probably moved these body parts when going back and forth or by the described cremation activities that took place beside the grave before remains were pushed in. The correlation between rank on the spatial analysis results list and distance is displayed in Figure 2-6. Again, it shows most DNA reassociated elements high in rank on the list and in close distance to the matching body. A higher rank, on the other hand—at least in these very few cases—does not necessarily indicate a proportionate increase in distance and vice versa.

Discussion

The results indicate that spatial analysis of the distribution of disarticulated remains within a mass grave may help solve commingling problems by suggesting probable reassociation matches in ranked order. Minimally, it will provide an objective testing strategy to implement during laboratory analysis. Spatial analysis of excavation survey data from mass grave BA05 found that 88% of the DNA-reassociated matches were the closest in physical distance to each other and that the median between the disarticulated parts was only 0.29 m. It may be assumed that most matching disarticulated remains that have so far failed to produce a DNA sequence in BA05 likewise are ranked high on the generated lists and were recovered near their matching element. When one is considering the numerous possible matches for each body part within BA05, narrowing down the possibilities to a few most likely matching candidates could dramatically assist reassociation efforts. The same would hold true for all mass graves, especially primary ones, excavated and recorded in a similar manner.

Without knowledge of the spatial relationships of the body parts, mortuary personnel will not know which disarticulated remains were near each other in the grave. In the authors' experiences, mortuary personnel either examine remains recovered from mass graves in a more or less random fashion as the cases are removed from storage—often starting with complete bodies and then moving to body parts where little or no reassociation is attempted—or the entire collection of hundreds (or thousands) of elements are laid out so the examiner can walk around between cases trying to piece together disarticulated parts. In this manner, reassociation possibilities primarily rely on the examiner's memory. These methods are not a prudent use of time and energy, and under such circumstances, managers are forced to consider the benefits of reassociation efforts.

Although spatial analysis cannot identify matching body parts on its own, it does provide a list of the most likely candidates in ranked order. A focused effort can then be made such that the nearest disarticulated body part is examined first, the next closest, second, and so on. Or, depending on what additional reassociation methods the examiner wishes to employ (e.g., pair matching, conjoining fracture, articular surface comparison, metric analysis), the first several most likely candidates could be removed from storage and examined together. In addition, the recovery data themselves provide an electronic remains inventory that, at bare minimum, will give mortuary personnel an idea of the number and types of remains that may be related to the case they are working on.

Logically, spatial analysis would have more success with remains recovered from primary graves than those recovered from secondary depositional events where remains were removed from their original context and further disarticulated. Additional research into spatial distributions in secondary graves will give a better estimate of the probabilities encountered in such cases. The more intentional commingling a group of bodies is subjected to, the more difficult it will be to reassociate disarticulated body parts. Nevertheless, Cabo et al. (2012) have demonstrated that even with intense postburial disturbances, spatial associations can be distinguished and the data utilized to resolve comingling issues.

Although a large number of bodies may have been disposed of in a mass grave, the number of remains that need to be queried during spatial analysis may be reduced through careful recording of body depositional events during excavation. A query run on remains recovered from a single deposit, as opposed to all the bodies recovered from the whole grave, may prove to be very helpful in narrowing down the number of probable matching remains. Indeed, with the exception of testing all recovered remains for DNA matches, focusing attention on remains from a single deposit at a time would assist all methods of reassociation.

Survey Codes

The use of excavation survey data (originally intended for the production of maps and a basic evidence inventory) for spatial analysis requires coding specifically adapted to this purpose. ICTY total station survey codes were used to record body and body part positions during the excavation of mass grave BA05. Afterward, a spatial analysis of the remains distribution within the grave was conducted, during which certain limitations of the adopted ICTY codes became apparent.

Although the ICTY codes are proficient enough for mapping purposes, they were found at times to be misleading when presenting a skeletal inventory of incomplete remains. For example, using the ICTY codes, a lower leg disarticulated due to a mid-shaft fracture of the femur would have only two points taken on it—the ankle and knee—whereas the fracture point of the distal femur would not be recorded (the ICTY codes provide codes only for joints and not the end points of disarticulated limbs due to fractures). A later review of the codes for this body part would mislead one to assume only the lower leg is present although half the femur is also articulated.

The ICTY codes not only created inaccurate inventories but also caused some confusion during spatial analysis, requiring additional research of the formal written excavation logs, sketches, and photos. As a result, the ICTY codes have since been augmented with additional codes (Table 2-4) that have now been incorporated into ICMP's standard operating

Table 2-4: Additional Suggested Total Station Survey Codes

Code Entry	Element
CFRG	Cranial Fragments
MAND	Mandible
RHUM	Right Humerus
RULN	Right Ulna
RRAD	Right Radius
LHUM	Left Humerus
LULN	Left Ulna
LRAD	Left Radius
RFEM	Right Femur
RTIB	Right Tibia
RFIB	Right Fibula
LFEM	Left Femur
LTIB	Left Tibia
LFIB	Left Fibula
- - - - P	Proximal End
- - - - D	Distal End
- - - - F	Fracture Point
- - - - V	Virtual Point*
SPINT	Spine Top
SPINB	Spine Bottom
SPINI	Spine Inflection Point
- - - - FI	Fracture Inflection

*Used only for shoulder and pelvic points (e.g., LSHOV, RPELV).

procedures for surveying of mass graves. Limitations of the ICTY codes and the additions that made for accurate inventory and smooth running of the spatial analysis are detailed in the following text. The standard ICTY codes are still used, with the exception of the central body point (CPOI)—omitted because it really does not assist in mapping or spatial analysis. This set of 14 codes makes up the standard points taken. The additional codes in Table 2-4 are used to clarify the inventory and assist spatial analysis in the case of incomplete remains.

To better represent a cranium that is fragmented, the code CFRG (**C**ranial **Frag**ments) is used. Coding in this manner will notify both a surveyor who is later making a map and mortuary personnel that what is present is a fractured, and possibly incomplete, skull. The code MAND is used for a disarticulated **Mand**ible. If only a portion of the mandible is recovered, a left/right designation can be added.

As noted, one problem with the ICTY codes found during the spatial analysis of BA05 is that incomplete or disarticulated limb ends are not clearly defined. With the ICTY codes, the humeral head of a complete disarticulated left arm would be recorded as a left shoulder (LSHO). A body missing the lower portion of its right leg would have a point recorded on the distal end of the right femur as a right knee (RKNE). Neither one of these points is technically the joint it is recorded to represent because the other bones that make up the joint are absent. Although the codes are adequate for mapping purposes, they force extra steps to be taken during analysis of the spatial relationships between disarticulated remains.

For example, when the ICTY code system is used to generate a list of bodies that a disarticulated left arm may belong to, a query between that arm's humeral head data point (LSHO) would be run against the other LSHO data points in the grave. Results would include not only the potential bodies missing a left arm, but also all the other disarticulated left arms in the grave (added to the results because of their recorded LSHO codes). These other arms would then have to be filtered out of the results.

To get around this additional step and make the spatial analysis program more user-friendly, additions to the coding system for incomplete or disarticulated limbs were made. Similar to the ICTY code system, when the end of a long bone needs to be recorded, a four-letter code is generated, starting with the side that element is from followed by the first three letters of the name of that bone. This is followed by either the suffix "P" for proximal or "D" for distal to indicate from which end of the bone the point is being recorded. The proximal end of the left humerus in the preceding example, instead of being recorded as LSHO, would have the code LHUMP (**L**eft **Hum**erus **P**roximal). The elbow and wrist of a left disarticulated arm would be recorded in the standard method (LELB and LWRI). The distal end of the right femur in the preceding example would be RFEMD (**R**ight **Fem**ur **D**istal), instead of RKNE. To locate possible matches for the disarticulated arm example, one would run the LHUMP data against all LSHO data points from the grave (only body trunks can have this code). For the body missing the lower right leg, its RFEMD data point would be run against RTIBP (**R**ight **Tib**ia **P**roximal) data points of disarticulated lower legs within the grave.

The additional codes listed in Table 2-4 better define disarticulated and fractured elements, allowing for a more accurate field inventory and narrowing the search parameters of potential reassociations by excluding misleading data points from the search. These codes should only be used to record disarticulated limb ends, whereas the standard 14 ICTY codes should be used for articulating joints. In this manner, it will be readily apparent which point on the limb needs to be used in the spatial analysis program and creates a more accurate inventory. Lower arms and legs consist of two long bones. If one needs to record a point on a disarticulated lower limb where both bones are present, we suggest using the ulna and tibia because these bones best articulate to their upper limb counterparts. The fibula and radius should be used if the other bone is absent.

Disarticulation may also occur at fracture points. The ICTY codes are incapable of demonstrating such trauma, forcing the surveyor to stop the recording points at the last joint prior to reaching the fracture. This gives an inaccurate representation of the remains present and will muddy all spatial analysis results. To overcome this, the surveyor should record fracture data points from long bones that are missing one end. These codes are to be understood as the end point of a long bone where the remainder of the bone is missing, and thus no joint, proximal, or distal long bone point could be taken. The fracture point will again be coded by using the side from which the element came, the first three letters of the fractured long bone, then the letter "F" to indicate it is a fracture point, followed by a "P" or "D" suffix denoting the point as the proximal or distal end of that bone (Table 2-4). Because spatial analysis is aimed at assisting in the reassociation of disarticulated remains, perimortem and postmortem fractures are coded the same way. Trauma analysis, as well as all final remains analysis, should be conducted during mortuary analysis.

The hypothetical example in Figure 2-7 illustrates how these fracture codes are used. An otherwise complete body is missing a right arm from mid-shaft humerus down. The regular shoulder point is taken on the body (RSHO), but the elbow is missing—only half the humerus is present. In such a case, a point will be taken on the distal end of the existing proximal section of humerus where the fracture/disarticulation took place. Thus, that point on the body

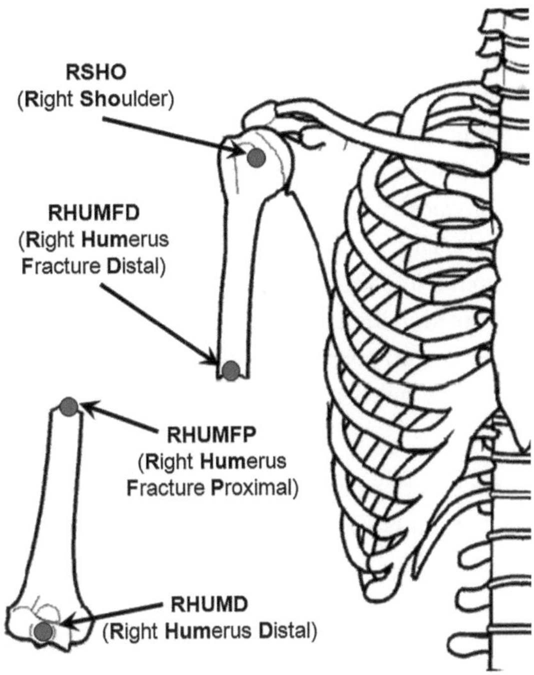

Figure 2-7
Demonstration of survey codes for a right arm disarticulated at mid-shaft humerus due to a fracture. A spatial query search for the missing distal humerus would involve the codes RHUMFD and RHUMFP.

would be recorded as RHUMFD (**R**ight **Hum**erus **F**racture **D**istal end of bone). It is important to understand that a distal designation is given to this **f**racture point because it represents the most **d**istal end of that section of right humerus. The proximal end of this humerus has already been recorded as the right shoulder (RSHO) because it articulates with the body and so does not receive a "proximal" designated point. In an effort to locate the missing lower portion of arm, one would run a spatial analysis query from the body's RHUMFD point to all RHUMFP (**R**ight **Hum**erus **F**racture **P**roximal end of bone) points recorded in the grave. This point represents the **f**racture (and most **p**roximal point) on the disarticulated distal section of a humerus. Only distal ends of humeri disarticulated due to a fracture of the shaft can have this proximal code. However, it will be unknown whether the missing portion of arm consists of the distal humerus with lower arm or just the distal section of humerus (the lower arm being disarticulated from this distal humerus at the elbow).

The query that is run to try to match the disarticulated bone is therefore between the fracture points on the humerus shaft—the point of separation (see Figure 2-7). If the fracture was clean on both bone ends, the fracture pattern can be articulated, and all other possible disarticulated fractured distal humeri can be excluded from consideration. If the articulating distal humerus is absent the lower arm, a second query may be run, this time searching from the distal end of the right humerus (RHUMD) to all possible right proximal ulnae (RULNP) and perhaps radii (RRADP).

In the BA05 inventory data, it was noted that sometimes shoulder and pelvic points on bodies were absent. These survey points were sometimes not recorded because the surveyor felt that not enough of the joint remained present on the body to justify its recording. For example, a surveyor may have omitted taking a shoulder point from a body missing its left arm and scapula. Because the body physically did not have a complete shoulder (only the clavicle remained), no point was taken. This scenario does not present too difficult a problem for mapping purposes, but without a left shoulder data point recorded from the body, reassociation analysis cannot be attempted. Although disarticulated left arms have data points recorded from their proximal ends, there is no corresponding shoulder point on the body available for the spatial analysis program to be queried against. The same would hold true for a body missing one side of its pelvis.

To overcome the lack of a shoulder or pelvic joint to query during spatial analysis, the surveyor needs to record a "virtual point" on the body where the joint would have been. Minor location inaccuracies should present little, if any, difference in the generated list of possible matches from a spatial analysis of the data. To denote the presence of a virtual point, the regular code is followed by the suffix "V" (e.g., LSHOV, RPELV) (see Table 2-4).

An additional concern was how to accurately record the bodies that separated at the spine. From the authors' experience working in mass graves, disarticulation of the spinal column often occurs at the cervical and lumbar regions. Disarticulation occurs regularly enough at the lumbar or lower thoracic region that bodies will often be categorized in evidence logs as "upper" or "lower" bodies (to further confuse the body versus body part classification debate). Likewise, heads often disarticulate with a couple of cervical vertebrae attached. Checking vertebral shape and the articulation between vertebrae offers a good platform for reassociating upper and lower bodies and cranium. To assist mortuary workers in these efforts of reassociation, we suggest that the additional total station codes, listed in Table 2-4, be used to identify the points of disarticulation on a spine: SPINT (**Spin**e **T**op) and SPINB (**Spin**e **B**ottom).

Determination of "top" or "bottom" depends on the anatomical orientation of the body part in question. A lower body consisting of legs, a complete pelvis, and several vertebrae would have a SPINT point recorded on the uppermost vertebrae. A thorax consisting of only thoracic vertebrae and ribs would have a SPINT point recorded on its T1 and a SPINB on T12. A cranium with a couple of cervical vertebrae attached would have the following points recorded on it: CRAN (**Cran**ium) and SPINB (indicating the last attached vertebrae). The presence of SPIN points would indicate to mortuary personnel that reassociation via vertebrae may be possible.

A final suggestion to augment the ICTY codes is the inclusion of an "inflection point." At times, spinal columns and fractured long bones are bent in such a manner that a surveyor making a map may question the accuracy of a recorded point. If a body is bent doubled-over itself in the grave, the mapped connection line made between the cranial point and the central pelvis point representing the spinal column would look absurdly short, perhaps only several centimeters long. The same would hold true for a fractured long bone in a limb radically bent at an impossible angle.

The inclusion of a point where the spinal column or radically bent long bone doubles back on itself would create a more understandable map. Although inflection codes are not used for spatial analysis (radical inflection may be present, but disarticulation is not), the inclusion of an inflection point will denote the presence of the extreme bend, possibly assisting mortuary personnel in their postmortem analysis. To indicate a spinal column inflection point, as indicated in Table 2-4, an "I" is added to the end of the regular SPIN code (SPINI). In an effort to keep survey time short, the surveyor should record fracture inflection points only when the bend is so great that he or she knows it may cause confusion during map generation. A fracture inflection point is recorded by adding an "I" instead of a distal or proximal suffix after the regular fracture code (e.g., LFEMFI). Thus, a left femur fractured midshaft and radically bent would have three points recorded on it: LPEL, LFEMFI, and LKNE (LFEMD if the lower leg is absent) (Figure 2-8).

Figure 2-9 illustrates the approximate location of most of the additional survey codes described previously. As explained, some of the codes can be combined when confronted with fractures and inflection points. Although not all the combinations are reflected in the figure, the illustration serves as a reference to help visualize survey possibilities. Although the list of

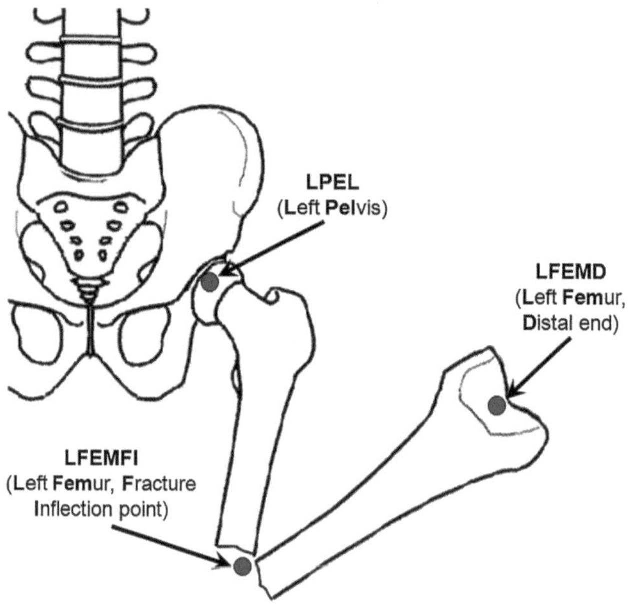

Figure 2-8
Demonstration of survey codes for a left femur inflection point due to a mid-shaft fracture. The purpose of recording inflection points is to assist in mapping, not for conducting spatial queries.

combined ICTY and suggested augmented survey codes appears lengthy, ICMP personnel using the new code system during excavation of several mass graves have found them to be very manageable. Most recorded points on a body will consist of the original 14 ICTY codes. The additional codes we suggest here are only used when remains are disarticulated or when the standard codes cannot accurately represent the elements present. It is suggested that the surveyor use a list of the codes and an illustration like Figure 2-9 as a reference in the field. We have found it convenient to hang the codes directly on the total station tripod for quick reference.

All codes suggested here are just those: suggestions. We have found these codes to satisfactorily work in *realistic* international situations involving complex mass graves, and we feel they reach a level of accuracy that serves both the investigation and identification goals of the various organizations we have worked for without exceeding timelines and budgets. However, if investigation organizers decide that smaller elements not represented within our suggested coding system are to receive the same attention as larger, more complete elements, additional codes could be created by using the same system proposed here. For example, a disarticulated **l**eft **han**d may be coded LHAN.

Whatever the codes decided on, the important point to keep in mind is that all codes must be *consistently* applied to all remains recovered for the spatial analysis program to be *consistently* helpful. The same coding system should be consistently applied to all the graves

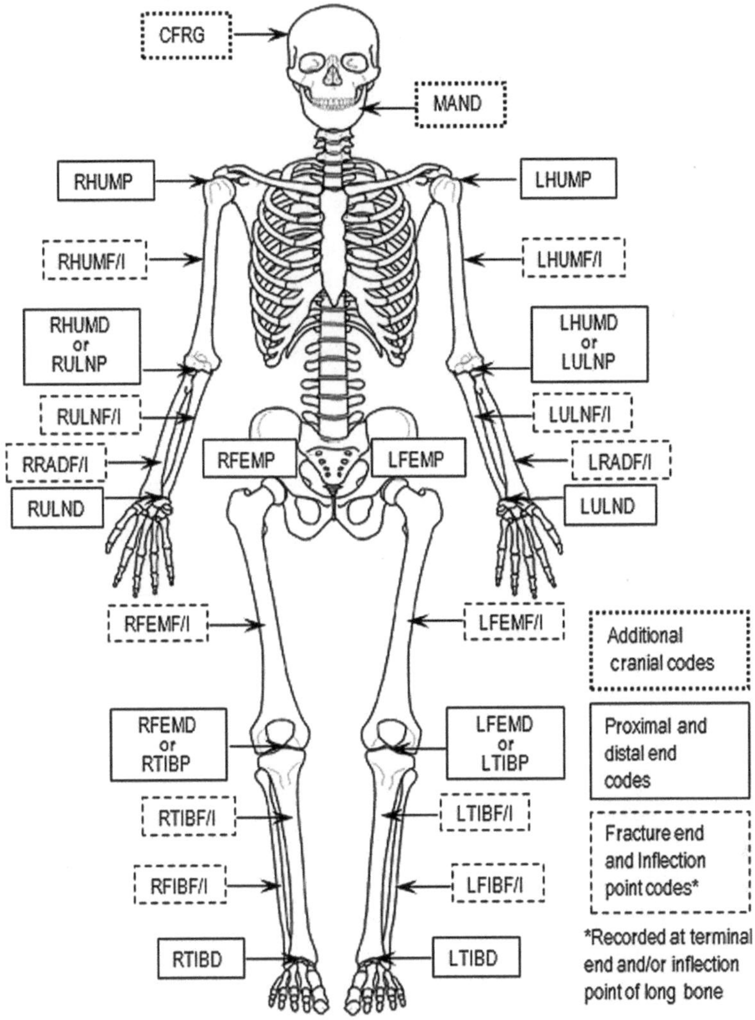

FIGURE 2-9
Illustration of suggested additional survey codes.

scheduled for excavation. If all graves created during a conflict are to be excavated, then the work will most likely take several years and be done by different personnel making up the excavation teams. Thus, standard survey codes must be decided on *prior* to excavation of the first grave and be consistently applied over the entire course of work. If not, there will be a build-up of conflicting codes that will inhibit reassociations. Changes in survey codes will only complicate the identification process, inhibit accurate spatial analysis, and create inconsistencies in the evidence log. Inconsistent recording of survey points is akin to inconstancies of recording evidence at a crime scene: the more that are introduced, the weaker the evidence. The adage "garbage in, garbage out" applies.

It should be noted that spatial analysis can be run using data containing only ICTY-type codes. However, as shown, these codes are limited. The analyst will have to spend extra time filtering the data, which would most likely involve searching through secondary sources such as field exhumation notes/body exhumation forms and photographs. Ideally, the analyst would be someone working in the mortuary who could run a spatial query on a particular case immediately after it is found to be missing an element. It is postulated that the use of only ICTY-coded data would slow down such a process to the point that running a query in the mortuary would not be beneficial. Although this does not exclude the possibility of running queries outside the mortuary prior to autopsy, the suggested additional codes proposed here, if properly implemented during excavation, would allow for direct field data transfer into the mortuary.

On a final note, although we have suggested a set of codes to augment the ICTY recording system, we recognize that computer technology is constantly advancing at a pace such that these codes are likely to become obsolete in the future. This is the main reason we are not providing the algorithm we used for our study. We can envision platforms such as computer tablets preprogrammed with a skeletal homunculus running total stations where one only needs to touch the screen to differentiate between a B, BP, or GBP. Limb joints, disarticulation points, fractures, and radical inflections will be defined with simple touches to the screen. Instead of having to download the recorded points to a separate program for manipulation, maps will be generated in real time as the remains, artifacts, and grave features are uncovered at the grave. Perhaps a spatial analysis of the data could be run while still in the field, giving the mortuary team advance notice of possible reassociations.

Although our suggested codes are destined to become antiquated, the idea of spatial analysis will continue to be relevant and useful regardless of the platform used. Whoever develops the next generation of total station data loggers/tablets for use in mass graves will still need to program algorithms that best capture the spatial data of disarticulated remains. With that in mind, this study provides enough insight into the strategy of resolving commingling problems with excavation-generated three-dimensional data that competent programmers will be able to construct their platforms successfully.

Conclusion

The combination of numerous bodies and taphonomic conditions, to include time afforded to decomposition and intentional disturbance or destruction of remains within a mass grave context, can all contribute to disarticulation and commingling. Although there is wide agreement that careful excavation is necessary and can contribute to mortuary analysis of remains, few examples exist of excavation data being applied within the laboratory. The spatial analysis of remains distribution within a grave is one method of bridging the gap between field and mortuary activities. By providing a list that ranks the most likely reassociations by distance from each other, spatial analysis can assist mortuary personnel with the reassociation of disarticulated body parts.

During the excavation of mass grave BA05, ICTY survey codes were used to record body and body part positions. A spatial analysis of the remains distribution within the grave was conducted using DNA matching results as a control. Results for the relatively complex grave show that the spatial analysis provides good evidence that certain bodies and body parts belong together. In secondary mass graves or other complex situations, the probability would be expected to be less. In such complex cases, analysis by separate deposits of human remains within the grave, as opposed to spatial searches involving all elements within the whole grave, will most likely prove to be a useful strategy. To create a more accurate inventory and easier spatial analysis queries, we have suggested a number of additional survey codes to augment the standard ICTY codes.

Ensuring a good documentation process in the field, and data flow from field to the mortuary, will result in a detailed field inventory of recovered remains—useful as evidence, for planning of mortuary processes, and for quick first rough estimates of remains represented in a grave—and can assist in reassociation of disarticulated remains. The concept of using spatial data to help assist in problems of commingled remains is not mind-boggling, nor should its implementation be complex. The only necessary elements are consistent coding during survey of remains with an eye toward spatial analysis and a plan to use the analysis during autopsy. The authors encourage the creation of the next generation of field hardware and software and look forward to seeing how these tools help tackle the problems of commingled remains.

Acknowledgments

The authors would first like to thank Sharna Daley for her tremendous assistance with the first edition of this study, of which she was a coauthor. Although she declined to take part in the second edition, her work is well represented within this study. All authors were employed by the International Commission on Missing Persons (ICMP) during the initial development of this study, and we would like to thank ICMP for the continued cooperation and interest that led to completion of this work.

References

Bass, W.M., Birkby, W.H., 1978. Exhumation: The method could make the difference. FBI Bull. 47, 6–11.

Buikstra, J.E., Gordon, C.C., Hoyme, L.S., 1984. The case of the severed skull: Individuation in forensic anthropology. In: Rathbun, T.A., Buikstra, J.E. (Eds.), Human Identification: Case Studies in Forensic Anthropology. Charles C. Thomas, Springfield, IL, pp. 121–135.

Byrd, J.E., Adams, B.J., 2003. Osteometric sorting of commingled human remains. J. Forensic Sci. 48 (4), 717–724.

Cabo, L.L., Dirkmaat, D.C., Adovasio, J.M., Rozas, V.C., 2012. Archaeology, mass graves, and resolving commingling issues through spatial analysis. In: Dirkmaat, D.C. (Ed.), A Companion to Forensic Anthropology. Wiley-Blackwell, Malden, MA, pp. 175–196.

Dirkmaat, D.C., Adovasio, J.M., 1997. The role of archaeology in the recovery and interpretation of human remains from an outdoor forensic setting. In: Haglund, W.H., Sorg, M.H. (Eds.), Forensic Taphonomy. CRC Press, Boca Raton, FL, pp. 39–64.

Dirkmaat, D.C., Cabo, L.L., 2012. Forensic anthropology: Embracing the new paradigm. In: Dirkmaat, D.C. (Ed.), A Companion to Forensic Anthropology. Wiley-Blackwell, Malden, MA, pp. 3–40.

Dirkmaat, D.C., Cabo, L.L., Ousley, S.D., Symes, S.A., 2008. New perspectives in forensic anthropology. Yearbook Phys. Anthropol. 51, 33–52.

Haglund, W.D., 2001. Archaeology and forensic death investigations. Historic Archaeol. 35 (1), 25–38.

Hanson, I., Sterenberg, J., Wessling, R., 2000. Survey procedures. ICTY forensic field team Bosnia. 2000 field season. ICTY forensic field team Bosnia and Croatia 2000. Manuscript on file, Exhumation and Examinations Division. International Commission on Missing Persons, Sarajevo, Bosnia and Herzegovina.

Jessee, E., Skinner, M., 2005. A typology of mass grave-related sites. Forensic Sci. Int. 152 (1), 55–59.

Morse, D., Crusoe, D., Smith, H.G., 1976. Forensic archaeology. Am. J. Phys. Anthropol. 35 (1), 35–38.

Owsley, D.W., 2001. Why the forensic anthropologist needs the archaeologist. Historic Archaeol. 35 (1), 25–38.

Rodriguez III, W.C., 2005. Methods and Techniques for Sorting Commingled Remains: Anthropological and Physical Attributes. Paper presented at the 57th Annual Meeting of the American Academy of Forensic Sciences, New Orleans, LA.

Skinner, M., 1987. Planning the archaeological recovery of evidence from recent mass graves. Forensic Sci. Int. 34 (4), 267–287.

Tuller, H., Đurić, M., 2006. Keeping the pieces together: Comparison of mass grave excavation methodology. Forensic Sci. Int. 156 (2–3), 192–200.

Tuller, H., Hofmeister, U., Daley, S., 2005. The Importance of Body Deposition Recording in Event Reconstruction and the Reassociation and Identification of Commingled Remains. Paper presented at the 57th Annual Meeting of the American Academy of Forensic Sciences, New Orleans, LA.

Ubelaker, D.H., 2002. Approaches to the study of commingling in human skeletal biology. In: Haglund, W.D., Sorg, M.H. (Eds.), Advances in Forensic Taphonomy: Methods, Theory, and Archaeological Perspectives. CRC Press, Boca Raton, FL, pp. 331–351.

Wagner, S.E., 2008. To Know Where He Lies: DNA Technology and the Search for Srebrinica's Missing. University of California Press, Berkeley, CA.

Wright, R., 1992. Correlation between cranial form and geography in Homo sapiens: CRANID—a computer program for forensic and other applications. Archaeol. Oceania 27 (3), 128–135.

Wright, R., 2003. Program NN_ICMP.EXE: A computer program for nearest neighbours spatial analysis of forensic exhumations. Manuscript on file, Exhumation and Examinations Division. International Commission on Missing Persons, Sarajevo, Bosnia and Herzegovina.

Wright, R., 2005. Archaeology of mass graves. In: Hunter, J., Cox, M. (Eds.), Forensic Archaeology: Advances in Theory and Practice. Routledge, Oxon and New York, pp. 137–158.

CHAPTER 3

Recovery Methods for Cremated Commingled Remains: Analysis and Interpretation of Small Fragments Using a Bioarchaeological Approach

Stephan Naji[1], Camille de Becdeliévre[2], Sélim Djouad[3], Henri Duday[1], Aurélie André[1,4], Stéphane Rottier[1]

[1]Université de Bordeaux, UMR PACEA, France [2]University of Belgrade, Department of Archaeology, Laboratory for Bioarchaeology, Serbia [3]Hadès–Bureau d'investigations archéologiques, France [4]Service Archéologique de la Ville de Lyon, France

Introduction

The purpose of this chapter is to consider the limits and contributions of gross analyses of commingled cremated human remains from a bioarchaeology perspective integrating the use of a geographic information system database. The experience of bioarchaeologists with archaeological cremations in various chronological and cultural contexts allowed them to develop and test several protocols depending on the degree of bone fragmentation or the number of bodies involved in a deposit. Burnt bones discovered in burial urns, for example, are often reduced to fragments rarely exceeding a few centimeters, deformed, and discolored by heat, desiccation, anthropogenic manipulations, or taphonomic phenomena (McKinley 1993; Van Andriga et al. 2013). For these reasons, anthropologists have often underestimated the potential for cremains, stemming from a lack of training in osteology or archaeological techniques. In addition, the interpretative potential inherent to these small fragments has been generally underestimated up until the recent publication of comprehensive books in forensic anthropology dedicated to cremains (Fairgrieve 2008; Symes et al. 2008), or interpretative protocols in archaeology (Duday et al. 2000; McKinley 1993, 1994). Because cremated remains from archaeological contexts are probably the most complex to analyze, implementing bioarchaeological protocols to forensic death scenes or skeletal identification is one of the most essential recent advances in forensic anthropology (Symes et al. 2008) and provides critical insights into crime scene contexts and interpretation of data. In addition, biological anthropologists are now increasingly involved in litigation of commercially cremated remains over disputed identity, excessive commingling, or negligent cremation

Commingled Human Remains. http://dx.doi.org/10.1016/B978-0-12-405889-7.00003-4

practices (Schultz et al. 2008; Warren and Van Deest, this book, Chapter 11). In these particular instances, the forensic approach is closest to bioarchaeology in dealing with dry, small, burnt fragments and should thus systematically draw from their mutual experiences (Duday and Guillon 2006).

Documentation

Recovery

Recovery of cremains should follow standard bioarchaeology excavation protocols and should be recorded by layers defined by all the fragments that can be removed without disturbing the underlying level (Duday 2009; Fairgrieve 2008). It is necessary to identify as many remains as possible *in situ* during field recovery because additional fragmentation may occur during recovery, transport, and laboratory analysis. Excavation, recording, and collecting methods are thus critical to efficiently integrate even the smallest fragments into the overall analysis. Investigation sites of fragmented cremated remains should be excavated following a grid system in order to document the location of every fragment (Figure 3-1). In archaeological contexts, empirical tests have demonstrated that the most efficient grid is between 20 × 20 to 30 × 30 cm (Bel 1996). The largest fragments (> 3 cm) can be individually located and should be geo-referenced, while the smallest (< 3 cm) can be grouped by grid square. The goal is to identify whether or not a meaningful arrangement is present in order to exploit the potential spatial distribution of cremains. Sieving should be adapted to the field context.

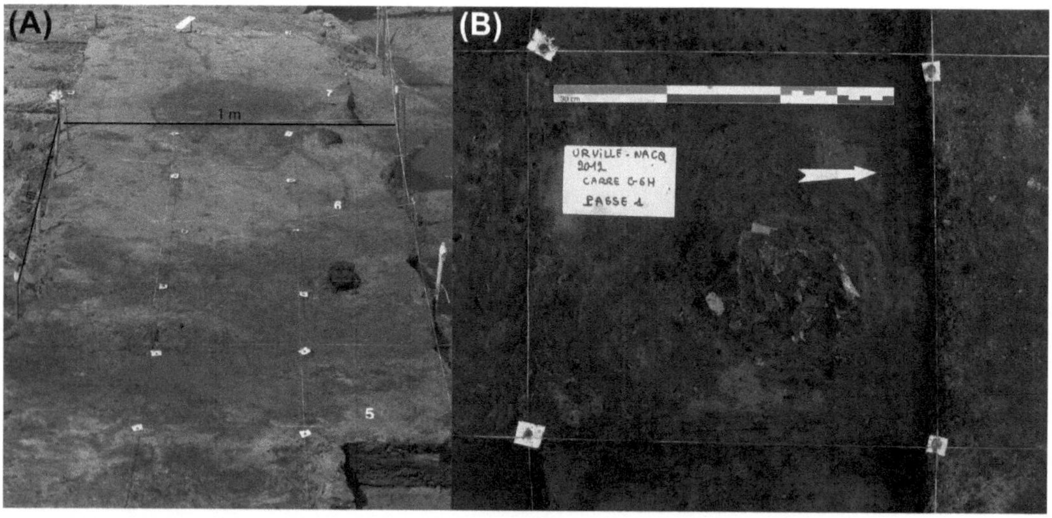

Figure 3-1
Excavation grid. (A) Oblique view of excavation grid for cremation area. (B) Overhead view of a square with cremains concentration. Iron Age site of Urville-Nacqueville, France. *(Source: Photos S. Rottier.)*

Identification

To optimize identification, multiple observations are needed on surface aspect, morphology, internal organization, and section shape simultaneously. In several archaeological studies, the identification rate of burnt fragments has been regularly reported above 80% for fragments heavier than 1.5 g (André et al. 2013; Van Andriga et al. 2013, fig. 386). It is therefore necessary to push the identification process beyond the traditional skeletal analysis, which consists of sorting cranial, postcranial, and indeterminate fragments (Devlin and Herrmann 2008). The cremains should be sorted by anatomical regions: "head," "trunk," "upper limb," "lower limb," or by bone types ("diaphysis," "flat bone," "epiphysis–short bone") when precise sorting is not possible. Here, we underline key anatomical features helpful in identifying cremains:

Cranial vault: This flat bone has characteristic bubble-like spherical lacunae homogeneously distributed and of comparable diameter in the diploe. During cremation, the two tables crack and get separated, often ripping away part of the diploe. This specific anatomical feature is characteristic even for fragments under 2 mm (Figure 3-2).
Teeth: Enamel easily fissures because of its high mineral content that creates a differential expansion with dentin when heated. Enamel can then easily fragment during post-depositional movement. Dentin, however, is much more resistant because of its mineral content. Dentin looks smoother and denser than bone and will often exhibit fine surface fissures. Most dental fragments greater than 1 mm are thus identifiable. Root shape,

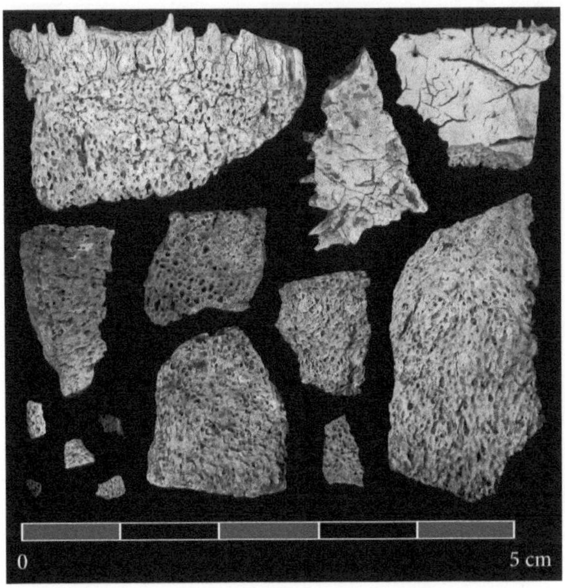

Figure 3-2
Cranial vault. Surface aspect of compact bone and diploe on burnt cranial vault remains. Archaeological site of Al Claus (Varen, Tarn-et-Garonne, France). *(Source: Photo by S. Djouad, 2013.)*

when partially preserved, can be used to determine exact tooth type. For immature individuals, dental germs are often well preserved, probably because of the thermal protection given by the surrounding alveolar bone, and can thus be easily identified (Figure 3-3).

Vertebrae: The body is characterized by two distinct features: thin compact bones exhibiting some degree of "large" (millimetric) porosity on the circumference, and upper and lower articular surfaces that exhibit finer (micrometric) porosity. Trabecular bone is relatively light and is mainly organized according to a gradient grid from the center toward the upper and lower surfaces. Posterior arches are identifiable because of their typical morphology and articular facets, which also allow differentiating between vertebral types (Figure 3-4). Vertebrae can fragment but deform only slightly. These criteria enable us to correctly identify fragments greater than 5 mm. Below that size, fragments are usually classified in the "epiphysis–short bone" category.

Ribs: Identifying ribs is unambiguous because of their flat bone organization and trabecular small-grid pattern, stretched in the direction of the bone's main axis. Outer and inner tables are often found separated and will fragment in a multitude of smaller pieces. Even worn down, however, ribs are still identifiable—even 2 mm long fragments (Figure 3-5). This organization does slightly change posterior of the neck and head angle. For these fragments, the external morphology is usually enough to properly identify the piece.

Figure 3-3

Dentin. Surface aspect of burnt teeth fragments. Archaeological site of Al Claus (Varen, Tarn-et-Garonne, France). *(Source: Photo by S. Djouad, 2013.)*

Figure 3-4

Vertebrae. Surface aspect of vertebral bodies and neural arches. 1. Articular process; 2. Nonarticular surface of vertebral body; 3. Epiphyseal ring; 4. Articular surface of vertebral body. Archaeological site of Al Claus (Varen, Tarn-et-Garonne, France). *(Source: Photo by S. Djouad, 2013.)*

Figure 3-5

Ribs. Surface aspect of skeletal trabeculae from burnt rib fragments. Archaeological site of "La ZAC Technopole" (Metz, Moselle, France). *(Source: Photo by S. Djouad, 2013.)*

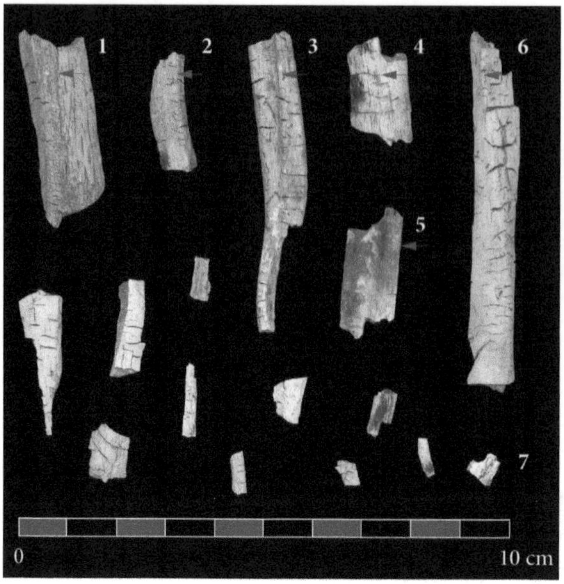

Figure 3-6
Diaphyses. Surface aspect of burnt long bones' diaphyses. 1. Femur, *linea aspera* (posterior-lateral view); 2. Tibia, anterior border (anterior view); 3. Fibula, anterior border (anterior view); 4. Ulna, posterior border (posterior-medial view); 5. Radius, interosseous crest (anterior view); 6. Ulna, interosseous crest (anterior-lateral view); 7. Indeterminate fragments. Archaeological site of Al Claus (Varen, Tarn-et-Garonne, France). *(Source: Photo by S. Djouad, 2013.)*

Long bones (upper and lower limbs): Long bones such as the humerus or metatarsals are composed of a diaphysis and two ends. Except for the clavicle, long bones contain trabecular bone only in their distal and proximal fourth (i.e., about half the total length of the bone). A long bone central part without trabecular bone tends to retract, deform, and fragment during combustion. Because long bones' diaphyses are usually composed of relatively thick cortical bone, most millimetric fragments can thus be classified as "undetermined diaphysis" (Figure 3-6). Discriminating between each long bone requires cautious identification of characteristic external morphology (e.g., section) because taphonomic processes will impact the shape of the bone. Proximal and distal ends can be identified by looking at the internal trabecular organization in addition to external morphology. Articular surfaces are thin and smooth with a trabecular network that gets denser as it reaches the external surface (Figure 3-7). Indeterminate fragments are classified in the "epiphysis–short bone" category.

Short bones: Short bones such as the carpal or tarsal bones are composed of a volume of trabecular bone enclosed by a thin layer of compact bone. During combustion, short bones tend to retract and fragment. Determination is mainly based on articular morphology and trabecular organization. Bones can thus be classified in the corresponding category (upper limb, lower limb, or indeterminate limb). Indeterminate fragments are, however, classified in the "epiphysis–short bone" category (Figure 3-7).

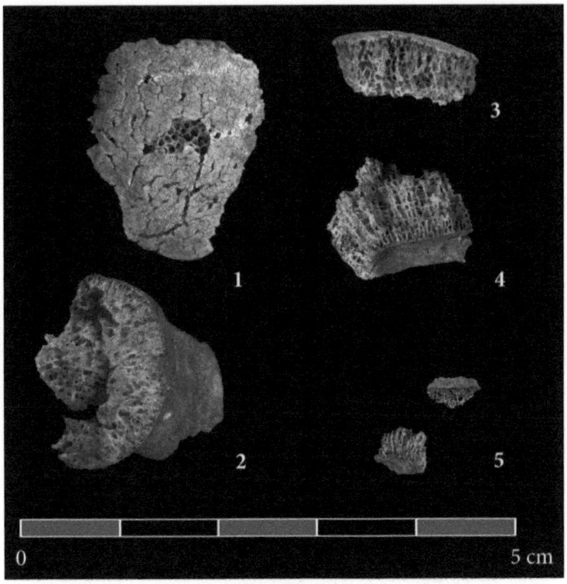

Figure 3-7

Epiphyses. Surface aspect and sections of burnt articular ends.1. Humerus, proximal end; 2. Humerus, fragment of *trochlea*; 3. Femur, fragment of femoral head; 4. Tibia, fragment of distal end; 5. Short bone-epiphysis, indeterminate fragments. Archaeological site of Al Claus (Varen, Tarn-et-Garonne, France). *(Source: Photo by S. Djouad, 2013.)*

Flat bones: Flat bones such as the scapula or ilium are composed of two tables of compact bones with trabecular bones in between. In some instances, the tables can be attached (e.g., infra-spinous fossa of the scapula). During combustion, flat bones tend to retract, and the tables can get separated. Flat bones can always be identified because even when the trabecular part is destroyed, their internal print is always visible regardless of the fragment's dimension (Figure 3-8). Precise identification of flat bone requires the identification of additional gross features.

Documentation

The analysis of highly fragmented, commingled remains requires crossing weight and spatial analyses to address differential fragmentation and the structure of the deposit, and to evaluate the depositional and postdepositional dynamic of cremains. These steps can be achieved only if they are planned prior to the excavation and fully integrated into the field protocol.

To address these issues, we are proposing two different tools: a recording spreadsheet and the use of a GIS database. Of course, this procedure is only necessary if a spatial structure is suspected. If the assemblage is known to be random, such as in commercial cremations, spatial documentation could be limited to simpler variables.

Figure 3-8
Flat bones. Surface and skeletal *trabeculae* aspect of burnt flat bones. 1. Right iliac wing near the anterior inferior iliac spine; 2. Indeterminate fragments. Archaeological site of "La ZAC Technopole" (Metz, Moselle, France). *(Source: Photo by S. Djouad, 2013.)*

Recording forms: Here, we present a spreadsheet used in archaeological context dedicated to recording cremains by weight (http://www.pacea.cnrs.fr/Classeurs-Excel-Cremation.html). The goal of this form is to look at skeletal representation and vertical or horizontal distribution of cremains, and to explore the overall organization of the deposit (Duday et al. 2000; Van Andriga et al. 2013). Each fragment's information is entered on the spreadsheet by stratigraphic level (column) and by anatomical region (lines). When fragments cannot be positively associated with a specific bone, they should be classified into the broader categories: "flat," "short–epiphysis–trabecular," or "diaphysis." Smaller fragments (< 5 mm) cannot always be identified and should be recorded and weighted as a group. The spreadsheet automatically generates several graphs estimated from the fragments' weight, which is more reliable than the fragments' number (Duday et al. 2000).

Mapping the site: GIS databases can be used to integrate dynamically contextual information by adding additional layers of data (e.g., topographic maps, altitudes, soils). Because direct input of individual geographical coordinates for each fragment is time consuming and may be unrealistic in forensic crime scenes, proper digital photographs can be used as a basis for the GIS mapping. Each photograph must correspond to one grid square and, if necessary, to a stratigraphic level of the remains (Figure 3-1). Geographical coordinates of the corners of the grid must be recorded to properly position the entire deposit. A 3D (X, Y, Z) representation of the skeletal deposit is then possible if Z

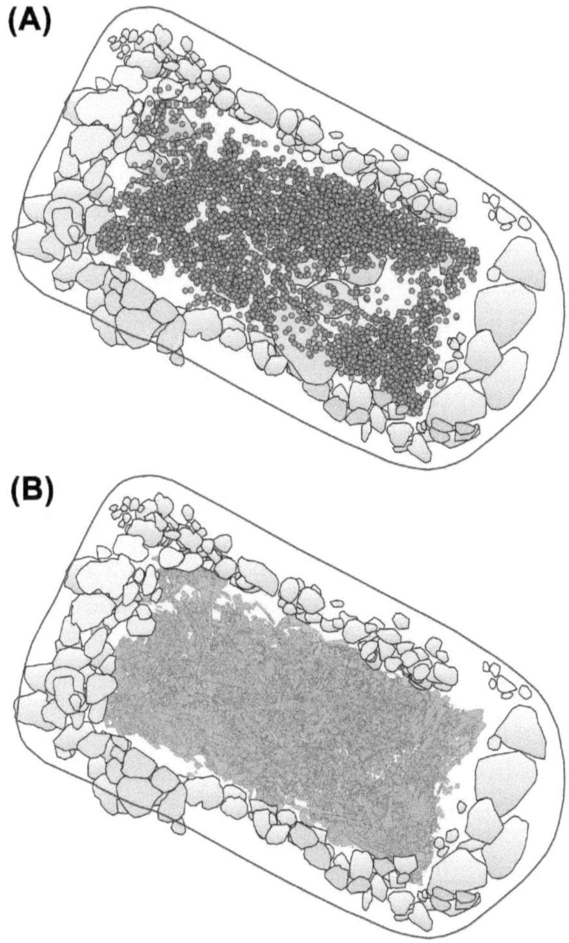

FIGURE 3-9
Archaeological site of "La Truie Pendue" (France). (A) Map of bone's upper layer represented by a centroid. (B) Corresponding map of vector-based drawing of the same layer of bone. *(Source: C. de Becdelièvre.)*

coordinates are recorded by fragment, grid, or layer, depending on the precision of analyses required. When this first step is complete a full map can be re-created from the digital pictures in the laboratory. Actually drawing each fragment (using vector-based drawing software) or only using an average "centroid" for each remain depends on the resources available and the investigation goals (Figure 3-9). If needed, most GIS packages include a geo-referenced scanning option to convert photos into geo-referenced documents. A centroid can then be assigned to each fragment (either manually or using automated built-in algorithms) to obtain a proper dynamic map of the cremains. GIS protocols should be defined according to the excavation's goal and prior to the actual recovery of the cremains to optimize data recording during excavation.

Analyses

MNI

A primary task when confronted with commingled human remains, cremated or not, is to establish how many individuals are present. Analysis of commingled cremains should focus first on macroscopic observation and their statistical treatment, especially as they are applicable in the field. Other analyses may be possible, such as DNA or elemental signature (Schultz et al. 2008), to match fragments to specific individuals, but in addition to cost and time issues related to these approaches, DNA is usually destroyed above 600°C and very often even below (Walker et al. 2008). Because we are mainly considering small burnt fragments, the use of elaborate methods (Adams and Konigsberg 2004, Konigsberg and Adams, this book, Chapter 9) to estimate the number of individuals present in a commingled assemblage is usually not possible.

We can conclude that more than one individual is present using the following criteria: (a) the identification of two identical bones; (b) an age incompatibility; (c) a major size difference (here we emphasize "major" because of potential differential heat retractions); and (d) more rarely, from pathological inconsistencies in cases of diagnosed systematic disease such as advanced syphilis or bone cancer (Demangeot 2008; Duday et al., 2000; Villena i Mota et al. 1996).

If none of these indicators are observable, the average weight of skeletal remains is the only way to estimate the number of individuals present. The mean average weight recorded in crematoriums today ranges from 1,760.3 g to 3,379 g (Bass and Jantz 2004; Depierre 2010; May 2011; Van Deest et al. 2011). Any greater mass of cremains should be investigated as evidence of more than one individual. Any smaller mass of cremains may indicate some selection process. These two statements also depend on the health status of the subject. For example, these weight ranges are not true when the subject has developed ankylosing spondylitis (then the weight can be greater; Duday 2009) or when the individual had osteoporosis (then the weight can be lower; Van Andringa et al. 2013). The weight index of identified anatomical regions should, however, be taken into account, as well as the sex and age if possible, to help discriminate between these two categories.

Finally, GIS mapping of biological data has proven effective to help evaluate the minimum number of individuals (MNI) or minimum number of elements (MNE) in bioarchaeological contexts (Devlin and Herrmann 2008; Herrmann 2008; Marean et al. 2001). Multicriteria requests in the database can help to isolate specific bodies or body parts disturbed by postdepositional processes (e.g., segments of the vertebral column) (Figure 3-10).

Biological Profile

Because we are dealing with small fragments, a conservative approach should be adopted in order to avoid false positives due to overconfident estimations that could misguide the

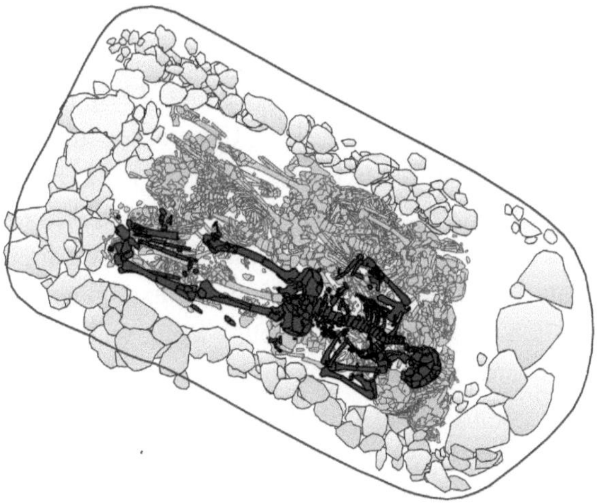

FIGURE 3-10

Identification of skeletal parts using GIS multicriteria requests by bone type. *(Source: C. de Becdelièvre.)*

medical examiner. In most cases, sex and age diagnoses will be very limited. Studies using total cremains weight to discriminate between sexes (Van Deest et al. 2011) should be considered tentative at best, even if the complete recovery of cremains is attested.

Age estimation will be mostly limited to subadults if growing dental remains or epiphyses are identifiable. For adults, traditional estimators will be even worse on cremains than on unaltered bones. One approach using cementum annulation counting on the dental root can be attempted, however, when temperature of combustion is below 600°C (Gocha and Schutkowski 2013). This approach, when properly implemented (Naji et al. in press; Wittwer-Backofen et al. 2004; Wittwer-Backofen 2012), can significantly help narrow down age categories.

Some pathologies are observable on small fragments, particularly degenerative lesions and trauma that are readily identifiable (Bohnert 2002; Reinhard 1994) and may be helpful in some cases (trauma) to narrow down the cause of death. In some rare instances, specific pathologies can be used when target populations are preferentially or exclusively male or female, such as internal frontal hyperostosis, which occurs most often in menopausal women (Van Andriga et al. 2013).

Temperature of Cremation

Several authors have published scales defining bone colors and density in order to evaluate cremation stages and temperature. A general relationship and basic pattern are accepted between thermal-induced changes and the temperature and duration of heating (Devlin and Herrmann 2008; Fairgrieve 2008; Shipman et al. 1984; Susini 1988; Walker et al. 2008). As long as the analyst understands that color does not uniquely depend on temperature, but rather on both temperature and duration of the combustion, these scales can be used to evaluate some of the fire's parameters (Figure 3-11). Temperature affecting bones is, of course, linked to several parameters such as the amount of oxygen available (Périnet 1982), the layers surrounding a body (clothing, amount of fat) (Bass and Jantz 2004; Christensen 2002; Holck 1986), and the actual position of the body in relationship to the fire (Binford 1972; Herrmann 1972; Symes et al. 2008). Duration is dependent on combustion mode and whether or not someone is "assisting" the combustion by feeding the fire and by manipulating the remains so that they are constantly exposed to the most intense part of the pyre. For example, when oxygen is available (oxidation), cremains are often very white. On the other hand, when oxygen is not available (reduction), cremains usually are brownish-black. In high-temperature exposure, "fresh" cadavers often result in very deformed bones of white-gray-blue colors (de Becdelievre et al. 2014a). In addition to bone colors, the examination of warping, cracking, fracturing, and fragmentation has been used to reconstruct the original physical circumstances of the cremation. If simultaneously analyzed, these indicators, beyond being an impediment to the understanding of the deposit, actually provide valuable clues regarding the depositional and postdepositional

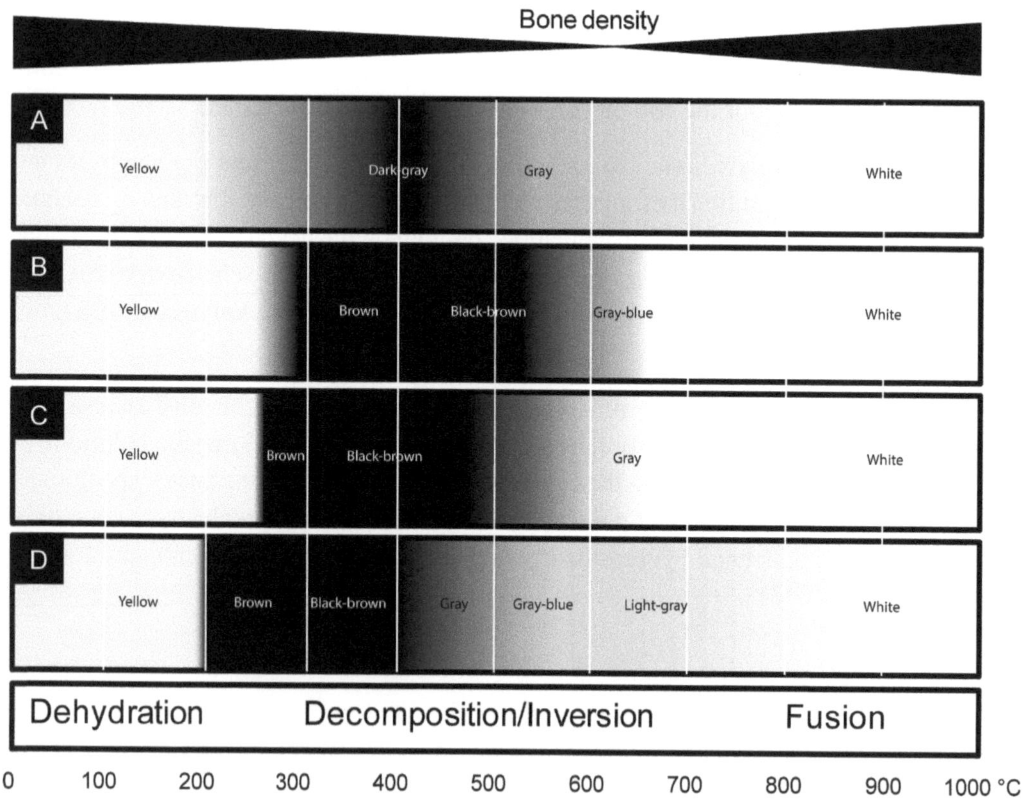

FIGURE 3-11
Illustration of color changes during combustion, in relation to bone density and chemical transformation. *(Source: Adapted from A: Holck 1986; B:Wahl 1981; C: Susini et al. 1988; D: Hummet et al. 1988.)*

history of the cremains. Exploring color distribution can help document several parameters such as fuel and oxidant, state of cadavers prior to incineration, intensity and dynamic of combustion, and "processing" and "management" of the fire (de Becdelievre et al. 2014a;b).

Interpretation

The purpose of the excavation and recording protocols presented in the preceding sections is to evaluate and analyze weight, size, degree of fragmentation, representation by anatomical regions, and spatial distribution of every fragment uncovered (Duday et al. 2000; Duday 2009). The goal of the analyses is to identify potential biases in skeletal representations within an assemblage and understand and interpret spatial organization of cremains deposits. The initial assessment is necessary to identify the number of victims present at a scene, especially when there is little prior information such as in a house fire, or random discovery of a crime scene with cremains. Estimating the presence or absence of individual elements also indicates if part of the body was removed or processed at a different location. The second interpretative step addresses issues of postdepositional manipulations of the remains in order to highlight the motivation to voluntarily hide, displace, or increase the destruction of the remains. In bioarchaeology, the goal of analysis is often to understand funerary rituals, whereas in a forensic context, the goal is to understand how an accident or a crime scene could have produced a commingled assemblage.

Representation of Anatomical Regions

For individuals of adult size, the proportion of each skeletal element or region has been documented in relation to total skeleton weight. In most cases, the study conducted by Lowrance and Latimer (1957) and modified by Duday et al. (2000) summarizes most of the known range variation in skeleton weight from modern crematorium to archaeological sites. Using this information allows us to evaluate if each region is homogeneously represented or if there is a significant bias. Of course, weight indices are different for children, and references should be adapted accordingly. Unfortunately, very few publications are available on this topic (Trotter and Hixon 1974). Contrary to general beliefs, weight variations generated by heat on bone type do not have a real influence on proportions of various anatomical regions and thus on their interpretations (André et al. 2013; Trotter and Peterson 1962). We can therefore identify information from specific graph patterns generated by the record sheet Figure 3-12 and compare them to reference values (Table 3-1). In the example proposed in Figure 3-12, we can see that in the lower layers (1–5), the head (solid black) is overrepresented and the lower limbs (solid gray) are underrepresented, whereas in the lower layers (6–9) the pattern is reversed. The trunk (horizontal lines) and upper limbs (diagonal lines) are more or less homogeneously represented throughout the layers and correspond to the expected frequencies.

Figure 3-12: Proportional Fragment's Weight Distribution by Anatomical Regions (y-Axis) and Stratigraphic Layer (x-Axis)*

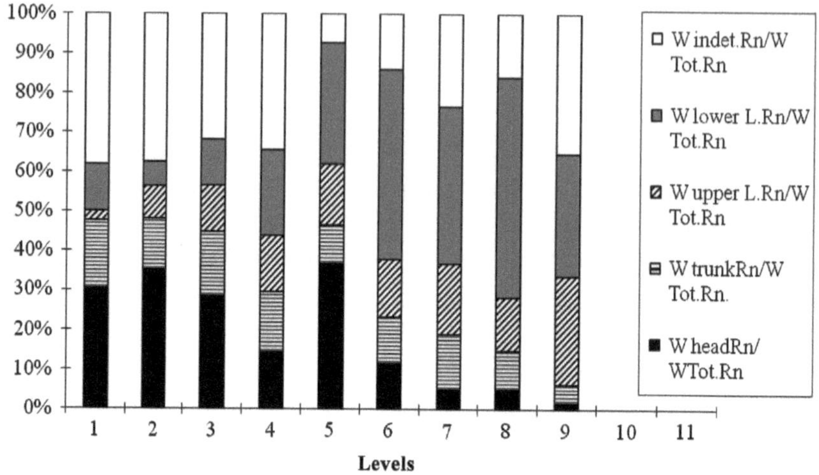

*W = weight; L = limb; R = level of excavation. Ex: "W lower L.R_1/W Totl.R_1" = the weight of the lower limbs fragments for the level R_1 divided by the weight of the total number of fragments for level R_1. *(Source: Modified from van Andringa et al. 2013.)*

TABLE 3-1: Summary Values for Reference Weight Data Adapted from Lowrance and Latimer (1957)*

	Weight (Average in g.)	Weight (Standard Deviation)	Weight (Relative)
Skeleton	2882	365	
Head	588.2	99.6	20.41%
Trunk	488.5	89.36	16.95%
Upper limb	510.43	100.88	17.71%
Lower limb	1298.7	219.78	45.06%

*For detailed individual anatomical elements, see van Andringa et al. 2013, fig2b:13.

Spatial Distribution of Cremated Remains

The identification of anatomic organization in the distribution allows us to address the issue of handling (or absence of handling) of the remains during or after combustion. The goal is to characterize the depositional dynamic by integrating all contextual variables of the assemblage (whether a crime scene or an archaeological site) and to interpret it. The record sheet generates graphs by layers of excavation providing information on the vertical distribution of cremains within the structure. For example, in archaeological contexts of urn burials, we can identify the sequence of cremains deposition within the receptacle (Figure 3-13). In this example, the x-axis represents the excavation levels of an assemblage from the Porta Nocera cemetery in Pompeii, from top (level 1) to bottom (level 11) (Van Andriga et al. 2013). The y-axis represents the cumulative frequency of fragments found by level and by anatomical

Figure 3-13: Cumulative Frequency Diagrams (by Percentage, y-Axis) of the Distribution by Anatomical Area and by Stratigraphic Layer (x-Axis)*

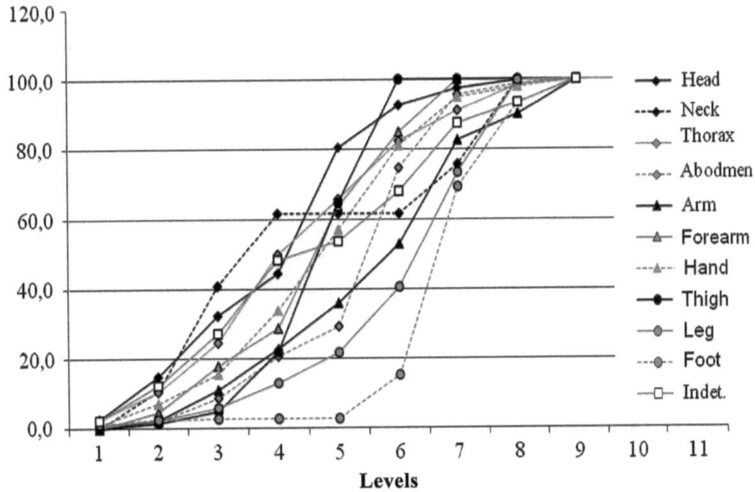

*Archaeological site of Pompeii, Porta Nocera, Tomb 32. *(Source: Modified from van Andringa et al. 2013.)*

regions. We can see that the distribution pattern is not random, with upper body fragments (head, neck, and thorax) being predominant in the top levels and lower body fragments (thigh, leg, and foot) being predominant in the bottom levels. The assemblage was thus purposefully constituted by collecting body parts in a determined pattern, probably starting with the toes and finishing with the head. This pattern implies that the remains were not displaced during the cremation and that the body was in an anatomical position identifiable (in this particular case, probably lying extended on a pyre) by the person who collected the bones.

A more thorough spatial analysis can be implemented using a GIS database. The simplest step is to perform a multicriteria request by bone type in the database in order to help identify anatomical connections within commingled assemblages to distinguish individual skeletons and sometimes interpret their original positions. A complementary approach to understand skeletal movement is the very tedious task of trying to systematically conjoin fragmentary cremains within an assemblage or between different areas. The efficiency of reconstructing bones, or rather parts of bones, from fragments has been demonstrated on several occasions in archaeological contexts in order to show the dispersion of one skeleton in various funerary structures (André et al. 2013; Duday 2009, fig. 139:147).

Performing simple database queries within a defined zone of the assemblage allows one to easily locate various body parts (e.g., a disturbed segment of vertebral column, a group of hand and foot bones) or try assigning them to a specific individual of the skeletal assemblage (Figure 3-10). Identifying osteological connections is a simple way to consider a cadaver's decomposition dynamic and thus address the body's original state prior to the cremation.

Additional GIS tools ("flux analyses") now provide the ability to map directions and distances of cremains' movement, providing new perspectives to discuss taphonomy (Rodier 2011, fig. 3.13). Thus, by assimilating the human body to a map, which is one of the bases of the archaeothanatology approach (Duday 2009), the compared topography of first order (anatomical connection) and second order (contiguous articulation) osteological relationships allows the tracking of cremains' movement, direction, and distance in space. Interpreting these movements in a forensic context can aid in understanding how the commingled assemblage has evolved through time, either naturally because of taphonomy or artificially because of human disturbances.

The nature and size of the burnt assemblage from the French Neolithic collective burial of "La Truie Pendue" (Passy-Véron, France), with more than 16,000 commingled and fragmented cremains, prompted the development of a GIS-based analysis to understand the cremains' spatial distribution within the deposit (de Becdelievre et al. 2014a). The deposit demonstrated intense heat signatures, differential colorations, deformations, fractures, and fragmentations. Tracking anatomical articulations using the GIS database revealed several fragmentation levels across the assemblage. The upper layers were mainly composed of highly fragmented cremains (Figure 3-14), while the deeper layers contained 13 complete skeletons (Figure 3-15). The differential fragmentation was evaluated through GIS by coupling weight analyses to the automated computation of the cremains surface area by anatomical regions (Figure 3-16). The search for anatomical connections indicated an initial body deposit in the lower levels in several close time periods. This spatial organization suggested the presence of at least two distinct funeral levels when the deposit was set on

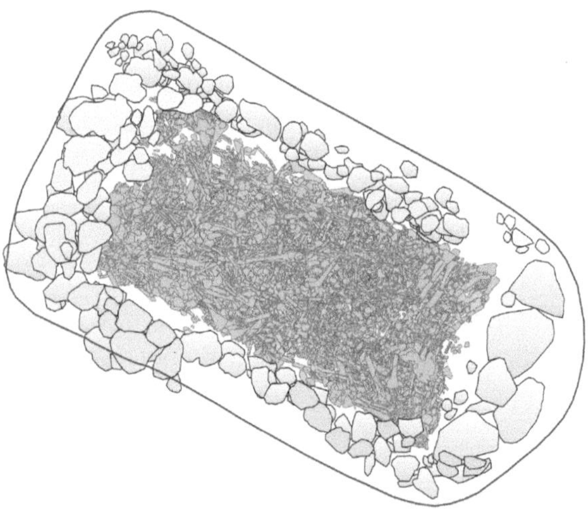

FIGURE 3-14
Vector map of articulated skeletons of the surface level of the archaeological site of "La Truie Pendue" (Yonne, France). *(Source: C. de Becdelièvre.)*

fire. In order to test this hypothesis, investigators explored the vertical distribution of small hand and foot bones across the assemblage by creating a series of spatial analyses in the GIS database (de Becdelievre et al. 2014a). Because several superimposed cadavers were deposited on the upper levels, the accumulation of small bones due to gravity (percolation) should be noticeable at the bottom of the first level, which delimitates the older deeper level.

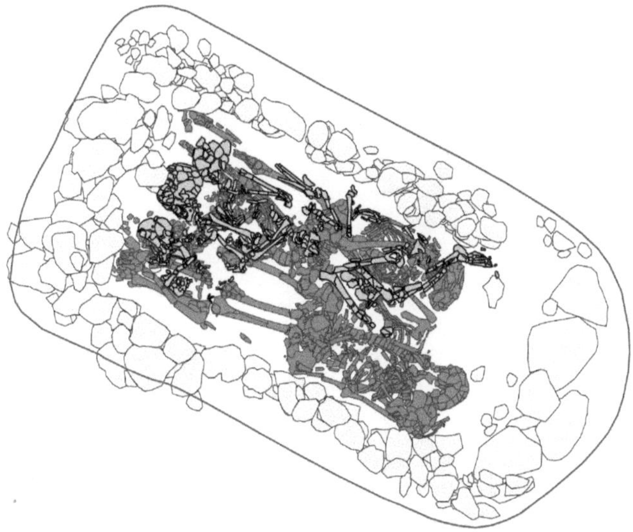

FIGURE 3-15
Vector map of articulated skeletons of the deepest level of the archaeological site of "La Truie Pendue" (Yonne, France). *(Source: C. de Becdelièvre.)*

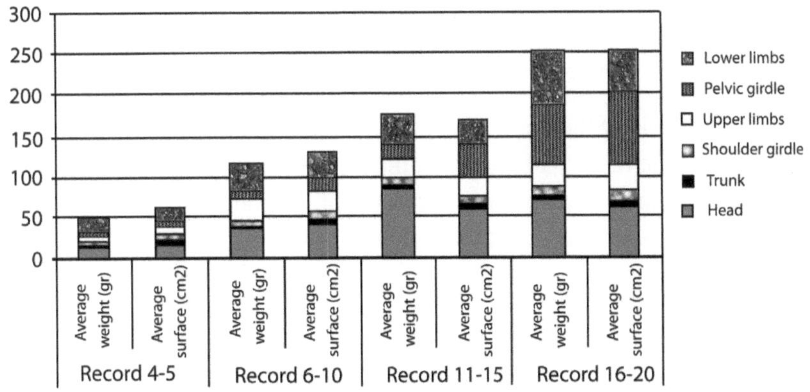

FIGURE 3-16
Fragmentation by weight and anatomical regions. Archaeological site of "La Truie Pendue" (Yonne, France). *(Source: C. de Becdelièvre.)*

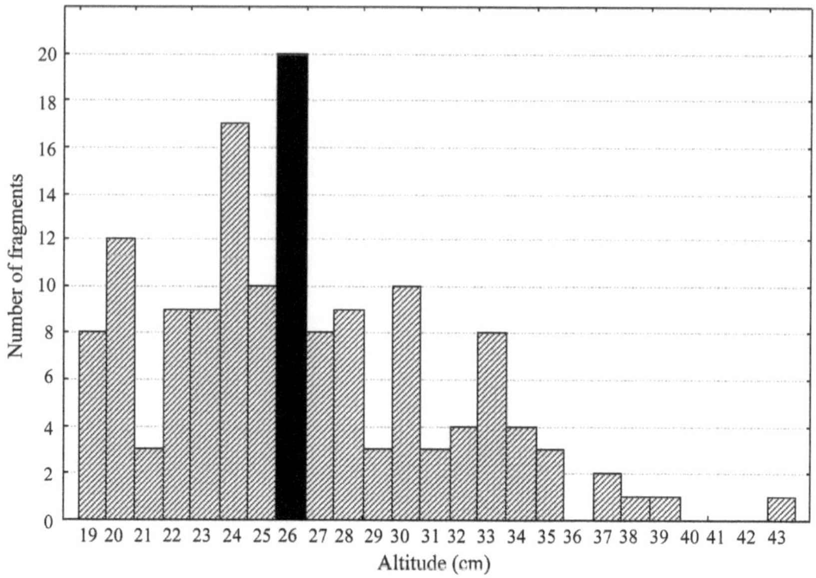

FIGURE 3-17

Histogram of fragmented feet cremains by archaeological levels. Archaeological site of "La Truie Pendue" (Yonne, France). In black, first level of bone accumulation. *(Source: C. de Becdelièvre.)*

The identification of accumulated bones under the layer of highly fragmented cremains and above the layer of articulated skeletons (Figure 3-17) confirmed the presence of a horizontal border within the assemblage (level 26 in solid black) at the time of the cremation, implying differential combustion environments: oxygenated in the upper levels and reductive in the lower ones.

In a forensic context, the comparative analysis of bone fragment density can be helpful, as demonstrated by the study conducted by Bontrager and Nawrocki (2008) on the Fox Hollow farm (Indiana). By crossing several lines of evidence, including spatial distribution of small bones unaffected by cremation, investigators hypothesized that some of the victims were burned in a dry state after being first decomposed and collected (Bontrager and Nawrocki 2005, 2008).

Using an integrated analysis of the deposit's spatial organization, we can explore various hypotheses and infer on the history of the assemblage, the chronology of deposits, decomposition modes, and initial cadaver state prior to combustion. Beyond a simple data plot, GIS spatial analyses tools enable a dynamic interpretation of burnt commingled skeletal assemblages.

Combustion Dynamic

A spatial approach of bone physical alterations (e.g., colors, warping, fragmentation) has been advocated as the most efficient way to reconstruct the temperatures that damaged bones and to understand corpse processing on an archaeological pyre (Duday et al. 2000) as well as a means to understand "the intention behind the use of fire" (Weitzel and McKenzie 2008). This

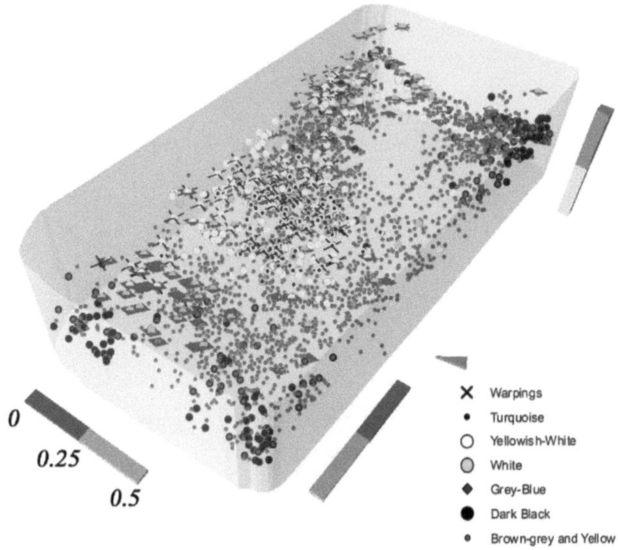

FIGURE 3-18

Distribution of bone color by depth of fragments. Archaeological site of "La Truie Pendue" (Yonne, France). *(Source: C. de Becdelièvre.)*

can only be done if both temperature and duration of combustion are simultaneously considered within the context of discovery.

To illustrate this point, anthropologists investigated the combustion environments of the archaeological site of "La Truie Pendue" (previously discussed) as indirect evidence of the assemblage distribution. All the cremains were plotted in three dimensions by heat colors and warping stages (de Becdelievre et al. 2014a). The data cloud offers a visual color gradient suggesting a decreasing diffusion of heat in the structure (Figure 3-18). Data also illustrate significant association of colors and warping stages indicative of a specific combustion pattern such as an intense fire fed by an oxygenated environment and organic matter from the surrounding decomposing cadavers. Cremains were then summarized by color groups, and their centroids' coordinates were interpolated (closer neighbors) using a kernel density model which smooth the data to highlight spatial patterns. "Bright" colors (e.g., white, turquoise) were used as proxy for oxygenated heat conditions, whereas "dark" colors (e.g., black) indicated reductive heat conditions (Fairgrieve 2008; Herrmann 1972; Lisowski 1968; Périnet 1982; Walker et al. 2008). The resulting models of heat diffusion within the assemblage (Figure 3-19) clearly depict the presence of a single hearth located in the upper part of the assemblage with a westward diffusion of heat. The models illustrate the differential combustion environment and thus the two-stage filling process of the structure. The fire intensely burned the upper (oxygenated) layer, while an obstacle obstructed the heat diffusion downward. This obstacle seems to be a sediment-filling level separating the assemblage.

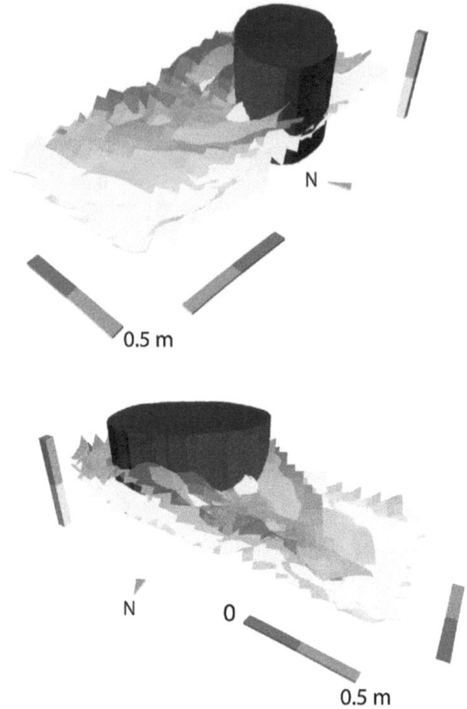

FIGURE 3-19
Three-dimensional model of combustion. Archaeological site of "La Truie Pendue" (Yonne, France). Legend: dark gray = very high intensity; gray = high; light gray = medium; white = low *(Source: C. de Becdelièvre.)*

The skeletons from the deeper layers, protected from the destructive action of fire, remained anatomically connected and exhibited dark colors indicative of a "rather reductive" heating environment. The intense fragmentation observed in the upper levels could have resulted from the "manipulation" of the last corpses during the "assisted" combustion where body parts were replaced in the hottest part of the pyre throughout the cremation. This stage was followed by the deposition of a layer of stones mixed with sediment, sealing the access to the dead (de Becdelievre et al. 2014a). This fire appears to be an integral part of a whole procedure designed to seal the grave and is thus more intentional than accidental.

Summary

To summarize our approach, we recommend the following steps when investigating commingled cremated remains, especially when highly fragmented:

Recovery: Excavation should be conducted by stratigraphic layers (2–5 cm), using a grid system (20 × 20 or 30 × 30 cm). Remains > 3 cm should be identified and mapped

individually *in situ*, whereas remains < 3 cm should be mapped by grid square and identified in the lab. If needed, remains can be geo-referenced.
Analysis: Fragment identification, weight, and count > 5 mm should be recorded by anatomical regions in the proposed form (http://www.pacea.cnrs.fr/Classeurs-Excel-Cremation.html). If needed, a GIS database by fragment can be set up, especially if additional variables such as bone color or size are necessary for spatial analyses.
Bone frequency and bone distribution by anatomical region are evaluated using graphs generated by the record form. MNI by exclusion of identical morphological features, age, size, pathological incompatibility, or by proportional weight is then estimated.
Additional analyses using the GIS database can be performed to complete the MNI estimation, to understand the spatial distribution of fragments, to investigate the combustion's dynamic in the structure, and to evaluate the assemblage history for body depositions.
Interpretation: Potential biases in the assemblage are indicative of pre- or postdeposition handling (e.g., destruction or transport of body parts). Spatial distribution of fragments can reveal precombustion body position (e.g., extended) or tampering during or after combustion. Combustion's dynamic can yield information on burial structure (e.g., open or closed) and the state of the bodies prior to cremation (e.g., dry or "fresh").

Concluding Remarks

Dealing with commingled remains is a laborious task. Dealing with burnt commingled remains is often a task researchers tend to avoid altogether. Forensic anthropologists cannot choose to avoid this type of crime scene and must therefore be aware of the most efficient field and laboratory methods available to properly recover evidence. Anthropologists who are familiar with cremains quickly become the most expert in osteology because morphological variations at their disposal are scarce and altered due to fragmentation and warping. The form presented here has been tested on many archaeological sites with great success. Homogenous recording and classification criteria are now available for large-scale comparative studies and identification of larger burial patterns in cultures dominated by cremation rituals. The lessons learned from these analyses should be integrated into the forensic discipline to push the limits of crime scene interpretation. Of course, many forensic contexts may not be suitable for such a detailed approach mainly due to time constraints. Yet, some examples, such as the Hollow Farm case previously cited, illustrate the need for elaborate investigation options.

A proper bioarchaeological approach to commingled remains, whether cremated or not, is useful to test hypotheses and interpret the nature of the deposit, the chronology of body deposition, manipulation of remains, taphonomy, and even the preservation stage of the body prior to the fire. Spatial analyses, when integrated with contextual data, can give us clues on the nature of the fire (e.g., combustion atmosphere type and cadaver conservation), the location of the fire, diffusion of heat, and even the type of fire (e.g., flaming/smoldering or laminar/turbulent) or the duration of combustion pre- or postflashover. By systematically addressing these questions, forensic anthropologists can efficiently contribute to the recovery, analysis, and interpretation of commingled cremains.

Acknowledgments

We would like to thank Drs. Bradley Adams and John Byrd for inviting us to contribute to this new edition of their central book on commingled remains methodology. We also thank Sandrine Thiol (Institut National de Recherches Archéologiques Préventives) for providing some of the original archaeological data from "La Truie Pendue" (Passy, France). Finally, our thanks to F. Santos (Université de Bordeaux) for the webpage hosting the inventory forms.

References

Adams, B.J., Konigsberg, L.W., 2004. Estimation of the most likely number of individuals from commingled human skeletal remains. Am. J. Phys. Anthropol. 125, 138–151.

André, A., Leahy, R., Rottier, S., 2013. Cremated human remains deposited in two phases: Evidence from the necropolis of the Tuileries Site (Lyon, France: 2nd century AD). Int. J. Osteoarchaeol. DOI: 10.1002/oa.2317.

van Andringa, W., Duday, H., Lepetz, S., 2013. Mourir à Pompéi: fouille d'un quartier funéraire de la nécropole romaine de Porta Nocera (2003–2007). (Vol. 1-2). École française de Rome, Roma.

Bass, W.M., Jantz, R.L., 2004. Cremation weights in east Tennessee. J. Forensic Sci. 49, 901.

de Becdelievre, C., Rottier, S., Thiol, S., Saligny, S., 2014a. Understanding the use of fire in a Neolithic collective grave: spatial analyses of fire-induced alterations on human bone remains from the site of La Truie Pendue. In prep.

de Becdelievre, C., Rottier, S., Thiol, S., Santos, F., 2014b. From fire-induced alterations on human bones to the original circumstances of the fire: an integrated approach of human cremains drawn from a Neolithic collective burial. In prep.

Bel, V., 1996. Etude spatiale de sept incinérations primaires gallo-romaines de la région lyonnaise. Bulletins et Mémoires de la Société d'Anthropologie de Paris 8, 207–222.

Binford, L.R., 1972. An analysis of cremations from three Michigan sites. In: Binford, L.R., Quimby, G.I. (Eds.), An Archaeological Perspective. Seminar Press, New York, pp. 373–382.

Bohnert, M., 2002. Diagnosis of a Captive-Bolt Injury in a Skull Extremely Destroyed by Fire. National Emergency Training Center, Emmitsburg, MD.

Bontrager, A.B., Nawrocki, S.P., 2005. A taphonomic analysis of burned remains from the Fox Hollow serial homicide site. Am. J. Phys. Anthropol. S 40, 68–69.

Bontrager, A.B., Nawrocki, S.P., 2008. A taphonomic analysis of human cremains from the Fox Hollow farm serial homicide site. In: Schmidt, C.W., Symes, S.A. (Eds.), The Analysis of Burned Human Remains. Academic Press, San Diego, CA, pp. 211–226.

Christensen, M.,A., 2002. Experiments in the combustibility of the human body. J. Forensic Sci. 47, 466–470.

Van Deest, T.L., Murad, T.A., Bartelink, E.J., 2011. A re-examination of cremains weight: Sex and age variation in a Northern California sample. J. Forensic Sci. 56, 344–349.

Demangeot, C., 2008. Le dénombrement des défunts dans les ensembles funéraires: problèmes théoriques, paramètres quantitatifs: application à la sépulture collective du dolmen des Peirières à Villedubert. Ph.D. dissertation, 844p University of Bordeaux, France.

Depierre, G., 2010. Des crémations en milieu à haute technologie aux incinérations du passé. Apports méthodologiques et réalités archéologiques Ph.D. dissertation, 734p. University of Bourgogne, France.

Devlin, J.B., Herrmann, N.P., 2008. Bone color as an interpretive tool of the depositional history of archaeological cremains. In: Schmidt, C.W., Symes, S.A. (Eds.), The Analysis of Burned Human Remains. Academic Press, San Diego, CA, pp. 109–128.

Duday, H., 2009. The Archaeology of the Dead. Oxbow Books, Oxford.

Duday, H., Depierre, G., Janin, T., 2000. Validation des paramètres de quantification, protocoles et stratégies dans l'étude anthropologique des sépultures secondaires à incinération. L'exemple des nécropoles protohistoriques du Midi de la France. In: Archéologie de la Mort, Archéologie de la Tombe au premier Age du Fer, vol. 5, pp. 7–29. Actes du XXI Colloque International de l'AFEAF, Lattes.

Duday, H., Guillon, M., 2006. Understanding the circumstances of decomposition when the body is skeletonized. In: Schmitt, A., Cunha, E., Pinheiro, J. (Eds.), Forensic Anthropology and Medicine. Humana Press, Totowa, NJ, pp. 117–157.

Fairgrieve, S.I., 2008. Forensic Cremation: Recovery and Analysis, 206p. CRC Press, Boca Raton, FL.

Gocha, T.P., Schutkowski, H., 2013. Tooth cementum annulation for estimation of age-at-death in thermally altered remains. J. Forensic Sci. 58, S151–S155.

Herrmann, B., 1972. Zur Beurteilung von Kohlenstoffverfärbungen bei Leichenbränden. Ausgrabungen und Funde 17, 275–277.

Herrmann, N.P., 2008. GIS applied to bioarchaeology: An example from the Rio Talgua Caves in Northeast Honduras. J. Cave Karst Stud. 64, 17–22.

Holck, P., 1986. Cremated Bones: A Medical-Anthropological Study of an Archaeological Material on Cremation Burials. University of Oslo, Oslo.

Lisowski, F.P., 1968. The investigation of human cremations. In: Anthropologie und Humangenetik. Festschrift zum 65. Geburtstag von Karl Saller. Hrsg. vom Inst. für Anthropologie und Humangenetik der Univ. München. Gustav Fischer Stuttgart, Stuttgart, pp. 76–82.

Lowrance, E.W., Latimer, H.B., 1957. Weights and linear measurements of 105 human skeletons from Asia. Am. J. Anat. 101, 445–459.

Marean, C., Abe, Y., Nilssen, P., Stone, E., 2001. Estimating the minimum number of skeletal elements (MNE) in zooarchaeology: A review and a new image-analysis GIS approach. Am. Antiquity 66, 333–348.

May, S.E., 2011. The effects of body mass on cremation weight. J. Forensic Sci. 56, 3–9.

McKinley, J.I., 1993. Bone fragment size and weights of bone from modern British cremations and the implications for the interpretation of archaeological cremations. Int. J. Osteoarchaeol. 3, 283–287.

McKinley, J.I., 1994. Bone fragment size in British cremation burials and its implications for pyre technology and ritual. J. Archaeol. Sci. 21, 339–342.

Naji, S., T. Colard, B. Bertrand, J-P. Bocquet-Appel, and J. Blondiaux. In press (accepted, 2014) Cementochronology, to cut or not to cut? Int. J. Paleopathol.

Périnet, G., 1982. Détermination des températures de cuisson des ossements humains. Les dossiers: Histoire et Archéologie 86, 96–97.

Reinhard, K., 1994. Cremation in Southwestern North America: Aspects of taphonomy that affect pathological analysis. J. Archaeol. Sci. 21, 597–605.

Rodier, X., (ed.). 2011 Information spatiale et archéologie. Errance. Paris. Available from http://livre.fnac.com/a3721918/Xavier-Rodier-Information-spatiale-et-archeologie

Schultz, J.J., Warren, M.W., Krigbaum, J.S., 2008. Analysis of human cremains: Gross and chemical methods. In: Schmidt, C.W., Symes, S.A. (Eds.), The Analysis of Burned Human Remains. Academic Press, San Diego, CA. pp. 75–94.

Shipman, P., Foster, G., Schoeninger, M., 1984. Burnt bones and teeth: An experimental study of color, morphology, crystal structure and shrinkage. J. Archaeol. Sci. 11, 307–325.

Susini, A., 1988. Etudes des caractéristiques biophysiques des tissus calcifiés humains (os, émail, dentine) soumis à des traitements thermiques: Applications anthropologiques et médicales. Ph.D. dissertation. Université de Genève, Switzerland.

Symes, S.A., Rainwater, C.W., Chapman, E.N., Gipson, D.R., Piper, A.L., 2008. Patterned thermal destruction of human remains in a forensic setting. In: Schmidt, C.W., Symes, S.A. (Eds.), The Analysis of Burned Human Remains. Academic Press, San Diego, CA. pp. 15–54.

Trotter, M., Hixon, B.B., 1974. Sequential changes in weight, density, and percentage ash weight of human skeletons from an early fetal period through old age. Anat. Record 179, 1–18.

Trotter, M., Peterson, R.R., 1962. The relationship of ash weight and organic weight of human skeletons. J. Bone Joint Surg. 44, 669–681.

Villena i Mota, N., Duday, H., Houët, F., 1996. Hiérarchie et fiabilité des liaisons ostéologiques par symétrie et contiguïté articulaire dans l'étude des sépultures anciennes. Bulletin et Mémoire de la Société d'Anthropologie de Paris 8, 373–384.

Walker, P.L., Miller, K.W.P., Richman, R., 2008. Time, temperature, and oxygen availability: an experimental study of the effects of environmental conditions on the color and organic content of cremated bone. In: Schmidt, C.W., Symes, S.A. (Eds.), The Analysis of Burned Human Remains. Academic Press, San Diego, CA, pp. 129–144.

Weitzel, M.A., McKenzie, H.G., 2008. Fire as a cultural taphonomic agent: Understanding mortuary behavior at Khuzhir-Nuge XIV, Siberia. In: Schmidt, C.W., Symes, S.A. (Eds.), The Analysis of Burned Human Remains. Academic Press, San Diego, CA, pp. 185–199.

Wittwer-Backofen, U., 2012. Age estimation using tooth cementum annulation. In: Bell, L.S. (Ed.), Forensic Microscopy for Skeletal Tissues, Methods in Molecular Biology. Humana Press, Totowa, NJ, pp. 129–143.

Wittwer-Backofen, U., Gampe, J., Vaupel, J.W., 2004. Tooth cementum annulation for age estimation: Results from a large known-age validation study. Am. J. Phys. Anthropol. 123, 119–129.

CHAPTER 4

More Pieces of the Puzzle: F.B.I. Evidence Response Team Approaches to Scenes with Commingled Evidence

Richard B. Marx[1], Michael J. Hochrein[2], Ann D. Fasano[1]
[1]*Supervisory Special Agent, Laboratory Division, Evidence Response Team Unit, Federal Bureau of Investigation, Quantico, VA,* [2]*Special Agent, Laurel Highlands Resident Agency, Federal Bureau of Investigation, Pittsburgh, PA*

Introduction

Since the establishment of the Federal Bureau of Investigation's (FBI's) Evidence Response Team (ERT) Unit in 1993, ERT teams across the United States have been involved in the documentation and collection of evidence from scenes large and small. One hundred and forty-one teams, composed of more than 1,200 members, have been formed within the 56 FBI field offices, or divisions. Single or combined ERT teams, in either federal cases or as requested assistance in state or local investigations, have participated in more than 1,000 crime or search scenes per year. FBI ERTs have been deployed internationally to sites in Africa, the Middle East, the Balkans, Central Asia, and Southeast Asia. Those domestic and international operational deployments have included natural disasters, terrorist bombings, terrestrial crashes, war zones, and mass graves in which the remains of the victims are intrinsically commingled. Regardless of the size of the scenes, similar fundamental approaches toward scene management and evidence collection have proven imperative in making sense of sometimes confusing situations.

Perhaps there is no other crime scene setting where the documentation of the three-dimensional position of fragmented and commingled evidence is more critical than that involving multiple or mass deaths. Such scenes may consist of the burial of two or more homicide victims in a common grave, or they could entail extremely fragmented remains over several acres of a crash scene. In both types of scenes, the identification of individual bone fragments in their environmental contexts preserves the patterns and relationships between evidence. These relationships, and patterns formed, are defined during the final stages of actions that were physically or behaviorally controlled. The act or reason for the final position of the evidence or remains is initially controlled by human behavior and/or the laws of physics. Both controls have been the subject of a myriad of research. For example, the

Commingled Human Remains. http://dx.doi.org/10.1016/B978-0-12-405889-7.00004-6

positioning of victims' bodies is many times the result of conscious or subconscious efforts of the killer(s). Brooks (1985), Burgess and Ressler (1985), Douglas et al. (1986), Douglas and Munn (1992a,b), Keppel (2005), Lundrigan and Canter (2001), Rajs et al. (1998), Ressler et al. (1985), and Rossi (1982) are just a representative few of the studies addressing the psychology behind victim selection, crime scene selection, and victim treatment that are ultimately reflected in the positioning of a body and other evidence. In cases involving clandestine burials, suspects go beyond affecting site selection and victim body position to also create and affect the space in which the body or bodies are concealed. Hochrein (1997, 2002) discusses spatial evidence, or geotaphonomic characteristics, that are created and influenced by conscious and subconscious subject behavior. Several authors have discussed the physics behind the patterned distribution of evidence in explosive or collision events; they include Anker and Taylor (1989), Barrie and Hudson-Walker (1970), Bergen-Henengouwan (1973), Gable (1968), Hellerich and Pollak (1995), Hill (1989), Kreft (1970), Matteson (1974), Min and Jia (1992), Steele (1983), and Swegennis (1987) to, again, name a few. In postblast, or postcrash, settings the controlling factor is, at some point, the physical dynamics of explosion that involve known forces on known volumes and materials, resulting in predictable patterns in which exploded materials are distributed. When the final position of crash debris and human remains, as well as environmental features that could have affected their flight on the way to those positions, are recorded precisely, research and predictive models represented by the aforementioned references are possible or confirmed. In the same vein, the precise mapping of body position and associated evidence in a multiple victim interment may reveal the human behavior that affected when, why, and how each individual was placed in the common burial. Often, however, crime scene investigators are faced with pressure from superiors or coworkers who believe the piece-plotting of evidence is pointless because they believe fragmentation occurs randomly, or all evidence in a clandestine grave was deposited contemporaneously. To overcome outside pressures to compromise during collection efforts, FBI ERT members receive training throughout their FBI careers that emphasizes the efficient yet complete recovery of evidence. Regardless of the magnitude of the scene, the same efforts toward quality and quantity of information gathering are attempted.

This chapter presents the FBI ERT concept and basic operational guidelines. It then presents two cases to illustrate how those guidelines were followed and how the extra effort toward three-dimensional mapping of human remains and associated evidence can aid in the interpretation, reconstruction, and presentation of a crime or disaster scene. Both cases involve multiple victims and represent a middle ground between cases of a single victim and those constituting large-scale mass disasters.

FBI Evidence Response Team Operational Guidelines and Responsibilities

The quality and quantity of evidence collected at any crime scene is directly impacted by the amount of preparation by crime scene investigators toward potential responses. As previously mentioned, FBI ERT members are required to apply fundamental techniques of crime scene management, evidence collection, and documentation to each and every site they process. In large and small scenes, personnel duties and responsibilities are clearly defined, and basic stages involving the organization of the search for potential evidence are well known to all ERT members. The size and magnitude of the crime scene may affect the number of personnel deployed to the scene, and the type of crime being investigated may require different forensic tools, but the basis for duties, assignments, and organization of the search remain the same. It may take only a handful of personnel to process a vehicle used in a crime. A major postblast or transportation crash scene could involve multiple ERT teams from numerous field offices. For example, 480 FBI ERT members worked over 11 months with 24 federal, state, and local agencies in processing 1.8 million tons of debris from the World Trade Center in New York City in the aftermath of the September 11, 2001, terrorist attacks (Figure 4-1). In response to the events of that same day, 137 ERT members were utilized toward the collection of evidence from the Pentagon crime scene. At the same time 96 ERT team members were utilized at the crash of Flight 93 near Shanksville, Pennsylvania.

Certain personnel duties and responsibilities are necessary in almost any major search operation. The following duties and responsibilities are typically crucial to ensure that search efforts are conducted in an organized and methodical fashion. It is important to note it may not be feasible to have one person assigned to each duty. It is relatively common for one person to

Figure 4-1
Joint FBI and NYPD forensic recovery operations utilizing physical searching and mechanical sifting of debris for human remains from the 9/11 World Trade Center terrorist attack. Search conducted on Staten Island, NY, from September 11, 2001 to August 9, 2002.

perform two or more duties. For all positions, interest and attitude of personnel are paramount concerns. Training and experience will be used to their best potential only when team members possess a positive attitude. This human side of Evidence Response Teams is significant due to the long hours and attention to detail often required of personnel. The following lists the major team assignments as well as corresponding general duties and responsibilities:

1. ERT team leader
2. Photographer and photographic log recorder
3. Sketch preparer
4. Evidence recorder/custodian
5. Evidence recovery personnel
6. Specialists (as required)

ERT Team Leader

The ERT team leader has the overall responsibility at the scene to ensure that communication, assessments, and responsibilities are conducted thoroughly and completely. The team leader assumes control upon arrival at the scene and is cognizant of safety issues that may affect team members. This may be as simple as having extra police officers or agents at the scene or as complex as prearranging military assets and personnel in a war-torn region. After the scene is secured and any safety issues are addressed, the team leader, usually assisted by the photographer, will conduct a preliminary walkthrough of the scene with the purpose of evaluating potential evidence and preparing a written narrative. After the scene has been evaluated, the team leader will brief other members of the team, establish a search pattern, and make appropriate assignments to team members. A command post should be created outside the crime scene. The command post could be located in a building, under a pop-up tent, inside a motor vehicle, or could even be located under a shady tree. The purpose of the command post is to maintain a designated area where the exchange of information can take place between the team leader and investigative personnel. The command post is also the point where coordination between all law enforcement agencies occurs. The team leader maintains these responsibilities throughout the entire process and should continually reevaluate the efficiency of the search during the entire course of the operation. After the search has been completed and a final survey and inventory review have been completed, it is the team leader's responsibility to release the scene.

Photographer and Photographic Log Recorder

The ERT photographer should make every effort to document the scene before it is entered by other team members. This should include the photography of any victims, crowds, or motor vehicles that may be considered part of the scene. The photographer is required to photograph the entire scene with overall, medium, and close-up coverage, using measurement scales for examination-purpose-quality photos when appropriate. All items of evidence must be photographed before they are moved. This will require communication and cooperation between other team components to include the sketch preparer, evidence recorder/custodian, and evidence recovery personnel. Cooperation among these ERT team components remains important when numbering and identifying items of evidence. Each item of evidence collected will have one number assigned to it and should be identified using the same nomenclature on all logs created at the scene. Using a different description on logs can become confusing when testifying in court. A room described on a log as the family room and later described as a den on another log can lead one to wonder if there were actually two rooms. In the case of multiple skeletal remains, the confusion could be even greater. All latent fingerprints and other impression evidence are photographed with and without scale before any lifts and/or casts are removed. Every photograph must be documented by the photographic log recorder on a photo log, which should also include a photo sketch. The photo sketch depicts the item photographed and its relationship within the scene along with the angle and direction of the camera at the time of the photograph.

Sketch Preparer

The sketch preparer is responsible for determining the scope of the scene and the selection of equipment used for mapping. The ERT sketch preparer determines if two-dimensional measurements are sufficient or if three-dimensional documentation is required. The sketch preparer determines if hand measurement tools, total station, or three-dimensional scanning equipment is utilized. The availability of the equipment, the environment being mapped, and the type of presentation required in court will assist the sketch preparer in determining the suitable method. Regardless of the type of sketch or equipment used, any prepared sketch must follow certain guidelines and contain specific information. The ERT sketch preparer must diagram the immediate scene and orient the sketch direction with north. Evidence item numbers and nomenclature must be coordinated with the other ERT team components. Adjacent buildings, rooms, furniture, and so on need to be indicated as appropriate. The sketch preparer should obtain appropriate assistance for operating equipment such as total stations and three-dimensional scanners. It is very difficult for one person to operate this equipment, and training is necessary for all operators. Even simple measuring with hand measurement tools is more efficient with assistance. The sketch preparer will determine the scale to be utilized. Whether the scene is depicted in feet and inches or metric measurements, the measurements must be consistent, and the sketch preparer must ensure consistency throughout the mapping process.

Evidence Recorder/Custodian

The ERT evidence recorder/custodian is responsible for the overall coordination of the documentation, packaging, and preservation of all evidence obtained at the scene. The evidence recorder/custodian is responsible for maintaining an evidence recovery log, which reflects the description, date, times, location, and individual collecting of each item of evidence. The evidence recorder/custodian receives and records all evidence from the evidence recovery personnel and is responsible for coordinating numbering and nomenclature of items with all other components of the team. The ERT evidence recorder/custodian maintains the chain of custody by maintaining control of the evidence, from the scene to the transmittal of the evidence to the case investigator, property room, or crime lab, per agency guidelines.

Evidence Recovery Personnel

The ERT evidence recovery personnel are responsible for locating and collecting items of evidence at the scene. These ERT members are also responsible for ensuring that each item collected has been photographed and documented in the sketch before it is moved from the scene and that the numbering and nomenclature of evidence are consistent with the other components. The evidence recovery personnel mark each package of evidence with their initials and date when collecting items. This is normally witnessed by a second individual who also initials and dates the packaged item. This process ensures the availability of at least one evidence recovery member if testimony is later required at a court hearing or trial. The evidence recovery personnel are required to keep the ERT team leader apprised of any significant evidence located throughout the search. The evidence recovery personnel ensure they are appropriately dressed (gloves, Tyvek, mask, etc.) to avoid any contamination issues while operating within the crime scene.

Specialists

Bringing in expertise from outside services is sometimes necessary and prudent. The field of forensic science is so broad today that no agency will have every form of specialty service available from among its ranks. Typically, specialists are brought in from industry, the academic community, private scientific laboratories, and similar concerns. The Evidence Response Team program has more than 1,200 members nationwide, and several members have formal education in more than one listed specialty, but these individuals are not always available or in a specific geographic area where they can respond to every case. When one is dealing with outside specialists, some pertinent aspects to consider are:

- The competency and reliability of the specialist
- The ability of the specialist to work within law enforcement guidelines at a scene
- The role of the specialist in presenting expert testimony in court

Specialists should be identified before they are needed in an actual case. A current contact list should be maintained if possible. The ERT team leader should meet with these individuals to determine the best manner to jointly conduct search planning, operations, and follow-up activity. Some examples of specialty assistance to be considered are described next.

Medical Examiner/Pathologist/Coroner

The medical examiner/pathologist/coroner role at a crime scene will vary by jurisdiction. Some states and counties are part of the coroner system. The coroner may or may not have a medical background and may have a staff that includes pathologists or may contract out the work. It is important to be familiar with the system responsible for a crime scene. In some jurisdictions, a pathologist will respond to the scene; in some jurisdictions, the medical examiner's office will send one of its investigators; and in some jurisdictions, there is no response to the scene. The important point to remember in all these scenarios is that the deceased is the responsibility of those medical examiner/pathologist/coroner jurisdictions and that the remains should not be touched without their approval. Regardless of which system is in place, the medical examiner/pathologist/coroner is responsible for the postmortem examination.

Forensic Odontologist

The forensic odontologist can be very useful in the identification of the victim. The forensic odontologist is capable of comparing ante- and postmortem dental records and rendering identification, and he or she is extremely useful when dealing with skeletal and decomposed remains. The forensic odontologist normally conducts these comparisons at the morgue or a dental office. The forensic odontologist should be utilized at the scene of arson where burned teeth can be preserved before transport of the remains; he or she can more easily identify burned teeth within the scene. The teeth of victims in postarson scenes can be easily destroyed and lost during movement of the remains. Forensic odontologists responded to the tsunami disaster of 2004 in Phuket, Thailand, and assisted in many of the identifications made there. Three acceptable methods of identification were accepted in Thailand for the Tsunami victims: dental, DNA, and fingerprint comparisons.

Forensic Anthropologist

The forensic anthropologist can identify skeletal portions of human remains and, using the skeletal remains, can determine factors such as age, race, stature, and gender, which are very useful in the identification of the remains. The forensic anthropologist can also assist in determining if skeletal remains are human or animal. In the case of mass or commingled graves, the forensic anthropologist can sort the skeletal remains and group the remains by victim. Forensic anthropologists can assist in identifying tool marks on bone and in determining whether they are caused by animals or weapons. These specialists can assist in determining whether damage to the skeletal remains occurred ante-, peri-, or postmortem.

Forensic Entomologist

The forensic entomologist is useful in the collection, preservation, and identification of various insects located within the general area of the human remains. The forensic entomologist is able to assist in estimating the time of death by studying the development of the collected specimens and determining the environmental conditions over a specified period of time.

Forensic Botanist

The forensic botanist, like the entomologist, is able to assist in estimating the time of death after collecting and identifying plant life found within the general area of human remains. The forensic botanist also requires local environmental conditions to assist in the estimation of time of death. This specialist can further assist in determining plant material associated with the remains that is not consistent with the area where the remains were recovered.

Forensic Blood Pattern Analyst

Using acceptable scientific methods, the forensic blood pattern analyst is able to enter a bloody crime scene and analyze various groups and shapes of bloodstains. Through this analysis, identification of various types of stains, the velocity required to create the stain, and the direction of travel can be determined. The forensic blood pattern analyst can assist the investigation by offering a re-creation of the events and identifying types of instruments used to create the pattern.

Geologist

The geologist can assist the investigation with issues relating to rock and soil. During the recovery of human remains, the geologist can advise on the consistency of soil as the grave is excavated and identify any soil and/or rock that are not consistent with the local region. This specialist can be useful in determining data obtained through the use of ground-penetrating radar or other geophysical prospecting methods.

Surveyor

A surveyor or surveying crew is useful in mapping utilizing the total station. A surveyor can also assist in locating local maps and topographic maps.

Engineer

Engineers can be of assistance in cases such as deep well excavations, mine shafts, or post-blast scenes where large structures have collapsed or partially collapsed. They have expertise in shoring, bracing, evaluating, and lifting structural components.

Bomb Technician

The bomb technician can be called to assist in cases where an explosive device is present or intelligence reports the possibility of such devices. The bomb technician can sweep the scene for primary and secondary devices. This specialist has render-safe capabilities and can conduct the render-safe technique at the site or transport the device to another location for detonation.

Crime Laboratory Examiner

The crime laboratory examiner is generally trained in several or one specific discipline such as DNA, trace evidence, firearms and tool marks, chemistry, etc. Depending on the circumstances of the case and local policy, it may be advantageous to request a crime laboratory examiner to respond to the scene or to consult with the examiner over the telephone. The crime laboratory examiner can assist in providing information on the proper collecting, packaging, and transmittal of specific types of evidence.

Safety Officer

The safety officer is trained in the use of various detection devices to measure hazardous gases such as carbon monoxide and methane. This specialist is also OSHA trained and can advise team members regarding the mandate to wear steel-toed shoes, helmets, protective eyewear, levels of Tyvek, etc. The safety officer received training in confined space and, like the engineer, can assist in partial or full building collapses.

Hazmat Specialist

The Hazmat specialist is trained in the detection and mitigation of all hazardous materials, including chemical, biological, and nuclear materials. Personnel should not enter any suspected Hazmat scene before it has been cleared by a Hazmat specialist. This specialist is also trained in the collecting and shipping of evidence from a hazardous environment.

The 12-Step Approach to Crime Scene Processing

Organization of the crime scene search process is paramount to any successful search. The FBI Evidence Response Teams are trained in a basic 12-step process as described here:

1. Preparation: Preparation requires training and maintaining adequate supplies and equipment to conduct the crime scene search. ERT teams are required to accumulate packaging and collection materials necessary for typical search circumstances. A list of required supplies and equipment is maintained, and teams put together response kits for various types of scenes such as latent fingerprints, recovery of human remains, DNA collection, etc. Each ERT team member receives training in completing computerized and preformatted logs and administrative worksheets. Prior to the search, legal documents and ramifications are discussed among the team. This may involve reviewing the search warrant for familiarization of the items and types of items to be seized. The ERT team leader is preselected, and assignments to other positions are generally predetermined. Specialized vehicles are stocked with supplies and equipment to handle a variety of circumstances to include communications, shelter, lighting, etc. Each ERT team member is issued a variety of clothing and protective gear to cover a wide range of weather conditions. Safety equipment such as steel-toed boots, gloves, helmets, eye protection, and

respirators is issued to each team member. In the event of extended operations like those of the 9/11 attacks, a rotation of ERT teams is developed. On several remote and overseas deployments, food and water were made part of the load-out package. Several ERT teams maintain their own medically trained personnel or draw medical personnel from other entities within the FBI. Local medical resources and adequate hospitals are identified prior to all deployments. Prior to arrival at the scene, communication is usually established with services of an ancillary nature (e.g., medical examiner, prosecuting attorney, and other specialists as required) so that questions that surface during the investigation may be resolved.

2. Approach scene: Upon initial arrival at the scene, be alert for evidence and be cautious concerning transient evidence, foot/tire impressions, and trace evidence. Make certain to protect evidence if necessary from contamination or loss. Extensive notes should be taken immediately; the notes can be written or dictated. Consideration of the safety of all personnel is paramount.
3. Secure and protect: Take control of the scene immediately and determine the extent to which the scene has been protected. Obtain information from personnel who have knowledge of the original condition of the scene, including first responders, medical personnel, any witnesses, and/or surviving victims. Designate one person in charge for final decision making and problem resolution. Take extensive notes and do not rely on memory. Keep out unauthorized personnel and record times and names of all personnel entering or leaving the scene.
4. Preliminary survey: Cautiously walk through the scene and maintain administrative and emotional control. Select a narrative technique (written, audio, or video). Have the designated photographer take preliminary photographs. Delineate the extent of the search area and initially expand the perimeter. Organize methods and procedures to be utilized and recognize special problem areas. Identify, protect, and document transient physical evidence. Determine personnel and equipment needs and make specific assignments. Develop a general theory of the crime based on current information. Take extensive notes to document the scene and describe the physical and environmental conditions as well as personnel movements.
5. Evaluate physical evidence possibilities: This evaluation begins upon arrival at the scene and becomes detailed in the preliminary survey stage. Ensure that the collection and packaging materials and equipment are sufficient. Focus first on evidence that could be lost and leave the least transient for last. Ensure all personnel consider the variety of possible evidence, not only evidence within their specialties. Search the easily accessible areas and progress out to view locations, always being aware of hidden items. Evaluate whether evidence appears to have been inadvertently moved or whether the scene appears to be contrived.
6. Narrative: The narrative is a running, general-terms description of the condition of the crime scene. The narrative describes the scene in a "general to specific" reference scheme. Use a systematic approach to the narrative. Nothing is too insignificant to record if it catches one's attention. Under most circumstances, do not collect evidence during the

narrative. Use photographs and sketches to supplement, not substitute, for the narrative. The narrative should include case identifier; date, time, and location; weather and lighting conditions; and condition and position of evidence.

7. Photography: Photograph the crime scene as soon as possible and prepare a photographic log that records all photographs and a description and location of evidence. Establish a progression of overall, medium, and close-up views of the crime scene. Photograph from eye level to represent the normal view. Photograph the most fragile areas of the crime scene first. Photograph all stages of the crime scene investigation, including discoveries, before the evidence is moved. Photograph the evidence in detail, and include a scale with the photographer's name and the date. When a scale is used, first take the photograph without the scale. Photograph the interior crime scene in an overlapping series using a normal lens, if possible. Overall photographs may be taken using a wide-angle lens. Photograph the exterior crime scene, establishing the location of the scene by a series of overall photographs including a landmark. Photographs should have 360 degrees of coverage. Consider aerial photography when possible. Photograph entrances and exits from the inside and the outside. Photograph evidence twice, taking a medium-distance photograph that shows the evidence and its position to other evidence. The second photograph is a laboratory examination-quality close-up photograph that includes a scale and fills the frame. Prior to entering the scene, attempt to acquire prior photographs, blueprints, or maps of the scene.
8. Sketch: The sketch establishes a permanent record of items, conditions, and distance and size relationships. Sketches supplement the scene photographs and the narrative description. Sketch number designations should coordinate with the evidence log number designations. Sketches are normally not drawn to scale; however, the sketch should have measurements and details to complete a drawn-to-scale diagram if necessary. The sketch should include case identifier; date, time, and location; identity and assignments of personnel involved in the sketch; dimensions of the rooms, furniture, doors, and windows; distances between objects, persons, bodies, entrances, and exits; measurements showing the location of evidence; and a key, legend, compass orientation, scale, scale disclaimer, or a combination of these features.
9. Conduct crime scene search: Use a search pattern (grid, strip, or spiral) and search from the general to the specific for evidence. Be alert for all evidence and carefully search entrances and exits. Wear latex or cotton gloves at all times to avoid leaving fingerprints. To avoid contamination, do not excessively handle the evidence after recovery. Label and seal all evidence packages at the crime scene. Obtain known standards (e.g., fiber samples from a known carpet). Make a complete evaluation of the crime scene.
10. Record and collect physical evidence: Photograph all items before collection and document on the photographic log. Mark evidence locations on the sketch and complete the evidence log with notations for each item of evidence. As previously set forth, have one person serve as evidence custodian. Two persons should observe the evidence in

place during recovery and mark evidence for identification. Do not mark directly on the evidence due to the potential loss of fingerprints and DNA; place identifying marks on packaging. Constantly check paperwork, packaging, and other information for errors.

11. Final survey: The final survey is a review of all aspects of the search. Discuss the search with all personnel and ensure that all documentation is correct and complete. Photograph the scene showing the final condition. Ensure that all evidence is secured and that all equipment is retrieved. Ensure that hiding places or difficult access areas have not been overlooked.
12. Release: Release the crime scene after the final survey. Documentation for the release of the crime scene should include the time and date of release, to whom released, and by whom released. Ensure that the evidence is collected according to legal requirements, documented, and marked for identification. If a search warrant was used, leave a copy of the warrant and receipt. Consider the need for specialists (e.g., a blood pattern analyst or medical examiner) to observe the scene before it is released. Once the scene is released, reentry may require a warrant, so the scene should be released only when all personnel are satisfied that the scene was searched correctly and completely. Only the person in charge should release the scene.

The following case histories are typical of situations to which FBI ERTs as well as other law enforcement agencies respond on a daily basis across the world. They serve here to present the applications of the preceding guidelines and responsibilities toward efficiently and accurately putting together the often mixed and confusing pieces of crime scene puzzles.

Commingling within Cold Case Exhumations

The likelihood of commingling due to multiple interments in clandestine graves related to homicidal behavior is not uncommon. The closest we come in the contemporary United States to criminal instances of mass graves are investigations of homicides in which two or more victims were killed and interred contemporaneously or in the same feature. In ongoing research first presented in 1999, one of the authors reviewed 920 homicide cases in which victims' remains were reported as buried (Hochrein et al. 1999). Of those 920 cases dating from 1951 to 1997, 143 (15%) were reported as involving the burial of two or more persons. Of those 143 cases, 55 (6% of the total cases reviewed and 38% of those involving multiple homicides) describe the burial of multiple victims in common graves. Examples include the triple homicide committed by Christopher Hightower in 1991. The common grave of two of his victims was found near Barrington, Rhode Island, two months after their murders. Tony Carruthers used a recently dug grave shaft in a Memphis, Tennessee, cemetery to conceal the bodies of three of his victims beneath a legitimate burial in 1994. In 1990, cult leader Jeffrey Lundgren directed the murders and mass burial of five of his followers on a farm in Kirkland, Ohio. And serial killers Dean Corll and Elmar Henley buried 17 of 26 victims beneath a

Galveston, Texas, boat shed during the early 1970s. Reinecke and Hochrein (2008) describe the burial of four homicide victims in one shallow pit feature.

Unlike the case presented next, commingling can also involve human with nonhuman animal remains. Reinecke and Hochrein (2008:44) mention an instance of naturally occurring nonhuman animal remains found within a clandestine human burial. Consider another clandestine burial excavated by Hochrein and the FBI's Pittsburgh Evidence Response Team in which nonhuman animal remains were intentionally added to further conceal a homicide victim's body. In that scene, an adult male victim was buried in a shallow grave for approximately eight months. The site selected for concealing the remains was historically used to discard deer, dog, cat, and other animal carcasses as well as general household refuse. Beneath an accumulation of debris and nonhuman bones, suspects dug a small pit and forced the victim's corpse into it. Nonhuman bones were placed within the pit and placed on top of it to further conceal the criminal interment.

At that scene, as well as general searches for remains or missing persons, the use of a mobile telephone's secure email and digital photography capabilities was very helpful. Investigators, uncertain whether a particular bone might be human, were able to take close-up anterior, posterior, proximal, and distal photographs of questioned bones, with scale. The images were then emailed to qualified experts who could advise, in real time, the species or if collection of the bones was warranted for further examination.

Case Example: The Red-Headed Woman

In Reinecke and Hochrein (2008), a clandestine, multiple homicide burial was presented as an example of, or potential for, commingling. In the current example, the authors present a cold case homicide investigation in which two legitimate funerary burials were encountered in the same excavation feature.

In 2007 FBI ERT Pittsburgh Division assistance was requested in a cold case homicide dating to 1950. During the spring of that year, the recently deposited body of an adult Caucasian female was found by a mushroom hunter along an embankment of Route 522 between Berkeley Springs, West Virginia, and Hancock, Maryland. Attempts to identify the nude, strangled, and battered victim were unsuccessful in spite of intensive efforts by the West Virginia State Police, Maryland State Police, FBI, as well as considerable media coverage. The mystery of Jane Doe, christened "The Red-Headed Woman," captured the local community's interest and compassion, as reflected in a full-page article in the December 29, 1951, edition of the *Charleston Gazette:*

> *Meanwhile news of the discovery spread like wildfire over the surrounding countryside. Before Drs. H.D. Powers and J.H. Armentrout of Martinsburg arrived to perform an autopsy at 11 p.m., more than 500 persons had already viewed the body. Several hundred others gathered outside the mortuary along with newspaper reporters from nearby communities. (Hill 1951:2m)*

Other accounts of the case further suggest the interest this investigation garnered:

> *So, on May 13, after 2000 people had viewed the body in Berkeley Springs, Helsley arranged to take the corpse to Newton D. Baker Veterans Hospital in Martinsburg. There it was put in cold storage and rolled out whenever relatives of missing persons came to see it. (Douglas 2000)*

The abandonment of the body along a heavily trafficked thoroughfare, near the intersection of three state boundaries, did not aid in limiting the possible geographic origins of the victim. An autopsy report prepared in 1950 and reviewed over the years contained biological details about the decedent including those of taphonomic relevance if her remains could be located in the more recent cold case investigation. For example the victim was described as 65 inches (165 cm) tall and 125–130 pounds (57–59 kg). She displayed antemortem scars from medical procedures but no evidence of fractures ante- or perimortem. Superficial abrasions were found over her head, face, and neck, and there were numerous "punctuate", or puncture wounds over her forearms, back, and thighs. During autopsy, the victim's skull cap was removed. It was the conclusion from the early morning autopsy that the unidentified white female was struck with numerous blows from a blunt object and strangled.

The community of Berkeley Springs seemed to adopt the Red-Headed Woman as one of their own, with viewings and a proper burial in a local cemetery, albeit the potter's field, or indigent, section of those facilities. In 2007, the West Virginia State Police resurrected the investigation through that agency's Cold Case Unit and in light of DNA technology discovered and developed since the homicide took place. With recent Internet postings of the case, two families came forward to the state police with hopes that Jane Doe might be their relative who went missing prior to the 1950 discovery of the decedent's body along the interstate. With a source of DNA to which the victim's might be compared, but no biological exemplars or associative evidence preserved from the 1950 investigation, the victim's remains had to be located. In 2007, the state police initially identified the cemetery in which the victim was interred but not the specific burial plot. Unfortunately, the care and interest the community took in Jane Doe did not include a permanent grave marker. Again, the undaunted efforts of the WVSP cold case investigator paid off in his location of research by a local historian who happened, in 2003, to take on a review of the cemetery's records as a project. The historian made the following notation in records for a plot identified only as "Red Headed Woman":

> *... However, I discovered the following information. It happened in May of 1950. An unidentified woman was murdered on Grocer's Hill. Which is on Route 522 between Berkeley Springs, WV and Hancock, MD. The only way to "identify" her when spoken of (sic) was because of her red hair.*

When the state police investigator visited the cemetery, he found the referenced area and plot but no markers. By comparing known marked graves and plots, and measuring approximate distances parallel to those plots, he identified an approximately 40 square foot (sqft) area (3.72 square meter [sqm]) in which he thought the grave could be located. In a review of the cemetery records, it appeared that there were no other graves in that area believed to hold the Red-Headed Woman. Using geotaphonomic indicators, soil probes, and core samplers, FBI ERT identified the precise position of a subsurface anomaly consistent with a possible grave feature. In that area located by the Cold Case Unit investigator there was a subtle, rectangular, 5.5 ft × 6 ft (3.07 sqm) depression. This anomaly appeared on the lower portion of the northern slope of a hill. Likewise, consistent with burials in the mid-twentieth century, and burials of the indigent in general, probing did not identify a concrete or other type of burial vault in which coffins or caskets are now often required to be "sealed." The notoriety of the case suggested the individual would have been interred within a casket. Probing and coring determined the compression-depression anomaly was further characterized by a void or area of lesser subterranean compaction consistently encountered 24–36 in (61–91 cm) below ground surface. Field tests of cored soil samples for pH, phosphorus, nitrogen, and potassium levels revealed the anomaly was less acidic than control samples. Another difference between the grave fill and undisturbed soils at the same level was slightly higher amounts of phosphorus.

Two months after the preliminary field survey, the West Virginia State Police applied for and received an order of exhumation for the above-described plot location. Exhumation, from the Latin *ex* meaning "out of" and *humus* or "ground," is the lawful disinterment of a ritually or officially buried body from a legally recognized grave. As Aggrawal (2001) points out, this distinction from the recovery of a body from a clandestine grave designed to hide evidence has legal repercussions. An exhumation requires a judicial, or court, order, whether for criminal or civil investigations. In the order obtained in this case, the judge found that with the development of new scientific and forensic techniques, such as DNA analysis, probable cause existed that could provide for identification of the Jane Doe victim. The judge issued an order that the plot identified by the Cold Case Unit and FBI ERT be exhumed to allow for examination of the unidentified female's remains for the purpose of DNA analysis and comparisons.

Unlike that of a clandestine grave, the excavation of a legitimate burial under an order of exhumation is conducted with assumptions that limit the amount of detailed archaeological excavation typically necessary to uncover geotaphonomic evidence of how and when the burial took place (Hochrein 1997, 2002). The known legitimacy of a cemetery burial (outside those situations in which homicide suspects have buried the remains of their victim(s) under or above that of legitimate ceremonial burial) negates the need to examine for, and collect, possible evidence of the cemetery gravedigger's work. As previously referenced, in 1996, Tony Von Carruthers was convicted in the murder of three individuals whom he buried alive beneath a legitimate burial in the Rose Hill Cemetery in Memphis, Tennessee (*State v. Carruthers* 2000). During testimony in a 2003 federal trial, New

Jersey's DeCalvacante crime family capo, Anthony Rotondo, described "double decker" burials. These involved his associates allegedly burying their victims in the same casket or grave as a legitimate burial (Rudolph 2003). The means and method by which a legitimate burial took place are typically a matter of record performed as a service, not as a means of concealing a crime. Adherence, however, to archaeological protocols cannot be completely ignored, as was demonstrated in the scene described next, and as should be followed in the event of commingled funerary remains.

The excavation to exhume remains believed to be those of the Red-Headed Woman began with ERT members trained in specific techniques being assigned duties of photography, excavation, mapping, maintenance of logs, and so on. The team leader oversaw the safety and needs of the team and assisted state police personnel. The ERT that responded to this scene consisted of members from the FBI Pittsburgh Division, which has as its territory all of West Virginia and the western half of Pennsylvania. The excavation was directed by a team member who had postgraduate training and professional experience as an archaeologist before joining the FBI. West Virginia State Police also participated as excavators and took possession of human remains removed during the exhumation.

Opening photographs documented the original condition of the scene on the date of exhumation following the confirmation of a subsurface anomaly using the soil probes, core sampler, and geotaphonomic indicators identified during the preliminary survey. Three-dimensional mapping using electronic total station technology recorded the site's topography and relationship to marked graves within the cemetery. An approximately 6.5 ft × 4.5 ft (2.72 sqm) grid unit was marked on the surface using paint. (It could also have been indicated using string and chaining pins or stakes.) This guide for what would be an exploratory trench was oriented perpendicular and across the center of the rectangular anomaly. Gross, or shovel, excavation began within the defined trench to determine the sides of a burial shaft, and to reach a depth at which more precise excavation techniques would be employed. In the excavation of clandestine graves, which are typically more shallow, archaeologists attempt to preserve internal stratification and pit boundaries in order to recognize geotaphonomic evidence such as tool marks and subsurface cracking or desiccation. In those scenes, an excavation window is initially dug near the center of the anomaly, but is much smaller than a trench in order that it can be systematically expanded toward the interfaces of the pit edge and undisturbed soils where tool marks are often preserved (Clark 2011; Hochrein 2002). The window, like the exhumation trench, also helps to determine the top of buried evidence within the grave. In Jane Doe's legitimate burial, the construction of a grave shaft by hand or heavy equipment was a given. The potential matching of the digging implement(s) to those associated with a suspect did not apply. The exploratory trench in this case served its purpose of revealing the textural and color differences between the undisturbed soils and those within a burial shaft. Through periodic monitoring with core samples, the gross excavation with shovels switched to small

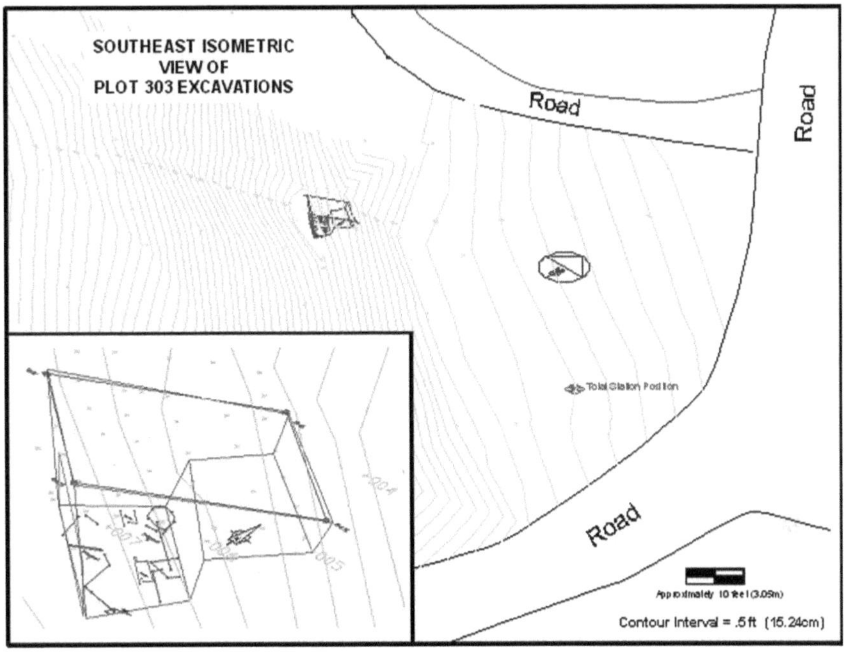

Figure 4-2
Isometric view, facing northwest, of the 2007 exhumation site compiled from total station raw data, and demonstrating the slope into which Burials 1 and 2 were originally dug.

hand tools and a vacuum when the buried remains were determined to be within approximately 6 in (15 cm) of the excavation floor.

As mentioned, in addition to photography from the outset of the exhumation, three-dimensional mapping of the scene was accomplished with electronic total station technology (Figure 4-2). This is one of the most efficient means of spatially documenting the position of remains within subterranean contexts—an especially critical factor when commingled remains might be involved. For this scene, a primary datum was established 53 ft (16 m) northeast of the suspected cemetery plot. From that vantage, the northing, easting, distance, and elevations were recorded for the site's general topography, relationship to marked graves, and evidence or features encountered during excavation.

Detailed excavation first revealed the skeletal remains of a single adult individual 3.95 ft (1.2 m) below surface. There was one problem, however; this skeleton exhibited fairly robust features, and the only clothing that appeared to survive was a segment of leather belt and a leather work boot on the right foot. The likelihood that this was Jane Doe quickly evaporated. The preliminary survey did not reveal any other burials in the vicinity of that area recorded as containing Jane Doe's 1950 plot. Could the records have been incorrect? Could these remains be those of an individual buried above Jane Doe? The age of this burial appeared to be relatively older than 1950 given the presence of corroded cut nails from an otherwise disintegrated wooden container and the complete disintegration of clothing other than the leather mentioned previously. The depth of the base of the contained remains at 4.3 ft (1.3 m) below surface opened the possibility this individual could have been placed above another in a burial shaft dug to a standard 6 feet (1.8 m). Further core sampling beneath the remains, however, substantiated the underlying stratigraphy was undisturbed.

Using the established grid or trench, the excavation was expanded across, and perpendicular to, the orientation of the burial shaft, systematically removing 5- to 10-cm (1.97- to 3.94-in) arbitrary horizontal and vertical levels at a time. Again, this procedure was used in an attempt to locate the north wall of the burial shaft, while ensuring that larger pieces of container or remains would be noticed. When decomposed wood or other cultural materials were identified in core samples, excavation switched to the use of smaller hand tools. The remains of a single individual were first encountered but found to be partially represented. They consisted of the right foot (contained in a boot), right fibula, tibia, femur, right pelvis, right radius, humerus scapula, and ribs, as well as a few vertebrae. At first, the archaeologist wondered if perhaps the interment may have undergone what Brothwell (1987:23-26) termed "tumbled bone." This condition was found in York's Jewbury Cemetery. There, the funerary remains were found to be in disarray or out of alignment in spite of their context within well-cut graves and containers. Brothwell suggested the remains may not have been buried immediately, allowing for movement of the skeletal elements in relatively decomposed remains. Media and investigative accounts of the Red-Headed Woman investigation related the following timeline between her discovery and interment:

May 10, 1950	04:00 p.m.	Body found and estimated to have been dead 48–96 hours
May 10, 1950	12:00–3:00 a.m.	Autopsy in mortuary
May 13, 1950		Body placed in cold storage at Veteran's Hospital
May 23, 1950		Body returned to mortuary and buried that afternoon

Boddington (1987:27–42) encountered similar disturbances to skeletons in an Anglo-Saxon Cemetery near Raunds, Northamptonshire, England. It was concluded that the number of correlated factors involved, including decomposition from soil, water, and chemical conditions of the grave, to treatment of the body within the casket made it difficult to explain what caused bone tumble or movement. As it could have related to the Red-Headed Woman's burial, the grave was dug on a significant slope. Media photographs of the burial site from 1950 depict a steep slope. The 2007 total station survey accomplished during the exhumation confirmed the same (approximately 28° slope). Ultimately, "bone tumble" as an explanation for the position of the partial skeleton in the cemetery setting believed to hold the Red-Headed Woman was ruled out. The correct anatomical orientation of the skeletal elements, along with the ill-preserved remnants of corresponding clothing elements and a level wooden container, suggested the remains were disturbed after their burial rather than before or during inhumation. Archaeologically and anatomically, their position was consistent with that of an individual laid horizontally on his or her back within a container within a burial shaft. In both the historical and forensic instances, the *in situ* documentation of remains and associated features through formal archaeological excavation was critical toward recognizing this context.

Further lateral excavation in search of the northern wall of the burial shaft for Individual 1 did not encounter that geotaphonomic feature. Rather, the remains of a second burial and individual were found at approximately the same level as those of Burial/Individual Number 1. It became clear that the burial of Individual Number 2 had intruded into that of Individual Number 1 (Figures 4-3 and 4-4). Approximately 8 in (20.3 cm) to the left, or north, of Individual Number 1 and slightly downslope, a metal handle and disintegrated remains of a fabric lined, wooden casket were encountered. The casket handles were octagonal short bars with lugs, arms, and tips (Hacker-Norton and Trinkley 1984:8–10). Within that container were the much more gracile remains of an individual consistent with the recorded 1950 burial of Jane Doe, or the Red-Headed Woman. Additionally, the cranium of Individual 2 was cut, resulting in a separate cranial cap indicative of an autopsy.

An unfortunate fact of forensic archaeology projects, unlike the archaeology of funded academic research projects, is that they more often than not fall under relatively severe time and budgetary constraints. In spite of their literal involvement in matters of life and death,

Figure 4-3
Plan view of Burials/Individuals 1 and 2 excavated to that degree at which they could be defined as two separate individuals from which respective DNA exemplars could be sampled.

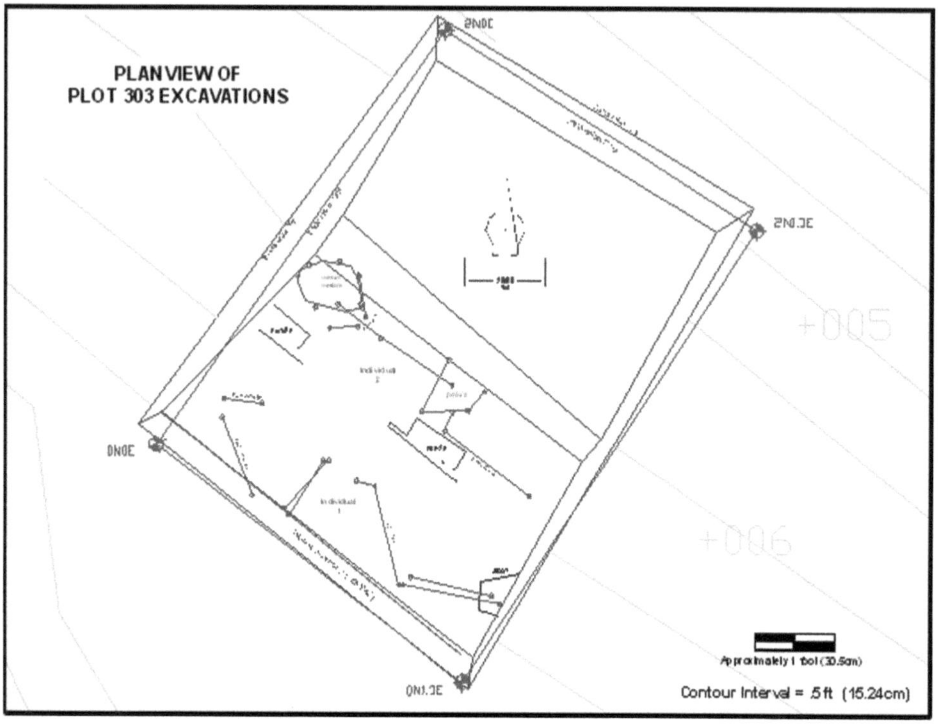

Figure 4-4
Plan view total station diagram of Individuals/Burials 1 and 2 depicting the more prominent elements of each skeleton and burial container.

crime scene investigators are often under pressure to collect evidence as efficiently as possible to limit the expense of manpower and supplies, as well as to return affected property as soon as feasible to persons who may have no involvement or association with the investigation. The author made the decision at this scene to expose only enough of Individual 2 to confirm it was the Red-Headed Woman's burial and to collect recommended skeletal elements for DNA analyses (Figure 4-3). The bones that are preferred for DNA testing are described in Boyer (2012:466) as those, such as long bones, from which a window of bone may be cut from their diaphyses. This preference is then followed by the cranial vault, ilium, or phalanges.

Unlike the forensic excavation of a clandestine grave, the upper levels of fill from the original and intrusive burial shafts were not entirely screened. Within 6 in (15 cm) of the remains, quarter-inch (6.35 mm) sieves were used. Again, the goal of the court-ordered exhumation was to locate and sample remains of Jane Doe, aka the Red-Headed Woman. Because the act of her ceremonial burial was not part of a criminal incident, the content of the shaft fill was grossly examined but not fully screened. As a result, smaller fragments associated with Individual 1 could have been mixed in the fill of the second shaft from the 1950 gravedigger's actions. If these fragments had been large, they would have been found during the shovel excavation phase of the exhumation. Within

6 in (15 cm) of Individual 2, such fragments would have been noticed through screening. The absence of any portion of a mandible or cranium for Individual 1 suggested those bones may have been inadvertently removed en masse during the intrusive 1950 excavation if not looted from the grave. Cemeteries routinely use borrowed fill to infill shafts. Because a mound of dirt next to an open grave during a ceremony is not aesthetically desirable, the fill is sometimes taken from the site, combined or dumped with spoils from other cemetery excavations, and then later returned to fill in the grave following the funeral ceremony. The Red-Headed Woman's burial ceremony may have been anticipated to be a local public event given the attention the investigation garnered. Care may have been taken to move the shaft spoils before the ceremony. In this case, the remains of Individual Number 1 may have been removed during the construction of Individual Number 2's (Jane Doe's) grave and relocated to a communal spoils pile. When fill was brought to infill Jane Doe's burial, it may have been selected from another area of the cemetery spoils pile. This was suggested by the presence of synthetic ribbon in the upper levels of the fill. Also, no fragmented bone was noticed during the gross excavation phase.

Ultimately, at the cemetery scene, Individual 2 was determined to be Jane Doe/Red-Headed Woman through the location of the grave, physical anthropological characteristics including the taphonomic evidence of a sawed cranium from an autopsy, and historical accounts of the burial. Likewise, the comparatively elaborate characteristics of Individual Number 2's casket were not consistent with that for an indigent buried in the potter's field section of a cemetery.

A nonforensic, nonarchaeological, less systematic excavation of the Red-Headed Woman's burial site may have resulted in damage to, and mixing of, Individuals 1 and 2. Heavy equipment could easily have torn through the disintegrated wooden containers of each burial. The soil stains, into which the wood of the containers had decomposed, would have given little indication to a heavy equipment operator that he had intruded into a burial. In fact, this sort of gross, reckless excavation probably resulted in the partial removal of Individual 1's burial in 1950. Without the use of strict archaeological protocols, commingled remains, even in a funerary setting, can be further confused. Clearly, the application of FBI ERT guidelines at this scene prevented further commingling. The sampled remains were selected, removed, and packaged along the same guidelines provided in Unidentified Human Remains Collection Kits maintained by all FBI ERT teams. West Virginia State Police submitted sampled remains from both Individuals 1 and 2 to two accredited institutions. Unfortunately, the profiles did not match those from either of the donating families. In spite of this disappointing outcome, the Red-Headed Woman's DNA record is preserved for future comparisons.

Case Example: Recovery of Multiple Victims from an Airplane Crash

The United States is obviously no stranger to natural, accidental, and criminally motivated mass disasters. The smallest of these scenes may involve only a few individuals but can

Figure 4-5
Aerial photograph of the Goldman, Missouri crash site demonstrating the remote and rugged terrain.

entail hundreds or thousands of pieces dispersed over several acres, or concentrated within the more confined area of a deep impact crater. An example of the first type of scene resulted from the October 16, 2000, crash of a small aircraft carrying Missouri governor Melvin Carnahan, his son Roger Carnahan, and the governor's campaign aide, Christopher Sifford.

During the evening of October 16, 2000, weather conditions combined with equipment problems and pilot error to cause the governor's Cessna 335 to barrel into a heavily wooded hillside (Figure 4-5) near Goldman, Missouri, at an estimated speed of more than 300 knots (345 miles per hour [556 kmph]). A small impact crater [5 ft (1.5 meters) wide, 10 ft long (3.0 meters), and 4 ft (1.2 meters) deep] and a stand of sheered trees evidenced the point of impact for the fixed-wing aircraft. Approximately 100 ft (30.5 meters) away from the crater, in the apparent direction of travel, were the twisted and abbreviated remnants of the cockpit and fuselage, which came to rest against a stand of trees (Figure 4-6). With the exception of the horizontal stabilizers and the aft upper fuselage skin, the airframe structure separated into small- (6 × 6 × 12 in [15 × 15 × 30 cm]) and medium-sized (12 × 12 × 24 in [30 × 30 × 60 cm]) pieces of debris (NTSB 2002). The distance from the furthest piece of wreckage, a right engine crankshaft, was 900 ft (274.3 meters). A small amount of debris landed as far as 100 ft (30.5 meters) behind the impact crater. The maximum width of the debris field was 250 ft (76.2 meters).

Figure 4-6
General view, from the beginning of the debris field, out and up toward the area at which the aircraft entered the tree line.

An often ignored, or less often considered, dimension of the terrestrial mass disaster site is that of elevation. At the Carnahan crash site, the problems associated with debris and remains landing in the tree canopy were compounded by the area's steep terrain (Figure 4-7). Another three-dimensional aspect on any wooded crash site is recording evidence that will help to reconstruct flight dynamics before and after impact. Specifically, the height of damaged and undamaged trees combined with the orientation (right and left) of aircraft parts on the ground helps to determine the attitude at which the aircraft entered the canopy and impacted, as well as whether it was right-side up or upside down. With information collected by the Missouri State Highway Patrol as well as the St. Louis and Springfield Division Evidence Response Teams, the National Transportation Safety Board investigators were able to create a three-dimensional model of the airplane flight path through the trees. They determined the airplane was in a 16° to 18°, right-wing-down attitude during its entry into the trees. Although no computerized video reconstruction is included in the NTSB's Aircraft Accident Brief for this crash, at least one figure depicts a side view of the broken tree tops left in the aftermath of the crash (NTSB 2002).

The volume of evidence previously mentioned as well as that of crash victims, including crew and passenger positions and their proximity to localized aircraft damage (i.e., holes in the fuselage or blast-related evidence), can become overwhelming in any setting, let alone

Figure 4-7
General view of an arborist used to retrieve plane parts and human remains from the tree canopy.

those complicated by rough terrain and thick woods. Without sophisticated mapping technology such as the electronic total station, the collection of spatial data that may reflect patterns in the distribution of otherwise commingled evidence would be difficult and incomplete. Two weeks prior to the crash of Governor Carnahan's airplane, the FBI's St. Louis Division ERT sponsored a medicolegal field school in the recovery of human remains. One of two final practical exercises in that school involved the search, mapping, and recovery of evidence from the simulated crash of a small fixed-wing aircraft using search and recovery protocols described in Dirkmaat et al. (2001). Attendees from across the United States, and especially the state of Missouri, utilized a combination of mapping techniques from the simplest to most sophisticated (Figure 4-8). They recorded the positions of 400 simulated human remains, plane parts, and topography across a debris field encompassing 52,800 square feet (4,905 square meters). The Terrestrial Mass Fatality Scene Protocol introduced in that training includes four steps: (1) search and location effort; (2) total station data collection and assignment of field specimen numbers; (3) photographic documentation; and (4) physical evidence collection and preservation (Dirkmaat et al. 2001:4–6). Some of the attendees of that school found themselves as first responders at the scene of their governor's death. Their experience and training in the above-mentioned protocols in collaboration with the FBI ERT members' familiarity with ERT guidelines, as well as the

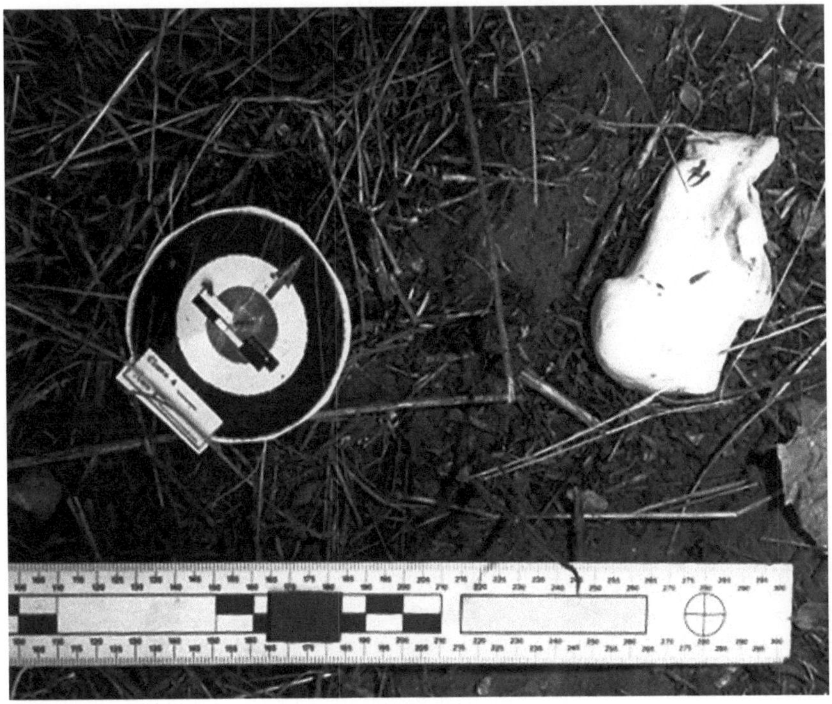

Figure 4-8

Close-up view of scales used in a training scenario to size and orient mock human remains (in this case, a plastic calcaneus) within the crash scene. The circular scale serves as a label, scale, and compass when the arrow is oriented to the north.

Highway Patrol's expertise in total station mapping, caused the joint agency team of responders to realize the efficiency and accuracy of using such methods and technology. As a result, the Terrestrial Mass Fatality Scene Protocol was easily applied in the scheme of the general FBI ERT methods outlined previously.

First applied in a commercial air disaster at the crash site of United Flight 427 near Pittsburgh, Pennsylvania, in September 1994 (Dirkmaat et al. 1995), electronic total stations, or laser measuring devices, are now required by the NTSB in the documentation of mass transportation disasters. The Missouri Highway Patrol combined the FBI ERT training they received little more than a week before, and their expertise in using multiple total stations for highway accident reconstructions, to maximize the information they could get from the Goldman, Missouri, crash site. Shortly after meeting with various investigative teams, two total stations were brought to the crash site. One was devoted to recording the position of human remains marked by search teams, while the second was devoted to mapping the location of diagnostic airplane parts identified by FAA and corporate engineers. The remaining nondiagnostic airplane debris would be collected using a reference system of 30 sectors established across the scene.

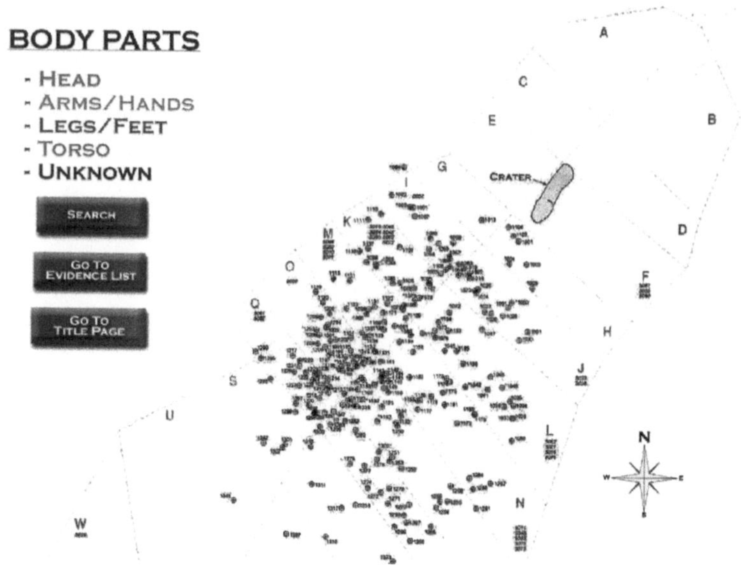

Figure 4-9
Interactive total station diagram showing the distribution of human remains across the crash site.

The dedication of two total stations was well conceived and seamlessly applied in the previously described method. However, the use of the technology would later reveal another complication that may arise in documenting different categories of commingled evidence. The numbering system used by the total station operators was not mutually exclusive. This meant that a piece of human remains numbered, for example, "1505" corresponded to that shot recorded by one total station, while a piece of aircraft might also be assigned "1505" using the second total station dedicated to aircraft components and other nonhuman remains evidence. A problem occurred in merging the information obtained by the two machines because there was not a mutually exclusive numbering system. This was corrected by the FBI's Operational Projects Unit when each total station's raw data were sent in from the field. However, respective, exclusive numbering systems applied to each type of crash evidence in the field could have saved time devoted toward interpreting the data.

As shown in the first case history, problems are encountered in most scenes of commingled evidence. It is the formulation, application, and maintenance of appropriate recovery methodologies that will lessen the impact of those problems or allow for their correction. The contextual recovery of evidence at the Goldman, Missouri, crash site served as the basis for the NTSB's reconstruction and conclusions regarding this accident (NTSB 2002). The data collected not only were accurate but also allowed the FBI's Operational Projects Unit, for the first time in a mass disaster scene, to create an interactive computerized crime scene diagram.

Investigators interested in the description of a particular piece of human remains or aircraft part could simply position the arrow on the computer screen over the item number on a two-dimensional plan view and receive a written description. By double-clicking on the same number or position, investigators would see a digital image of the fragment. Maps of human remains could be separated from nonhuman evidence and were coded by body part (Figure 4-9). Unlike the sector or grid system method of collection, the piece plotting of each fragment ensured the evidence was not commingled. The impact on future air disaster investigations includes an ability to study the aforementioned patterns created by the distribution of human remains and debris.

Conclusions

The two cases presented here, as examples of the application of formal guidelines by FBI ERTs, demonstrate complications that may arise in dealing with commingled evidence including human remains. More so, they demonstrate the value and efficiency of such planned, structured methodologies toward compiling accurate reconstructions of seemingly chaotic collections of evidence. Gone should be the days when medical examiners and the experts they employ are presented with bags of bones simply picked up from a scene. Where investigators once relied on such experts to help solve crimes solely from clues found on the bodies, we can now collect as much, if not more, from subtle clues contained in the recorded contexts of those remains. In cases such as the commingled legitimate burials previously described, or that of a clandestine mass grave presented in Reinecke and Hochrein (2008), three-dimensional data can offer, among other information, (1) the sequence in which victims were deposited, (2) whether or not the decedents were mutilated, shot, or otherwise damaged peri- or postdeposition, (3) postburial disturbances such as attempts to relocate or further conceal bodies, and (4) the relocation or absence of evidence due to bioturbation. Similarly, the mass collection of evidence from general areas throughout a crash scene is no longer acceptable in light of developed protocols and applications of laser technologies as seen in the aforementioned air crash investigation. The three-dimensional documentation through total station or scanner technologies of individual items commingled at a crash site may offer insight into (1) flight and impact dynamics, (2) peri- or postimpact explosions versus in-flight explosions, (3) passenger and crew positions, and (4) postimpact disturbances via human or nonhuman scavenging. The patterns left in the aftermath of natural and man-made disasters or criminal conduct are as unique as the factors that caused them. Only by collecting evidence in a manner which allows us to analyze all the evidence offered in a scene in context can we begin to accumulate data sets that are comparable between crime scenes or mass disaster scenes. The ability to compare evidence patterns between more and more scenes will lead to an ability to more accurately create interpretive models toward solving crimes and perhaps predictive models for preventing future events.

Acknowledgments

The authors would like to thank each and every member of the FBI ERT for their efforts and dedication. Special thanks are offered to members of the St. Louis, Springfield, and Pittsburgh teams as well as the West Virginia State Police and the Missouri Highway Patrol. Their efforts contributed to the successful resolution of the cases presented herein. Likewise, the expertise of those specialists who work within the FBI Laboratory and the FBI's Operational Projects Unit has helped to continuously advance FBI ERT's in the manner in which data is collected and interpreted.

References

Aggrawal, A., 2001. Exhumation-medical and legal aspects. Anil Aggrawal's J. Forensic Med. Toxicol. 2 (2). http://www.anilaggrawal.com/ij/vol_002_no_002/ug002_002.html (accessed February 4, 2013).

Anker, R., Taylor, F., 1989. The trajectories of falling parts following in-flight breakup. Proceedings of the Twentieth International Seminar of the International Society of Air Safety Investigators Forum. ISASI 22, 133–140.

Barrie, H.J., Hudson-Walker, N., 1970. Incidence and pathogenesis of fractures of the lumbar transverse processes in air crashes. Aerosp. Med. 41, 805.

Bergen-Henengouwan, S.G., 1973. Aircraft Wreckage Trajectory Analysis User Manual. Aeronautical and Mechanical Engineering Department, Southern Alberta Institute of Technology, Calgary, Alberta.

Boddington, A., 1987. Chaos, disturbance and decay in an Anglo-Saxon cemetery. In: Boddington, A., Garland, A.N., Janaway, R.C. (Eds.), Death, Decay and Reconstruction, Approaches to Archaeology and Forensic Science. Manchester University Press, Manchester, UK, pp. 27–42.

Boyer, D., 2012. DNA identification and forensic anthropology: Developments in DNA collection analysis and technology. In: Dirkmaat, D. (Ed.), A Companion to Forensic Anthropology. Wiley Blackwell, New York, pp. 462–476.

Brooks, P., 1985. Crime scene and profile characteristics of organized and disorganized murderers. FBI Law Enforcement Bull. August.

Brothwell, D., 1987. Decay and disorder in the York Jewbury Skeletons. In: Boddington, A., Garland, A.N., Janaway, R.C. (Eds.), Death, Decay and Reconstruction, Approaches to Archaeology and Forensic Science. Manchester University Press, Manchester, UK, pp. 22–26.

Burgess, A.W., Ressler, R.K., 1985. Sexual Homicide Crime Scenes and Patterns of Criminal Behavior. Final Report, Boston City Health and Hospitals Department, Boston, MA.

Clark, M.D., 2011. Toolmark identification of a mattock to a clod of soil from a grave. J. Forensic Sci. 56 (1), 241–243.

Dirkmaat, D.C., Hefner, J.T., Hochrein, M.J., 2001. Forensic Processing of the Terrestrial Mass Fatality Scene: Testing New Search, Documentation, and Recovery Methodologies. A paper presented at the American Academy of Forensic Sciences 53rd Annual Meeting, Seattle, WA.

Dirkmaat, D.C., Quinn, A., Adovasio, J.M., 1995. New methodologies for search and recovery. Disaster Management News, National Foundation for Mortuary Care. December, pp. 1–2.

Douglas, J., 2000. The Redhead Murder Case. The Morgan Messenger, May 24, 2000 as reprinted May 24, 2007. http://www.morganmessenger.com/news/content/story-4265 (accessed May 17, 2013).

Douglas, J.E., Munn, C., 1992a. Violent crime scene analysis: Modus operandi, signature and staging. FBI Law Enforcement Bull. 61 (2), 1–10.

Douglas, J.E., Munn, C., 1992b. Violent crime scene analysis. Homicide Invest. J. Spring 63, 69.

Douglas, J.E., Ressler, R.K., Burgess, A.W., Hartman, C.R., 1986. Criminal profiling from crime scene analysis. Behav. Sci. Law 4 (4), 401–421.

Gable, W.D., 1968. Pathology patterns in aircraft accident investigators. Aerosp. Med. 39, 638.

Hacker-Norton, D., Trinkley, M., 1984. Remember Man Thou Art Dust: Coffin Hardware of the Early Twentieth Century. Chicora Foundation, Columbia, SC.

Hellerich, U., Pollak, S., 1995. Airplane crash: Traumatologic findings in cases of extreme body disintegration. Am. J. Forensic Med. Pathol. 16, 320–324.

Hill, I.R., 1989. Mechanism of injury in aircraft accidents: A theoretical approach. Aviat. Space Environ. Med. 60 (7), A18–A25.

Hill, J.A., 1951. Brutal murder of redhead near Maryland line one of state's most baffling unsolved crimes. Charleston Gazette. December 23, 1951, p. 2m.

Hochrein, M.J., 1997. Buried crime scene evidence: The application of geotaphonomy in forensic archaeology. In: Stimson, P., Mertz, C. (Eds.), Forensic Dentistry. CRC Press, Boca Raton, FL, pp. 83–99.

Hochrein, M.J., 2002. An autopsy of the grave: Recognizing, collecting, and preserving forensic geotaphonomic evidence. In: Haglund, W.D., Sorg, M. (Eds.), Advances in Forensic Taphonomy: Method, Theory, and Archaeological Perspectives. CRC Press, Boca Raton, FL, pp. 45–70.

Hochrein, M.J., Gabra, J., Nawrocki, S.P., 1999. The buried body cases content analyses project: Patterns in buried body investigations. Proc. Am. Acad. Forensic Sci. V, 212–213.

Keppel, R.D., 2005. Serial offenders: Linking cases by modus operandi and signature. In: James, S.H., Norby, J.J. (Eds.), Forensic Science: An Introduction to Scientific and Investigative Techniques, second ed. CRC Press/Taylor & Francis Group, Boca Raton, FL, pp. 605–614.

Kreft, S., 1970. Who was at the aircraft's controls when the fatal accident occurred? Aerospace, Pathology. College of American Pathologists Foundation, Chicago, IL, p. 96.

Lundrigan, S., Canter, D., 2001. Spatial patterns of serial murder: An analysis of disposal site location choice. Behav. Sci. Law 19 (4), 595–610.

Matteson, F.H., 1974. Analysis of wreckage patterns from in-flight disintegrations. J. Safety Res. 6, 60–71.

Min, J.X., Jia, M.Z., 1992. Correlation of trauma and cause of death to accident reconstruction: A case of a flight accident report. J. Forensic Sci. 37 (2), 585–589.

National Transportation Safety Board, 2002. Aircraft Accident Brief: Accident Number CHI01MA011; Cessna 335, N8354N. Missouri, Hillsboro, October 16, 2000. http://www.ntsb.gov/publictn/2002/AAB0202.pdf.

Rajs, J., Lundstrom, M., Brobery, M., Lidberg, L., Lindquist, O., 1998. Criminal mutilation of the human body in Sweden: A thirty year medico-legal and forensic psychiatric study. J. Forensic Sci. 43 (3), 563–580.

Reinecke, G.W., Hochrein, M.J., 2008. Pieces of the puzzle: FBI evidence response team approaches to scenes with commingled evidence. In: Adams, B.J., Byrd, J.E. (Eds.), Recovery, Analysis, and Identification of Commingled Human Remains. Human a Press, Totowa, NJ, pp. 31–55.

Ressler, R.K., Burgess, A.W., DePue, R.L., Douglas, J.E., Hazelwood, R.R., Lanning, K.V., Lent, C., 1985. Crime scene and profile characteristics of organized and disorganized murderers. FBI Law Enforcement Bull. 54, 18–25.

Rossi, D., 1982. Crime scene behavioral analysis: Another tool for the law enforcement investigator. Police Chief January, 152–155.

Rudolph, R., 2003. Mafia turncoat tells of 'over/under' coffins. Star Ledger, October 8, 2003. http://wwwnj.com/sopranos/ledger/index.ssf?/stories/mafiosi_20031008sl_coffin (accessed May 13, 2013).

State of Tennessee v. Tony V. Carruthers and James Montgomery, December 11, 2000. www.caselaw.findlaw.com/tn-supreme-court/1406494.html

Steele, R.M.G., 1983. Trajectory Plots of Aircraft Debris Following In-Flight Break-up. Unpublished Master's of Science thesis. Cranfield Institute of Technology, England.

Swegennis, R.W., 1987. Impact angles and velocities. In: Carver, B. (Ed.), Safety Investigation: Investigative Techniques. Department of the Air Force, Washington, D.C., pp. 1–16.

CHAPTER 5

The Use of Radiology in Mass Fatality Events

Mark D. Viner

The Inforce Foundation, Cranfield University Forensic Institute, United Kingdom, St. Bartholomew's and The Royal London Hospitals, London, United Kingdom

History

Since very shortly after the announcement by Wilhelm Conrad Röntgen of his discovery of "A New Type of Ray" in December 1895, radiology has been widely used to assist in the analysis and identification of human remains (Röntgen 1895). The applications of the use of X-rays first suggested by Levinsohn, Angerer, and Bordas (Brogdon and Lichtenstein 2011; Goodman 1995; Levinsohn 1899) still comprise the main methods by which medical imaging contributes to the identification and investigative process. Radiological imaging has the advantage of enabling the examination of remains in a variety of states of decomposition from fully fleshed to completely skeletonized. In an era when the invasive nature of some forensic medical procedures is increasingly at odds with the acceptable norms of society (Clarke 2000), it affords the opportunity to obtain a considerable amount of data without the need to clean and completely deflesh the remains, and it provides the investigative team with a rapid method of triage and classification by answering a number of fundamental questions:

- Determination of human versus nonhuman remains
- Recognition of commingling
- Evaluation of the biological profile (age, sex, stature, and ancestry)
- Recognition of embedded/hidden foreign objects
- Interpretation of trauma
- Positive identification of individuals by comparison of antemortem and postmortem radiological data

Human versus Nonhuman

In most cases involving animal bones that are brought to the attention of forensic investigators, a simple visual examination is all that is necessary for the trained anatomist or osteologist to determine nonhuman characteristics. In some cases, however, the most distinctive parts of the bones, the articular surfaces, may be missing due to fragmentation, decomposition, or

Commingled Human Remains. http://dx.doi.org/10.1016/B978-0-12-405889-7.00005-8

animal activity. In such cases, radiographic examination of the bone structure and trabecular pattern can be useful in distinguishing human from nonhuman remains (Brogdon 2011b; Chilvarquer et al. 1987).

Recognition of Commingling

In cases involving large amounts of fragmented remains, such as a mass fatality incident, remains may be commingled and mixed with large amounts of debris and artifacts. Physical examination of such remains, particularly in cases of fire damage where there is a uniformity of discoloration of all samples retrieved, is both difficult and time-consuming. In such cases, radiological examination can prove useful both in determining the presence of one or more individuals, but also in identifying and locating small body parts, especially teeth, which may otherwise be overlooked in the absence of a thorough and time-consuming fingertip search (Goodman and Edelson 2002; Kahana et al. 1997; Viner et al. 1998; Viner and Lichtenstein 2011). Its use for this purpose in forensic archaeological investigations is discussed in greater detail later in this chapter.

Age Estimation

The development and maturation of the skeleton from birth through childhood, puberty, adolescence, and early adulthood provides reliable age indicators. The appearance and fusion of primary and secondary ossification centers within the developing skeleton follows a predetermined chronological pattern and, in the same way that a physical examination of the defleshed skeleton can determine age at the time of death, so can skeletal radiography deliver the same information in the case of less decomposed remains. There are a number of radiological standards for determination of bone age throughout the first two decades of life, based on the appearance and fusion of the secondary ossification centers. One of the last epiphyses to fuse is the medial end of the clavicle, normally occurring during mid to late 20s.

In addition to dental development, one of the most useful examinations in determining the age of children is radiography of the hand and wrist, although examination of the knee, foot, and ankle can also be helpful (Greulich and Pyle 1959; Hansman 1962; Hoerr et al. 1962; Pyle and Hoerr 1955; Scheuer and Black 2004). In the mature skeleton, the degenerative changes that begin to appear at the margins of the articular surfaces of major joints at around age 40 allow the experienced radiologist to estimate adult age within the range of +/– 5 to 10 years (Brogdon 2011b). Calcification of the costal cartilage associated with the ribs and sternum may be readily visualized in people over 50, although it is sometimes observed in younger subjects (Mora et al. 2001). Although chest radiography demonstrates this calcification, its specificity as an aging method is reduced due to similar amounts of mineralization throughout adulthood (McCormick 1980). It is, however, a quick, inexpensive method to obtain a general age estimate that can be used along with other anthropological examinations (e.g., pubic symphysis morphology).

Sex Determination

Differentiation of sexes by skeletal radiology is unreliable until after puberty because the features that distinguish male from female are not sufficiently developed until this point (Krogman and Iscan 1986). Although on examination the appearance of the male skeleton is more substantial than the female, being generally heavier and the long bones of greater length/size, it is the examination of certain specific bones that is most useful in determining the sex of an individual. In particular, the shape, size, and geometry of the pelvis (Kurihara et al. 1996; Rogers and Saunders 1994; Sutherland and Suchey 1991), skull, and mandible (Bass 1990; Kurihara et al. 1996) and patterns of calcification of the costal (Navani et al. 1970), tracheobronchial, thyroid, and arytenoid cartilages (Kurihara et al. 1996) can be used to determine sex from skeletal remains by radiological means (Brogdon 2011b). These methods have traditionally relied on the physical examination and measurement of skeletal elements that requires full skeletization to have occurred. Advances in and applications of multidetector CT scanning have permitted the use of 3D radiological images for the assessment of fleshed remains using these methods. Most recently, these radiological methods have permitted validation and refinement of the methodology by access to large-scale modern samples of known demographic profile (Edwards et al. 2013).

Stature Estimation

Physical anthropologists are able to make estimations of stature by direct measurement from unfleshed human remains. The length of the femur is usually used because this measurement has been shown to be reliable (Trotter and Gleser 1952, 1958). In the case of fleshed remains, the same measurements can be made very accurately by using radiological methods. CT scanning, which uses data acquired throughout a 360-degree rotation of an X-ray beam, is able to provide highly accurate measurements.

Measurements can also be made using two-dimensional (planar) radiographs provided that correction for magnification is made. This can be achieved by means of an adapted radiographic technique, applying a simple correction factor, or utilizing modern imaging techniques (Beningfield et al. 2003; Bryan 1979; Jenkins 1980).

Determination of Ancestry

Determination of ancestry is challenging, especially when the remains are badly decomposed or skeletonized. Similar methods to those used by physical anthropologists to determine ancestry from skeletal remains can be applied radiographically with fleshed remains. In particular, examination of the skull and mandible (Bass 1990; Fischman 1985), the distal end of the femur (Craig 1995), and the ratio of long-bone length can be useful in determination of population ancestry (Krogman and Iscan 1986).

Recognition of Embedded/Hidden Objects and Interpretation of Trauma

The use of X-ray imaging can be utilized to detect and retrieve hazardous objects, personal effects, projectiles, aircraft parts, and other artifacts and forensic evidence, especially when body fragmentation is extensive (Figure 5-1). It can assist with determination of the cause/ manner of death, document trauma, negate the requirement for invasive autopsy, permit anthropological assessment without the requirement for defleshing, and, of course, establish identification through positive matching of postmortem and antemortem data (Gould 2003; Viner 2001a, 2001b; Viner et al. 2003; Viner & Lichtenstein 2011). It has proved particularly useful in mass fatality incidents resulting from air disasters (Alexander and Foote 1998; Mulligan et al. 1988; Viner et al. 1998), explosions, and terrorist incidents including suicide attacks (Harcke et al. 2002; Kahana et al. 1997; Nye et al. 1996; Society of Radiographers 2005; Viner and Lichtenstein 2011; Viner et al. 2006). Radiological methods have also been employed extensively in the investigation of mass graves, war crimes, and human rights abuses involving the exhumation of buried human remains (Gould 2003; Loe and Brady 2010; Tonello 1998; Viner 2001a). In such incidents, the systematic application of radiology has proved essential to the investigation and identification of victims.

Positive Identification of Individuals by Comparison of Antemortem and Postmortem Radiological Data

Some of the methods of identification (such as fingerprint analysis) depend on the integrity of the soft tissues of remains (Brogdon et al. 2003). In some cases involving skeletonization,

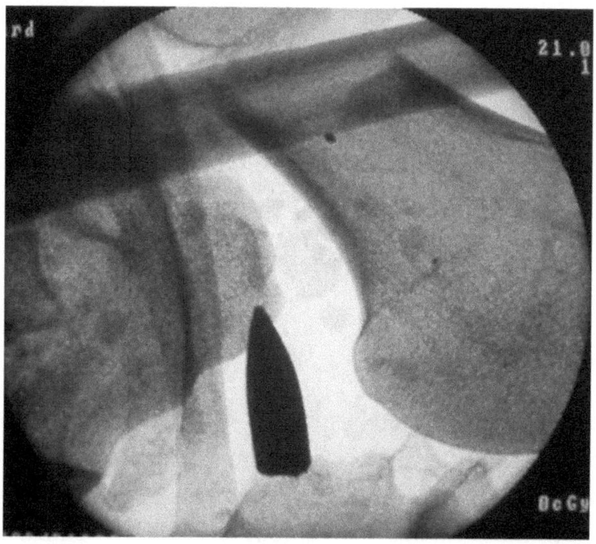

Figure 5-1
Fluoroscopic image of commingled human remains recovered from a crime scene reveals the presence of ballistic evidence.

fragmentation, decomposition, incineration, mutilation, or other disfigurement, identification by means of the skeleton and highly resilient dentition assumes a greater importance, and it is here that X-ray imaging comes into its own. Such incidents are often characterized by damage to the soft tissues caused by fire or water or severe disarticulation due to explosion or rapid deceleration injury.

Radiological identification of human remains requires specific and unique findings on postmortem images to be matched exactly with antemortem images of the individual. In some cases, identification can be made from a series of relatively common or nonspecific pathological anatomical changes that appear in identical locations in ante- and postmortem images. In other cases, a single unique feature is sufficient (Brogdon 2011a). In 1927, Culbert and Law made the first identification of human remains by comparison of antemortem and postmortem radiographs of the frontal sinuses. The degree of human variation in sinus patterns, based on size, asymmetry, outline, partial septia, and supraorbital cells, makes effective comparison for identification possible (Christensen 2005; Kirk et al. 2002; Marlin et al. 1991; Nambiar et al. 1999; Smith et al. 2010).

Medical imaging has long been used for the identification of human remains and is well documented (Binda et al. 1999; Buchner 1985; Craig 1995; Jensen 1991; Kahana and Hiss 1997; Murphy et al. 1980; Sanders et al. 1972; Schwartz and Woolridge 1977). Radiology is used extensively in anthropological and odontological assessment of postmortem and antemortem radiographs, records, or other images for concordance because they represent an excellent source of data for comparison of anatomical features (Figures 5-2A and 5-2B). Many specific cases have been reported in which radiology has played the leading role in the identification of human remains (Goodman and Edelson 2002; Greulich and Pyle 1959; Kahana et al. 1997; Viner and Lichtenstein 2011). Binda et al. (1999) even report on a case where radiology proved to be more accurate than DNA.

Radiographs taken for medical purposes are often required by statute to be retained for long periods of time. In the United Kingdom, for example, the Department of Health requires that radiographs are retained for eight years, and longer in the case of children (until the patient reaches their 25th year), and three years following death (Dimond 2002). In many cases, particularly in privately run clinics, radiographs are routinely given to the patient for safe keeping, and thus may be in existence for much longer than the statutory period. With the advent of digital imaging and the decreasing cost of digital storage, many institutions are retaining medical images far beyond their previously applied practice for X-ray film. Records are thus, on the whole, fairly accessible.

The last assessment of the frequency of medical and dental X-ray examinations undertaken by the National Radiological Protection Board (NRPB) in the United Kingdom for the year 2001–2002 showed an overall examination rate of 700 examinations per 1,000 head of population per annum. Of this figure, 31% were dental radiography examinations, with a total 480 examinations per 1,000 head of population being medical X-ray exams. This

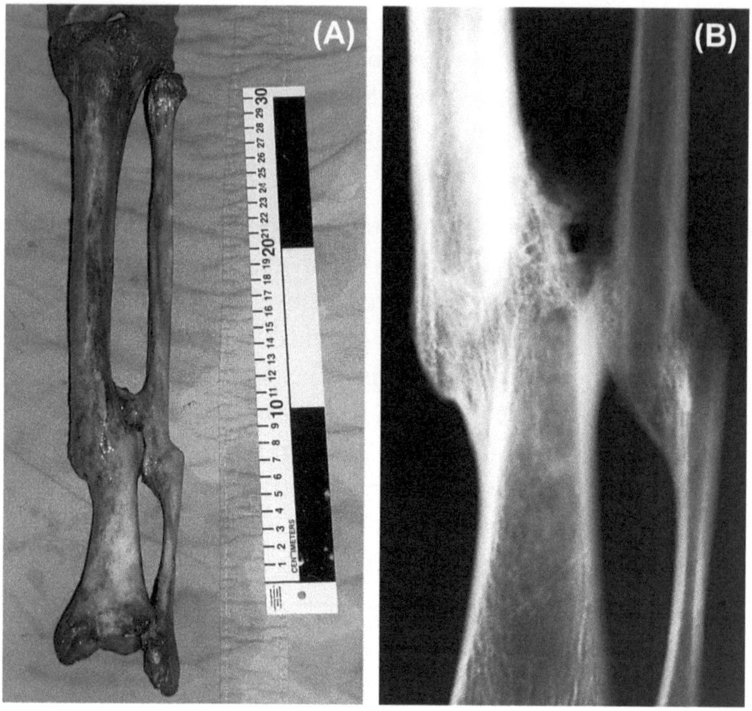

Figure 5-2
A previously healed fracture of the tibia and fibula (A) offers the possibility of identification by radiology because such trauma will usually have been well documented at the time of the original injury and throughout the healing process. This subject was later identified by comparison of the postmortem radiograph (B) with an antemortem film.

figure was almost exactly half of the rate for medical examinations in the United States and European countries including Germany, Belgium, and Luxemburg. The majority of examinations were conventional X-ray studies (68%) with the majority of these being teeth, chest, and limb radiographs, which accounted for 76% of all conventional examinations. A further 14% were pelvis, spine, and hip examinations. CT examinations represented 7% of the total, with 45% of these being head and neck, 34% abdomen and pelvis, and 14% chest (European Commission 2008). This position echoes Brogdon's evaluation of the distribution of radiologic examinations by body part and modality in the United States undertaken during the same period. As Brogdon asserts, examinations of the chest demonstrate consistency of bony structures over time, and extremities may contain useful radiographic identifiers due to previous injury, degenerative change, or malformation (Brogdon 2011a). All of the preceding points to a wealth of useful antemortem data being available to the investigator. This repository of information is often overlooked but offers the possibility of obtaining a clear and decisive identification if postmortem and antemortem data can be located and matched.

As demonstrated by the NRPB study, radiographic examinations of the skull have dramatically declined since the advent of CT scanning, and antemortem radiographic data is thus less likely to be available. However, positive identification can be established by CT either by comparison with other CT scans or by using the CT "Scout View" or scanogram to compare with conventional radiographs (Brogdon 2011a; Reichs and Dorion 1992; Thali et al. 2011).

Imaging Modalities

Until recently, much forensic examination of the deceased carried out in the medical examiner's office or incident mortuary has relied on traditional X-ray technology, which is little changed from the time of Röntgen. In recent years, however, some of the newer technologies that have been available within hospitals and clinics have been used for the forensic examination of the deceased, and their use in forensic investigation is increasing rapidly. Most significantly, they have included the latest generation of CT scanning equipment: multi-detector computed tomography scanning (MDCT) and magnetic resonance imaging (MRI) (Bisset et al. 2002; Brookes et al. 1996; Thali et al. 2003; Thali et al. 2009).

All of the imaging modalities described in this chapter rely on the principles of the absorption of X-ray photons to demonstrate differentiations in atomic structure of the subject under examination. To achieve a satisfactory result, the operator must be conversant with the physical principles of X-ray interaction with matter and have a sound knowledge of human anatomy.

Contrast and density on the resultant image depend on the chemical composition of the subject under examination, the energy of the X-ray photons (determined by the peak kilovoltage [kV] applied across the X-ray tube), and the number of photons reaching the film or digital detector (determined by the milliamperage [mA] applied to the coil of the X-ray tube, the time of the exposure, and the distance of the film or receptor from the X-ray source). It is essential to match the kV applied to the body part under examination to achieve an optimum result. Even small variations can enable visualization of anatomical structures that would otherwise be missed, particularly in the juvenile skeleton.

The examination technique, imaging system (be it either film or digital technology), and other factors, including the structure of the examination table, will introduce a number of additional variables that all need to be taken into account to produce the optimum result. In the case of the photographic image, these factors also depend on the availability of consistent processing conditions that rely on accurate temperature control, regular replenishment of appropriate chemicals, and control of development time. For these reasons, it is desirable that examinations are conducted by a trained radiographer and are undertaken on equipment that has been regularly and appropriately maintained and is subject to a regular quality control program. As Brogdon (2011a:157) points out: "…[T]he person who actually positions and exposes the roentgenograms is absolutely critical to the success of the entire endeavour. The educated, experienced, and sophisticated eye of the radiologist or other professional observer may be required to detect and interpret the subtle nuances recorded on the film, but without adequate technical support, that eye will be blinded."

Modern digital equipment gives the illusion of being easier to operate and more forgiving than conventional film-based imaging, with exposure being apparently less critical. However, Brogdon's observation applies equally, if not more so, to digital radiography where valuable information can be missed due to poor technique and failure to select the correct exposure factors.

Discussion of all the available imaging modalities is not possible here, and the following text focuses on those techniques that may be more commonly used in the examination of commingled human remains resulting from mass fatality incidents.

Radiography

The two-dimensional radiograph, as demonstrated by Röntgen, still remains as the method of choice for the examination of the skeleton. It delivers a high-quality image of skeletal structures, and can be relatively easily and cheaply acquired and replicated. The radiograph is in essence a "shadow-gram"—a still-life image produced by radiation emerging from a subject and striking an image receptor (photosensitive digital plate or sheet of film) (Figure 5-3).

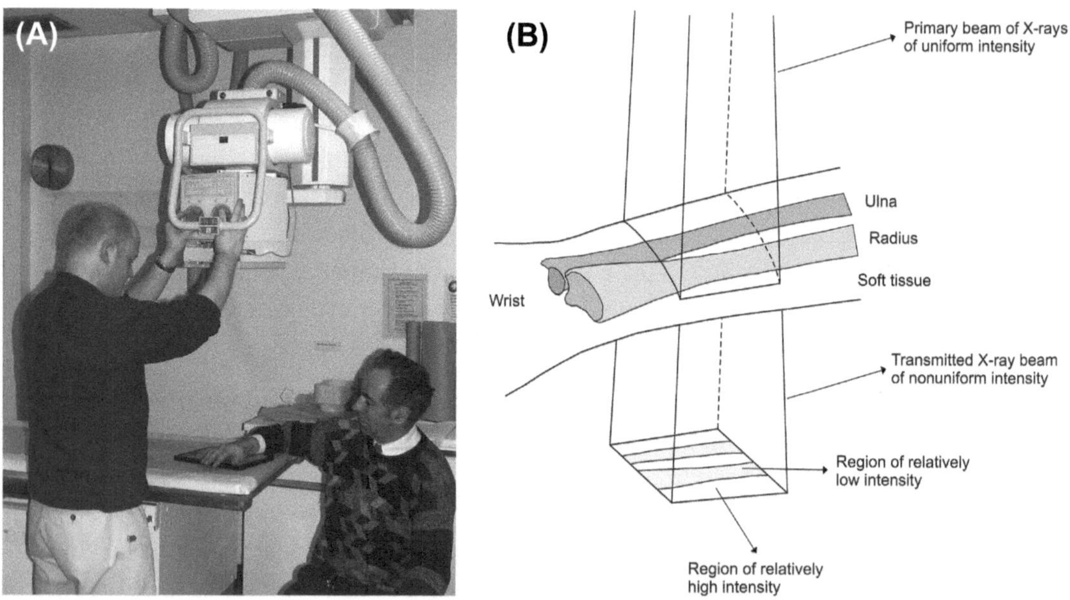

Figure 5-3
(A) Radiography examination of the wrist showing position of X-ray tube, body part, and detector. (B) The basic principles of radiography.

In recent years, technological advances have allowed traditional film-based systems to be replaced by digital technology. Digital images offer enormous benefits to medical and forensic applications. They can be relatively easily acquired without the need for use of photographic chemicals and equipment. The recording methods require a decreased radiation dose and have a wider dynamic range than film, resulting in the ability to demonstrate both soft tissue and bony structures from the same image data by altering the display factors. This makes digital imaging an ideal method for detailed examination of fragmented remains with tissue; the same image data can be used to display soft tissue structures, nonmetallic foreign bodies, bony detail, and metallic foreign bodies by simple adjustment of the display parameters.

Digital images can also be superimposed over one another, allowing accurate comparison of antemortem and postmortem data. The fact that digital information can be sent electronically speeds up and simplifies this process, dramatically facilitating rapid identification of the remains of an individual from antemortem data recovered thousands of miles away.

Current systems fall broadly into two categories: computed radiography (CR) and digital radiography (DR). In the process of computed radiography, a photostimulable phosphor plate replaces the film and screens within the X-ray cassette. The examination is performed in an identical manner to the traditional X-ray examination, and following exposure, the cassette is placed in a CR reader (Figure 5-4A). The reader withdraws the plate, scans it, and converts the data stored on it into a digital image. The entire process takes a similar amount of time to the conventional film-based process, but the end result is a digital image (Emerton et al. 2005).

With digital radiography, a flat-panel X-ray detector replaces the X-ray cassette (Figure 5-4B). The examination is performed in the same way as conventional and CR imaging, but the image appears almost instantly on a monitor following the exposure (Lawinski et al. 2005). Aside from the increase in speed and productivity, this process offers significant advantages for forensic

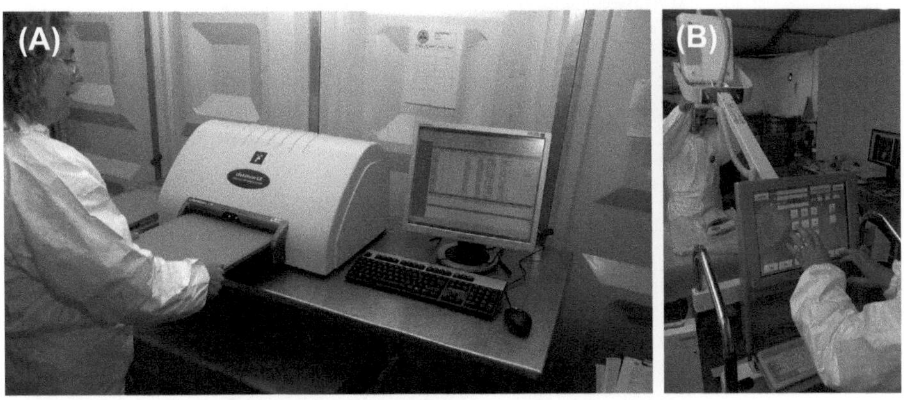

Figure 5-4

Two options for digital radiography: (A) computed radiography (CR) and (B) direct digital radiography (DR).

work. First, with DR, there is no need to remove the plate following exposure to be able to view the image. Thus, with cases that are difficult to position or for commingled remains where structures may overlie one another, making interpretation difficult, the subject can be repositioned immediately, thus improving accuracy and minimizing examination time. Second, where foreign body removal is required (e.g., ballistic material or traces of explosive devices), the same image can be instantly replicated with a radiopaque pointer used to highlight the subject. The item can then be retrieved by the pathologist with the aid of sequential radiographs.

Digital radiography can be successfully employed as a triage tool, providing a series of survey radiographs covering an entire body bag. This imaging will allow for the identification of small fragments of bone, teeth, personal effects, and possible items of evidence among debris. However, the static nature of the image and the limitations of the gantry systems currently available reduce its flexibility for identification of superimposed structures and result in a complex process for retrieval of items under X-ray control. In cases where it is likely to be a requirement to retrieve small items of evidence from bags containing commingled remains, or when assisting the pathologist in locating and retrieving evidential items from within the soft tissues, a combination of DR and fluoroscopy (described later) should be considered to be the gold standard. Modern DR equipment is now highly portable and can be run from a generator offering a field-deployable solution (Figure 5-5).

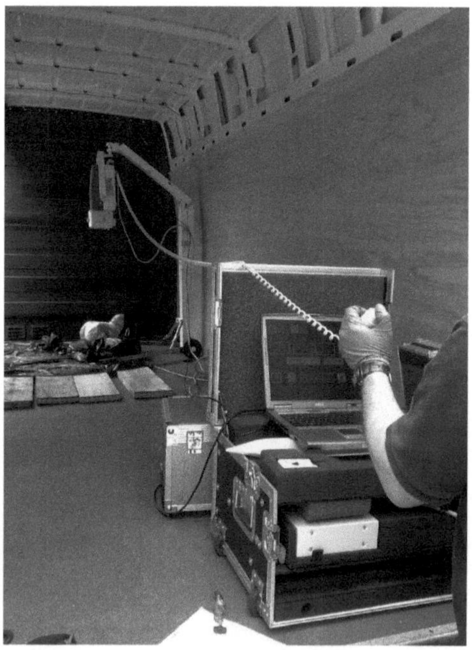

Figure 5-5
Mobile digital radiography equipment can be used for field work. In this case, the unit is being operated in the back of a van and powered by a small generator.

Film Radiography

The use of film-based systems may provide a simple, low-cost solution in situations in which access to digital equipment and the required infrastructure may be problematic or prohibitively expensive. Simple x-ray equipment can be easily configured to run from a generator, and films can be processed manually in a darkroom or using a field-deployable X-ray processing machine. This capability is particularly useful in remote locations and where radiography is required to be deployed at the recovery site. The film is developed using a standard photographic process, resulting in a negative image in which the dark areas represent those areas of the subject through which a greater number of X-ray photons have been transmitted.

Since the early days of radiography, it has been common for the majority of the image to be formed not by radiation, but by light emitted by phosphorescent "intensifying screens" placed on either side of the sheet film in a cassette. These screens emit light in proportion to the number and energy of the X-ray photons absorbed within them. Although this considerably reduces the exposure time and thus radiation dose, it can introduce a degree of unsharpness to the image. For this reason, a wide range of screen types is available, both for general and more detailed skeletal work, where the unsharpness is minimized within the intensifying screens. For optimum trabecular detail, nonscreen film may be used, and this is the type of examination favored for the examination of samples in a lead-lined cabinet X-ray machine where such minute detail may prove to be of value. For the majority of examinations, and certainly in the mass casualty situation, the speed and ease of use of a film/screen combination will suffice.

Fluoroscopy

One of Röntgen's earliest observations was that of a fluoroscopic image (Burrows 1986). In fluoroscopy, a continuous "beam" of radiation is directed at and passes through the subject under examination. The emergent rays strike a fluorescent screen that emits light in proportion to the energy of the incident X-ray photons falling on it. This image, visible to the naked eye, is amplified several thousand times via an "image intensifier" and is recorded and projected on to a computer screen via a closed-circuit TV system (Figure 5-6).

The resultant image is viewed in "real time." As the apparatus is moved over the subject, the image seen reflects the movement over the subject, thus allowing rapid coverage of a scene in the same way that a video camera can be panned over a landscape. Alternatively, the apparatus can remain stationary, and any movement of the subject will be detected and demonstrated on the image.

Fluoroscopy offers significant advantages to the investigator, particularly in the examination of commingled human remains following a mass fatality incident. The real-time nature of the examination makes it particularly suitable for rapid examination of body bags as a triage method. The resultant image, derived from the relative density of objects, rather than their appearance, makes it a simple matter to identify even small fragments of bone and teeth

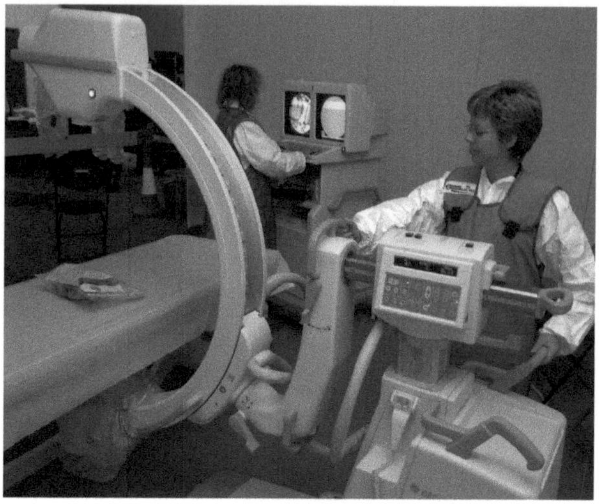

Figure 5-6
C-Arm mobile fluoroscopy unit.

among debris, personal effects, and possible items of evidence from fire, crash, explosion, and other disaster scenes. Employing fluoroscopy as the first stage of the examination process in a mass fatality incident also permits the presence of any hazardous material (sharp objects or unexploded ordnance) to be detected and located, thus reducing the potential hazard at subsequent stages of the process.

The use of a mobile C-Arm fluoroscope allows the X-ray tube and detector to be rotated and angled to give better visualization of superimposed structures, which can be particularly useful when examining fragmented, commingled human remains. It is also useful for rapid retrieval of small objects (e.g., ballistic material) under X-ray control. Without fluoroscopy (and appropriate protective equipment), location and removal of these objects would otherwise be difficult and time consuming.

Fluoroscopy does, however, have its limitations in terms of image quality and the total amount of information that can be permanently recorded on a single image. In this respect, it is best suited to use as an initial triage tool, to be supplemented by further examination using digital radiography (International Association of Forensic Radiographers 2004; Tonello 1998; Viner et al. 2006; Viner and Lichtenstein 2011).

Digital X-Ray Scanography

An alternative method, which offers the combined advantages of digital imaging and fluoroscopy, is the use of digital X-ray scanography. The Lodox Statscan® was originally developed for examining suspected diamond smugglers in the mines of South Africa. This machine employs a digital version of the "scanogram" technique described earlier (Figures 5-7A and 5-7B).

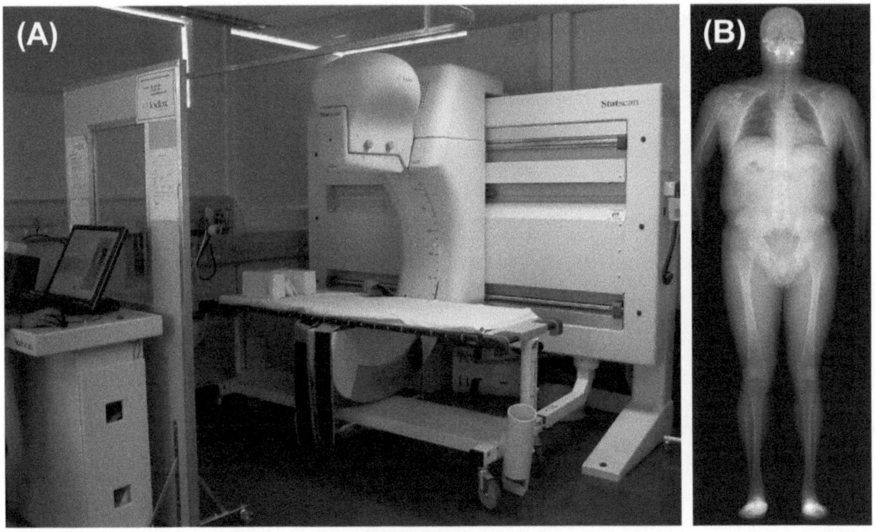

Figure 5-7
Digital X-ray scanography. The Lodox Statscan (A) gives a full-body digital scanogram in just 13 seconds (B).

A narrow slit beam of radiation passes rapidly over the subject, and the resultant image is recorded using digital technology employing 12 solid-state detectors in a linear array detector. An entire body can be examined from head to toe in approximately 13 seconds, and the gantry can be rotated through 90 degrees (and any angle in between) to give a lateral or oblique image (Beningfield et al. 2003).

The Statscan has been employed very successfully for investigation and management of polytrauma in shock trauma centers in the United States, Europe, and Africa. It has most recently been applied to great effect in forensic pathology units in South Africa and the United States. However, due mainly to its high cost, the application of this machine for forensic use is currently limited to high-volume centers and is in its early stages. Despite this, it clearly offers significant advantages over conventional X-ray techniques.

Dental Radiography

One of the most useful tools available to the investigator in a mass casualty situation is the use of dental radiography. Identification by odontological means still remains one of the major primary methods of identification in mass fatality incidents, despite advances in DNA technology. Comparison of dental radiographs is an important tool for the forensic odontologist. The production of dental X-ray images is rapid, cost effective, and simple, and it can be achieved without the need for complex equipment. The principles are identical to those of skeletal radiography and can be accomplished with plain film (without the use of intensifying screens), computed radiography, or direct digital systems. Recent advances in battery technology have permitted the development of hand-held dental X-ray units which offer a field deployable solution that has been used to great effect in mass casualty situations (Pittayapat et al. 2012).

One of the problems associated with dental comparisons is the postmortem replication of antemortem images. The most common examinations performed by dentists upon their patients are the intra-oral "bite-wing" projections and extra-oral panoramic survey view (Hart and Wall 2002). The bite-wing projection relies on the subject being able to hold an intra-oral film in position in the mouth by biting on a card support attached to the film. Achieving an exact replication of this view can be very difficult during postmortem analysis for obvious reasons.

The panoramic, or "orthopantomographic," technique produces a single film showing the entire dentition, mandible, maxillae, and maxillary sinuses on the same image (Figure 5-8). The examination is performed using a technique known as rotational tomography in which the X-ray tube and film rotate around a series of fulcrum points that follow the line of the mandible. Structures that are not in the same plane as the fulcrum are blurred out so that superimposition of the structures is avoided (Mason and Bourne 1998). Since Siemens plc ceased production of its Zonarc®, all currently available orthopantomography equipment operates on the principle that the patient is able to sit or stand in the erect position. This single factor makes replication of the orthopantomograph image very difficult to undertake postmortem, and results in the requirement for a series of intra-oral radiographs to be undertaken. An alternative method for achieving a comparable projection to that obtained using orthopantomography that is currently in use in clinical dentistry and under evaluation for postmortem identification is Cone Beam and Multi-detector CT scanning (Jackowski et al. 2006; Rocha Sdos et al. 2003; Thali et al. 2006).

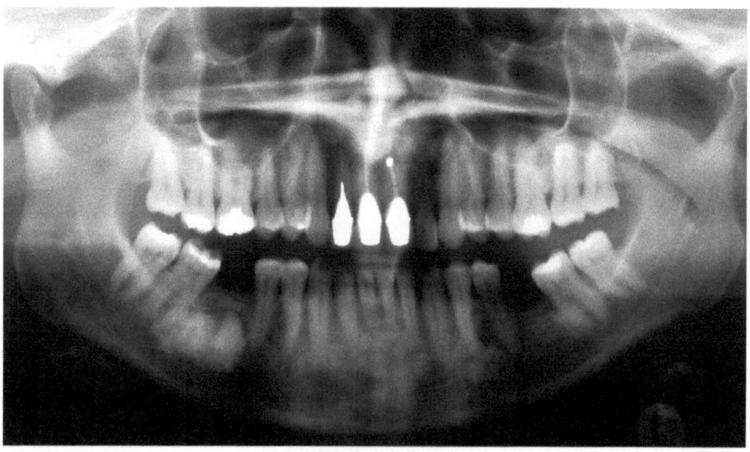

Figure 5-8
Orthopantomograph: Standard panoramic X-ray view of the dentition routinely performed in general dental practice.

CT Scanning

Computed axial tomography (CAT) scanning was developed in the 1970s by a British scientist, Godfrey Hounsfield, working for the EMI Corporation. Hounsfield applied the physics of rotational tomography but went a stage further so that the tube and X-ray detector gantry rotated about a single axis in the body. X-ray detectors replaced film and continuously took a series of measurements while the gantry rotated. A computer analyzed the data recorded and reconstructed it as a digital image of an axial "slice" of the subject displayed on an image matrix on a CRT screen. Each pixel was allocated a level on a gray scale that corresponded to the level of radiation transmitted through the body at that location and thus the relative density of the subject. These values are now known as Hounsfield units (HUs), and the scale, in which the density level corresponding to 0 is equivalent to water (mid gray), spans from dense air −1024 units (black) to bone > +400 units or greater to dense metallic objects, etc., +3071(white). Initially deployed as a tool for imaging the head, it enabled radiologists to accurately examine the brain for the first time without the overlying features of the bony skull obscuring vital soft tissue information.

CT scanning, as it is now known, has enormously benefited from advances in technology and computer processing power. Modern CT units make use of a large number of detectors to simultaneously record the image data (Figures 5-9A and 5-9B). The entire body can now be scanned by such multi-detector (MDCT) scanners in a matter of seconds, and images can be reconstructed in any plane: axial, coronal, sagittal, or oblique. While MDCT scanning is a routine tool in clinical medicine, it has only relatively recently been employed in postmortem and forensic examination. Since the early 2000s there has been a rapid expansion in the number of centers of forensic medicine routinely using CT scanning, and there is a rapidly increasing body of literature demonstrating its efficacy at postmortem examination (Baglivo et al. 2013) and its ability to gather data that may otherwise be impossible to collect. The ability of CT scanning to undertake 3D and multiplanar reconstructions offers the pathologist and anthropologist the opportunity to examine the underlying skeletal structure of fleshed remains, visualizing trauma, degenerative processes, and articular surfaces and taking accurate measurements (Thali et al. 2000; Thali et al. 2003). There are at present a number of studies being undertaken worldwide to evaluate the possibilities of CT for forensic examination and identification and, in recent years, CT scanners have been deployed in the investigation of multiple casualty incidents (O'Donnell et al. 2009; Rutty et al. 2007).

Radiation Protection

Within three months of Röntgen's announcement, reports of the harmful effects of X-rays began to appear in the literature (Burrows 1986). Early experimenters and practitioners, however, took no steps to protect themselves against the effects of radiation. X-ray rooms and X-ray tubes were unshielded and emitted radiation in all directions. It was a common practice

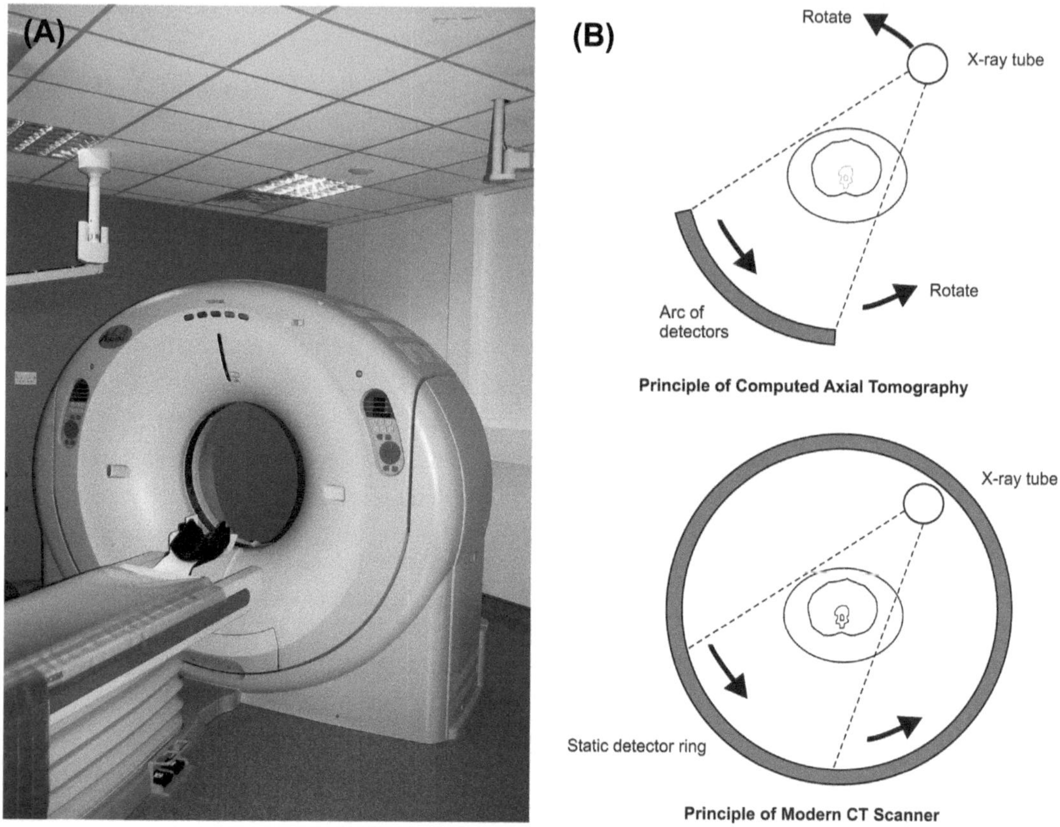

Figure 5-9
(A) Modern scanner gantry housing rotating tube and static ring of detectors. (B) The basic principles of computed axial tomography.

among early radiographers and radiologists to test the X-ray tube and determine the exposure required by taking an exposure of their own hand prior to each examination (Burrows 1986). In the United Kingdom, documentation of radiation injuries by Dr. John Hall-Edwards and Ernest Wilson led to the publication of a safe code of practice by Dr. Hall-Edwards in 1908. Both men later died of their radiation-induced injuries.

Adequate protection and codes of practice did not become commonplace until the 1920s, and it was not until 1928 that the International Congress of Radiology in Stockholm adopted the third revised report of the British Radiological Protection Committee as the basis for international regulations (International X-ray Protection Committee 1928). It was not until the 1950s that it was understood that the low levels of radiation exposure used in diagnostic radiology represented a danger to patients. This resulted in the adoption of the radiation protection regulations that are now in use, based on the risk to patients and operators from late effects of radiation following low-level exposure (Engel-Hills 2006).

There is no absolute evidence of a threshold below which no damage occurs. Even the lowest doses may cause damage to cells, which might later lead to malignancy or hereditary effects if the cells irradiated are the germ cells in the gonads (Engel-Hills 2006). For this reason, radiation exposures should be limited and controlled by appropriate international, national, and state regulations, codes of practice, and schemes of work. X-ray and imaging equipment should be regulated, adequately maintained and inspected, and subject to regular quality control programs. Radiation workers should be appropriately trained in the use of such equipment for the purpose for which it is employed. This is particularly important for fluoroscopy, where the radiation exposure received by the operators can be significantly increased by the use of poor technique and by inexperienced operators using the equipment for longer periods than are necessary to gather the required information.

Provided that appropriately qualified personnel are involved in planning, commissioning, and operating the equipment, most X-ray techniques can be performed safely in "field" conditions encountered in incident mortuaries following mass fatality incidents or during large-scale criminal investigations. The imaging equipment routinely required in such investigations (fluoroscopy, digital and digital dental radiography, and even CT scanning) is available in mobile or portable form and is routinely employed in military field hospitals or domiciliary and veterinary radiological practices. There is therefore no logistical reason why incident mortuaries cannot benefit from the resources required to undertake a thorough investigation. Some recent developments in technology have made portable X-ray units more accessible, and there is an increasing tendency for them to be used by untrained operators in uncontrolled conditions. The ability to take the X-ray unit out of its specially designed protective environment places a greater responsibility on the user to ensure that appropriate controls are put in place to protect himself/herself and others.

Application of Radiographic Methods to Mass Fatalities

Whatever modalities are employed, the examination of commingled and/or fragmented remains, particularly from large-scale incidents, will require systematic application of imaging so as to maximize the information gained while minimizing the time taken and prevent delays in the examination process. In planning the forensic protocol to include the use of radiological imaging, the following principles should be applied (International Association of Forensic Radiographers 2004):

- Imaging will be useful as an initial screening tool at triage to determine the nature of the remains. This includes the presence of hazardous material, the remains of more than one individual, and the presence of significant material and artifacts (e.g., personal effects and forensic evidence). It also will be useful to locate and retrieve small, unassociated body fragments (e.g., teeth).

- Aside from dental radiography, the use of radiography for identification is likely to play a relatively small (but important) role in the identification process.
- Radiographic comparison views for identification will require accurate positioning and exposure. This time-consuming process cannot be undertaken successfully until after the initial examination or search process is complete (Viner and Lichtenstein 2011). It is thus advisable to triage recovered remains so that detailed skeletal radiography for identification is undertaken only when indicated rather than as part of the routine forensic protocol.

Imaging requirements for mass fatality investigation are thus best described along the same lines as for the management of major trauma in the emergency room (Figure 5-10):

- Primary survey: Initial triage and assessment
- Secondary survey: Standard examination of specific body parts (e.g., dentition)
- Tertiary examinations: Specific examinations performed in response to findings during primary or secondary surveys or during pathology, odontology, or anthropology assessment

The manner in which these requirements are met will greatly depend on the imaging methodologies employed. In the majority of cases where radiography or fluoroscopy is used, separate imaging examinations will need to be conducted at each stage to acquire the necessary radiological data. If MDCT is used, it may be possible simply to conduct one imaging examination at the start of the mass fatality DVI process and to review and evaluate the same data set at each stage of the process to gather the required information. For this reason, the following section describes (1) a conventional approach and (2) an investigation using MDCT.

Conventional Approach

Primary Survey (Triage)

The purpose of the primary survey is to undertake an initial assessment of the remains. This should be considered essential in all cases but is particularly important for circumstances involving extensive fragmentation, decomposition, or intermixing with debris. In some cases, the use of either computed radiography (CR) or direct digital radiography (DR) will deliver a high-quality image that can be subsequently evaluated by the pathologist, anthropologist, and odontologist without the need for further examination. The digital nature of these images will allow display of both hard and soft tissues, as well as metallic and nonmetallic artifacts and personal effects. In the absence of CR or DR, plain film radiography techniques will offer an alternative, but without the benefits of a digital image. DR has the advantage of being a far more rapid technique than film or CR, and it is particularly suited to use in the mass fatality situation when speed is of critical importance. Direct digital radiography should therefore be considered to be the modality of choice in such cases.

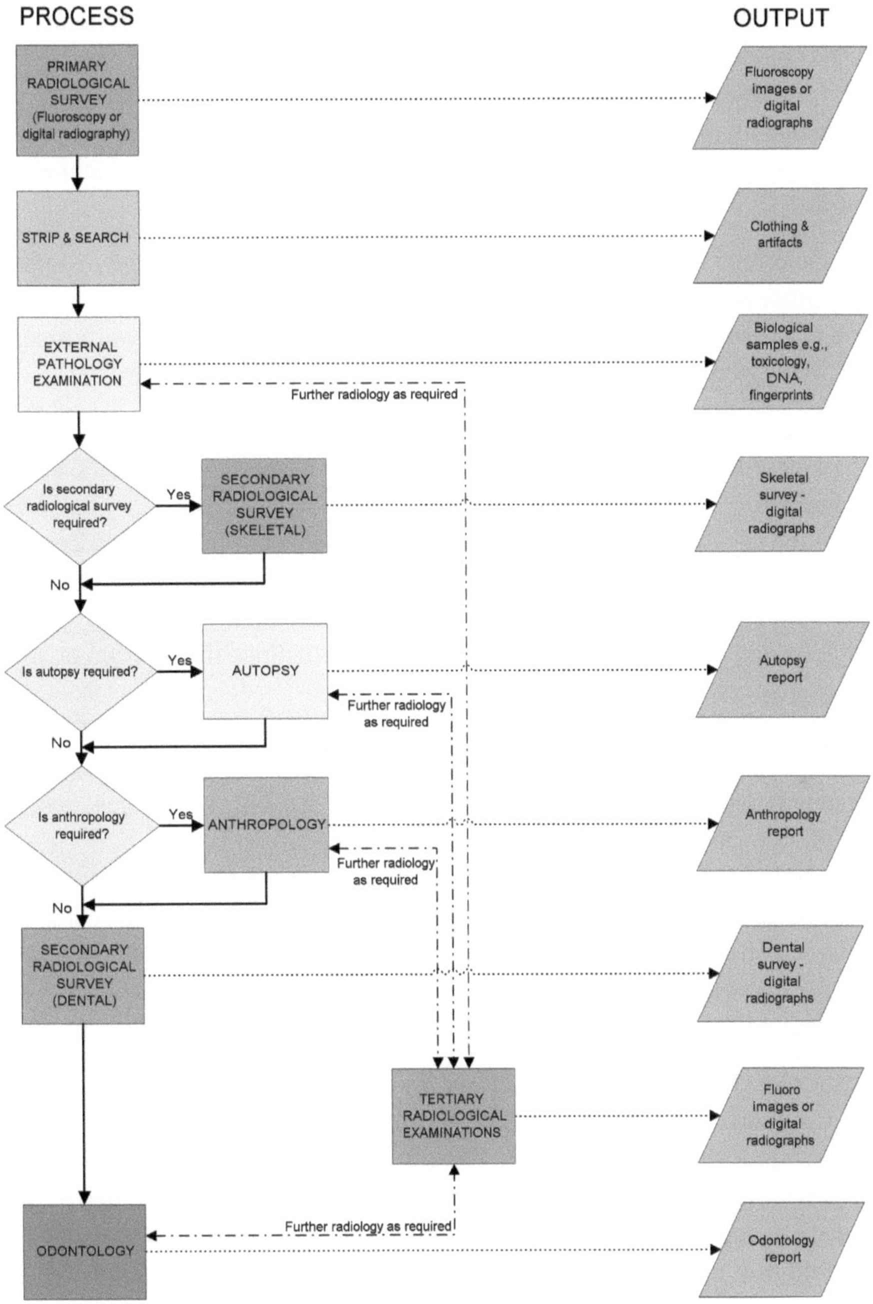

Figure 5-10

Flowchart showing how radiology contributes to the examination of human remains in mass fatality investigations at each stage.

In the absence of DR and particularly in cases in which large quantities of remains are recovered and commingled with one another and other evidential material, the advantages of fluoroscopy for mass fatality situations will become apparent at triage. The "real-time" nature of the fluoroscope image will enable rapid location and retrieval of items of interest, and the ability to rotate the C-Arm of the fluoroscope will enable superimposed structures to be more easily identified.

In all cases, the primary radiographic survey should be considered to be the first phase of the investigative process, particularly when examining remains from a crime scene. Imaging examination of the sealed body bag will yield all or some of the following information about the contents of the body bag:

- Recognition of body parts with discernible anatomical landmarks that can be used for body part identification, which is especially useful in cases of fragmentation and decomposition.
- An indication of whether the remains of more than one individual are present.
- The location and nature (if possible) of any hazardous material—unexploded ordnance, metallic sharps, glass, etc.
- The location and degree of skeletal trauma. This may include the location of any projectile fragments with possible associated bony injury.
- The location of unassociated teeth and other small body parts useful for identification.
- The location of personal effects (e.g., jewelery, cigarette lighters, keys, wallets). This may be particularly useful in cases of burned or exhumed remains, where these artifacts may be difficult to locate.
- The presence of any unique identifying features (e.g., prosthetic hip replacement) that may require further radiographic investigation following autopsy and/or odontology.
- The presence of previous healed fractures and other pre-existing pathological or anatomical features that may be useful for identification purposes.
- The presence of dental work (e.g., fillings, bridges, crowns, root canal treatments).

The information obtained from the primary survey should be recorded on a report form to aid subsequent pathology, anthropology, and odontology examinations. Examples of recording forms are shown in Figures 5-11A and 5-11B. If fluoroscopy is used, it is recommended that the entire examination is recorded using video or similar technology. Although hard or soft-copy images should be taken of significant findings, fluoroscopy is a dynamic real-time examination, and it is advisable that the process is undertaken by a radiographer along with a forensic pathologist, radiologist, or anthropologist and appropriate law enforcement personnel to ensure continuity. The use of DR or CR as a primary survey tool will result in a series of hard- or soft-copy images as a permanent record.

In cases with a large amount of fragmented and/or commingled remains, a primary survey of body bags using digital radiography can be used to construct an image database to aid the identification process. Images can be categorized and filed according to observed anatomical

(A)

Site Code ______________

Body Number______________

RADIOLOGY PRIMARY SURVEY:
ARTIFACT/PATHOLOGY LOCATION DIAGRAM

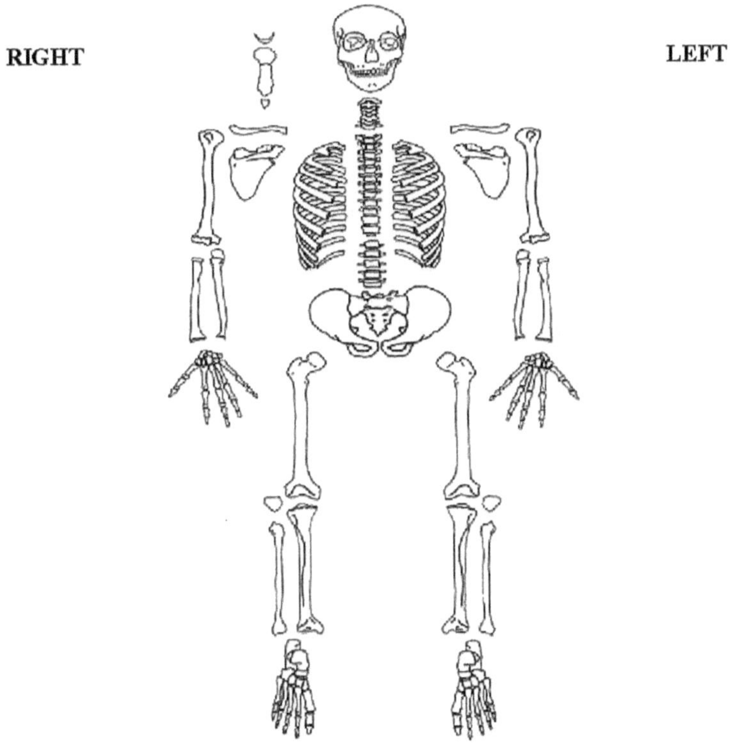

KEY: (#1, #2 etc for multiple examples. Location: ?)

A: Intact Bullet	D: Cartridge Case	G: Needle	J: Jewellery	M: Metal (Unknown)
B: Bullet Fragment	E: Whole Round	H: Knife or Blade	K: Key	N: Radio / Remote
C: Shrapnel	F: Razor Blade	I: Glasses	L: Watch	O: Other (describe)

Recorded By ______________

MR22 PAGE 2 Signature ______________

Date ______________

Figure 5-11
Examples of primary survey recording forms designed by the Inforce Foundation and the Association of Forensic Radiographers for use in the investigation of human remains exhumed from mass graves. The two forms allow the location of artifacts and pathology to be indicated anatomically (A) and on a grid system (B) as appropriate.

(B)

Site Code ________________

Body Number________________

RADIOLOGY PRIMARY SURVEY: ARTIFACT LOCATION DIAGRAM

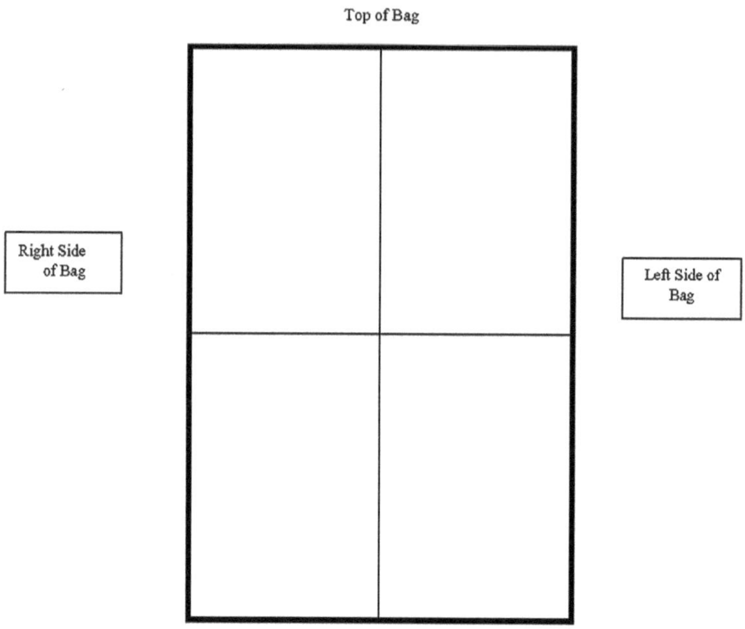

KEY: (#1, #2 etc for multiple examples. Location: ?)

A: Intact Bullet	D: Cartridge Case	G: Needle	J: Jewellery	M: Metal (Unknown)
B: Bullet Fragment	E: Whole Round	H: Knife or Blade	K: Key	N: Radio / Remote
C: Shrapnel	F: Razor Blade	I: Glasses	L: Watch	O: Other (describe)

Recorded By ________________

MR22 PAGE 1 Signature ________________

Date ________________

Figure 5-11 (Continued)

parts, facilitating rapid retrieval for later comparison with antemortem radiographs should this prove necessary. It should be remembered that radiographs produced at the primary survey stage will not be of sufficient quality to permit accurate evaluation by a radiologist due to the random nature of the anatomical positioning of the body parts within the body bag. Further radiography examinations may be required as part of the investigative process as detailed in the following sections. These examinations, performed subsequent to the primary survey, should in all cases be correctly anatomically positioned so that the resultant radiographs replicate as far as possible the standard views that would be undertaken on a live subject.

Secondary Survey (Standard Radiographic Examination)

The secondary survey should be undertaken after the initial strip and search and external examination so that standard positions can be replicated without overlying clothing and other artifacts. In most cases, examinations can be undertaken following autopsy, but this will depend on the precise nature of the examinations to be performed. Examinations of the skull, for example, are in most cases best undertaken prior to the cranial vault being opened.

The use of imaging to obtain standard projection radiographs as a routine part of the examination protocol should be restricted to those cases that are likely to yield the greatest benefit from the deployment of resources required. In the case of a mass fatality investigation, advances in other identification methods (e.g., DNA) have largely negated the need for the full skeletal survey examination deployed in previous incidents (Mulligan et al. 1988; Nye et al. 1996). In such cases, secondary surveys are now usually restricted to routine dental surveys as a means of collecting postmortem data for later comparison with antemortem films. Because the incidence of dental X-ray examinations and availability of dental records in Western populations is high, the likelihood of such antemortem data being available makes the routine dental survey worthwhile. In other populations, where dental treatment is either rare or poorly documented, it may be decided that a routine dental radiography survey is not indicated. However, there may be value in routinely taking radiographs of the mandible in the region of the third molar to provide data for age estimation.

The precise requirements for dental radiography surveys will be determined by the working practices of the forensic odontologist. In the absence of a presumptive identification with antemortem data for comparison, a full sequence of intra-oral peri-apical films showing the entire dentition, together with bilateral bite wing examinations, represents a thorough survey from which comparison can be made with antemortem data. In the case of large-scale examinations involving multiple fatalities, the secondary dental survey represents a significant and time-consuming part of the postmortem data collection process. A team approach involving odontologists and experienced dental radiographers and nurses working together in the incident mortuary can greatly increase the speed of the identification process and negate the requirement for body parts to be examined elsewhere (Viner and Lichtenstein 2011).

Similar to the dental images, there may be other indications for including a series of cranial and postcranial projections in the routine postmortem examination protocol. For example, in the case of examining the remains from suspected atrocity crimes, the possibility of systematic antemortem torture and/or beatings may indicate routine examination of body parts, such as skull, limbs, and ribs, for evidence of healed or healing fractures at the time of death (Tonello 1998; Viner 2001c).

In all events, the precise protocol deployed will depend on a number of factors unique to the circumstances surrounding the death of the individuals. The protocol will thus need to be agreed in consultation with the coroner, medical examiner, odontologist, anthropologist, radiologist, and radiographer to achieve the maximum benefit while limiting examination time and resources.

Tertiary Examinations (Special Circumstances)

As described earlier, a range of medical imaging techniques and examinations may be useful in determining the identity of an individual or his/her anthropological profile or in determining the cause and manner of his/her death. The techniques employed will vary from case to case and will be determined by the nature, or suspected nature, of the incident under investigation. In most instances, the requirement for further specific imaging will be determined as a result of data obtained at primary radiological survey or from the pathological, odontological, anthropological, or crime scene examinations. Again, one should remember that radiographs produced at the primary survey stage will not be of sufficient quality to permit accurate evaluation by a radiologist due to the random nature of the anatomical positioning of the body parts within the body bag. The following are possible indications for radiography:

- Any unique skeletal features or pathological conditions seen during the primary survey or identified during examination by the pathologist, anthropologist, or odontologist that may be useful for identification.
- To replicate poor quality antemortem dental radiographs by undertaking subsequent examinations using substandard angulations to facilitate accurate comparison.
- In cases in which evidence of trauma identified by the pathologist, anthropologist, or odontologist may indicate further imaging investigations to determine the nature of the injury or weapon used.
- To detect, locate, and retrieve items of forensic evidence seen during the primary survey but not located during examination by the pathologist.
- For those cases that are proving difficult to identify via other means, a full skeletal survey may be useful in determining age, sex, stature, etc., or for detecting unique skeletal features that have been previously documented in antemortem records.
- To document injuries and injury patterns for the purposes of the criminal investigation or as a means of negating the requirement for full autopsy where the cause of death is known.

In the last two cases, imaging examinations may be particularly useful in cases of fleshed remains where anthropological examination is difficult.

Mass Fatality Investigation Using MDCT

In recent years, multi-detector CT scanning has been applied to the forensic examination of the deceased. While CT scanning has been in clinical use since 1971, shortly after its invention by Godfrey Hounsfield, it is only relatively recently that this technology has been applied within the postmortem setting, due mainly to financial constraints and availability.

It is now in widespread use for the examination of the deceased at centers in Switzerland, Japan, and Denmark and on a smaller scale in many other countries across the globe. The volume of research papers involving MDCT has risen exponentially, and the field has recently been able to establish an international society and journal.

As with many forensic procedures for the investigation of death, trauma, and identification of the deceased, MDCT can potentially be applied within the mass fatality setting. This use has been recognized by a number of authors, but it is only relatively recently that the technology has been applied to the systematic analysis of human remains in mass fatality incidents. There are as yet very few incidents in which MDCT has been employed; the volume of data documenting its use in cases involving fragmentation and commingling is small. However, in two well-documented cases, it is clear that MDCT has proved its effectiveness as a tool that in certain circumstances can combine the primary and secondary surveys. With appropriate scanning protocols, it also offers the opportunity for the data acquired during this examination to be re-examined to provide additional information in place of a separate tertiary imaging examination. The methods employed in these two cases were identical to the extent that MDCT was used for the initial examination. In one case, a mobile-trailer-mounted MDCT scanner attended the disaster mortuary after a five-vehicle road traffic incident. Five out of six bodies were successfully imaged by MDCT with an examination time of around 15 minutes per body. Subsequent full radiological analysis took around one hour per case (Rutty et al. 2007).

In the other case, a static CT unit, installed within the Victorian Institute of Forensic Medicine, Melbourne, Australia, was employed to examine the remains of all deceased individuals and fragmented remains admitted to the mortuary following devastating bush fires in 2009. The contents of 255 body bags were examined in the 28 days following the fires and were CT scanned in their body bags using established protocols. Images were reviewed by teams of radiologists experienced in forensic imaging. A total of 164 missing persons was included in the DVI process, with 163 deceased individuals eventually identified. CT contributed to this identification in 161 persons. CT was utilized in the initial triage of each bag's contents. If radiological evaluation determined that bodies were incomplete, then this information was provided to search teams who revisited the scenes of death. CT was helpful in differentiation of human from nonhuman remains, determination of sex, and age estimation. Specific identifying features detected on CT included the presence of disease, medical devices, and 274 everyday metallic items associated with the remains of 135 individuals. CT scanning provided useful information prior to autopsy by flagging the presence of nonhuman remains, at the time of autopsy by assisting in the localization of identifying features in heavily disfigured bodies, and after autopsy by retrospective review of images for clarification of issues that arose at the time of pathologist case review (O'Donnell et al. 2009).

In both cases, the workflow was the same: the bodies or body parts underwent an initial MDCT scan and the image data resulting from this scan was utilized for the same purposes as the primary and secondary (skeletal) surveys, and where necessary, the data could be used in place of any tertiary examinations needed. However, in neither case was the MDCT data used for the secondary (dental) survey, although the authors of the studies recognized the potential for MDCT data to be used for odontological identification. A study by Kirchhoff et al. (2008) sounded a note of caution on this point and highlighted the problems associated with streak artifacts and difficulties of image interpretation. The value of MDCT for postmortem dental identification is still being evaluated, and technological advances have minimized the presence of streak artifacts caused by metallic amalgam restorations that are present on earlier scans.

The advantage of MDCT is that it has the potential to replace all three of the stages outlined earlier in this chapter. The digital nature of the technology enables accurate discrimination between hard and soft tissues and artifacts made from a range of different materials. Triangulation from a continuous sequence of X-ray transmissions through 360 degrees provides for accurate location and measurement of anatomical structures, artifacts, ballistic material, etc. The vast data sets acquired can permit reconstruction in any plane, thus negating the need for accurately positioned comparison views, and the data can be shared, transmitted, displayed, and read remotely.

There are, however, some significant disadvantages. MDCT scanners are expensive to purchase and have high maintenance costs for servicing and replacement of X-ray tubes. They require a three-phase power supply and a lead-shielded scan room and separate control area. Although the actual process of scanning is rapid, there is additional body handling and significant time required for scan reconstruction and interpretation. While the initial scan may negate further radiological examination in most cases, intra-oral radiography for dental identification and the use of either fluoroscopy or digital radiography for rapid location and removal of ballistic material cannot currently be entirely ruled out. It is perhaps for these logistical reasons that CT scanning has not yet been more widely used in mass fatality response. Mass fatality plans either need to incorporate the use of existing CT scanning facilities into the disaster mortuary (predisposing the use of static locations) or make use of mobile technology. Mobile (trailer-mounted or containerized) CT scanners offer a possible one-stop solution for the emergency mortuary and have been adopted by national DVI teams, including Denmark and the United Kingdom (Leth 2007). Geography and/or cost may preclude others from adopting the same approach, and there will thus be a continued reliance on more conventional imaging methods.

These challenges associated with CT scanning have been recognized by the Disaster Victim Identification Working Group of the International Society of Forensic Radiology and Imaging (ISFRI) in its position statement on the use of radiology in disaster victim identification:

> *The modality used will be dependent upon the equipment available at the time and the question to be answered as part of the DVI process. It can include the use, either singularly or in combination or radiographs (plain film, computed or digital radiography), fluoroscopy, computed tomography or dental radiography. Currently Magnetic Resonance Imaging (MR) is not considered a modality for use in DVI unless the only ante-mortem imaging available for comparison is MR. (Rutty et al. 2013)*

Case Studies

United Nations International Criminal Tribunal Investigations of Mass Graves in Croatia, Bosnia, and Kosovo, 1996–2002

During the period from 1996 to 2002, the forensic teams of the Office of the Prosecutor for the United Nations International Criminal Tribunal for the Former Yugoslavia (ICTY) exhumed and examined several mass graves in Croatia, Bosnia Herzegovina, and Kosovo as part of their investigation into alleged war crimes and crimes against humanity. Several mass graves, with wide variations in size and content, were exhumed, and the human remains were examined in mortuaries employing a modified mass fatality protocol. Although the exhumation process was generally painstakingly carried out to the highest standards of forensic archaeology, some of the exhumed remains were unavoidably commingled. This was particularly true in "secondary" graves containing remains of individuals which had been "robbed" (i.e., disinterred) from the primary graves and subsequently reburied in another location in an attempt to conceal them (Brown 2006). Radiography played an important role in the examination of the remains from these graves. Fluoroscopy, radiography, and dental radiography were used, sometimes in "field" conditions, and were employed according to the following protocol.

Primary Survey

The primary survey (triage) was performed using fluoroscopy in all cases. All body bags were examined using a mobile C-Arm fluoroscope by a radiographer and pathologist or anthropologist working together. Fluoroscopy proved invaluable in the location of hazardous material, including a number of live hand grenades and ammunition, razor blades, and other sharp objects. Its primary value was the location of projectile fragments (e.g., bullets and shrapnel), allowing the pathologists to locate and retrieve these at autopsy as well as locate personal effects, many of which carried identifiable markings. The examination of commingled remains using fluoroscopy enabled rapid evaluation of the contents of body bags and facilitated fast separation of human bone from soil, stones, and other artifacts.

Secondary Survey

Secondary surveys were performed only in specific circumstances. The incidence of any dental work among the population was generally very low and did not usually warrant a full dental radiography survey. In most cases, the secondary survey was limited to an oblique projection of both mandibular rami for age determination. In some specific investigations, however (where dental records were known to be available), a full-mouth dental radiography series was undertaken. In other investigations in which systematic antemortem assault was alleged, a radiographic examination of the rib cage and extremities was undertaken to look for evidence of trauma and healing fractures (Figure 5-12).

Tertiary Examinations

Fluoroscopy: The nature of the exhumed remains often rendered the physical location of items seen at primary survey difficult to locate during autopsy, particularly when these lay in clothing or decomposing tissue. Fluoroscopy was frequently employed during autopsy to locate and retrieve these items under X-ray control.

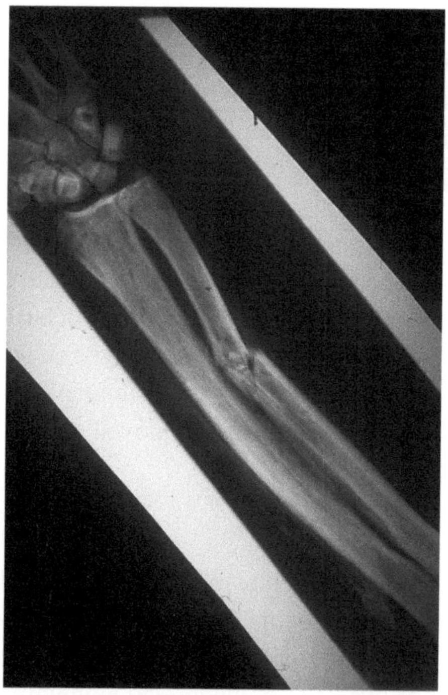

Figure 5-12
Secondary surveys may sometimes be used to document perimortem injuries, as in this case showing a defensive fracture of the radius and ulna.

Radiography: Radiography was undertaken in a number of cases to document identifying features seen during the primary survey or at autopsy or anthropological examination. It was regularly employed to examine epiphyseal plates in young adults to assist with age determination and, in some cases, it proved possible to establish identity by comparison of postmortem radiographs with antemortem films (Figure 5-13). Generally, however, the incidence of antemortem films being available for comparison proved to be very low. Plain film radiography using high-definition techniques was also employed in some cases to determine whether bony trauma was associated with projectile fragments, particularly in cases in which the exact nature of the injury could not be determined simply by physical examination.

London Bombings, July 7, 2005

On July 7, 2005, three terrorist bombs exploded on underground trains and another bomb on a bus in London. Fifty-six people were killed in these explosions, and several hundred people were injured. Fifty-six bodies were recovered from the scenes of the explosion together with a large number of fragmented remains.

In accordance with the London Resilience Mass Fatality Plan, the Association of Forensic Radiographers (AFR) mobilized its forensic radiography response team and equipment, some

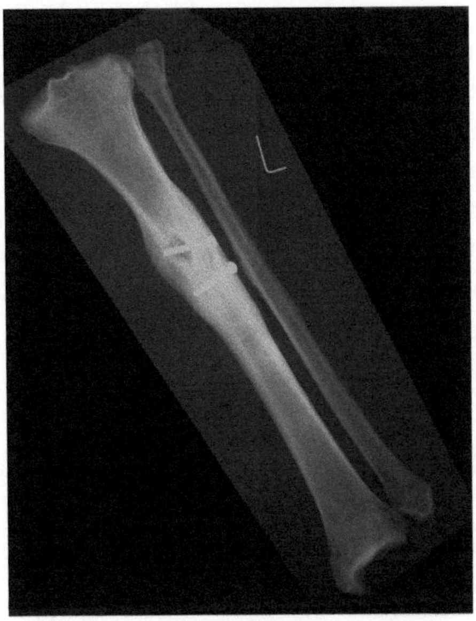

Figure 5-13

Identifying features seen during the primary survey such as this healed fracture with two orthopaedic screws *in situ* were radiographed in true AP and lateral projections for the purpose of identification as a tertiary examination.

of which was provided on loan by the medical supply industry. A total of 27 radiographers worked in teams of between six and eight people for 12 hours per day during the subsequent 11 days (Viner and Lichtenstein 2011; Viner et al. 2006). Two mobile C-Arm fluoroscopy units, a DR unit, and a CR unit, together with plain film radiography and dental radiography, were deployed according to the following protocol.

Primary Survey

Fluoroscopy was employed for the primary survey (triage) of the bodies. Two radiographers, working together with a pathologist, examined each case documenting any identifying features, injuries, personal effects, and hazardous objects and printing hard-copy images via a thermal printer. The average examination time was ten minutes.

Both digital radiography and computed radiography were employed for the primary survey of the body parts. The use of CR was abandoned after the first day because DR proved to be almost ten times faster than CR in this application. Two radiographers examined each case using correct anatomical positioning where possible, which was facilitated by the use of transparent body-part bags in many cases. Images were stored on a workstation accessible to the pathologist and anthropologist for evaluation, and written to CD-ROM as a permanent record.

The use of digital technology allowed images to be displayed to evaluate both soft-tissue and bony elements and facilitated rapid triage of commingled body parts for anthropological analysis and DNA testing. In many cases, subsequent radiography for analysis of bony elements was not required due to the high-definition nature of the images and the use of correct anatomical positioning. In this case, due to the rapid identification of victims by other means, it did not prove necessary to utilize the digital image database for comparison with antemortem skeletal radiographs. However, a number of dental fragments were recovered as part of the primary survey and, in most cases, further radiography of these parts was not required because the information obtained at primary survey was sufficient for odontological analysis and identification to be made.

Secondary Survey

Dental radiography was undertaken as a routine part of the identification process using conventional intra-oral film radiography. Teams of experienced dental radiographers worked in conjunction with the forensic odontologists to undertake dental surveys *in situ*, shortening the odontological examination time.

Tertiary Examinations

Tertiary examinations of identifiable skeletal pathology were undertaken as part of the identification process, none of which contributed to a positive identification.

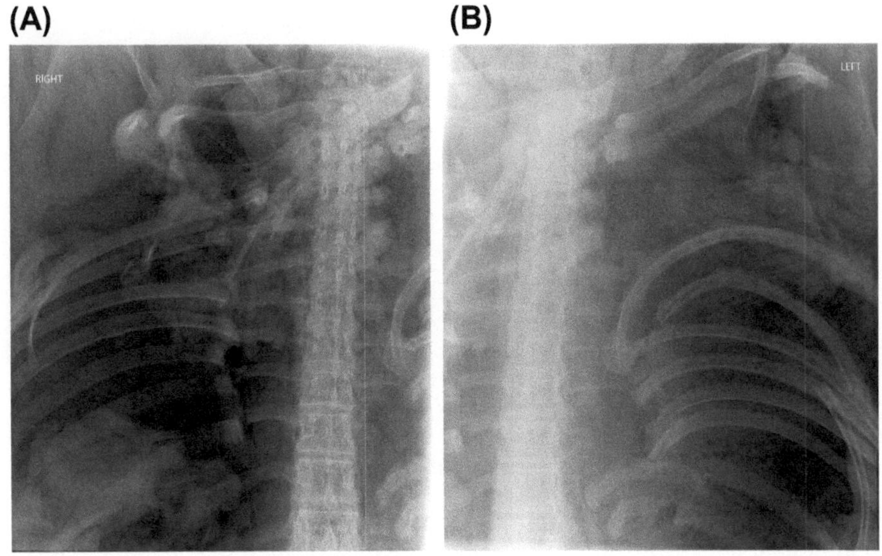

Figure 5-14
Radiographs of the ribs of one of the suspected suicide bombers reveal fractures on the right side (A) and dislocations on the left side (B) of the chest, providing information regarding the direction of the blast.

Following the initial victim identification process, a number of further examinations of fragmented remains were undertaken using both CR and DR. In certain cases, missing body parts identified by DNA were reconciled with the cadaver and then examined both radiologically and anthropologically to identify and document trauma patterns. These examinations provided the investigating team with further information and evidence regarding the nature, location, and direction of the blast (Figures 5-14A and 5-14B).

Commonwealth War Graves Commission and Oxford Archaeology, 2009

In 2009, Oxford Archaeology undertook an exhumation of several mass graves on behalf of the Commonwealth War Graves Commission. The graves contained the remains of 250 Australian and British soldiers killed in the Battle of Fromelles in 1916. The human remains and artifacts were examined in a bespoke temporary mortuary at the grave site employing a modified mass fatality protocol. Radiography played an important role in the examination of the remains from these graves. Digital radiography was deployed in "field" conditions and was employed according to the following protocol.

Primary Survey

The primary survey (triage) was performed in all cases using DR radiography. The initial radiography enabled rapid evaluation of the contents of body bags and facilitated fast

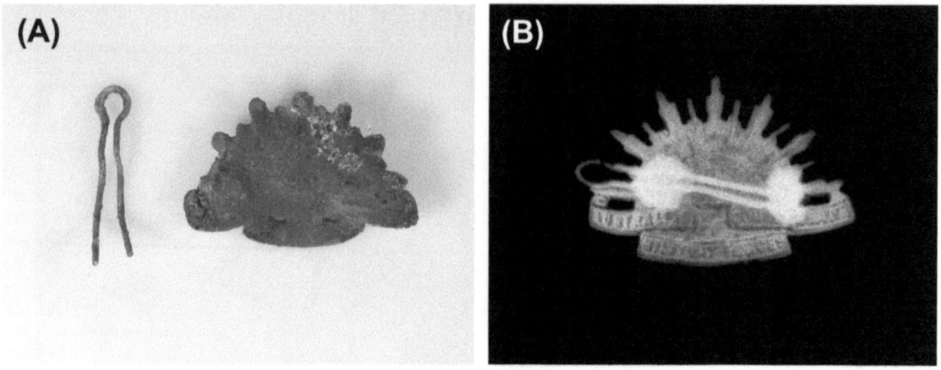

Figure 5-15
Corroded artifact exhumed with remains from the mass grave (A) is revealed as an Australian Army "Rising Sun" badge (B). *(Source: Images courtesy of Oxford Archaeology.)*

separation of human bone from soil, stones, and other artifacts. It also helped to identify small personal effects and military insignia, which proved invaluable to the identification process. The "real-time" information from the radiography examination enabled the exhumation teams to make minor modifications to the exhumation protocol to locate and identify clothing components that also proved useful in separately identifying British and Australian soldiers.

Secondary Survey

Secondary surveys using DR radiography were performed only in specific circumstances. The incidence of dental interventions among the cohort was unexpectedly high with many restorations, although the lack of antemortem records did not warrant a full dental radiography survey. In some cases, oblique projections of both mandibular rami proved useful for age determination.

Tertiary Examinations

Due to the lack of any antemortem radiological records, tertiary examinations did not prove useful for identification. However, radiography proved invaluable for the examination of archaeological "finds." In many cases, radiography was able to identify corroded personal effects, enabling an appropriate conservation process to be adopted (Figures 5-15A and 5-15B). These personal effects contributed significantly to the identification process.

Conclusion

The science of medical imaging has developed rapidly over the last century since Röntgen's announcement of the discovery of X-rays and is continuing to develop at a rapid pace with each leap forward in computer technology. Medical imaging has an important and increasing role in forensic investigation, both in determining the cause of death or injury and in the identification of the deceased. There is no one technique that will deliver all the answers, and its contribution to the analysis and identification of commingled human remains will depend on the timely application of the most appropriate techniques. Close collaboration between investigators, pathologists, odontologists, anthropologists, and the radiology professionals (radiologists, radiographers, and physicists) is essential if the maximum benefit is to be obtained.

References

Alexander, C.J., Foote, G.A., 1998. Radiology in forensic identification: the Mt Erebus disaster. Australas. Radiol. 42 (4), 321–326.

Baglivo, M., Winklhofer, S., Hatch, G.M., Ampanozi, G., Thali, M.J., Ruder, T.D., 2013. The rise of forensic and post-mortem radiology—Analysis of the literature between the year 2000 and 2011. J. Forensic Radiol. Imaging 1 (1), 3–9.

Bass, W.M., 1990. Forensic anthropology. In: Fierro, M.F. (Ed.), CAP Handbook for Postmortem Examination of Unidentified Remains: Developing Identification of Well Preserved, Decomposed, Burned, and Skeletonised Remains. College of American Pathologists, Skokie, IL, Chapter 8.

Beningfield, S., Potgieter, H., Nicol, A., van As, S., Bowie, G., Hering, E., Latti, E., 2003. Report on a new type of trauma full-body digital X-ray machine. Emerg. Radiol. 10 (1), 23–29.

Binda, M., Cattaneo, C., Bogoni, A., Fattorini, P., Grandi, M., 1999. Identification of human skeletal remains: forensic radiology vs DNA. Radiol. Med. Torino 97 (5), 409–411.

Bisset, R.A., Thomas, N.B., Turnbull, I.W., Lee, S., 2002. Postmortem examinations using magnetic resonance imaging: four year review of a working service. BMJ 324 (7351), 1423–1424.

Brogdon, B.G., 2011a. Radiological identification of individual remains. In: Thali, M.J., Viner, M.D., Brogdon, B.G. (Eds.), Brogdon's Forensic Radiology, second ed. CRC Press, Boca Raton, FL, pp. 153–176.

Brogdon, B.G., 2011b. Radiological identification: anthropological parameters. In: Thali, M.J., Viner, M.D., Brogdon, B.G. (Eds.), Brogdon's Forensic Radiology, second ed. CRC Press, Boca Raton, FL, pp. 85–106.

Brogdon, B.G., Lichtenstein, J.E., 2011. Forensic radiology in historical perspective. In: Thali, M.J., Viner, M.D., Brogdon, B.G. (Eds.), Brogdon's Forensic Radiology, second ed. CRC Press, Boca Raton, FL, pp. 9–24.

Brogdon, B.G., Vogel, H., McDowell, J., 2003. A Radiologic Atlas of Abuse, Torture and Inflicted Trauma. CRC Press, Boca Raton, FL.

Brookes, J.A., Hall-Craggs, M.A., Sams, V.R., Lees, W.R., 1996. Non-invasive perinatal necropsy by magnetic resonance imaging. Lancet 348 (9035), 1139–1141.

Brown, A.G., 2006. The use of forensic botany and geology in war crimes investigations in N E Bosnia. Forensic Sci. Int. 163 (3), 204–210.

Bryan, G.J., 1979. Diagnostic Radiography, third ed. Churchill Livingstone, Edinburgh.

Buchner, A., 1985. The identification of human remains. Int. Dent. J. 35 (4), 307–311.

Burrows, E.H., 1986. Pioneers and Early Years: A History of British Radiology. Colophon Ltd, Alderney, Chanel Islands.

Chilvarquer, I., Katz, J.O., Glassman, D.M., Prihoda, T.J., Cottone, J.A., 1987. Comparative radiographic study of human and animal long bone patterns. J. Forensic Sci. 32 (6), 1645–1654.

Christensen, A.M., 2005. Testing the reliability of frontal sinuses in positive identification. J. Forensic Sci. 50 (1), 18–22.

Clarke, Lord Justice, 2000. Thames Safety Enquiry, HMSO, London, pp. 91–92.

Craig, E.A., 1995. Intercondylar shelf angle: a new method to determine race from the distal femur. J. Forensic Sci. 40 (5), 777–782.

Culbert, W.L., Law, F.M., 1927. Identification by comparison of roentgenograms of nasal accessory sinuses and mastoid processes. JAMA (88), 1632–1636.

Dimond, B., 2002. Legal Aspects of Radiography and Radiology, Blackwell Science, Oxford, pp. 58–67.

Edwards, K., Viner, M.D., Schweitzer, W., Thali, M.J., 2013. Sex determination from the foreman magnum. J. Forensic Radiol. Imaging 1 (4), 186–192.

Emerton, D., Honey, I., McKenzie, A., Blake, P., Annett, D., Lawinski, C., Cole, H., 2005. Computed Radiography Systems for General Radiography, (CR) Comparative Report, Edition 2, Report 05081. NHS Purchasing and Supply Agency, Her Majesty's Stationary Office London.

Engel-Hills, P., 2006. Radiation protection in medical imaging. Radiography 12 (2), 153–160.

European Commission, 2008. European Guidance on Estimating Population Doses from Medical X-Ray Procedures Annex 1-DD Report 1 Review of Recent National Surveys of Population Exposure from Medical X-Rays in Europe. European Commission, Strasbourg.

Fischman, S.L., 1985. The use of medical and dental radiographs in identification. Int. Dent. J. 35 (4), 301–306.

Goodman, N.R., Edelson, L.B., 2002. The efficiency of an X-ray screening system at a mass disaster. J. Forensic Sci. 47 (1), 127–130.

Goodman, P.C., 1995. The new light: discovery and introduction of the X-ray. Am. J. Roentgenol. 165 (5), 1041–1045.

Gould, P., 2003. X-ray detectives turn images into evidence. Diagn. Imaging (Special Edition).

Greulich, W.W., Pyle, S.I., 1959. Radiographic Atlas of Skeletal Development of the Hand and Wrist. Stanford University Press, Stanford, CA.

Hall-Edwards, J., 1908. On X-ray dermatitis and its prevention. Arch. Roentgen Ray 13, 243–248.

Hansman, C.F., 1962. Appearance and fusion of ossification centers in the human skeleton. Am. J. Roentgenol. Radium. Ther. Nucl. Med. 88, 476–482.

Harcke, H.T., Bifano, J.A., Koeller, K.K., 2002. Forensic radiology: response to the Pentagon Attack on September 11, 2001. Radiology 223 (1), 7–8.

Hart, D., Wall, B.F., 2002. Radiation Exposure of the UK Population from Medical and Dental X-Ray Examinations. National Radiological Protection Board-W4, Chilton.

Hoerr, N.L., Pyle, S.I., Francis, C.C., 1962. Radiological Atlas of the Foot and Ankle. Charles C. Thomas, Springfield, IL.

International Association of Forensic Radiographers, 2004. Radiography facilities for temporary emergency mortuaries in the event of a mass fatality incident. London. www.iafr.org.uk/.

International X-Ray Protection Committee, 1928. International recommendations for X-ray and radium protection. Br. J. Radiol. 1, 358–363.

Jackowski, C., Aghayev, E., Sonnenschein, M., Dirnhofer, R., Thali, M.J., 2006. Maximum intensity projection of cranial computed tomography data for dental identification. Int. J. Legal Med. 120 (3), 165–167.

Jenkins, D., 1980. Radiographic Photography and Imaging Processes. MTP Press Ltd., Lancaster, England.

Jensen, S., 1991. Identification of human remains lacking skull and teeth. A case report with some methodological considerations. Am. J. Forensic Med. Pathol. 12 (2), 93–97.

Kahana, T., Hiss, J., 1997. Identification of human remains: forensic radiology. J. Clin. Forensic Med. 4 (1), 7–15.

Kahana, T., Ravioli, J.A., Urroz, C.L., Hiss, J., 1997. Radiographic identification of fragmentary human remains from a mass disaster. Am. J. Forensic Med. Pathol. 18 (1), 40–44.

Kirchhoff, S., Fischer, F., Lindemaier, L., Herzog, P., Kirchhoff, C., Becker, C., Bark, J., Reiser, M.F., Eisenmenger, W., 2008. Is post-mortem CT of the dentition adequate for correct forensic identification? Comparison of dental computed tomography and visual dental record. Int. J. Legal Med. 122, 471–479.

Kirk, N.J., Wood, R.E., Goldstein, M., 2002. Skeletal identification using the frontal sinus region: a retrospective study of 39 cases. J. Forensic Sci. 47 (2), 318–323.

Krogman, W.M., Iscan, M.Y., 1986. The Human Skeleton in Forensic Medicine, second ed. Charles C. Thomas, Springfield, IL.

Kurihara, Y., Kurihara, Y., Ohashi, K., Kitagawa, A., Miyasaka, M., Okamoto, E., Ishikawa, T., 1996. Radiologic evidence of sex differences: is the patient a woman or a man? Am. J. Roentgenol. 167 (4), 1037–1040.

Lawinski, C., McKenzie, A., Cole, H., Blake, P., Honey, I., 2005. Digital Detectors for General Radiography: A Comparative Technical Report 05078. NHS Purchasing and Supply Agency, Her Majesty's Stationary Office, London.

Leth, P., 2007. The use of CT scanning in forensic autopsy, For. Sci. Med. Pathol., DOI: 10.1385/Forensic Sci. Med. Pathol.:3:1:65.

Levinsohn, 1899. Beitraz zur feststellung der identitat. Arch. Krim. Anthrop. 2, 221.

Loe, L., Brady, K., 2010. Remembering Fromelles, Br. Archaeol. Issue 111, March/April. http://www.archaeologyuk.org/ba/ba111/feat6.shtml.
Marlin, D.C., Clark, M.A., Standish, S.M., 1991. Identification of human remains by comparison of frontal sinus radiographs: a series of four cases. J. Forensic Sci. 36 (6), 1765–1772.
Mason, R., Bourne, S., 1998. A Guide to Dental Radiography, fourth ed. Oxford University Press, Oxford.
McCormick, W.F., 1980. Mineralization of the costal cartilages as an indicator of age: preliminary observations. J. Forensic Sci. 25 (4), 736–741.
Mora, S., et al., 2001. Applicability of the Greulich and Pyle standards. Pediatr. Res. 50, 624–812.
Mulligan, M.E., McCarthy, M.J., Wippold, F.J., Lichtenstein, J.E., Wagner, G.N., 1988. Radiologic evaluation of mass casualty victims: lessons from the Gander, Newfoundland, accident. Radiology 168 (1), 229–233.
Murphy, W.A., Spruill, F.G., Gantner, G.E., 1980. Radiologic identification of unknown human remains. J. Forensic Sci. 25 (4), 727–735.
O'Donnell, C., Lino, M., Mansharan, K., Leditscke, J., Woodford, N., 2009. Contribution of post-mortem multidetector CT scanning to identification of the deceased in a mass disaster: experience gained from the 2009 Victorian bush fires. Forensic Sci. Int. 205 (2011), 15–28.
Nambiar, P., Naidu, M.D., Subramaniam, K., 1999. Anatomical variability of the frontal sinuses and their application in forensic identification. Clin. Anat. 12 (1), 16–19.
Navani, S., Shah, J.R., Levy, P.S., 1970. Determination of sex by costal cartilage calcification. Am. J. Roentgenol. Radium Ther. Nucl. Med. 108 (4), 771–774.
Nye, P.J., Tytle, T.L., Jarman, R.N., Eaton, B.G., 1996. The role of radiology in the Oklahoma City bombing. Radiology 200 (2), 541–543.
Pittayapat, P., Jacobs, R., De Valck, E., Vandermeulen, D., Willems, G., 2012. Forensic odontology in the disaster victim identification process. J. Forensic Odontostomatol. 30 (1), 1–12, July.
Pyle, S.I., Hoerr, N.L., 1955. Atlas of Skeletal Development of the Knee. Charles C. Thomas, Springfield, IL.
Reichs, K., Dorion, R.B.J., 1992. The use of computed tomography (CT) scans in the analysis of frontal sinus configuration. Can. Soc. Forensic Sci. J. 25, 1.
Rocha Sdos, S., Ramos, D.L., Cavalcanti Mde, G., 2003. Applicability of 3D-CT facial reconstruction for forensic individual identification. Pesqui Odontol. Bras. 17 (1), 24–28.
Rogers, T., Saunders, S., 1994. Accuracy of sex determination using morphological traits of the human pelvis. J. Forensic Sci. 39 (4), 1047–1056.
Röntgen, W.C., 1895. A new kind of ray. Phys-Med. Ges. (137), 132–141.
Rutty, G.N., et al., 2007. The role of mobile computed tomography in mass fatality incidents. J. Forensic Sci. 52 (6), 1343–1349.
Rutty, G.N., et al., 2013. Use of radiology in disaster victim identification: positional statement of the members of the Disaster Victim Identification working group of the International Society of Forensic Radiology & Imaging, May. J. Forensic Radiol. Imaging 1 (4), 218.
Sanders, I., Woesner, M.E., Ferguson, R.A., Noguchi, T.T., 1972. A new application of forensic radiology: identification of deceased from a single clavicle. Am. J. Roentgenol. Radium Ther. Nucl. Med. 115 (3), 619–622.
Scheuer, L., Black, S., 2004. The Juvenile Skeleton. Academic Press, London.
Schwartz, S., Woolridge, E.D., 1977. The use of panoramic radiographs for comparisons in cases of identification. J. Forensic Sci. 22 (1), 145–146.
Smith, V.A., Christensen, A.M., Myers, S.W., 2010. The reliability of visually comparing small frontal sinuses. J. Forensic Sci. 55 (6), 1413–1415.
Society of Radiographers, 2005. Radiographers help identify London Bombing victims. Synergy. September 1, pp. 1–2.
Sutherland, L.D., Suchey, J.M., 1991. Use of the ventral arc in pubic sex determination. J Forensic Sci. 36 (2), 501–511.
Thali, M.J., et al., 2000. Improved vision in forensic documentation: forensic 3D/CAD-supported photogrammetry of bodily injury internal structures to provide more leads and stronger practical forensic evidence. Paper presented at the International Society of Optical Engineering: 3D Visualisation for Data Exploration and Decision Making, Washington, D.C.

Thali, M.J., Dirnhofer, R., Vock, P. (Eds.), 2009. The Virtopsy Approach: 3D Optical and Radiological Scanning and Reconstruction in Forensic Medicine. CRC Press, Boca Raton, FL.

Thali, M.J., Markwalder, T., Jackowski, C., Sonnenschein, M., Dirnhofer, R., 2006. Dental CT imaging as a screening tool for dental profiling: advantages and limitations. J. Forensic Sci. 51 (1), 113–119.

Thali, M.J., Preiss, U., Bollinger, S., 2011. Dental scan and body CT imaging as a screening tool for identification. In: Thali, M.J., Viner, M.D., Brogdon, B.G. (Eds.), Brogdon's Forensic Radiology, second ed. CRC Press, Boca Raton, FL, pp. 149–152.

Thali, M.J., Yen, K., Schweitzer, W., Vock, P., Boesch, C., Ozdoba, C., Schroth, G., Ith, M., Sonnenschein, M., Doernhoefer, T., Scheurer, E., Plattner, T., Dirnhofer, R., 2003. Virtopsy, a new imaging horizon in forensic pathology: virtual autopsy by postmortem multislice computed tomography (MSCT) and magnetic resonance imaging (MRI)—a feasibility study. J. Forensic Sci. 48 (2), 386–403.

Thali, M.J., Yen, K., Schweitzer, W., Vock, P., Ozdoba, C., Dirnhofer, R., 2003. Into the decomposed body-forensic digital autopsy using multislice-computed tomography. Forensic Sci. Int. 134 (2–3), 109–114.

Tonello, B., 1998. Mass Grave Investigations. Paper presented at Imaging, Science & Oncology, British Institute of Radiology.

Trotter, M., Gleser, G.C., 1952. Estimation of stature from long bones of American whites and Negroes. Am. J. Phys. Anthropol. 10, 463–514.

Trotter, M., Gleser, G.C., 1958. A re-evaluation of estimation of stature based on measurements of stature taken during life and of long bones after death. Am. J. Phys. Anthropol. 16, 79–123.

Viner, M.D., 2001a. Forensic investigation: the role of radiography. Eur. Radiol. Supplement to Volume 11 (2), 95.

Viner, M.D., 2001b. Forensic investigation: the role of radiography in forensic medicine. ISRRT Newsletter 37 (2), 4–7.

Viner, M.D., 2001c. The radiographers role in forensic investigation. Hold Pusten: J. Norwegian Soc. Radiog. (9/2001), 1–3.

Viner, M.D., Cassidy, M., Treu, V., 1998. The Role of Radiography in a Disaster Investigation. Paper presented at Imaging, Science & Oncology, British Institute of Radiology.

Viner, M.D., Hoban, W., Rock, C., Cassidy, M.T., 2003. The Role of Radiography in the Investigation of Mass Incidents. Paper presented at the American Academy of Forensic Sciences, 55th Scientific Meeting, Chicago, IL.

Viner, M.D., Lichtenstein, J.E., 2011. Radiology in mass casualty situations. In: Thali, M.J., Viner, M.D., Brogdon, B.G. (Eds.), Brogdon's Forensic Radiology, second ed. CRC Press, Boca Raton, FL, pp. 177–198.

Viner, M.D., Rock, C., Hunt, N., Mackinnon, G., Martin, A.W., 2006. Forensic Radiography: Response to the London Suicide Bombings on 7th July 2005. Paper presented at the American Academy of Forensic Sciences, 58th Scientific Meeting, Seattle, WA.

CHAPTER 6

A Practical Method for Detecting Commingled Remains Using Epiphyseal Union

Maureen Schaefer
Michigan State University, Department of Radiology, Division of Anatomy

The utility of epiphyseal union as a means of estimating the chronological age of juvenile remains is well known and documented. Less thoroughly investigated, however equally valuable, is the application of epiphyseal union in the recognition and sorting of commingled remains (Buikstra et al. 1984; L'Abbe 2005; Owsley et al. 1995; Schaefer and Black 2007; Schaefer 2008a). Detection of commingled remains is most easily accomplished through the recognition of duplicate elements within an assemblage, e.g., two left femora. In the absence of repeated elements, however, commingling episodes are more difficult to recognize and rely on the anthropologist to detect discrepancies between skeletal elements within the assemblage. Inconsistencies often include variation in size and shape of bilateral elements, disproportionate upper and lower body measurements, or discrepancies in the age, sex, or racial attributes of materials within the assemblage (Buikstra et al. 1984; Byrd and Adams 2003; L'Abbe 2005; Owsley et al. 1995; Snow 1948; Snow and Folk 1970). In much the same way, status of epiphyseal union can serve as a tool to recognize incongruities in the maturity level of different elements (Schaefer and Black 2007; Schaefer 2008a). This technique is useful for identifying commingling episodes between juvenile remains mixed with that of either additional juvenile or adult material. Although discrepancies between juvenile and adult material may seem obvious, they are less conspicuous if the juvenile skeleton has approximated full maturity, and many epiphyseal elements would be expected to display complete union.

The ability to detect discrepancies in the developmental status of juvenile material nearing maturity requires an understanding of the association between union phases of different epiphyses (Schaefer and Black 2007; Schaefer 2008a). Three lines of evidence can be used to guide this understanding: (1) the sequence in which epiphyses initiate union; (2) the sequence in which epiphyses complete union; and (3) an understanding of interphase relationships such as what epiphyses should, or should not, complete before others begin. When phase associations between epiphyses are understood, the documented patterns can serve as a reference

Commingled Human Remains. http://dx.doi.org/10.1016/B978-0-12-405889-7.00006-X

from which to recognize potentially incompatible material. Epiphyseal elements that do not conform to the documented patterns are evidence indicating the presence of more than one individual.

Sequences of beginning and complete union, as well as interphase relationships, have been previously documented in the form of "sequence trees" and "antenna diagram" figures (see Appendix 6-1).

Although these figures demonstrate potential combinations of incongruent fusing sequences from which to recognize commingled remains, they concentrate on documenting a range of acceptable variation that is presented within fusing sequences among different individuals. The extensive documentation of variation helps to ensure that individuals who display less common but acceptable fusing patterns are not erroneously labeled as commingled. The layers of detail provided within the figures, however, may disable the quick recognition of a misplaced bone. The aim of this chapter is to present a user-friendly epiphyseal recording form that quickly highlights areas of possible incongruent fusing patterns. Once suspect areas are recognized, then the sequence trees and antenna diagram can be referenced to add support to or reject suspicions. This process of quick recognition followed by more detailed investigation is demonstrated using two sample cases. And last, the utility at which the method can determine the presence of misplaced elements is tested on 14 artificially commingled individuals.

Background Information

Phase relationships among the epiphyses were defined using a Bosnian sample, including 256 identified male individuals between the ages of 14 and 30 who lost their lives during the fall of Srebrenica. Data were collected on 21 epiphyses, including:

- Proximal, medial, and distal humerus
- Proximal and distal radius
- Proximal and distal ulna
- Proximal and distal femur, greater and lesser trochanter
- Proximal and distal tibia
- Proximal and distal fibula
- Ischial tuberosity, iliac crest, and tri-radiate complex
- Medial clavicle
- Coraco-glenoid complex and acromion process

The boundaries that constitute most epiphyses are easy to recognize, with the exception of the ischial tuberosity. The exact location in which the tuberosity terminates and the ramus begins is difficult to ascertain because the ramal epiphysis develops as an extension of the tuberous epiphysis. To promote scoring consistency within this study, researchers designated the inferior border of the tuberosity as the area in which the epiphysis begins to "pinch" to form the beginning of the ramus. For an illustration see Schaefer 2008b, p. 539.

Each epiphysis for which information was recorded was scored according to a three-phased approach:

- Phase 0—Open or no union
- Phase 1—Active union (union had initiated, but parts of an epiphyseal line were retained)
- Phase 2—Complete union (line of fusion was no longer present, although an epiphyseal scar could remain)

Phasing data was evaluated using the crosstabs procedure available from SPSS. The procedure individually cross-referenced the 21 epiphyses with each of the remaining 20 epiphyses, to produce a total of 210 3 × 3 charts. The frequencies with which each of the three phases occurred within the sample for the two epiphyses under investigation were displayed in chart form. Table 6-1 demonstrates one of these 3 × 3 charts and compares the results of the proximal humerus with those of the proximal fibula. An understanding of how each individual epiphysis relates to the other epiphyses was thus established.

It was then possible to determine the sequence with which the epiphyses unite according to each developmental phase. When Table 6-1 was used as an example, the sequence of union for the proximal humerus and proximal fibula could be established. To determine *beginning* union, researchers compared the number of individuals whose proximal fibula displayed some form of union (phases 1 or 2) but their proximal humerus remained open (phase 0; n = 5) to the number of individuals whose proximal humerus displayed union (phases 1 or 2) but their proximal fibula remained open (phase 0; n = 2). More individuals demonstrated the proximal fibula initiating union prior to the proximal humerus (n = 5 versus n = 2), so this represents the *modal* sequence pattern. Because two individuals did not conform to that pattern, however, some degree of variation was present in the established sequence order.

Establishing the sequence of complete union was done using the same method but considering different variables. The number of individuals whose proximal fibula had completed union (phase

Table 6-1: Frequency Distribution of No Union (phase 0), Active Union (Phase 1), and Complete Union (Phase 2) in Relation to the Proximal Fibula and Proximal Humerus

Phase		Prox Fib			
		0	1	2	Total
Prox Hum	0	28	4	1	33
	1	2	7	32	41
	2	0	0	134	134
Total		30	11	167	208

2) while their proximal humerus had not (phases 0 or 1; n = 33) were compared to the number of individuals whose proximal humerus had completed union whereas their proximal fibula had not (phases 0 or 1; n = 0). No individuals displayed the latter sequence pattern, and therefore, in this sample, the proximal fibula always completes union prior to the proximal humerus.

Foundations for Understanding Epiphyseal Union Sequencing

Epiphyseal growth plates are strategically located in bony areas that require growth in either length or in width: these may include the proximal and distal ends of a long bone or the medial and lateral borders of irregular bones such as the scapula. Longitudinal growth at the proximal and distal ends of a long bone is generally unequal, and one end favors growth more readily (Bisgard and Bisgard 1935). The end that contributes more significantly toward length expansion is commonly referred to as the growing end, whereas the end that contributes less toward overall growth is known as the nongrowing end. The designation of growing versus nongrowing ends is, of course, a misnomer in that both ends do indeed contribute to overall longitudinal growth; however, their contributions are not equal.

Longitudinal growth at the end of a long bone continues until some point during adolescence when ossific deposition begins to outpace chondral expansion of the epiphyseal plate. The growth plate begins to narrow and the metaphyseal ends of the epiphysis and diaphysis approximate one another. When ossification bridges the gap between the epiphysis and the diaphysis, longitudinal growth at that location is no longer possible. Thus, bony ends that exhibit later epiphyseal fusing times have a window of growth opportunity that extends beyond that of their earlier uniting counterparts. Epiphyses that fuse late during adolescence represent the growing ends of long bones, whereas those that unite earlier represent the nongrowing ends.

Reference to growing and nongrowing ends of long bones can also be extended to entire joint complexes. Epiphyseal ends that participate in the formation of a joint work together as a unit to ensure that functionality of the joint is maintained. It is likely that joint functionality requires participating epiphyses to share similar growth patterns, such as union times, so that one epiphyseal end does not have the opportunity to outgrow that of another (Bisgard and Bisgard 1935). Thus, an epiphysis that forms the growing end of one long bone will articulate with the growing end of a second long bone so that the joint itself can be referred to as a growing joint.

The shoulder, wrist, and knee represent the growing joints, whereas the elbow, hip, and ankle display reduced growth velocity (Pritchett 1991, 1992, 1997). As a general rule, it can be stated that the epiphyses of the elbow, hip, and ankle unite earlier than the epiphyses of the shoulder, wrist, and knee (Stewart 1979). This means that variations in the sequence order between the growing and nongrowing end epiphyses are not expected.[1] For example, the proximal humerus should not begin or complete union prior to the distal tibia beginning or

[1] The distal fibula presents an exception to this general rule in that it is part of the *nongrowing* ankle, and yet it is reported to vary in the sequence in which it completes union with epiphyses of the wrist and knee.

completing union, respectively. On the other hand, epiphyses comprising the nongrowing joints commonly display variation in the order in which they begin and/or complete union. For example, the distal tibia and proximal radius vary in the sequence in which they begin and complete union. Likewise, epiphyses forming the growing joints of the knee, wrist, and shoulder are also likely to display significant variation in the order in which they undergo union. Understanding this inherent relationship between the growing versus nongrowing joint complexes and epiphyseal fusing sequences can serve as a foundation from which to recognize incompatible maturity levels among osseous material.

Although this knowledge presents a useful tool for the quick recognition of incompatible maturity levels between long bone osseous elements, it does not take into account epiphyses of irregular bones, such as the pelvis or scapula. Thus, more detailed analysis is required.

Designing a Recording Form

One extremely quick and easy method to help with the recognition of incongruent union progression is to design a recording form that lists the epiphyses in the general order in which they are expected to unite (Appendix 6-2). In that way, a normal epiphyseal phase distribution would be expected to progress from more mature to less mature epiphyses moving from top to bottom of the page. If, however, an early fusing epiphysis (listed toward the top of the page) is observed to be less mature than that of a late fusing epiphysis (listed toward the bottom of the page), then this display of nonsequential maturity should alert the recorder to a potential problem.

The recording form presented here is based on an earlier piece of work that determined *modal* sequence patterns for the sequence in which the epiphyses initiate union, as well as the sequence in which the epiphyses complete union (Appendix 6-1) (Schaefer and Black 2007). The order in which the epiphyses appear on the recording form has been altered from the sequence in which they appear in the *modal* pattern, however, to accommodate a more user-friendly document. Alterations in the sequence order could be made without compromising the integrity of the information because of the range of sequence variation that was encountered when originally describing this pattern. Any adjustments that were made to the order in which the epiphyses are listed on the recording form were justified in that they represented areas in which variations were documented in the original modal pattern.

Beginning and *complete* union sequence patterns were amalgamated into a single arrangement to create a user-friendly recording form. In addition, the epiphyses were regrouped according to the joint in which they belong. Grouping according to joint complexes helps to streamline documentation efforts in that the recorder can move more systematically through the skeleton.

Complete amalgamation onto a single recording form was not possible, however, due to the extended window of fusing activity displayed by some epiphyses. The ischial tuberosity, for example, always began union prior to the epiphyses of the knee; however, it always completed union after the knee epiphyses. The same scenario was also shown to be true with another pelvic epiphysis in that the iliac crest always began union prior to the distal ulna, but it did not complete union until after this element. Thus, the order in which those epiphyses are listed on the form can reflect only one sequence pattern. Asterisks included alongside the named pelvic epiphyses alert the user to this inconsistency.

A problem also arose when attempting to rearrange the epiphyses into joint complexes. Fusion of the coracoid process interrupts the synchronized union of the epiphyses of the elbow, in that the coracoid process is shown to begin and complete union after the distal humerus and proximal ulna while at the same time displaying the opposite pattern of that of the proximal radius. The recording sheet could document only one pattern, so it listed the coracoid process after that of the elbow epiphyses. This inconsistency does not cause much concern, however, in that observations regarding the coracoid process and the proximal radius that appear within the sequence trees were based on such few individuals that their significance cannot be weighted too heavily. Future research that utilizes a larger number of early adolescents will likely prove that any sequence patterns between the coracoid process and the proximal radius are variable because they unite at similar ages (Schaefer 2008b).

It should also be noted on the recording form that the greater and lesser trochanters were combined with the proximal femur and described as constituting the hip. While the greater and lesser trochanters do not actually contribute to the formation of the hip joint complex itself, previous research demonstrates that they display synchronized union times to that of the proximal femur, and thus, they were grouped together for the sake of simplicity (Schaefer 2008b).

Two Examples Demonstrating Use of the Recording Form

Two examples are provided to demonstrate how the recording form can be used to identify potentially incompatible maturity levels between epiphyses. Use of the sequence trees and antenna diagram as a reference to justify whether areas of potential discrepancy should be further addressed is also described.

The assemblages within both examples were designed to mimic a typical commingling scenario that was commonly encountered during identification efforts in Bosnia Herzegovina. Mass graves associated with the Fall of Srebrenica were especially complex due to the secondary and even tertiary nature of the burials in which remains had been exhumed and reburied in more clandestine areas.

Exhumation and reburial were accomplished with backhoes that disrupted the already-decomposing bodies, dividing them into many components. When transferred to secondary graves, the remains mixed with the bodies and partial remains of other individuals. As a result, the remains that have since been exhumed by archaeologists are often incomplete and/or frequently contain commingled elements. The artificially generated assemblages within these examples were designed to replicate this type of scenario, i.e., the skeletal remains of a single individual that might also include elements from a second individual. The assumption, therefore, is that the remains belong to a single individual, unless a suspicious element is detected.

Example 1

Table 6-2 displays the epiphyseal fusing status of the bones present within a potentially commingled individual. When one examines the phase distribution continuum, an

TABLE 6-2: A Completed Epiphyseal Recording Sheet Demonstrating the Distribution of Phases Associated with Example 1 in the Text

EPIPHYSIS	PHASE	Notes
acetab	2	
elbow		
d hum	2	
p uln	2	
p rad	2	
corocoid	NP	
m hum	2	
ankle		
d tib	NP	
d fib	NP	
hip		
p fem	1	
l troch	1	
g troch	1	
isch	2	
knee		
d fem	0	
p tib	NP	
p fib	NP	
acromion	NP	
wrist		
d rad	2	
d uln	2	
iliac crest	1	
shoulder		
p hum	2	
m clavicle	NP	

Bones present: pelvis, humerus, radius, ulna, femur.
NP = not present.

TABLE 6-3: Areas of Concern within the Epiphyseal Recording Sheet Associated with Example 1

EPIPHYSIS	PHASE	Notes
acetab	2	
elbow		
d hum	2	
p uln	2	
p rad	2	
corocoid	NP	
m hum	2	
ankle		
d tib	NP	
d fib	NP	
hip		Hip epiphyses do not vary in complete sequence order with the ischial tuberosity, distal radius, distal ulna, or proximal humerus
p fem	1	
l troch	1	
g troch	1	
isch	2	
knee		Wrist epiphyses and p hum never complete union prior to the distal femur beginning union
d fem	0	
p tib	NP	
p fib	NP	
acromion	NP	
wrist		
d rad	2	
d uln	2	
iliac crest	1	
shoulder		
p hum	2	
m clavicle	NP	

Bones present: pelvis, humerus, radius, ulna, femur.

inconsistency in numeric sequencing is clearly noticed at the hip and distal femur (Table 6-3). The elbow epiphyses, which are listed earlier in the sequence than the hip epiphyses, display complete union (Phase 2), whereas the epiphyses of the hip display active union (Phase 1). This progression is natural in that epiphyses occurring higher on the page should display more advanced maturity to those located lower on the page. Conversely, the epiphyses listed lower in the sequence should display delayed maturity to those listed higher on the page. This is not the case, however, in that three of the epiphyses listed below the actively uniting hip—namely, the distal radius, distal ulna, and proximal humerus—display advanced maturity or complete union (Phase 2). This disruption in the overall continuum of phase distribution warrants further investigation into the likelihood of this display.

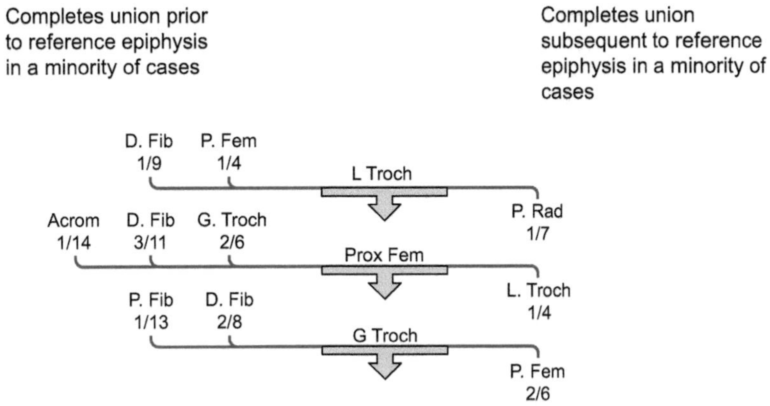

Figure 6-1

A selected segment within the sequence tree diagram demonstrating epiphyses that vary in their complete sequence order with the lesser trochanter, proximal femur, and greater trochanter. For further explanation as to how to read the diagram, refer to Appendix 6-1.

The active status of the hip epiphyses in contrast to the complete status of the wrist epiphyses and shoulder epiphysis is questionable; thus, the sequence tree representing complete union should be consulted (Appendix 6-1). When one investigates the epiphyses that vary in the order in which they complete fusion with the epiphyses of the hip (proximal femur and greater and lesser trochanters), neither the distal radius, distal ulna, nor the proximal humerus is listed (Figure 6-1). It is also noted that the ischial tuberosity is not found to vary in its complete sequence order with the epiphyses of the hip, despite the current display. The inconsistency with the ischial tuberosity is not as noticeable on the recording form, however, because the hip and the ischial tuberosity are sequentially placed on the page.

Even without use of the recording form or sequence tree diagram, this disruption in normal sequencing between the hip and shoulder/wrist epiphyses should be evident in that the basic premise that growing end joints (shoulder and wrist) should not complete union prior to a nongrowing joint (the hip) has been compromised.

A second observation that is distinctly identified as suspicious is that the distal femur exhibits open union (Phase 0), whereas the epiphyses of the wrist (distal radius and distal ulna) display complete union (Phase 2) (Table 6-3). Variability in the sequence in which the distal femur and wrist epiphyses complete union has been documented; however, this is not the case in regard to the order in which they begin union. Thus, the wrist epiphyses should not display any evidence of union prior to that of the distal femur. In addition, the demonstration of phase extremes (open versus complete) among epiphyses that are listed so close together seems suspicious. This line of evidence requires knowledge as to what epiphyses can complete union prior to another epiphysis beginning union. This type of information is provided within the antenna diagram (Appendix 6-1). Owing to the design of the diagram, the question to address

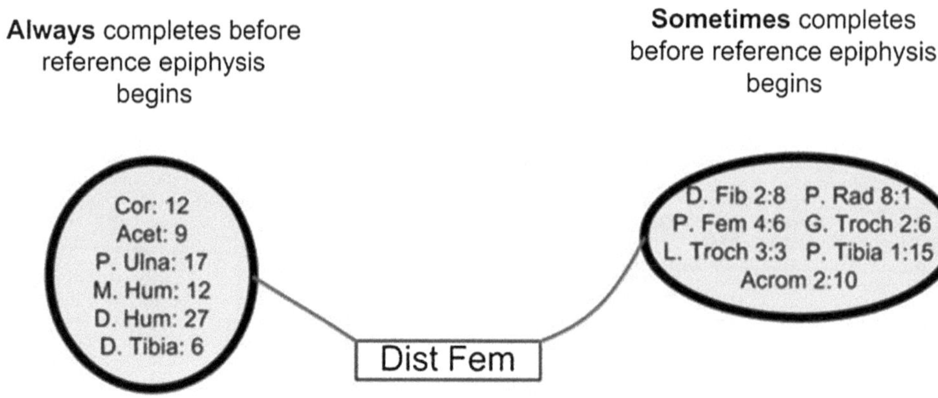

Figure 6-2
A selected segment within the antenna diagram demonstrating epiphyses that always or sometimes complete union prior to the distal ulna, distal radius, or proximal humerus beginning union. For further explanation as to how to read the diagram, refer to Appendix 6-1.

is, "Does the distal radius, distal ulna, or proximal humerus always or sometimes complete union prior to the reference distal femoral epiphysis?" The answer is no (Figure 6-2), thus it is unlikely that this epiphyseal display belongs to that of one individual. In conclusion, two lines of evidence support suspicions that the maturity status of the femur is not compatible with that of the other epiphyses.

Example 2

Table 6-4 displays the union status of a second potentially commingled individual to demonstrate use of the recording form. When analyzing the phase distribution tabulated on the recording form, one distinctly notices that the numeric phases do not arrange themselves in a completely sequential fashion in that phase 1s are interspersed between that of phase 2s, as well as between phase 0s. This distribution pattern is not discordant, however, in that the epiphyses progress from that of mature, to fused or fusing, to that of fusing or open, and finally to that of immature or open epiphyses. Although the epiphyses are not listed in numeric order, this assemblage still displays natural progressive maturity among the epiphyses; thus, no concerns for further investigation have been alarmed. In addition, if we consider our basic premise for sequencing, no concerns are highlighted in that all the nongrowing epiphyses display advanced maturity to their growing counterparts.

Testing the Method

The utility in which the recording form can be used to alert users to areas of maturational discrepancies was tested on additional artificially commingled individuals. If areas of concern

TABLE 6-4: A Completed Epiphyseal Recording Sheet Demonstrating the Distribution of Phases Associated with Example 2 in the Text. No Areas of Concern were Identified.

EPIPHYSIS	PHASE	Notes
acetab	2	
elbow		
d hum	2	
p uln	2	
p rad	2	
corocoid	2	
m hum	2	
ankle		
d tib	2	
d fib	1	
hip		
p fem	2	
l troch	1	
g troch	2	
isch	1	
knee		
d fem	0	
p tib	1	
p fib	0	
acromion	0	
wrist		
d rad	0	
d uln	0	
iliac crest	0	
shoulder		
p hum	0	
m clavicle	0	

Bones present: pelvis, scapula, humerus, radius, ulna, tibia, fibula, femur, clavicle.

were highlighted within the recording sheet, further investigation utilizing the sequence trees and antenna diagram was warranted. The analyzed results were then compared to known results to determine whether this method could accurately identify potentially misplaced bones.

Fifteen artificially commingled assemblages, derived from a modern Portuguese population (subset of the Scheuer collection housed at the University of Dundee), were used for this investigation. The assemblages themselves had been arranged over five years before to test an earlier application of this work that employed Bayesian analysis to support or reject suspicions of commingling (Schaefer 2008a). Thus, only the epiphyseal phasing data that were recorded from the assemblages were utilized for this current analysis. The assemblages themselves were not viewed again. When the assemblages were originally designed, any number of skeletal elements from that of a single individual could be included with one or more additional bones being replaced from that of another individual. The replacement element(s), however, had to be of a different maturity level than the original element; otherwise, the test could not possibly discriminate between individuals.

Epiphyseal phases associated with each element present within the 15 assemblages were transcribed onto a recording sheet and are presented in Table 6-5. Case 3 was not included because it was already presented in the previous section as Example 1. The correct answers, methodological predictions, and reasoning behind the prediction are presented in Table 6-6.

In each of the 14 cases, the recording form was able to recognize an area of potential concern that encouraged use of further documentation to support or reject suspicions. Not all of the

TABLE 6-5: Epiphyseal Phase Distributions Associated with the Skeletal Elements Present in 14 Artificially Commingled Assemblages

EPIPHYSIS	Case 1	Case 2	Case 4	Case 5	Case 6	Case 7	Case 8	Case 9	Case 10	Case 11	Case 12	Case 13	Case 14	Case 15
acetab	2	NP	NP	NP	2	NP	2	NP	2	NP	2	2	2	NP
elbow														
d hum	2	NP	2	2	2	2	NP	2	2	2	2	NP	2	2
p uln	2	2	2	2	2	NP	NP	2	NP	NP	2	NP	NP	NP
p rad	2	1	2	NP	2	NP	NP	2	NP	NP	NP	NP	NP	1
corocoid	2	2	1	NP	2	1	NP	NP	1	NP	2	1	NP	2
med hum	2	NP	2	2	2	2	NP	2	2	2	2	NP	2	2
ankle														
d tib	2	0	NP	0	2	NP	2	0	NP	2	NP	2	2	NP
d fib	1	NP	NP	NP	NP	0	2	NP	NP	2	1	NP	2	NP
hip														
p fem	2	1	NP	1	2	1	2	NP	2	1	2	2	2	2
l troch	2	0	NP	0	2	0	2	NP	2	1	2	2	2	2
g troch	2	0	NP	1	2	1	2	NP	2	1	2	2	2	2
isch	2	NP	NP	NP	2	NP	1*	NP	2	NP	2	2	1	NP
knee														
d fem	2	0	NP	0	2	0	2	NP	2	1	2	2	2	2
p tib	1	0	NP	0	1	NP	1	0	NP	2	NP	2	2	NP
p fib	1	NP	NP	NP	NP	0	2	NP	NP	1	1	NP	2	NP
acromion	2	2	0	NP	2	1	NP	2	0	NP	2	0	NP	2
wrist														
d rad	2	0	2	NP	2	NP	NP	2	NP	NP	NP	NP	NP	0
d uln	2	0	2	0	2	NP	NP	2	NP	NP	0**	NP	NP	NP
iliac crest	1	NP	NP	NP	1	NP	0	NP	1	NP	1	1	0	NP
shoulder														
p hum	2	NP	2	0	2	2	NP	2	2	0	2	NP	0	2
m clavicle	NP	NP	NP	NP	NP	NP	NP	0	NP	NP	1	NP	NP	1

NP= not present.

* isch tub begins union prior to the knee; however it completes after the knee.

** iliac crest begins union prior to the d ulna; however it completes after the d ulna.

Table 6-6: Misplaced Element Predictions Associated with Each of the 14 Commingled Assemblages. The Reasoning Behind the Prediction as Well as the Correct Answer are Also Included

Case	Answer	Prediction	Reasoning
1	tib & fib	same	d fib does not vary in complete sequence with the isch, d femur, d rad, or p hum (d fib should not be phase 1); p fib and p tib do not vary in complete sequence with the d rad or p hum (p fib and p tib should not be Phase 1)
2	scapula	same	acrom does not vary in beginning sequence with the d tib or vary in complete sequence with the p rad (acrom should be Phase 0); acrom is not listed as an epiphysis that sometimes completes prior to the d tib, l or g troch or p tib beginning (acrom should not be Phase 2)
4	scapula	same	cor does not vary in complete sequence with the d rad, d ulna or p hum (cor should be Phase 2); d rad, d ulna and p hum are not listed as epiphyses that sometimes or always complete prior to the acrom beginning union (acrom should not be Phase 0)
5	tib & fem	tibia	m hum is not listed as an epiphysis that always or sometimes completes prior to the d tib beginning union (d tib should not be Phase 0)
6	tibia	same	p tib does not vary in complete sequence with the d rad or p hum (p tib should be Phase 2)
7	humerus	same	p hum does not vary in complete sequence with the acro, p fib, d fem, g troch, l troch, d fib or cor (p hum should not be Phase 2)
8	pelvis & tib	pelvis	d fem is not an epiphysis that completes union before the iliac crest begins (iliac should not be Phase 0); isch does not vary in complete sequence with the d fem or p fib (isch should not be Phase 1)
9	tibia	same	d tib does not vary in beginning or complete sequence with the d rad, d ulna or p hum (d tib should be Phase 2); p tib does not vary in beginning sequence with the d rad, d ulna or p humor vary in complete sequence with the d rad or p hum (p tib should be Phase 2)
10	scapula	same	acrom does not vary in beginning sequence with the p hum and isch is not an epiphysis that sometimes completes before the acrom begins (acrom should not be Phase 0); cor does not vary in complete sequencewith the p fem, g & l troch, isch, d fem, p hum (cor should be Phase 2)
11	tibia	same	p tib is not an ep that sometimes completes before the p hum begins and the p tib does not vary in complete sequence with the p fem, and g & l trochs (p tib should not be Phase 2)
12	fib & ulna	same	d ulna does not vary in complete sequence with the p hum (should be Phase 2); d fib does not vary in complete sequence with d fem, acrom, or p hum (d fib should be Phase 2); p fib does not vary in complete sequence with the p hum (p fib should be Phase 2)
13	scapula	same	cor does not vary in complete sequence with the p fem, g & l troch, d fem, p tib, d tib or isch (cor should be Phase 2); d fem and p tib are not epiphyses that sometimes complete before the acrom begins (acrom should not be Phase 0)

Continued

Table 6-6: Misplaced Element Predictions Associated with Each of the 14 Commingled Assemblages. The Reasoning Behind the Prediction as Well as the Correct Answer are Also Included—cont'd

Case	Answer	Prediction	Reasoning
14	pelvis & hum	same	d fem is not an epiphysis that completes union before the iliac crest begins (iliac should not be Phase 0); d fem and p tib are not epiphyses that sometimes complete before the p hum begins (p hum should not be Phase 0)
15	rad & clav	radius	p rad does not vary in complete sequence with the p fem, g troch, d fem, acrom, or p hum (p rad should be Phase 2); d fem and p hum are not epiphyses that sometimes complete before the d rad begins (d rad should not be Phase 0)

misplaced elements within the assemblage were detected, however. In three of the cases, a second commingled element was not identified. This finding can most likely be attributed to the reduced number of elements that were present within some of the assemblages. Every epiphysis adds to the puzzle that describes an individual's overall skeletal maturity; thus, the more pieces that are missing, the more ambiguous the picture. If only a vague understanding of the individual's maturity level is captured, then it is less likely that commingled elements will oppose the union pattern of the other material present.

The clavicle (Case 15), in particular, is noted as a difficult bone to single out as a misplaced element, due to the delayed time frame in which it undergoes fusion. Once all of the epiphyses investigated in this study have completed union, the clavicle still has the potential to be open, fusing, or completely united. Thus, elimination based on the fusing status of other epiphyses within this method is not possible.

Discussion

The current chapter provides a means to help with the initial recognition of epiphyseal material whose maturity level may be out of sync with that of other material. The method introduced here is most applicable in situations of "small-scale commingling" where one can assume the presence of a single individual, with the possibility that some outside skeletal material may have been included. This situation may arise in burials (such as mass graves) where clothing or some other wrapping material preserves the continuity of most skeletal elements; however, a region where the clothing is deficient loses its connection with the rest of the body. Bony material from a second individual may then inadvertently become confused as belonging to that of the first individual.

When one is dealing with this type of situation, or any other in which the possibility of commingled elements may exist, it is recommended that the epiphyseal recording sheet presented here is filled out during skeletal analysis as part of typical epiphyseal data transcription. If any incongruence is noted in the flow of epiphyseal maturation from top of the page to bottom of the page, then a "red flag" is alerted, and further consultation with the sequence tree and antennae diagrams is advised. If the epiphyseal pattern displayed between bony elements within the skeletal collection has not been described within the diagrams, the possibility that the incongruent element does not belong to the individual should be considered. Further testing via nuclear DNA matching can confirm whether the suspicious element belongs to that of another individual.

The three nondetected commingled elements in the examples highlight an important concept in the application of this method. This method's strength comes from its ability to segregate commingled skeletal elements based on incompatible relationships. Lack of a red flag signal does not conclusively indicate a lack of commingling because commingled elements may still be present from another individual exhibiting a similar (i.e., compatible) state of epiphyseal union.

It must also be stressed that this method does not positively confirm that a suspicious bone does not belong to an individual. Although one can be confident that some combinations of epiphyseal states should never occur, it is possible that a single individual's legitimate fusing pattern has not been described within the reference materials presented here, and thus, an element might be mistakenly identified as that of a second individual. To lessen potential errors, one should consult pattern frequencies reported within the reference materials to avoid placing overconfidence in predictions that are based on few examples. Certainty of a match or mismatch can be achieved through nuclear DNA tests.

Appendix 6-1

Sequence Tree Diagrams

Sequence tree diagrams demonstrate the overall sequence in which epiphyses begin and complete union (Schaefer 2008a; Schaefer and Black 2007; Schaefer et al. 2009). Each figure displays a modal sequence pattern, as demonstrated by a majority of individuals in the sample, in addition to all observed variations to that pattern. The modal sequence pattern is represented by the central "tree trunk" within the figure and demonstrates progressive maturity from top to bottom. Variations to the modal pattern are demonstrated through the use of "tree branches." Each "branch" signifies the extent of variation that occurs in relation to the reference "trunk" epiphysis. The "twig" projections extending from the branches identify those epiphyses that exhibit the minority pattern; those positioned to the left of the trunk were occasionally observed to commence/complete union **before** the referenced "trunk" epiphysis, whereas those located to the right were sometimes observed to commence/complete **after** the referenced "trunk" epiphysis. Also listed in association with each twig epiphysis is the frequency with which that pattern was observed to occur, that is, the number of individuals that displayed the alternative pattern in relation to the total number of cases utilized for defining the sequence. This provides an indication as to the confidence that we can assign to that pattern. Epiphyses that have no "branches" extending from their "trunk" were not seen to exhibit any variation in sequence order to that of the modal pattern in this sample. Likewise, any epiphysis not listed within a branch did not vary in its union sequence with the reference "trunk" epiphysis.

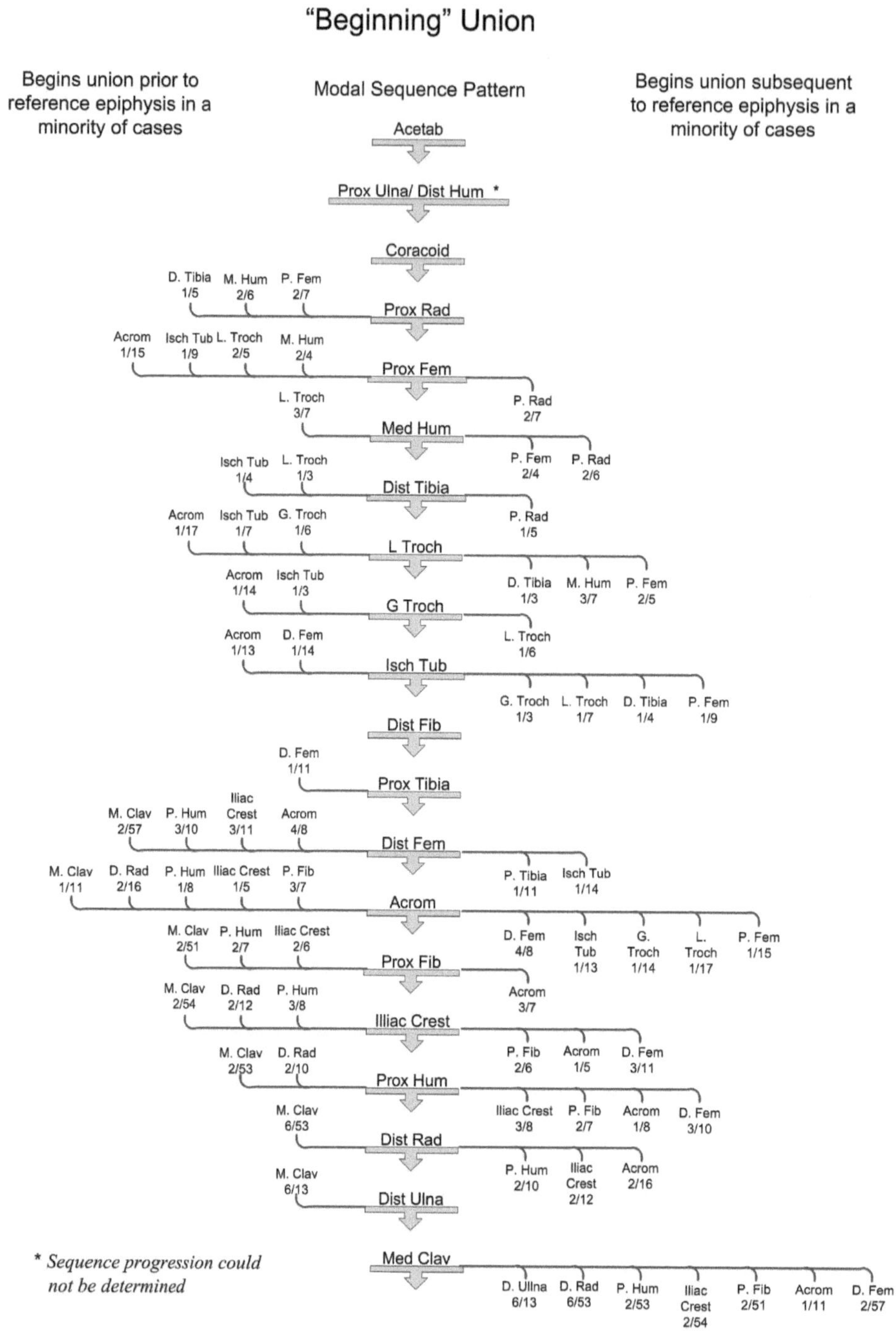
"Beginning" Union
Begins union prior to reference epiphysis in a minority of cases
Modal Sequence Pattern
Begins union subsequent to reference epiphysis in a minority of cases
Acetab
Prox Ulna/ Dist Hum *
Coracoid
D. Tibia 1/5
M. Hum 2/6
P. Fem 2/7
Prox Rad
Acrom 1/15
Isch Tub 1/9
L. Troch 2/5
M. Hum 2/4
Prox Fem
P. Rad 2/7
L. Troch 3/7
Med Hum
P. Fem 2/4
P. Rad 2/6
Isch Tub 1/4
L. Troch 1/3
Dist Tibia
P. Rad 1/5
Acrom 1/17
Isch Tub 1/7
G. Troch 1/6
L Troch
D. Tibia 1/3
M. Hum 3/7
P. Fem 2/5
Acrom 1/14
Isch Tub 1/3
G Troch
L. Troch 1/6
Acrom 1/13
D. Fem 1/14
Isch Tub
G. Troch 1/3
L. Troch 1/7
D. Tibia 1/4
P. Fem 1/9
Dist Fib
D. Fem 1/11
Prox Tibia
M. Clav 2/57
P. Hum 3/10
Iliac Crest 3/11
Acrom 4/8
Dist Fem
P. Tibia 1/11
Isch Tub 1/14
M. Clav 1/11
D. Rad 2/16
P. Hum 1/8
Iliac Crest 1/5
P. Fib 3/7
Acrom
D. Fem 4/8
Isch Tub 1/13
G. Troch 1/14
L. Troch 1/17
P. Fem 1/15
M. Clav 2/51
P. Hum 2/7
Iliac Crest 2/6
Prox Fib
Acrom 3/7
M. Clav 2/54
D. Rad 2/12
P. Hum 3/8
Illiac Crest
P. Fib 2/6
Acrom 1/5
D. Fem 3/11
M. Clav 2/53
D. Rad 2/10
Prox Hum
Iliac Crest 3/8
P. Fib 2/7
Acrom 1/8
D. Fem 3/10
M. Clav 6/53
Dist Rad
P. Hum 2/10
Iliac Crest 2/12
Acrom 2/16
M. Clav 6/13
Dist Ulna
Med Clav
D. Ullna 6/13
D. Rad 6/53
P. Hum 2/53
Iliac Crest 2/54
P. Fib 2/51
Acrom 1/11
D. Fem 2/57
* Sequence progression could not be determined

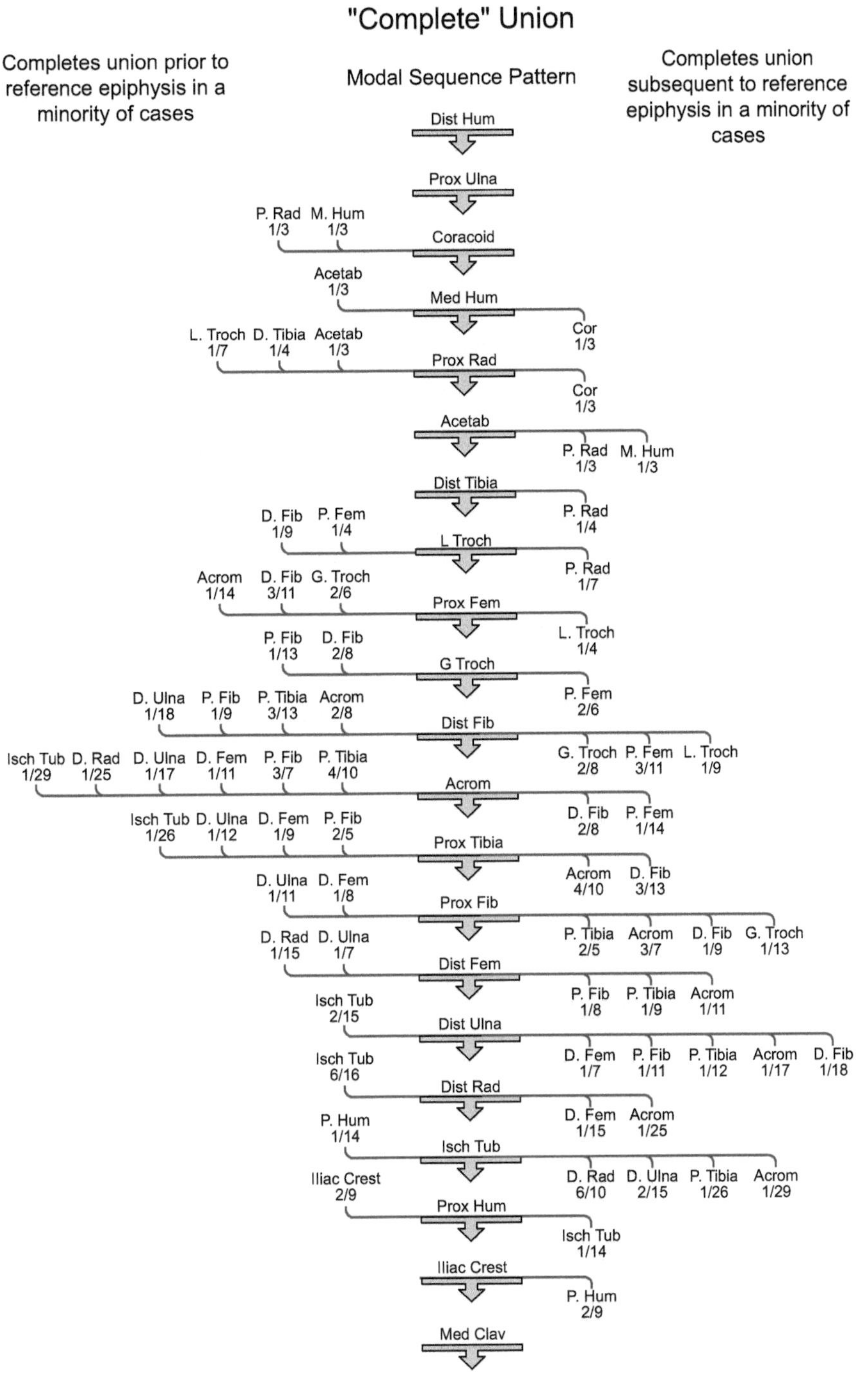
"Complete" Union
Completes union prior to reference epiphysis in a minority of cases
Modal Sequence Pattern
Completes union subsequent to reference epiphysis in a minority of cases
Dist Hum
Prox Ulna
P. Rad 1/3
M. Hum 1/3
Coracoid
Acetab 1/3
Med Hum
Cor 1/3
L. Troch 1/7
D. Tibia 1/4
Acetab 1/3
Prox Rad
Cor 1/3
Acetab
P. Rad 1/3
M. Hum 1/3
Dist Tibia
P. Rad 1/4
D. Fib 1/9
P. Fem 1/4
L Troch
P. Rad 1/7
Acrom 1/14
D. Fib 3/11
G. Troch 2/6
Prox Fem
L. Troch 1/4
P. Fib 1/13
D. Fib 2/8
G Troch
P. Fem 2/6
D. Ulna 1/18
P. Fib 1/9
P. Tibia 3/13
Acrom 2/8
Dist Fib
G. Troch 2/8
P. Fem 3/11
L. Troch 1/9
Isch Tub 1/29
D. Rad 1/25
D. Ulna 1/17
D. Fem 1/11
P. Fib 3/7
P. Tibia 4/10
Acrom
D. Fib 2/8
P. Fem 1/14
Isch Tub 1/26
D. Ulna 1/12
D. Fem 1/9
P. Fib 2/5
Prox Tibia
Acrom 4/10
D. Fib 3/13
D. Ulna 1/11
D. Fem 1/8
Prox Fib
P. Tibia 2/5
Acrom 3/7
D. Fib 1/9
G. Troch 1/13
D. Rad 1/15
D. Ulna 1/7
Dist Fem
P. Fib 1/8
P. Tibia 1/9
Acrom 1/11
Isch Tub 2/15
Dist Ulna
D. Fem 1/7
P. Fib 1/11
P. Tibia 1/12
Acrom 1/17
D. Fib 1/18
Isch Tub 6/16
Dist Rad
D. Fem 1/15
Acrom 1/25
P. Hum 1/14
Isch Tub
D. Rad 6/10
D. Ulna 2/15
P. Tibia 1/26
Acrom 1/29
Iliac Crest 2/9
Prox Hum
Isch Tub 1/14
Iliac Crest
P. Hum 2/9
Med Clav

Antenna Diagram

The antenna diagram illustrates interphase relationships between the epiphyses. Located along the central body of the diagram is a list of epiphyses that serve as a reference from which to describe phase relationships. The reference epiphyses are connected to a bubble, via an antenna, which identifies a further list of epiphyses. Those listed in bubbles located on the left of the page are epiphyses that have been identified as **always** completing union prior to initiation of union of the reference epiphysis, whereas those listed in the bubbles toward the right of the page are those that **sometimes** complete union prior to initiation of the reference epiphysis. The epiphyses that **never** complete union prior to initiation of the reference epiphysis are understood through their exclusion because they are the epiphyses not listed within either the right or left bubble.

Also included within each bubble is the number of observations from which the data were extracted. Thus, the bubbles on the left portray the number of individuals who display completion of the named epiphysis while at the same time displaying open union of the reference epiphysis. The bubbles on the right display a ratio; the first number represents the number of individuals displaying completion of the named epiphysis while at the same time displaying open union of the reference epiphysis, and the second number represents the frequency in which the two epiphyses were observed to be simultaneously in the process of uniting. The frequency at which various patterns were observed to occur provides an indication as to the confidence that one can assign to that pattern.

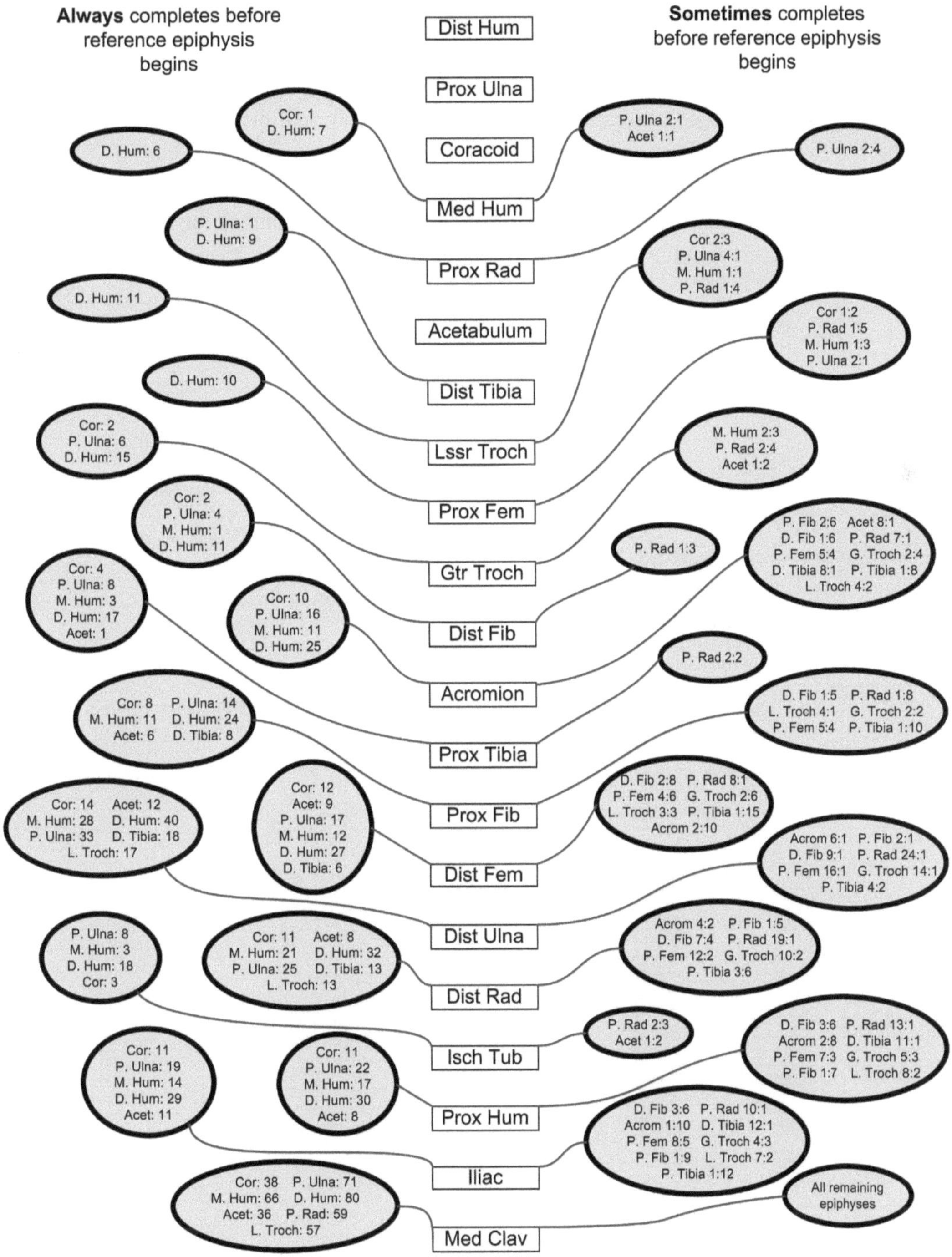

Always completes before reference epiphysis begins
Sometimes completes before reference epiphysis begins
Dist Hum
Prox Ulna
Coracoid
Med Hum
Prox Rad
Acetabulum
Dist Tibia
Lssr Troch
Prox Fem
Gtr Troch
Dist Fib
Acromion
Prox Tibia
Prox Fib
Dist Fem
Dist Ulna
Dist Rad
Isch Tub
Prox Hum
Iliac
Med Clav
Cor: 1 D. Hum: 7
D. Hum: 6
P. Ulna: 1 D. Hum: 9
D. Hum: 11
D. Hum: 10
Cor: 2 P. Ulna: 6 D. Hum: 15
Cor: 2 P. Ulna: 4 M. Hum: 1 D. Hum: 11
Cor: 4 P. Ulna: 8 M. Hum: 3 D. Hum: 17 Acet: 1
Cor: 10 P. Ulna: 16 M. Hum: 11 D. Hum: 25
Cor: 8 P. Ulna: 14 M. Hum: 11 D. Hum: 24 Acet: 6 D. Tibia: 8
Cor: 14 Acet: 12 M. Hum: 28 D. Hum: 40 P. Ulna: 33 D. Tibia: 18 L. Troch: 17
Cor: 12 Acet: 9 P. Ulna: 17 M. Hum: 12 D. Hum: 27 D. Tibia: 6
P. Ulna: 8 M. Hum: 3 D. Hum: 18 Cor: 3
Cor: 11 Acet: 8 M. Hum: 21 D. Hum: 32 P. Ulna: 25 D. Tibia: 13 L. Troch: 13
Cor: 11 P. Ulna: 19 M. Hum: 14 D. Hum: 29 Acet: 11
Cor: 11 P. Ulna: 22 M. Hum: 17 D. Hum: 30 Acet: 8
Cor: 38 P. Ulna: 71 M. Hum: 66 D. Hum: 80 Acet: 36 P. Rad: 59 L. Troch: 57
P. Ulna 2:1 Acet 1:1
P. Ulna 2:4
Cor 2:3 P. Ulna 4:1 M. Hum 1:1 P. Rad 1:4
Cor 1:2 P. Rad 1:5 M. Hum 1:3 P. Ulna 2:1
M. Hum 2:3 P. Rad 2:4 Acet 1:2
P. Rad 1:3
P. Fib 2:6 Acet 8:1 D. Fib 1:6 P. Rad 7:1 P. Fem 5:4 G. Troch 2:4 D. Tibia 8:1 P. Tibia 1:8 L. Troch 4:2
P. Rad 2:2
D. Fib 1:5 P. Rad 1:8 L. Troch 4:1 G. Troch 2:2 P. Fem 5:4 P. Tibia 1:10
D. Fib 2:8 P. Rad 8:1 P. Fem 4:6 G. Troch 2:6 L. Troch 3:3 P. Tibia 1:15 Acrom 2:10
Acrom 6:1 P. Fib 2:1 D. Fib 9:1 P. Rad 24:1 P. Fem 16:1 G. Troch 14:1 P. Tibia 4:2
Acrom 4:2 P. Fib 1:5 D. Fib 7:4 P. Rad 19:1 P. Fem 12:2 G. Troch 10:2 P. Tibia 3:6
P. Rad 2:3 Acet 1:2
D. Fib 3:6 P. Rad 13:1 Acrom 2:8 D. Tibia 11:1 P. Fem 7:3 G. Troch 5:3 P. Fib 1:7 L. Troch 8:2
D. Fib 3:6 P. Rad 10:1 Acrom 1:10 D. Tibia 12:1 P. Fem 8:5 G. Troch 4:3 P. Fib 1:9 L. Troch 7:2 P. Tibia 1:12
All remaining epiphyses

Appendix 6-2

A blank epiphyseal recording sheet is provided for use by the reader. Phase information from either the right or left epiphyses can be recorded because minimal difference should exist between the two sides (Albert and Greene 1999; Schaefer 2008b; Schmeling et al. 2004). If a difference does exist, first decide whether the two sides belong to the same individual by using morphological comparison. If they belong together, record that of the more advanced epiphysis because this mimics the method in which the original data were collected (Schaefer and Black 2007).

Epiphyseal Recording Sheet for Maturational Sequence Analysis

Phase description

0 = open or no union

1 = active union; union has initiated, but the epiphyseal line is still visible

2 = complete union; line of fusion is no longer present, although an epiphyseal scar could remain

EPIPHYSIS	PHASE	Notes
acetab		
elbow		
d hum		
p uln		
p rad		
corocoid		
m hum		
ankle		
d tib		
d fib		
hip		
p fem		
l troch		
g troch		
isch *		
knee		
d fem		
p tib		
p fib		
acromion		
wrist		
d rad		
d uln		
iliac crest **		
shoulder		
p hum		
m clavicle		

* isch tub begins union prior to the knee; however it completes after the knee.

** iliac crest begins union prior to the d ulna; however it completes after the d ulna.

Bones present ____

References

Albert, A.M., Greene, D.L., 1999. Bilateral asymmetry in skeletal growth and maturation as an indicator of environmental stress. Am. J. Phys. Anthropol. 110, 341–349.

Bisgard, J., Bisgard, M., 1935. Longitudinal growth of long bones. Arch. Surg. 31, 568–578.

Buikstra, J.E., Gordon, C.C., St. Hoyme, L., 1984. The case of the severed skull: Individuation in forensic anthropology. In: Rathbun, T.A., Buikstra, J.E. (Eds.), Human Identification: Case Studies in Forensic Anthropology. Charles C. Thomas, Springfield, IL, pp. 121–135.

Byrd, J.E., Adams, B.J., 2003. Osteometric sorting of commingled human remains. J. Forensic Sci. 48 (4), 717–724.

L'Abbe, E.N., 2005. A case of commingled remains from rural South Africa. Forensic Sci. Int. 151 (2–3), 201–206.

Owsley, D.W., Ubelaker, D.H., Houck, M.M., Sandness, K.L., Grant, W.E., Craig, E.A., Woltanski, T.J., Peerwani, N., 1995. The role of forensic anthropology in the recovery and analysis of Branch Davidian Compound victims: Techniques of analysis. J. Forensic Sci. 40 (3), 341–348.

Pritchett, J., 1991. Growth plate activity in the upper extremity. Clin. Orthop. Related Res. 268, 235–242.

Pritchett, J., 1992. Longitudinal growth and growth-plate activity in the lower extremity. Clin. Orthop. Related Res. 275, 274–279.

Pritchett, J., 1997. Growth and growth prediction of the fibula. Clin. Orthop. Related Res. 334, 251–256.

Schaefer, M.C., 2008a. Patterns of epiphyseal union and their use in the detection and sorting of commingled remains. In: Adams, B.J., Byrd, J.E. (Eds.), Recovery, Analysis and Identification of Commingled Human Remains. Humana Press, Totowa, NJ, pp. 221–240.

Schaefer, M.C., 2008b. A summary of epiphyseal union timings in Bosnian males. Int. J. Osteoarchaeol. 18 (5), 536–545.

Schaefer, M.C., Black, S.M., 2007. Epiphyseal union sequencing: Aiding in the recognition and sorting of commingled remains. J. Forensic Sci. 52 (2), 277–285.

Schaefer, M.C., Black, S.M., Scheuer, L., 2009. Juvenile Osteology: A Laboratory and Field Manual. Elsevier, San Diego, CA.

Schmeling, A., Schulz, R., Reisinger, W., Muhler, M., Wernecke, K.D., Geserick, G., 2004. Studies on the time frame for ossification of the medial clavicular epiphyseal cartilage in conventional radiography. Int. J. Legal Med. 118, 5–8.

Snow, C.C., 1948. The identification of the unknown war dead. Am. J. Phys. Anthropol. 6, 323–328.

Snow, C.C., Folk, E.D., 1970. Statistical assessment of commingled skeletal remains. Am. J. Phys. Anthropol. 32, 423–427.

Stewart, T.D., 1979. Essentials of Forensic Anthropology: Especially as Developed in the United States. Charles C. Thomas, Springfield, IL.

CHAPTER 7

Application of Portable X-ray Fluorescence (XRF) for Sorting Commingled Human Remains

Alexandra Perrone, Janet E. Finlayson, Eric J. Bartelink, Kevin Dennis Dalton
Department of Anthropology, California State University, Chico, CA

Introduction

Commingled human skeletal remains present complex challenges for medicolegal investigations. In cases of commingling, it is important to accurately segregate the remains of each individual represented and then make a determination of the number of individuals present. Forensic anthropologists are uniquely qualified to make assessments regarding commingling because they routinely employ laboratory methods such as identifying duplicated skeletal elements, visual and osteometric pair-matching of bilateral elements, evaluation of joint congruity between articular surfaces, skeletal age comparisons, and assessment of corresponding pathological changes and taphonomic modifications between different skeletal elements (Byrd and Adams 2003; Cheverko 2013; Murad and Murad 2000; Schaefer 2008; Schaefer, this book, Chapter 6; Ubelaker 2002). Other methods for resolving commingled remains, such as nuclear and mitochondrial DNA testing, involve destructive, costly, and time-consuming techniques (Damann and Edson 2008; Mundorff et al. 2008; Mundorff et al., this book, Chapter 12; Yazedjian and Kešetović 2008). Although these methods are highly accurate for identification, time and resource limitations, as well as cultural beliefs by a decedent's family, may negate the use of destructive analytical methods in some contexts.

Recent research using X-ray fluorescence (XRF) spectrometry has shown promise in determining whether a set of remains belongs to a single or multiple individuals by analyzing elemental concentrations in human bones (Gonzalez-Rodriguez and Fowler 2013). One advantage to this approach is that it has the potential to provide an inexpensive, rapid, and nondestructive method for assessing small-scale cases of commingling. The development of portable XRF (pXRF) technology has opened the possibility to apply the method to both complete and fragmentary remains not only in a laboratory setting, but also allowing for analyses in the field.

Commingled Human Remains. http://dx.doi.org/10.1016/B978-0-12-405889-7.00007-1

X-Ray Fluorescence Spectrometry

XRF spectrometry is a nondestructive method of elemental analysis that uses primary X-rays to bombard the surface of a sample with radiation. X-rays interact with matter in three ways: scattering through the material, being absorbed by an atom, or transmitting through the material. X-ray fluorescence is a product of absorption. When an X-ray is absorbed, it can cause atoms to become ionized (Pollard et al. 2007). If an X-ray strikes an inner-shell electron of an atom with enough energy to dislodge it, an inner shell vacancy (e.g., in the K, L, M, N orbitals) is created. As a result, the atom becomes unstable. In order to restore stability to the atom, an outer-shell electron fills the inner-shell position (Figure 7-1). The movement of the outer-shell electron to the inner-shell releases a lower-energy secondary fluorescent X-ray. Some secondary fluorescent X-rays escape and are measured by the XRF instrument's detector, providing a means to characterize the elements in the sample (Pollard et al. 2007). The energy of the detected fluorescent X-ray is used to identify the elements in the sample, whereas the intensity of the X-ray reflects the concentration of the detected elements. Finally, computer software is used to interpret the detector output. XRF analysis provides output in two formats, including a visual spectrum showing the concentration peaks for each element as well as an elemental concentration chart. One way to analyze the visual representation is through spectra overlay, which allows for the simultaneous comparison of two samples by

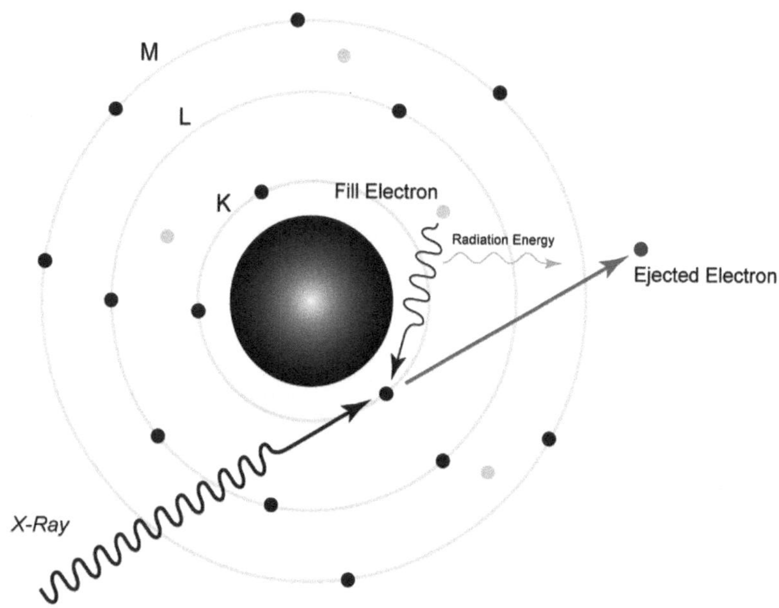

Figure 7-1
Diagram of an ejected electron from an atom in the K shell caused by a primary excitation X-ray. The vacancy is filled by an electron from another shell, which emits a secondary fluorescent X-ray.

overlaying their elemental concentration peaks (Figure 7-2). In the second type of output, the elemental concentration chart provides raw values reported in, or easily converted to, parts per million.

XRF spectrometry is most commonly conducted in a laboratory setting with a stationary unit. The recent introduction of portable XRF (pXRF) now enables analysis in either a stationary position on a stand or in the field, in which the equipment can be transported to the sample. This allows for the analysis of large and intact samples that might not otherwise be easily transported to laboratories. This also opens up the possibility of avoiding destructive preparation procedures such as powdering or cutting a bone to fit within the small sample chamber of a stationary XRF unit. Portable XRF has recently been integrated for use at archaeological sites and outdoor forensic scenes (Shackley 2011; Trombka et al. 2002). Although XRF has the benefit of being a nondestructive method, it is generally able to detect only elements from fluorine (atomic number = 9) to uranium (atomic number = 92) within the periodic table, with an even more limited range among many pXRF units (Shackley 2011). To detect elements of low atomic number (eg. phosphorous) samples should be analyzed under vacuum. This minimizes the absorption of X-rays caused by the presence of air (Christensen et al. 2012).

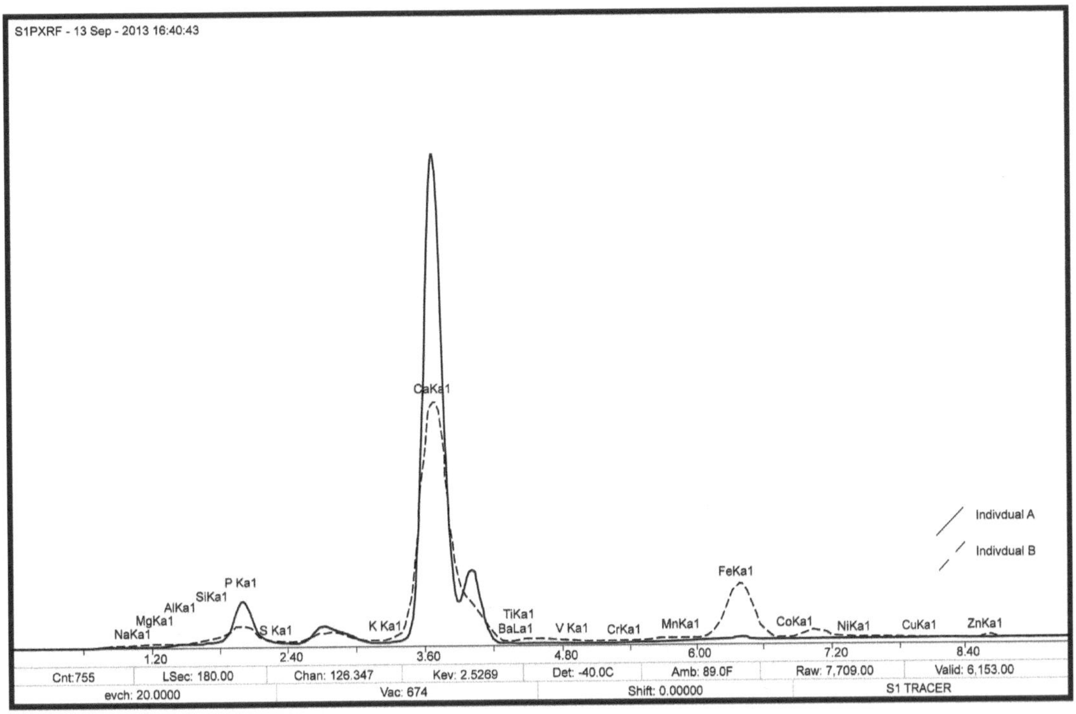

Figure 7-2

Spectral overlay of elemental concentrations in skeletal elements from two individuals.

Use of XRF on Human Skeletal Remains

The use of XRF for elemental analysis dates back to 1909, and has been utilized for archaeological applications since the 1960s (Shackley 2011). While XRF analysis in archaeology has typically focused on geological materials such as obsidian, it has also been used to chemically analyze bone and other tissues. Recently, XRF has become a more significant tool in forensic anthropology and odontology for chemical analysis of dental resin (Bush et al. 2007) as well as the discrimination of human osseous and dental remains from other material (Christensen et al. 2012). In addition, its application for the segregation of commingled human bone has recently been demonstrated. For example, Gonzalez-Rodriguez and Fowler (2013) conducted XRF analysis on a sample of five archaeological human skeletons and were able to successfully differentiate skeletal elements between individuals for scenarios involving between two and four individuals.

Human bone continually remodels throughout life replacing an average of 5% to 10% of the skeleton each year in adults (Kini and Nandeesh 2012). During bone remodeling, new minerals are introduced into newly formed bone based on the chemical environment of the body (Darrah 2009). Teeth, however, do not remodel and retain the elemental concentrations incorporated at the time of tooth formation. Although the mineral content of human bone is composed of many different elements, those most commonly detected and used from XRF analysis include potassium, calcium, iron, magnesium, phosphorus, zinc, strontium, and lead (Christensen et al. 2012; Fulton et al. 1986; Gonzalez-Rodriguez and Fowler 2013).

Individual differences in bone mineral composition may be associated with *in vivo* uptake from food and drinking water, for example, the uptake of strontium and barium, which can substitute for calcium in bioapatite (Burton and Price 2000). Other differences in bone mineral composition can be associated with metabolic function or other means of absorption such as inhalation and chemical exposure (Swanston et al. 2012). In addition, postmortem contamination (i.e., diagenesis) may also affect the elemental concentrations in human bones and teeth that have been buried (Burton and Price 2000). For example, soil adhering to the cortical surface can contaminate the outer layer of bone, and elements contained within groundwater and soil from the burial environment may chemically exchange with bone, thus affecting elemental concentrations. Due to the occurrence of individual variation in trace element incorporation in the human body, pXRF analysis has the potential to establish whether a set of human skeletal remains belongs to a single or multiple individuals. Therefore, the use of pXRF in commingled human remains cases introduces the possibility of cost-effective, timely, and successful segregation of skeletal material in challenging contexts such as small-scale disasters or domestic cases with a small number of victims.

Materials and Methods

This study evaluates the utility of pXRF spectrometry in detecting intraskeletal and interskeletal variation in elemental concentrations in human remains to test whether the method can

Table 7-1: Composition of the Sample

Sample	Sex	Context	Condition
1	Male	Donation	Fleshed
2	Male	Surface	Skeletal
3	Male	Surface	Skeletal
4	Male	Surface	Skeletal
5	Male	Buried	Skeletal
6	Female	Surface	Fleshed
7	Female	Surface	Skeletal
8	Male	Buried	Skeletal
9	Male	Surface	Skeletal
10	Male	Surface	Fleshed
11	Male	Surface	Skeletal
12	Male	Surface	Skeletal
13	Male	Surface	Skeletal
14	Male	Surface	Skeletal
15	Female	Surface	Skeletal
16	Male	Surface	Skeletal
17	Male	Surface	Skeletal
18	Male	Buried	Skeletal
19	Male	Surface	Skeletal
20	Male	Surface	Skeletal

accurately segregate the bones of two or more individuals. For pXRF to be effective in sorting commingled skeletal remains, there must be greater variation in elemental concentrations *between* individuals than *within* individuals. To test this hypothesis, elemental concentrations were compared between individuals to assess whether the method can be used to resolve cases of small-scale commingling.

XRF analysis was conducted on 20 adult skeletons (18+ years of age) from the donated human skeletal collection at the California State University, Chico Human Identification Laboratory (Table 7-1). The sample derives from donated, closed forensic anthropology cases, as well as one willed body donor and one historic pioneer burial dating to the late 1800s. All individuals included in the sample were recovered from outdoor surface or buried contexts, with the exception of the willed body donation. For the fleshed remains cases (n = 4), the remains were processed using water maceration or a dermestid beetle colony. The remaining individuals were primarily skeletal or completely skeletonized when discovered, including 13 found as surface remains and three as buried remains. These skeletons were selected based on their overall completeness, and none represented cases of commingling.

Where possible, 10 bones and one tooth from each skeleton were selected for pXRF analysis including:

- Enamel surface of the maxillary first molar (n = 16)
- Mental eminence of the mandible (n = 17)
- Shaft of the fourth rib (n = 19)
- Body of the fifth lumbar vertebra (n = 19)
- Midshaft of the humerus (n = 20)
- Midshaft of the ulna (n = 19)
- Midshaft of the radius (n = 17)
- Midshaft of the femur (n = 20)
- Midshaft of the tibia (n = 18)
- Midshaft of the fibula (n = 17)
- Metacarpal shaft (n = 17)

Left elements were selected for analysis, but the right side was used when the left was not available. When the first maxillary molar was absent or showed evidence of dental restoration, a second molar (or the closest tooth position) was sampled. When the fourth rib was not available, a first, second, or third rib was sampled. If the first metacarpal was absent, the next closest metacarpal was used, or in a few cases, a carpal or metatarsal. For some individuals, a few skeletal elements were missing, so sample sizes varied from 16 to 20 elements per individual. The skeletal elements selected represent the major anatomical regions of the skeleton and should account for expected variation within a single individual. Furthermore, in order to fully cover the pXRF sensor, the authors analyzed the flattest surface of each element.

Prior to analysis, each bone was cleaned with 100% ethanol and air-dried to minimize surface contamination. However, surface contamination effects should be minimal because X-rays penetrate a few millimeters beyond the surface (Shackley and Dillian 2002; Shackley 2011:8). The surface of the pXRF sensor was cleaned in a similar fashion between each scanned element. Specimens were analyzed in the CSU, Chico Archaeology Laboratory using a Bruker Tracer IV Series pXRF machine with S1 PXRF software v. 3.8.30 (Bruker AXS Handheld, Inc.) (Figure 7-3). Each sample was scanned without a filter for 180 seconds. An X-ray tube operating at a voltage of 15 kV and the highest available current was used. A vacuum pump was used to evacuate the pXRF device. This allowed for more precise measurements of lighter elements by removing air, which can absorb X-ray radiation (Shackley 2011:30). Elemental concentrations were measured in reference to a mudrock calibration file (a recommended standard for bone), and converted to parts per million (ppm). Concentration values for all detected chemical elements from each sample were exported into Microsoft Excel for data processing.

Repeated measures ANOVA tests were computed to gain an understanding of intraskeletal variation in chemical concentrations (i.e., comparing chemical element concentrations between bones of the same individual). ANOVA tests were then used to compare chemical element

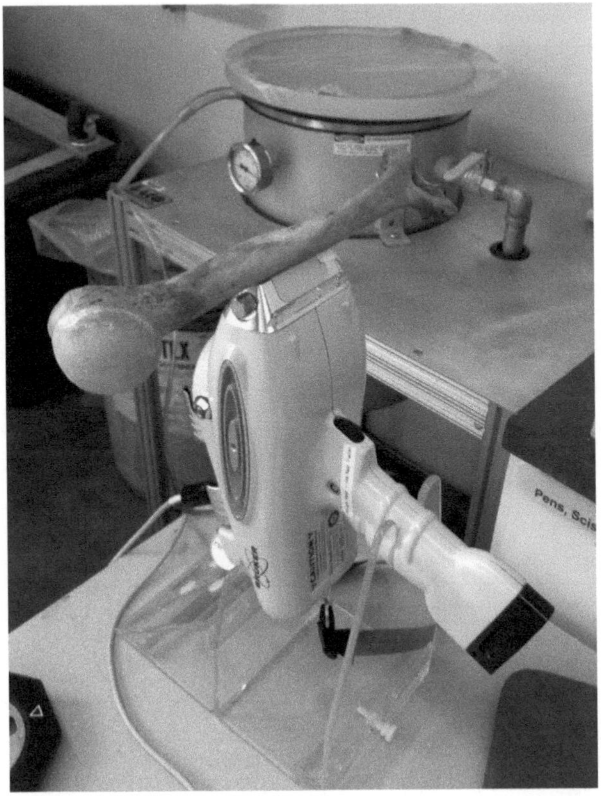

Figure 7-3
Portable XRF setup for scanning human bone samples.

concentration values between individuals. For each chemical element detected, 95% confidence intervals were created. The confidence intervals were produced using values compiled from all scanned skeletal elements for each individual. Two-person combinations were used to simulate small-scale commingling scenarios. All possible two-person combinations were first generated, and then each combination was compared. The proportion of cases of commingling that could be accurately detected (i.e., the proportion of cases that did not overlap in their 95% confidence intervals) was derived from the two-person comparisons, as well as the failure rate. All statistical analyses were computed with SPSS v. 20, with statistical significance set at $\alpha = 0.05$.

Results

Fifteen elements were detected in high enough concentrations to be measured by the pXRF: sodium (Na), magnesium (Mg), silicon (Si), phosphorus (P), potassium (K), calcium (Ca), titanium (Ti), vanadium (V), chromium (Cr), manganese (Mn), iron (Fe), cobalt (Co), nickel (Ni), copper (Cu), and zinc (Zn). Elemental concentrations for some skeletal elements fell below detection limits and were assigned a value of zero. Table 7-2

Table 7-2: Descriptive Statistics for Elemental Concentrations (in ppm) by Skeletal Element

Element		Na	Mg	Si	P	K
Mandible (n = 17)	Mean	810.2	27923.5	25133.4	366136.4	2828.0
	SD	714.1	8615.4	3034.0	125080.4	1736.7
Rib (n = 19)	Mean	786.9	28814.1	25141.0	397017.0	1779.0
	SD	1264.8	10362.3	4786.9	159793.5	930.6
Humerus (n = 20)	Mean	512.03	31674.95	24477.58	425678.12	1752.50
	SD	688.66	8680.91	2516.31	137521.92	801.83
Radius (n = 17)	Mean	860.1	26637.7	23719.2	337426.1	1639.4
	SD	900.1	9198.4	2446.5	118127.7	817.5
Ulna (n = 19)	Mean	680.7	31070.2	24153.3	416087.5	1605.6
	SD	645.9	10313.4	2425.7	160275.4	677.7
Femur (n = 20)	Mean	1341.7	27532.5	23387.6	334661.3	1703.3
	SD	1885.9	11159.7	4330.1	168697.1	898.8
Tibia (n = 18)	Mean	809.5	28033.2	24598.8	385716.8	1677.5
	SD	901.0	10379.6	2551.8	179305.5	1018.7
Fibula (n = 16)	Mean	1493.7	26735.7	22985.3	305913.3	1356.9
	SD	1903.8	10313.7	4312.7	141272.2	780.8
L5 (n = 18)	Mean	2233.9	17529.1	27074.9	247306.6	1637.6
	SD	1578.4	12504.9	5295.7	178499.2	1080.9
Metatarsal (n = 17)	Mean	876.3	28101.0	24551.6	363494.5	1543.0
	SD	918.1	11124.2	3388.0	193779.4	594.1
Enamel (n = 16)	Mean	674.5	49672.5	24635.1	617991.3	1352.4
	SD	1194.1	49359.9	2099.1	237398.6	484.6

provides means and standard deviations for each elemental value and for each bone type and tooth.

Intraskeletal Variation

Elemental concentration values may vary within the skeleton due to differences in remodeling rates between bones. For example, skeletal elements that are less dense (e.g., having thinner cortical bone) remodel at faster rates than elements with denser cortical bone. To evaluate whether elemental concentration values vary significantly between skeletal elements, repeated measures ANOVA tests were computed (enamel samples excluded). ANOVA results indicate significant differences in elemental concentrations only for Mg (p = .031). A post-hoc Bonferroni test indicates statistically a significant

Ca	Ti	V	Cr	Mn	Fe	Co	Ni	Cu	Zn
252097.0	462.4	92.0	10.5	341.5	2323.9	2.3	81.5	59.6	225.9
22982.0	115.4	19.9	11.0	171.0	2479.5	0.9	15.7	24.7	126.8
249199.8	404.5	87.7	12.2	393.5	2824.2	2.5	80.1	62.5	254.7
34555.6	355.0	31.0	15.5	291.9	3906.3	1.4	22.5	32.9	200.2
258889.87	400.14	89.53	13.25	320.62	2120.83	2.24	79.57	59.88	232.29
19676.27	165.58	19.80	30.88	98.69	2263.97	0.77	13.43	19.57	94.82
251830.9	387.6	102.0	26.2	326.4	1535.4	2.0	85.6	68.8	265.7
25946.3	124.1	19.1	30.1	105.6	2920.4	1.0	15.0	24.0	142.2
263281.9	412.8	98.8	16.7	408.2	1854.5	2.2	85.1	63.8	239.5
22898.3	176.8	14.6	19.9	235.4	4422.3	1.6	14.8	21.8	176.7
243540.3	360.8	93.6	10.7	361.1	1919.3	2.1	78.4	64.5	270.3
60576.0	156.2	30.4	13.3	233.4	3248.2	0.8	26.1	30.5	126.8
251723.9	333.8	89.4	9.6	325.7	1012.7	1.8	81.0	49.3	162.3
25609.9	155.7	13.6	11.1	162.0	862.7	0.4	13.6	16.9	52.9
239783.5	350.9	96.8	19.0	422.1	1517.8	2.1	81.8	63.6	251.1
65172.2	127.8	31.2	22.7	327.3	3649.1	0.9	23.9	29.6	146.6
226961.8	560.8	100.1	25.4	357.9	2647.9	2.4	84.8	68.1	256.0
48102.7	385.7	32.5	12.6	193.4	3432.0	1.3	24.0	27.3	134.8
250600.5	380.9	98.7	16.6	329.2	1230.7	2.0	84.8	59.6	207.2
29213.1	184.1	14.7	12.2	94.7	1859.4	0.7	13.9	17.6	79.7
249535.6	227.8	53.3	1.0	253.9	1653.0	2.0	56.4	59.7	330.0
45304.6	101.4	20.8	4.0	56.4	600.9	0.1	53.3	41.2	92.6

difference in Mg concentration values between L5 and the ulna. These results suggest that chemical elements may be differentially incorporated or retained in different bones, reflecting variation in bone metabolic processes as well as variation in remodeling rates within the skeleton (Brätter et al. 1977). However, variation between elements is minimal, and in the case of Mg, no intraskeletal difference was identified when the L5 was removed from analysis ($p = .855$).

Interskeletal Variation

The primary focus of this research is to establish whether more variation exists in elemental concentration values *between* the skeletal elements of different individuals versus *within* the skeletal elements of individuals. To assess whether interskeletal variation is greater than intraskeletal variation, ANOVA tests were computed. The results indicate greater interskeletal variation for 14 of the 15 chemical elements ($p \leq .05$), demonstrating that elemental concentrations vary significantly between individuals. Only Na concentration values were not significantly different ($p = .14$).

To simulate small-scale commingling scenarios, 95% confidence intervals were created for each individual based on the range of variation in chemical elemental concentrations in his or her skeleton. Confidence intervals were first examined to identify the chemical elements that showed the greatest discrimination between individuals (i.e., having the greatest chance of detecting commingling based on the smallest degree of overlap in 95% confidence intervals). Confidence intervals for Si, P, K, Ca, Mn, Fe, and Co showed the greatest potential for resolving commingling (Figures 7-4 through 7-10). In contrast, Na, Mg, V, Cr, Ni, Cu, Ti, and Zn showed a significant degree of overlap and are not considered further. Tables 7-3 through 7-9 provide the results of all comparisons of 95% confidence intervals for Si, P, K, Ca, Mn, Fe, and Co, respectively, as well as the failure rates for resolving commingling in all possible two-person commingling scenarios. The percentage of cases for which commingling could be resolved (i.e., where pairs of individuals could be discriminated based on nonoverlapping confidence intervals) varied from 0% to 84.2% (failure rates varied from 15.8% to 100%). Overall, the highest percentage of cases that could be resolved for commingling were from Si and Mn (35.5% and 35.3%, respectively), followed by K (28.2%), Ca (27.4%), Co (24.2%), P (20.8%), and Fe (16.6%). These results indicate that individuals can be accurately segregated only if their 95% confidence intervals for a single chemical element do not overlap with that of other individuals; thus, the method *should not* be used to associate remains with overlapping confidence intervals. However, significant differences between individuals for more than one elemental concentration provide an even stronger basis for recognizing commingling. For example, Individual #1 could be segregated from Individual #6 based on only one chemical element (K) but could be segregated from Individual #18 based on five different chemical elements (Si, K, Mn, Fe, and Co).

For an actual commingling scenario, different chemical elemental concentrations in bones that are clearly associated with the same individual can be used to create a confidence interval, and then potentially commingled elements can be tested to determine whether they fall within or outside that confidence interval. Skeletal elements that fall within the confidence interval may or may not belong to the same individual, whereas elements that fall outside the confidence interval are unlikely to be from the same individual. As a test, the skeletal elements for each of the 20 individuals were randomly assigned to one of two groups. Confidence intervals were calculated for Si, P, K, Ca, Mn, Fe, and Co for each individual. In 100% of comparisons, the confidence intervals overlapped between sets of bones from the same individual. In other words, no errors were detected. This comparison provides additional assurance that elemental concentrations show a much lower level of intraskeletal variation than interskeletal variation, thus providing a potentially robust approach for detecting commingling when confidence intervals do not overlap.

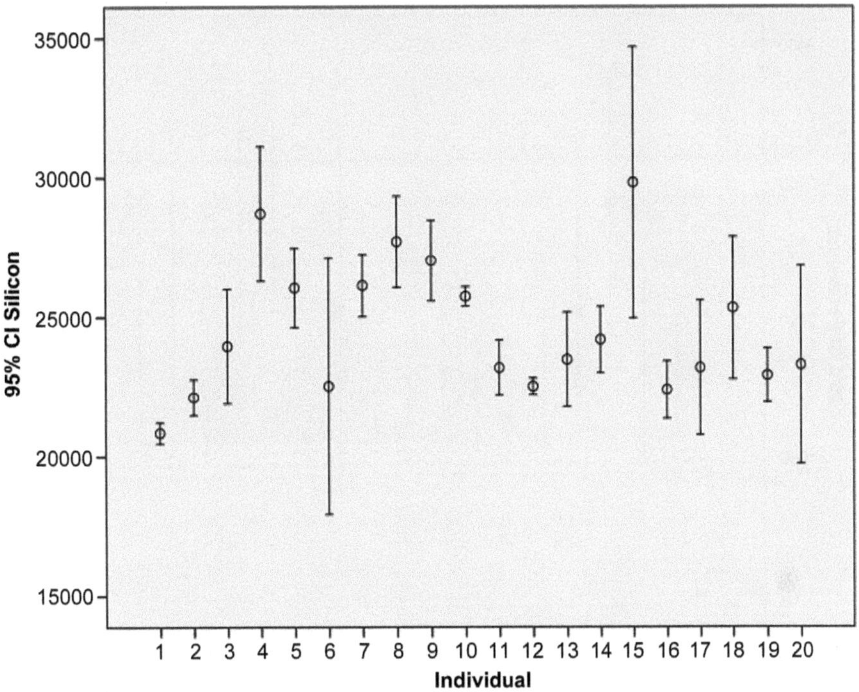

Figure 7-4
Elemental concentration distribution of Si in skeletal elements from the study sample (95% confidence interval).

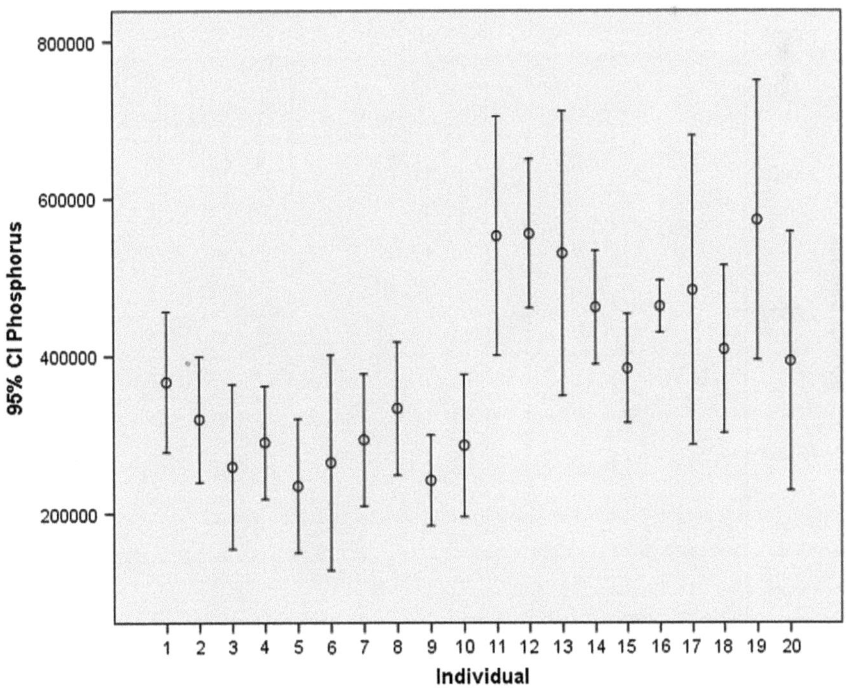

Figure 7-5
Elemental concentration distribution of P in skeletal elements from the study sample (95% CI).

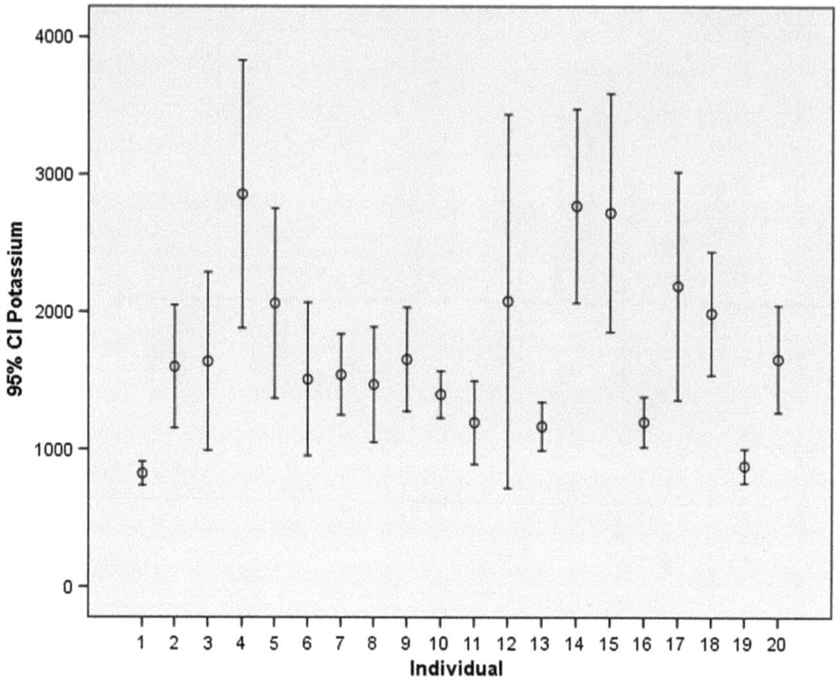

Figure 7-6
Elemental concentration distribution of K in skeletal elements from the study sample (95% CI).

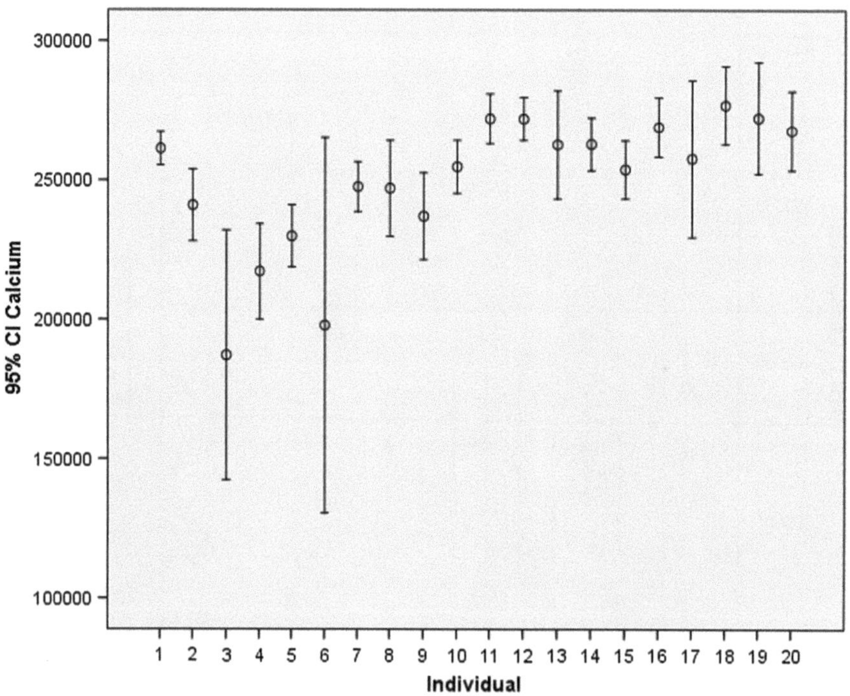

Figure 7-7
Elemental concentration distribution of Ca in skeletal elements from the study sample (95% CI).

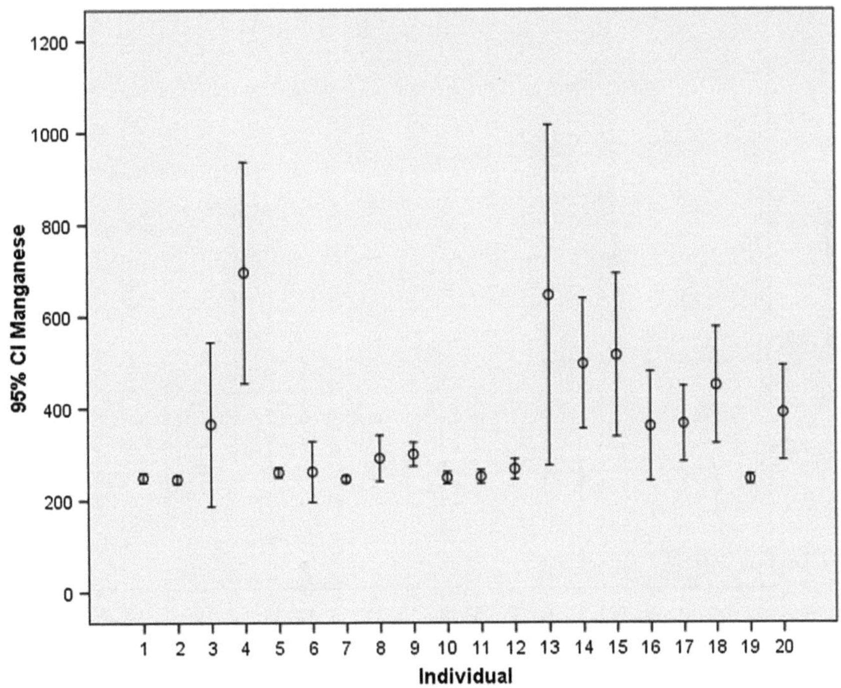

Figure 7-8
Elemental concentration distribution of Mn in skeletal elements from the study sample (95% CI).

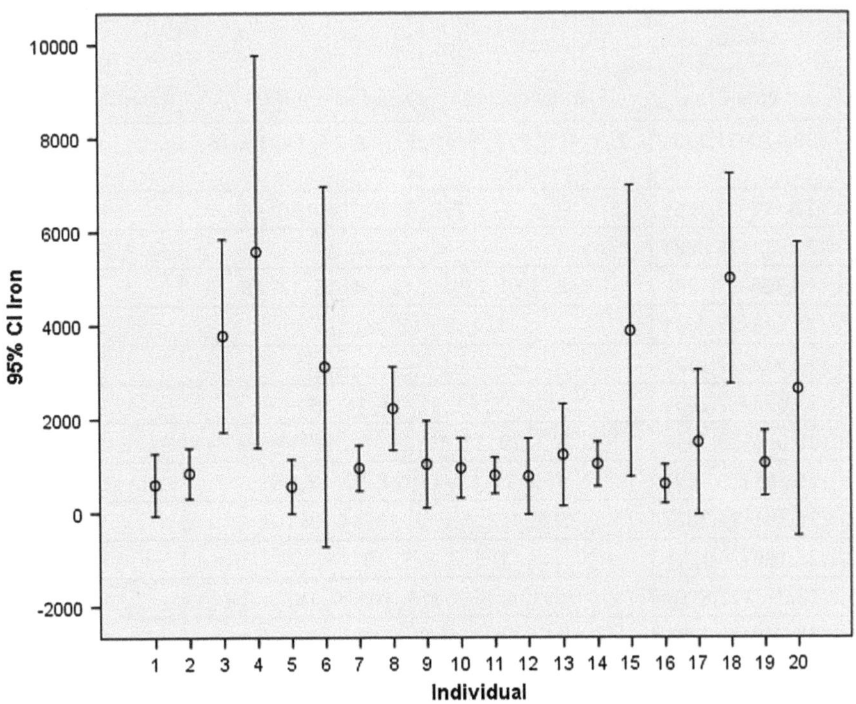

Figure 7-9
Elemental concentration distribution of Fe in skeletal elements from the study sample (95% CI).

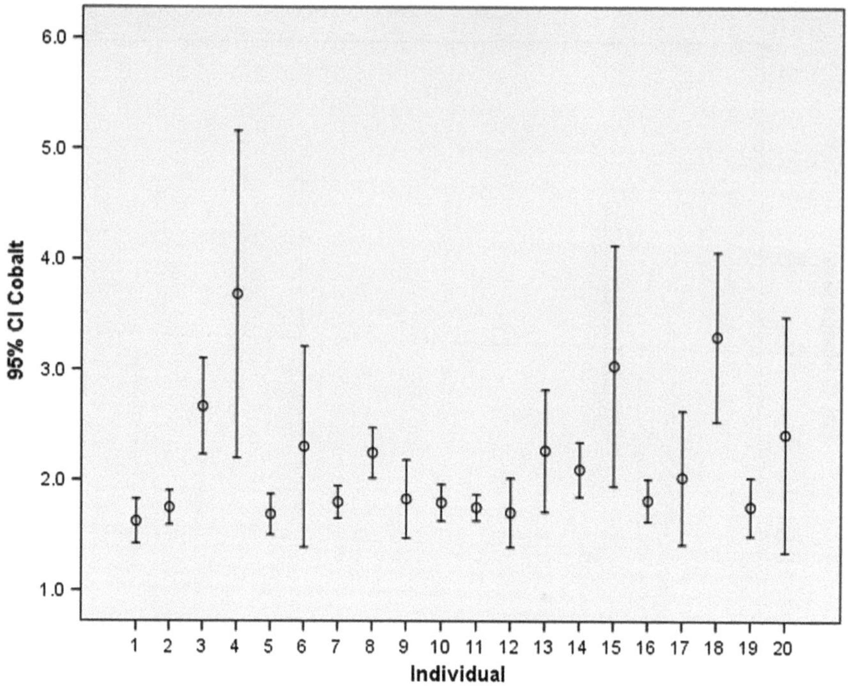

Figure 7-10
Elemental concentration distribution of Co in skeletal elements from the study sample (95% CI).

Table 7-3: Detection of Commingling Based on 95% Confidence Intervals for Si

Individual	95% CI	Individuals Segregated at α = 0.05	No. of Unresolved Cases	% Failure Rate
1	(20,470–21,233)	2, 3, 4, 5, 7, 8, 9, 10, 11, 12, 13, 14, 15, 18, 19	4/19	21.1
2	(21,489–22,776)	1, 4, 5, 7, 8, 9, 10, 14, 15	10/19	52.6
3	(21,911–26,008)	1, 4, 8	16/19	84.2
4	(26,300–31,124)	1, 2, 3,10, 11, 12, 13, 14, 16, 17, 19	8/19	42.1
5	(24,633–27,465)	1, 2, 11, 12, 16, 19	13/19	68.4
6	(17,938–27,117)	---------------------------------	19/19	100.0
7	(25,025–27,243)	1, 2, 11, 12, 13, 16, 19	12/19	63.2
8	(26,066–29,341)	1, 2, 3, 10, 11, 12, 13, 14, 16, 17, 19	8/19	42.1
9	(25,583–28,469)	1, 2, 11, 12, 13, 14, 16, 17, 19	10/19	52.6
10	(25,391–26,087)	1, 2, 4, 8, 11, 12, 13, 14, 16, 19	9/19	47.4
11	(22,196–24,171)	1, 5, 7, 8, 9, 10, 15	12/19	63.2
12	(22,215–22,819)	1, 4, 5, 7, 8, 9, 10, 14, 15	10/19	52.6
13	(21,785–25,172)	1, 4, 8, 9, 10	14/19	73.7
14	(23,003–25,376)	1, 2, 4, 8, 9, 10, 12	12/19	63.2

Table 7-3: Detection of Commingling Based on 95% Confidence Intervals for Si —cont'd

Individual	95% CI	Individuals Segregated at α = 0.05	No. of Unresolved Cases	% Failure Rate
15	(24,955–34,683)	1, 2, 11, 12, 16, 19	13/19	68.4
16	(21,351–23,425)	4, 5, 7, 8, 9, 10, 15	12/19	63.2
17	(20,764–25,589)	4, 8, 9	16/19	84.2
18	(22,775–27,877)	1	18/19	94.7
19	(21,941–23,875)	1, 4, 5, 7, 8, 9, 10, 15	11/19	57.9
20	(19,734–26,836)	--------------------------------	19/19	100.0

Table 7-4: Detection of Commingling Based on 95% Confidence Intervals for P

Individual	95% CI	Individuals Segregated at α = 0.05	No. of Unresolved Cases	% Failure Rate
1	(277,883–456,710)	12	18/19	94.7
2	(239,667-399,650)	11, 12, 16	16/19	84.2
3	(154,478–364,377)	11, 12, 14, 16, 19	14/19	73.7
4	(218,506–362,109)	11, 12, 14, 16, 19	14/19	73.7
5	(149,673–319,981)	11, 12, 13, 14, 16, 19	13/19	68.4
6	(127,559–401,894)	12, 16	17/19	89.5
7	(209,462–377,768)	11, 12, 14, 16, 19	14/19	73.7
8	(248,873–418,005)	12, 16	17/19	89.5
9	(184,582–299,628)	11, 12, 13, 14, 15, 16, 19	12/19	63.2
10	(196,024–376,820)	11, 12, 14, 16, 19	14/19	73.7
11	(401,234–704,310)	3, 4, 5, 7, 9, 10	13/19	68.4
12	(461,080–650,333)	2, 3, 4, 5, 6, 7, 8, 9, 10	10/19	52.7
13	(349,477–711,744)	9	18/19	94.7
14	(389,765–534,155)	3, 4, 5, 7, 9, 10	13/19	68.4
15	(315,217–453,655)	9	18/19	94.7
16	(430,159–496,245)	2, 3, 4, 5, 6, 7, 8, 9, 10	10/19	52.7
17	(287,089–680,355)	--------------------------------	19/19	100.0
18	(302,129–515,315)	--------------------------------	19/19	100.0
19	(395,618–750,406)	3, 4, 5, 7, 9, 10	13/19	68.4
20	(229,308–558,460)	--------------------------------	19/19	100.0

Table 7-5: Detection of Commingling Based on 95% Confidence Intervals for K

Individual	95% CI	Individuals Segregated at α = 0.05	No. of Unresolved Cases	% Failure Rate
1	(737–910)	2, 3, 4, 5, 6, 7, 8, 9, 10, 13, 14, 15, 16, 17, 18, 20	3/19	15.8
2	(1,153–2,018)	1, 19	17/19	89.5
3	(992–2,287)	1, 19	17/19	89.5
4	(1,882–3,830)	1, 7, 8, 10, 11, 13, 16, 19	11/19	57.9
5	(1,370–2,753)	1, 13, 16, 19	15/19	78.9
6	(953–2,066)	1	18/19	94.7
7	(1,248–1,839)	1, 4, 14, 19	15/19	78.9
8	(1,052–1,891)	1, 14, 19	16/19	84.2
9	(1,277–2,033)	1, 14, 19	16/19	84.2
10	(1,227–1,571)	1, 4, 14, 15, 19	14/19	73.7
11	(891–1,499)	4, 14, 15, 18	15/19	78.9
12	(718–3,436)	--------------------------------	19/19	100.0
13	(992–1,343)	1, 4, 5, 14, 15, 17, 18, 19	11/19	57.9
14	(2,064–3,478)	1, 7, 8, 9, 10, 11, 13, 16, 19	10/19	52.6
15	(1,854–3,591)	1, 10, 11, 13, 16, 19	13/19	68.4
16	(1,015–1,381)	1, 4, 5, 14, 15, 18, 19	12/19	63.2
17	(1,358–3,019)	1, 13, 19	16/19	84.2
18	(1,542–2,439)	1, 11, 13, 16	15/19	78.9
19	(756–1,003)	2, 3, 4, 5, 7, 8, 9, 10, 13, 14, 15, 16, 17, 18, 20	4/19	21.1
20	(1,269–2,046)	1, 14, 19	16/19	84.2

Table 7-6: Detection of Commingling Based on 95% Confidence Intervals for Ca

Individual	95% CI	Individuals Segregated at α = 0.05	No. of Unresolved Cases	% Failure Rate
1	(255,328–267,232)	2, 3, 4, 5, 7, 9	13/19	68.4
2	(228,150–253,882)	1, 11, 12, 16, 18	14/19	73.7
3	(142,356–232,031)	1, 7, 10, 11, 12, 13, 14, 15, 16, 18, 19, 20	7/19	36.8
4	(199,968–234,363)	1, 7, 10, 11, 12, 13, 14, 15, 16, 18, 19, 20	7/19	36.8
5	(218,747–241,080)	1, 10, 11, 12, 13, 14, 15, 16, 18, 19, 20	8/19	42.1
6	(130,526–265,210)	-----------------	19/19	100.0
7	(238,682–256,534)	11, 12, 16, 18	15/19	78.9
8	(229,929–264,245)	--------------------------------	19/19	100.0
9	(221,483–252,707)	1, 11, 12, 14, 16, 18, 20	12/19	63.2
10	(245,322–264,348)	3, 4, 5	16/19	84.2
11	(263,137–281,056)	2, 3, 4, 5, 7, 9	13/19	68.4

Table 7-6: Detection of Commingling Based on 95% Confidence Intervals for Ca —cont'd

Individual	95% CI	Individuals Segregated at α = 0.05	No. of Unresolved Cases	% Failure Rate
12	(264,356–279,787)	2, 3, 4, 5, 7, 8, 9, 10, 15	10/19	52.6
13	(243,330–282,196)	3, 4, 5	16/19	84.2
14	(253,424–272,453)	3, 4, 5, 9	15/19	78.9
15	(243,397–264,262)	3, 4, 5, 12	15/19	78.9
16	(258,408–279,718)	2, 3, 4, 5, 7, 9	13/19	68.4
17	(229,578–285,927)	------------------	19/19	100.0
18	(262,946–291,004)	2, 3, 4, 5, 7, 9	13/19	68.4
19	(252,379–292,461)	3, 4, 5	16/19	84.2
20	(253,548–282,036)	3, 4, 5	16/19	84.2

Table 7-7: Detection of Commingling Based on 95% Confidence Intervals for Mn

Individual	95% CI	Individuals Segregated at α = 0.05	No. of Unresolved Cases	% Failure Rate
1	(239–260)	4, 13, 14, 15, 17, 18, 20	12/19	63.2
2	(236–254)	4, 13, 14, 15, 17, 18, 20	12/19	63.2
3	(187–544)	--------------------------------	19/19	100.0
4	(455–936)	1, 2, 5, 6, 7, 8, 9, 10, 11, 12, 17, 19	7/19	36.8
5	(250–271)	4, 13, 14, 15, 17, 18, 20	12/19	63.2
6	(196–328)	4, 14, 15, 18	15/19	78.9
7	(239–253)	4, 13, 14, 15, 17, 18, 20	12/19	63.2
8	(241–341)	4, 14	17/19	89.5
9	(274–326)	1, 2, 4, 10, 11, 14, 15, 18, 19	10/19	52.6
10	(236–262)	4, 13, 14, 15, 17, 18, 20	12/19	63.2
11	(236–266)	4, 13, 14, 15, 17, 18, 20	12/19	63.2
12	(246–290)	4, 14, 15, 18, 20	15/19	73.7
13	(275–1,015)	1, 2, 5, 7, 10, 11, 19	12/19	63.2
14	(355–638)	1, 2, 5, 6, 7, 8, 9, 10, 11, 12, 19	8/19	42.1
15	(338–693)	1, 2, 5, 6, 7, 8, 9, 10, 11, 12, 19	8/19	42.1
16	(242–480)	--------------------------------	19/19	100.0
17	(284–448)	1, 2, 4, 5, 7, 10, 11, 12, 19	10/19	52.6
18	(323–577)	1, 2, 5, 7 10, 11, 12, 19	11/19	57.9
19	(235–256)	4, 13, 14, 15, 17, 18, 20	12/19	63.2
20	(287–493)	1, 2, 5, 7, 10, 11, 12, 19	11/19	57.9

Table 7-8: Detection of Commingling Based on 95% Confidence Intervals for Fe

Individual	95% CI	Individuals Segregated at α = 0.05	No. of Unresolved Cases	% Failure Rate
1	(-62–1,259)	3, 4, 8, 18	15/19	78.9
2	(305–1,377)	3, 4, 18	16/19	84.2
3	(1,715–5,843)	1, 2, 5, 7, 10, 11, 12, 14, 16	10/19	52.6
4	(1,383–9,770)	1, 2, 5, 7, 11, 14, 16	12/19	63.2
5	(-18–1,138)	3, 4, 8, 18	15/19	78.9
6	(-724–6,962)	--------------------------------	19/19	100.0
7	(468–1,436)	3, 4, 18	16/19	84.2
8	(1,329–3,118)	1, 5, 11, 16	15/19	78.9
9	(104–1,958)	18	18/19	94.7
10	(315–1,585)	3, 18	17/19	89.5
11	(406–1,176)	3, 4, 8, 18	15/19	78.9
12	(-40–1,579)	3, 18	17/19	89.5
13	(138–2,317)	18	18/19	94.7
14	(559–1,506)	3, 18	17/19	89.5
15	(765–6,984)	--------------------------------	19/19	100.0
16	(196–1,019)	3, 4, 8, 18	15/19	78.9
17	(-45–3,041)	--------------------------------	19/19	100.0
18	(2,751–7,230)	1, 2, 5, 7, 9, 10, 11, 12, 13, 14, 16, 19	7/19	36.8
19	(357–1,749)	18	18/19	94.7
20	(-489–5,762)	--------------------------------	19/19	100.0

Table 7-9: Detection of Commingling Based on 95% Confidence Intervals for Co

Individual	95% CI	Individuals Segregated at α = 0.05	No. of Unresolved Cases	% Failure Rate
1	(1.4–1.8)	3, 4, 8, 14, 15, 18	13/19	68.4
2	(1.6–1.9)	3, 4, 8, 15, 18	14/19	73.7
3	(2.2–3.1)	1, 2, 5, 7, 9, 10, 11, 12, 16, 19	9/19	47.4
4	(2.2–5.2)	1, 2, 5, 7, 9, 10, 11, 12, 16, 19	9/19	47.4
5	(1.5–1.9)	3, 4, 8, 15, 18	14/19	73.7
6	(1.4–3.2)	--------------------------------	19/19	100.0
7	(1.7–1.9)	3, 4, 8, 15, 18	14/19	73.7
8	(2.0–2.5)	1, 2, 5, 7, 10, 11, 12, 16, 19	10/19	52.6
9	(1.4–2.2)	3, 4, 18	16/19	84.2
10	(1.6–2.0)	3, 4, 8, 18	15/19	78.9

Table 7-9: Detection of Commingling Based on 95% Confidence Intervals for Co—cont'd

Individual	95% CI	Individuals Segregated at α = 0.05	No. of Unresolved Cases	% Failure Rate
11	(1.6–1.9)	3, 4, 8, 18	15/19	78.9
12	(1.4–2.0)	3, 4, 8, 18	15/19	78.9
13	(1.7–2.8)	--------------------------------	19/19	100.0
14	(1.8–2.3)	1	18/19	94.7
15	(1.9–4.1)	1, 2, 5, 7, 10, 11	13/19	68.4
16	(1.6–2.0)	3, 4, 8, 18	15/19	78.9
17	(1.4–2.6)	--------------------------------	19/19	100.0
18	(2.5–4.1)	1, 2, 5, 7, 8, 9, 10, 11, 12, 14, 16, 19	7/19	36.8
19	(1.5–2.0)	3, 4, 8, 18	15/19	78.9
20	(1.3–3.5)	--------------------------------	19/19	100.0

Discussion and Conclusion

The commingling of human remains continues to be a major challenge in forensic anthropology casework. Although scenarios such as mass fatality incidents and mass grave contexts will continue to require a much more comprehensive approach to commingling, there are an increasing number of nondestructive tools available for smaller-scale cases of commingling. The use of pXRF produced promising results, indicating that it has the potential for the gross sorting of commingled remains; however, the method should not be used to associate remains that have overlapping chemical concentration values (Gonzalez-Rodriguez and Fowler 2013). Further, accurate segregation rates may be lower for scenarios involving a large number of commingled individuals. Gonzalez-Rodriguez and Fowler's (2013) pXRF study obtained high correct classification rates using elemental ratios (e.g., Pb/Ca, Zn/Fe, and Sr/Pb) of five medieval coffin burials. However, it is unknown whether these ratios would successfully distinguish between individuals in modern contexts. In the current study, the pXRF unit was unable to detect Sr and Pb, two key elements used by Gonzalez-Rodriguez and Fowler (2013).

Little evidence of intraskeletal variation was identified in the sample. In fact, no significant interelemental differences were found when the L5 was removed from the analysis for comparisons of Mg. Thus, the greatest differences in elemental concentration values were found between individuals, especially for Si, P, K, Ca, Mn, Fe, and Co.

Another confounding factor not evaluated in the current study is the influence of diagenesis on elemental concentration values. Remains that have been buried or exposed on the surface for long periods of time may have incorporated elements through chemical exchange with the surrounding soil and groundwater, and through incorporation of contaminants into the cortical surfaces and pore spaces of bone. This should be evaluated in future research to determine whether human remains buried in the same context tend to show more similar elemental concentration values due to diagenesis.

Acknowledgements

The authors would like to thank Dr. Brad Adams and Dr. John Byrd for their kind invitation to contribute this chapter, and for their invaluable advice on this research. In addition, we thank Dr. Antoinette Martinez and Dr. Georgia Fox of California State University, Chico, for their permission to use the XRF and for their support of this research.

References

Brätter, P., Gawlik, D., Lausch, J., Rösick, U., 1977. On the distribution of trace elements in human skeletons. J. Radioanal. Chem. 37, 393–403.

Burton, J.H., Price, T.D., 2000. The use and abuse of trace elements for paleodietary research. In: Ambrose, S.H., Katzenberg, M.A. (Eds.), Biogeochemical Approaches to Paleodietary Analysis. Kluwer Academic/Plenum Publishers, New York, pp. 159–171.

Bush, M.A., Miller, R.G., Prutsman-Pfeiffer, J., Bush, P.J., 2007. Identification through X-ray fluorescence analysis of dental restorative resin materials: A comprehensive study of noncremated, cremated, and processed-cremated individuals. J. Forensic Sci. 52, 157–165.

Byrd, J.E., Adams, B.J., 2003. Osteometric sorting of commingled remains. J. Forensic Sci. 48, 717–724.

Cheverko, C., 2013. The use of joint surface pathology to reassociate commingled human remains in forensic anthropology. Proc. Am. Acad. Forensic Sci. 14, 402–403.

Christensen, A.M., Smith, M.A., Thomas, R.M., 2012. Validation of X-ray fluorescence spectrometry for determining osseous or dental origin of unknown material. J. Forensic Sci. 57, 47–51.

Damann, F.E., Edson, S.M., 2008. Sorting and identifying commingled remains of U.S. war dead: The collaborative roles of JPAC and AFDIL. In: Adams, B.J., Byrd, J.E. (Eds.), Recovery, Analysis, and Identification of Commingled Human Remains. Humana Press, Totowa, NJ, pp. 301–315.

Darrah, T.H., 2009. Inorganic trace element composition of modern human bones: Relation to bone pathology and geographical provenance. Unpublished dissertation. Department of Earth and Environmental Sciences, University of Rochester, Rochester, NY.

Fulton, B.A., Meloan, C.E., Finnegan, M., 1986. Reassembling scattered and mixed bones by trace element ratios. J. Forensic Sci. 31, 1455–1462.

Gonzalez-Rodriguez, J., Fowler, G., 2013. A study on the discrimination of human skeletons using X-ray fluorescence and chemometric tools in chemical anthropology. Forensic Sci. Int. 231 (407), e1–497e6.

Kini, U., Nandeesh, B.N., 2012. Physiology of bone formation, remodeling, and metabolism. In: Fogelman, I., Gnanasegaran, G., van der Wall, H. (Eds.), Radionuclide and Hybrid Bone Imaging. Springer, Berlin, pp. 29–57.

Mundorff, A.Z., Shaler, R., Bieschke, E., Mar-Cash, E., 2008. Marrying anthropology and DNA: Essential for solving complex commingling problems in cases of extreme fragmentation. In: Adams, B.J., Byrd, J.E. (Eds.), Recovery, Analysis, and Identification of Commingled Human Remains. Humana Press, Totowa, NJ, pp. 285–299.

Murad, T.A., Murad, T.D., 2000. The postmortem fate of Pat Gregory: A disinterred Native American. J. Forensic Sci. 45, 488–494.

Pollard, M., Batt, C., Stern, B., Young, S.M.M., 2007. Analytical Chemistry in Archaeology. Cambridge University Press, Cambridge, UK.

Schaefer, M., 2008. Patterns of epiphyseal union and their use in the detection and sorting of commingled remains. In: Adams, B.J., Byrd, J.E. (Eds.), Recovery, Analysis, and Identification of Commingled Human Remains. Humana Press, Totowa, NJ, pp. 221–240.

Shackley, M.S. (Ed.), 2011. X-Ray Fluorescence Spectrometry (XRF) in Geoarchaeology. Springer, New York.

Shackley, M.S., Dillian, C., 2002. Thermal and environmental effects on obsidian geochemistry: Experimental and archaeological evidence. In: Loyd, J.M., Origer, T.M., Fredrickson, D.A. (Eds.), The Effects of Fire and Heat on Obsidian. Cultural Resources Publication, Anthropology Fire-History, U.S. Bureau of Land Management, Sacramento, CA, pp. 117–134.

Swanston, T., Varney, T., Coulthard, I., Feng, R., Bewer, B., Murphy, R., Hennig, C., Cooper, D., 2012. Element localization in archaeological bone using synchrotron radiation X-ray fluorescence: Identification of biogenic uptake. J. Archaeol. Sci. 39, 2409–2413.

Trombka, J.I., Schweitzer, J., Selavka, C., Dale, M., Gahn, N., Floyd, S., Marie, J., Hobson, M., Zeosky, J., Martin, K., McClannahan, T., Solomon, P., Gottschang, E., 2002. Crime scene investigations using protable, non-destructive space exploration technology. Forensic Sci. Int. 129, 1–9.

Ubelaker, D.H., 2002. Approaches to the study of commingling in human skeletal biology. In: Haglund, W.D., Sorg, M.H. (Eds.), Advances in Forensic Taphonomy: Method, Theory, and Archaeological Perspectives. CRC Press, Boca Raton, FL, pp. 355–378.

Yazedjian, L., Kešetović, R., 2008. The application of traditional anthropological methods in a DNA-led identification process. In: Adams, B.J., Byrd, J.E. (Eds.), Recovery, Analysis, and Identification of Commingled Human Remains. Humana Press, Totowa, NJ, pp. 271–284.

CHAPTER 8

Osteometric Sorting

John E. Byrd, Carrie B. LeGarde
Central Identification Laboratory, Joint POW/MIA Accounting Command

Assemblages of commingled human remains present special problems for the identification process. Complete biological profiles of individuals cannot be developed until the remains have been segregated into individuals. Cause and manner of death cannot be fully evaluated without access to segregated, complete skeletons. Segregation is also a goal for reasons extending beyond the need for comprehensive analysis, as in forensic applications when remains must be returned to next of kin for disposition. Although the presence of soft tissue can, in some cases, usefully inform the process (e.g., hair color and texture, skin tone), most of the information used to resolve commingling is obtained from the skeleton. Charles Snow (1948) provided an early comprehensive overview of methods for sorting commingled skeletons that is still relevant today, although it predates some important new technologies such as DNA analysis. The primary categories of information used to sort commingled remains are age, articulation, visual pair matching, size (osteometric sorting), robusticity ("build"), taphonomy, and DNA profile data. Osteometric sorting is but one of the many tools available to the anthropologist for sorting commingled remains. Descriptions of these methods are given elsewhere in this volume as well as previous publications (Adams and Byrd 2006; Byrd 2008; Byrd and Adams 2009; Snow 1948; Ubelaker 2002) and therefore are not repeated here.

An additional tool that can be invaluable in sorting commingled remains is the process of elimination (Adams and Byrd 2006). Most authors neglect this important aspect of segregating remains despite its fundamental relevance. However, before bones can be assigned to an individual on the basis of a process of elimination, one must be certain that the case includes only a specific, known number of individuals. We might say that such cases exhibit *epistemic closure* (De Cornulier 1988), meaning that the circumstances of the case permit one to make strong inferences on negative evidence. An example of the use of process of elimination is a case in which we have two commingled individuals and seek to associate a left femur. One of the individuals has a right femur, but it is found to be of a size too large to match the left femur. We conclude that it must associate with the other individual because that is the only rational choice remaining post-analysis: the second individual is the only one *with no evidence against the association*. Following Snow, we advocate the systematic use of all the aforementioned methods to sort commingled remains. Each step in

Commingled Human Remains. http://dx.doi.org/10.1016/B978-0-12-405889-7.00008-3

the sorting process is documented and can (in principle) be replicated by other anthropologists (Adams and Byrd 2006; Byrd and Adams 2003).

The segregation of commingled remains is a form of inductive inference and should be viewed as a series of tests of possible associations between bones. The tests—which probe the evidence *against* an association—are performed using the methods previously listed, with some methods being inherently more powerful than others. But the ability of a test to correctly segregate bones depends on more than the power of a statistical model; it will also be determined by the attributes of the case specimens themselves. For example, some articulations are more reliable than others for testing the association of adjoining bones (Adams and Byrd 2006; Puerto et al., this book, Chapter 14). Unreliable articulations are those for which bones from different individuals can appear to fit with high frequency. (The reverse—adjoining bones from a single individual not articulating—can be considered rare to nonexistent.) A test involving an "unreliable" articulation can nonetheless yield a convincing rejection (and subsequent segregation) when the fit is extremely poor (e.g., the bones cannot articulate). What we seek through our probing are *severe tests* (Mayo 1996; 2003; 2004), that is, tests that follow the *severity principle*. Mayo states, "The intuition underlying the severity principle is a familiar one: we have a good indication that we are correct about a claim or hypothesis…just to the extent that we have ruled out the ways we can be wrong in taking the claim or hypothesis to be true" (Mayo 2003:101). Thus, confidence in the negative test result with an unreliable articulation is based on the fact that an extremely poor fit between two adjoining bones (from the same individual) will be a rare-to-nonexistent event. The rarity of a negative test result when the bones originate in one person grants the high severity. Further illustration is offered in the case of a match (accepting the null hypothesis), where low severity results when bones from individuals of similar size are in the assemblage. Low severity is inferred in this circumstance because the probability of associating bones from multiple individuals is high (due to the inability of the method to segregate bones from similar-sized people). Tests based on statistical hypotheses are capable of providing a measure of how strong the evidence is against the null hypothesis (of an association). Statistical tests also permit one to measure the *severity* of the test, as defined by Mayo (Mayo 1996; 2003; 2004; Mayo and Spanos 2006). Osteometric sorting utilizes statistical tests and thus supports evaluation of severity.

It should be clear at this juncture that we recommend a statistical approach in line with "classical" or "frequency" statistics. These statistics are designed to support probing the possible associations by offering tests capable of providing evidence of the falsity of null hypotheses, where the latter are defined in a manner germane to the specific problem. These statistics are typically straightforward and easy to interpret. Inherent in this approach is an asymmetry in the potential conclusiveness of results, such that rejections of a null are clearly interpretable, but failure to reject is not interpretable without supporting information beyond the test. It is possible to obtain inconclusive results. Because sampling error must be accounted for, models based on small samples will more often yield inconclusive results. One alternative approach is to utilize Bayesian models (cf. O'Brien and Storlie 2011). Bayesian methods are based on a fundamentally different philosophy—dubbed "probabilism" by Deborah Mayo—that seeks to assign probabilities to the primary working hypotheses. These models combine the prior probability of the hypothesis with its likelihood based on the data at hand. What results from this calculation is a posterior probability that the hypothesis is true. The advantage of this approach should be that informative prior information is contributing to the statistical calculation. An important difference from frequentist principles is that the data inform the result only through the likelihood function, so that no explicit or implicit accounting is made for sampling error. The posterior probability is based on the prior information, the model selected for use, and the data at hand. This probability is interpreted as the best available indicator of the truth of the hypothesis. In the context of osteometric sorting, one would presumably choose the association with the highest posterior probability when given choices. There is no prescription for when to reject an association based on a posterior probability, although one can invent any convention he or she likes. See Chapter 9 in this volume (Konigsberg and Adams) for an interesting discussion of various approaches to osteometric pair matching.

We do not favor Bayesian methods because there is typically no probative prior information incorporated into osteometric sorting and because they do not (by design) control for sampling error. There are also general concerns with probabilism that are too lengthy to discuss here. In most cases, each hypothesis of an association between two bones will be assigned equal priors. Thus, if there are four possible combinations to be examined, they are each assigned a prior probability of 0.25. Although this solution is pragmatic (and commonly adopted in Bayesian analyses in other contexts), it guarantees that no useful role will be played by the prior information. All influence is then focused on the likelihoods. Given this, it makes more sense to drop the Bayesian analysis and develop a likelihood-based solution to the problem. Comparison of likelihoods alone has the advantage of providing a very direct way to highlight the evidence for each hypothesis as given in the data. However, one must still determine how to make inferences from these comparisons. Some advocate adhering to the Law of Likelihood, and simply choose the hypothetical association with the strongest likelihood ratio as the correct association. Others, the current authors included, would admonish that one must establish cutoff values for likelihood ratios, below which one must conclude the evidence is ambiguous. Royall (1997), for example, recommends likelihood intervals 1:8 (read as parameter values within the interval have a likelihood ratio more than 1/8 when compared to the most likely value) and 1:32, as meaningful. A simplistic approach in which one simply chooses the hypothesis with the strongest likelihood ratio—without regard for how strong it actually is—will lead to uncontrollable errors in an unreliable procedure. Controlling for error with cutoff values will prevent this problem and yield a workable solution. This workable solution will respond to the same attributes in the data that our classical models do, and will yield similar results in which errors are controlled at comparable levels (see Lew 2013). We prefer the classical models based on the t-test for their familiarity and simplicity. However, it is not the only solution.

Osteometric sorting depends on the strong correlations among the sizes of the bones of the skeleton. A large humerus is associated with a large femur, a large metatarsal, etc. This isometric reality is exploited in the sorting process by formally comparing the sizes of two bones. Byrd and Adams (2003) have proposed that we test the statistical null hypothesis that the two specimens are of a size to have originated in the same individual. The original proposal relied on the use of prediction intervals, following the Neyman-Pearson approach to hypothesis testing (c.f. Neyman and Pearson 1933). This chapter expands beyond the use of prediction intervals and presents a means of assessing the strength of evidence obtained in a particular test as well as a means of comparing the strength of evidence for competing sorting options in a given analysis. These approaches require the calculation of statistical models from a large reference data set appropriate to the population of interest. This chapter presents three basic approaches to osteometric sorting: (1) comparison of left and right bones using models that key on shape; (2) comparison of adjoining bone with models responding to the correlation of corresponding regions at joints (see Buikstra et al. 1984); and (3) comparison of the sizes of bones with the use of regression models. Each approach is described here following a brief description of the reference data.

Data Sources and Analytical Methods

Statistical models employed for hypothesis testing are only as good as the reference data they are built upon. Reference data should be appropriate to the problem at hand, meaning that they are representative of the same population as the case specimens in question, can be considered a random sample with regard to the attributes measured, and were collected according to a standard protocol. Because the ancestry and sex of commingled individuals are often unknown prior to sorting, reference data for osteometric sorting should be representative of multiple populations and both sexes. The reference data used in this study were developed at the Central Identification Laboratory, Joint POW/MIA Accounting Command (JPAC/CIL) for broad applications in research and casework. The data are primarily composed of postcranial measurements. Included are the standard measurements found in the Forensic Databank at the University of Tennessee, Knoxville (Moore-Jansen et al. 1994) as well as new measurements designed to be taken on fragmented bones. The numbering scheme for new measurements was designed to integrate with the forensic databank. A considerable portion of the reference data consists of Forensic Databank data generously provided by Dr. Richard Jantz. The individuals in the reference data set are as listed in Table 8-1.

Statistical calculations (described later) were performed using SPSS (2000), Microsoft Excel (2002), and the Resampling Stats Add-in for Excel (2006) as follows. Regression models were calculated in SPSS. Comparisons to the t-distribution and normal distribution were made in Microsoft Excel. Bootstrap analyses were conducted in Microsoft Excel using the add-in

Table 8-1: Reference Sample Organized by Collection, Race, and Sex

Collection	Sex	Black	White	Asian	Mex	Total
CIL	F	0	1	0	0	1
	M	5	55	5	0	65
CMNH-HT	F	2	2	0	0	4
	M	7	7	0	0	14
SI-TERRY	F	14	10	0	0	24
	M	14	2	0	0	16
UT-BASS	F	3	9	0	0	12
	M	4	7	0	0	11
FDB	F	12	46	0	0	58
	M	17	108	0	0	125
ICMP	F	0	0	0	0	0
	M	0	41	0	0	41
HARV-PEA	M	0	0	0	2	2
	F	0	0	0	3	3
TOTAL		78	288	5	5	376

Abbreviations: *CIL*, JPAC Central Identification Laboratory
CMNH-HT, Cleveland Museum of Natural History Hamann-Todd collection
SI-TERRY, Smithsonian Institution Terry collection
UT-BASS, University of Tennessee Bass collection
FDB, University of Tennessee Forensic Data Bank
ICMP, International Commission on Missing Persons
HARV-PEA, Harvard University Peabody Museum

produced by Resampling Stats. Details of these statistical analyses are presented in the appropriate sections below. All measurements used in this paper are defined in Appendix 8-1, Table 8-8.

Models for Osteometric Sorting

The basic principle underlying osteometric sorting is that two bones that are of sizes more disparate than observed in most humans are likely to be commingled. In this, as in most forensic applications, we are working from the general patterns known to exist in the relevant population(s) to the specific patterns seen in case specimens. This approach can be contrasted with the more common goal of statistical analysis in science: to infer general population characteristics from the specific characteristics of samples. Thus, osteometric sorting depends first on our ability to formally characterize normal size and shape relationships among skeletal elements. This is accomplished by utilizing estimates of population parameters such as the mean and standard deviation calculated from the reference data. These parameters are then used to formulate the null hypothesis of a "typical" size (and/or shape) relationship that is subjected to significance testing as described by Fisher (1958). The null hypothesis in these tests is closely grounded to the baseline of interest: normal bone size relationships.

Conclusions are primarily supported by having rejected a null hypothesis, because accepting the null in and of itself does not prove an association. The models are built from the reference data to address the problems encountered in the case (utilizing measurements that can be taken from the case specimens). An effort has been made to keep the statistical models as simple as possible. Simplicity serves two interests: the first is to avoid common problems with complex models, such as overfitting; the second is to make the method accessible to case analysts using only an osteometric board, calipers, and a spreadsheet. All the calculations can be done with a scientific calculator if necessary.

Paired Elements

Models for comparison of right- and left-paired bones were developed that emphasize shape. These models respond to many of the same attributes that make visual pair matching (Adams and Byrd 2006) possible and in most cases perform equally well. Measurements of length and of girth at numerous positions along each bone are utilized. Where length measurements are not available (due to fragmentation), models utilizing only girth measurements are calculated. These models take the general form

$$D = \sum (a_i - b_i) \tag{8-1}$$

where a is the right-side bone measurement i, and b is the left side bone measurement i for each of the measurements included in the comparison. The null hypothesis of no difference is tested by comparing the value of D against "0" (no difference) and using the reference data standard deviation of D. The deviation from "0" divided by the reference data standard deviation is evaluated against the t-distribution with two tails to obtain a p-value. A low p-value provides a measure of the strength of evidence against the null, which can also be taken as evidence for how atypical the case specimens are assuming they originate in the same individual. The 0.10 significance level is recommended for most applications of this test but recognize that the cutoff must be determined according to the needs of the investigation. (It is also worth emphasizing the need to use the test result in conjunction with independent lines of evidence.) This method has performed well in all test applications but would benefit from a larger reference sample.

Example 1

A left and right femur were randomly selected from the reference sample to serve as an example. Five measurements were chosen in this case (Figure 8-1), as listed in Table 8-2.

We regard this result as relatively easy to interpret because we can expect disparities between a left and right femur this large to be rare-to-nonexistent events when the bones are from the same individual. These bones would be segregated.

Subsequent to the original publication of the pair-matching models in Byrd (2008), LeGarde (2012) carried out a large validation study of this general approach in order to explore the effects of skeletal asymmetry on osteometric sorting. The study was rigorous in that it

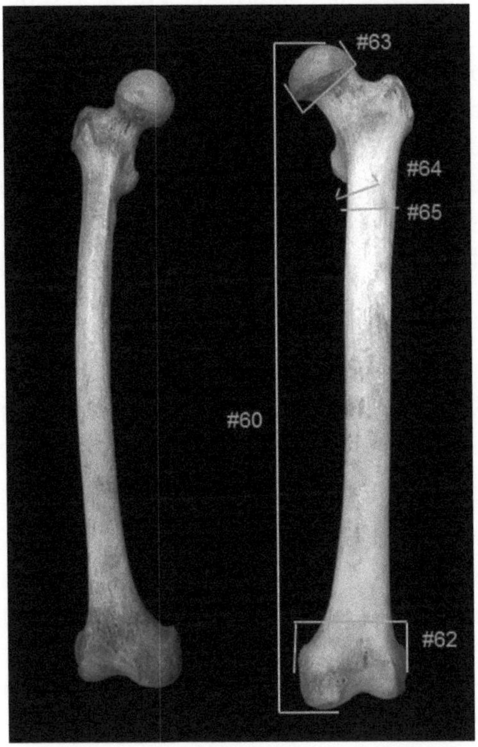

Figure 8-1
Measurements used in Example 1 (see also Appendix 8-1) *(Source: Photograph by Charity Barrett.)*

Table 8-2: Measurement Values and Statistics from Comparison of Randomly Chosen Left and Right Femurs in Example 1

Measurement*	Left	Right
60. Total length (mm)	505	448
62. Distal epiphysis breadth (mm)	82	86
63. Maximum diameter femur head (mm)	50	47
64. A-P subtrochlear diameter (mm)	29	27
65. M-L subtrochlear diameter (mm)	32	35
D	55.0	
Reference sample standard deviation (N = 67)	3.99	
t [calculated as (D – 0)/3.99]	13.8	
p (from t-distribution, d.f.=66, 2 tails)	0.000	

*Measurement numbers correspond to Moore-Jansen et al. (1994).

included a new measurement for the humerus believed to reflect directional asymmetry and included a test sample size larger than the original reference sample. The measurement in question was the maximum diameter of the humerus along the deltoid tuberosity. This measurement was designed by the senior author to facilitate testing for asymmetry related to handedness and has not been utilized in osteometric sorting. The test sample size varied from 118 to 151 specimens, depending on availability of measurements, as compared to the reference data which had a maximum size of 92 individuals but less for some models. LeGarde designed her study to examine the impact of directional asymmetry under circumstances where one would expect to see some degree of negative impact (e.g., models based on the humerus and radius) as well as where one expected minimum impact (e.g., models based on the femur). She added further rigor by adopting a leave-one-out protocol. Each test specimen was pulled from the data used to generate the models and evaluated as an independent test. While the Byrd–Adams data included individuals from throughout the 20th century and from multiple skeletal collections, LeGarde utilized the modern Bass Collection at the University of Tennessee, Knoxville for her study. Thus, there was opportunity for collection bias/temporal trends to introduce additional error into the test results.

LeGarde's results generally show little negative impact of asymmetry on osteometric sorting when following the general method given in Byrd (2008). The paired bone models for the humerus (12 models) yielded a mean error of 10% when using a cutoff value of $p = 0.10$. The models for the radius (six models) yielded an average error of 11.25% based on the same cutoff. The femur models (two) yielded an error rate of 6.3%. In total, the mean error rate in her study was 9.2%, not counting some breakouts by sex. Thus, it appears that when applied to the modern Bass Collection, the approach recommended by Byrd (2008) performs essentially as expected. This is not to say that there are not interesting patterns discovered by LeGarde that merit further examination. Subsequent papers will highlight that information. For readers interested in a simpler, faster approach (though less powerful) to osteometric pair matching, see Thomas et al. (2013). Numerous pair-matching models are provided in Appendix 8-1.

Articulating Bone Portions

Models for comparison of adjoining bones are calculated using the difference in sizes of adjoining portions as their basis (see Buikstra et al. 1984, for an original example of this approach applied to vertebrae). For example, the innominate and femur are compared by subtracting the maximum diameter of the femur head (measurement #63 in Moore-Jansen et al. 1994) from the maximum diameter of the acetabulum (measurement described in Adams and Byrd 2002). The model takes the general form

$$D = c_i - d_j \tag{8-2}$$

where measurement i of bone c is subtracted from measurement j of bone d. The null hypothesis that the two specimens are of an appropriate size to have originated in one individual is evaluated by comparing the D value obtained from the case specimens to the mean D value calculated from the reference data. The deviation of D from the reference data mean, divided by the reference data standard deviation, is evaluated against the t-distribution with two tails to obtain a p-value. A low p-value provides a measure of the strength of evidence against the null, which can also be taken as evidence for how atypical the case specimens are if we assume that they originate in the same individual. The 0.10 significance level is recommended, but larger or smaller significance levels can be assigned depending on the circumstances of the investigation.

Example 2

A femur and tibia were randomly selected from the reference sample to serve as an example. Two measurements, one taken from the distal femur and the other the proximal tibia (Figure 8-2), were used as the basis for the statistical test. Table 8-3 presents the data and results.

This result provides strong evidence that the two bones are not from the same individual. The decision to sort them apart depends on the cutoff value chosen by the analyst along with other factors (such as independent lines of evidence, an evaluation of alternative associations, etc.). Numerous models for articulations are given in Appendix 8-1.

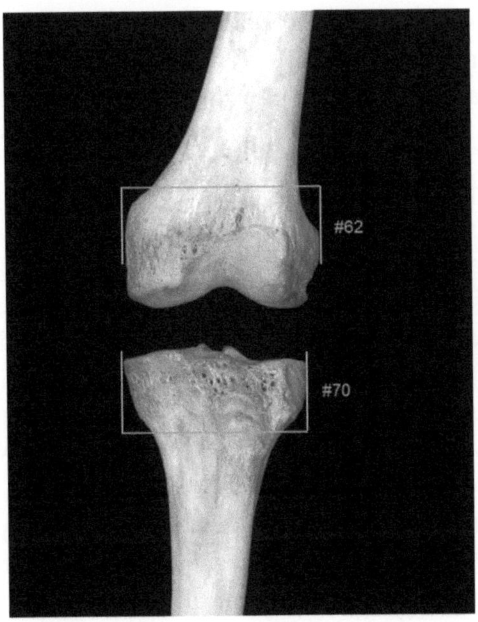

Figure 8-2
Measurements used in Example 2 (see also Appendix 8-1) *(Source: Photograph by Charity Barrett.)*

Table 8-3: Measurement Values and Statistics from Comparison of Randomly Chosen Femur and Tibia in Example 2

Measurement*	Value
62. Femur distal epiphysis breadth (mm)	85.0
70. Tibia proximal epiphysis breadth (mm)	84.0
D	1.0
Reference sample mean (N= 270)	5.2
Reference sample standard deviation	2.2
t [calculated as (*D* – 5.2)/2.2]	1.91
p (from t-distribution with d.f.=269, 2 tails)	0.057

*Measurement numbers correspond to Moore-Jansen et al. (1994).

Other Bone Portions

Models for comparison of different bone sizes are generally more complex in their derivation. After experimenting with numerous approaches, Byrd and Adams (2003) settled on the following linear combination as an acceptable index for bone size. The available measurements on a bone are simply summed and the natural logarithm of this sum is the value used in regression models. Because length measurements typically show the highest correlations with one another, models including length measurements perform best. The addition of breadths and girth measurements into the indices offers a slight, but noticeable improvement in the statistical models. A surprising finding is that models utilizing several breadth and girth measurements, with no length measurements, perform nearly as well in some cases as those including lengths. This fact has great significance when working with highly fragmented assemblages.

Byrd and Adams (2003) originally advocated using the 90% prediction interval as the basis for the hypothesis tests. If the point representing the two bones fell within the prediction interval, then the null hypothesis of association was accepted; otherwise, it was rejected. There was no measure of how good or poor the "fit" of the case specimens was relative to the regression model. This Neyman-Pearson approach is reasonable and simple to implement. However, it is recommended here to derive the t-value from the case specimens using the following model, modified from the confidence interval model provided by Giles and Klepinger (1988)

$$t = |y^{\wedge} - y_i| / \left[(\text{S.E.}) \times \sqrt{\left[1 + (1/\text{N}) + (x_i - x)^2 / (\text{N} \times S_X{}^2) \right]} \right] \qquad (8\text{-}3)$$

where $y^\wedge$ is the predicted value from the regression model, y_i is the dependent variable value of the case specimen, S.E. is the regression model standard error, N is the sample size used in calculation of the regression model, x_i is the independent variable value of the case specimen, x is the reference sample mean for the independent variable, and S_x is the reference sample standard deviation of the independent variable. We recommend this approach because it yields a p-value, which measures the strength of evidence against the null (see Lew 2013 for a discussion of the evidential meaning of the p-value). Note that the confidence interval model from which this formula was derived is shaped as a hyperbola, centered on the regression model line. The hyperbolic shape is sensitive to sample size and reflects the increasing uncertainty of regression model predictions as the independent variable value becomes more distant from the mean value (see Neter and Wasserman 1974). At large sample sizes ($N>200$), whence the lines of the hyperbola become flat, a simpler model can be derived by using the difference between the case specimen dependent variable value and the predicted value divided by the standard error of the estimate. The value resulting from this calculation can be compared to the t distribution.

Example 3

A humerus and a femur from two individuals, designated "A" and "B," were randomly selected from the reference sample. Comparisons were made (see Table 8-4) as though the true association of the bones was unknown and there were only two individuals commingled in the case. For ease of presentation, only one measurement for each bone (Figure 8-3) was used rather than the combinations recommended in Byrd and Adams (2003).

Assuming that epistemic closure holds for this case, we are faced with two courses of action: (1) segregate humerus A from femur A, which forces the segregation of humerus B from femur B; or (2) segregate humerus A from femur B along with humerus B from femur A. Because the association of humerus B with femur A is rejected with $p = 0.001$, we would recommend the second of the two courses of action here. Where epistemic closure does not

Table 8-4: Model and Statistics for Comparison of Right and Left Femora in Example 3

Measurement*	Value	
40. Maximum length humerus (HUM) (mm)	A. 348mm	B. 324mm
60. Maximum length femur (FEM) (mm)	A. 505mm	B. 468m
Regression model: HUM = 0.647(FEM) + 28.335		
N	274	
R	0.932	
F	1804.702	
P	0.001	
S.E. (standard error)	9.590	
X (mean FEM)	461.257	
S_{FEM} (standard deviation FEM)	43.541	
HUM A & FEM A	t: 0.735	p: 0.463
HUM B vs. FEM B	t: 0.742	p: 0.459
HUM A vs. FEM B	t: 1.756	p: 0.080
HUM B vs. FEM A	t: 3.228	p: 0.001

*Measurement numbers correspond to Moore-Jansen et.al. (1994).

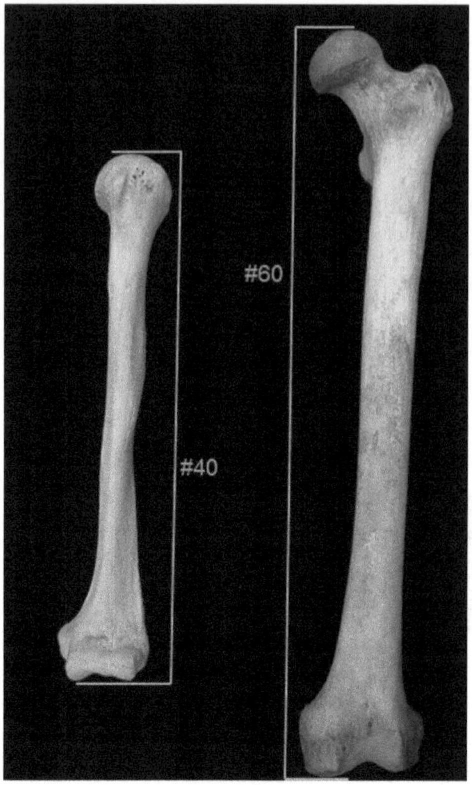

Figure 8-3
Measurements used in Example 3 (see also Appendix 8-1) *(Source: Photograph by Charity Barrett.)*

hold, we can still confidently segregate the As from the Bs. It is the subsequent associations that will be uncertain (i.e., the association has low severity due to the possibility of multiple individuals of approximately the same size). Further evaluation of decisions in which multiple options must be simultaneously considered is discussed next. Numerous regression models for sorting are provided in Appendix 8-1.

Assessment of Results

Sorting commingled remains is an inductive process. From an assemblage of bones with varying elements, sizes, shapes, and conditions, one must proceed stepwise through the assemblage using a variety of "probes" to infer whether each pair of bone specimens could have originated in the same individual. One does not seek a numeric probability of correct association because each segregation decision is either correct or incorrect. Rather, confidence is built by having subjected the sorting options to severe tests (see Mayo 1996; 2003; 2004). Some tests are more powerful (e.g., visual pair matching, osteometric pair matching, comparison of DNA profiles) than others (e.g., assessment of age in adults, comparison of taphonomy). In the end, we are hopefully left with segregated skeletons for which there is a high degree of confidence that every bone attributed to each skeleton originated from the same individual. There will rarely be *absolute* certainty in the resulting segregations because induction, by its nature, does not lead to absolutes. However, inductive processes in science do lead to conclusions that are highly reliable (i.e., able to withstand scrutiny, exhibit low error rates). How reliable are the results of osteometric sorting?

Osteometric sorting proceeds by testing the null hypothesis that two bones under consideration are of a size (and, to some extent, shape) that could have originated in the same individual. Such tests are repeated as often as necessary to segregate the assemblage of bones. Byrd and Adams (2003) originally proposed the use of the prediction interval of a regression model as a basis for the test, where all case values falling outside the prediction interval were rejected. This Neyman-Pearson–type approach to hypothesis testing requires one to choose the prediction interval value (generally 90% or 95%) in advance, and then react only to whether the case values fall within or outside the interval. This approach has some notable limitations. First, it ignores important information, such as how far outside the interval a set of case specimens fall. If their test value was within the prediction interval, was it close to the boundary, or near the value expected under the statistical model? Second, the original approach provides no objective method of assessing the family of results that are obtained when more than two bones are included in a test or when results of multiple tests must be evaluated. The method of hypothesis testing is here redirected to a form more in line with Fisher's (1958; 1959) significance testing.

Assessment of the results of a single test is straightforward: one relies on the p-value, which indicates how often we should expect to see bone measurement values as disparate as observed in the case specimens when the bones originate in a single individual. A low p-value (e.g., $p < 0.10$) is interpreted to mean we do not expect to find bones of the sizes seen in this case unless the bones are commingled from two individuals or an unlikely event has occurred (e.g., bones from an individual on the edge of normal human variation). Because unlikely events are infrequent, it is rational to opt for the first interpretation. More complex is the issue of what to do with the multiple p-values resulting from multiple comparisons. The recommended solution is a modification of Fisher's omnibus statistic, originally offered as a means of combining results of multiple chi-squared tests (Fisher 1958:99–101). Fisher noted:

> *When a number of quite independent tests of significance have been made, it sometimes happens that although few or none can be claimed individually as significant, yet the aggregate gives an impression that the probabilities are on the whole lower than would often have been obtained by chance. It is sometimes desired, taking account only of these probabilities, and not of the detailed composition of the data from which they are derived, which may be of very different kinds, to obtain a single test of the significance of the aggregate, based on the product of the probabilities observed. The circumstance that the sum of a number of values of* X^2

is itself distributed in the X^2 distribution with the appropriate number of degrees of freedom, may be made the basis of such a test (Fisher 1958:99)

Fisher's method called for using twice the summation of the natural log of the respective p-values, with sign reversed, to obtain a new statistic. This statistic was itself compared to the chi-squared distribution to get a single p-value for the aggregate. Because we are not using chi-squared tests in osteometric sorting, Fisher's method is not directly applicable to the problem of assessing the multiple test results.

The tests performed in osteometric sorting utilize the t-distribution. We can devise an omnibus test applicable to our test results that is similar to Fisher's chi-squared version by first using the same basic statistic

$$O = \sum - \ln (pi) \tag{8-4}$$

which is the summation of the natural log of each p-value, with sign reversed. Note that we do not double the value as did Fisher. We next calculate the mean and standard deviation of the omnibus statistic from the reference data. For application here, the add-in Resampling Stats for Excel was used to sample p-values from the reference data (where each individual's p-value was derived from application of a test to their measurement values), with replacement, for several 1000 trial runs. P-values from combinations of two, three, four, and six of the trials were randomly associated with one another to create a simulation of the test, but where no bones are commingled (i.e., the null hypothesis is true). Thus, bootstrap estimates of the mean and standard deviation of the omnibus statistic were derived. The omnibus statistic calculated from the reference skeletal data is at least approximately normally distributed (see Figure 8-4). It has been observed that the mean tends to be very close to (slightly less than) the number of tests in the aggregate, and the standard deviation tends to be very close to the square root of the number of tests. One can conservatively substitute these values for the sample statistics. Mean and standard deviation estimates for the omnibus statistic are then used to derive a z-score for each aggregate of test results. The z-score is compared to the normal distribution to obtain the overall p-value. This should be viewed as a one-sided test because we are only interested in significantly high values of O. An alternative manner for obtaining the p-value is to use the bootstrap distribution; however, experimentation suggests that the normal distribution is simpler to use and gives approximately the same result.

The severity of tests used in osteometric sorting can be measured using the procedure given by Mayo (1996:194) under her Rule of Rejection: severity is 1 minus the probability of getting a statistical value as large as obtained, assuming that the bones are not commingled (the condition represented by the reference data). Thus, the smaller the p-value obtained, the greater the severity of the test. It is clear that the severity obtained in a test is determined by the power of the test *and* the scale of the difference observed in the case

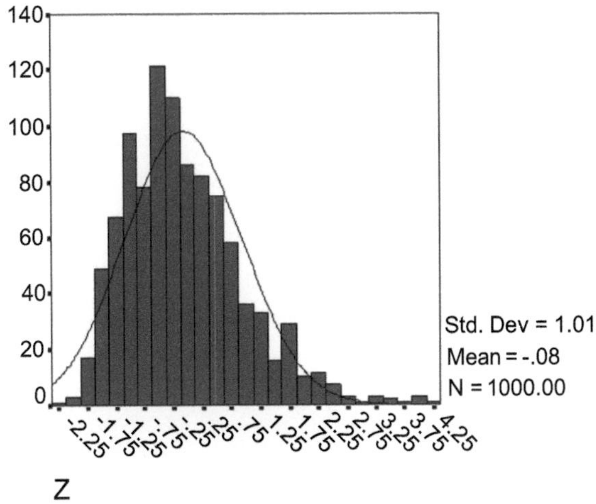

Figure 8-4
Z-scores calculated from the omnibus statistic. This example used data from comparison of the distal femur to the proximal tibia. P-values were calculated from the reference data and then sampled 1,000 times with replacement. This process was repeated six times to generate 1,000 randomly selected groupings of p-values. Z-scores were calculated using the value O minus 6, divided by the square root of 6.

specimens. Severity can be achieved even with weak tests so long as the case specimens exhibit sufficient disparity in their values (relative to one another). Osteometric tests predictably lack severity when the sizes of the commingled individuals are approximately the same, but can be very severe indeed when the body sizes are disparate. There will be for each test a degree of body size disparity at which osteometric tests will sort all measured bones with no error (severity = 1).

Example 4

Eleven airmen who were killed in 1944 when their B-24 bomber crashed into the jungle of Papua New Guinea were extensively commingled. Careful field recovery revealed that in some instances partially articulated skeletons could be recovered as a unit and that remains of the respective individuals were distributed in the site according to where they had been positioned in the aircraft. Two left innominates (AL and I-07L) and two right innominates (AR and BR) from one area within the site needed to be segregated in the laboratory. One of the left innominates (I-07L) was already associated with a partial skeleton. Fragmentation precluded the application of visual pair matching. Due to the fragmentation, only one measurement (#59A, see Figure 8-5) could be taken on all four bones. The standard deviation for the difference between left and right innominates for measurement #59A was calculated from the reference data. This value along with the value for D (see Equation 8-1) was used to test the null hypothesis (of no difference) for each of the possible pairings of the bones. Note that in this case we have two possible courses of action and a total of four pairings to evaluate: AL and AR are paired along with I-07L and BR, or AL and BR along with I-07L and AR. We can objectively evaluate each course of action by testing the null hypothesis that selections combine two p-values expected by chance if the bones are correctly paired. Table 8-5 presents the results of the tests.

In this instance we have a clear interpretation of the results. Course of Action #1 is well within the limits of reasonable expectation for bones originating in a single individual. In

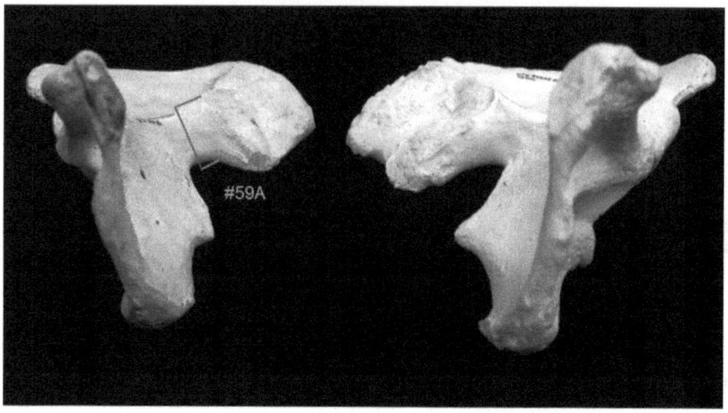

Figure 8-5
Measurements used in Example 4 (see also Appendix 8-1) *(Source: Photograph by Charity Barrett.)*

Table 8-5: Comparison of Right and Left Innominates from Example 4

Measurement*	Value	
59A. Max. thickness ilium at sciatic notch (mm)	AL: 21.6	AR: 23.2
	I-07L: 29.8	BR: 29.7
	Course of Action #1	
AL & AR	t: 1.13	p: 0.265
I-07L & BR	t: 0.070	p: 0.944
	Course of Action #2	
AL & BR	t: 5.70	p: 0.000
I-07L & AR	t: 4.64	p: 0.000
O (COA #1)	z: 1.39	p: 0.668
O (COA #2)	z: 25.98	p: 0.000

*Measurement described in Adams and Byrd (2002).

contrast, Course of Action #2 is outside such limits, and it would be irrational to choose these associations. The severity of the test of Course of Action #2 is 0.9999.

Example 5

Remains of two Marines killed in action in 1943 on Tarawa were accidentally discovered during construction activities in 1999. The disturbance of the grave resulted in extensive commingling of the remains. After the legs had been sorted into two sets of limbs, there was a need to associate the lower limbs with hip and abdomen portions. This problem could be addressed by osteometric comparison of the diameter of the acetabulum (measurement #59E) from one of the innominates with the maximum diameter of the femur head (measurement #63) from a femur representing each limb set (Figure 8-6). Only one of the hip sets could be measured due to fragmentation. The data and statistics are presented in Table 8-6.

We have strong support for the segregation of the innominate from femur #2, which is notably smaller than femur #1. Because there are only two individuals involved in the case (i.e., we have epistemic closure), by process of elimination we can associate the second set of limbs to the second set of hips. The simplicity of the problem negated the need for an omnibus test. The severity of the second test is 0.9999.

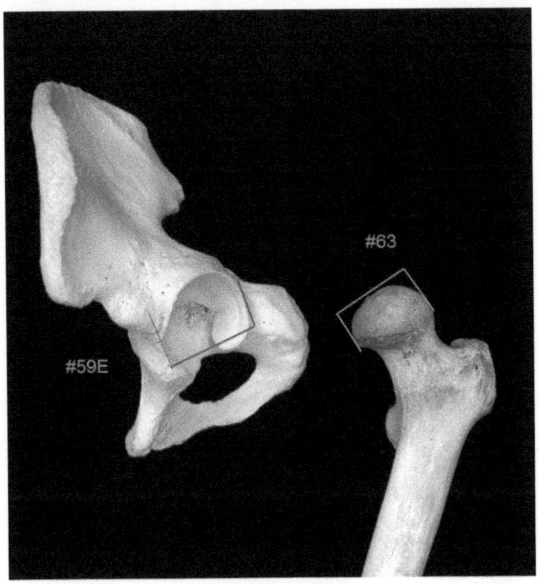

Figure 8-6
Measurements used in Example 5 (see also Appendix 8-1) *(Source: Photograph by Charity Barrett.)*

Table 8-6: Statistics from Comparison of Innominate and Femur from Example 5

Measurement*	Values	
59E: Max diameter of the acetabulum (mm)	innom#1: 66	
63: Max diameter of femur head (mm)	fem#1: 53.7	fem#2: 46.9
Innom#1 & femur #1	t: 1.578	p: 0.117
Innom#1 & femur #2	t: 5.640	p: 0.000

*Measurement numbers correspond to Moore-Jansen et al. (1994) or Adams and Byrd (2002).

Example 6

This example is taken from the case involving the B-24 aircraft crash that was described previously. Two sets of unassociated radii (designated A and B) were known to belong to either of two individuals represented by partial skeletons (I-09 and I-11). Osteometric sorting was attempted to resolve the problem. A simple linear regression model relating one measurement (Figure 8-7) of the radius (#47C) to two measurements of the humerus (#41 and #41A) was calculated from the reference data. As prescribed in Byrd and Adams (2003), the measurements for each bone were summed and the natural log taken to create the variables RAD and HUM, with HUM being the independent variable. Next, a series of

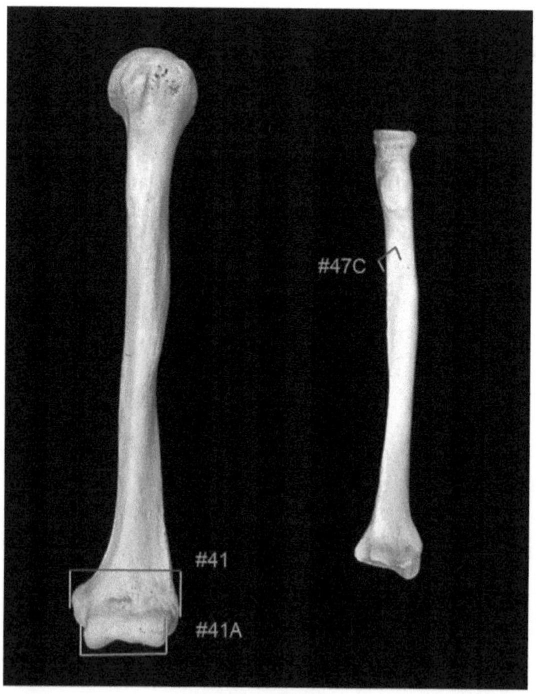

Figure 8-7
Measurements used in Example 6 (see also Appendix 8-1) *(Source: Photograph by Charity Barrett.)*

four tests were conducted comparing the regression model predicted values for the two humeri to the measurement values for the two radii. In each instance, we tested the null hypothesis that the radius was of the expected size, given the size of the humerus and the regression model statistics. Following the four tests of possible associations, the omnibus statistic was used to test each of the two possible courses of action in sorting. Results are presented in Table 8-7.

Upon viewing these results, one can be tempted to reject COA#2 on the basis that we are only interested in large positive z-scores, and the z-score for COA#2 is appreciably larger than that of COA#1. We cannot, however, interpret the results in this simplistic manner. Despite the larger z-score and corresponding smaller p-value, COA#2 is still well within the range of results we expect to obtain by chance when bones are legitimately associated. The severity of the test of Course of Action #1 is only 0.207, and only 0.590 for

Table 8-7: Model and Statistics from Comparison of Humerus and Radius from Example 6

Measurement*	Value	
41. Epicondylar breadth humerus (mm)	I-09: 66	I-11: 61.5
41A. Capitulum-trochlear breadth humerus (mm)	I-09: 45.4	I-11: 41.6
47C. Minimum diameter diaphysis radius (mm)	A: 11.8	B: 11.0
HUM	I-09: 4.71	I-11: 4.64
RAD	A: 2.47	B: 2.4
Regression model: RAD = 1.099(HUM) − 2.737		
N	164	
R	0.801	
F	291.9	
P	0.000	
S.E. (standard error)	0.762	
x (mean HUM)	4.67	
S_{HUM} (standard deviation HUM)	0.091	
Course of Action #1		
HUM I-09 &. RAD A	t: 0.402	p: 0.688
HUM I-11 vs. RAD B	t: 0.493	p: 0.623
Course of Action #2		
HUM I-09 vs. RAD B	t: 0.514	p: 0.608
HUM I-11 vs. RAD A	t: 1.41	p: 0.161
O (COA#1)	z: −0.818	p: 0.793
O (COA#2)	z 0.230	p: 0.410

*Measurement numbers correspond to Moore-Jansen et al. (1994) or Byrd and Adams (2003).

Course of Action #2. No sorting is possible based on the osteometric results in this example.

Conclusion

Segregation of commingled remains is a process of induction whereby bones are systematically compared to one another in a series of tests. Confidence in results is greatest when the tests are severe. Less than severe test results must be combined with other lines of evidence before segregation is done. Osteometric sorting is an important sorting tool that permits objective assessments of the severity of its tests. The application of osteometric sorting in case work at the JPAC/CIL is currently done in an ad hoc manner, where the appropriate statistical models (utilizing measurements available in the case specimens) are calculated from the reference data as the need arises. Osteometric comparisons of paired bones and adjoining bones are most advantageous when sorting large assemblages where it is impractical to make visual comparisons of every possible match. Further, this method is superbly suited to computer automation. We hope to develop an approach whereby all available measurement values for the case specimens are entered in advance, and all relevant comparison results can be produced as the analysis proceeds, without having to generate the statistical models for each comparison as separate steps for the anthropologist. As specimens are sorted apart by the various methods described in this chapter, they can be eliminated from consideration within the software application.

Appendix 8-1

This appendix presents models and statistics that can be applied to whole and fragmented bones in case assemblages. The measurements used are described in Table 8-8. Measurements are numbered and defined as in Moore-Jansen et al. (1994), Adams and Byrd (2002), and Byrd and Adams (2003) unless otherwise noted.

Paired Elements

Use Equation 8-1 to calculate D with the sets of measurements listed (Table 8-9) for each bone. Next, compare the value of "$|D - 0|$/standard deviation" to the t-distribution as a two-sided test with N – 1 degrees of freedom.

Articulating Bone Portions

Calculate the value for D as indicated in Table 8-10 (based on Equation 8-2). Next, compare the value of "$|D - \text{mean}|$/standard deviation" to the t-distribution as a two-sided test with N – 1 degrees of freedom.

Table 8-8: Measurements

Measurement	Definition
Scapula	
39B. Max. br. glenoid fossa	The maximum breadth of the glenoid fossa. Place one flat surface of the jaw of the calipers on the anterior side of the glenoid fossa and place the flat surface of the other jaw on the posterior side with both jaws oriented parallel to the long axis of the bone.
Humerus	
40. Max. length	The maximum length of the humerus taken on the osteometric board.
41. Epicondylar br.	The maximum breadth of the distal humerus taken on the osteometric board.
41A. Capitulum-trochlea br.	The breadth of the capitulum and trochlea at the distal humerus. One end of the sliding calipers is positioned parallel to the flat, spool-shaped surface of the trochlea, and the other end is moved until it comes into contact with the capitulum.
42. Max. vertical diam., head	Place the point of the fixed jaw of the sliding calipers on the most superior point of the head of the humerus on the perimeter of the articular surface. Place the movable jaw so as to find the maximum diameter without moving the fixed jaw from its position.
42A. A-P br., head	The maximum breadth of the humeral head taken in the anterior-posterior direction on the articular surface. This measurement is taken perpendicular to the vertical diameter of the humeral head.
44B. Min. diam. diaph.	The minimum diameter of the humeral diaphysis taken in any direction perpendicular to the shaft. This measurement should be taken on the oval part of the shaft, superior to the flattening observed around the olecranon fossa and the lateral supercondylar ridge. Often it is found near midshaft.
Radius	
45. Max. length	The maximum length of the radius taken on the osteometric board.
46. Sag. diam. midshaft	The sagittal diameter of the diaphysis taken at midshaft with sliding calipers.
47. Trans. diam. midshaft	The transverse diameter of the diaphysis taken at midshaft with sliding calipers.
47A. Max. diam. radial tub.	The maximum shaft diameter on the radial tuberosity. Position the calipers around the tuberosity and rotate the bone until the maximum distance is obtained.
47B. Max. diam. diaph. distal to radial tub.	The maximum shaft diameter distal to the radial tuberosity, positioned along the interosseous crest. The bone should be rotated to find the maximum distance.
47C. Min. diam. diaph. distal to radial tub.	The minimum shaft diameter anywhere distal to the radial tuberosity. The bone may be rotated to find the minimum distance.
47D. Max. diam. radial head	Position the calipers around the radial head and rotate the bone until the maximum distance is obtained.
Ulna	
48. Max. length	The maximum length of the ulna taken on the osteometric board.
49. Dorso-volar diam.	The diameter taken perpendicular to the transverse diameter at the same position along the diaphysis.
50. Transverse diam.	The diameter taken in the transverse dimension at the point of maximum expression of the interosseus crest.
51A. Min. diam. along interosseus crest	Locate the minimum diameter of the diaphysis along the portion of the bone that includes the interosseous crest. This measurement may not necessarily include the interosseous crest, but should be taken on that part of the shaft that exhibits the crest.

Continued

Table 8-8: Measurements—cont'd

Measurement	Definition
51C. Br. distal end of semi-lunar notch	This is a measure of only the distal surface of the semilunar notch (the base). To obtain the distance, position one end of the calipers within the radial notch (approximate midpoint), roughly parallel to the shaft. Apply the other end of the calipers to the medial edge of the semilunar notch.
Innominate	
59A. Max thickness sciatic notch	The maximum thickness of the ilium at the sciatic notch. Place the fixed jaw of the sliding caliper on the anterior surface of the ilium adjacent to the apex of the auricular surface. Close the flat surface of the movable jaw onto the posterior surface.
59E. Max. diam. acetabulum	The maximum diameter of the acetabulum. Move the jaws of the sliding calipers around the perimeter of the acetabulum to find the maximum value.
Femur	
60. Max. length	The maximum length of the femur taken on the osteometric board.
62. Epicondylar br.	The breadth of the epicondylar region of the distal femur taken on the osteometric board.
63. Max. diam. head	The maximum diameter of the femur head taken with sliding calipers.
64. A-P subtrochlear diam.	The anterior-posterior diameter of the femur taken in the subtrochlear region.
65. Trans. subtrochlear diam.	The transverse diameter of the femur taken in the subtrochlear region.
68E. Max. diam. along linea aspera	The maximum shaft diameter at any point along the linea aspera. As the bone should be rotated to obtain the maximum distance, the measurement does not necessarily have to include the linea aspera.
Tibia	
69. Max. length	The condylar-malar length of the tibia.
70. Max br. prox. epiphysis	The maximum breadth of the proximal tibia taken on the osteometric board.
71. Max. br. distal epiphysis	The maximum breadth of the distal tibia taken on the osteometric board.
72. Max. diam. nut. foramen	The maximum diameter of the tibia at the nutrient foramen taken with sliding calipers.
73. Trans. diam. nut. foramen	The transverse diameter of the tibia taken at the nutrient foramen.
74B. Min. A-P diam. distal to popliteal line	Locate the smallest anterior-posterior distance at any point on the tibial shaft.
Fibula	
75. Max. length	The maximum length of the fibula taken on the osteometric board.
76. Max. diam. midshaft	The maximum diameter of the fibula at midshaft, taken with sliding calipers.
Talus	
79. Min. br. art. surface	The minimum diameter of the articular surface of the talus. Place the flat surfaces of the jaws of the sliding calipers on either side of the articular surface with the jaws (approximately) parallel to the long axis of the bones. Close the jaws to take the minimum value.

Table 8-9: Statistics for Comparison of Paired Elements

Element	Measurements	N	Standard Deviation
Humerus	#40, #41, #42	113	5.28
Radius	#45, #46, #47	100	3.56
Ulna	#48, #49, #50	93	3.60
Femur	#60, #62, #63, #64, #65	67	3.99
Tibia	#69, #70, #71	87	3.68
Fibula	#75, #76	71	2.99
Fragmented Bones			
Humerus	#44B	73	0.72
Radius	#47A, #47B, #47C	52	1.34
Ulna	#49, #50, #51A	45	1.62
Femur	#64, #65	123	1.75
Tibia	#72, #73, #74B	44	2.62

Table 8-10: Models and Statistics for Comparing Bones from Selected Joints

Joint	*D*	N	Mean	Standard Deviation
Shoulder	(#42A - #39B)	159	6.61	2.35
Elbow 1	(#41A - #47D)	156	20.99	2.38
Elbow 2	(#41A - #51C)	166	20.49	2.39
Hip	(#59E - #63)	176	9.66	1.67
Knee	(#62 - #70)	270	5.20	2.20
Ankle	(#71 - #79)	147	17.91	2.85

Other Bone Portions

Use the listed measurements to calculate the variable values given in Table 8-11. Next, enter the independent variable value from the first case specimen into the regression model equation in Table 8-12 to obtain the predicted value for the dependent variable. The predicted value of the dependent variable, the actual value of the dependent variable (from the second case specimen), the actual value of the independent variable, the mean and standard deviation values of the independent variable (from Table 8-11), the standard error of the regression model (from Table 8-12), and the sample size (from Table 8-12) are entered into Equation 8-3 to obtain the value for t. This value is then compared to the t-distribution as a two-sided test with N – 2 degrees of freedom (where N is taken from Table 8-12).

Table 8-11: Variables

Variable	Measurements	N	Mean	Standard Deviation
HUM	LN(#40 + #41 + #42)	291	6.08	0.08
HUMFG	LN(#41A + #44B)	169	4.13	0.10
RAD	LN(#45 + #46 + #47)	282	5.61	0.11
RADFG	LN(#47A + #47B + #47C)	181	3.84	0.11
ULN	LN(#48 + #49 + #50)	277	5.68	0.10
ULNFG	LN(#49 + #50 + #51A)	177	3.73	0.12
FEM	LN(#60 + #62 + #63)	277	6.38	0.08
FEMFG	LN(#64 + #65 + #68E)	161	4.49	0.11
TIB	LN(#69 + #70 + #71)	277	6.23	0.10
TIBFG	LN((#72 + #73 + #74B)	180	4.44	0.12

Table 8-12: Models

Model	N	R	p	Standard Error
RAD=1.01(HUM) - 0.52	264	0.93	0.000	0.03
ULN=0.994(HUM) - 0.35	259	0.93	0.000	0.03
HUM=0.95(FEM) + 0.02	255	0.95	0.000	0.03
RAD=1.03(FEM) - 0.93	248	0.92	0.000	0.03
ULN=0.99(FEM) - 0.65	239	0.91	0.000	0.04
TIB=1.02(FEM) - 0.29	255	0.96	0.000	0.02
HUM=0.88(TIB) + 0.57	252	0.94	0.000	0.03
RAD=1.00(TIB) - 0.61	249	0.96	0.000	0.03
ULN=0.97(TIB) - 0.37	242	0.96	0.000	0.03
RAD=1.01(ULN) - 0.13	261	0.99	0.000	0.02
Fragmented Bones				
RADFG=0.96(HUMFG) - 0.14	161	0.89	0.000	0.05
ULNFG=1.07(HUMFG) - 0.68	160	0.88	0.000	0.06
HUMFG=0.87(FEMFG) + 0.22	139	0.85	0.000	0.06
RADFG=0.93(FEMFG) - 0.37	141	0.85	0.000	0.06
ULNFG=0.96(FEMFG) - 0.60	142	0.79	0.000	0.08
TIBFG=1.02(FEMFG) - 0.15	144	0.90	0.000	0.05
HUMFG=0.77(TIBFG) + 0.72	152	0.85	0.000	0.06
RADFG=0.83(TIBFG) + 0.14	162	0.84	0.000	0.06
ULNFG=0.88(TIBFG) - 0.18	165	0.82	0.000	0.07
RADFG=0.81(ULNFG) + 0.83	172	0.87	0.000	0.06

References

Adams, B.J., Byrd, J.E., 2002. Interobserver variation of selected postcranial measurements. J. Forensic Sci. 47 (6), 1193–1202.

Adams, B.J., Byrd, J.E., 2006. Resolution of small-scale commingling: a case report from the Vietnam War. Forensic Sci. Int. 156 (1), 63–69.

Buikstra, J.E., Gordon, C.C., St. Hoyme, L., 1984. The case of the severed skull: individuation in forensic anthropology. In: Rathbun, T.A., Buikstra, J.E. (Eds.), Human Identification: Case Studies in Forensic Anthropology. Charles C. Thomas, Springfield, IL, pp. 121–135.

Byrd, J.E., 2008. Models and methods for osteometric sorting. In: Adams B.J., Byrd, J.E. (Eds.), Recovery, Analysis, and Identification of Commingled Human Remains. Humana Press, Totowa, NJ, pp. 199–220.

Byrd, J.E., Adams, B.A., 2003. Osteometric sorting of commingled human remains. J. Forensic Sci. 48, 717–724.

Byrd, J.E., Adams, B.A., 2009. Analysis of commingled human remains. In: Blau, S., Ubelaker, D. (Eds.), Handbook of Forensic Anthropology and Archaeology. Left Coast Press, Walnut Creek, CA, pp. 174–186.

De Cornulier, B., 1988. "Knowing whether", "knowing who", and epistemic closure. In: Meyer, M. (Ed.), Questions and Questioning. Walter de Gruyter Press, Berlin, pp. 182–192.

Fisher, R.A., 1958. Statistical Methods for Research Workers, thirteenth ed. Hafner Publishing Company, Inc., New York, NY. Rev.

Fisher, R.A., 1959. Statistical Methods and Scientific Inference. Hafner Publishing Company, Inc., New York, NY.

Giles, E., Klepinger, L., 1988. Confidence intervals for estimates based on linear regression in forensic anthropology. J. Forensic Sci. 33 (5), 1218–1222.

LeGarde, C.B., 2012. Asymmetry of the Humerus: The Influence of Handedness on the Deltoid Tuberosity and Possible Implications for Osteometric Sorting. M.A. Thesis, Forensic Anthropology. The University of Montana, Missoula.

Lew, M.J., 2013. To P or not to P: On the evidential nature of P-values and their place in scientific inference. arXiv:1311.0081v1 [stat.ME] 1 Nov.

Mayo, D., 1996. Error and the Growth of Experimental Knowledge. University of Chicago Press, Chicago, IL.

Mayo, D., 2003. Severe testing as a guide for inductive learning. In: Kyburg Jr., H.E., Thalos, M. (Eds.), Probability Is the Very Guide of Life: The Philosophical Uses of Chance. Open Court, Chicago, IL, pp. 89–118.

Mayo, D., 2004. An error-statistical philosophy of evidence. In: Taper, M., Lele, S. (Eds.), The Nature of Scientific Evidence: Statistical, Philosophical, and Empirical Considerations. University of Chicago Press, Chicago, IL, pp. 79–118.

Mayo, D., Spanos, A., 2006. Severe testing as a basic concept in a Neyman-Pearson philosophy of induction. Br. J. Philos. Sci. (57), 323–357.

Microsoft Excel 2002. Microsoft Corporation, 2001.

Moore-Jansen, P.M., Ousley, S.D., Jantz, R.L., 1994. Data Collection Procedures for Forensic Skeletal Material. Report of Investigations no. 48. University of Tennessee, Department of Anthropology, Knoxville, TN.

Neter, J., Wasserman, W., 1974. Applied Linear Statistical Models: Regression, Analysis of Variance, and Experimental Designs. Richard D. Irwin, Inc, Homewood, Il.

Neyman, J., Pearson, E.S., 1933. On the problem of the most efficient tests of statistical hypotheses. In: Joint Statistical Papers. Cambridge University Press, Cambridge. 1967. First published in Philosophical Transactions of the Royal Society (A), 231, 289–237.

O'Brien, M., Storlie, C.B., 2011. An alternative bilateral refitting model for zooarchaeological assemblages. J. Taphonomy (9), 245–268.

Resampling Excel Add-in, Version 3.2. Resampling Stats, Inc., 2006.

Royall, R.M., 1997. Statistical Evidence: A Likelihood Paradigm. Chapman & Hall/CRC, Boca Raton, FL.

Snow, C., 1948. The identification of the unknown war dead. Am. J. Phys. Anthropol. 6, 323–328.

SPSS for Windows, Version 10.1.0. SPSS, Inc., 2000.

Thomas, R.M., Ubelaker, D.H., Byrd, J.E., 2013. Tables for the metric evaluation of pair matching of human skeletal elements. J. Forensic Sci. 58 (4), 952–956.

Ubelaker, D., 2002. Approaches to the study of commingling in human skeletal biology. In: Haglund, W.D., Sorg, M.H. (Eds.), Advances in Forensic Taphonomy: Method, Theory, and Archaeological Perspectives. CRC Press, Boca Raton, FL, pp. 331–351.

CHAPTER 9

Estimating the Number of Individuals Represented by Commingled Human Remains: A Critical Evaluation of Methods

Lyle W. Konigsberg[1], Bradley J. Adams[2]

[1]*Department of Anthropology, University of Illinois, Urbana-Champaign,* [2]*Department of Forensic Anthropology, Office of Chief Medical Examiner, New York City*

Introduction

Much of the literature that deals with various quantification techniques comes from faunal analysis. Generally, there are two goals of these techniques when working with animal remains. The first is to quantify the deposited/recovered faunal assemblage and from these data extrapolate information about past hominid behavior. The results of such studies attempt to draw conclusions concerning human diet, animal procurement strategies, and predator–prey relationships (Lyman 1987). The second goal is directed toward quantifying the recovered faunal assemblage to reconstruct the living community of animals. The results of these types of studies attempt to draw conclusions concerning faunal turnover and succession, reconstruction of paleoenvironmental conditions, and geographic faunal patterns (Lyman 1987). When one is working with commingled human remains, the goal of quantification is obviously to estimate the total number of dead, and many of the techniques developed for faunal analysis are not appropriate. Exceptions are the minimum number of individuals (MNI) and the Lincoln Index (LI). In paleodemographic studies, estimation of the number of individuals is critical for the interpretation of past cultures, whereas in the forensic context, it is vital for the identification process and for possible criminal trials.

In general, most discussions concerning the quantification of commingled human remains revolve around the MNI. Certainly one of the reasons for the popularity of the MNI is the ease of its calculation. Another reason is that physical anthropologists may not be familiar with other options. Research has shown that the Lincoln Index is a viable option for dealing with human remains, and one that is not significantly more complicated than the MNI in its calculation (Adams 1996). A more statistically accurate modification of the LI has been presented; it is called the most likely number of individuals, or MLNI (Adams and Konigsberg 2004). As such, a significant portion of this chapter discusses the MLNI in place of the LI.

Commingled Human Remains. http://dx.doi.org/10.1016/B978-0-12-405889-7.00009-5

These alternatives to the MNI provide physical anthropologists with more analytical power when dealing with commingled remains.

The MLNI can be calculated rather simply using a computer spreadsheet with either single or multiple elements (see http://konig.la.utk.edu/MLNI.html), and as a consequence, there have now been a number of applications (Hufthammer et al. 2011; L'Abbé et al. 2008; Nagaoka et al. 2012; Suby and Guichón 2010). The key difference between the MNI and the MLNI is that the MLNI estimates the *original* number of individuals represented by the osteological assemblage, whereas the MNI estimates only the *recovered* assemblage and, as the name implies, reflects a bare minimum estimate. In cases of taphonomic loss, this distinction can be quite important because the values presented by the MNI may provide misleading number estimates. The MLNI, on the other hand, will present a more accurate estimate of the original population size that can be used for paleodemographic or forensic purposes. Furthermore, it is possible to provide confidence intervals with the MLNI, but not with the MNI.

Factors Affecting Quantification: Bone Preservation and Scale of the Incident

There are two critical components to consider when determining the appropriate quantification technique: bone preservation and scale of the incident. Preservation is probably the most important of the two. Extremely fragmentary or poorly preserved remains may not be amenable to any meaningful quantification techniques. In these situations, the MNI is the best quantification technique to utilize, but the results will tend to underestimate the true population of dead. Regarding the scope of the incident, most commingled sites can usually be considered to be either small-scale or large-scale. Everything else being equal, it will usually be easier to determine the number of individuals with small-scale incidents. Large-scale scenarios become more complicated from both an analytical and logistical perspective (Byrd et al. 2003). Obviously, it will be much easier to deal with a small-scale incident involving five people as opposed to a large-scale incident involving 500.

Taphonomy is defined as the "science of the laws of embedding or burial" (Lyman 1994:1). An accurate understanding and recognition of the potential taphonomic changes that can occur to skeletal remains prior to recovery is essential for a meaningful interpretation of the assemblage, especially for quantification studies. In both forensic and archaeological scenarios, it is very possible that there will be less than 100% recovery of the skeletal elements deposited at a site. Whether data loss occurs from chemical breakdown of the bone, transport away from the site, or recovery bias, some degree of data loss is nearly impossible to avoid. Lyman (1987, 1994) outlines four general taphonomic effects that occur after death: disarticulation, scattering/dispersal, fossilization, and mechanical alteration. At each of these stages, there is the potential for data loss. In addition, bone assemblages can still undergo detrimental changes after recovery unless adequate measures are implemented for their curation. While the concerns for taphonomic loss may be less in the forensic context than the archaeological context, it is still a common occurrence.

With human remains, disarticulation generally occurs as the result of animal scavenging or the natural putrification process. It is also possible as a result of traumatic events, such as a plane crash or explosion. Scattering or dispersal may occur simultaneously with disarticulation, but is expressed in varying degrees depending on the distance between previously articulated elements. This could range from only a few millimeters to many miles. With remains deposited on the surface, dispersal may result from animal scavenging, but it is also possible that intentional site tampering may occur, resulting in further commingling and data loss. Several such examples of clandestine body removal and mass grave relocation have been documented in the former Yugoslavia (Skinner et al. 2002).

Fossilization refers to the changes that occur as the result of the associated soil matrix, and it also includes surface weathering. Gordon and Buikstra (1981), for example, have shown how the pH level of the soil is directly related to the state of preservation encountered at mortuary sites. Mechanical alteration results in fragmentation and/or abrasion due to mechanical or physical processes (e.g., fluvial transport and compression). Fragmentation occurs by the loading of force on a bone and its failure to withstand the pressure, whereas abrasion is the result of frictional forces on the bone surface. Mechanical alteration can occur at any time between death (possibly associated with death) and recovery. Bone porosity and density are important factors for preservation during both fossilization and mechanical alteration. Several studies have shown that larger and denser bones have a better chance of survival than the delicate elements (Brain 1976; Lyman 1993; Waldron 1987; Willey et al. 1997). As stated before, remains sustaining a significant amount of fragmentation or alteration will complicate the quantification process.

Quantification Techniques

Minimum Number of Individuals (MNI)

The MNI is arguably the most popular method of quantification in any type of commingled osteological analysis. Many researchers credit T.E. White (1953) with its initial use for abundance studies in archaeology. For interpreting population size from a skeletal assemblage, the MNI (as the name suggests) presents the minimum estimate for the number of individuals that contributed to the sample. To deal with fragmentary remains, one can use specific segments of an element (e.g., distal femur) for the calculation of the MNI. Every fragment must share a unique landmark to ensure that fragments do not originate from the same skeletal element. The basic principle of an MNI estimate is to avoid counting the same individual twice.

Unless all of at least one type of skeletal element are recovered and identified, the MNI will underestimate the original (i.e., true) number of individuals represented by the remains. In their discussion of faunal remains, Fieller and Turner (1982:56) wrote "...the very presence of

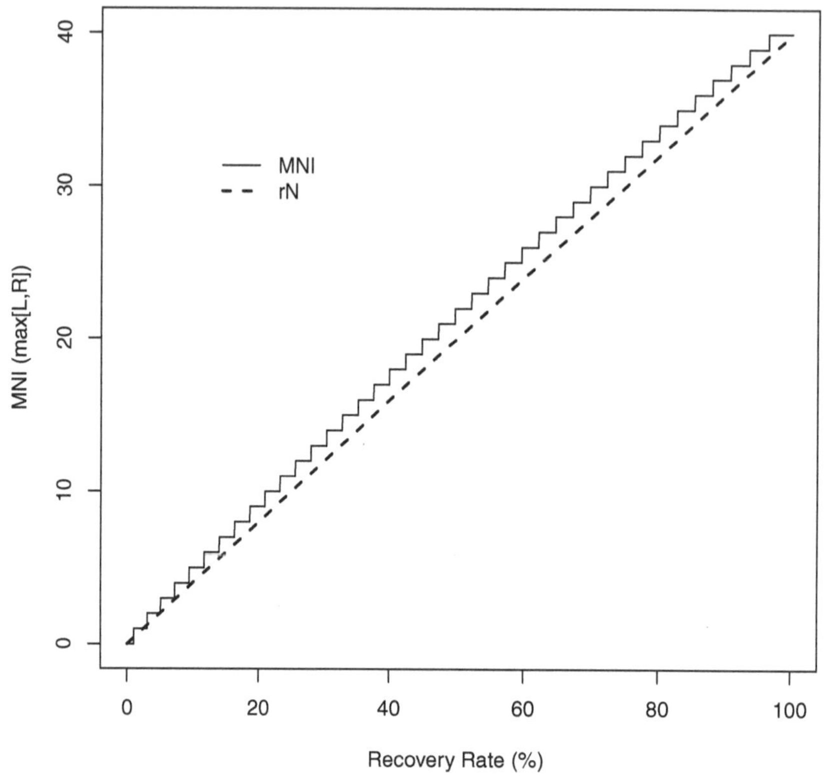

Figure 9-1
Analytical calculation of the MNI against recovery rate based on an actual size of 40 individuals.

unmatched bones indicates that the MNI estimate is necessarily an underestimate of the number comprising the death assemblage." The MNI simply states how many individuals would have been necessary to provide the recovered skeletal elements but may not be a reflection of the original death population. Because the MNI varies depending on the recovery rate, it may be of limited interpretive value in some instances.

Figure 9-1 shows the results of analytical calculations of the MNI against recovery rates of 0.01% to 99.99% in steps of 0.01% with an actual number of individuals equal to 40. The probability function for the MNI is

$$\Pr(MNI = m) = \Pr(m \mid N, r)^2 + 2 \sum_{x=0}^{m-1} \Pr(x \mid N, r) \tag{9-1}$$

where the probabilities on the right hand are the binomial probabilities based on N (here equal 40) and the recovery probability r. Letting L be the number of left bones and R be the number of right bones, the first term on the right side is the probability that $L = R = m$, which is just the square of the probability that $L = m$ (or equivalently $R = m$). The second term is the probability that $L = m > R$ (or equivalently $R = m > L$, which explains the multiplication by two). To draw Figure 9-1, we took the MNI from Equation 9-1 that had the highest probability given $N = 40$ and the current value of r (the recovery probability). This produces the step function labeled MNI in Figure 9-1, which is a step function because the MNI has a discrete distribution (there are no "partial counts" of bones). For comparison, Figure 9-1 also shows rN, which is a reasonable approximation to the MNI when N is relatively large. As is clear from Figure 9-1, the value of the MNI is a fairly direct indication of the representation of skeletal elements. Granted that the original population estimate determined through the recovery of ancient remains can almost never be verified, but the general trend of the MNI's behavior proves the need for caution with its use as a quantifier of abundance. Even in circumstances of near complete recovery, it will still be an underestimate of the original population.

Calculation of the MNI

The most common derivation of the MNI used for the analysis of human remains is simply calculated by sorting the bones by side and element and then taking the greatest number as the estimate. In other words, it is the most repeated element after sorting by element and side, Max (L, R), as we assumed in drawing Figure 9-1. It is equivalent to assuming that all of the less frequently observed bones are paired with the more frequently observed bones, and subsequently, provides a rather unlikely estimate in situations in which the recovery is less than 100%. There is another variant of the MNI, sometimes referred to as the grand minimum total, that will usually provide higher estimates than the standard MNI estimate. It is calculated as $L + R - P$, where P signifies the number of bone pairs. With this quantification technique, unpaired bones from different sides are assumed to come from different individuals. Take, for example, a scenario in which femora were the most numerous elements recovered from a site. There were 145 lefts, 130 rights, and 95 pairs within this group. The MNI derived as Max (L, R) would be 145, and the grand minimum total would be 180.

Lincoln Index (LI) and the Most Likely Number of Individuals (MLNI)

The Lincoln Index (LI) has been most commonly utilized and discussed concerning zooarchaeological remains and population studies of living animals (Allen and Guy 1984; Chapman 1951; Chase and Hagaman 1987; Fieller and Turner 1982; Horton 1984; Klein and Cruz-Uribe 1984; Plug 1984; Ringrose 1993; Seber 1973; Turner 1980, 1983, 1984; Turner and Fieller 1985; Wolter 1990; and many others). The LI was first developed for population studies of living animals based on capture-recapture techniques, and was later adapted for application to zooarchaeological faunal assemblages. The most likely number of individuals (MLNI) is a slight variation of the LI that improves the accuracy of the estimates (Adams and

Konigsberg 2004). Although Adams and Konigsberg (2004) referred to this calculation as the *MLNI,* it is actually the maximum posterior probability for the number of original individuals after integrating across a uniform prior for the recovery probability (as explained in Adams and Konigsberg where they cited Roberts [1967]). With both the LI and MLNI, it is critical that elements can be accurately pair-matched.

The theoretical basis of the LI and MLNI is that it can be used on populations in which all of the animals (living or dead) need not be observed in order to still derive accurate estimates of the original population. This has particular utility with archaeological samples or in forensic situations when the recovery of major skeletal elements is less than 100%. When one is working with the LI or MLNI, it is important that probabilities of sampling the left sides and of sampling the right sides within individuals are independent.

Calculation of the LI

In capture-recapture studies of living animals, a group of n_1 animals is initially trapped. These animals are then tagged and returned to the wild. Sometime later, a second group of n_2 animals is captured. The number of tagged animals that is recaptured from the initial catch is then counted as m. With the assumption that the proportion of initially tagged animals present in the second sample is roughly the same for the entire population, the estimated population size ($\dot{N}$) can be derived by Equation 9-2

$$\hat{N} = n_1 n_2 / m \tag{9-2}$$

The formula from the capture-recapture studies has been adapted for the same purpose of determining population size with zooarchaeological faunal remains. By using the bones of dead animals, the technique can achieve results similar to those obtained from living animals. As previously stated, the goal of the implementation of the LI is to estimate the actual population that is represented by the skeletal assemblage, that is, the size of the community at death instead of at recovery.

When working with skeletal elements, one calculates the LI based on pair matching. Pair matching involves the comparison of right and left elements to determine whether they are from a single individual. The bones from one side of the skeleton, e.g., left (L), are analogous to the initial stage of the capture-recapture procedure (n_1). The bones from the other side of the skeleton, e.g., right (R), are analogous to the second stage of the capture-recapture procedure (n_2). The number of elements that can be matched from the right and left sides as coming from the same individual (P) is analogous to the recapture of initially tagged animals (m). An estimate of the original death assemblage (LI) represented by the skeletal elements is determined by Equation 9-3

$$LI = LR/P\,. \tag{9-3}$$

Calculation of the MLNI and Confidence Intervals

A simple modification to this formula is recommended by Seber (1973) to account for possible sample bias. Adams and Konigsberg (2004) have shown that this formula represents the maximum likelihood estimate and refer to it as the most likely number of individuals, or MLNI. It is simply calculated as

$$MLNI = \left\lfloor \frac{(L+1)\,(R+1)}{P+1} - 1 \right\rfloor, \tag{9-4}$$

where $\lfloor\ \rfloor$ is the floor function that removes any decimal points. The floor function was incorrectly dropped by Nikita and Lahr (2011), and they instead rounded to the nearest integer so that some of their estimates are one individual too high. Although both the LI and the MLNI will provide similar results in most situations, it is recommended that MLNI should be used in all circumstances because it was derived specifically to remove bias from the estimate. Using the previous example with 145 left, 130 right, and 95 pairs of femora, we determine the resulting MLNI estimate would be 198 individuals. This value is considerably higher than both the Max (*L, R*) MNI value of 145 and the grand minimum total of 180. The MLNI equation, using the hypergeometric probability function, is currently available in an Excel™ spreadsheet for instances involving single elements or multiple elements; see http://konig.la.utk.edu/MLNI.html.

With the MLNI, it is possible to calculate confidence intervals, a feature not possible with MNI estimates. An approximate confidence interval can be calculated using the following variance equation

$$v^* = \frac{(L+1)\,(R+1)\,(L-P)\,(R-P)}{(P+1)^2\,(P+2)} \tag{9-5}$$

For example, an approximate 95% CI can then be calculated as MLNI $\pm\ 1.96\sqrt{v^*}$. Remember that the lower limit of the CI should never be reported as less than the MNI (grand minimum total) value of $L + R - P$.

Because the number of individuals, *N*, follows a discrete distribution, it is not statistically accurate to give customary confidence intervals, such as 95% intervals discussed previously. Adams and Konigsberg (2004) discuss a more appropriate technique called the highest density region (HDR; see Lee 1997:49), which is preferable to classical confidence intervals. For more information on the HDR and its calculation, see Adams and Konigsberg (2004) and the website http://konig.la.utk.edu/MLNI.html.

Comparison of the MNI and MLNI

In situations in which accurate pair matching is possible, the MLNI will provide more accurate results than the MNI. Table 9-1 shows the behavior of the MNI and MLNI with

Table 9-1: Quantification Estimates Derived from Differing Population Sizes and Recovery Rates[a]

Original Population	Recovery Rate 10% MLNI		20% MLNI[d]		30% MLNI		50% MLNI		70% MLNI		90% MLNI	
	MLNI	MNI[c]	MLNI[d]	MNI	MLNI	MNI	MLNI	MNI	MLNI	MNI	MLNI	MNI
10	2.6 (2.2)[b]	1.5 (0.9)	5.8 (3.6)	2.7 (1.1)	8.3 (4.1)	3.8 (1.3)	10.0 (3.3)	5.9 (1.3)	10.0 (1.6)	7.8 (1.1)	10.0 (0.4)	9.5 (0.7)
20	6.5 (4.4)	2.7 (1.3)	14.7 (7.9)	4.9 (1.6)	19.8 (9.4)	7.1 (1.7)	20.0 (5.7)	11.2 (1.9)	20.1 (2.2)	15.27 (1.6)	20.0 (0.5)	18.7 (1.0)
50	25.6 (13.7)	6.1 (1.9)	51.3 (25.5)	11.6 (2.4)	55.8 (23.8)	16.8 (2.8)	51.1 (8.0)	27.0 (2.9)	50.0 (3.0)	36.9 (2.6)	50.0 (0.8)	46.2 (1.7)
100	73.6 (33.2)	11.7 (2.6)	114.1 (53.5)	22.3 (3.4)	107.7 (32.1)	32.6 (3.8)	101.0 (10.4)	52.8 (4.1)	100.0 (4.4)	72.6 (3.6)	100.0 (1.1)	91.8 (2.4)
150	134.4 (60.5)	17.0 (3.2)	170.0 (70.9)	32.8 (4.3)	156.7 (36.2)	48.2 (4.6)	150.9 (12.6)	78.3 (4.9)	150.0 (5.1)	108.1 (4.5)	150.0 (1.4)	137.0 (3.0)

[a] Each value is based on 1,000 computer-simulations. Note how the MLNI value estimates the true population at low recovery rates while the MNI does not reflect the true population.

[b] Number in parentheses is the standard deviation.

[c] MNI is derived by the Max (L,R) method.

[d] MLNI is derived as $\left\lfloor \frac{(L+1)(R+1)}{(P+1)} - 1 \right\rfloor$.

differing population sizes and recovery rates. Note that the MLNI estimates are very accurate when recovery rates reach 50%, whereas the MNI estimates are still quite low. Robson and Regier (1964) suggest that bias in the MLNI will be negligible if the number of pairs is greater than seven.

Test for the Accuracy of Visual Pair Matching

The primary danger involved with the use of the MLNI for quantification from skeletal elements is the misidentification of pairs. Because of the multiplicative nature of these techniques, it is more vulnerable than other methods to fragmentation and misidentification of pairs. In extremely fragmentary situations, thorough pair matching may be impossible, and the MLNI should not be used. With good preservation, the step of visual pair matching will be substantially facilitated by accurate field excavation notes, consideration of general morphology, and taphonomic similarities. Of course, extensive osteological experience will be one of the most important factors for an accurate analysis.

Because accurate pair matching is critical to the use of the MLNI, it was necessary to examine this facet of the technique more in depth. In theory, any paired element in the body could be used for the calculation of the MLNI. In practice, though, particular parts of the skeleton will be more useful than others. Important criteria to consider for choosing appropriate skeletal elements are their size, presence of distinct morphological traits, potential for age and sex determination, and likelihood of survival. To examine the reliability of visual pair matching of the same element type (e.g., right and left femora), an experimental test was performed using an archaeologically recovered assemblage of well-preserved human skeletal remains originating from intact burials. The accuracy of visual pair matching was tested using only gross morphological characteristics (i.e., osteometric comparisons were not included).

To perform a verifiable test of gross pair-matching abilities, a random sample was drawn from an archaeological skeletal collection housed at the University of Tennessee, Knoxville. Larson Cemetery (39WW2) is an Arikara site associated with the Post-contact Variant of the Coalescent Tradition (Owsley 1994; Owsley et al. 1977). Initial occupancy at Larson is suspected to have begun about A.D. 1680 and to have ended by A.D. 1700 (Johnson 1994). Larson Cemetery was excavated during the 1966–1968 field seasons under the direction of William M. Bass through the University of Kansas. A total of 621 individuals were recovered (Owsley et al. 1977). Based on the demographic analysis of the remains, the cemetery appears to have been the sole repository for the village dead (Bass and Rucker 1976).

Two computer-generated lists simulated a 60% recovery sample of tibiae, femora, and humeri from both adult and subadult primary burials from Larson Cemetery, one derived from an original population of 15 individuals and one from 30 individuals. The samples drawn for the test consisted of both complete and fragmentary elements. The randomly selected elements were commingled on a table without any assistance by the observer (BJA), and any identifying labels (e.g., catalog numbers) were covered. These procedures removed any chance of bias to the observer during the test. Furthermore, the simulated recovery rate of 60% was also unknown to the observer.

Conjoining of fragmentary remains should be attempted prior to pair matching. After all potential matches between fragments are exhausted, pair matching should then be performed. Morphological indicators to use in the visual matching process include length, robusticity, muscle markings, epiphyseal shape, and general symmetry between elements. Taphonomic variables include the state of preservation (e.g., degree of weathering and color), presence of burning, presence of cut marks, and presence of animal damage. Because of the potential variation that is possible from differential preservation, taphonomic indicators should not be weighted as heavily as gross morphological features during pair matching.

Although limited to a relatively small number of individuals, results of the Larson Cemetery pair-matching test suggest that visual pair matching can be accurately performed by experienced osteologists (Tables 9-2 and 9-3). It was found that it is more likely for errors in pair matching to occur from overlooking true pairs, as opposed to the pairing of unrelated elements. It is suspected that this tendency may change if the sample size is substantially increased because variation between individuals may not be as obvious. The main reason for any difficulty in pair matching is that fragmentation, even minimal, can obliterate key areas used for identifying a match. Overall, the Larson Cemetery pair-matching test provided encouraging results, but additional validation experiments would be warranted.

Table 9-2: Results of the 15 Individual Tests for Visual Pair Matching

Element	Pairs	Unpaired Lefts	Unpaired Rights
Femur	6	3	3
Tibia	4	3	3
Humerus	3* (4)	4* (3)	6* (5)

*Indicates that an error was made and the number in parentheses is the correct answer.

Table 9-3: Results of the 30 Individual Tests for Visual Pair Matching

Element	Pairs	Unpaired Lefts	Unpaired Rights
Femur	11	4	10
Tibia	10* (11)	9* (8)	8* (7)
Humerus	11* (12)	9* (8)	7* (6)

*Indicates that an error was made and the number in parentheses is the correct answer.

Test Application of the MNI and MLNI: Larson Village

Commingled skeletal remains from Larson Village (39WW2) were utilized as a test for quantification using the MNI and MLNI. Larson Village is an Arikara site that is associated with Larson Cemetery (described previously). Larson Village was excavated during the summers of 1963 and 1964 as a salvage program of the Smithsonian Institution River Basin Surveys. Although 29 circular lodge depressions were visible on the ground surface at the village site, only three were completely excavated (Lodges 1, 21, and 23).

Initial discovery of scattered burials on the lodge floors led to suspicion of an epidemic disease (smallpox) as a cause (see Bass and Rucker 1976), but subsequent analysis revealed extensive perimortem trauma suggesting warfare (Owsley et al. 1977). The state of the skeletons encountered within the lodges was a clear indication that intentional burial did not occur. It appeared as though the individuals were massacred and placed within the lodges or were left to decompose where they were killed. The majority of the remains were discovered on the floor of Lodge 21 (Figure 9-2). Owsley et al. (1977:121) state in their analysis of the warfare evident at the site, "Due to disturbance and mixture of the skeletons … it was necessary to treat the bones as if they came from an ossuary."

The bones from Larson Village were generally in an excellent state of preservation and exhibited minimal fragmentation, weathering, or abrasion. There was extensive commingling that appears to have been largely the result of carnivore scavenging. This was demonstrated by numerous examples of tooth puncture marks on the bones. A study by Hudson (1993) showed that limb bones tend to dominate animal-scavenged assemblages. This is an important pattern to acknowledge, especially for quantification techniques such as the MLNI that rely

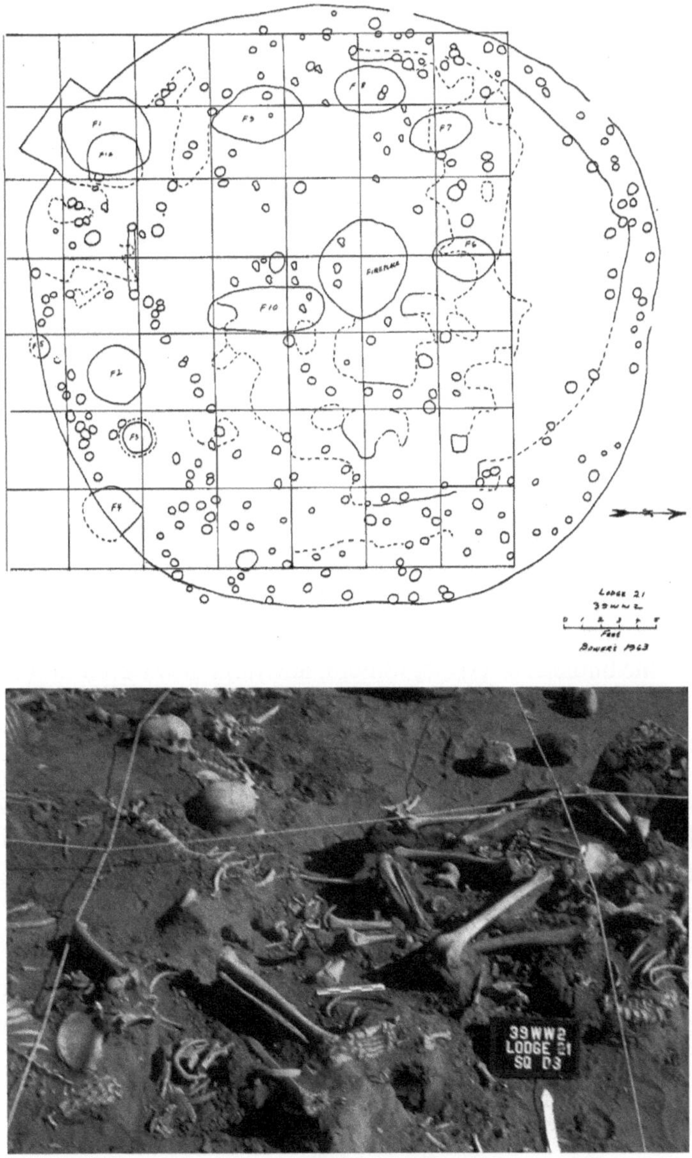

Figure 9-2
Original excavation map of Lodge 21 showing features (top) and a photograph of a section of Lodge 21 showing commingled skeletons (bottom).

on paired elements. Similarly, Marean and Spencer (1991) showed through an actualistic study of carnivore ravaging that the ends of limb bones are often destroyed although the shafts are preserved. When carnivore activity is apparent, they stress the need to include long bone shafts into quantification procedures and not to rely solely on the more easily identifiable epiphyses.

A second agent responsible for disarticulation at Larson was the human factor. Many elements showed evidence of cut marks, suggesting that parts of the victims' bodies were removed as trophies. Scalping and dismemberment of victims during warfare were not uncommon events on the Great Plains, as is evident by the literature documenting this type of trauma from the ethnographic and osteological record (Catlin 1989; Denig 1961; Grinnell 1910; Hollimon and Owsley 1994; Olsen and Shipman 1994; Owsley 1994; Owsley et al. 1977; Willey 1990). Scalping may be the most widely recognized type of mutilation associated with Native American warfare, but hands, feet, heads, noses, and limbs were also removed from the recently deceased as trophies. Sometimes the violence and dismemberment were quite extensive, as is exemplified by the Crow Creek massacre where one-fourth of the victims were decapitated (Willey 1990). At Larson Village, there is evidence that heads, hands, and possibly feet were removed from several individuals. These disarticulated parts would most likely have been transported away from the massacre site, creating a systematic bias (nonrandom) and providing a viable rationale for excluding these elements from any type of quantification study.

To observe the estimates generated by the MNI and the MLNI regarding Lodge 21, four paired elements were selected for study. Sorting and visual pair-matching procedures were performed on all of the humeri, os coxae, femora, and tibia discovered in the lodge. The MNI results derived by Max (*L*, *R*) from these elements revealed an estimate of 43 individuals based on the counts of the femur (Table 9-4).

Calculation of the MLNI provided a higher population estimate. All of the MLNI point estimates derived for each of the four elements inventoried from Lodge 21 are between 49 and 51 individuals (Table 9-4). By assuming independence and combining the estimates from each of the four elements, an approximate 95% HDR (confidence interval) of 48–52 individuals was derived with a point estimate of 50 individuals. A formatted spreadsheet available at http://konig.la.utk.edu/MLNI.html calculates MLNI and HDR values from single elements or multiple elements. The slightly higher MLNI estimate (approximately seven more than the

Table 9-4: Visual Pair-Matching Results and Population Estimates from Lodge 21 (Larson Village)

Element	Pairs	Total Lefts	Total Rights	MLNI	MNI (Max *L*, *R*)
Tibia	20	30	34	**50** (44–62)*	34
Os coxa	29	37	39	**49** (47–55)	39
Humerus	22	31	37	**51** (46–62)	37
Femur	31	43	36	**49** (48–54)	43
Combined				**50** (48–52)	43

*Number in parentheses represents the approximate 95% HDR (confidence interval). The lower limit of the interval cannot be less than $L + R - P$.

MNI) provides evidence for the high recovery rate achieved at Larson Village, but it also shows that data loss did occur and that the MNI is an underestimate of the true population.

Results from the Larson Village analysis are reasonably supportive of Badgley's (1986) view toward the MNI, which suggests that in situations of good preservation, near complete recovery, and deposition resulting from a single event, the MNI estimates will be close to the original population. Similarly, in this type of situation the MLNI results should be extremely accurate, and agreement between the two techniques can be used to prove that a high degree of recovery was achieved. It is considered advisable to compute the MLNI whenever it is feasible because it will be much more accurate than the MNI when recovery is not quite so complete.

Alternative Methods for Estimating the Number of Individuals

Recently, Nikita and Lahr (2011) and Nikita (2012) suggested alternative methods of estimating what they refer to as the "initial number of individuals" or the "original number of individuals" that attempt to remove some of the computational burden of forming the MLNI. In reality, their methods have a much higher computational burden because they replace direct analytical results with computer simulation; because none of the methods they have described produce a full distribution of N, their methods may be of limited utility. The simulation methods described in Nikita and Lahr (2011) do provide a standard deviation for the estimates of N, but because the full posterior distribution for N is often quite asymmetric, a mean and standard deviation do little to characterize the distribution. In their Table 5, they calculate Chapman's N (the MLNI for L, R, and P counts of a single element) where "alteration" is induced by reducing the left and right bone counts by a percentage while leaving the count of paired bones unaffected. This makes little sense because it is equivalent to saying that a proportion of the left and right bones become unrecognizable but that the number of paired bones stays the same.

What Nikita and Lahr (2011) essentially portray in their simulations is a crude form of what is known as approximate Bayesian computation, or ABC (Beaumont et al. 2002; Boattini et al. 2013; Konigsberg and Frankenberg 2013; Pritchard et al. 1999; Ray and Excoffier 2009; Tavaré et al. 1997; Tsutaya and Yoneda 2013; Turner and Van Zandt 2012). In ABC, one simulates data using parameter values from a prior distribution and then accepts those parameter values as samples from the posterior distribution of the parameters, provided that the simulated data are "close enough" to the actual data. In Nikita and Lahr's (2011) case, rather than setting a threshold for "close enough," they form a grid of possible parameter values and simulate at each grid point. They then select the grid point that produces simulated data closest to the observed data and do this "for about 20 times" (Nikita and Lahr 2011:633) to average across iterations.

We can adapt Nikita and Lahr's (2011) method so that it is a true ABC method. To do so, we begin with the common assumption that the recovery probability (one minus Nikita and Lahr's "loss") is a "nuisance" parameter (Cormack 1992; Roberts 1967). Dennis (1996:1097) defines nuisance parameters as those "parameters that are unknown but not of direct interest to the investigator." This leaves N as the only parameter to be estimated because the recovery probability is unknown and "not of direct interest." For our initial example, we use $L = 53$, $R = 58$, and $P = 18$. These are the observed counts for femora from the Jebel Moya site given in Nikita and Lahr's Table 2. This is a site with remains that were not commingled, so the actual number of skeletons excavated (N=153) is known, as is the number of pairs for any given element. Nikita and Lahr consequently use the remains from this site as a test case for estimating N. As a prior for N, we used

$$N \sim \lfloor U(0,251) \rfloor + L + R - P, \tag{9-6}$$

where $U(0, 251)$ is random uniform deviate between 0 and 251, and the use of the "floor" function truncates the deviates so that $\lfloor U(0,251) \rfloor$ is the set of integers from 0 to 250, each with a probability of 1/251, and these represent the number of individuals from whom no femora were sampled. The number 251 is used to set an upper bound (at 250) for the number of individuals from whom neither a left nor a right femur was sampled. Setting the boundary lower will truncate the posterior distribution of N, whereas setting the boundary higher is wasteful because very few draws from the prior will be accepted. Conditional on the observed L and R values and the value of N simulated from Equation 9-6, we then simulated a count for the number of pairs (P^*) out of the hypergeometric distribution based on the simulated number of individuals and the observed L and R counts. In the first run of simulation, we accepted an iteration of the simulation only if $P^* = P$, in which case the simulated value of N was stored. We ran this simulation until there were 50,000 stored values of N.

Figure 9-3 shows the histogram (as vertical lines) for the distribution of simulated N values. Also shown is the analytical solution (as a heavy line) using the hypergeometric distribution "normalized" so that the sum of $Pr(P|L, R, N)$ from $N = L + R - P$ to $N = L + R - P + 250$ was 1.0. This is labeled as "Hypg (uniform N)" because it assumes a uniform distribution for N starting at the MNI. Technically, this is an improper prior because it should run out to $N = \infty$, but the support from the data falls off rapidly, so there is no danger in truncating the prior at 343 (the MNI of $L + R - P$, or 93, plus 250). Also shown is the analytical solution where there is the assumption of a uniform prior for the recovery probability [labeled "Hypg (uniform recovery)" and shown with a dotted line], which is the basis for the MLNI (Chapman's estimator). Note that the simulation recovers the analytical posterior distribution of N under a uniform prior for N, because this is literally how the simulation was run. Because we required that the simulated number of pairs equaled the observed number of pairs, very few (only about 4%) of the simulations were accepted. In ABC, one typically relaxes the requirement that the simulated data are identical to the actual data because this is typically an unattainable goal. If we require only that the simulated P be in the range of 17 to 19 (inclusive), then about 12% of the simulations are accepted. For a required range of 16–20, the acceptance rate rises to 20%, and for a range of 15–21, the acceptance rate rises to 29%. As we become more "liberal" in the

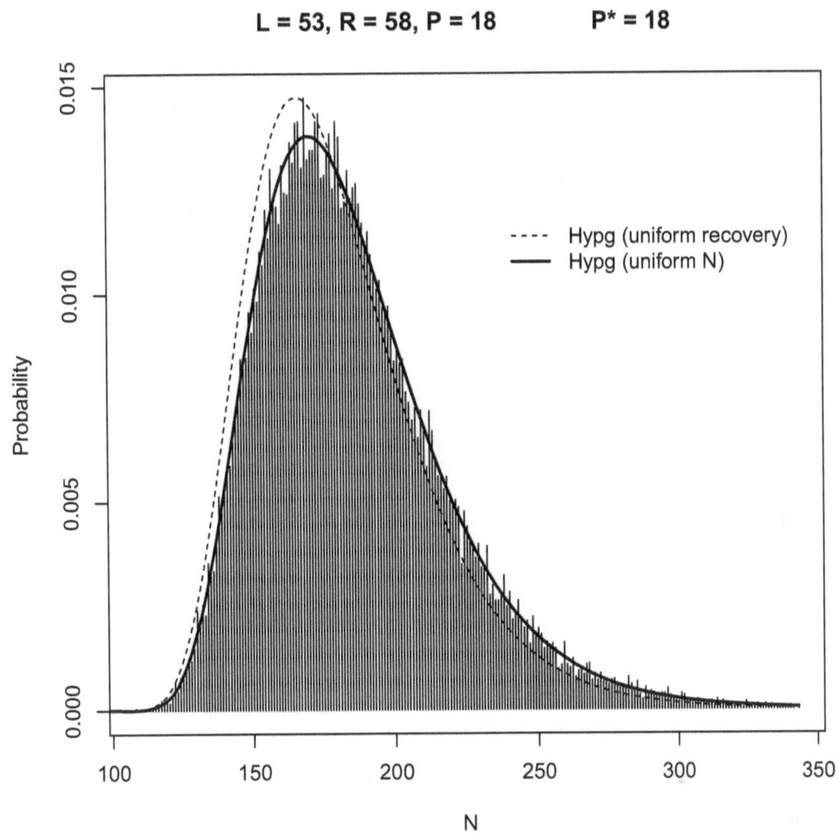

Figure 9-3

Approximate Bayesian computation (ABC) of the number of individuals in which the simulated number of counted bone pairs (P^*) must equal the observed count. "Hypg (uniform recovery)" is the analytical result assuming a uniform prior for the recovery probability and a hypergeometric distribution for the number of bone pairs. "Hypg (uniform N)" assumes a uniform distribution for the number of individuals.

range of simulations that we will accept, the distribution of simulated values becomes "heavier" in the tails. This is shown in Figure 9-4 for the 15–21 range on *P*.

The ABC method is often referred to as a "likelihood-free" method because it does not require the likelihood function. As such, one would not ordinarily be able to compare the results from ABC to analytical results calculated from the likelihood function because the likelihood function does not exist in closed form. This means that in Figures 9-3 and 9-4, we ordinarily would not be able to draw the two curves based on the likelihood function from the hypergeometric distribution. As such, the usual path in ABC analyses is to start with a high "tolerance" for accepting simulations and then move to lower tolerances, stopping at the point where the approximate posterior distributions do not change substantially. But this all begs

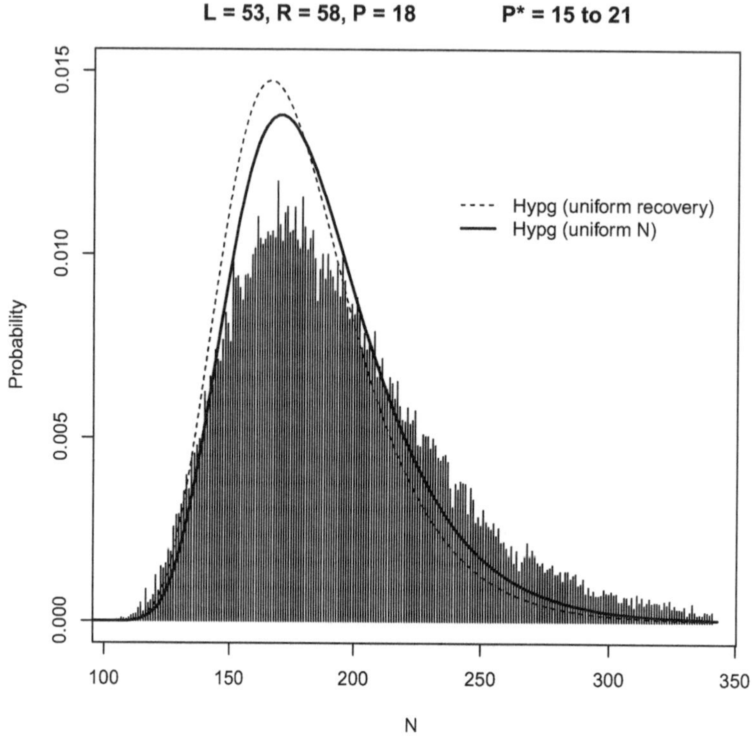

Figure 9-4
As in Figure 9-3, but allowing the simulated pair counts to range as far as three above or below the actual count. Note how the histogram from ABC (the vertical lines) has begun to "grow" in the tails relative to the analytical calculations.

the question why one would use a "likelihood-free" method (or Nikita and Lahr's cruder simulation method) for a model where the likelihood function is well understood and easy to evaluate. In fact, we see no rationale for replacing the straightforward calculations that underlie the MLNI with any computer simulation method.

Some Comments on Counting Pairs of Bones

There is one possible benefit of using the ABC method, which is that it allows for some "play" in the number of counted bone pairs because simulations need not exactly reproduce the number of pairs to be accepted. Failure to recognize some pairs increases the estimated *N*, but similarly overcounting pairs (in other words, counting more pairs than actually exist in the recovered bones) will decrease the estimated *N*. When the number of recovered bones is high, then the ability to count pairs using only visual matching becomes less of a reasonable option. For example, in Nikita and Lahr's example from Jebel Moya, with 58 right femora and 53 left femora, there are 3,074 ($R \times L$) possible pairings to be checked if one systematically considers all possible pairs. This could be decreased by first size sorting the bones, but even so, one's ability to systematically consider plausible pairings is impeded as sample size increases. As a consequence, there has been some discussion of methods for automating the counting of pairs using measurements of antimeres (Byrd 2008; Lyman 2006; Nikita and Lahr 2011; O'Brien and Storlie 2011; Thomas et al. 2013). These methods differ both in how asymmetry between antimeres is measured and in how information on potential pairing is interpreted. Before turning to various asymmetry measures, we first examine how such information is used.

Most methods use a reference sample of known paired bones to obtain information on the similarity between a homologous measurement or measurements on left and right bones. Nikita and Lahr (2011:632) do not use a reference sample but instead consider all possible pairings in a commingled sample and "[i]f all the pairwise differences lie below a maximum acceptable level (user-defined), then the right and the left element under examination are given in the output as a potential pair." Their method is essentially used as a way to "prescreen" possible pairs so that one does not waste time trying to visually match bones of different sizes and/or shapes. Of the other methods available, they almost all use a "frequentist" approach (classical statistical hypothesis testing) that pairs two bones, measures the departure between those bones, and then compares that departure to the reference sample to decide whether the observed departure is equal to or greater than that expected from the paired bones in the reference sample. This is clearest in Byrd's (2008:203) work, where he writes that "[a] low p-value provides a measure of the strength of evidence against the null, which can also be taken as evidence for how atypical the case specimens are assuming they originate in the same individual." In contrast to the frequentist approach, O'Brien and Storlie (2011) adopt an implicitly Bayesian approach that calculates the posterior probabilities. We will argue here that the frequentist approach to the problem of forming (and counting) pairs is useful while the Bayesian approach is decidedly not.

Before turning to our argument in favor of the frequentist approach, we first need to consider the various measures that have been used in the past to measure similarity among actual pairs as well as among potential pairs. Perhaps the simplest measure is Byrd's (2008:Eq. 10.1) sum of right minus left measurements. This measure has the advantage that under the central limit theorem, it should be normally distributed, but it has the disadvantage that a value of zero indicates symmetry only if one is using a single bone measurement on the left and right sides. With two or more measurements per side, measurements that are larger on the right may be "balanced" by measurements that are larger on the left. Recognizing this, Thomas et al. (2013) argued for using what they referred to as the "M statistic," which is

$$M = \frac{2|x_L - x_R|}{x_L + x_R}, \tag{9-7}$$

where x_L and x_R are homologous measurements on the left and right sides. The absolute value in the numerator takes care of the problem of having left and right sides canceling one another out when there are multiple measurements. However, Thomas et al. (2013) presented their "M statistic" for a single measurement only on the left and right sides, so the problem of sides "canceling out" is not an issue. Unlike Byrd's simple measure, Thomas et al.'s measure will have a folded normal distribution because of the absolute value. Because of this more complicated distribution, they give a table of 90th and 95th empirical percentile values from their reference data. And while Thomas et al. (2013:954) note that "M is similar to the measure of standardized asymmetry developed by Van Valen," their "M statistic" is identical to a fluctuating asymmetry measure that Palmer and Strobeck (1986) refer to as "Index 2." This is a commonly used measure in the literature on fluctuating asymmetry.

Lyman (2006) suggested using the Euclidean distance between two measurements on the left and two on the right, or

$$\sqrt{(x_{L1} - x_{R1})^2 + (x_{L2} - x_{R2})^2}, \tag{9-8}$$

where the subscripted numerals give the "variable numbers" on the two sides. If we assume that measurements are correlated only between the sides and that homologous measurements have equal variances across the sides, then

$$\sum_{k=1}^{t} \left(\frac{x_{Lk} - x_{Rk}}{\sigma_k^2} \right)^2 \tag{9-9}$$

should have a chi-squared distribution with t degrees of freedom, where t is the number of homologous measurements measured on both the left and right sides. Equation 9-9 is just the squared Euclidean distance scaled by the variances.

O'Brien and Storlie (2011) used the most elaborate of the methods discussed here for assessing departures between known left and right pairs and possible pairs. Some of their description of methods differs slightly from the R code they provide as their appendix B.1. Our description here follows the R code and points out where O'Brien and Storlie's description differs from the code. Within their reference sample of known pairs, O'Brien and Storlie form vectors within individuals that are the right-side measurements subtracted from the left-side measurements. We write these as row vectors $\mathbf{d}_i = \mathbf{X}_{iL} - \mathbf{X}_{iR}$, where i indexes individuals within the reference data. Stacking these vectors into the $i \times t$ matrix $\mathbf{D}$ and finding the vector of column means $\boldsymbol{\mu}$ gives the average difference between left and right sides within measurements. In their text, O'Brien and Storlie claim that they assume $\boldsymbol{\mu} = 0$, but such is not the case in their R code, where they also have an error in that they pass the $\mathbf{D}$ matrix where they intended the vector of mean differences. From the $\mathbf{D}$ matrix, O'Brien and Storlie also calculate the $t \times t$ variance–covariance matrix $\boldsymbol{\Sigma}$. They then give the multivariate probability density function for observing a vector $\mathbf{d}$ given $\boldsymbol{\mu}$ and $\boldsymbol{\Sigma}$. Given that they use this density function to calculate posterior probabilities, we can ignore any constants and instead write the density as a proportion. This gives

$$f(\mathbf{d} \mid \boldsymbol{\mu}, \Sigma) \, \alpha \exp\left(-0.5(\mathbf{d} - \boldsymbol{\mu})' \Sigma^{-1} (\mathbf{d} - \boldsymbol{\mu}) \right). \tag{9-10}$$

Now for a sample of commingled bones we can use Equation 9-10 for all pairings. As an example, we can use O'Brien and Storlie's reference data from their Table 2 and reuse a portion of their reference data as a test case. Specifically, for the test case, we use the right-side bone measurements from individuals 1–3 (21271R, 40082R, and 42162R) and the left sides from individuals 1–6 (the left-paired bones from the previously listed individuals plus 42174L, 53505L, and 8255L). Although it is tempting to use simulated data from O'Brien and Storlie (2011; for example that in their Table 4) as the test case, these data were simulated under a different model (one that assumed equal mean measurements) than is actually used analytically in O'Brien and Storlie's approach. Applying Equation 9-10 between all pairings produces the 6×3 matrix (where rows represent left-side bones and columns represent right-side bones)

$$\mathbf{L} = \begin{bmatrix} 5\times10^{-3} & 5\times10^{-167} & 7\times10^{-52} \\ 4\times10^{-172} & 10^{-2} & 0 \\ 2\times10^{-63} & 0 & 9\times10^{-2} \\ 3\times10^{-46} & 10^{-176} & 6\times10^{-65} \\ 2\times10^{-24} & 3\times10^{-82} & 10^{-96} \\ 6\times10^{-12} & 3\times10^{-167} & 4\times10^{-42} \end{bmatrix},$$

where zero entries are less than the smallest double precision number (10^{-324}). We refer to this matrix as the **L** matrix because it contains entries that are proportional to the probabilities of getting observed data conditional on model parameters, so the elements are likelihoods. Now we can convert the preceding matrix to a column stochastic matrix by dividing each element by its appropriate column total to get

$$f(\mathbf{x}_L|\mathbf{x}_R) = \begin{bmatrix} 1 & 0 & 0 \\ 0 & 1 & 0 \\ 0 & 0 & 1 \\ 0 & 0 & 0 \\ 0 & 0 & 0 \\ 0 & 0 & 0 \end{bmatrix}, \tag{9-11}$$

or we can divide each element by its appropriate row total to get the row stochastic matrix

$$f(\mathbf{x}_R|\mathbf{x}_L) = \begin{bmatrix} 1 & 0 & 0 \\ 0 & 1 & 0 \\ 0 & 0 & 1 \\ 1 & 0 & 0 \\ 1 & 0 & 0 \\ 1 & 0 & 0 \end{bmatrix} \tag{9-12}$$

Equation 9-11 gives the posterior probability of left-bone measurements conditional on right-bone measurements (or really, the differences between measurements), and Equation 9-12 gives the posterior probability of right-bone measurements conditional on left-bone measurements. Equation 9-11 was arrived at using equal priors (of 1/6) that each of the left bones would have been paired with a given right bone, whereas Equation 9-12 was arrived at using equal priors (of 1/3) that each of the right bones would have been paired with a given left bone. These priors are then "updated" by the likelihoods to arrive at posterior probabilities.

The preceding Bayesian approach from O'Brien and Storlie (2011) suffers from two problems. First, there is the problem of how to interpret the two sets of posterior probabilities (one conditioned on the right-side bones and one conditioned on the left-side bones). O'Brien and Storlie (2011) take the rather ad hoc approach of forming two matrices, one of which has the maxima by element and the other the minima. They then "threshold" values from either their matrix of maxima or their matrix of minima to decide which bones may potentially be paired. The second, and greater, problem with their Bayesian approach is the same one that has been discussed concerning interpretation of posterior probabilities within discriminant function analysis (Ousley and Jantz 2012; Ousley et al. 2009). Specifically, in the discriminant function setting, there may be a high posterior probability that an individual is from a particular group even if that individual is "atypical" for the group. In the current setting, we may find that a left and right bone have a high posterior probability of being from the same individual even if there is great disparity between the potentially paired bones. In discriminant function analysis, one would use the "typicality probability" to assess this problem, where the typicality probability is the probability of getting a Mahalanobis distance equal to or greater than the observed distance if the individual was actually from the stated group. This approach can be easily applied to O'Brien and Storlie's (2011) method, which converts the analysis from a Bayesian one to a frequentist one. Typicality probabilities can be found using either the chi-square distribution, the F distribution, or a parametric bootstrap (Konigsberg et al. 2009). We use the simplest method here, which is the chi-square, even though it is only asymptotic (i.e., it assumes a large reference sample, which is not the case here). The Mahalanobis distance between a "case" (here, the left minus right measurements for a given pair) and the centroid (here, the vector of mean differences for known pairs, or $\boldsymbol{\mu}$) is asymptotically distributed as a chi-square with the number of degrees of freedom equal to the number of homologous measurements (in this case, six). The Mahalanobis distance is

$$(\mathbf{d}-\boldsymbol{\mu})'\boldsymbol{\Sigma}^{-1}(\mathbf{d}-\boldsymbol{\mu}) \tag{9-13}$$

which is already available as part of the calculation in Equation 9-10. Applying this to the current problem gives the following matrix of Mahalanobis distances

$$\begin{bmatrix} 11 & 766 & 236 \\ 789 & 9 & 1746 \\ 288 & 1683 & 5 \\ 210 & 810 & 296 \\ 109 & 375 & 442 \\ 52 & 767 & 191 \end{bmatrix}$$

When these Mahalanobis distances are referred to a chi-square distribution with six degrees of freedom, the corresponding typicality probabilities are

$$\begin{bmatrix} 0.0883 & 0 & 0 \\ 0 & 0.1736 & 0 \\ 0 & 0 & 0.5438 \\ 0 & 0 & 0 \\ 0 & 0 & 0 \\ 2\times10^{-9} & 0 & 0 \end{bmatrix}$$

This matrix shows that the last three left bones cannot be paired with any of the right bones, and the first three left bones can be paired with the first three right bones.

The decisions we might make about which bones to pair with one another using the typicality probabilities do not differ from what we would decide using the posterior probabilities conditioning on the right-side measurements. But let us consider a second example in which we use the right bones from individuals 1–3 (21271R, 40082R, and 42162R) and the left sides from individuals 4–9 (42174L, 53505L, 8255B, 8263B, 8363B, and 8403B). In this case, there are no truly paired bones. The posterior probabilities conditioning on the right sides are

$$f(\mathbf{x}_L|\mathbf{x}_R)=\begin{bmatrix} 0 & 0 & 0 \\ 0 & 1 & 0 \\ 1 & 0 & 0 \\ 0 & 0 & 0 \\ 0 & 0 & 0 \\ 0 & 0 & 1 \end{bmatrix},$$

and conditioning on the left sides are

$$f(\mathbf{x}_R|\mathbf{x}_L)=\begin{bmatrix} 1 & 0 & 0 \\ 1 & 0 & 0 \\ 1 & 0 & 0 \\ 0.91 & 0 & 0.09 \\ 0 & 0 & 1 \\ 0 & 0 & 1 \end{bmatrix}$$

None of the typicality probabilities from this second example are greater than 10^{-6}, showing that it would be extremely unlikely to get the observed departures (or greater departures) between any of the left bones paired with any of the right bones if those pairs had actually originated from the same individual.

Final Considerations

Data loss from skeletal assemblages can occur as a result of many distinct processes (i.e., taphonomic forces). Haglund and Sorg published two edited volumes dealing precisely with forensic taphonomy (Haglund and Sorg 1997, 2002) showing that data loss is possible in both ancient and recent contexts. Any study that attempts to draw conclusions based on commingled human remains needs to implement the most appropriate quantification technique available.

This chapter has discussed three different quantification techniques: the MNI, the LI, and the MLNI. For human skeletal remains, the most common option employed by physical anthropologists for the purpose of estimating the original population size has been the MNI. The results revealed through computer simulation and the analysis of an actual commingled assemblage show that the MLNI is the best estimator of the original death assemblage, not the MNI. The strength of this technique is that it can account for taphonomic biases, which are an inherent part of archaeological samples and forensic contexts, with negligible effects to the estimate. The MLNI provides a more realistic reconstruction of past population counts from commingled situations and supplies researchers with more accurate figures from which to present demographic results and/or to establish identifications. The MNI should still be reported, but alongside the MLNI instead of alone. Similar results between the MNI and MLNI only provide added support for the reliability of the estimates and a high recovery rate. Discrepancies between the two methods demonstrate the MNI's correlation with the recovery rate and its inability to estimate the original population when data loss has occurred.

This chapter has also examined approximate Bayesian computation (ABC) as an alternative to analytical use of the MLNI. This application was suggested as a formalization of the ad hoc procedures used by Nikita and Lahr (2011). We find little utility in ABC for this setting because the direct calculation of the likelihood for the MLNI is straightforward. The one possible advantage to using ABC is that it can allow for uncertainty in the number of counted pairs. It consequently expands highest posterior density regions for the estimated number of individuals relative to the MLNI which does not account for uncertainty in pair counts.

Overall, positive results were found for the reliability of visual pair matching with selected skeletal elements from a relatively small number of individuals. If fragmentation is extensive or preservation is extremely poor so that accurate pair matches are impossible to determine, the MLNI for multiple elements is prone to gross miscalculations due to the multiplicative nature of the procedure. In situations of recovery greater than 50%, good preservation, and at least seven pairs, the use of the MLNI provides an accurate assessment of the actual population that contributed to the recovered osteological assemblage. It is also possible to apply confidence intervals to these estimates, a feature not available with the MNI. Visual pair matching does become increasingly difficult as the size of an assemblage increases, and it is for this reason that various authors (Byrd 2008; Byrd and Adams 2003; Lyman 2006; Nikita and Lahr 2011; O'Brien and Storlie 2011) have proposed metric methods for forming matches, or for reducing the number of potential bone pairs to assess visually. Kendell and Willey (2014:100) have been particularly critical of the LI and MLNI when applied to large samples, writing that their chapter "refutes one assertion of LI and MLNI calculations, namely, the assumption that loss of elements is random (Adams & Konigsberg, 2008, p. 245)." Neither the LI nor the MLNI is actually based on "the assumption that loss of elements is random," but rather that sampling of left and right sides is independent. This is made clear in Adams and Konigsberg (2004:141) where they write "…we assume independence for sampling of rights and lefts…."

Kendell and Willey do make a compelling argument that right and left sides are ordinarily not sampled independently because of correlation between the sides. For example, an individual with high bone mineral density on the left would be expected to have high bone mineral density on the right so that the probability of sampling the left and right bones is increased for that individual. Ultimately, such left/right correlations decrease the LI and the MLNI from their true values. In a "worst-case scenario" where the correlation between sides is at its maximum ($\rho = 1$), the number of pairs will equal $\min(L,R)$, and both the LI and the MLNI will equal $\max(L,R)$, which is the traditional MNI. This relationship can be difficult to understand, so we examine it in more detail using the final two figures in this chapter.

The limiting case in which the correlation between sides is at its maximum of 1.0 can mislead one's intuition, as one might mistakenly assume that perfect correlation mandates that no unpaired bones are sampled. This mistaken assumption comes from thinking that the correlation is for the sampling events themselves, so that if a left bone is sampled, then the paired right must be sampled; conversely, if the left bone is not sampled, then the right bone from the same body cannot be sampled. The correlation instead comes from the relationship between the "latent traits" for the left and right sides. These latent traits can be thought of as continuously distributed traits that influence whether a given left-side bone is sampled and whether a given right-side bone is sampled. These latent traits could include, for example, bone mineral density, age at death, and other factors specific to the bones. We assume that the left and right sides each have a standard normal distribution (with a mean of zero and variance of one), and in our original use of the MLNI, we also assumed that the latent traits were uncorrelated. On each of the latent traits, we establish a "threshold" so that if the latent trait for a particular bone is above the threshold, then the bone enters the sample. We used a threshold of 0.7 for the left side (equivalent to a sampling probability of about 0.24 from the upper tail of the normal) and 0.5 for the right (a sampling probability of about 0.31). Figure 9-5 shows a single simulation where the bivariate correlation was assumed to equal 0.999. The figure shows a 95% isodensity ellipse with its means at 0,0 and with a correlation of 0.999 and variances in both directions of 1.0. We then simulate 500 (bivariate) cases, compare the simulated latent traits to the thresholds, and count the number of individuals with no observed bones (350), the number with the left bone but not the right observed (0), the number with both bones observed (116), and the number with the right bone observed but not the left (34). The MNI from this example is $116 + 34 = 150$, the number of right bones. The MLNI is $117 \times 151 \div 117 - 1 = 150$, identical with both the MNI and the LI.

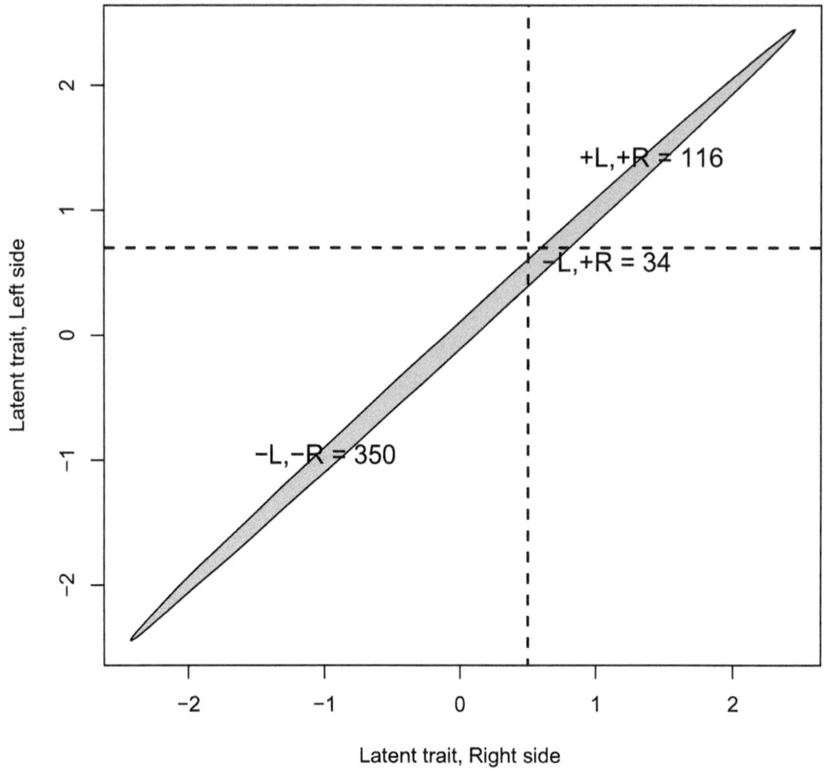

Figure 9-5
Simulation of sampling left and right bones from 500 individuals in which the latent traits for sampling bones have a standard bivariate normal distribution with a correlation of 0.999. The gray ellipse is the 0.95% isodensity ellipse, and sampling thresholds are at 0.5 (vertical dashed line) for the right side and 0.7 (horizontal dashed line) for the left side. Counts are given for "*–L,–R*" (neither bone sampled), "*+L,+R*" (both bones sampled), and "*–L,+R*" (only right bone sampled).

Figure 9-6 shows the relationship between the MLNI and MNI under the "ideal" case where there is no correlation between sides, an intermediate case where the correlation between sides is 0.7, and the scenario from the previous paragraph where the correlation is 0.999. To draw this figure, we simulated 1,000 replicates at each correlation value, and within each replicate, we simulated 500 individuals. We then calculated the MLNI and max(L,R) (the traditional MNI) for each replicate and plotted them in the figure, enclosing the simulations at correlations of 0.0 and 0.7 within their convex hulls and plotting the line of identity for simulations at a correlation of 0.999. Note that at a correlation of 0.0, the convex hull is centered vertically (for the MLNI) near the actual number of individuals (500). The median MLNI from these simulations was 496. The MNI is (as the name implies) a minimum estimate, having a median value of 154. At the correlation value of 0.7, the MLNI estimates have dropped considerably to a median of 223, while at the unrealistically high correlation value of 0.999, the MLNI and

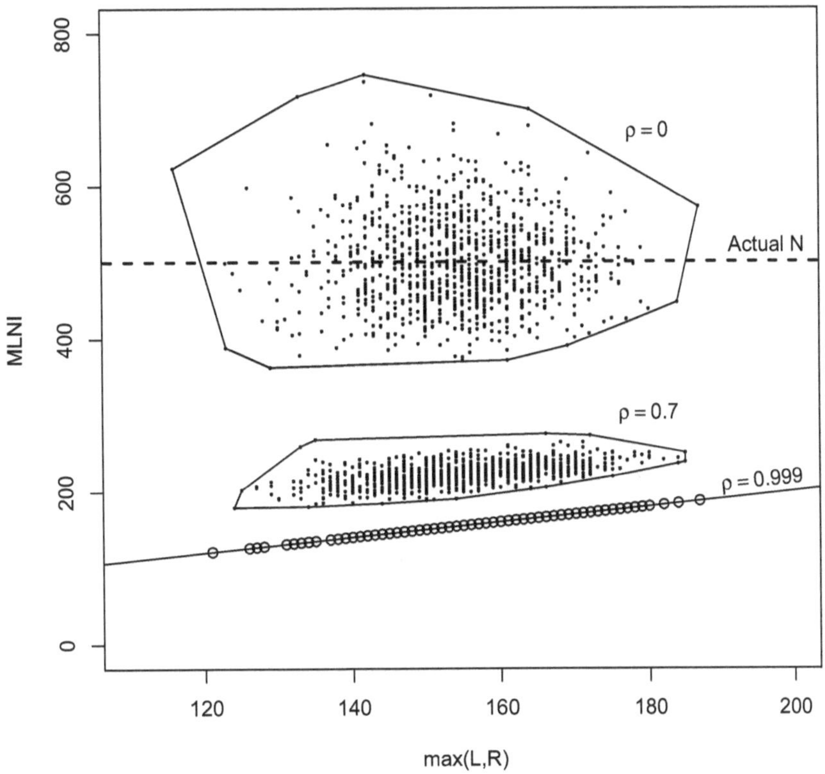

Figure 9-6
Simulations as in Figure 9-5, but with 1,000 iterates of sampling from 500 individuals at left, right correlation values of 0.0, 0.7, and 0.999. The iterates for correlation values of 0.0 and 0.7 are enclosed by their convex hulls, while the iterates for correlation values of 0.999 are indicated with a line of identity.

MNI are identical, having a median of 154. Were we to choose the traditional MNI over the MLNI in an actual setting, we would be guilty of substituting an estimator that we know gives us an underestimate, versus an estimator that may be giving us an underestimate if the correlation between left and right sides is high.

References

Adams, B.J., 1996. The Use of the Lincoln/Peterson Index for Quantification and Interpretation of Commingled Human Remains. Unpublished master's thesis. Department of Anthropology, University of Tennessee, Knoxville.

Adams, B.J., Konigsberg, L.W., 2004. Estimation of the most likely number of individuals from commingled human skeletal remains. Am. J. Phys. Anthropol. 125 (2), 138–151.

Adams, B.J., Konigsberg, L.W., 2008. How many people? Determining the number of individuals represented by commingled human remains. In: Adams, B.J., Byrd, J.E. (Eds.), Recovery, Analysis, and Identification of Commingled Human Remains. Springer, Totowa, NJ, pp. 241–255.

Allen, J., Guy, J.B.M., 1984. Optimal estimations of individuals in archaeological faunal assemblages: how minimal is the MNI? Archaeol. Oceania. 19, 41–47.

Badgley, C., 1986. Counting individuals in mammalian fossil assemblages from fluvial environments. Palios 1, 328–338.
Bass, W.M., Rucker, M.D., 1976. Preliminary Investigation of Artifact Association in an Arikara Cemetery (Larson Site), Walworth County, South Dakota. National Geographic Research Reports, 1968 Projects.
Beaumont, M.A., Zhang, W., Balding, D.J., 2002. Approximate Bayesian computation in population genetics. Genetics 162 (4), 2025–2035.
Boattini, A., Castrì, L., Sarno, S., Useli, A., Cioffi, M., Sazzini, M., et al., 2013. mtDNA variation in East Africa unravels the history of Afro–Asiatic groups. Am. J. Phys. Anthropol. 150, 375–385.
Brain, C.K., 1976. Some principles in the interpretation of bone accumulations associated with man. In: Isaac, G.L., McCown, E.R. (Eds.), Human Origins. W.A. Benjamin, Menlo Park, CA, pp. 97–116.
Byrd, J.E., 2008. Models and methods for osteometric sorting. In: Adams, B.J., Byrd, J.E. (Eds.), Recovery, Analysis, and Identification of Commingled Human Remains. Springer, Totowa, NJ, pp. 199–220.
Byrd, J.E., Adams, B.J., 2003. Osteometric sorting of commingled human remains. J. Forensic Sci. 48 (4), 717–724.
Byrd, J.E., Adams, B.J., Leppo, L.M., Harrington, R.J., 2003. Resolution of large-scale commingling issues: lessons from CILHI and ICMP. Proceedings of the Paper presented at the 55th Annual Meeting of the American Academy of Forensic Sciences, Chicago, IL.
Catlin, G., 1989. North American Indians. Viking, New York, NY.
Chapman, D.G., 1951. Some properties of the hypergeometric distribution with applications to zoological sample census. Univ. Calif. Public. Stat. 1, 131–159.
Chase, P.G., Hagaman, R.M., 1987. Minimum number of individuals and its alternatives: a probability theory perspective. OSSA 13, 75–86.
Cormack, R.M., 1992. Interval estimation for mark-recapture studies of closed populations. Biometrics 48, 567–576.
Denig, E.T., 1961. Five Indian Tribes of the Upper Missouri. University of Oklahoma Press, Norman, OK.
Dennis, B., 1996. Discussion: should ecologists become Bayesians? Ecologol. Appl. 6, 1095–1103.
Fieller, N.R.J., Turner, A., 1982. Number estimation in vertebrate samples. J. Archaeol. Sci. 9, 49–62.
Gordon, C.C., Buikstra, J.E., 1981. Soil pH, bone preservation, and sampling bias at mortuary sites. Am. Antiquity 46 (3), 566–571.
Grinnell, G.B., 1910. Coup and scalp among the Plains Indians. Am. Anthropol. 12, 296–310.
Haglund, W.D., Sorg, M.H. (Eds.), 1997. Forensic Taphonomy: The Postmortem Fate of Human Remains. CRC Press, Boca Raton, FL.
Haglund, W.D., Sorg, M.H. (Eds.), 2002. Advances in Forensic Taphonomy: Method, Theory, and Archaeological Perspectives. CRC Press, Boca Raton, FL.
Hollimon, S.E., Owsley, D.W., 1994. Osteology of the Fay Tolton site: implications for warfare during the Initial Middle Missouri Variant. In: Owsley, D.W., Jantz, R.L. (Eds.), Skeletal Biology in the Great Plains: Migration, Warfare, Health, and Subsistence. Smithsonian Institution Press, Washington, D.C., pp. 345–353.
Horton, D.R., 1984. Minimum numbers: a consideration. J. Archaeol. Sci. 11, 255–271.
Hudson, J., 1993. The impacts of domestic dogs on bone in forager camps. In: Hudson, J. (Ed.), From Bones to Behavior. Southern Illinois University, Carbondale, IL, pp. 301–323. Occasional Paper No. 21.
Hufthammer, A.K., Bratbak, O.F., Indrelid, S., 2011. A study of bone remains and butchery patterns from medieval mass-hunting of reindeer in the South Norwegian mountain districts. Quaternary Int. 238 (1), 55–62.
Johnson, C.M., 1994. A Chronology of Middle Missouri Plains Village Sites. National Museum of Natural History, Smithsonian Institution. Washington, D.C. Unpublished report submitted to the Department of Anthropology.
Kendell, A., Willey, P., 2014. Crow Creek bone bed commingling: relationship between bone mineral density and minimum number of individuals and its effect on paleodemographic analyses. In: Osterholtz, A.J., Baustian, K.M., Martin, D.L. (Eds.), Commingled and Disarticulated Human Remains. Springer, New York, NY, pp. 85–104.
Klein, R.G., Cruz-Uribe, K., 1984. The Analysis of Animal Bones from Archeological Sites. University of Chicago Press, Chicago, IL.

Konigsberg, L.W., Algee-Hewitt, B.F.B., Steadman, D.W., 2009. Estimation and evidence in forensic anthropology: sex and race. Am. J. Phys. Anthropol. 139 (1), 77–90.

Konigsberg, L.W., Frankenberg, S.R., 2013. Bayes in biological anthropology. Am. J. Phys. Anthropol. 152 (S57), 153–184.

L'Abbé, E.N., Loots, M., Keough, N., 2008. The Matjes River Rock Shelter: a description of the skeletal assemblage. South Afr. Archaeol. Bull. 63 (187), 61–68.

Lee, P.M., 1997. Bayesian Statistics: An Introduction, second ed. Oxford University Press, New York, NY.

Lyman, R.L., 1987. Zooarchaeology and taphonomy: a general consideration. J. Ethnobiol. 7, 93–117.

Lyman, R.L., 1993. Density-mediated attrition of bone assemblages: new insights. In: Hudson, J. (Ed.), From Bones to Behavior. Center for Archaeological Investigations, Carbondale, IL, pp. 324–341.

Lyman, R.L., 1994. Vertebrate Taphonomy. Cambridge University Press, Cambridge.

Lyman, R.L., 2006. Identifying bilateral pairs of deer (*Odocoileus* sp.) bones: how symmetrical is symmetrical enough? J. Archaeol. Sci. 33 (9), 1256–1265.

Marean, C.W., Spencer, L.M., 1991. Impact of carnivore ravaging on zooarchaeological measures of element abundance. Am. Antiquity 56 (4), 645–658.

Nagaoka, T., Abe, M., Shimatani, K., 2012. Estimation of mortality profiles from non-adult human skeletons in Edo-period Japan. Anthropol. Sci. 120 (2), 115–128.

Nikita, E., 2012. Estimation of the original number of individuals using multiple skeletal elements. Int. J. Osteoarchaeol. http://dx.doi.org/10.1002/oa.2252.

Nikita, E., Lahr, M.M., 2011. Simple algorithms for the estimation of the initial number of individuals in commingled skeletal remains. Am. J. Phys. Anthropol. 146 (4), 629–636.

O'Brien, M., Storlie, C.B., 2011. An alternative bilateral refitting model for zooarchaeological assemblages. J. Taphonomy (9), 245–268.

Olsen, S.L., Shipman, P., 1994. Cutmarks and perimortem treatment of skeletal remains on the Northern Plains. In: Owsley, D.W., Jantz, R.L. (Eds.), Skeletal Biology in the Great Plains: Migration, Warfare, Health and Subsistence. Smithsonian Institution Press, Washington, D.C., pp. 377–387.

Ousley, S.D., Jantz, R.L., 2012. Fordisc 3 and statistical methods for estimating sex and ancestry. In: Dirkmatt, D.C. (Ed.), A Companion to Forensic Anthropology. Wiley-Blackwell, London, pp. 311–329.

Ousley, S., Jantz, R., Freid, D., 2009. Understanding race and human variation: why forensic anthropologists are good at identifying race. Am. J. Phys.l Anthrop. 139 (1), 68–76.

Owsley, D.W., 1994. Warfare in coalescent tradition populations of the Northern Plains. In: Owsley, D.W., Jantz, R.L. (Eds.), Skeletal Biology in the Great Plains: Migration, Warfare, Health and Subsistence. Smithsonian Institution Press, Washington, D.C., pp. 333–344.

Owsley, D.W., Berryman, H.E., Bass, W.M., 1977. Demographic and osteological evidence for warfare at the Larson Site, South Dakota. Plains Anthropol. 13, 119–131.

Palmer, A.R., Strobeck, C., 1986. Fluctuating asymmetry: measurement, analysis, patterns. Annu. Rev. Ecol. Systematics 17, 391–421.

Plug, I., 1984. MNI counts, pits and features. In: Hall, M., Avery, G., Avery, D.M., Wilson, M.L., Humphreys, A.J.B. (Eds.), Frontiers: Southern African Archaeology Today. British Archaeological Reports International Series 207, Oxford, pp. 357–362.

Pritchard, J.K., Seielstad, M.T., Perez-Lezaun, A., Feldman, M.W., 1999. Population growth of human Y chromosomes: a study of Y chromosome microsatellites. Mol. Biol. Evol. 16 (12), 1791–1798.

Ray, N., Excoffier, L., 2009. Inferring past demography using spatially explicit population genetic models. Hum. Biol. 81 (3), 141–157.

Ringrose, T.J., 1993. Bone counts and statistics: a critique. J. Archaeol. Sci. 20, 121–157.

Roberts, H.V., 1967. Informative stopping rules and inferences about population size. J. Am. Stat. Assoc. 62 (319), 763–775.

Robson, D.S., Regier, H.A., 1964. Sample size in Petersen mark-recapture experiments. T. Am. Fish. Soc. 93, 215–226.

Seber, G.A.F., 1973. The Estimation of Animal Abundance and Related Parameters. Griffin, London.

Skinner, M.F., York, H.P., Connor, M.A., 2002. Postburial disturbance of graves in Bosnia-Herzegovina. In: Haglund, W.D., Sorg, M.H. (Eds.), Advances in Forensic Taphonomy: Method, Theory, and Archaeological Perspectives. CRC Press, Boca Raton, FL, pp. 293–308.

Suby, J.A., Guichón, R.A., 2010. Los restos óseos humanos de al colección de la Misión Salesiana "La Candelaria" (Río Grande, Argentina). Magallania Chile 38 (2), 151–164.

Tavaré, S., Balding, D.J., Griffiths, R.C., Donnelly, P., 1997. Inferring coalescence times from DNA sequence data. Genetics 145 (2), 505–518.

Thomas, R.M., Ubelaker, D.H., Byrd, J.E., 2013. Tables for the metric evaluation of pair–matching of human skeletal elements. J. Forensic Sci. 58 (4), 952–956.

Tsutaya, T., Yoneda, M., 2013. WARN: an R package for quantitative reconstruction of weaning ages in archaeological populations using bone collagen nitrogen isotope ratios. In: arXiv preprint. Available from http://arxiv.org/abs/1304.2468.

Turner, A., 1980. Minimum number estimation offers minimal insight in faunal analysis. OSSA 7, 199–201.

Turner, A., 1983. The quantification of relative abundances in fossil and subfossil bone assemblages. Ann. Trans. Mus. 33, 311–321.

Turner, A., 1984. Behavioural inferences based on frequencies in bone assemblages from archaeological sites. In: Hall, M., Avery, G., Avery, D.M., Wilson, M.L., Humphreys, A.J.B. (Eds.), Frontiers: Southern African Archaeology Today. British Archaeological Reports International Series 207, Oxford, pp. 363–366.

Turner, A., Fieller, N.R.J., 1985. Considerations of minimum numbers: a response to Horton. J. Archaeol. Sci. 12, 477–483.

Turner, B.M., Van Zandt, T., 2012. A tutorial on approximate Bayesian computation. J. Math. Psychol. 56 (2), 69–85.

Waldron, T., 1987. The relative survival of the human skeleton: implications for palaeopathology. In: Boddington, A., Garland, A.N., Janaway, R.C. (Eds.), Death, Decay, and Reconstruction. Manchester University Press, Manchester, pp. 55–64.

White, T.E., 1953. A method of calculating the dietary percentage of various food animals utilized by aboriginal peoples. Am. Antiquity 4, 396–398.

Willey, P., 1990. Prehistoric Warfare on the Great Plains: Skeletal Analysis of the Crow Creek Massacre Victims. Garland, New York, NY.

Willey, P., Galloway, A., Snyder, L., 1997. Bone mineral density and survival of elements and element portions in the bones of the Crow Creek Massacre victims. Am. J. Phys. Anthropol. 104, 513–528.

Wolter, K.M., 1990. Capture-recapture estimation in the presence of a known sex ratio. Biometrics 46, 157–162.

CHAPTER 10

Assessment of Commingled Human Remains Using a GIS-Based and Osteological Landmark Approach

Nicholas P. Herrmann[1], Joanne Bennett Devlin[2], Jessica C. Stanton[3]

[1]*Department of Anthropology and Middle Eastern Cultures, Cobb Institute of Archaeology, Mississippi State University;* [2]*Department of Anthropology, University of Tennessee;* [3]*Tennessee Valley Archaeological Research , Huntsville*

Introduction

The quantification of fragmentary human remains offers a challenge for physical and forensic anthropologists. Physical anthropologists frequently borrow methods and quantification techniques developed by zooarchaeologists to assess such collections. Traditionally, zooarchaeological examinations deal with highly fragmentary, commingled samples from numerous contexts. As such, the archaeofaunal literature is rich with analytical approaches to assess these complex assemblages. However, the appropriate application of zooarchaeological approaches to human bone assemblages is uncertain.

The present study examines the commingled, burned human remains from the Walker–Noe site (15Gd56) in Garrard County, Kentucky. The site is a small, early Middle Woodland Adena crematory located on the southern periphery of the Bluegrass physiographic region of the state. Extreme fragmentation of the remains precludes the use of a simple elemental coding system to generate a skeletal inventory. Osteological coding systems like Standards (Buikstra and Ubelaker 1994) or Osteoware (Wilczak and Dudar 2012) would be ineffective in capturing the fragment diversity and anatomical positions of the cranial and postcranial fragments. This chapter details the application of two quantification methods adapted to document the Walker–Noe cremated remains. One approach is based on bone landmarks (Landmark Analysis), whereas the other employs the analysis of fragment shapes within a geographic information system (GIS analysis). These two approaches to address commingling issues have roots in zooarchaeological analytical techniques. The Landmark approach is a logical extension of White's (1953) MNI estimation in which the most abundant element is determined using the most frequent landmark. The GIS approach was originally developed by zooarchaeological researchers (Marean et al. 2001) to provide both a minimum number of elements (MNE) and

Commingled Human Remains. http://dx.doi.org/10.1016/B978-0-12-405889-7.00010-1

minimum number of individuals (MNI) estimate. The two methods presented in this study have applications for both bioarchaeology and forensic anthropology. The physical anthropologist needs tools to accurately quantify the number of elements and individuals recovered from a commingled context, whether prehistoric, historic, or forensic.

Issues of Fragmentary and Commingled Human Remains

Though several measures exist for quantifying individuals represented in an assemblage, most frequently, biological anthropologists seek to estimate the minimum number of individuals (MNI). Simply, the MNI is generated by sorting elements to side of the body and recognizing the highest value as an indicator of the number of individuals present (Grayson 1984). This generates an approximation of the minimal number of individuals represented in the assemblage but cannot be considered as a reflection of the size of the population that produced the recovered assemblage. Estimations of the original population size are possible (see Adams and Konigsberg 2004; Konigsberg and Adams, this book, Chapter 9); however, extreme bone fragmentation limits the accuracy of such approaches and renders pair matching impossible. For most examinations of extremely fragmentary remains, the estimation of the MNI is an appropriate approach.

At the core of MNI assessments must lay an accurate determination of the minimum number of skeletal elements (MNE) present in a collection. Seemingly straightforward, the relationship between the MNE and MNI is, in practice, a complex one. The MNE is defined as a derived quantitative measure (Lyman 1994) and, as such, requires explicit definition as to its calculation. Lyman presents multiple examples of MNE definitions that would result in several different estimates. Similarly, MNI calculations based on elemental coding systems are susceptible to the same problems of over- or underestimation as the MNE. Given the basic practice of sorting and coding elements by context and side of body, and recognizing the highest count as indicative of the context-specific MNI, it is apparent how such values can underrepresent or potentially inflate the MNI if the context-specific values are simply summed. Adams and Konigsberg (2004) proposed a technique for estimating the most likely number of individuals (MLNI) as a variation of the Lincoln Index (LI). However, these techniques, predominantly based on pair matching, are poorly suited to extremely fragmented and cremated assemblages, as noted by Adams and Konigsberg (2004). Further, in an overview of methods for interpreting cremated remains, Mayne Correia and Beattie (2002) illustrate the lack of a cohesive analytical approach to estimating the MNI from cremated remains.

Osteological data collection manuals are lacking in coding systems for highly fragmented and taphonomically modified deposits. Buikstra and Ubelaker's (1994) osteological standards manual does provide for analysis of commingled remains, but the system is primarily useful when dealing with large fragments. Elements are to be coded according to the presence of specific percentages for the diaphysis (in thirds) and articular ends for long bones. Whole cranial elements and specific axial elements or groups of midline bones are to be recorded as such. The database recording structure presented in the standards manual (Buikstra and Ubelaker 1994) does allow for bone identification, element completeness, MNI count (based on identifiable elements), and demographic parameters. While providing a good structure for complete or near-complete skeletal recording, the methods presented in the standards manual (Buikstra and Ubelaker 1994) do not provide enough detail for highly fragmentary remains, cremations, or large commingled samples.

Church and Burgett (1996) and Burgett (1990) adapted a zooarchaeological coding system in an attempt to capture the variation in extremely fragmentary human remains. Burgett (1990) initially developed this information recording and retrieval system to document *in situ* commingled and fragmentary faunal remains. Church and Burgett (1996) describe the coding system as an alphanumeric identification hierarchy within which element, portion, and segment of the bone are identified. In addition to the identification hierarchy, Church and Burgett (1996) incorporate basic bone properties and taphonomic attributes. The properties fields constitute size, age, sex, fusion/development, and pathological conditions. The taphonomic attributes include weathering, gnawing, modification, breakage, burning, and trauma. Although this system deals with fragmentary remains far better than the Standards (Buikstra and Ubelaker 1994) approach for human remains, it still has several shortcomings. The element, portion, and segment identification hierarchy can often become cumbersome when dealing with small identifiable fragments. The analyst decides whether an element is included in the calculation of the MNE or MNI. Small fragments typically do not represent the entire coded specimen and are given a "partial" or "fragment" segment code within this system. Clearly, the inclusion of partial/fragment codes in the summary analysis would result in overestimations of both the MNE and MNI, while excluding these specimens could seriously underestimate the MNE and MNI for fragmentary samples. This is problematic given that an accurate estimation of the number of individuals represented in an assemblage is often crucial to the interpretation of site formation processes. Often with cremated and extremely fragmentary commingled remains, it is possible to identify very small fragments to side and exact position. However, these identifications may not be such that can be incorporated into an existing database or calculation system. Absent in the literature to date is a detailed recording system in biological anthropology that allows an analyst to accurately assess and estimate the MNE and MNI for highly fragmented or cremated commingled human remains.

Many of the problems considered herein are confronted in the techniques associated with landmark quantification and the GIS-based methods developed by Marean and colleagues (Abe et al. 2002; Marean et al. 2001). The landmark-based approach is familiar to bioarchaeologists and forensic anthropologists in that visual comparison for element presence can be quickly done on a limited number of remains to determine the MNI. The system proposed here is for dealing with hundreds, if not thousands, of fragments that present a diverse set of landmarks. These would be difficult to quantify visually or to lie out on a table. Thus, this method provides a systematic approach to landmark recording.

The GIS-based approach advanced by Marean and colleagues also provides a systematic approach to visually recording each fragment. These researchers developed a customized

ArcView extension, *BoneEntryGIS*, which utilizes an element-specific GIS to calculate MNE estimates. In effect, this approach facilitates a systematic means to overlay all identifiable elements, thereby generating a count of the minimum number of each element present in an assemblage. By "identifiable," we mean that the fragment can be sided and specifically positioned on a bone template. As average fragment size decreases, the number of placeable fragments will likely decrease, especially for long bones as compared to cranial elements.

For the Walker–Noe site, we use this approach as a means to overcome the inadequacies of traditional inventory systems in managing fragmentary and highly modified remains such as cremated samples. The GIS approach provides a visual inventory and an efficient method to quantify the MNE. In the present discussion, we focus on the cranial elements of an archaeologically derived assemblage from the Walker–Noe site. In an attempt to thoroughly document both the number of individuals represented in the collection and taphonomic attributes of heat exposure as an indicator of cremation practice, identifiable bone fragments were digitized and assessed with ESRI ArcGIS 10 in the spirit of the *BoneEntryGIS* software extension. The new ESRI ArcGIS platform provides many of the functions of *BoneEntryGIS* within the toolbox, which allows for the batch conversion, organization, and summation of the various shapefiles and grids. The results highlight the utility of this system for documenting highly fragmentary and taphonomically modified human remains, while also identifying potential problems in the application of this technique to human bone assemblages from both archaeological and forensic contexts.

Walker–Noe (15Gd56)

As previously mentioned, the Walker–Noe site (15Gd56) represents a small, early Middle Woodland period mound situated in the south-central Bluegrass region of Kentucky (Figure 10-1), supported by radiocarbon dates spanning from 170 B.C. to A.D. 130 (Pollack et al. 2005). Excavations at the site were conducted during the fall of 2000. Ceramics and lithic artifacts associate activity at the mound with the Adena culture. The radiocarbon dates firmly place the Walker–Noe site within the Middle Woodland period of the eastern United States. Adena is typically considered an Early Woodland culture throughout much of the Ohio River Valley; however, Late Adena does extend into the Middle Woodland period (see Anderson and Mainfort 2002; Clay 1998, 2002; Railey 1990). Commonly, Adena mounds identified in Kentucky are characterized by extended interments with few cremations within large mounded burial facilities (Railey 1990). Walker–Noe can be considered an "event-centered" site à la Clay (1998, 2002), but it is not an accretional mound. Walker–Noe appears to have been a short-use facility where the local population cremated their dead (see Pollack et al. 2005).

The extensive presence of cremains at Walker–Noe suggests a fairly unique crematory pattern from that of other documented Woodland period mounds both in design and in use

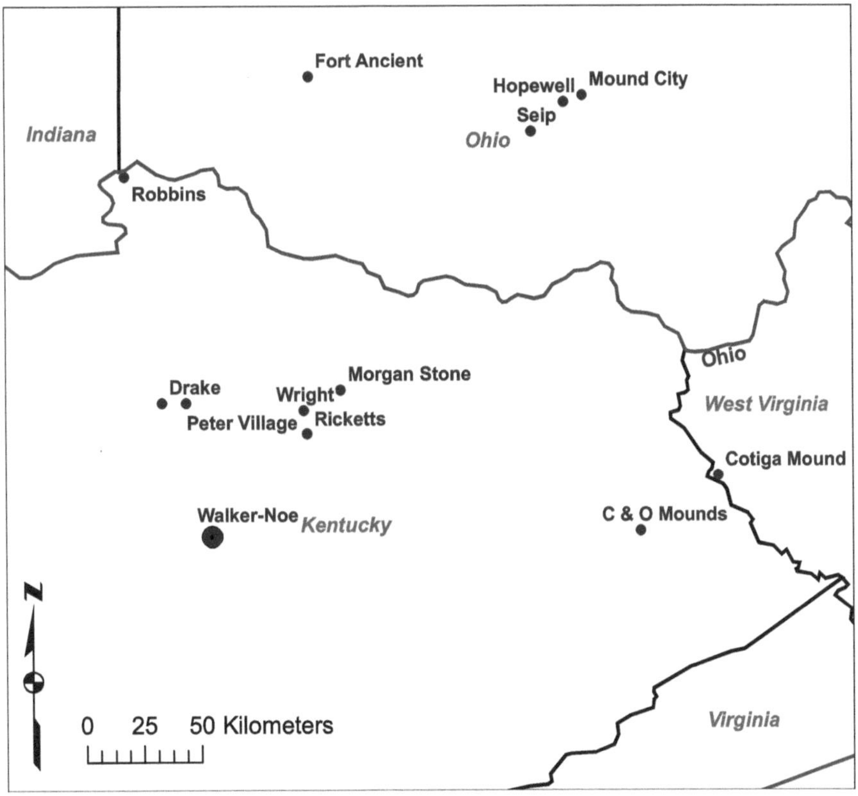

Figure 10-1
Map of Adena sites found near the Kentucky Bluegrass region *(Source: Modified from Pollack et al. 2005.)*

in this region. In particular, Walker–Noe is rather distinct in the apparent existence of *in situ* cremations evidenced by substantial burned soils. The site is marked by a centrally located feature, a 1.25-square-meter deposit five centimeters in depth of burned clay loam (Figure 10-2). The area of burned soil surrounding the central feature contained large amounts of fire-cracked dolomite (150 kilograms in total). Concentrations of cremated bone were identified directly above and around the central burned area. In addition, aggregations of burned bone were present in peripheral regions of the site. All skeletal material was located in association with wood charcoal, ash, and burned soils (Pollack et al. 2005). Several recovered projectile points/knives (PP/Ks) demonstrated attributes that suggest a contextual association with the cremation practices at the mound. Six PP/Ks did not exhibit any use-wear, interpreted to represent their preparation as ceremonial objects. However, two PP/Ks demonstrated heat alteration, indicating direct association with cremation practices. The Walker–Noe mound has been posited as a primary site for both cremation and interment, as supported by excavation and artifactual evidence (Pollack et al. 2005).

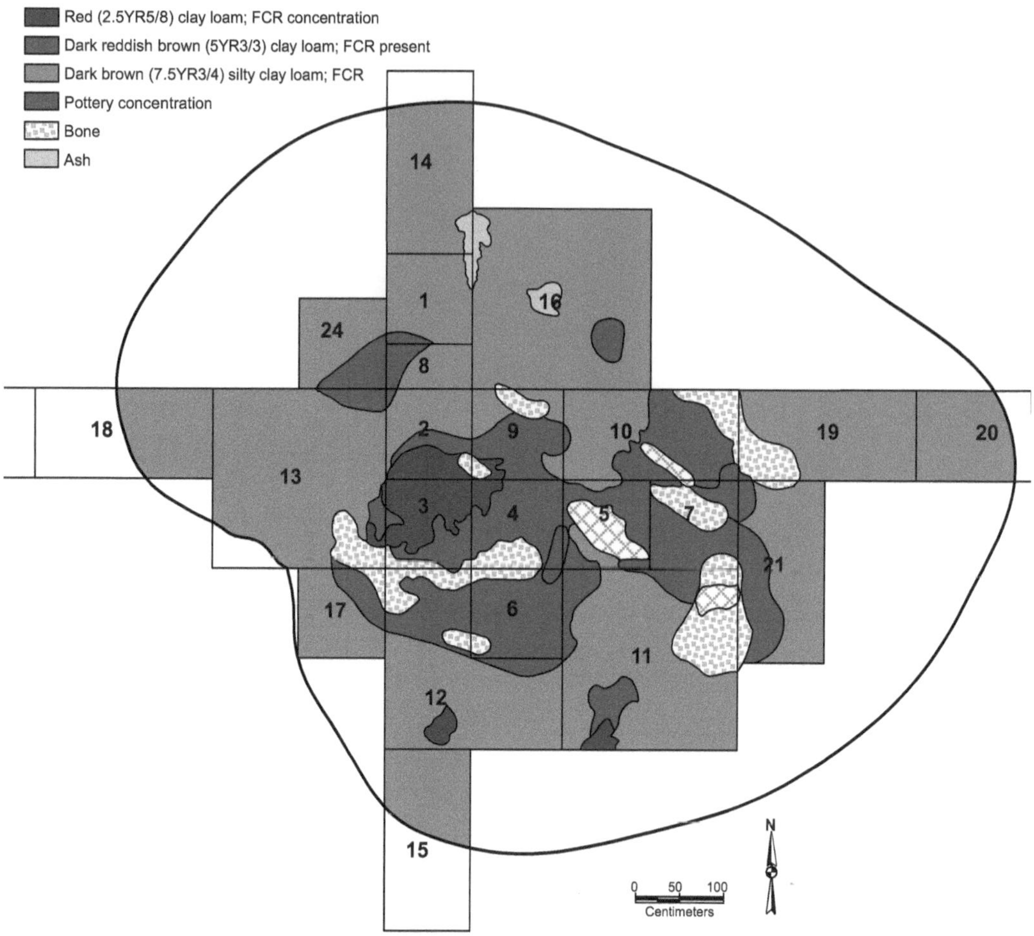

Figure 10-2
Plan map of the Walker-Noe mound *(Source: Modified from Pollack et al. 2005.)*

Walker–Noe Skeletal Analysis

A thorough examination and analysis of the human remains recovered at Walker–Noe is crucial in characterizing the mound as a crematory. Fieldwork yielded over 18 kilograms of charred and calcined human bone. The majority of fragments are less than three centimeters in diameter, with nearly all specimens exhibiting classic characteristics of extensive heat alteration, extreme fragmentation, and particular surface colors. All elements exhibit burning on both the internal and external surfaces. Little variation in color was noted across the cremation sample, with nearly all fragments displaying surface colors of gray and whitish gray, which is evidence of calcination. Surface colors associated with incomplete combustion of the organic components (i.e., browns and blacks) were not observed. In addition, fragments display extreme shrinkage and moderate degrees of warping, though the latter does vary throughout the assemblage. In addition, surface cracking and fracturing are apparent on the majority of specimens, on both endocranial and ectocranial surfaces. The condition of the Walker–Noe skeletal material reflects a thorough incineration process. The consistency of these heat alteration attributes across the sample may be indicative of intentional processing and/or repeated exposure.

Preliminary assessments of the osseous material from Walker–Noe demonstrated that identifiable cranial fragments far exceeded recognizable postcranial elements, and the bone fragments examined in this study represent the commingled remains of numerous individuals (Bennett Devlin et al. 2006; Herrmann et al. 2005; Herrmann et al. 2014). We suspect that identification of cranial fragments over postcranial remains is common in most archaeologically derived cremains. The concentration of discrete and recognizable hard-tissue features of the skull compared to undifferentiated features of long bone shafts makes the use of cranial fragments more appropriate. Given this pattern, the present analysis incorporates data only from select cranial material, but GIS templates and landmark codes were developed for the major cranial and postcranial elements. The images and the element outline shapefiles are also available for download at the website http://130.18.228.15/BoneTemplates.html.

Landmark Analysis

The first approach employed to quantify Walker–Noe is referred to as the "Landmark Method." Giovas (2009) provides an excellent example of this type of analysis for the zooarchaeological examination of a mollusk shell collection. As modified to human remains, sets of traditional and nontraditional boney landmarks that correlate to explicitly defined points on the skeleton were developed for 17 elements. These elements included seven cranial elements (frontal, maxilla, zygomatic, mandible, temporal, parietal, and occipital), the shoulder girdle and arm (clavicle, scapula, humerus, radius, and ulna), and the pelvic girdle and legs (innominates, femur, tibia, fibula, and calcaneus). The landmarks correlated to explicitly defined points on the bone. The number of landmarks ranged from nine on the calcaneus to 36 on the occipital. The approach of looking at nontraditional osseous landmarks or measures is similar to the osteometric sorting method proposed by Byrd and Adams (2003), Byrd (2008), and Byrd and LeGarde (this book, Chapter 8) with the goal of capturing as much information as possible within a limited number of observations. Each identifiable fragment is assessed to determine side (if possible) and any applicable landmarks are recorded. For the Walker–Noe analysis, a simple check box interface was developed for the cranial elements (Figure 10-3). However, a drop-down menu based on identified element was coded in Microsoft Access which also presents a visual interface of the landmarks selected and would be useful in a larger-scale analysis. Regardless of the method of coding, a query can then easily be conducted to determine the most frequently identified landmark and establish the MNE for each element included in the query. The element with the highest MNE can therefore be used as the landmark-based MNI.

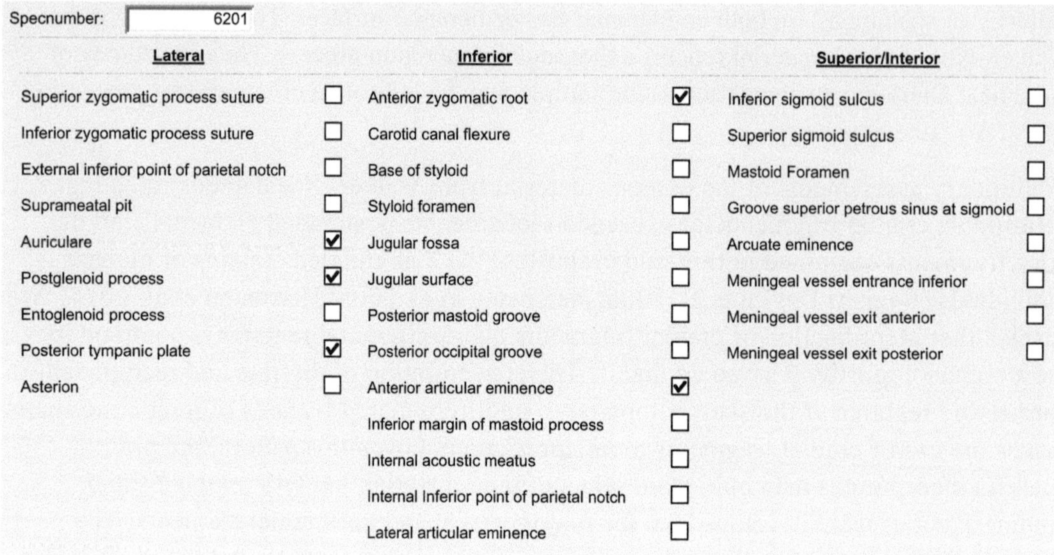

Specnumber: 6201

Lateral		Inferior		Superior/Interior	
Superior zygomatic process suture	☐	Anterior zygomatic root	☑	Inferior sigmoid sulcus	☐
Inferior zygomatic process suture	☐	Carotid canal flexure	☐	Superior sigmoid sulcus	☐
External inferior point of parietal notch	☐	Base of styloid	☐	Mastoid Foramen	☐
Suprameatal pit	☐	Styloid foramen	☐	Groove superior petrous sinus at sigmoid	☐
Auriculare	☑	Jugular fossa	☐	Arcuate eminence	☐
Postglenoid process	☑	Jugular surface	☐	Meningeal vessel entrance inferior	☐
Entoglenoid process	☐	Posterior mastoid groove	☐	Meningeal vessel exit anterior	☐
Posterior tympanic plate	☑	Posterior occipital groove	☐	Meningeal vessel exit posterior	☐
Asterion	☐	Anterior articular eminence	☑		
		Inferior margin of mastoid process	☐		
		Internal acoustic meatus	☐		
		Internal Inferior point of parietal notch	☐		
		Lateral articular eminence	☐		

Figure 10-3
Example of the temporal bone check box interface developed in Microsoft Access.

The MNE based on the landmark analysis was 40 on the right temporal and 39 on the left temporal. Both MNE values were based on the internal auditory meatus. This landmark is located on the dense petrous portion and highly identifiable by an experienced osteologist; therefore, it is not surprising that this feature represents the landmark-based MNI. Because only the temporal was used in the Landmark Method, the higher of the two MNE values is used as the MNI value.

GIS Analysis

The examination of the fragmentary human remains was conducted in several stages. Bone fragments were initially sorted into three categories of cranial, postcranial, and indeterminate elements. When possible, fragments were identified to particular element, although they were not sorted to side of the body. Due in part to this result, we focus on several craniofacial elements: frontal, zygomatic, maxilla, temporal, and mandible. These elements were selected for several reasons: (1) they have a high likelihood of recovery; (2) these elements are readily identifiable (by osteologists) in fragmentary form; and (3) these four craniofacial elements possess multiple features that facilitate recognition of small, cremated fragments as a particular portion of the bone. The last of these criteria is the most important given the concept of digitizing the fragment into an osteological GIS (or more appropriate an Osteological Information System [OIS]).

Shapefile templates of the major skeletal cranial elements were created according to the methods described by Abe and Marean (n.d.). First, the underlying composite image with the various surface views was created within Adobe Photoshop. For cranial elements, element views were selected that displayed both endocranial and ectocranial surfaces as well as other important elemental surfaces. For postcranial elements, four anatomical views of the long bones (anterior, posterior, medial, and lateral) were included; for irregular bones, specific views that captured the entire surface morphology were selected. For paired elements, these images were flipped horizontally to create the antimere image. The composite images were then georeferenced to four coordinate points within Erdas Imagine. The coordinate points are visible as the four symbols on the images (see Figures 10-4 and 10-5 for examples). The images were converted to a 1-bit grid and then changed to a shapefile to capture the perimeter of the bone surfaces. The element shapefile could then be edited, cut, and coded based on the observed fragments. Fragmentary specimens were initially identified to one of four bones of the craniofacial skeleton. Fragments were separated based on field data. Subsequent examination sought to identify the particular area or region of the bone that the fragment represents. A substantial number of fragments were identifiable to a particular bone but did not contain specific features to facilitate identification to an exact location and were not digitized. A total of 396 specimens were subjected to further assessment (see Table 10-1). These specimens were identifiable to an exact location on the complete bone, herein referred to as "placeable." Researchers were able to "place" 112 frontal, 45 zygomatic, 59 left and 58 right maxillae, 122 mandibular, and 153 left and 141 right temporal fragments to a particular location on the

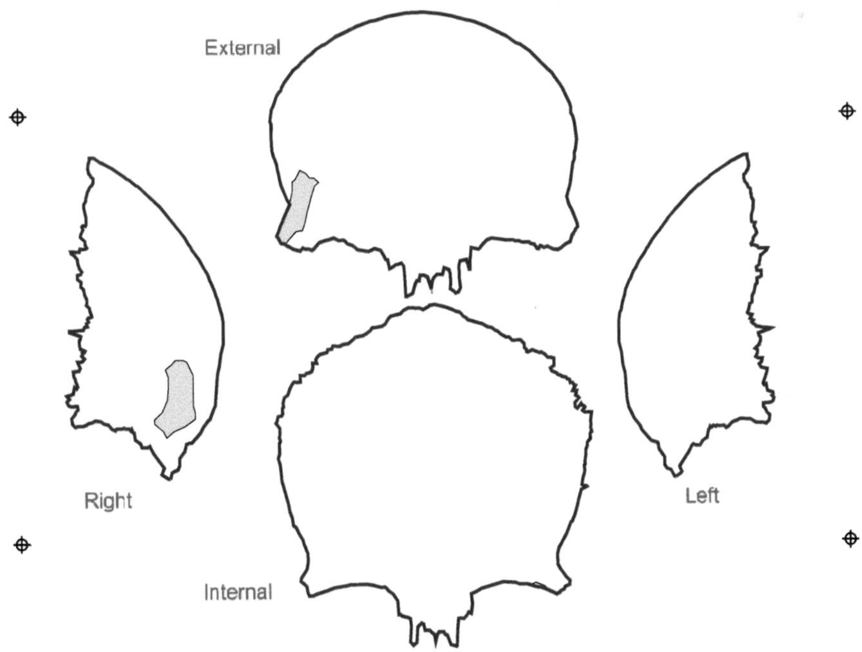

Figure 10-4
Frontal bone template with single placed fragment digitized.

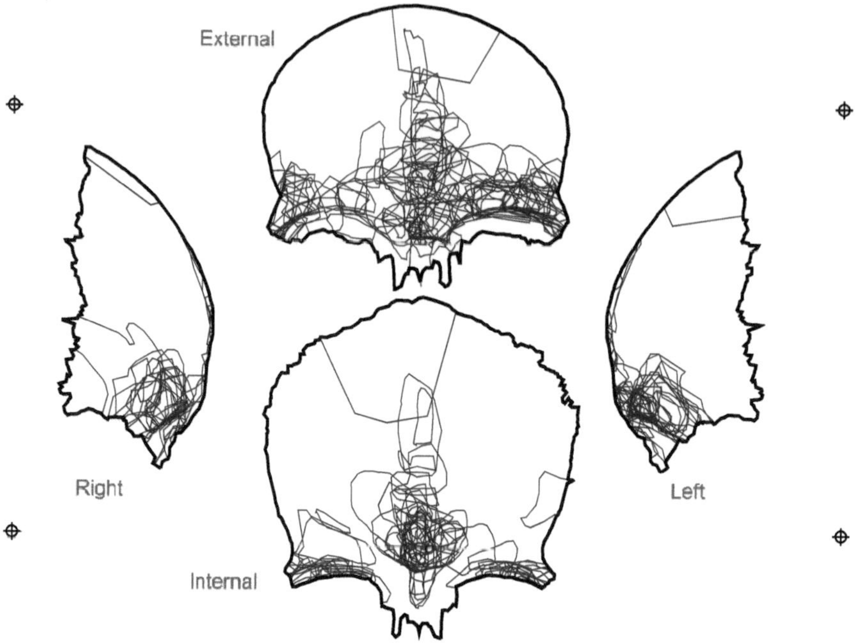

Figure 10-5
Outlines of all placed frontal bone fragments from Walker-Noe.

Table 10-1: Lab and Munsell Color and MNE Estimate for the GIS and Landmark (LM) Approaches by Elements

Element	Placed	Mean Color	Extreme Light Color	Extreme Dark Color	MNE (GIS)	MNE (LM)
Frontal	112	4.4YR6.5/2.8	4.2YR7.9/4.3	7.8YR4.0/1.2	26*	-
Malar (R/L)	23/22	4.7YR6.4/2.8	3.3YR8.4/4.3	3.8YR5.1/1.4	17/16	-
Maxillae (R/L)	59/58	4.8YR6.2/2.9	3.3YR8.1/4.7	3.8YR4.5/1.2	20/21	-
Mandible	122	4.4YR6.6/3.0	3.2YR8.5/4.4	1.5YR4.9/1.2	21	-
Temporal (R/L)	153/141	4.5YR5.8/2.8	3.3YR8.0/4.3	1.9RP3.2/0.5	38/41	40/39
Total	690				41	40

*Please see discussion of MNE determination in text.

respective element. In addition, these fragments were macroscopically assessed in terms of surface colors, level of distortion, apparent degree of shrinkage, and overall fracture and cracking patterns. Each of these placeable fragments was assigned a specimen identification number as dictated by the *BoneEntryGIS* protocol, which incorporated the field specimen (FS) number to enable consideration of fragment distribution across the site and site formation processes.

GIS Results and Discussion

The 690 placeable fragments were digitized using ArcGIS following the approach of Marean et al. (2001) whereby skeletal fragments were recorded by location on two-dimensional representations of the complete element. Figure 10-4 illustrates the process involved in "placing" a single fragment of the frontal bone. The overall shape, location, and dimensions of the fragment are recorded as the specimen is positioned on the appropriate images that illustrate all views of the element. Each entry is saved as a shapefile, which can be merged (or layered) to demonstrate the density (i.e., numbers present) at a particular skeletal location. Figure 10-5 illustrates all the data cells for identifiable fragments of frontal bone. Note the overlapping outlines of fragments. This information can then be interpreted and quantified as representing the number of elements present. Further, data such as fracture pattern, external and internal color, and other traditional human skeletal characteristics (pathology and discrete variants) can be recorded into a linked database. Data concerning recovery location may also be managed in this system. This technique generates a system that enables quantification of the MNI (and MNE) and allows collection and management of data illustrative of taphonomic processes, undoubtedly facilitating interpretation of numerous aspects of site use and formation. Although time-intensive, the GIS system as used here provides the means to accurately quantify fragmentary and taphonomically modified skeletal material.

Surface colors were assessed on all identifiable specimens using an X-rite CA22 spectrophotometer. This handheld device systematizes color evaluation by measuring an area approximately 6 mm in diameter (approximately 28 mm^2) on samples greater than 1/4 inch and relays color data to a host computer running Matchrite ColorDesigner software with a D65 illuminant (the daylight illuminant). As illustrated in Table 10-1, major ectocranial surface colors were noted and are represented as an average across the sample in the Mean Color column. Color data were recorded in the L*a*b* (Lab) color system, a numerical-based system that represents colors in terms of three dimensions. The extreme light and dark colors were also noted, as they are indicative of more unique heat exposure situations. Lab color values were then converted to Munsell colors (Munsell Soil Color Charts 2000) using the Munsell Color Conversion software (version 12.113a; http://wallkillcolor.com).

Based on a weighted consideration of the number of identifiable fragments for each of the six cranial elements, a GIS-based MNI of 41 individuals is indicated. Each craniofacial element was assessed individually, as illustrated in Figure 10-6 and reported in Table 10-1. The highest density of "placeable" fragments per element, signified by an increasingly darker color, reflects specimen overlap (i.e., fragment redundancy). The variation in MNE values noted for the individual elements examined reflects the fragmentation process due to thermal damage. For example, fragments from the orbital margin of the frontal are highly identifiable and placeable. However, delaminated endocranial surfaces of the frontal and fragments of the frontal plate are not locationally distinct and, as such, these fragments could rarely be

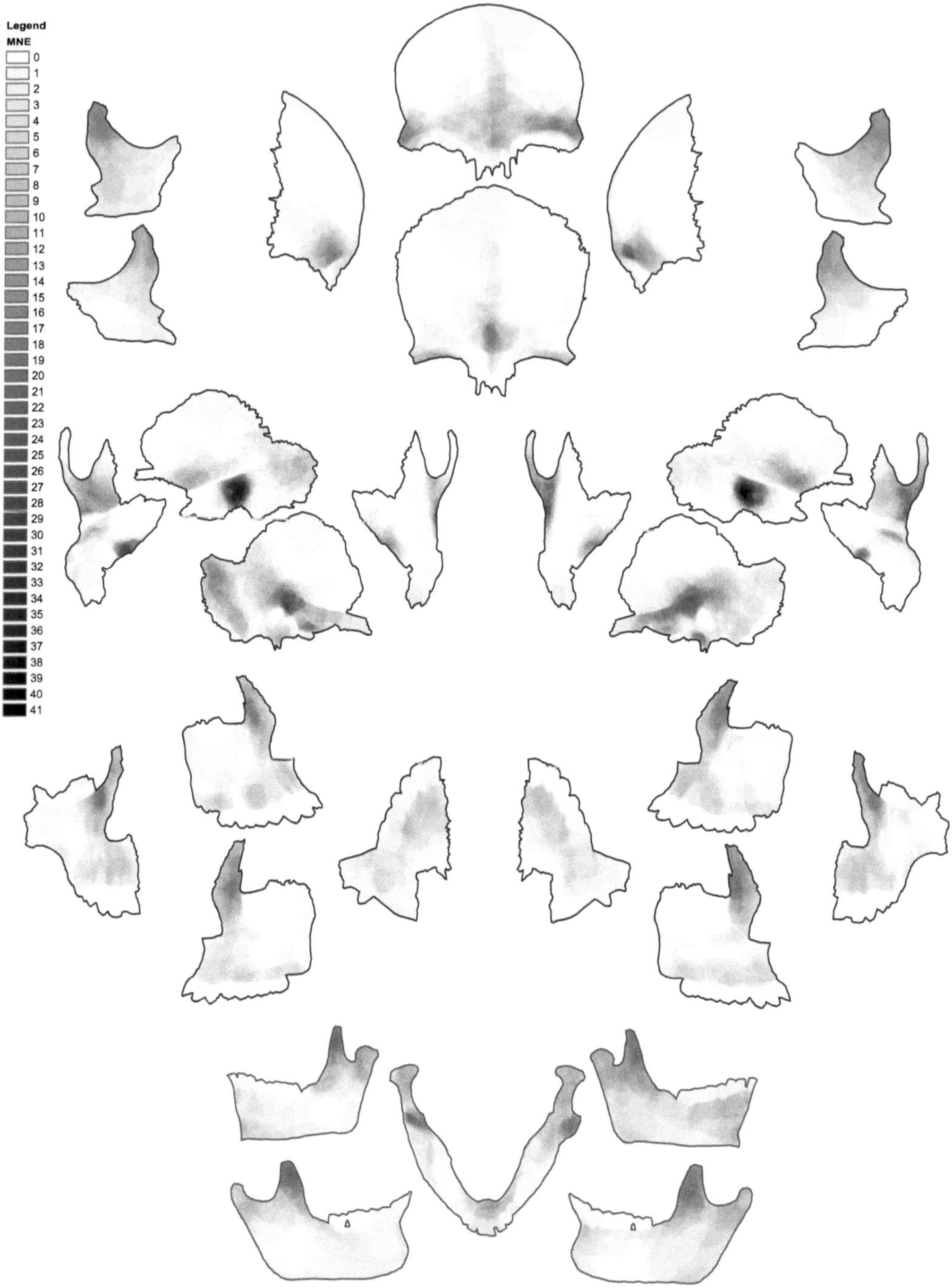

Figure 10-6
Composite image of all cranial elements examined in this study.

specifically placed. The parietal bone was not selected for this study for these exact reasons. The temporal bone offers ubiquitous unique surface morphology and dense bone, which resulted in the highest number of placeable fragments. Not surprisingly, the temporal bone has the highest MNE value and is the basis for the MNI estimate.

The GIS analysis of the frontal fragments indicates a maximum of 26 shared locations, or cells, within the GIS indicating the minimum number of elements recovered from the site. Zygomatic specimens support a minimum number of 17 elements. Fragments of the mandible and right maxilla indicate 21 elements, while the left maxilla suggests a minimum of 20 elements present. The temporal bone GIS method produced MNE values of 38 and 41 for the right and left side, respectively. Although element MNE values range from 17 to 41, the highest values are for the two dense temporal bones, and the reduced values represent the more delicate facial skeleton elements.

As previously stated, the frontal bone has the next highest MNE value, with a value of 26, as compared to the temporal bone values. The other facial elements fall near an MNE of 21. Although the frontal bone MNE value is closer to the temporal estimates, digitizing fragments onto the frontal template proved difficult on the lateral view, specifically at the orbital margin. This area on the template represents the entire depth of the frontal bone from nasion to the zygomatic process. The ability of the observer to accurately "place" or digitize a frontal bone fragment on either an anterior or posterior view is relatively simple. Determining accurate outlines of the same fragment in a lateral view was difficult and we suspect that digitization errors have resulted in the higher MNE estimate for the frontal bone based on the lateral view as compared to other facial elements. The compression of three-dimensional distance across two-dimensional space may lead to digitizing problems for any analyst. We would argue that areas encompassing substantial depth should be identified and eliminated from the final MNE determination. Recent three-dimensional technologies would allow for the capture of all fragments either by computer tomography or by three-dimensional laser scanning. The scanned fragments could then be placed on a generalized three-dimensional element template. Such an approach would eliminate the problem associated with digitizing onto a two-dimensional template.

Comparison of Landmark and GIS Analyses

As seen in Table 10-1, the MNI for Walker–Noe is 41 based on the GIS MNE of the temporal bone. The Landmark approach is consistent with the GIS-based approach with MNE values of 40 and 39 for the right and left, respectively. The Landmark approach produces only marginally higher right counts (+1) and slightly lower left counts (–2). A review of all the landmarks suggests that the count differences vary across the fragment and suggest that the digitization process captures some regions better than the Landmark approach, but landmarks can be placed in locations that would not show up in the two-dimensional images in the GIS approach. For our study, the digitization and landmark recording were conducted independently of each other, and the results helped us refine the positioning of the landmarks for future studies. We do feel that some landmarks should be thought of as fuzzy landmarks (Valeri et al. 1998) similar to craniometric landmarks identified on CT scans. These points can be viewed as occupying an area that is difficult to specifically identify on bone fragments due to morphological variability from individual to individual (fragment to fragment) and, in the case of Walker–Noe, warping related to incineration. A good example is the internal auditory meatus location, which can fragment into several pieces that are identifiable and placeable. This situation would require that the internal auditory meatus presence be noted but may, in fact, not overlap in the OIS/GIS.

Of interest is that the high representation of cranial fragments at Walker–Noe may also result from the common practice at Adena mortuary sites of including isolated crania, or trophy heads, in the burial context (Fenton 1991; Webb and Baby 1957). However, the *in situ* relationship of the skeletal material on the central platform is unknown due to a prior disturbance. No cutmarks were observed on any cranial elements, while several fragments did have surface fractures and cracking suggestive of a dry bone cremation. As such, it may be desirable to calculate an MNE from postcranial elements to compare with the cranial value. However, as previously stated, identification of highly fragmented postcranial elements is more difficult than cranial element recognition. In a recent study of the spatial distribution of skeletal material at Walker–Noe, the authors (Herrmann et al. 2014) found that cranial elements are disproportionally located near the clay platform with postcranial material underrepresented across the mound. This would support the interpretation that the deposit was primarily composed of crania to the exclusion of postcranial elements. Thus, the deposit may have been a series of isolated crania with a limited number of complete inhumations or bone bundles that included postcranial elements.

Conclusion

The initial cursory examination of the material from the Walker–Noe site indicated an MNI of less than 10 (Sharp et al. 2003). With application of the methods described here, the value increased tremendously, suggesting an MNI of around 41 individuals with the OIS/GIS- and Landmark-based approaches producing similar results for both sides of the temporal bone, ranging from 41 to 38 elements. Additional data concerning each fragment can be collected during the laboratory analysis, and such information can be project-specific and allow the recorder to address specific research questions. In this case, we recorded surface modification and color changes related to heat. The implications for site use at Walker–Noe are directly impacted by findings from this study.

Two methods were employed in this study. The Landmark Method uses a set of defined boney landmarks that are coded in a Microsoft Access database. This was done in this study using a check box interface, although a multiselect drop-down interface has also been developed for use in larger-scale analyses. The database can be queried to determine the landmark with the highest frequency or the landmark-based MNE. The second method is the GIS approach. This method requires that the shape and extent of each placeable fragment is recorded as a shapefile within ArcGIS. These shapefiles can then be rasterized and summed to determine the number of overlaps on each element, which is the GIS-based MNE.

Although the GIS technique cannot be criticized for artificially inflating the values, it can, however, be faulted on several levels: (1) the length of time involved in identifying and recording data for each fragment is extreme; (2) it relies on elements that include clearly identifiable and unique attributes; and (3) to be accurate and effective, the analysis must be completed exclusively by skilled osteologists. Although there may appear to be limitations to this image-based approach, in particular with regard to individual and population morphological variations, these concerns are manageable. Cranial and postcranial templates for infants and younger subadults should be developed separate from the adult templates. The database can be formulated to enable compilation of major skeletal parameters, such as age distinctions (e.g., between adults and older subadults) or sexual dimorphism. Age and morphological variation do not impact the digitization of fragments. In effect, size and shape particulars are disregarded during the digitizing process, as all are reproduced onto the same generalized element created for the system. The element shapefiles produced in this approach reflect a standardized presence of the bone fragments, while the linked database provides fragment-specific information for user queries. A key to this approach is template creation and selection. Specific element surfaces with significant depth should be reviewed and possibly eliminated from the final templates to reduce the potential for MNE inflation due to fragment placement errors.

The Landmark approach provides a means of rapidly assessing a series of elements as compared to the more time-intensive GIS-based approach. Of consideration is that the spatial/locational data available from the landmark distribution is more limited than the full spatial attributes of the GIS approach. The key with the Landmark approach is it removes the potential error associated with digitizing the fragment and limits the analyst to a manageable number of features to examine, which is important for large fragmentary collections.

The use of specific landmarks or digitizing fragments will likely result in higher counts for assemblages than those generated using more traditional quantification approaches. Both the Landmark and GIS approaches presented in this chapter allow for accurate estimation of the number of elements and individuals represented. While the use of the Landmark method is faster, the GIS-based system provides a systematic means for tracking patterns across an assemblage that is not possible with the former method. Therefore, the decision of which method(s) to use is highly dependent on the scale of analysis and the questions being asked.

Acknowledgments

We would like to thank David Pollack, the Kentucky Archaeological Survey, and the William S. Webb Museum of Anthropology at University of Kentucky for access to the Walker–Noe skeletal material. Curtis Marean of Arizona State University provided the *BoneGISEntry* extension and manual. Jonathan Bethard and Anne Kroman assisted in sorting the Walker–Noe material, and Sherri Turner performed data entry. The William M. Bass Endowment provided funding for the X-rite CA22 spectrophotometer.

References

Abe, Y., Marean, C., n.d. *Bone Entry GIS and Bone Sorter Manual: For recording, Sorting, and Analyzing Bones Using GIS.* Unpublished manual distributed with the BoneEntryGIS software extension.

Abe, Y., Marean, C., Nilssen, P., Assefa, Z., Stone, E., 2002. The analysis of cutmarks on archaeofauna: A review and critique of quantification procedures, and a new image-analysis GIS approach. Am. Antiquity 67, 643–663.

Adams, B.J., Konigsberg, L.W., 2004. Estimation of the most likely number of individuals from commingled human skeletal remains. Am. J. Phys. Anthropol. 125 (2), 138–151.

Anderson, D., Mainfort, R. (Eds.), 2002. The Woodland Southeast. The University of Alabama Press, Tuscaloosa.

Bennett Devlin, J., Herrmann, N., Pollack, D., 2006. GIS analysis of commingled and cremated bone. Poster presented at the 71st Annual Meeting of the Society for American Archaeology, San Juan, Puerto Rico.

Buikstra, J.E., Ubelaker, D.H. (Eds.), 1994. Standards for Data Collection from Human Skeletal Remains, Proceedings of a Seminar at The Field Museum of Natural History (Arkansas Archeological Survey Research Series No. 44), Spiral ed. Arkansas Archeological Survey, Fayetteville.

Burgett, G., 1990. The bones of the beast: Resolving questions of faunal assemblage formation processes through actualistic research. Unpublished dissertation. Department of Anthropology, The University of New Mexico, Albuquerque.

Byrd, J.E., 2008. Models and methods for osteometric sorting. In: Adams, B.J., Byrd, J.E. (Eds.), Rccovery, Analysis, and Identification of Commingled Human Remains. Humana Press, Totowa, NJ, pp. 199–220.

Byrd, J.E., Adams, B.J., 2003. Osteometric sorting of commingled human remains. J. Forensic Sci. 48, 717–724.

Church, M., Burgett, G., 1996. An information recording and retrieval system for use in taphonomic and forensic investigations of human mortalities (abstract). Proc. Am. Acad. Forensic Sci. 48th Sci. Meeting 2, 167–168.

Clay, B., 1998. The essential features of Adena ritual and their implications. SE Archaeol. 17, 1–21.

Clay, B., 2002. Deconstructing the Woodland Sequence from the Heartland: A review of recent research directions in the Upper Ohio Valley. In: Anderson, D., Mainfort Jr., R. (Eds.), The Woodland Southeast. University of Alabama Press, Tuscaloosa pp. 162–184.

Fenton, J.P., 1991. The Social Uses of Dead People: Problems and Solutions in the Analysis of Post Mortem Body Processing in the Archaeological Record (Mortuary Analysis). Unpublished dissertation. Columbia University, New York.

Giovas, C.M., 2009. The shell game: Analytic problems in archaeological mollusc quantification. J. Archaeol. Sci. 36 (7), 1557–1564.

Grayson, D.K., 1984. Quantitative Zooarchaeology. Academic Press, New York.

Herrmann, N., Bennett Devlin, J., Pollack, D., 2005. GIS analysis of the cremated skeletal material from the Walker–Noe site, Kentucky. Am. J. Phys. Anthropol. Suppl. 40, 11.

Herrmann, N., Bennett Devlin, J., Stanton, J., 2014. Bioarchaeological Spatial analysis of the Walker-Noe Crematory (15GD56). In: Osterholtz, A.J., Baustian, K.M., Martin, D.L. (Eds.), Commingled and Disarticulated Human Remains: Working Towards Improving Theory, Method, and Data. Springer, New York. pp. 51–66.

Lyman, R.L., 1994. Vertebrate Taphonomy. Cambridge University Press, Cambridge.

Marean, C., Abe, Y., Nilssen, P., Stone, E., 2001. Estimating the minimum number of skeletal elements (MNE) in zooarchaeology: A review and a new image-analysis GIS approach. Am. Antiquity 66, 333–348.

Mayne Corriera, P., Beattie, O., 2002. A critical look at methods for recovering, evaluating and interpreting cremated human remains. In: Haglund, W., Sorg, M. (Eds.), Advances in Forensic Taphonomy: Method, Theory and Archaeological Perspectives. CRC Press, Boca Raton, FL, pp. 435–450.

Munsell Soil Color Charts, 2000. Munsell Soil Color Charts. Munsell Color GretagMacbeth, New York.

Pollack, D., Schlarb, E., Sharp, W., Tune, T., 2005. Walker–Noe: An early middle Woodland Adena mound in Central Kentucky. In: Applegate, D., Mainfort Jr., R. (Eds.), Woodland Period Systematics in the Middle Ohio Valley. The University of Alabama Press, Tuscaloosa, pp. 64–74.

Railey, J., 1990. Woodland period. In: Pollack, D. (Ed.), Archaeology of Kentucky: Past Accomplishments and Future Directions. Kentucky Heritage Council, Frankfort, pp. 247–374.

Sharp, W., Pollack, D., Schlarb, E., Tune, T., 2003. Walker–Noe: A Middle Woodland Mound in Central Kentucky. Paper presented at the 68th Annual Meeting of the Society for American Archaeology, Montreal, Canada.

Valeri, C.J., Cole, T.M., Lele, S., Richtsmeier, J.T., 1998. Capturing data from three-dimensional surfaces using fuzzy landmarks. Am. J. Phys. Anthropol. 107 (1), 113–124.

Webb, W.S., Baby, R., 1957. The Adena People. No. 2. Papers in Archaeology. Ohio Historical Society, Columbus.

White, T.E., 1953. A method of calculating the dietary percentage of various food animals utilized by aboriginal peoples. Am. Antiquity 18 (4), 396–398.

Wilczak, C.A., Dudar, J.C. (Eds.), 2012. Osteoware Software Manual, vol. I. Smithsonian Institution, Washington, D.C.

CHAPTER 11

Human Cremation: Commingling and Questioned Identity

Michael W. Warren, Traci L. Van Deest
University of Florida, C. A. Pound Human Identification Laboratory, Department of Anthropology, Gainesville, FL

Introduction

Medicolegal issues involving commercially cremated human remains (i.e., cremains) are almost universally related to the commingling of more than one decedent within a single urn. When family members or loved ones find materials in the cremains that, at least to them, do not belong, the identity of the decedent represented by the cremains is called into question. This situation is complicated by the fact that commercial cremation of human remains, as it is currently practiced in North America and most of Western Europe, results in the inevitable commingling of the remains of more than one dead body—if not demonstrably, at least at trace levels. Locard's Principle of Exchange, also known as the theory of transfer, tells us that if two objects are in contact with one another, evidence of that contact will remain once the objects are no longer in contact (Saferstein 2009). In light of how cremations are performed (a single retort is used for countless cremations), commingling is inevitable and will occur to some degree in every cremation. The extent of commingling is contingent upon several factors, including the specific protocol used by the cremationist and the design of the retort and processor. If this is the case, how can commingling be detected by anthropologists, and to what degree is it a problem? Furthermore, if commingling is expected, why has the issue of commingled cremains become an important legal issue?

To answer these questions and others, this chapter discusses in greater detail the factors that lead to commingling of cremains and the circumstances and situations in which commingling in cremation becomes a legal issue.

Finally, it is important to describe analytical approaches to the analysis of cremated remains because it is different than standard forensic osteological analyses. A better understanding of the cremation process and subsequent examination of cremains is useful for the anthropologist, attorney, and other interested parties in considering how commingling might be described to a jury or arbitrator, who ultimately must decide if the degree of commingling is incidental to the normal cremation process or the result of negligent cremation practice.

Commingled Human Remains. http://dx.doi.org/10.1016/B978-0-12-405889-7.00011-3

While the assessment of cultural artifacts is qualitative, weights can be used to estimate the portions of the biological profile, such as sex and stature of the purported individual. Cultural artifacts should be described in detail, using the categories described by Warren and Schultz (2002), discussed later. The methodology for determining commingling in cremains is primarily qualitative, focusing on a discussion of the probative value of evidence in determining if demonstrable commingling exists and to what extent.

As the reader will see, experience plays a role in interpreting each piece of evidence because cremations present many challenges which are not typically a part of the skeletal analyses conducted by forensic anthropologists. What biological and artifactual evidence might we expect to survive the cremation process? What types of biological and artifactual evidence should we expect to find after the remains have been processed at the facility? Equally important, what types of evidence would we not expect to find, and what does that tell the investigator?

As cremation has become more popular (Davies 2005; Murad 1998), the cremation and funeral home industry has become the target of civil litigation. Issues such as the commingling of the remains of more than one decedent, improper cremation practice, disputed identity of remains, and improper disposal are becoming increasingly popular courtroom topics. Several class-action suits of note have involved literally hundreds of plaintiffs—each with potentially millions of dollars at stake (Bass and Jefferson 2003; Iverson 2001; Maples and Browning 1994). Several of these cases have received national media attention, such as the Tri-State Crematory case (Steadman et al. 2008). As a result, crematories and funeral homes have been placed under public scrutiny as industry standards and practices are developed and instituted.

When individuals have some reason to believe that the cremated remains in their possession are not those of their loved one or that more than one person is represented, legal counsel will often consult with forensic experts to perform scientific analyses that might help resolve the dispute. Since cremains are principally composed of the fragmented remains of the skeleton, the expert usually takes the form of a forensic anthropologist who is a specialist in skeletal anatomy, morphology, and taphonomy. Taphonomy literally refers to burial laws, but in a biological sense it covers all of the processes that occur to a body after death. The anthropologist performs an examination of the cremated remains using microscopy, radiography, and other methods to find clues that might lead to identification. These clues generally come from two sources: (1) the biological remains, consisting of osseous (bony) and dental fragments, and 2) nonosseous artifacts. In almost every case, the evidence for identity is presumptive. This is due to the loss of positive lines of evidence such as DNA and fingerprints during the cremation process. Only in rare cases are dental or medical implants present which have survived the extreme environment of the cremation retort and are still available for comparison to antemortem radiographs, thus providing a positive line of evidence for identification.

Along with the anthropologist, a multidisciplinary team of experts may be required, each bringing a different area of expertise to bear in the analysis of the cremains and associated artifacts. The expertise of a forensic odontologist is often warranted, particularly for cases in which significant dental artifacts are found. The odontologist will recognize the types of dental artifacts altered by heat within cremains and be able to better assess the antemortem dental records and radiographs than the anthropologist.

The Inevitability of Commingling in Cremation

To understand the relevant findings in a forensic analysis of cremains, as well as the inevitable issue of commingling, one must have a thorough understanding of the cremation process (for a complete description of the cremation process, see Bohnert et al. 1998; Murad 1998; Schultz et al. 2008). The process begins when the body is placed into an empty cremation retort, generally within a cremation container of flammable material such as cardboard or fiberboard. The body is subjected to a direct flame and burns at temperatures ranging between 1400°F and 1800°F (760°C and 982°C) in the cremation chamber. The duration of the cremation cycle is generally between one and two hours. The specific protocol depends on the type of equipment, the size of the body, and whether or not the cremation is being performed in a preheated retort. The goal is calcination of the remains, which is the process of removing all water and organic matter within the body by using intense heat.

After the body has been incinerated, the retort door is opened, and the chamber is allowed to cool. When the chamber has cooled to a temperature low enough for the cremationist to safely work, the cremains are removed from the retort with a long-handled wire-bristle brush or hoe. Most retorts are built with a catchment area near the door into which the fragments fall as they are raked forward by the cremationist, eventually ending up in a receptacle beneath the door. At this point, the cremationist will usually remove easily detected, larger foreign objects, including orthopaedic appliances, casket hardware, and magnetic debris. The cremains are then further reduced to smaller particulates within a post-cremation processor, known by various names, such as cremulator, pulverizer, or simply, processor. This processor reduces the calcined bone fragments to small particles and ash suitable for inurnment or scattering (Warren and Schultz 2002).

The aforementioned Locard's Principle of Exchange tells us that it is impossible, even under ideal conditions, to introduce a body into an enclosed space and then remove it without leaving evidence of it having been there. Obviously, the cremation retort does not present ideal conditions. During cremation, it becomes an extremely volatile environment, in which fragments of calcined bone are blown about by large volumes of combustion air added to the retort to maintain the fire needed for the process. When the cremated bone fragments and ash are removed from the retort by the cremationist, it is difficult for even the most well-trained and conscientious cremationist to perfectly clean out the deeper recesses of the retort floor. This fact is recognized by state-level legislation related to cremation (see following text). The retort is a relatively large space, and the areas in the back corners are difficult to reach with the standard issue long-handled broom and hoe. The cremation chamber is unlit, so the back areas are dark,

Figure 11-1
Corner of the inside of a retort following a cremation.

making bone fragments and artifacts difficult to see and remove (Figure 11-1). Additionally, the retort remains hot during retrieval of the cremains, and is intentionally kept at a relatively high temperature if another body is to be cremated. These challenges can lead to mistakes and lapses in procedure, which may result in demonstrable commingling as opposed to the inevitable trace amounts of commingling that are to be expected as a part of the cremation process.

Factors That May Lead to Excessive Commingling

Aside from the normal degree of commingling expected during a well-performed cremation, a number of other factors can lead to excessive amounts of commingling. Although commercial cremation has been practiced in North America since the 19th century (Prothero 2001), it has been within the past few decades that it has gained wide acceptance. The funeral industry, while currently closely regulated by various governmental agencies, began practicing cremation with relatively little oversight in the late 1800s (Prothero 2001). Few, if any, industry standards were established at its inception in the United States. Therefore, there were no prohibitions in the early days of crematory operations against several practices that are uniformly considered unprofessional by current standards, such as cremating more than one body simultaneously. In response, the funerary industry has been proactive in seeking remedies for earlier shortcomings, and many states have passed legislation that controls and permits action against crematories guilty of improper practices.

For example, Arizona has passed laws that permit disciplinary action against crematories for "using a retort for any purpose other than the cremation of human remains," "cremating more than one dead human body at the same time in the same retort without the express written consent of the authorizing agents," and "introducing a second dead human body into a retort before reasonable efforts have been made to remove all fragments of the cremated remains from the preceding cremation without the express written consent of the authorizing agents" (Arizona State Legislation 32-1398). This legislation specifically addresses the intentional commingling of human remains during the cremation process.

The inevitability of commingling is acknowledged in the legislation by specifically referencing "incidental and unavoidable residue remaining in a retort after a cremation" (Arizona State Legislation 32-1398). Florida has also enacted laws that recognize the "unintentional commingling of the residue of the cremation process" (Florida State Legislation 497.608). The Florida statute continues on to state, "The operator of a cinerator facility shall establish written procedures for the removal of cremated remains, to the extent possible, resulting from the cremation of a human body and the postcremation processing, shipping, packing, or identifying of those remains" (Florida State Legislature 497.608). This implies that even the most thorough efforts to remove all material from the retort will never be completely successful.

Another source of excessive commingling is simply the result of poor cremation practice and procedures. The process requires vigilance and good effort. Although some crematories are "direct cremation" businesses, most cremationists are associated with funeral homes, and many cremationists are licensed funeral directors. In fact, most of the cremains examined by the senior author of this chapter have been conducted in the proper manner, and no evidence of wrongdoing can be found. However, some show evidence of haphazard procedure, such as insufficient temperature and/or duration, failure to remove magnetic debris, inadequate documentation, and other signs that introduce doubt into the families of the decedents, resulting in legal action and the involvement of forensic experts.

How Commingling Is Detected

Cremains contain both biological remains and cultural or material items related to a person's identity. The analysis of cremated remains is focused on finding evidence for identity that corresponds to the known biological profile of the decedent and any evidence that records the decedent's life history, as well as the circumstances surrounding the remains at the time of cremation. The analysis involves careful examination of every fragment and artifact contained within the urn.

As most forensic anthropologists are well versed in the analysis of relatively complete human skeletal remains, the analysis of cremains in such an extreme state of fragmentation presents challenges. Although Warren et al. (1999) briefly discuss the steps to a cremation analysis, these steps are discussed in greater detail here. The equipment needed to properly complete a cremation analysis as described here includes photographic and radiographic equipment, microscopes or some ability to examine the remains under magnification, scales, and testing sieves (Figure 11-2).

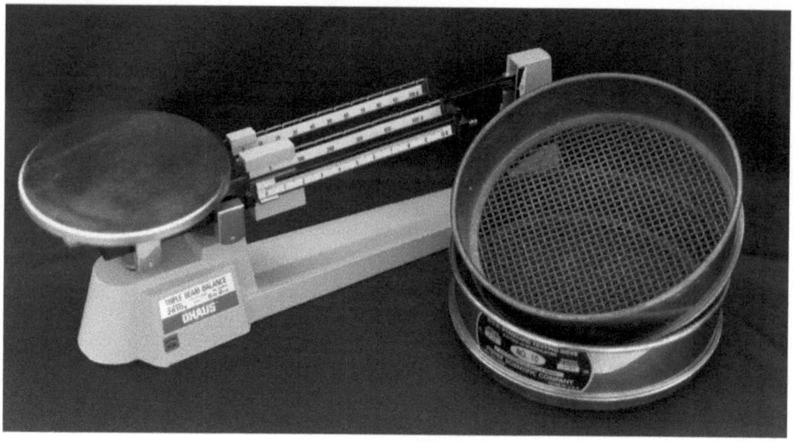

Figure 11-2
Balance and sieves used during cremains analysis.

First, as in any forensic case, all containers and accompanying materials need to be documented photographically and with written notes. In addition, photographs of the containers and contents should be taken as the containers are opened and the contents removed. Once the container(s) is opened and documented, the remains should be weighed and the general color, condition, and any accompanying items or items visible within the remains should be noted and imaged. In the event that a cremation tag is present, the tag should be documented through written and photographic evidence.

Once the remains are weighed and their conditions are fully described in written notes, the remains should be separated using standard sieves; generally standard sieves No. 18, 10, and 5 are used (Figure 11-2). This results in the separation of remains in four particulate size categories: >4 mm, >2 mm, >1 mm, and <1 mm (Figure 11-3), in comparison to unprocessed cremated remains (Figure 11-4). At this time, any cultural items present and visually identifiable should be removed from the remains with provenience maintained.

When one is radiographing the remains, it is useful to place a small metal grid, cut to the size of the shallow boxes used in the analysis, to allow for easy recovery of any radiopaque items within the remains. These items may be useful for the identification process and to detect any appreciable level of commingling. On occasion, identifiable bone fragments can be distinguishable on radiographs.

The next step in the analysis is to remove all radiolucent items from the remains, using the metal grids as a location guide. Each type of artifact should be kept separately, with particulate size noted. This will aid in the identification of cultural items and the separation of these items based on the five categories established by Warren and Schultz (2002): medical, dental, personal, mortuary, and miscellaneous.

After all materials distinguished on radiographs are removed, each fragment greater than 1 mm in size is examined under magnification, with the use of a standard dissection microscope as

Figure 11-3
Particulate sizes of sorted processed cremains: >4 mm, >2 mm, >1 mm, and <1 mm. Scale is in centimeters.

needed. Although they are extremely fragmented, a well-trained osteologist, especially one well versed in the changes to skeletal and dental remains resulting from heat exposure, will be able to identify portions of the cranial vault and dentition, if present. Additionally, under magnification, all other nonosseous materials can be found and removed from the biological remains for identification and use in determining commingling as well as identity.

Finally, the remains are placed under ultraviolet light. It has been noted in the literature that human cremains will fluoresce following heat exposure and/or cremation, but not all remains will fluoresce (Warren et al. 1999). Although fluorescence of burned and cremated bone from exposure to ultraviolet light is known, the underlying reason for the fluorescence is still unknown.

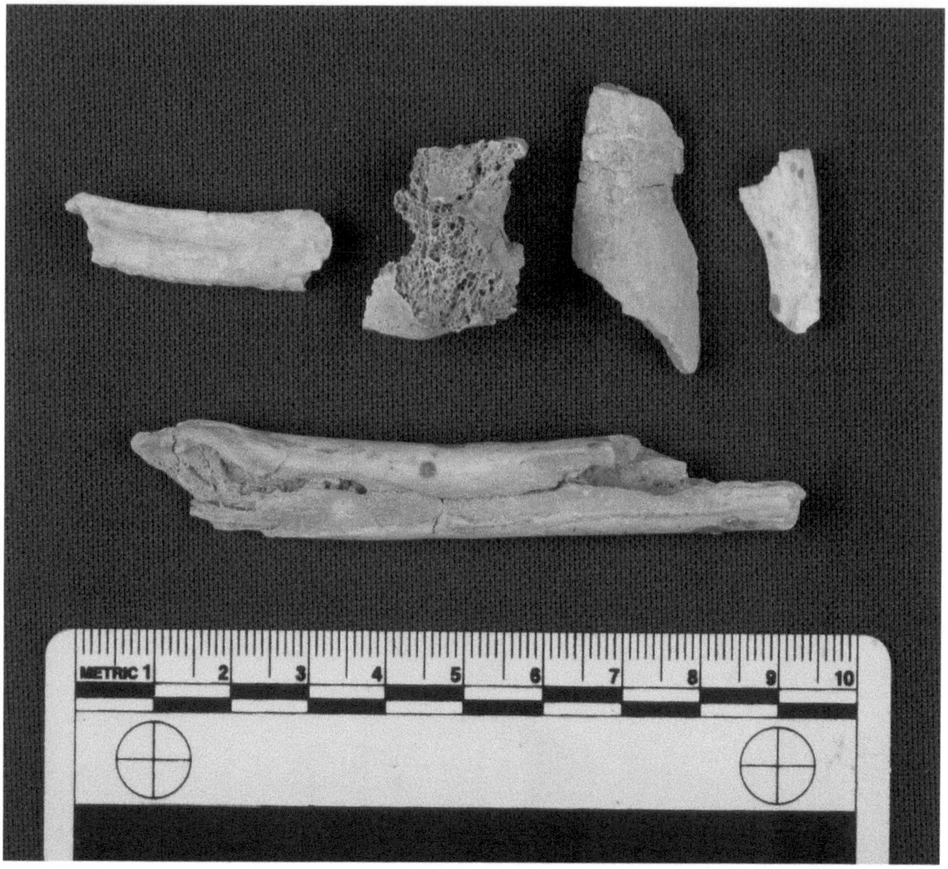

Figure 11-4
Examples of fragments of unprocessed cremated remains. Scale is in centimeters.

Examination of remains that have been reduced to less than 1 mm is even more limited than the larger particulate sizes. Diagnostic fragments are rare, as are identifiable items, in this size range. The use of analytical methods to assess the chemical constituents can help to identify if the "ash" is consistent with human remains or another material. These chemical analyses can be employed should the examiner suspect that foreign material has been presented with, or in lieu of, human cremains. Recently, several researchers have begun to characterize the chemical constituents of burned and cremated human remains, as well as other visually similar materials (Bergslien et al. 2008; Brooks et al. 2006; Christensen et al. 2012; Schultz et al. 2008). Analysis of the bone mineral crystal structure, as opposed to chemical composition, has also proven promising in distinguishing burned bone from other materials (Bergslien et al. 2008).

The Biological Remains

The biological component of cremated remains consists of literally thousands of small, calcined bone and tooth fragments. Although osseous structure of cortical and trabecular bone

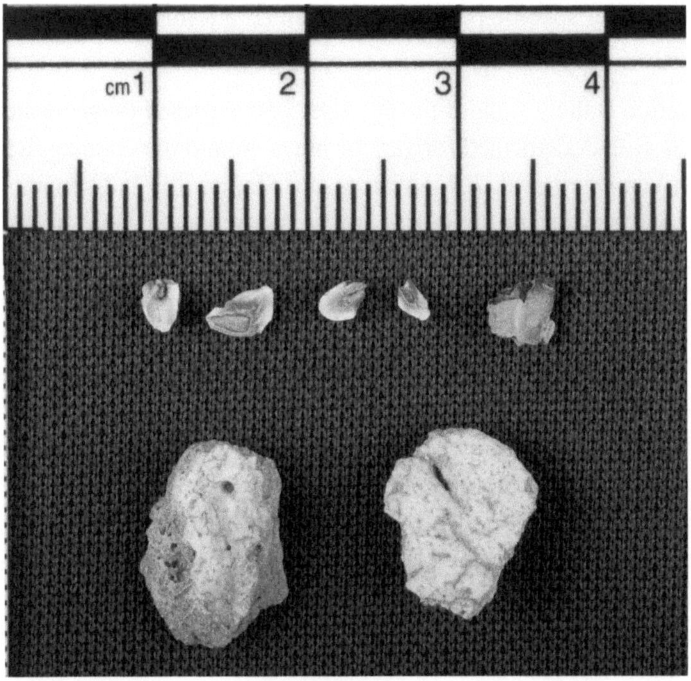

Figure 11-5
Cranial and dental fragments from processed cremains. Scale is in centimeters.

organization is present, almost all of the fragments are unidentifiable to element and even to whether the remains are human or nonhuman. Although it may not be possible to state solely from the presence of trabecular and cortical bone that the remains are those of the purported decedent, they will establish whether the material under analysis contains biological remains.

Factors affecting the presence of diagnostic bone fragments should be kept in mind. For example, the type and condition of the processor used in the pulverization process of the cremation can greatly impact the size of the fragments present after processing. To compare, a small amount of unprocessed cremated remains can be seen in Figure 11-4. For example, when a hammer mill type of processor is used, the fragments tend to be larger because they are processed only to the point at which they fall through the perforations in the drum (Warren and Schultz 2002). A rotary blade processor, more common currently, is time dependent and will process the remains as long as the machine is running, usually between 30 and 60 seconds. In this case, the condition of the blade will impact the survivability of diagnostic fragments. A worn blade will allow for more identifiable fragments than a new or relatively unworn blade (Warren and Schultz 2002).

Therefore, information gleaned from the osseous remains usually results in only general statements about concordance of the remains with known information about the decedent. For example, if the decedent had teeth, one would typically find tooth enamel fragments among the cremains (Figure 11-5). An edentulous decedent should not contain numerous tooth enamel fragments; this is presumptive evidence of commingling. More specific information is rare, although evidence of specific pathology or skeletal anomalies is occasionally found (Warren et al. 1999).

A second consideration is the weight of the remains. The expected range of the weight of cremated remains is well documented for various areas around the country (Bass and Jantz 2004; Sonek 1992; Van Deest et al. 2011; Warren and Maples 1997). Cremains weight has been correlated to several aspects of the biological profile. Warren and Maples (1997) state that stature has the highest correlation to cremains weight of the variables they examined, providing regression equations for calculations. Van Deest et al. (2011) show a significant difference in the weights of males and females, as well as a weak negative relationship to age. Bass and Jantz (2004) also show lower cremains weights with advanced age. In terms of cremains weight and commingling, if the weight of the cremated remains grossly exceeds the expected range of male individuals, the investigator can only reach the conclusion that more than one decedent may be represented or that the material presented for analysis is not human cremated remains. In cases involving a female decedent, weights well into the male range may also indicate commingling, but variation in female cremains weights and the overlap with the male weight distribution should be considered before reaching this conclusion. If the weight is considerably less than the expected range, several possibilities exist: either all remains are not present, or the remains are those of a smaller body than the purported decedent.

One must keep in mind that the consideration of weights necessarily relies on the assumption that all of the remains are present. This problem is particularly vexing because it is common for cremated remains to be divided among family members. Although research into cremains weight indicates correlations with aspects of the biological profile, more research is needed to examine the full range of cremains weights from a number of different crematories due to the demonstrated differences in mean weights between different crematoria and different regions (Bass and Jantz 2004; Birkby 1991; Sonek 1992; Van Deest et al. 2011; Warren and Maples 1997).

Personal Identification in Cremains Analysis

In order for an identification to be attempted as the second phase of the examination in the case of cremated remains, antemortem information is necessary. This can be accomplished by providing a questionnaire or interrogatory to the decedent's family or legal representative. Because this process may involve court orders and other forms of legal wrangling, it should begin as soon as the expert is contacted and retained. Collection of antemortem data from the family members of the decedent is, of course, a familiar process to anthropologists working in human identification, particularly in human rights work. Here, the context is different, resulting in a slightly different inquiry.

Following is a reasonable list of questions that might bear fruit in establishing identity and/or determining whether commingling exists:

- Was the decedent male or female?
- What was the decedent's age at death?

- What was the decedent's height?
- What was the decedent's weight?
- What was the cause and manner of death?
- List surgical procedures and surgeon of record.
- List dental procedures and dentist of record.
- Did the decedent have any natural teeth remaining? Dentures or partial plates?
- Was the decedent embalmed prior to cremation (i.e., was there a "viewing" or "wake")?
- What clothing was on the body during cremation?
- Was the decedent cremated in a cardboard container, a wooden "cremation casket," a standard wooden casket, or without container or casket?
- Were any foreign objects cremated with the decedent (e.g., CDs, stuffed animals, flower arrangements)?
- Have the cremains been in an urn since cremation? What type? Was there a small memorial urn?
- Are all of the cremains present?

For cases in which chemical analysis is chosen as an examination method, it may also be helpful to know information about the decedent's life history. Case studies and research have shown that chemicals and elements associated with certain occupations (e.g., industrial workers with high chemical exposure) or foreign materials that may have persisted within the body during life (such as projectiles or medical implants) can be detected in the chemical composition of bone and cremated remains (Brooks et al. 2006; Schultz et al. 2008; Warren et al. 2002).

The crematory may be asked to answer some of the following questions:

- What is the brand of retort?
- Is the floor cast or brick?
- How old is the retort?
- Has the floor been replaced?
- What tools did the cremationist use to remove the cremains from the retort?
- Does the cremationist open the retort and stir the remains during the cremation cycle?
- What type of processor was used to pulverize the cremains?
- Was a magnet used to retrieve ferrous material from the cremains?
- Is the cremationist experienced? Did he receive training from the retort manufacturer?
- Was a cremation "tag" used, and should it be with the cremains?
- If possible, enclose a copy or original of the temperature readout during the cremation cycle.
- When was the last EPA or OSHA inspection of the retort and/or facilities?
- Are there local inspectors?

The use of the questionnaire may provide answers as to the biological information of the individual and the state of the remains at the time of cremation, such as the presence of clothing and personal effects. This will inform the anthropologist as to what cultural artifacts would be expected in the cremains analysis. For example, Florida state statute dictates that a form of "proper identification be placed in the container or urn containing the cremated remains" (Florida State Legislation 497:171). This indicates that a forensic expert examining remains cremated within the state of Florida would expect to find some form of accompanying identification, such as a cremation tag.

The questioning of family about the medical and life history of a decedent is common practice for death investigations, but one should keep in mind that much of this information about a decedent may be coming from memory of family or loved ones. As such, things such as height, weight, and medical/dental history should be viewed with the inherent bias of information recall in mind. In some cases, medical and dental records may be provided at the time of analysis or later based on court order and should be used for comparison at the completion of the examination of the remains. Here, experience in the analysis of cremains is important because the examiner must know which aspects of the medical, dental, and mortuary history would be likely to survive the cremation process. Some pathological conditions or treatments are more likely to produce evidence than others (Warren et al. 1999). Medical and dental records may be subpoenaed by the legal counsel for whom the examiner is consulting, if not already freely provided. Using the biological profile and history of the putative decedent, one can generate a list of expected and unexpected findings. The following fictitious list might be relevant for a male decedent who died post-operatively from a heart bypass surgery and who was embalmed prior to the cremation of his body within a cremation casket. If the decedent died while still in possession of his natural dentition, then enamel and root fragments would be placed in the "expected" list and artificial porcelain-like fragments would be included in the "unexpected" list.

Expected Biological and Artifactual Evidence	Present	Absent
Bone structure (e.g., cortical, trabecular, foramina)	X	
Diagnostic bone fragments	X	
Natural dental fragments (e.g., roots, enamel fragments)	X	
Hospital bracelet	X	
Hospital gown snaps		X
Ligation clips		X
Skin-closure staples	X	
Sternotomy sutures	X	
Mortuary injector needles	X	
Coffin hardware (e.g., screws, staples, brads)	X	
Jewelry (including lumps of yellow metal and gemstones)		X
Unexpected Biological and Artifactual Evidence		
Porcelain or composite artificial dental fragments (e.g., dentures, crowns, pontics)	X	
Dental posts, bridgework, other metallic dental prostheses		X
Clothing snaps, hooks, claps, zippers		X
Pacemaker and defibrilator wires		X
Embolism filters		X
Arterial stents		X
Artificial heart valves		X
Bra hook and clasps		X

The list can be exhaustive provided the examiner gets good compliance with the request for antemortem information. The presence or absence of each finding can be considered presumptive evidence that either partially refutes or confirms the identity of the decedent. Mixed results (e.g., artifacts are present in both the expected and unexpected lists) suggest commingling of the remains of more than one individual.

How Commingling Becomes a Legal Issue

A primary reason leading to litigation is the lack of understanding by the public, and by extension, the family of the decedent about the cremation process. The grieving family may have preconceived notions about what the remains should look like, and are not told about the inevitability of commingling at some level. Many families receive an urn from the funeral home containing their loved one's cremains and never open the container. In cases when the urn is opened, some families compare what they are seeing with a preconceived expectation that does not match what is in front of them. There may be a perception there are not enough cremains, or they may feel no "emotional attachment" when viewing the cremains. People may be confused because the cremains do not look like ash but something else. This insecurity is compounded when a funeral home or crematory is publicly accused of misdeeds or has shown evidence of mishandling remains.

Legal action often follows when parents examine the cremains of a child. The cremains of children are smaller in weight and volume and are often hand-processed, resulting in less reduction and larger bone fragments. Children have accrued less medical and dental artifacts than adults. When the parents examine their child's cremains and find remnants of denture material, surgical clips, or other artifacts, it is readily apparent that either they have the wrong set of cremains or the cremains of their child are commingled with those of an adult. It is this type of demonstrable commingling that proves problematic for the cremation industry and often results in attorneys utilizing the expertise of scientists to help resolve the issue.

In summary, two things are certain: (1) commingling will occur with every cremation, and (2) legal issues will be resolved by the amount and quality of demonstrable commingling identified by forensic experts. The jury or mediator will be the arbiter of whether the cremationist was conscientious and thorough in the performance of the cremation, or whether the commingling is evidence of improper or negligent cremation practices.

How Is Commingling Described to a Jury?

The forensic consultant is an objective expert. Findings relevant to the case are disclosed to counsel whether the evidence supports or refutes the case for commingling, negligence, mistaken identity, or any other legal issue. Legal counsel, judges, and juries should be provided with a description of the cremation process and the inevitability of incidental commingling whenever possible in order to make a well-informed decision on any legal matter involving cremains and possible commingling of such remains. It should be emphasized that a small amount of commingling does not necessarily imply poor cremation practices and is, in fact, to be expected. Forensic cases involving cremated remains are usually within the civil legal system, not the criminal system. As such, the position of the opposing attorneys can present to the court the same amount of commingling evidence using two very different viewpoints. Attorneys for the crematory/funeral home tend to present evidence for commingling by reporting the weight of the artifacts and biological material as a (small) percentage of the overall weight of the cremains. For example, inconsistent artifacts may "weigh about the same as a dime" or "weigh less than 1% of the total cremains weight." On the other hand, the family/decedent supporter's counsel may consider any demonstrable commingling as proof of improper practice or as introducing doubt as to the identity of the decedent.

Case Study

The following case study is representative of a typical cremation investigation. The case, which involves the cremated remains of a fetus that was spontaneously aborted at 4½ lunar months' gestation, illustrates the amount of information that can be gleaned from a small amount of bone fragments.

The senior author of this chapter examined the remains at the C.A. Pound Human Identification Laboratory at the University of Florida. The cremains were mostly white in color, completely calcined and brittle, and produced a metallic sound when percussed with an instrument. The size of the cremains fragments was most consistent with a commercially available rotary-bladed processor.

The total weight of the bag of cremains was 225.0 grams. This weight is significantly less than the published mean of approximately 2,430 grams for a mixed-sex sample of cremated adult remains, suggesting either that the remains were those of a subadult or that a portion of the cremains was not presented for examination. The weight of this case is also significantly more than the cremains weight of 3 grams for a fetus of roughly comparable gestational age as reported by Warren and Maples (1997).

Several intact bones were present that confirmed that the cremains were of human origin (Figure 11-6). An intact incus bone (one of the ear ossicles) was uniquely human in morphology. Among the cremains were several small but intact long bone diaphyses. An intact femoral diaphysis measured 23.5 millimeters, corresponding to a crown-to-heel length of approximately 19.64 millimeters using the established regression formulae of Fazekas and Kósa (1978), or alternatively, approximately 21.17 centimeters using published data from Warren (1999). This crown-to-heel length corresponded to a gestational age between four and five lunar months, or 16 to 20 weeks. The degree of development of seven intact vertebral elements of the neural arch, two complete ribs, three additional long bone fragments, and a

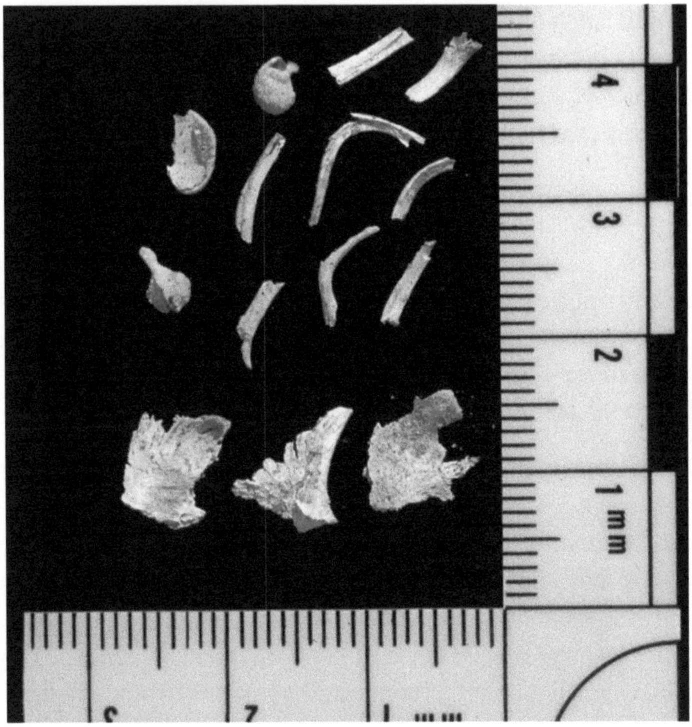

Figure 11-6
Fetal cremated remains.

partial sphenoid bone all corresponded to a fetal developmental age of four to five lunar months' gestation.

Two larger bone fragments were too large to be fetal material and represented commingled cremains from a previous cremation of an adult. No debris was found among the cremains, including staples or other casket hardware. Most importantly, no dental material was discovered, nor were any medical, dental, or mortuary artifacts noted.

A questionnaire similar to the one previously discussed filled out by the putative decedent's family, and provided by their legal counsel, provided the following information about the decedent. The decedent was a female who died of nonviable immaturity at 17 weeks' gestation. No surgical, medical, or dental procedures had been performed, and, of course, the decedent had no natural teeth. It was unknown whether the decedent was embalmed prior to cremation. The family reported that no clothing or foreign objects were cremated with the remains and that all of the cremains were presented for examination.

In this case, several complete bones, as well as primary ossification centers representing elements of the vertebral column were noted and confirmed that the cremains were those of a human. The size and morphology of the bones and elements were consistent with a human fetus between four and five lunar months' gestation, the developmental age of the putative decedent. In terms of commingling, two cortical bone fragments were too thick to represent fetal bones. The absence of dentition, as well as the absence of medical or dental artifacts, was consistent with expected findings for a fetus or infant.

One interesting note involved the cremains weight in this case. The cremains weight was more than the weights published for a decedent of similar age. However, the reference fetus documented in the published study (Warren and Maples 1997) was cremated in a stainless steel container placed within the retort. The presence of the two larger bone fragments in the case example presented here suggested that the fetus was most likely cremated on the floor of the retort and a small amount of unrelated ash and refractory material was added to the weight.

This case illustrates several points. First, doubt crept into the minds of the parents because they had no prior knowledge of the amount of cremains that should be expected after the cremation of a fetus. Second, it is easier to discover demonstrable commingling among the cremains of fetuses, infants, and children than it is among adults. This is due to both the lesser volume of material to be examined and the shorter time frame in which to accrue cultural artifacts related to life history. The presence of bone fragments diagnostic of gestational age, as well as the relatively small amount of commingling in this case, convinced the decedent's loved ones that the crematory had performed a conscientious and professional service, and they returned home satisfied with the conclusions of the analysis.

Conclusion

Contemporary commercial cremation represents an extreme taphonomic process that usually destroys all positive biological evidence of identity and leaves little in the way of scientific evidence that might help resolve legal issues of commingling and improper cremation practice. However, several recent legal cases have drawn the attention of forensic scientists, who have responded by producing a growing body of literature outlining case histories and research projects that seek to improve our understanding of the cremation process and its effect on the human body. These efforts are not directed at resolving commingling during cremation but are instead aimed at increasing our ability to discover the extent and nature of commingling as a part of the routine cremation process.

References

Arizona State Legislature. 32–1398. Crematories, disciplinary actions, acts of crematory. Accessed at: http://www.azleg.gov/FormatDocument.asp?inDoc=/ars/32/01398.htm&Title=32&DocType=ARS

Bass, B., Jefferson, J., 2003. Death's Acre. G.P. Putnam and Sons, New York.

Bass, W.M., Jantz, R.L., 2004. Cremation weights in East Tennessee. J. Forensic Sci. 49, 901–904.

Bergslien, E.T., Bush, M., Bush, P.J., 2008. Identification of cremains using X-ray diffraction spectroscopy and a comparison to trace element analysis. Forensic Sci. Int. 175, 218–226.

Birkby, W.H., 1991. The Analysis of Cremains. 43rd Annual Meeting of the American Academy of Forensic Science, Anaheim, CA.

Bohnert, M., Rost, T., Pollak, S., 1998. The degree of destruction of human bodies in relation to the duration of the fire. Forensic Sci. Int. 95, 11–21.

Brooks, T.R., Bodkin, T.E., Potts, G.E., Smullen, S.A., 2006. Elemental analysis of human cremains using ICP-OES to classify legitimate and contaminated cremains. J. Forensic Sci. 51, 967–973.

Christensen, A.M., Smith, M.A., Thomas, R.M., 2012. Validation of x-ray fluorescence for determining osseous or dental origin of unknown material. J. Forensic Sci. 57, 47–51.

Davies, D.J., 2005. Encyclopedia of Cremation. Ashgate Publishers, Burlington, VT.

Fazekas, I., Kosa, K., 1978. Forensic Fetal Osteology. Akademiai Kiado Publishers, Budapest, Hungary.

Florida State Legislature. 497.171. Identification of human remains. Accessed at: http://www.leg.state.fl.us/Statutes/index.cfm?App_mode=Display_Statute&Search_String=&URL=0400-0499/0497/Sections/0497.171.html

Florida State Legislature. 497.608. Liability for unintentional commingling of the residue of the cremation process. Accessed at: http://www.leg.state.fl.us/Statutes/index.cfm?App_mode=Display_Statute&Search_String=&URL=0400-0499/0497/Sections/0497.608.html

Iverson, K.V., 2001. Death to Dust: What Happens to Dead Bodies? Galen Press, Ltd., Tucson, AZ.

Maples, W.R., Browning, M., 1994. Dead Men Do Tell Tales: The Strange and Fascinating Cases of a Forensic Anthropologist. Broadway Books, New York.

Murad, T.A., 1998. The growing popularity of cremation versus inhumation: Some forensic implications. In: Reichs, K. (Ed.), Forensic Osteology: Advances in the Identification of Human Remains. Charles C. Thomas Publisher, Ltd., Springfield, IL, pp. 86–105.

Prothero, S.R., 2001. Purified by Fire: A History of Cremation in America. Health Press, Berkeley, CA.

Saferstein, R., 2009. Forensic Science: From Crime Scene to the Crime Lab. Pearson Prentice Hall, Upper Saddle River, NJ.

Schultz, J.J., Warren, M.W., Krigbaum, J.S., 2008. Analysis of human cremains: Gross and chemical methods. In: Schmidt, C.W., Symes, S.A. (Eds.), The Analysis of Burned Human Remains. Elsevier Academic Press, London, pp. 75–94.

Sonek, A., 1992. The Weight(s) of Cremains. 44th Annual Scientific Meeting of the American Academy of Forensic Sciences, New Orleans, LA.

Steadman, D.W., Sperry, K., Snow, F.L., Fulginiti, L., Craig, E., 2008. Anthropological investigations of the Tri-State Crematorium incident. In: Adams, B.J., Byrd, J.E. (Eds.), Recovery, Analysis, and Identification of Commingled Human Remains. Humana Press, Totowa, NJ, pp 81–96.

Van Deest, T.L., Murad, T.A., Bartelink, E.J., 2011. A re-examination of cremains weight: Sex and age variation in a northern California sample. J. Forensic Sci. 56, 344–349.

Warren, M.W., 1999. Radiographic determination of developmental age in fetuses and stillborns. J. Forensic Sci. 44, 708–712.

Warren, M.W., Falsetti, A.B., Hamilton, W.F., Levine, L.J., 1999. Evidence of arteriosclerosis in cremated remains. Am. J. Forensic Med. Pathol. 20, 277–280.

Warren, M.W., Falsetti, A.B., Kravchenko, I.I., Dunnam, F.E., Van Rinsvelt, H.A., Maples, W.R., 2002. Elemental analysis of bone: Proton-induced X-ray emission testing in forensic cases. Forensic Sci. Int. 125, 37–41.

Warren, M.W., Maples, W.R., 1997. The anthropometry of contemporary commercial cremation. J. Forensic Sci. 42, 417–423.

Warren, M.W., Schultz, J.J., 2002. Post-cremation taphonomy and artifact preservation. J. Forensic Sci. 47, 656–659.

CHAPTER 12

Marrying Anthropology and DNA: Essential for Solving Complex Commingling Problems in Cases of Extreme Fragmentation

Amy Z. Mundorff[1], Robert Shaler[2], Erik T. Bieschke[3], Elaine Mar-Cash[4]

[1]Assistant Professor, Anthropology, The University of Tennessee [2]Retired Professor of Biochemistry and Molecular Biology, Pennsylvania State University [3]Criminalist, San Diego Police Department [4]EMar Forensic Consulting

Introduction

On September 11, 2001, 10 terrorists using two planes attacked the World Trade Center (WTC) in New York City. Although the attack is often thought of as one large disaster, it was actually four separate events (two aircraft crashes and two building collapses) that occurred almost simultaneously and in the same general location. The initial events left 2,749 people dead from the planes' impacts and the subsequent building collapses. Others have since died from medical complications, increasing the current number of known victims of the WTC attack to 2,753. As of September 2013 (12 years after the WTC attack), nearly 22,000 pieces of human remains have been recovered, of which 13,703 have been identified. This translates to a male-to-female ratio nearly matching the number of missing victims, the number of identified victims, and the number of identified fragments (Figure 12-1). Jurisdiction for victim identification fell to the city of New York, and it became the job of the Office of Chief Medical Examiner (OCME) to identify the victims' remains. As might be expected with a disaster of this scale and with such extensive body fragmentation, the identification process was (and is to this day) an extremely complicated endeavor. The goal of this chapter is to highlight some of the initial challenges in victim identification and to point out the integral role that both anthropology and DNA played, particularly in the process of sorting out commingled human remains. Moreover, it was actually the combination of anthropology and DNA analysis that was essential for the more complex commingling problems.

This chapter proceeds in two sections. The first section provides a historical overview of the process used to identify victims' remains from the WTC disaster. This was an evolving process that adjusted over time, as new techniques were developed to address novel

Commingled Human Remains. http://dx.doi.org/10.1016/B978-0-12-405889-7.00012-5

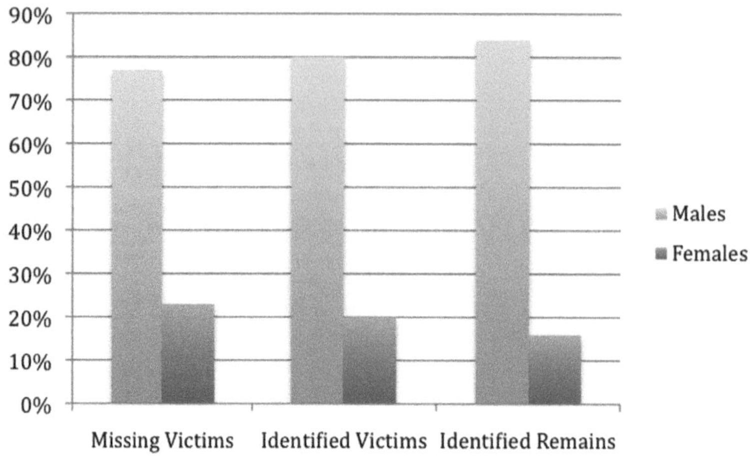

Figure 12-1
Ratio of male to female victims and identifications.

challenges. This section also focuses on the increasingly complex techniques used to extract DNA, as well as the processes implemented to address identification discrepancies. Specifically, it discusses the development of a "special projects group" to work on the more complex cases, and the Final Anthropological Review (FAR) program, which was implemented for quality control purposes. The procedures for both the special projects group and FAR highlight the importance of interdisciplinary collaboration in troubleshooting problem cases in any sizable mass fatality incident with extreme fragmentation.

The second section provides a series of case examples illustrating some mistakes encountered with the identification of WTC victims and how the problems were resolved. Overall, the work of the OCME and ancillary agencies involved in the identifications has been the highest possible quality given the current restrictions of the technology. Indeed, as discussed in the following sections, the science of DNA identification was pushed forward by the efforts and expertise of those working on this project. Also, the OCME has embraced an admirable policy of transparency, allowing both successes and setbacks to be openly discussed in a variety of scientific venues. The overriding purpose of this chapter is to provide future practitioners and policymakers a means of learning from the adaptations made during the early months of the WTC identification project as they plan and implement their own programs to prepare for future events.

Part I: Overview of WTC Identification Process

Victim identification following a mass fatality incident (MFI) is usually performed by a team of forensic specialists including odontologists, fingerprint examiners, pathologists, radiologists, and anthropologists. However, since the early 1990s, DNA has become an increasingly common means of identification for mass fatality victims, especially when traditional methods such as fingerprint and dental matching have been exhausted (Ballantyne 1997; Clayton et al. 1995; Corach et al. 1995; Fernando and Vanezis 1998; Goodwin et al. 1999; Hsu et al. 1999; Kahana and Hiss 1997; Leclair et al. 2004; Ludes et al. 1994; Olaisen et al. 1997). As DNA technology has evolved, its role in the identification of human remains from mass fatalities has grown. For example, in the 1996 ValuJet Flight 592 crash, the degree of fragmentation as well as logistical and technical limitations was considered to preclude the use of DNA in the identification process (Mittleman et al. 2000). However, just a few years later, DNA was the sole means of identification for the 155 victims of the 2000 Kaprun cable car fire in Austria (Meyer 2003). DNA has played a primary role in victim identification in the aftermath of events such as the crash of American Airlines Flight 587 in 2001, the Indonesia Tsunami disaster, the Madrid subway bombings in 2004, and the London subway bombings and Hurricane Katrina in 2005.

Following the 2001 WTC disaster in New York City, Mayor Giuliani mandated the identification of as many of the recovered remains as possible. This propelled DNA analysis to the center of the WTC identification process. Ultimately, DNA analysis was responsible for identifying the majority of the WTC remains. In fact, of the 13,723 fragments that have been identified to date (September 11, 2013), more than 90% have been identified using DNA alone. And of the 1,634 victims who have been identified to date, 886 have been identified solely by their DNA. Without DNA technology, more than half of the identified victims would not have been identified.

The Role of DNA in WTC Identifications

The many unique challenges of the WTC disaster meant that DNA would become increasingly important while the role of more traditional victim identification methods became comparatively limited. For example, the explosive force of the falling buildings extensively fragmented remains, limiting the application of fingerprint and dental matching, because these methods can be employed only to identify remains that retain either fingers or dentition. With an average victims-to-remains ratio of 1:8, based on 13,723 identified fragments and 1,634 identified victims, only a small proportion of those remains possessed identifying characteristics such as fingers or dentition. Because the vast majority of the remains lacked such identifying characteristics, DNA became an essential tool in the victims' identification effort. The value of DNA analysis in mass fatality identification, such as the events of September 11, 2001, results from its ability to identify fragments of human tissue and bone, regardless of the body part recovered or the size of the fragment.

DNA identifications were achieved by comparing unknown remains to known references. For example, personal items taken from or used by the missing person, such as stored blood, a toothbrush, or a razor blade, could be used as direct comparison references for victim remains. Concurrently, specimens such as buccal swabs from biological relatives were used to construct kinship pedigrees to compare with victim remains. But successful DNA analysis also requires a usable sample from the remains. This became increasingly problematic as the WTC remains began showing signs of extensive decomposition caused by the prolonged recovery process. Moreover, thermal conditions associated with "hot spots" at the recovery site and humidity from spraying the rubble with water in order to reduce temperatures to aid in the rescue process further degraded the DNA (Arismendi et al. 2004; Burger et al. 1999; Holland et al. 2003; Imaizumi et al. 2004). As time passed, the likelihood of obtaining intact and usable DNA from soft tissue faded, and those conducting the identifications began to see a growing possibility that DNA degradation might limit identification capabilities, leaving hundreds of individuals unidentified. Struggling to keep pace with the evolving conditions, DNA scientists conducted the process of victim identification in what can now be described as a series of distinct but overlapping phases.

Phase I utilized standardized DNA tests commonly employed at that time by forensic laboratories throughout the world. During this phase, short tandem repeat (STR) analysis was employed and, minimally, the 13 original loci used in the Combined DNA Index System (CODIS) were analyzed. This technology was a logical approach for analyzing the WTC remains because it had been extensively validated and represented a noncontroversial choice for analyzing samples that had been exposed to environmental insults. After only three weeks of testing, however, it was clear that a significant percent of the remains were giving either partial profiles (33%) or no profiles (28%) at all. At the conclusion of Phase I testing, nearly 60% of the remains were yielding poor DNA results that were not adequate for meeting the requirement for matching and identification.

While a significant percentage of remains did not yield DNA, 33% yielded partial profiles; in other words, while not sufficiently robust to satisfy STR identification protocols, nearly one-third of the cases provided usable DNA for the purposes of identification. In response, analysts devised strategies for extracting additional genetic information from the compromised remains.

Phase II involved re-examination of the original samples and additional research aimed at increasing the yield of analyzable DNA. This effort was successful, because soft tissue and bones originally yielding only partial profiles now yielded either full profiles or partial profiles with additional loci being observed. However, even following this process, many remains still did not yield a sufficient amount of usable DNA for valid identifications. This necessitated another testing strategy, which began Phase III of the victim identification effort.

Phase III began in November 2001 after it became clear that these partial DNA profiles would fall short of the threshold of statistical robustness established for identifications. Three DNA techniques previously unused in the WTC identification process were applied. First, building on a technique that was being developed prior to 9/11, a mini-STR test panel was created. Initially, a study was started with John Butler at the National Institute of Standards and Technology (NIST) to investigate using mini-STR analysis for the WTC samples. Although the initial study by NIST was marginally successful, the Bode Technology Group reprised the research in March 2002, developing a new mini-STR panel that delivered the first mini-STR results in December 2002. This new mini-STR panel was used to successfully identify thousands of remains. Second, Celera performed mitochondrial DNA sequencing for remains and reference samples. Third, research to develop a 70-loci single nucleotide polymorphisms (SNPs) panel by Gene Screen in Texas was used to test thousands of remains and reference samples. Each of these approaches supplemented traditional STR analysis, leading to new identifications that would not have been possible otherwise.

Challenges to the DNA Identification Effort

In addition to ongoing concerns regarding degraded DNA, other issues that could compromise identification efforts continually surfaced, such as unanticipated commingling and DNA contamination. Anthropologists and DNA analysts collaborated to address these problems by implementing two programs designed to add more rigorous quality control procedures at all stages of the victim identification effort (Budimlija et al. 2003). The first measure, the Anthropological Verification Project (AVP), focused efforts on the re-examination of *unidentified* remains for the purpose of discovering potential instances of commingling that may have been missed during the initial examination. The first few days following a mass fatality incident are characterized by overwhelming confusion and chaos (Biesecker et al. 2005; Fernando and Vanezis 1998; Moody and Busuttil 1994). Because of this, mistakes are most likely to occur early in the process, although they likely will go unnoticed for days, weeks, or even months. However, these mistakes can have a significant impact on the overall identification effort. The AVP (see Chapter 17 of this volume for more in-depth discussion on AVP) included the re-examination of 16,969 unidentified cases, of which 75 (0.044%) were flagged as *potentially* containing instances of missed commingling. More than half of these flagged cases had been processed through the mortuary within the first month of the disaster, and most (49%) were from September (Figure 12-2) (Mundorff 2009).

The second measure, the Final Anthropological Review (FAR), entailed the examination of *identified* remains as part of the reconciliation process prior to family notification (MacKinnon and Mundorff 2006). This program was designed and implemented in May 2002 in response to a single case in which commingling had been discovered *after* the remains had been identified (although they had not yet been released to the funeral home). The purpose behind its development was to ensure a final check of each identified fragment of human remains prior to approving its release. The FAR became a critical quality control measure aimed at discovering potential misidentifications stemming from mistakes originating from a variety of sources, many of which were unanticipated when the project began.

As part of this approach, a "special projects group" was formed in the DNA laboratory to handle various sample processing issues such as victim or reference sample contamination or

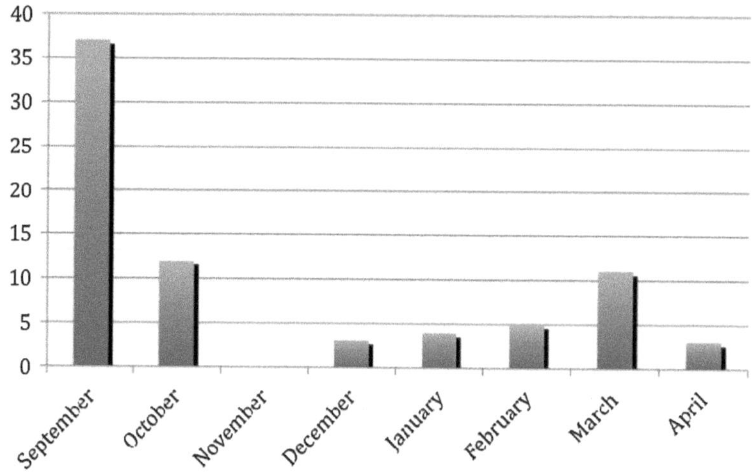

Figure 12-2
This chart presents the number of cases, by the month they were originally processed through the mortuary, that were later flagged as potentially containing missed instances of commingling. Nearly half were processed in the first few weeks following September 11.

mix-up, as well as to investigate "questionable identifications" resulting from these core problems (Budimlija et al. 2003). Also within the DNA laboratory, a "WTC data analysis group" was in place to bridge the gap between anthropologists and the "special projects group" in detecting and troubleshooting these core problems. In general, many of the problems addressed by this group had been revealed during the FAR examination as illogical identifications, such as two left feet for the same individual. The most frequent cause of these types of errors was DNA contamination or transcription mistakes. Once a problem case was discovered, the DNA laboratory along with the anthropologist and a medicolegal investigator (MLI) reviewed the case file and examined the remains, often resampling for new DNA analysis. This cooperative effort among DNA analysts, anthropologists, and MLIs resolved numerous errors, such as mislabeling and sampling problems in the mortuary, DNA contamination, laboratory equipment contamination, transcription errors, data entry mistakes, and problems with early antemortem sample collection.

Implementing the Final Anthropological Review

By early April 2002, the use of traditional identification methods, such as fingerprint and dental matching, slowed such that these were not a significant source of future identifications. It became clear that the majority of new identifications would come through DNA. No identification project to date had attempted to identify so many fragments by DNA alone, and DNA provided the ability to potentially link dozens of pieces of human remains to a single individual (Biesecker et al. 2005).

As the pace of DNA identifications increased, it became apparent that there were some problem identifications. Commingling and/or DNA contamination had occurred in some of the samples, and mistakes made during the initial collection of antemortem information from families complicated the identification process. At one point, it was estimated internally that tens of thousands of errors may have been made during the antemortem information collection (Hennessey 2002; 2008). For example, at the family assistance center (FAC), the New York Police Department (NYPD) collected personal reference and kinship samples and interviewed victims' families to collect data for the victim information forms. These forms recorded antemortem information about the victims that could later be used to assist identifications. Hundreds of federal temporary workers from the Disaster Mortuary Operational Response Team (DMORT) performed the data entry for thousands of these forms. Unfortunately, one-sixth of the initial information collected had to be corrected because of missing data, incorrectly recorded data, improper kinship sampling, or data entry errors (Biesecker et al. 2005; Cash et al. 2003). These challenges, along with others that occurred during the mortuary and laboratory stages, led to inevitable identification problems. Discovering and rectifying these problems became the main focus of both the DNA special projects group and the Final Anthropological Review team.

At the height of the WTC identification efforts, the OCME identified dozens of victims per day using DNA, and many of these individual identifications involved numerous small fragments. Every identification was finalized according to an established routine. First, the DNA lab matched a reference or kinship pedigree to human remains and sent this "DNA match report" to the MLI identification unit. Then, two medicolegal investigators further scrutinized the case information, checking, among other details, if any remains had been previously identified to the victim or if this was a new identification. The medicolegal investigators were also responsible for verifying all of the data in the case file, including the victim's biological information. In the early months of the recovery and identification effort, the process simply stopped at this point and the identified remains were released to the family. However, as some of the initial information collection problems became more apparent, policymakers determined that the identification process should also include a final quality control measure to catch potential errors; thus, the Final Anthropological Review was added just prior to releasing remains to funeral homes (MacKinnon and Mundorff 2006).

The medicolegal investigator and the anthropologist developed a new form for the FAR procedure that included specific information pertinent to a final verification of the identified remains. This information included the date of recovery, the case number, the name of the attending medical examiner, a brief description of the remains including what was sampled for DNA (bone, muscle, tooth, etc.), the date of identification, and the means of identification. If identified fragments were linked to a previously identified individual, information including descriptions of the previously identified fragments were included on the form. The form also indicated whether or not previously identified fragments were still curated at the OCME and could be re-examined, or if they had already been released to a funeral home. Each time a new piece or an aggregate of pieces (pieces from a single individual) was identified, the medicolegal investigator reviewing the new DNA match filled out the FAR form.

After the form had been completed, the anthropologist reviewed it for inconsistencies that could indicate a problem with the newly identified piece. Potential problems were flagged on the FAR form before the final examination of the remains. Take, for example, the circumstances in the following hypothetical case. First, the individual in question has already been successfully identified through several pieces of remains, including a partial right foot. Next, a new fragment is identified to that same individual and the case file indicates that this new piece is also a partial foot, but the paperwork lacks detailed information indicating which foot, right or left. Under these circumstances, the newly identified fragment's case file would be flagged so that during the final examination the anthropologist could determine if this preliminarily linked piece was an additional fragment of the previously identified right foot, if it was a left foot fragment, or if this was a duplicate body part (the same anatomical elements as the previously identified right foot). The final scenario (a duplicated body part) would indicate a problem with the identification.

After the FAR form had been reviewed and potential problem cases flagged, the anthropologist re-examined the human remains. Both the newly identified pieces as well as the previously identified pieces that were still curated at the OCME went through a final examination. In cases in which fragments had been previously identified and released to funeral homes and were, therefore, unavailable for re-examination, the anthropologist relied on the information from the original case file recorded on the FAR form and photographs. During the final examination, the anthropologist initially confirmed that the case number on the outside of the body bag matched the case number and remains inside the bag. When this confirmation was established, the anthropologist then looked for inconsistencies between the physical remains and their description in the paperwork, duplicated elements, or other discrepancies. This included confirming that the victim's biological profile matched the presumptively identified remains. If the identified victim was a female, did the remains appear to be from a female of the same approximate age? If there were any disagreements between the documentation and the remains being evaluated, duplication of body parts, conflict between the biological profiles, or any other questions regarding the potential validity of the identification, the identification was placed on hold. Once a case was placed on hold, the special projects group, the WTC data analysis group, and an anthropologist investigated it until the problem was resolved. Often this investigation included a detailed retrospective examination of the chain of custody for the reference sample used to establish the questionable identification. Other antemortem information collected to establish the identification was scrutinized, as was the information recorded in the remains' postmortem file. And, if needed, DNA was resampled and retested. Taken as a whole, these quality control measures revealed overwhelming accuracy within the system, and very few problems were found.

Part II: WTC Case Examples

Defining Case

This example is paradigmatic of all issues faced in subsequent problem cases and illustrates the importance of a holistic approach to troubleshooting identifications. It is also the case that alerted OCME staff to the need for more rigorous quality control procedures before final release of remains, and one that led to significant procedural changes, specifically the implementation of the Final Anthropological Review process. The discussion of this case is followed by a series of short case examples demonstrating the multidisciplinary teamwork among DNA specialists, medicolegal investigators, and anthropologists in detecting and solving complex commingling and contamination problems, transcription and data entry mistakes, and antemortem collection errors from the WTC disaster identification project.

After a disaster such as WTC, the decision regarding when to have a funeral and bury the remains can be wrenching. Families had been informed that because of the extreme fragmentation and the ongoing identification process, it was likely that victim remains would continue to be identified days, weeks, months, or even years later. Many were forced into a waiting game as they balanced the desire for a speedy funeral against the desire to lay to rest as much of the decedent's remains as possible. Often, families waited until a "significant amount" of remains had been identified before deciding to claim a loved one's remains. Therefore, it was not uncommon that, upon notification of an identification, families would request that OCME personnel provide them with an estimate of the percentage of identified remains from that victim.

In May 2002, the OCME notified a family that their missing family member's remains had been identified. In this particular case, the forensic anthropologist examined the remains in collaboration with a medicolegal investigator, at the family's request, to determine the percentage of identified remains. The victim's remains had been excavated from Ground Zero fairly early in the recovery process and were stored in a refrigerated unit for months pending identification. The remains consisted of two major portions: the top portion of a torso down to the fourth lumbar vertebra, and the lower portion of a torso, from the sacrum down. There was no fifth lumbar vertebra, which could have articulated the two halves together. At the time, it was not clear whether or not these two portions had been previously articulated by skin or soft tissue and had become disarticulated over time due to decomposition, or whether they had never been physically attached but were grouped together because they were assumed to be from the same individual at the time of recovery. It was not uncommon for two disparate portions of remains to be held together by skin only. For example, although a portion of hip might be attached to a foot by skin, all of the connecting leg bones and other soft tissue in between might be absent. In this case, the original medical examiner's notes stated that the body was in two separate portions (both of which were sampled for DNA) but made no mention of whether or not the remains were connected by skin or soft tissue. Of the two DNA samples, one was used to identify the remains, while the other sample failed to yield viable DNA.

During the interim between the time this body was recovered and the time it was identified, mortuary personnel had learned a great deal about the extent of the devastation at the disaster site. Complicated excavation procedures at Ground Zero combined with enormous fragmentation of the human remains produced far more commingling than had been initially recognized (Mundorff 2003). In response, more rigorous triage standards and examination techniques had been introduced after the first few weeks of recovery. This included, for example, a protocol that any remains not conjoined by soft tissue or able to be conjoined along skeletal fracture sites should be treated as separate remains, even if they appeared to be from the same individual. However, this particular body had been processed through the mortuary during the earliest stages and thus was not subjected to these more rigorous standards (MacKinnon and Mundorff 2006; Mundorff, this book, Chapter 17). The secondary examination revealed that these two pieces were not (or were no longer) attached by tissue, and possibly would not have been grouped together under the more rigorous triage and exam standards. The anthropologist and the medicolegal investigator recommended that the identification be placed on hold until both body portions had been retested for DNA. Interestingly, the medical examiner, though agreeing to the DNA reanalysis, believed that the two pieces represented a single individual. Subsequent DNA analysis confirmed the identification on the top portion of the torso but also revealed that the bottom portion belonged to a previously unidentified individual. The result of this inquiry led to the development and implementation of the AVP and FAR to address the need for more rigorous quality control procedures.

Additional Case Examples

This section highlights WTC case examples in which various problems with identified remains were encountered and solved using a multidisciplinary approach between anthropology and DNA. Several of the examples are simple, such as mislabeling, and others involve complex DNA investigations. Often, tracing the root of the problem was more complicated than solving the problem itself. However, understanding how the problems occurred helped to avoid similar errors in the future.

Example 1: Mislabeling in the Mortuary

When more than 22,000 cases and their corresponding DNA samples are processed, labeling errors are likely to happen. Two bone and two tissue samples were submitted to the DNA laboratory from the mortuary labeled with the case number 30776. The two bones were tested and yielded DNA profiles matching two different individuals. The tissue samples had not yet been tested because two different laboratories tested tissue and bone samples. Based on the bones' conflicting DNA results, all four samples were retested as part of the DNA conflict investigation. A sample audit was performed in parallel, and it was determined that case number 30777 (the next consecutive number) did not have DNA samples submitted. As a result, a bone sample from 30777 was taken independently of the reinvestigation. DNA results confirmed that the four samples originally labeled as case 30776 originated from two different individuals, one of which matched the DNA results from the recently sampled case 30777. Because case numbers were assigned consecutively in the mortuary, it was theorized that two of the four samples submitted as case number 30776 actually belonged to the next case, 30777, and the wrong barcode label had been affixed during examination. The curated remains for cases 30776 and 30777, as well as their corresponding DNA samples from the lab, were pulled from storage and inspected by the anthropologist and a DNA analyst. One of the DNA bone samples labeled as 30776 could be conjoined with the remains labeled 30777, confirming that this sample had been mislabeled as 30776 in the mortuary.

Example 2: Clerical Error in Case File

A partial body had been identified by dental comparison. The mortuary paperwork for this partial body indicated that a left arm, including the hand, was present. Months later, DNA matched a left hand to that same individual. While assessing the final anthropological review form, it was obvious that a left hand was being linked by DNA to an individual who, according to the case file, apparently already had a left hand attached to a previously identified partial body. However, the body had already been released, so there was no way to confirm that the hand attached to the body was indeed a left and not mistakenly a right. It was not uncommon to encounter right/left mix-ups on the paperwork from examination, and it was also not uncommon to encounter data entry errors where the form stated "right," but "left" was entered into the database. Anthropology confirmed during re-examination that the newly matched hand was left (and not mistakenly a right), and the DNA review indicated that the match was solid. However, during the review of the paperwork in the case file from the original partial body identification, a note was discovered from the police officer responsible for fingerprinting the "left" hand attached to the body. The note indicated that the hand was actually a right, not a left as described by the medical examiner. However, this information was not picked up during data entry, and therefore, the information was never corrected in the database to illustrate that the hand attached to the original body was actually a right. Consequently, the newly matched left hand was not a duplicate part, as it appeared, but merely a clerical error that was eventually sorted out during the review process.

Example 3: DNA Sample Contamination

A DNA match report was issued indicating that three fragments had been identified to the same individual. Due to the extreme fragmentation caused by the nature of the disaster, it was common for multiple remains to be linked by DNA to the same individual. In fact, many victims had dozens of fragments separately identified; one individual had more than 176. During the FAR documentation review, it was noticed that all three newly matched fragments were humeri and, specifically, two were described in the paperwork simply as "proximal left" without any other detail, while the third fragment was recorded as a "right shaft fragment." The two proximal left fragments both could have been small pieces of different portions from the same bone, or they could have been duplicate body parts; only a visual inspection of the remains could clarify this. The re-examination would also ensure there was not a transcription error, for example, recording "left" for "right" or "distal" for "proximal." However, this was not the case. In fact, upon examination, based on the bones' morphology it was apparent that the three humeri fragments were from at least two different individuals (Figure 12-3). Additionally, there were indeed two overlapping proximal left fragments. One of the proximal fragments was robust, possibly indicating male, while the other appeared gracile, possibly indicating female; either way, there were overlapping features present on both bones. All three cases were placed on hold until a resampling strategy was devised.

In the forensic biology laboratory, the DNA analyst responsible for WTC quality assurance was concurrently investigating a possible contamination problem during the high-throughput DNA testing process. During this investigation, a pattern emerged. Samples in the same well position, in sequentially numbered or processed trays, were giving the same DNA profiles (for example, tray 1 position A4 and tray 2 position A4 yielded the same profiles). Many of these samples on the affected trays gave conflicting results when compared to other samples from the same case number. High-throughput DNA testing took place in one of the contracting DNA laboratories; therefore, their procedures were reviewed, and it was determined that a new robotic pipetting instrument was the cause of the contamination. Insufficient washing of

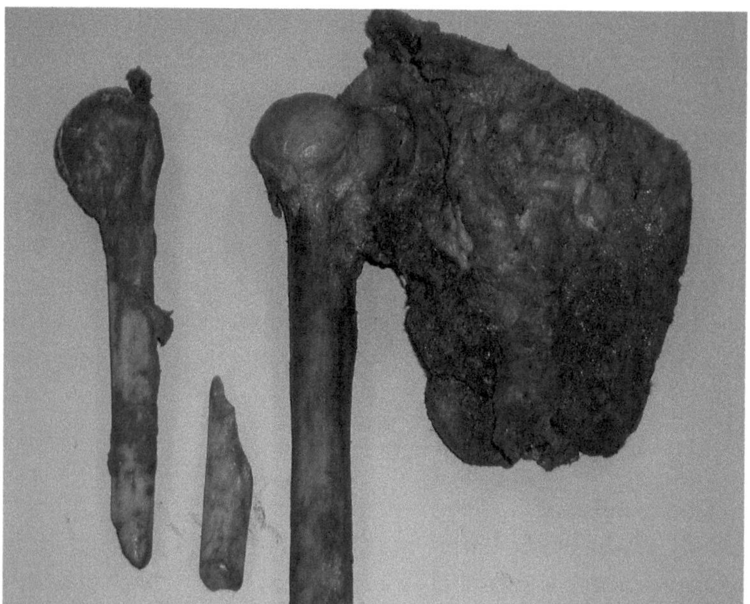

Figure 12-3
Two proximal left humeri and right humeral fragment. *(Source: Office of Chief Medical Examiner, New York City.)*

the pipette tips between processing of trays led to sample carryover from one tray to the next, even though the recommended number of washings was being employed. A common characteristic of this phenomenon was high amounts of DNA in the donor tray and a lower amount of the same DNA in the recipient tray. DNA testing using the liquid handling robots was stopped for approximately three months so that the problem and its solution could be identified.

After this systematic error was detected, the DNA quality assurance analyst collaborated with a representative from the vendor laboratory in order to resolve the issue. The first step taken in the corrective action was to remove the pipetting robot from the sample processing flow and replace it with a disposable tip system. The second measure taken was to perform a thorough review of the existing data in search of potentially affected samples. Samples that were deemed to be affected were retested. After subsequent retesting, a determination was made as to the reliability of the original results. Also, DNA profiles that were proven unreliable were invalidated and therefore no longer used for comparison. However, not all potentially affected samples were first detected during the DNA data review; several cases were instead detected during the FAR process, such as in the previous example presented. Based on the recommendations of the anthropologist, all three humeri were retested. DNA results confirmed that two of the fragments were consistent with their original results, whereas the third fragment originated from a different individual.

Example 4: DNA Sample Contamination

The mistake in the previous example was noted prior to visually examining the actual remains because the information in the paperwork indicated a conflict. In that case, there were two proximal left humeri fragments. The next example illustrates a similar problem; however, simply looking at the paperwork could not have revealed the mistake, as the case descriptions did not conflict with each other or any other identified remains. This problem could be discovered only by re-examining the actual remains. DNA matched two fragments to one individual. The documentation review of these two fragments made sense: one was a distal right femur, and the other was a distal left femur. There was no overlap between these elements, and no distal femora had been previously identified for this victim. However, when the fragments were visually examined during the FAR, it was noted that, morphologically, these two pieces were very different from each other: one was very large, and the other was very small (Figure 12-4). Hence, there was little possibility that they belonged to the same individual. The two pieces in question were placed on hold and resampled. Results from the DNA retesting confirmed that the two bones originated from two different individuals. As the original DNA results were investigated further, it was determined that the mistake also resulted from the systematic robotic pipetting error described in the previous example. However, this mistake would not have been discovered by only reviewing the documentation because on paper the identification made sense; only a re-examination of the actual remains would have caught this mistake.

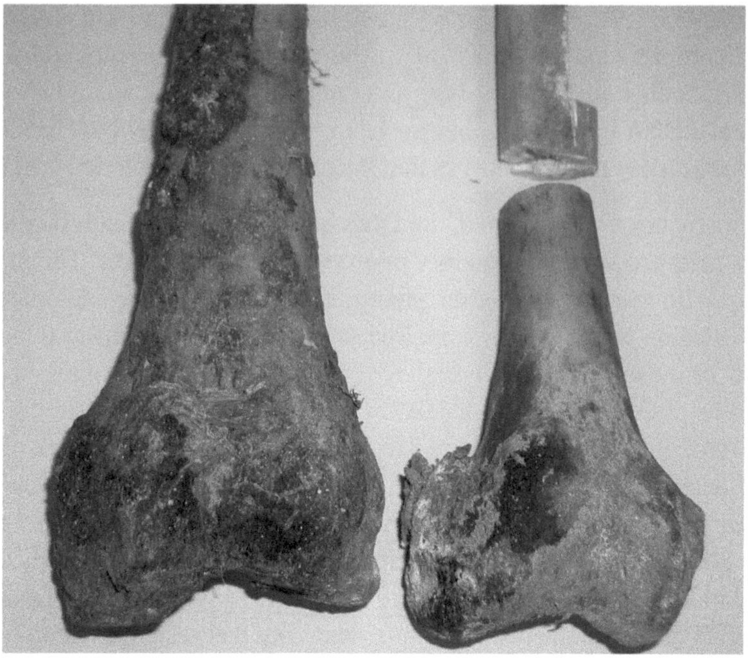

Figure 12-4
Right and left distal femora. *(Source: Office of Chief Medical Examiner, New York City.)*

Example 5: DNA Case Number Mix-up

Two hipbone fragments, case numbers 30709 and 85571, were identified by DNA as belonging to the same individual. Both were fragments, specifically recorded as ilium, with a significant amount of adhering decomposed soft tissue. Because both pieces were listed only as "fragment of ilium," they were flagged during the documentation review as indicating a need to ensure the fragments did not overlap. It was not uncommon for case descriptions to lack specific details such as right/left. More than 30 anthropologists from around the United States rotated through the OCME during the WTC victim identification project. Proficiency levels, especially when it came to experience with decomposed soft tissue obscuring bony landmarks, greatly varied. Therefore, although these pieces may have been easily recognized as ilium fragments, other specifics, such as side, may have been more challenging for the individual first examining the remains. The FAR examination revealed that the pieces overlapped; therefore, both cases were placed on hold and resampled for DNA testing (Figure 12-5). Retesting results for case 30709 confirmed the original identification results; however, case 85571 matched a different individual. In general, two separate reactions had to be performed to obtain a full STR DNA profile. The first reaction in the original test result for case 85571 yielded no DNA profile; however, the second reaction yielded the maximum result. This combination of data is unusual, as an analyst would expect to see consistent results from one reaction to the next. In conjunction with the DNA results, a review of the sample's chain of custody led the DNA analyst to

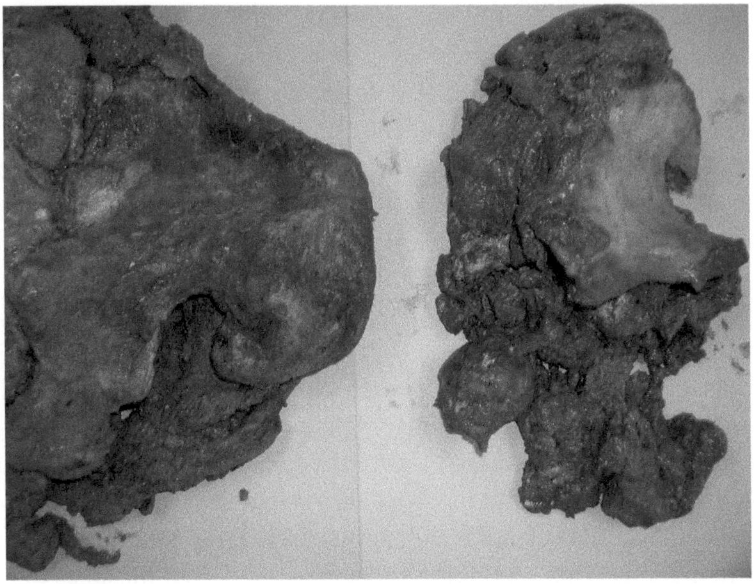

Figure 12-5
Overlapping ilium fragments. *(Source: Office of Chief Medical Examiner, New York City.)*

theorize that case 85571 had been mixed up with case 8571. Case 8571 matched the original, and the retest results for case 30709 and case 85571 were indeed from a different individual.

Example 6: Element Siding Mistake During Examination

Two separate right hands were recovered in February 2002, five months into the recovery process. When they arrived at the Medical Examiner's Office, both were fragmentary and in an advanced state of decomposition. Months later, both right hands were linked by DNA to the same individual. This was immediately flagged during the documentation review portion of the FAR because of their overlap in description. Re-examination proved that one of the hands was actually a left, and so no additional DNA testing was warranted. This mistake could have happened at a number of different points in the process, but it is impossible to pinpoint when it occurred. For example, there may have been a communication problem between the examiner and his or her scribe; this may also have been a transcription error in which the scribe wrote one thing when he or she meant to write another; or similar to the previous case, the decomposition and fragmentation could have been so extensive that it was not clear to the examiner processing the remains whether the hand was right or left. However, adding in a final verification of the remains ensured one last level of assurance before identification.

Example 7: DNA Sample Switch

During the FAR, it was discovered that a left distal femur (case number 308230) was matched by DNA to an individual who had already been identified by multiple remains, including a left distal femur (case number 308232). Because of the duplicate body part, the anthropologist initiated an investigation. During the course of this investigation, the DNA results and the DNA sample handling process were evaluated. It was hypothesized that a DNA sample switch had occurred between these two cases. Case 308232 was resampled and tested, confirming the initial results. Case 308230 was resampled and tested and subsequently matched a different individual. Thus, the new DNA result confirmed the hypothesis of sample mix-up that was noted during the final anthropological review because of duplicate elements.

Conclusion

In summary, because of the WTC disaster's scope and complex characteristics, including extreme fragmentation and commingling, ongoing interdisciplinary collaboration, specifically between anthropologists and DNA analysts, proved vital in the process of identifying victim remains. Through various examples, it has been shown that this collaboration should include those who collect and interpret scientific and nonscientific information at both the antemortem and postmortem levels. This continuing collaboration allowed mistakes to be detected and corrected. It also allowed systems to be adjusted to prevent the same mistakes from being repeated. This dynamic process pushed forward both the science of DNA identification and our understanding of the complexities inherent in managing the identification process in a disaster of this magnitude.

References

Arismendi, J.L., Baker, L.E., Matteson, K.J., 2004. Effects of processing techniques on the forensic DNA analysis of human skeletal remains. J. Forensic Sci. 49 (5), 930–934.

Ballantyne, J., 1997. Mass disaster genetics. Nat. Genet. 15 (4), 329–331.

Biesecker, L.G., Bailey-Wilson, J.E., Ballantyne, J., Baum, H., Bieber, F.R., Brenner, C., Budowle, B., Butler, J.M., Carmody, G., Conneally, P.M., Duceman, B., Eisenberg, A., Forman, L., Kidd, K.K., Leclair, B., Niezgoda, S., Parsons, T.J., Pugh, E., Shaler, R., Sherry, S.T., Sozer, A., Walsh, A., 2005. Epidemiology. DNA identifications after the 9/11 World Trade Center attack. Science 310 (5751), 1122–1123.

Budimlija, Z.M., Prinz, M.K., Zelson-Mundorff, A., Wiersema, J., Bartelink, E., MacKinnon, G., Nazzaruolo, B.L., Estacio, S.M., Hennessey, M.J., Shaler, R.C., 2003. World Trade Center human identification project: Experiences with individual body identification cases. Croat. Med. J. 44 (3), 259–263.

Burger, J., Hummel, S., Hermann, B., Henke, W., 1999. DNA preservation: A microsatellite-DNA study on ancient skeletal remains. Electrophoresis 20 (8), 1722–1728.

Cash, H.D., Hoyle, J.W., Sutton, A.J., 2003. Development under extreme conditions: Forensic bioinformatics in the wake of the World Trade Center disaster. Pac. Symp. Biocomput., 638–653.

Clayton, T.M., Whitaker, J.P., Maguire, C.N., 1995. Identification of bodies from the scene of a mass disaster using DNA amplification of short tandem repeat (STR) loci. Forensic. Sci. Int. 76 (1), 7–15.

Corach, D., Sala, A., Penacino, G., Sotelo, A., 1995. Mass disasters: Rapid molecular screening of human remains by means of short tandem repeats typing. Electrophoresis 16 (9), 1617–1623.

Fernando, R., Vanezis, P., 1998. Medicolegal aspects of the Thai Airbus crash near Kathmandu, Nepal: Findings of the investigating pathologists. Am. J. Forensic. Med. Pathol. 19 (2), 169–173.

Goodwin, W., Linacre, A., Vanezis, P., 1999. The use of mitochondrial DNA and short tandem repeat typing in the identification of air crash victims. Electrophoresis 20 (8), 1707–1711.

Hennessey, M., 2002. World Trade Center DNA Identifications: The Administrative Review Process. Paper presented at the International Symposium on Human Identification, Phoenix, AZ.

Hennessey, M., 2008. Data management and commingled remains at mass fatality incidents (MFIs). In: Adams, B., Byrd, J. (Eds.), Recovery, Analysis, and Identification of Commingled Human Remains. Humana Press, Totowa, NJ, pp. 337–356.

Holland, M.M., Cave, C.A., Holland, C.A., Bille, T.W., 2003. Development of a quality, high-throughput DNA analysis procedure for skeletal samples to assist with the identification of victims from the World Trade Center attacks. Croat. Med. J. 44, 264–272.

Hsu, C.M., Huang, N.E., Tsai, L.C., Kao, L.G., Chao, C.H., Linacre, A., Lee, J.C., 1999. Identification of victims of the 1998 Taoyuan Airbus crash accident using DNA analysis. Int. J. Legal Med. 113 (1), 43–46.

Imaizumi, K., Miyasaka, S., Yoshino, M., 2004. Quantitative analysis of amplifiable DNA in tissue exposed to various environments using competitive PRC assays. Sci. Justice 44, 199–208.

Kahana, T., Hiss, J., 1997. Identification of human remains: Forensic radiology. J. Clin. Forensic Med. 4 (1), 7–15.

Leclair, B., Fregeau, C.J., Bowen, K.L., Fourney, R.M., 2004. Enhanced kinship analysis and STR-based DNA typing for human identification in mass fatality incidents: The Swissair Flight 111 disaster. J. Forensic Sci. 49 (5), 939–953.

Ludes, B., Tracqui, A., Pfitzinger, H., Kintz, P., Levy, F., Disteldorf, M., Hutt, J.M., Kaess, B., Haag, R., Memheld, B., et al., 1994. Medico-legal investigations of the Airbus A320 crash upon Mount Ste-Odile, France. J. Forensic Sci. 39 (5), 1147–1152.

MacKinnon, G., Mundorff, A.Z., 2006. World Trade Center—September 11th, 2001. In: Thompson, T.J.U., Black, S.M. (Eds.), Forensic Human Identification: An Introduction. CRC Press, Boca Raton, FL, pp. 485–499.

Meyer, H.J., 2003. The Kaprun cable car fire disaster—Aspects of forensic organisation following a mass fatality with 155 victims. Forensic Sci. Int. 138 (1–3), 1–7.

Mittleman, R.E., Barnhart, J.S., Davis, J.H., Fernandez, R., Hyman, B.A., Lengel, R.D., Lew, E.O., Rao, V.J., 2000. The Crash of ValuJet Flight 592: A Forensic Approach to Severe Body Fragmentation. Miami-Dade County Medical Examiner Department, Miami, FL.

Moody, G.H., Busuttil, A., 1994. Identification in the Lockerbie air disaster. Am. J. Forensic Med. Pathol. 15 (1), 63–69.

Mundorff, A.Z., 2003. The Role of Anthropology During the Identification of Victims from the World Trade Center Disaster. Paper presented at the American Academy of Forensic Science, Chicago, IL.

Mundorff, A.Z., 2009. Human Identification Following the World Trade Center Disaster: Assessing Management Practices for Highly Fragmented and Commingled Human Remains. Ph.D. dissertation. Simon Fraser University, British Columbia, Canada.

Olaisen, B., Stenersen, M., Mevag, B., 1997. Identification by DNA analysis of the victims of the August 1996 Spitsbergen civil aircraft disaster. Nat. Genet. 15 (4), 402–405.

CHAPTER 13

Prioritized Sampling of Bone and Teeth for DNA Analysis in Commingled Cases

David Z.C. Hines[1], Matthew Vennemeyer[2], Sylvain Amory[1], René L.M. Huel[1], Ian Hanson[1], Cheryl Katzmarzyk[2], Thomas J. Parsons[1]

[1]International Commission on Missing Persons (ICMP)

[2]International Committee of the Red Cross (ICRC)

Introduction

Since its establishment in 1996, the International Commission on Missing Persons (ICMP) has provided extensive services in missing persons documentation, archaeological excavation, anthropological analysis, and identification of unidentified remains to governments in the Balkans, South America, Africa, Asia, and the Middle East. As of September 2013, the ICMP has collected 96,814 blood samples from family members of 32,023 reported missing persons and obtained nuclear short tandem repeat (STR) DNA profiles from 59,526 bone and tooth samples from unidentified human remains. As a result of large-scale DNA profile database comparisons and genetic kinship analysis, the ICMP has issued DNA match reports indicating the identity of more than 18,562 individuals.

Many of the sets of unidentified human remains tested by the ICMP come from secondary mass graves, where complex commingling of body parts occurred (Yazedjian and Kesetovic 2008). One of the largest sets of related cases and mass graves is associated with the 1995 fall of UN "Safe Area" Srebrenica to Bosnian Serb forces. In that event, a number of very large primary mass graves were created, which were exhumed several months later with heavy machinery and the fragmented body parts distributed to a large series of secondary mass graves scattered across the remote countryside. Accordingly, the identification program relied heavily on DNA testing to help reassociate separate skeletal elements or body parts and to identify individuals. Due to the complex commingling, the number of body parts identified by DNA was substantially higher than the number of unique individuals identified because many individuals were sampled more than once. Over a multiyear project, protocols combining anthropological examination and DNA sampling were optimized to reassociate the major body parts of a single individual so that largely complete sets of remains could be returned to families, as best as possible within the constraints of cost efficiency (Figure 13-1).

Commingled Human Remains. http://dx.doi.org/10.1016/B978-0-12-405889-7.00013-7

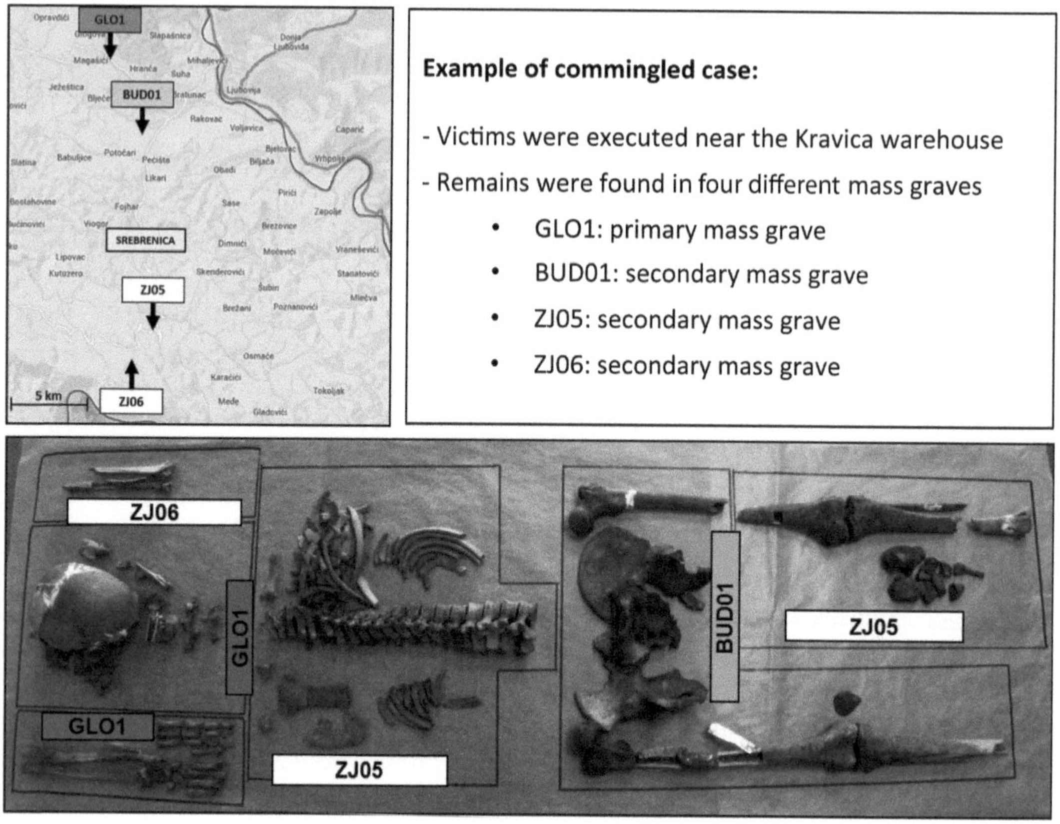

Figure 13-1
Reassociated remains of an individual recovered from four separate mass graves relating to the 1995 fall of UN Safe Area Srebrenica.

As a result of this DNA testing of an extremely wide range of isolated body parts, the ICMP has amassed a very large dataset regarding the relative DNA preservation within different skeletal elements. Skeletal remains were recovered over the course of many years, in a wide range of environmental contexts, and many of the remains tested were highly degraded. As a result, DNA testing sometimes failed due to insufficient preservation of DNA. However, ongoing refinement of DNA extraction methods has resulted in a highly efficient DNA extraction protocol currently in use at the ICMP, based on full demineralization of the bone sample, followed by purification by silica binding (Amory et al. 2012; Huel et al. 2012).

The correct selection of samples for DNA testing is critical to the identification process. Collecting unsuitable or superfluous samples adds to mortuary and laboratory workflow, causing additional expense, delays, and inconvenience. An optimal strategy thus seeks to minimize the number and maximize the quality of samples taken. Established practice has heavily focused on sampling dentition and dense, weight-bearing bone, but detailed recommendations have lagged. Mundorff et al. (2009) provide a good overview of established practice, highlighting the general positive correlation between bone density and DNA survival. However, published data is scattered and has been limited to a few areas of the skeleton (e.g., Alonso et al. 2001; Edson et al. 2004; Milós et al. 2007; Parsons and Weedn 1997; Perry et al. 1988; Prinz et al. 2007). Edson et al. (2004), for example, reported good results for mitochondrial DNA typing using the femur and tibia, the metatarsals, and the ribs (given an adequate specimen size), but only limited success with cranial fragments.

The few official guidelines that have been published are broad: the National Institute of Justice (2005) recommended sampling blood, deep skeletal muscle, organ samples, skin, bones, and teeth, but offered no more specific guidelines; the DNA Commission of the International Society for Forensic Genetics recommended dense cortical bone, preferably from long bones, or teeth, be used as samples from skeletonized remains (Prinz et al. 2007). Today, the femur remains the most agreed-upon site for sampling, but collecting femoral samples requires an autopsy saw. With that in mind, Mundorff et al. (2009, 2013) have argued that patellae, metatarsals, and foot phalanges should be sampled more often because these elements give high success rates as well. Collection of a phalanx, as Mundorff noted, is readily accomplished with a scalpel, even when the remains to be sampled are well fleshed or decomposing.

In this chapter, we present the relative success rates of DNA testing from various skeletal elements based on a uniform, highly effective DNA extraction method (Amory et al. 2012). This method results in up to a 91% success rate in obtaining DNA profiles from aged bone samples, depending on the skeletal element sampled. Based on the results of more than 11,650 DNA tests, we present a practical protocol for guiding effective sampling strategies for partial/commingled remains, depending on the body parts that may be encountered in any given case.

Methods

DNA testing success rates for nuclear STR loci were tabulated from more than 11,650 DNA tests of skeletal remains recovered throughout the Western Balkans. To ensure uniformity in interpretation, all these tests were performed using ICMP's most recent demineralization extraction protocol (Amory et al. 2012; Huel et al. 2012), and amplified using the Promega PowerPlex 16 multiplex STR kit. Amplifications were repeated a minimum of twice, with alleles considered as authentic only if present in at least two amplifications. For this evaluation, a test was classified as successful if reproducible results were obtained from a minimum of 11 autosomal loci and the sex indicating locus amelogenin.

Samples included in this study came from a wide range of environmental contexts. Most prevalent were samples coming from primary or secondary mass graves, but other samples came from such environments as caves, single burials, surface remains, or remains recovered from a watercourse. Cemetery sites and suspected historical cases (predating the conflicts of the 1990s) were excluded. For additional comparative purposes, three subsets of samples were considered: samples from cases found in mass graves (N = 2,941), primarily associated with the

1995 fall of Srebrenica; samples from cases found exposed on the surface, primarily from the forest floor and also dating to 1995 (N = 672); and samples from cases collected from the Drina river after water was released from a large dam, exposing large sections of riverbed. These samples came primarily from individuals killed and disposed of in the river in 1992 (N = 1,442).

Results

Assessment of the success rates for the various elements allowed categorization of sample success rates into four tiers (Figure 13-2; Table 13-1). The first tier, offering the best results, consisted of the **teeth**, the **talus**, the other **tarsals**, the **petrous portion of the temporal**, the **femur**, the **vertebrae**, the **tibia,** and the **metatarsal**. The second tier, offering moderate success rates, included the **os coxa**, the **fibula**, the **scapula**, the **mandibular body**, and the **metacarpal**. The third tier was successful less than half the time; it consisted of the **ribs, cranium**, and **humerus**. The fourth tier, consisting of the **clavicle, ulna**, and **radius**, was even less successful.

Samples labeled "cranium" or "cranial vault" consisted of an occipital, a parietal, or a frontal bone. Although the success rates for the occipital were slightly higher than the parietal and frontal bones, they did not differ as much as the temporal/petrous bone. The temporal/petrous had a significantly higher success rate for DNA extraction and was separated from the other cranial elements. Other elements, including the patella, also exhibited good results, but the number of patella samples in our study was too small (<10) to be highly informative. In general, our results were consistent with previous observations that bones that are larger or of higher density are better for DNA preservation, and weight-bearing bones are better than smaller, less dense bones, or bones that do not bear weight, with some exceptions (the carpals and metacarpals yield better results than the humerus, for example).

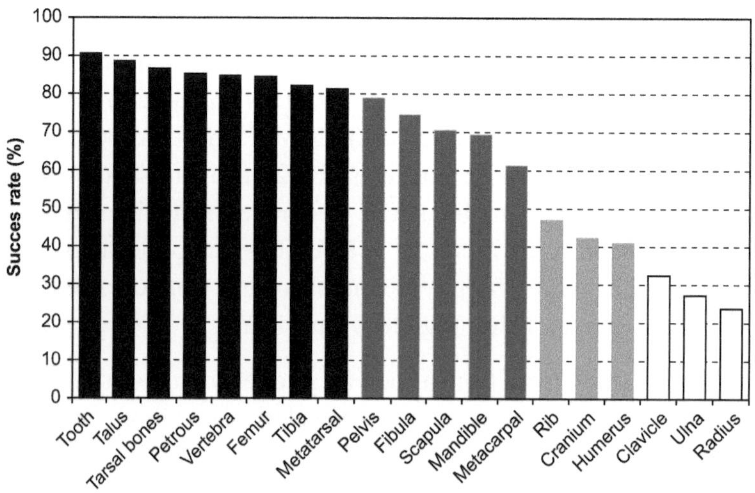

Figure 13-2
ICMP typing success rates. Shades of gray indicate the different tiers.

Table 13-1: ICMP Typing Success Rates

Element	Success Rate	Number of Samples
Teeth	91%	987
Talus	89%	36
Tarsals (except Talus)	87%	23
Petrous Temporal	86%	450
Femur	85%	1,866
Vertebra	85%	321
Tibia	82%	803
Metatarsal	82%	320
Os Coxa	79%	475
Fibula	75%	301
Scapula	71%	171
Mandibular Body	70%	335
Metacarpal	62%	91
Ribs	47%	178
Cranium	42%	494
Humerus	41%	2,295
Clavicle	33%	294
Ulna	27%	1,321
Radius	24%	864

Several researchers have reported taphonomic influence on the likelihood of obtaining DNA profiles. Milós et al. (2007) reported that environment and time since death affected the likelihood of obtaining DNA samples from a variety of elements representing three separate events and time periods (71% for 1992 cases to a high of 82% for 1999 cases). Although these findings were pertinent to nuclear DNA, mitochondrial DNA studies reported similar findings (Edson et al. 2004; Milós et al. 2007). Leney (2006) reported that both the element sampled and the weight of the sample affected the likelihood of success, and that environment (particularly heat and humidity) could be a factor.

Although the impact of environment can be difficult to assess, given the variables involved, the demineralization protocol (Amory et al. 2012) appears to greatly reduce the environmental impact seen by Milós et al. (2007). More than 5,055 samples used in the assessment came from three disparate types of sites—mass grave (Figure 13-3), underwater (Figure 13-4), and wooded surface (Figure 13-5)—created between 1992 and 1995 and recovered between 1996 and 2010. The mass grave dataset consisted of complete skeletons and many commingled elements recovered from nine large mass graves connected to a single event. The underwater site dataset consisted of body parts recovered from the bank of a drained river. The surface site dataset consisted of remains recovered from two similar surface sites. The success rates and rankings for the various elements remain quite consistent.

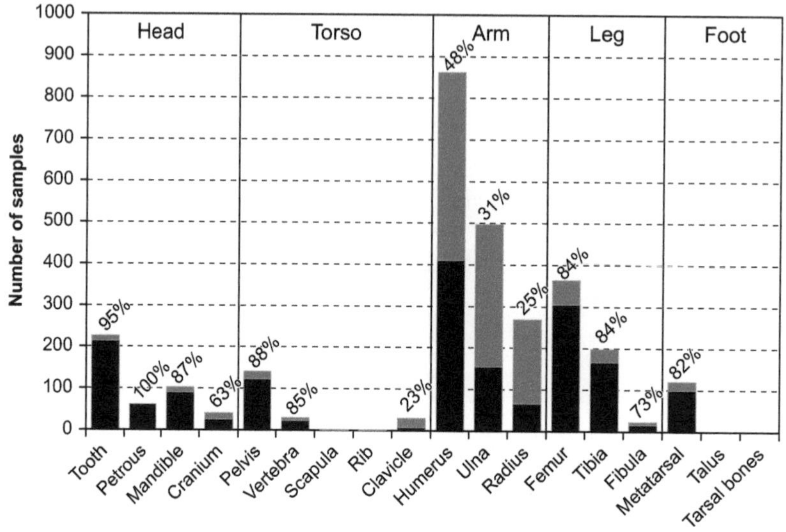

Figure 13-3

Mass grave typing success rates. N = 2,941. Black represents successful profiles; gray, failed profiles.

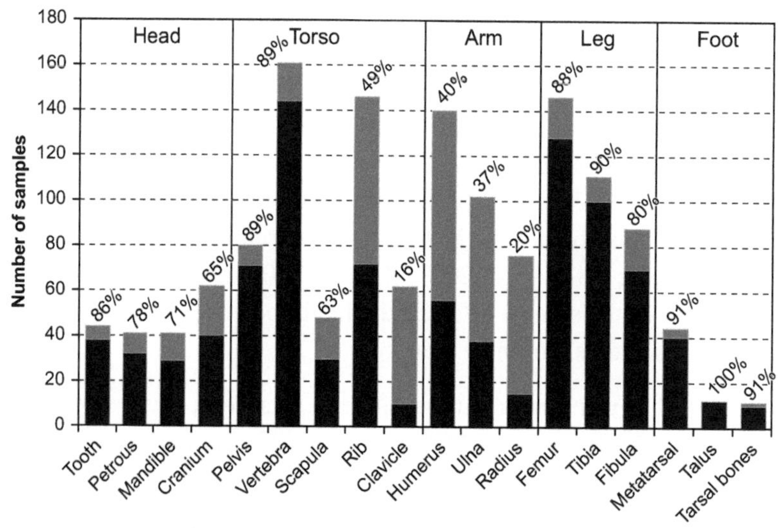

Figure 13-4

Underwater site typing success rates. N = 1,442. Black represents successful profiles; gray, failed profiles.

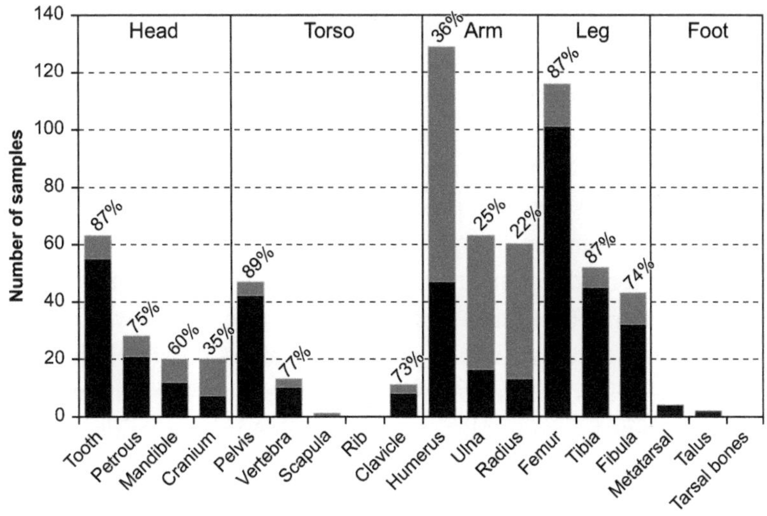

Figure 13-5

Surface site typing success rates. N = 672. Black represents successful profiles; gray, failed profiles.

Discussion

Determination of skeletal elements that are intrinsically the best for preservation of DNA is made difficult by the many additional variables that affect DNA preservation. Different studies may use methods of differing efficiency, making it hard to combine results across studies. Likewise, if an attempt is made to control for the variables of environmental conditions, or age of sample, it is difficult to obtain large sample sizes. The primary strengths of the dataset presented here are the large sample size for most elements and the uniform methods used. Of course, in this study, different skeletal elements of the same type may have substantially different DNA preservation due to environmental conditions, or relating to the sample age or characteristics of the individual. For example, although most tooth samples give full profiles, 9% of tooth samples in this analysis yielded insufficient DNA to produce any sort of reliable profile. The large sample sizes for most elements can be expected to average out the effects of sample-to-sample variation and provide a good basis for prediction of DNA preservation on the basis of the intrinsic propensity of different skeletal elements to preserve DNA.

Analysts may be faced with any sort of skeletal assemblage: not only complete bodies but also isolated body parts and/or commingled remains may be present. Accordingly, sampling strategies vary depending on the nature of the assemblage and the goal of the identification effort, and will incorporate factors other than success rates alone. The patella may have a high success rate (not shown in the preceding charts because of a < 10 sample size), but because it cannot generally be clearly matched to the bones with which it articulates, and is entirely destroyed during sampling, it is not a very desirable element to test in commingled cases. As another example of practical considerations, vertebrae have better DNA preservation than does the os coxa, but sampling a vertebra greatly damages its utility for physical reassociation.

Accordingly, the ICMP incorporated success rates into a priority-based sampling method that includes a variety of additional practical considerations. Rather than select samples based on success rates alone, the ICMP prioritizes bones from 1 to 6 based on DNA typing success rates, durability, ease of sampling, diagnostic nature, and usefulness for articulations and other reassociations. Priority 1 elements are most preferred and Priority 6 elements, least preferred. The analyst must also consider the circumstances of the recovery site, the resources and goals of the project, and any unique processing issues. A small site where three bodies are mixed together may call for a different sampling approach than a secondary grave containing hundreds of body parts. An effort to maximize unique identifications will require fewer samples than will an effort to reassociate as many elements as possible. The amount of time, staff, and resources available to the project will determine what goals are possible. In some cases, access to the remains for resampling in case of DNA testing failure may be difficult or impossible, due to distance or other considerations. In this case, it is wise to sample from a number of high-priority elements to maximize the chance for success.

Given all these considerations, and the unique nature of each assemblage, a well-trained physical anthropologist is essential to the sampling procedure. When selecting samples, the anthropologist must assess the circumstances of the recovery, evaluate the material present, and maintain a clear picture of the available resources and the goals of the identification process. Because DNA sampling is a destructive process, the anthropologist must also consider the forensic importance of skeletal characteristics in determining sites for sampling. Distinctive morphological features relating to age, sex, and stature must be avoided; for example, cross cuts of long bones destroy information on their length, which would have a detrimental effect on stature estimation and the ability to evaluate antimere pair-matching. Likewise, skeletal elements indicating antemortem or perimortem trauma, providing information on cause and manner of death, or skeletel elements providing distinguishing characteristics should be avoided for DNA sampling.

Following identification, comparison of the DNA identification with the anthropological findings is useful for quality control to catch potential labeling, coding, and association errors by comparing morphology and biological profile gathered from the skeleton to the profile of the missing person. Additionally, closely related missing persons may require anthropological resolution, because familial DNA analysis compares to living individuals rather than a known tissue sample from a missing person, and the ability to uniquely identify depends on the reference samples available. For example, same-sex siblings cannot be distinguished by DNA if kinship comparison is made only to their parents. If several missing persons are closely related, anthropological assessment may be essential to sort out their identities within the family unit. If several closely related persons are missing, but only one is reported as such, then familial DNA analysis may incorrectly associate an unidentified body with the reported missing person, when the body is actually a relative of the reported missing person. Anthropological review of identifications is essential to avoid such issues.

Following the return of DNA match reports, reassessing cases may identify errors of association that had gone unnoticed, or suggest new associations to be tested. The ICMP found that an average of 12% of cases receiving an element reassociated through DNA already had such an element included in the case, indicating commingling that had not been detected.

Protocols

Given that DNA testing is a destructive process, all examinations of the skeletal remains should be completed before sampling, including inventory, measurement, and photographs. After these examinations are completed, the analyst may prepare the required tools and equipment for sampling.

To prevent contamination, the analyst must clean tools before taking each sample. After a water rinse to remove adherent material, rinse the tool surface with a solution of 10% commercial bleach, or wipe with bleach, using a clean wipe each time. Finally, apply a rinse with ethanol. Hazards from bleach and ethanol are minimal, but risk assessments for chemical hazards should be undertaken and material safety data sheets (MSDS) or equivalent made available. Personal protective equipment (PPE) in the form of gloves, a mask, and safety glasses protects the analyst from any contaminants or foreign particles, and avoids contaminating the specimens with the analyst's DNA. If multiple samples are being taken, particularly in enclosed spaces, then particulate/fume extraction facilities should be used.

Each sample collected is given a unique sample code that is used throughout analysis. The code is used to link each sample with the case and individual bone from which it was excised, allowing for reassociation of even highly commingled assemblages. The ICMP uses a relatively complex sample coding convention that includes substantial information regarding the case that the sample came from. We have found this to be useful, for example, in tracking success rates by type of skeletal element, identifying transcription errors, and relaying processing instructions through the sample code alone without the need for reference to additional reference lists. Such an approach has the disadvantage of being somewhat more error-prone, but in our identification system, the additional information has proven useful overall in downstream case tracking and management. In any case, the importance of systematic quality control in ascribing and cross-checking sample identifiers, regardless of the labeling scheme used, cannot be overemphasized. In some laboratories, simpler labeling schemes may be better adapted to the requirements for separating or merging different body parts as commingled cases are resolved/reassociated, but the ICMP makes use of a custom database case tracking module that accommodates our labeling scheme and facilitates this process. Anthropology laboratories should devise robust sample labeling strategies amenable to robust chain of custody and case association and that work well with their particular work flow and protocols. In the following protocol description, ICMP's convention is presented as an example.

The basic ICMP sample code consists of several components: a **site code**, a **case number,** and a **side and element code.** To this may be appended, if applicable, an **element number,** a **sample number,** or a **reserve status code.** A simpler approach can reduce risk of transcriptional error, but the ICMP's approach, while initially appearing more cumbersome, has proven successful. Problems that would be associated with misidentification or incorrect siding of bones is less of a concern, given that ICMP protocols recommend against sampling fragmented material.

Site Code, Case Number, and Side and Element Code

Site code and case number are typically assigned outside the mortuary by the investigating authority. Given a body from site AJRØ1 with evidence number 86, represented as **AJRØ1/Ø86B,** a side and element code is appended to identify which element is sampled and what side of the body it is from. For example, a sample from the left femur of this case would be given the sample code **AJRØ1/Ø86B-LF.** The ICMP uses a standardized list of unique abbreviations to describe the bones.

> Priority 1 samples are the maxillary teeth (coded as MXT), mandibular teeth (MNT), petrous temporal (PT), os coxa/pelvis (P), femur (F), tibia (T), and metatarsal (MT).
> Priority 2 samples are the mandible (MN), vertebra (CV, TV, or LV), fibula (FB), and talus (TAL).
> Priority 3 samples are the occipital (OCP), scapula (SC), metacarpal (MC), patella (PAT), and the tarsals (except the talus) (TR).
> Priority 4 samples are the cranial vault (other than the occipital) (PR for parietal, else SK), the rib (RB), the humerus (H), the carpals (CR), and the hand and foot phalanges (HPH or FPH).
> Priority 5 samples are the clavicle (CL), radius (R), and ulna (U).
> Priority 6 samples are the facial bones (FC), the sacrum (SAC), and the sternum (manubrium or sternal body) (ST).

Elements not given here are listed later in Appendix 13-1.

Element Number

Some commingled cases may have several duplicate elements, each of which will be sampled. Either a separate case number is issued at this point for the commingled element, or an element number is used to distinguish between the same elements in a commingled assemblage. ICMP's internal software uses these numbers to generate new case numbers as identifications are made. For example, two left femora under one sample code are distinguished as:

> **AJRØ1/Ø86B-LF1**
> **AJRØ1/Ø86B-LF2**

Determination of a Sample Code for a Second Sample from the Same Bone

If the first DNA sample produced an unsuccessful DNA result, and another sample is selected from the same skeletal element, add the identifier **-2.** For example,

AJRØ1/Ø86B-RT1
AJRØ1/Ø86B-RT1-**2**

Reserve Samples

Spare samples that have no possibility of originating from a different individual are termed reserve samples. For example, a femur specimen from an articulated individual whose tooth has already been sampled is a reserve sample. A reserve sample is processed only if the most desirable sample fails to yield a DNA profile.

For only the reserve samples, add the identifier **–RES.** For example,

AJRØ1/Ø86B-LF-**RES**

Sample Preparation and Packaging

The container for the sample and the element from which the sample was taken must both be labeled. To label the sampled element, the analyst may use metal "Aluma-Boss" labels, or some other form of durable, indelible labeling retained with the element. This is particularly important if there is commingling within an assemblage. Before the sample is collected, the analyst photographs the element in its original condition, with a photo scale and label. After sampling, the analyst takes a second photograph including the sampled element with the extracted location clearly shown, the extracted sample, label with sample code, and a photo scale.

After the sample has been taken, it is placed in the appropriate sealable container, along with the label generated for the sample at the time of recording. The container should be labeled with the sample code in indelible ink and signature sealed so that any attempt to open the vial/sample bag/container is obvious. Each sample must be in its own container, with a unique specimen number. Do not expose the samples to conditions of elevated heat or humidity, if possible. (ICMP laboratories store DNA samples, once received for processing and analysis, at –20°C.) It is important that the specimen is completely dried before packaging, and breathable (e.g., paper) packaging should be used where practical. ICMP uses standardized paper envelopes with a proforma window to prompt proper recording of sample codes, site, date, collector, etc. If the sample is moist, it can be helpful to rinse with 95% or absolute ethanol and allow to air dry, to promote dehydration.

Sample Size

In practice, it is possible to obtain a profile from only a few hundred milligrams of sample. The ICMP prefers to collect larger samples, when possible, to ensure adequate useable

Figure 13-6
Cutting a window from a femur for a bone sample.

material is available. A sample of 15 to 25 grams is desirable. Four grams is minimal but acceptable. If circumstances are favorable and preservation is good, smaller samples may provide results and so may be taken, if there is no alternative. Larger samples may provide a better chance for DNA success with highly degraded remains through multiple extractions; they permit the DNA analyst to remove superficial layers that may be contaminated or have discoloration of PCR inhibitors. The ICMP has specific recommendations for sampling each element. In general, when one is sampling a large bone, such as a femur, a small portion of the bone (typically a window rather than a cross-section) is taken according to ICMP protocols (Figure 13-6). When sampling a small bone, such as a tarsal, the entire bone is sampled (except in the case of the calcaneus, for which the posterior half is sampled).

Avoid sampling areas where the bone is discolored. Discoloration may indicate exposure to materials or an environment that can cause DNA degradation. However, bone that is discolored but dense and intact may yield better results than bone that is sun-bleached, porous, or physically degraded. Avoid areas with individualizing or potentially identifying characteristics or sites of trauma. These may be useful for identification purposes or in determining the cause and manner of death.

Specific Recommendations

The specific application of ICMP recommendations differs depending on what elements are present in the assemblage and completeness of the assemblage. The general procedure is to preferentially sample the elements that are present based on their priority level. If contiguous bones are absent and/or the articulation of skeletal elements is questionable, additional samples may be submitted for DNA testing to help assess likely associations. For a case representing a single complete individual, analysts typically collect one main sample and another sample as a reserve, to be held in storage and processed only if the main sample does not yield a profile. This measure minimizes the need to reopen and resample examined cases, which may be impractical in some contexts—for example, if cultural practices encourage rapid reburial.

In the case of a body (defined by the ICMP as an assemblage consisting of the largely complete skeleton, 75% or more, of one individual), sample priority 1 bones, ideally at least two intact, healthy teeth, because these are readily sampled and are the most likely to offer a DNA profile. To ensure that only one individual is represented, take either two teeth from the maxilla or two teeth from the mandible, rather than one from each. Teeth are extracted whole, using dental pliers. Anterior molars or premolars are preferred, from either the maxilla or the mandible, not both. The full order of preference is as follows: first molar (left or right), second molar, third molar, first or second premolar, canine, incisors. If more than one tooth is selected, it is important that each tooth receive a separate sample code (i.e., one should be considered a reserve sample).

Because the high success rate of teeth is largely due to the enamel's protection of DNA from any contaminants, the teeth sampled should not have caries or postmortem damage, if possible. Avoid teeth with dental restorations because they are not only potentially useful for identification but have an increased risk of crown fracture, which may minimize DNA yield. Also, to minimize the likelihood of commingling, avoid sampling a loose tooth or teeth that have been replaced in the alveolar process.

If teeth are not available, or if a reserve sample is desired for a case classified as a body, take the sample from the femur, tibia, or os coxa (Figure 13-7). When one is sampling the femur, the first priority is a window of bone removed from the proximal anterior shaft below the plane of the lesser trochanter (black). The second priority is a window of bone removed from the distal anterior shaft (gray). When one is sampling the tibia, the first priority is a window of bone removed from the anterior proximal shaft (black). Second priority is a window of bone removed

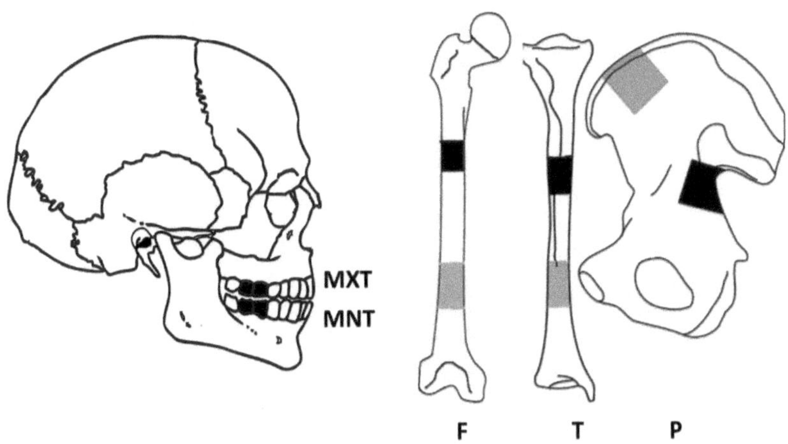

Figure 13-7
Sampling locations for a body.

from the distal anterior shaft (gray). When one is sampling the os coxa, the first priority is a rectangular section cut from the greater sciatic notch area (black), from beneath the preauricular sulcus to approximate mid-point of the sciatic notch (be sure to record sciatic notch sex determination values before taking the sample). The second priority is a rectangular section from the iliac crest near the anterior area (gray). A fantail blade should be used to cut os coxa samples.

If contiguous bones are absent and/or the connection of skeletal elements is questionable, additional samples may be submitted for DNA testing. Any subsequent samples are submitted separately. Never collect two samples under the same sample code. Doing so will result in the laboratory processing unnecessary samples and then being unable to link each sample with the bone that was processed to obtain it.

For a body part (defined by the ICMP as more than one bone, making up less than 75% of the skeleton but still representing one individual), the sample selected is dependent on the nature and condition of the remains. As with the body, when one is examining an incomplete body or body part, the appropriate course of action is to sample the highest-priority bones that are of good quality and intact.

Accordingly, a body part consisting of a skull or cranium should be sampled for, in order of priority: the teeth (MXT, MNT) or petrous temporal (PT), the mandible (MN), the occipital (OCP), the parietal (PR) or other bones of the vault (SK), and as a last resort the bones of the face (FC) (Figure 13-8).

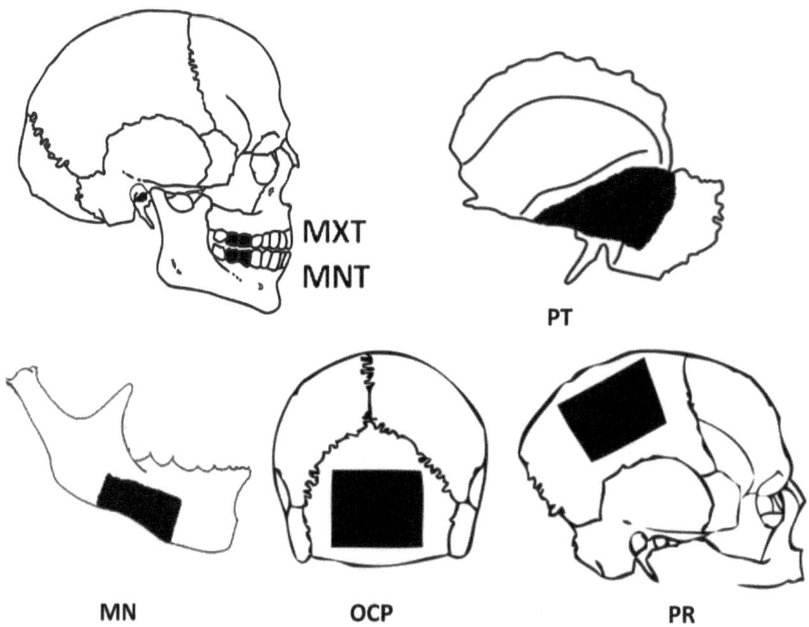

Figure 13-8
Sampling locations for a body part (skull or cranium).

When sampling the petrous temporal, cut the endocranial aspect of the petrous portion (black). In juveniles, particularly, this is much more likely to give a result than bones of the vault. When one is sampling the mandible, a window of the inferior mandibular body is sampled, leaving the alveolar process intact. When one is sampling the occipital, a relatively large sample should be taken that includes the external occipital protuberance. Avoid cutting through the cranial sutures or fractures. Owing to the relatively large sample size, an occipital bone is sampled only once. A similar approach is used for the parietal.

A body part consisting of the torso should be sampled for, in order of priority: the os coxa (P), vertebra (CV, TV, LV), scapula (SC), the rib (RB), the clavicle (CL), and sacrum (SAC) or sternum (manubrium or sternal body) (ST) (Figure 13-9). A complete cervical may be submitted, if possible; the transverse and spinous processes (black) are first priority for the thoracic and lumbar, with the bodies second priority (gray.) In sampling the scapula, the first priority is the acromion and spine (black); the second choice is the axillary border (gray). The glenoid cavity and coracoid may also be used. The vertebral half (black) of one of the middle ribs is a priority. A complete or mostly complete upper or lower rib (gray) is second priority for selection of rib samples. The clavicle is cross-sectioned, and the acromial and sternal ends are bagged together. A complete or mostly complete manubrium or sternal body may be sampled. Select the area(s) best preserved with the most cortical bone. The medial sacral crest and articular surfaces (black) are priority in sampling the sacrum.

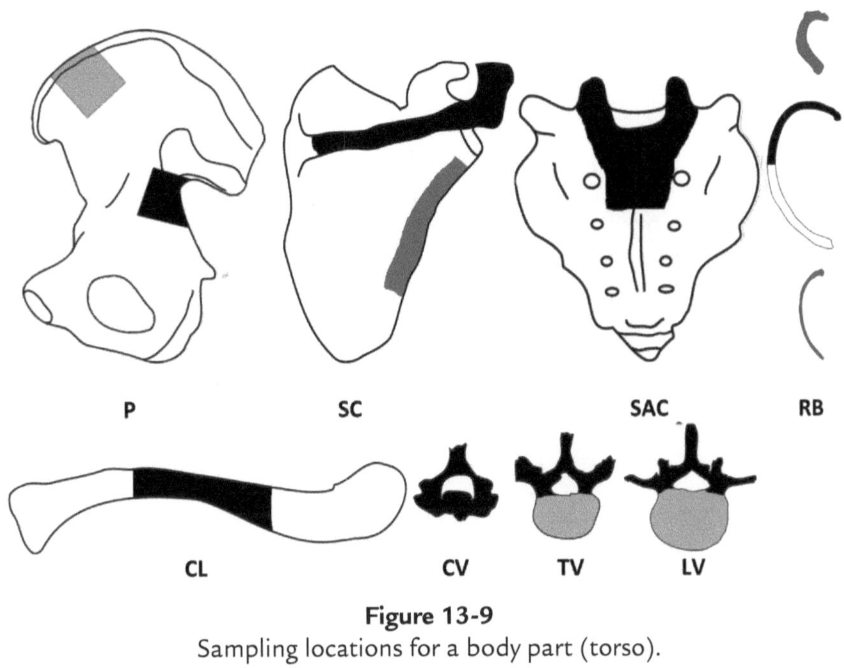

Figure 13-9
Sampling locations for a body part (torso).

Because success rates for the arm bones (humerus, ulna, and radius) are relatively poor compared to the hand bones (metacarpal, carpal, proximal phalanx), sampling arms is not a priority unless more suitable samples are not available. If skeletal elements from the hand are available and these hand bones are associated with the arm, then it is recommended that the hand bones be sampled as a priority over sampling an arm bone. Accordingly, a body part consisting of the arm and hand should be sampled for, in order of priority, the metacarpal (MC), the carpal (CR), the hand phalanx (HPH) or humerus (H), and the radius (R) or ulna (U) (Figure 13-10).

When one is sampling a hand, the preferred bones are the metacarpal and capitate, but priorities will vary depending on the available elements and the degree of preservation.

When one is sampling a metacarpal, the fourth metacarpal (black) is preferred. The third metacarpal (gray) may be substituted if the fourth is not available. When one is sampling a carpal, a complete capitate (black) is preferred. If one is not available, any of the larger carpals that are available can be substituted. When one is sampling hand phalanges, the first proximal phalanx (black) is preferred. The second choice is the second proximal phalanx (gray).

When one is sampling the humerus, the first priority is a window of bone from the distal medial shaft approximately 2 cm above the plane of the trochlea (black). Second priority is a window section at or near the proximal mid-shaft (gray). With respect to the radius and ulna, the first priority is a window of bone removed from the proximal shaft along the interosseous crest (black), and the second priority is a cross-section of the distal mid-shaft (gray).

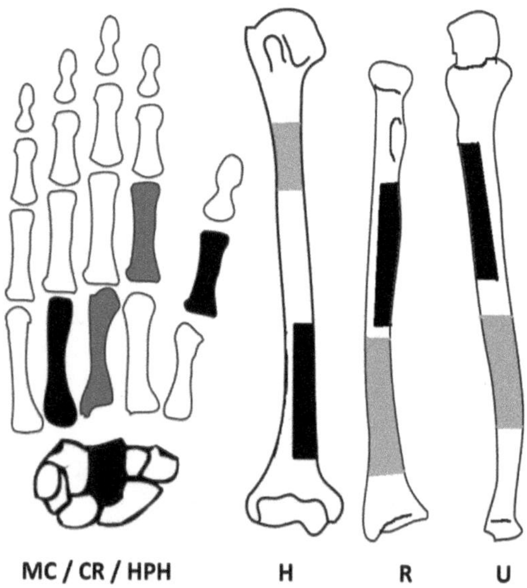

Figure 13-10
Sampling locations for a body part (arm and/or hand).

A body part consisting of the leg and foot should be sampled for, in order of priority: the femur (F), tibia (T), or metatarsal (MT); fibula (FB) or talus (TAL), patella (PAT) or tarsals other than talus (TR, CAL for calcaneus), or foot phalanx (FPH) (Figure 13-11).

When one is sampling the femur, the first priority is a window of bone removed from the proximal anterior shaft below the plane of the lesser trochanter (black). Second priority is a window of bone removed from the distal anterior shaft (gray). When one is sampling the tibia, the first priority is a window of bone removed from the anterior proximal shaft (black), and second priority is a window of bone removed from the distal anterior shaft (gray). A complete or mostly complete patella may be sampled. When one is sampling the fibula, a window of bone is removed from the distal shaft. In some cases, a cross-section of the shaft is necessary. If so, the proximal and distal ends are bagged together. Among the metatarsals, the fifth metatarsal (black) is preferred. The first metatarsal (gray) may serve as a substitute, if necessary.

Among the tarsals, the talus (striped) is preferred. If the calcaneus is sampled, the posterior body (black) is preferred. If a smaller tarsal is sampled, the preference is for a complete navicular (black) and then a complete cuboid (gray). If a foot phalanx is sampled, the first proximal phalanx (black) is preferred. The second proximal phalanx (gray) (or another large phalanx) may be an alternate.

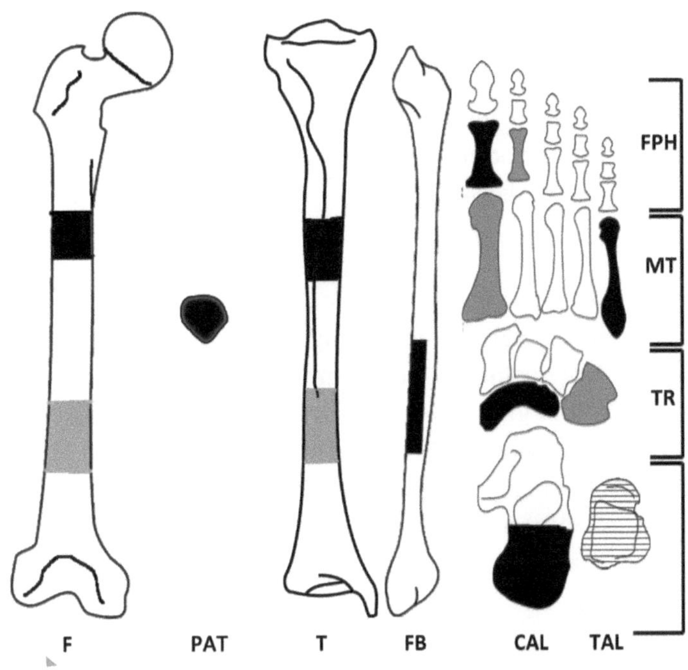

Figure 13-11
Sampling locations for a body part (leg and/or foot).

In the case of commingled remains, if skeletal elements can be physically reassociated, follow the selection procedure described for the appropriate body part. Unless considerable resources are available, sampling every bone slows down the lab, costs too much money, and takes too much time. Instead, work to maximize results. Do not sample bones that are unlikely to return DNA profiles, except in unusual cases—for example, if they are the basis for MNI. Our protocols state that it is not recommended to sample a complete bone or bone fragment that is not paired, articulated, or associated with another skeletal element. This is particularly important if remains are poorly preserved.

After Sampling

After the sample has been sealed and the chain of custody information completed, attach the chain of custody information to the sample container. The individual taking the sample completes the information, inserts the sample into the container, and uses evidence sealing with a signature to seal the container. This sealed container is then handed over to the person who will be submitting it to the DNA laboratory or processing facility. This person signs in the space provided (i.e., name, signature, and date) as confirmation of receipt, and then generates the appropriate chain of custody submission form for the DNA laboratory or processing facility. In this way, this submission form can contain the details of more than one sample that is being submitted for DNA analysis and record the transfers of these samples among the responsible parties.

Samples should be transferred in a sealed container, such as a lockable box. If the container cannot be locked, it should be sealed with evidence sealing tape with signatures across each opening and potential opening so that any effort to tamper with the container is evident. The DNA laboratory or processing facility may not accept items it receives with incomplete or illegible chain of custody information and/or missing, tampered, or incorrect signature seals may result in nonacceptance of the samples.

Conclusion

DNA analysis is an essential tool for identifying and reassociating commingled human remains, especially for large commingled assemblages. For such large challenges, DNA is the only practical solution, given its scalability. Its power and utility, however, pose new problems of scope. Analysts must be careful to not overburden laboratory facilities with more samples than the organization has resources to handle. The ICMP's prioritized sampling approach is effective and offers strategies for highly fragmented and commingled assemblages that maximize reassociation without overburdening the laboratory.

Appendices

Appendix 13-1 summarizes all sample codes. Appendix 13-2 summarizes all sampling locations.

Appendix 13-1

Region	Bone/Tooth Element	Priority	Sample Codes	Left	Right	Unsided
HEAD	Tooth–Mandible	1	MNT			
	Tooth–Maxilla	1	MXT			
	Temporal/Petrous	1	PT	LPT	RPT	UPT
	Mandibular Body	2	MN	LMN	RMN	UMN
	Occipital Bone	3	OCP			
	Parietal Bone	4	PR	LPR	RPR	UPR
	Skull–Other cranial vault	4	SK			
	Facial–cranial bones	6	FC			
TORSO	Os Coxa/Pelvis	1	P	LP	RP	UP
	Vertebra–Cervical	2	CV			
	Vertebra–Thoracic	2	TV			
	Vertebra–Lumbar	2	LV			
	Scapula	3	SC	LSC	RSC	USC
	Rib	4	RB	LRB	RRB	URB
	Clavicle	5	CL	LCL	RCL	UCL
	Sacrum	6	SAC			
	Sternum (Manubrium or Body)	6	ST			
ARM	Humerus	4	H	LH	RH	UH
	Radius	5	R	LR	RR	UR
	Ulna	5	U	LU	RU	UU
HAND	Metacarpal	3	MC	LMC	RMC	UMC
	Carpal	4	CR	LCR	RCR	UCR
	Phalanx–Hand	4	HPH	LHPH	RHPH	UHPH
LEG	Femur	1	F	LF	RF	UF
	Tibia	1	T	LT	RT	UT
	Fibula	2	FB	LFB	RFB	UFB
	Patella	3	PAT	LPAT	RPAT	UPAT
FOOT	Metatarsal	1	MT	LMT	RMT	UMT
	Talus	2	TAL	LTAL	RTAL	UTAL
	Tarsal (not Talus or Calcaneus)	3	TR	LTR	RTR	UTR
	Calcaneus	3	CAL	LCAL	RCAL	UCAL
	Phalanx–Foot	4	FPH	LFPH	RFPH	UFPH

Appendix 13-2

Skeletal Elements

The following sections summarize recommendations for first and second priorities for the collection of samples from the individual skeletal elements. A second priority location (indicated in gray) is provided, in case part of the skeleton or skeletal elements display possible identifying features, trauma, or other indicator of degraded DNA material. The forensic expert may choose to select the left- or the right-sided element, subject to the preservation or availability of the skeletal material.

Occipital Bone

A relatively large sample should be taken that includes the external occipital protuberance (Figure 13-12). Avoid cutting through the cranial sutures or fractures because this may compromise the integrity of the cranium, and they are used to confirm physical reassociations in cases of disarticulated and/or commingled remains. Be sure to record occipital protuberance sex determination values before taking the sample.

Owing to the relatively large sample size, an occipital bone is sampled only once.

Parietal Bone

A relatively large sample should be taken (Figure 13-13). As is the case with the occipital bone, avoid cutting through the cranial sutures or fractures because this may compromise

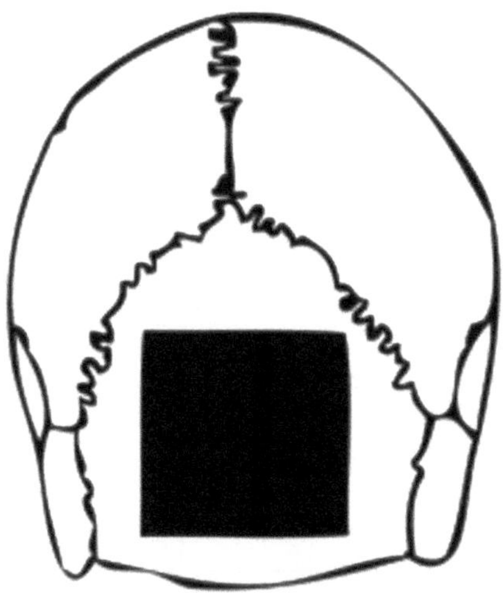

Figure 13-12
Location and relative size of an occipital bone sample (posterior view).

the integrity of the cranium, and they are used to confirm physical reassociations in cases of disarticulated and/or commingled remains.

Owing to the relatively large sample size, a parietal bone is sampled only once.

Temporal Bone

Cut the endocranial aspect of the petrous portion of the temporal bone (Figure 13-14).

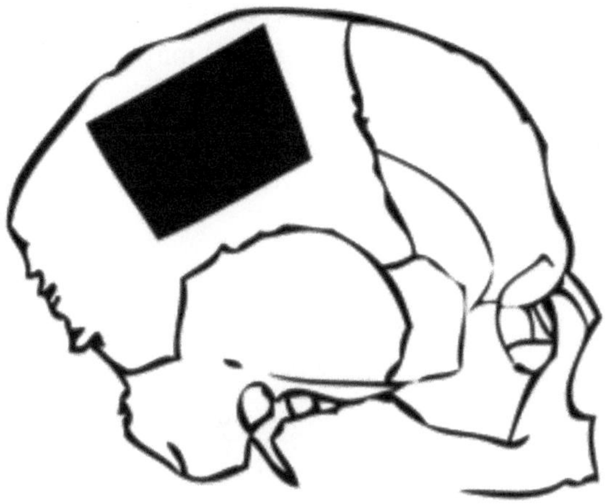

Figure 13-13
Location and relative size of a parietal bone sample. (A right parietal is illustrated, lateral.)

Figure 13-14
Location and relative size of a petrous temporal sample. (A right temporal is illustrated, endocranial view.)

In the case of a subadult cranium with thin vault bones, sampling of the petrous portion of the temporal bone is preferred rather than sampling the occipital or parietal bones.

Mandibular Body

A window of the inferior mandibular body is sampled, leaving the alveolar process intact (Figure 13-15).

Scapula

The first priority is the acromion and spine (black) of the scapula. The second choice is the axillary border (gray). The glenoid cavity and coracoid may also be used (Figure 13-16).

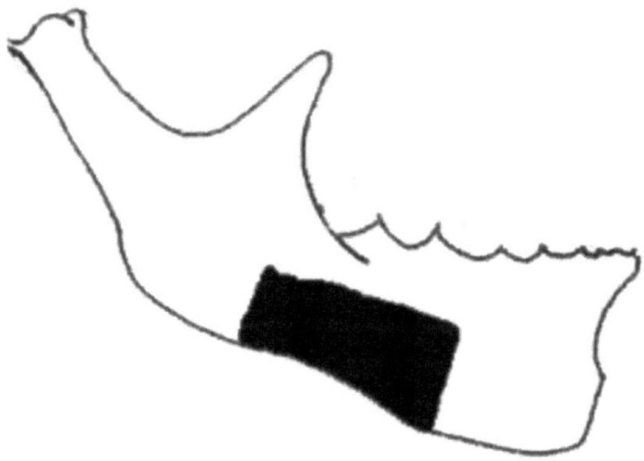

Figure 13-15
Location and relative size of a mandibular body sample. (A right half of the mandible is illustrated.)

Figure 13-16
Location and relative size of a scapula sample. (A right scapula is illustrated, posterior view.)

Clavicle

The clavicle is cross-sectioned, and the acromial and sternal ends are bagged together (Figure 13-17).

Sternum (Manubrium and Body)

A complete or mostly complete manubrium or sternal body may be sampled. The two may be fused. Select the area(s) best preserved with the most cortical bone.

Vertebrae (Cervical, Thoracic, and Lumbar)

The transverse and spinous processes (black) are first priority for the thoracic and lumbar vertebrae. The vertebral body (gray) is second priority. A complete cervical vertebra may be submitted, if possible. Vertebrae should be stacked to verify articulation before sampling (Figure 13-18).

Sacrum

The medial sacral crest and articular surfaces (black) are priority (Figure 13-19).

Ribs

The vertebral half (black) of one of the middle ribs is priority. A complete or mostly complete upper or lower rib (gray) is second priority for selection of rib samples (Figure 13-20). Ribs should be seriated before sample selection.

Figure 13-17
Location and relative size of a clavicular sample. (A right clavicle is illustrated, superior view.)

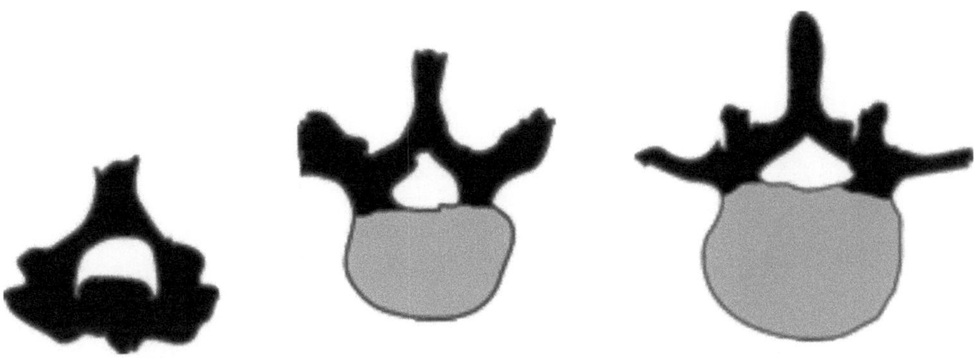

Figure 13-18
Location and relative size of vertebral samples. (Left to right, cervical, thoracic, and lumbar. The superior aspect is illustrated.)

Humerus

First priority is a window of bone from the distal medial shaft approximately 2 cm above the plane of the trochlea (black). Second priority is a window section at or near the proximal mid-shaft (gray) (Figure 13-21).

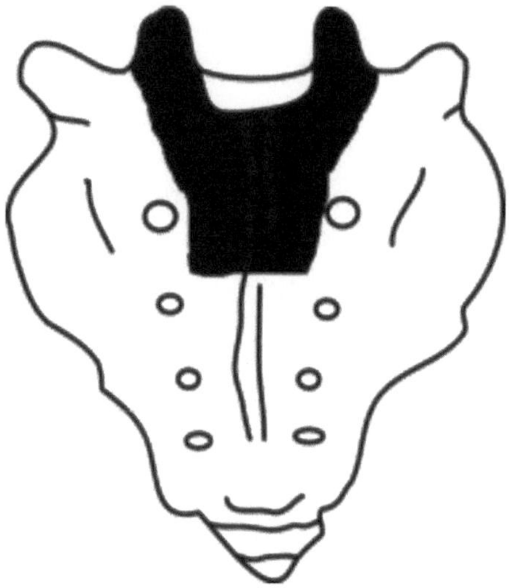

Figure 13-19
Location and relative size of a sacral sample. (The posterior aspect is illustrated.)

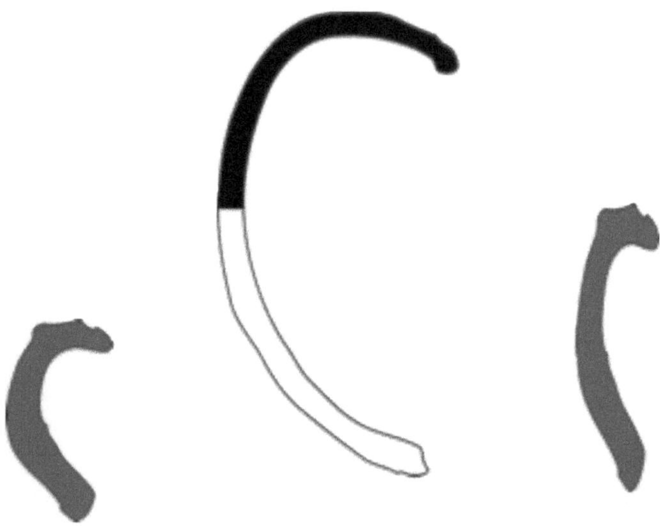

Figure 13-20
Location and relative size of a rib sample. (Right ribs are illustrated, left to right: upper, middle, lower. All are shown in superior view.)

Figure 13-21
Location and relative size of a humerus sample. (A right humerus is illustrated, anterior view.)

Radius and Ulna

The first priority is a window of bone removed from the proximal shaft along the interosseous crest (black). Second priority is a cross-section of the distal mid-shaft (gray) (Figure 13-22).

Hand Bones

The metacarpal and capitate are the preferred bones when one is sampling a complete hand. However, priorities will vary, depending on the available elements and the preservation (Figure 13-23).

Hand Phalanges

The first priority is the first proximal phalanx (black).

Second priority is the second proximal phalanx (gray) or another large hand phalanx.

Metacarpals

The first priority is a fourth metacarpal (black).

Second priority is a third metacarpal (gray).

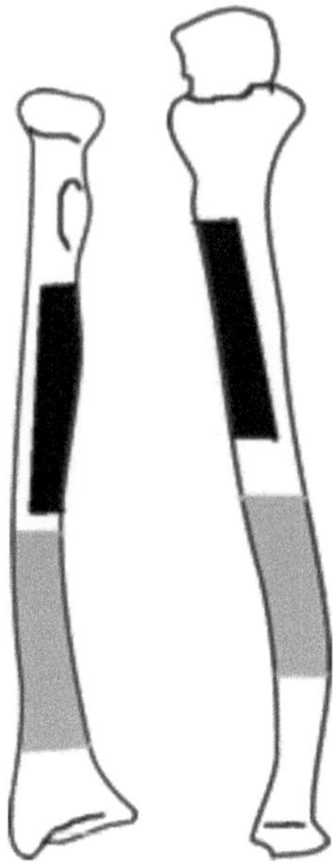

Figure 13-22
Location and relative size of samples for the radius and ulna. (Both right radius and right ulna are illustrated, anterior view.)

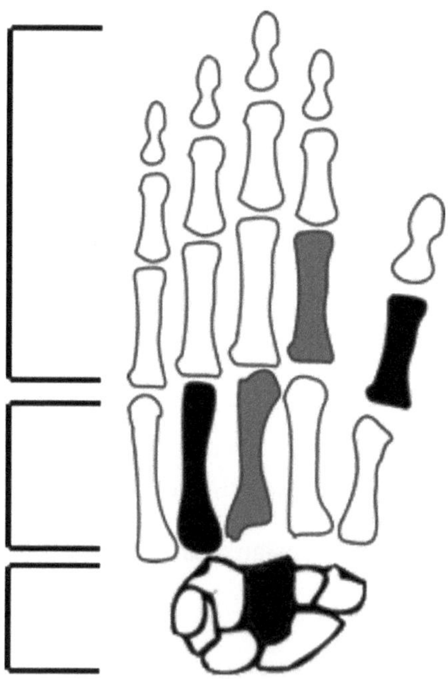

Figure 13-23
Location and relative size of hand samples. (A right hand is illustrated, palmar view.)

Carpals

The first priority is a complete capitate (black).

Any available larger carpal bones are second priority.

Os Coxa

The first priority is a rectangular section cut from the greater sciatic notch area (black). The superior border of the cut is beneath the preauricular surface and into the bone toward the arcuate line. The inferior border is approximately mid-point of the sciatic notch to avoid damaging the acetabulum. Be sure to record sciatic notch sex determination values before taking the sample. The second priority is a rectangular section from the iliac crest near the anterior area (gray) (Figure 13-24).

When an innominate sample is excised, use a fantail blade.

Femur

First priority is a window of bone removed from the proximal anterior shaft below the plane of the lesser trochanter (black). Second priority is a window of bone removed from the distal anterior shaft (gray) (Figure 13-25).

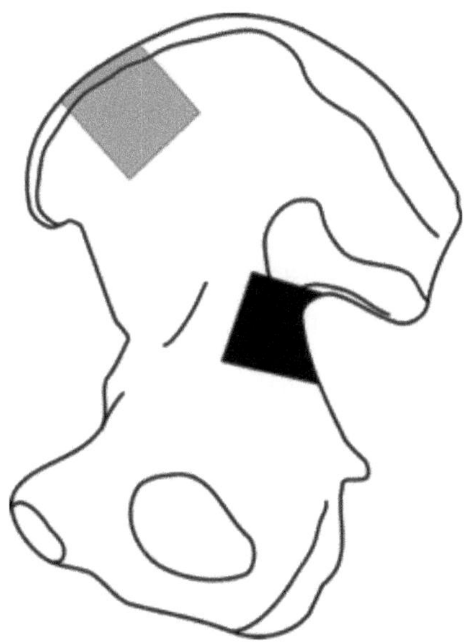

Figure 13-24

Location and relative size of an os coxa sample. (A right os coxa is illustrated, anterior view.)

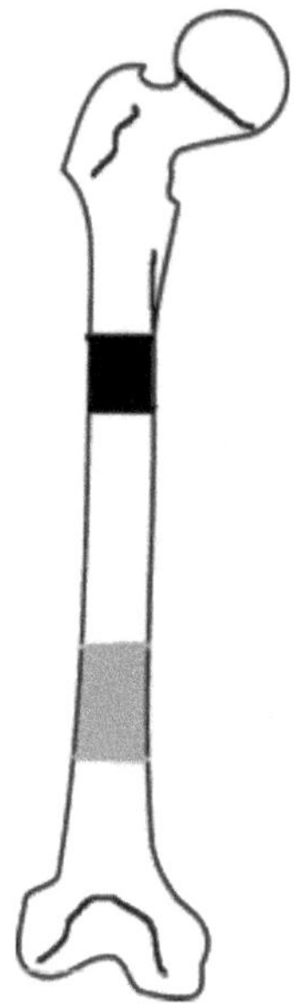

Figure 13-25
Location and relative size of a femoral sample. (A right femur is illustrated, anterior view.)

Patella

A complete or mostly complete patella may be sampled.

Tibia

The first priority is a window of bone removed from the anterior proximal shaft (black). Second priority is a window of bone removed from the distal anterior shaft (gray) (Figure 13-26).

Fibula

A window of bone is removed from the distal shaft. In some cases, a cross-section of the shaft is necessary. If so, the proximal and distal ends are bagged together (Figure 13-27).

Foot Bones

The metatarsal and talus are the preferred bones when one is sampling a complete foot. However, priorities will vary, depending on the available elements and the preservation (Figure 13-28).

Foot Phalanges

The first priority is the first proximal phalanx (black).

Second priority is the second proximal phalanx (gray) or another large foot phalanx.

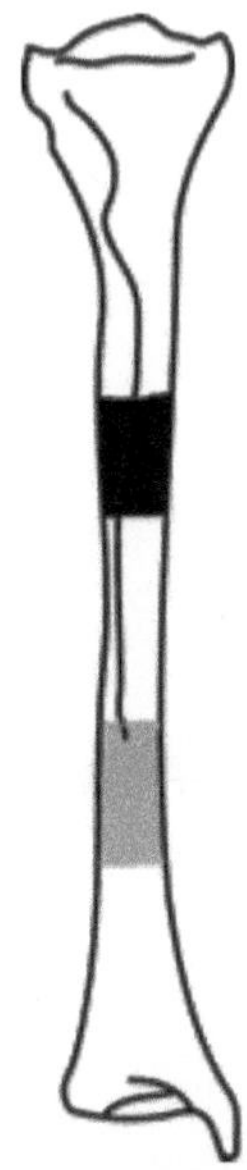

Figure 13-26
Location and relative size of a tibia sample. (A right tibia is illustrated, anterior view.)

Figure 13-27
Location and relative size of a fibula sample. (A right fibula is illustrated, anterior view.)

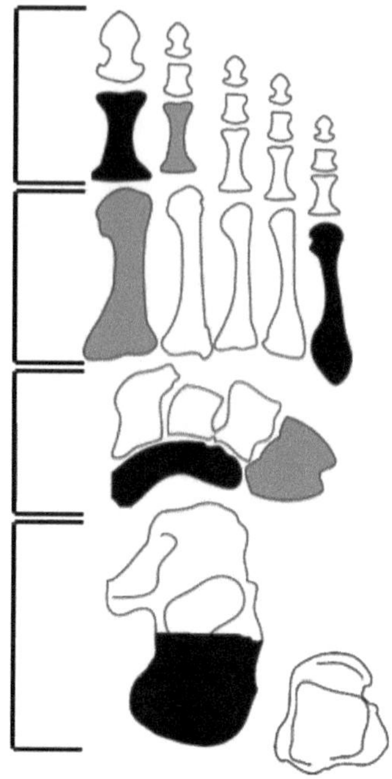

Figure 13-28
Location and relative size of foot samples. (A right foot is illustrated, dorsal view.)

Metatarsals

The first priority is a fifth metatarsal (black).

Second priority is the first metatarsal (gray).

Other Tarsals

The first priority is a complete navicular (black).

Second priority is a cuboid (gray).

Talus

A complete or mostly complete talus may be sampled.

Calcaneus

The posterior area or the body of the calcaneus (black) is first priority for the calcaneus.

References

Alonso, A., Andelinovic, S., Martin, P., Sutlovic, D., Erceg, I., Huffine, E., et al., 2001. DNA typing from skeletal remains: evaluation of multiplex and megaplex STR systems on DNA isolated from bone and teeth samples. Croat. Med. J. 42 (3), 260–266.

Amory, S., Huel, R., Bilić, A., Loreille, O., Parsons, T.J., 2012. Automatable full demineralization DNA extraction procedure from degraded skeletal remains. Forensic Sci. Int. Genet. 6 (3), 398–406.

Edson, S.M., Ross, J.P., Coble, M.D., Parsons, T.J., Barritt, S.M., 2004. Naming the dead: confronting the realities of rapid identification of degraded skeletal remains. Forensic Sci. Rev. 16 (1), 63–90.

Huel, R., Amory, S., Bilić, A., Vidović, S., Jasaragić, E., Parsons, T.J., 2012. DNA extraction from aged skeletal samples for str typing by capillary electrophoresis. Methods Mol. Biol. 830, 185–198.

Leney, M.D., 2006. Sampling skeletal remains for ancient DNA (aDNA): a measure of success. Hist. Archaeol. 40 (3), 31–49.

Milós, A., Selmanovic, A., Smajlovic, L., Huel, R., Katzmarzyk, C., Rizvic, A., et al., 2007. Success rates of nuclear short tandem repeat typing from different skeletal elements. Croat. Med. J. 48, 486–493.

Mundorff, A.Z., Bartelink, E.J., Mar-Cash, E., 2009. DNA preservation in skeletal elements from the World Trade Center disaster: recommendations for mass fatality management. J. Forensic Sci. 54 (4), 739–745.

Mundorff, A.Z., Davoren, J., Weitz, S., 2013. Developing an Empirically Based Ranking Order for Bone Sampling: Examining the Differential DNA Yield Rates Between Human Skeletal Elements Over Increasing Post Mortem Intervals. Document Number 241868. U.S. Department of Justice, Washington D.C.

National Institute of Justice, 2005. Mass fatality incidents: a guide for human forensic identification. Technical Working Group for Mass Fatality Forensic Identification (NCJ 199758), p. 79. U.S. Department of Justice, National Institute of Justice, Washington, D.C.

Parsons, T.J., Weedn, V.W., 1997. Preservation and recovery of DNA in postmortem specimens and trace samples. In: Haglund, W.D., Sorg, M.S. (Eds.), Forensic Taphonomy: The Postmortem Fate of Human Remains. CRC Press, Boca Raton, FL, pp.109–138.

Perry, W.L., Bass, W.M., Riggsby, W.S., Sirotkin, K., 1988. The autodegradation of deoxyribonucleic-acid (DNA) in human rib bone and its relationship to the time interval since death. J. Forensic Sci. 33 (1), 144–153.

Prinz, M., Carracedo, A., Mayr, W.R., Morling, N., Parsons, T.J., Sajantila, A., et al., 2007. DNA Commission of the International Society for Forensic Genetics (ISFG): recommendations regarding the role of forensic genetics for disaster victim identification (DVI). Forensic Sci. Int. Genet. 1, 3–12.

Yazedjian, L., Kesetovic, R., 2008. The application of traditional anthropological methods in a DNA-led identification project. In: Adams, B., Byrd, J. (Eds.), Recovery, Analysis, and Identification of Commingled Human Remains. Humana Press, Totowa, NJ, pp. 271–284.

CHAPTER 14

A Multidisciplinary Approach to Commingled Remains Analysis: Anthropology, Genetics, and Background Information

Mercedes Salado Puerto, Sofía Egaña, Mercedes Doretti, Carlos María Vullo

Argentine Forensic Anthropology Team (EAAF)

In a previous chapter by the authors (Egaña et al. 2008), we presented several challenging cases investigated by the Argentine Forensic Anthropology Team (EAAF[1]) involving commingled remains in the context of international human rights investigations in El Salvador, Zimbabwe, and Argentina. These examples described not only difficulties in the recovery of remains, but also obstacles in the identification process. Given the limitations of morphological reassociation, we concluded that identification and sorting based on anthropological analysis must be considered as preliminary in most cases and necessarily followed up by DNA testing. This is particularly true in cases involving: (1) highly commingled remains involving a large number of individuals; (2) "open" or virtually open cases, with a large list of potential candidates for remains; and (3) poor or unavailable antemortem information.

In this chapter, we present our reflections and lessons learned as a result of the incorporation of forensic genetics on a large scale in the commingled remains cases that EAAF has regularly worked on in the context of human rights investigations. Conclusions and recommendations are based on a methodological reassessment of the examination of remains, reassociation, and identification when applying forensic genetics in the analysis of commingled remains.

It is critical to understand the context of the investigations on which our reflections are based. We provide a brief description of the scenarios involved, as well as the methodological approaches in two historical events concerning the application of large-scale genetic analysis. We subsequently propose methodological recommendations concerning the study of commingled remains in such contexts.

[1] The EAAF is a nonprofit, nongovernmental organization that applies forensic sciences—especially anthropology, archaeology, genetics, and forensic pathology—to investigating violations of human rights and international humanitarian law.

Commingled Human Remains. http://dx.doi.org/10.1016/B978-0-12-405889-7.00014-9

Forensic Anthropology and the Investigation of Human Rights Violations

Since 1984, EAAF has worked on the recovery and identification of victims of human rights violations in different countries. Many of these cases include commingled remains. These investigations involve difficulties of various kinds, such as the challenges in recovering remains, their generally poor condition and preservation, and complications with accessing relevant historical information as well as the quality of this information.

Investigations are generally carried out years after the events took place, with little documentary or testimonial information available, outside the usual procedures used for investigations of common criminal cases, and with little or no support from the state to access and examine information. Historically, this led EAAF, and later, other nongovernmental forensic groups in Latin America, to enlarge the scope of the forensic investigation by including the compilation of historical information (both documentary and testimonial), the recovery of remains, and their analysis with the twofold objective of identifying individuals and clarifying the circumstances of death. These investigations include a final comprehensive forensic report provided to the official in charge of the investigation as part of a special commission of inquiry, a local court, or an international court. In each case, the investigative mechanism set in place may utilize the forensic findings for accountability processes, including prosecution.

Efforts in the Identification of the Disappeared in Argentina

Based on depositions made by the families of the victims, estimates range from 8,000 to 9,000 for the number of individuals who disappeared from 1976 to 1983 as a result of the last military regime in Argentina. Approximately 500 additional people disappeared and/or were assassinated prior to the military coup under an elected government, particularly in 1975. Since 1984, EAAF has had a primary role in the search, exhumation, and identification of people who were disappeared by the state during these periods. In Argentina, EAAF has always conducted its forensic work as expert witnesses for the local courts.

Initial EAAF Genetic Experience

At the end of the 1980s, it became possible to extract and amplify by PCR genetic material from bones. Between 1991 and 2003, laboratories in Argentina unsuccessfully tried to process bone samples submitted by EAAF. In a very small number of cases, bone samples taken by EAAF in Argentina, Ethiopia, and Haiti were processed by various laboratories working on a pro bono basis in the United States, United Kingdom, and Canada, achieving the first EAAF identifications confirmed by DNA analysis in 1991. Finally, in 2003, an existing private genetics laboratory in Argentina, LIDMO SRL, successfully began producing STR genetic profiles from bone samples submitted by EAAF. Partnering with LIDMO established genetic testing as more sustainable for the team.

Due to insufficient technical and financial resources, however, the ability to rely on genetic testing both in Argentina and often abroad was limited to the very few cases where EAAF had a *strong identification hypothesis* that required genetic confirmation and where DNA analysis was donated by the processing laboratories, or where EAAF obtained limited funding for the analysis.

Due to the complexity of the repression in Argentina, reaching a strong identification hypothesis demanded thorough historical research from EAAF, often requiring years of investigations, putting together interviews with survivors of illegal detention centers, testimonies from social and political activists as well as former members of political-military organizations, and documentary evidence such as cemetery records, death certificates, police and military records, and newspaper clippings, among other sources. When working abroad, EAAF shares the task of preliminary investigations with local NGOs, prosecutors' offices, and/or investigative bodies.

By 2005, EAAF had in its laboratories in Argentina about 600 skeletons under custody thought to correspond to disappeared people, but the team was still unable to formulate strong identity hypotheses for them. A new alternative was needed to significantly expand genetic testing.

The Latin America Initiative for the Identification of the Disappeared (LIID) in Argentina

The need to identify victims' remains of two major catastrophic events—the Balkan War and the September 11, 2001, attack on the World Trade Center in New York City—resulted in a significant upgrade in DNA technology. As a result, it increased the possibility of applying DNA testing to human rights cases in Latin America. Considering the existence of a common need in the region, in late 2004, EAAF contacted the Peruvian Forensic Anthropology Team (EPAF) and the Guatemalan Forensic Anthropology Foundation (FAFG) about forming a Latin American Initiative for the Identification of the Disappeared (LIID) with the aim of bringing large-scale genetic analysis to the region for human rights cases. In 2005, LIID was able to obtain an earmarked grant from the U.S. Congress. The grant was channeled through the Bureau of Democracy, Human Rights, and Labor of the U.S. Department of State and distributed to the three organizations in mid-2007.

EAAF's first year of LIID focused on trying to identify the close to 600 skeletal remains previously mentioned, collecting (through a national campaign) and processing an initial 5,000 blood samples from relatives of disappeared people, and setting up an EAAF DNA genetics laboratory for processing and training. At the same time, EAAF continued with the exhumation and anthropological analysis of 200 new individuals, to be genetically tested in the second year of the project.

Large-scale use of forensic genetics enabled the massive comparison of all the profiles obtained from bone samples with all family reference profiles that are part of the

EAAF-SDHN Genetic Bank.[2] This blind comparison not only allowed for a significant increase in the number of identifications, but also led to new information related to the historical research field and the possibility to generate new identity hypotheses from identifications in progress. That is to say, each identified person opened an "umbrella" of information about the possible identities of the remains that were buried during the same event, generating new lines of investigation.

Finally, large-scale genetic comparisons enabled EAAF to deal with major cases of commingled remains, including identification and intraskeletal reassociation, which had not been possible up until then. From the beginning of genetic testing under LIID in 2008 to the present, the remains of more than 130 people have been returned to their families after the identification and reassociation of intermixed bone elements. In addition, since using large-scale forensic genetics, EAAF has been working on more complex scenarios than those previously addressed (Doretti and Fondebrider 2012). We discuss them in the following sections.

Types of Scenarios

Human rights investigations are carried out in different contexts; however, they share some features in terms of:

- Time elapsed since the events took place: usually years.
- Condition of the remains: skeletonized or badly decomposed.
- Places where the remains were discovered: usually (1) known mass or individual graves, located in cemeteries, often buried as John and Jane Does, or in graves/pits located directly on clandestine military or police grounds; or (2) unattended/stored in medical service mortuaries, generally poorly preserved (loss of parts, commingled, incomplete, etc.); or (3) clandestine or unofficial burial places.
- State of preservation for remains: often commingled, fragmented, or burned due to several reasons, among which are both the circumstances of death and postmortem alterations.

In general, we can group the types of scenarios in which the investigations are conducted into several categories, depending on a number of criteria:

a. *Case type:* **open** versus **closed.**
   Depending on the scenario, the case type may include two factors:
   - Possible identities of the deceased (available list of victims)

[2] The EAAF-SDHN Genetic Bank includes the Data Bank of the Argentine Forensic Anthropology Team (EAAF) and the reference profiles obtained through a specific cooperative agreement between the Human Rights Secretariat (Ministry of Justice) and EAAF within the frame of the Latin American Initiative for the Identification of the Disappeared.

- Context of commingling (secondary graves versus disturbed primary graves)

Generally, the concept of "open/closed" is used to refer to a case depending on the availability of information about the *identities* of the victims—that is to say, whether or not the investigation has a list of the alleged victims who may be among the deceased or missing for a given case. The classic example of a closed case is a plane crash where the manifest of alleged victims is available.

We extend this concept in relation to the *context* in which the remains were *commingled.* We are not referring to the identities of possible victims, but to the reason for the intermixing of remains—that is to say, if the remains have been commingled by the *disturbance of a primary grave* (where the skeletons are intermingled without any skeletal elements introduced from other burials), or if it is a *secondary grave* in which the remains were transferred from one or more unknown primary burials. The first would be a closed context of commingling (intermixing of remains from a finite set of the same origin), and the second would be an open context of commingling (commingled remains from several original locations, without precise information about the primary contexts).

As an example, a grave containing the remains of victims of an explosion, where we *do not* have a list of people present at the explosion site, but where the remains have been *mixed by the explosion* at the recovery site, would be an open case in terms of identification but a closed context in regards to commingling.

The recovery and identification of the victims' remains of some of the cases that occurred during the latest Balkan War are typical examples of an open context of commingling, where secondary burials are the product of the disturbance of the original burial sites in order to hide the remains. Consequently, in these secondary graves, commingled remains from one or more primary graves related to an indeterminate number of individuals can be found.

Therefore, from now on, the terms **open/closed cases** will be used regarding the availability or not of a list of victims and **open/closed context of commingling** will refer to the circumstances in which the remains were mixed.

b. *Circumstance and time when remains were commingled:* We can divide these circumstances into two groups: pre-deposition or post-deposition. The first typically relates to the circumstances of the death (e.g., explosions, dismemberment, burning of the bodies), and the second to those circumstances derived from taphonomic processes (e.g., biotic and environmental factors), the accidental alteration of burial sites (e.g., building construction) or the intentional alteration (e.g., in order to conceal, destroy, damage the remains), as well as malpractice at the time of the exhumation or laboratory analysis of the remains.

c. *Time of intervention of forensic experts in the investigation of already commingled remains:* Intervening from the beginning (allowing for participation in planning a strategy for the collection of information, as well as recovery and analysis of remains), or when the investigation has already begun, at any stage after the recovery or laboratory analysis of remains.

d. *State of the remains:* Degree of fragmentation, mixing, preservation, or condition.
e. *Number of victims and characteristics:* Although there are common methodological guidelines, the methodological approach largely depends on the scale of the case, in terms of the quantity of bones (and represented individuals). Similarly, the demographic characteristics (biological profile) and personal characteristics (robusticity, antemortem pathologies, etc.) will influence the possibility of bone sorting and the specific methodological needs.
f. *Requests by the officials in charge of the investigation to be addressed by the forensic team:* Objectives set up by the investigative body in charge of the investigation for the forensic experts, regarding reassociation of commingled remains and identifications.

Clearly, in any of the cases listed here, there could be (and often are) mixed or combined situations within or between each of the categories. Finally, it should be noted that although general methodological guidelines exist for the recovery and analysis strategies for such cases, variations determined by the specific type of scenario should be considered in the planning and development of the investigation of each case.

Background Information

Preliminary information, or a "case history," is required for the reconstruction of the event under investigation, for methodological planning, and to determine the possibilities to accomplish the main forensic goals; among these, the identification of victims is of utmost importance. In human rights investigations, the group of forensic professionals is generally responsible for collecting such information. We again emphasize the *special nature of these types of investigations* and their differences with those conducted for "common" crimes, where the police or prosecutors are usually in charge of both the investigation and the handling of the case history.

We previously reflected on the difficulties in tracing and recovering the historical information of cases of human rights violations, both in regard to finding archives or related documents, as well as collecting antemortem information for the victims. This is due to the time elapsed, the context of secrecy and illegality of state repression (which generally involves the concealment or destruction of records), and, most commonly, the lack of primary witnesses of the events under investigation.

There are three main sources of information:

- *Documentary:* This type of information includes intelligence files, ID cards of disappeared people, fingerprint records for corpses and for disappeared persons, police records on removal of human remains, morgue and cemetery entry and exit records, death certificates, hospital records, private funeral homes, reports of disappearances to state and non-governmental agencies, official reports on exhumations of remains, etc.

- *Testimonial:* This type of information refers to data collected from interviews and testimonies given by survivors, witnesses, and relatives of missing persons. It includes both background and physical information about each disappeared person, as well as information about clandestine detention centers, political activist structures and relations, witnesses of kidnapping/death/burial, etc.
- *Visual material:* This type of information includes visual material referring to the victims, potential places of detention, and burial sites (e.g., historical aerial photography, satellite imagery, etc.)

The background information collected by anthropologists in this context refers solely *to circumstances of the victim's disappearance/death/burial* and his or her antemortem information, with the aims of identifying the remains, providing information regarding cause and manner of death, and reconstructing the events under investigation. *It does not include the investigation of those responsible* for such events. In most cases where EAAF takes part, the team's forensic report is part of a criminal investigation, and the judicial authority is responsible for the clarification of criminal responsibility.

There is an interesting discussion in the forensic community at large about when background information should be consulted by forensic experts working on a case, in order to avoid bias in the interpretation of evidence.We agree that it is necessary to avoid such bias, being cautious in selecting who will have access (and at which points in the process) to background information for a given case. However, taking into account the benefits obtained in several investigations conducted by EAAF, we highly recommend *integrating and reconciling preliminary information* with the rest of the analysis to help reach conclusions. Selecting a system for information flow (division of work, collection, analysis, and reconciliation) is part of the expertise of the forensic team working on a case, similar to the methodologies for recovery and analysis of remains.

Multidisciplinary Approach in Commingled Remains

The addition of large-scale genetic testing to EAAF's anthropological analysis of more than 20 investigations in Argentina involving commingled remains resulted in the systematization of new methodological approaches and procedures. In our view, if possible, these should be taken into account from the beginning of the analysis. We present here some of these approaches and procedures:

- Design a strategy for the systematic analysis of commingled remains, including steps to be followed in the anthropological analysis and the genetic testing, as well as the use of background information.
- Adopt standard protocols and forms.
- Create anthropology and genetics databases (or improvement of those already existing); this includes both programming a Laboratory Information Management System (LIMS) for traceability and the acquisition of software to compare genetic profiles for matching.

- Develop a structural organization of anthropology and genetics laboratories at a spatial level, division of staff tasks, and coordination between different areas.
- Develop a sampling strategy for genetic analysis, sampling by phases including:
  - Genetic analysis
  - Review of remains analysis with consideration of genetic results
  - Resampling of remains accordingly. In these cases, EAAF decided to sample until all possibilities of genetic testing in all cases were exhausted.
- Initiate genetic comparison of profiles (for both remains reassociation and identification) based primarily on STR profiles. In clearly closed commingling contexts, and at the end of the sorting process, reassociations could be made through mitochondrial DNA (mtDNA) analysis of bone elements showing highly degraded DNA characteristics to produce STR profiles and *after determining that unique mtDNA haplotypes allowed for discrimination among the individuals.*
- Use direct genetic matching for reassociation of remains, instead of kinship analysis.
- In bone samples that yield partial STR profiles after several processing attempts, assign a consensus STR profile. In the cases where different samples potentially belonging to the same individual show inconsistencies in some loci, the profile probabilities should be assessed statistically considering the possibility of allele dropout.
- Consensus profiles should not be generated by using different bone elements, but always derived from various samples of the same bone element. After a group of bone elements is detected to be reassociated, the bone sample showing the most complete STR profile may be selected for the purpose of kinship analysis to identify the victim. This criterion is limited in cases where biologically related individuals in a grave containing commingled remains could coexist.
- Conduct blind comparisons of genetic profiles, both for direct matching and kinship analysis. Although in some of these cases background information strongly indicated that they were closed contexts of commingling (commingled intragrave or intracemetery), we decided to confirm this information, proceeding to treat all cases as open contexts of commingling in the comparison of genetic information.
- Use a combination of *prior odds* with LR (likelihood ratio) for the calculation of *posterior probability* both for identification and for intraskeletal reassociation.
- Use a threshold of posterior probability: after the combination with prior probability, 99.99% as a reliable value to report an identification or an intraskeletal reassociation.
- Notify an identification to the investigative body in charge of the case and to his or her relatives as soon as the first bone element confirms a positive identification, not at the end of the sorting process. This may imply issuing initial and subsequent supplemental reports and leaving the case open until the sorting process is exhausted. The forensic team held meetings with courts and relatives of victims to explain the basis, process, and estimated time frame for results.

- Decide the final destination of the commingled remains that could not be reassociated at the end of the sorting process. In closed cases, after court approval, the team held consultations with the appropriate family groups or/and affected communities to decide on a disposition for the unidentified remains.

Many of these methodological strategies that we used in these cases of large-scale commingled remains were implemented from the beginning of the investigation. Other methodological decisions were made each time new challenges appeared. It is important to note that prior to 2008, there were few systematized and public experiences on this topic. At the same time, while these investigations were conducted, new improvements in the field of forensic genetics, particularly in recent years, took place (e.g., analysis of SNPs, Indels [insertion/deletion polymorphisms], new improved DNA extraction protocols, etc.).

Methodological Approach in the Analysis of Commingled Skeletal Remains

The procedures for examining commingled remains, incorporating all available information (historical, archaeological, anthropological, and genetic), which is currently used by EAAF, can be summarized as follows:

a. Create a *photographic record of the remains* in original containers, before starting the process of analysis, regardless of whether the remains are recovered by the same group or by other institutions/external agents. Photographic records are done throughout the entire process of analysis.
b. *Coding* is particularly important for commingled remains. The development of a coding system involves creating codes for bone elements and the samples derived from them. In cases of commingled remains, it is important that the bone element code preserves the information of the site, the grave (if appropriate), the skeletal assemblage (if appropriate), and the sequential number of bone elements, to access source information easily and to ensure traceability after the bone elements are moved for sorting. For example, one bone element code could come from Cemetery Site 2 (C2), grave 3 (G3), skeletal assemblage 1 (S1), and is the fifth element collected from this provenience; this code would appear as C2-G3-S1-0005. A similar coding system could be utilized for commingled remains received from a laboratory or other non-archaeological setting. For genetic samples, the original code for each bone element should be preserved, with an additional code describing the sample. If we extend the preceding example, the first bone sample (B1) collected from bone element C2-G3-S1-0005 would appear as C2-G3-S1-00005-B1. It is essential to avoid duplication in coding, and that the coding system is adequate in number and types of characters to avoid transcription errors, producing unique traceable codes. Also, in the case of genetic samples, for reasons of traceability we strongly suggest using barcodes.

c. Use *labels*. Each bone element should be labeled according to the chosen code, facilitating traceability and the subsequent reconstruction of the type and degree of commingling.
d. Record an *inventory* according to original containers (boxes or bags as used in the recovery), prior to the movement of remains for sorting.
e. Assess the *minimum number of individuals* or *Most Likely Number of Individuals* (MNI/MLNI) by using anthropological techniques.
f. In the *first phase of anthropological reassociation,* use variables such as age and sex, paired elements, joint match, overall morphology, continuity in the pattern of traumatic injury, consistency of specific antemortem features, consistency of postmortem changes, and so on.
g. The *first sampling for genetic analysis* should include at least the bone elements that indicate the MNI/MLNI and those that, because of a particular trait, have potential for identifications (e.g., bone pathology or relevant dental characteristics).
h. *Compare STR profiles* using direct matching (reassociation) and kinship analysis (identification).
i. *Reconsider* anthropological reassociations depending on genetic results.
j. Select *new samples* for genetic analysis and resampling in cases in which the initial processing failed or yielded partial results.
k. *Repeat stages* of sampling and anthropological analysis until the process is exhausted.
l. Evaluate the possibility of reassociating bone samples through *mtDNA* where the STR DNA profiling failed due to degradation of genetic material. At a genetic level, if it is a closed context of commingling, it is fundamental to assess the nonrepetition of mtDNA haplotypes using bone elements that have shown a unique STR profile. Different STR profiles indicate different individuals.
m. *Consider the case comprehensively* with anthropological analysis + genetic + background information (files, photos, recovery and laboratory reports in documentary archives). We recommend this is done after the sorting process is finished to avoid bias. Issue initial comprehensive forensic reports when there are positive identifications.
n. Where a closed context of commingling is certain, evaluate the possibility of making later reassociations through a *process of elimination*, at both anthropological and genetic levels.
o. Perform *individual analysis* using inventory and anthropological analysis of the reassociated remains as partial skeletons, after the possibilities of reassociation have been exhausted: biological profile, pathological analysis, and perimortem trauma. This includes nonbiological evidence associated with each individual.
p. Inventory the *unassociated remains.*
q. Inventory the *unassociated nonbiological evidence* or *artifacts.*

r. Compile *final expert reports,* which detail reassociated individuals (identified or not) and provide a comprehensive report of the case including inventories of unassociated remains and nonbiological evidence.

Anthropological Reassociation of Remains and Sampling for Genetic Analysis

It is important to consider that in the case of commingled remains, genetic analysis entails multiple objectives, such as contributing to the determination of the MNI present in the whole set, identification of the remains, and reassociation of bone elements belonging to the same person. The sampling strategy should consider all these aspects while at the same time reaching a balance between the amount and types of samples selected for the reassociation of each skeleton. This is what we may call an effective and efficient sampling strategy—that is to say, obtaining the maximum possible information with the minimum number of samples. Based on the experience of working with commingled remains, we propose conducting bone sampling for genetic analysis *in phases*, as described in the following sections.

Phase I: Sampling for Genetic Analysis

If schedule and budget allow, it is prudent (or ideal) to begin sampling for genetic analysis of the remains after steps (a) to (f) mentioned in the previous section have been completed. In this first phase of sampling, we attempt to include both the elements suitable to genetically determine the MNI (and therefore, the genetic profiles of each individual that will serve for identification purposes) and the optimum samples for reassociation of anatomical sections (body parts). However, due to time and financial constraints in this type of large-scale investigation, it is usually necessary to prioritize goals and complete all the objectives in stages over time.

Hence, we have applied an initial sampling strategy that includes those bone elements that define the MNI as diagnosed anthropologically, and sections carrying particular traits that make them more likely to be identified (e.g., bone pathology and relevant dental characteristics). Usually, this step can be solved with a smaller time investment than required by sampling for morphological reassociation of the set. The results of this genetic analysis will allow for:

a. Progress in matters of identification and sorting
b. Diagnosis of the general state of preservation of the genetic material (number of full, partial, and null STR profiles) and reconsideration of the sampling strategy if necessary
c. Confirmation or modification of the MNI as well as the reassociation of remains that were previously proposed anthropologically

Phase II: Sampling for Genetic Analysis

The second phase is performed after obtaining the genetic results from the samples tested in Phase I, and after the units of anthropological (i.e., morphological and osteometric) reassociation have been defined to a greater extent than in the previous phase. Because this sampling stage of genetic analysis depends on the scope and reliability of the morphological reassociations, as well as the results of Phase I, the options for retesting will primarily depend on two variables: the preservation of bone elements and the case scale (number of bones and individuals).

In cases of highly fragmented or incomplete bones, the number of elements to analyze will be higher than when dealing with complete bones, and it will include isolated pieces to a larger degree than articulated body parts. The grouping of bone elements into a larger unit will depend on the presence of bone elements in that set available for genetic analysis and on the success in obtaining genetic profiles.

The homogeneity in biological profiles and other features (sex, age, stature, robusticity, etc.) of the persons represented in these cases will impair and reduce the reliability of anthropological reassociations, even for sets of well-preserved and complete bone elements. The higher the homogeneity, the greater the need to sample for genetic analysis.

In cases in which bone elements are *well preserved* and, after utilizing the usual criteria of reassociation[3]—which define a major skeletal unit (body part)—have been applied, we have obtained positive results with a *crossed sampling* strategy. This strategy consists of carrying out the analysis of the remains (maximizing the information with the minimum number of samples), and is based on the high reliability of pair matching in anthropological reassociation, as well as certain fixed joints (axial plane: spine, sacro-coxal) or joints with certain pathologies and/or identifying features.

For paired bones, this strategy implies taking a sample for DNA analysis from one element and the subsequent reassociation of the pair via anthropological comparison. For example, to confirm the reassociation of the lower limbs of an individual, we would take a sample from the right femur, left tibia, and right fibula. If the results of the genetic reassociation were positive, we would anthropologically group the left femur, right tibia, and left fibula. Similarly, to confirm the grouping of the axial skeleton, it would be necessary to sample one of the bone elements of the spine or the pelvis, whenever there is continuity in the existence of articulated elements.

[3] Archeological information about the association *in situ* of the remains at exhumation: age and sex, paired elements, joint matching, general morphology, continuity in patterns of traumatic injury, consistency of specific antemortem features, consistency of postmortem changes, and preliminary investigation results (documental and testimonial sources).

In summary, sampling in phases implies a sequential strategy in which the next round of genetic analysis is determined depending on the previous results, always combining genetic and anthropological analyses.

Illustrating with Some of the Investigated Cases

To illustrate these considerations, we have selected a number of cases of commingled remains that EAAF has worked on in recent years. These are investigations in which EAAF intervened at different stages of the recovery and the analysis of the remains to identify the remains of disappeared persons in a context of human rights violations. Cases are grouped according to the cemetery or place of recovery. The minimum number of individuals (MNI) in Table 14-1

Table 14-1: Examples of Commingled Cases Investigated by EAAF

		Degree of Commingling*[a]			Degree Of Fragmentation/ Absence Of Bone Elements		
Case	**MNI (Final)**	**H**	**M**	**L**	**H**	**M**	**L**
Forensic Service (Argentina)	97	X[b]				X	
Avellaneda A8 (Argentina)	8		X				X
General Lavalle (Argentina)	13	X			X		
Rafael Calzada (Argentina)	15	X				X	
Río Medina (Argentina)	11	X			X		
San Andrés de Giles (Argentina)	5	X			X		
San Martin (Argentina)	35	X				X	
Tacanas (Argentina)	4			X			X
Transradio (Argentina)	4		X			X	
Ciudad Juárez (México)	18			X			X
Viejo Velazco (México)	2	X			X		

*H = high, M = medium, L = low

[a]Degree of commingling: H (*high*, bone elements with no association), M (*medium*, body parts + isolated bone elements), L (*low*, partial mixing of anatomical sections of various individuals).

[b]Commingled remains recovered in a nonscientific way between 1984 and 1985 from 12 cemeteries of Buenos Aires Province (Argentina) and transferred to the Forensic Service of La Plata to be analyzed. They remained there until 2003 when EAAF was authorized to analyze them. The cases have different degrees of commingling from medium (M) to high (H), depending on the original cemetery.

refers to the final estimate after the integration of genetic analysis. Later, we show how this MNI was modified in various stages of our research. In all these cases, the moment when commingling occurred was *post-depositional* and as a result of malpractice in the exhumation and the improper handling of the remains before the intervention of EAAF.

Types of Cases

In most of the cases, through documentary information, there was information on the time and circumstances that led to the commingling of the bones. In general, the remains had been exhumed in various cemeteries (where commingling took place), or they had been recovered on the surface, transferred to an official forensic institution (morgue) to be submitted for analysis by medical examiners, labeled, and placed in storage or reburied in another section of the same cemetery. Although theoretically—according to the definition previously developed—these were closed contexts of commingling (i.e., there was no certainty of inter-cemetery commingling), they were treated as open contexts in the genetic analysis, carrying out blind comparison of genetic profiles.

In all the cases described here, we were able to combine anthropological and genetic analysis until the reassociation possibilities were exhausted. Moreover, in several cases, there were records of previous analysis that had been made by medical examiners, so it was possible to trace back comparatively, rebuilding the trajectory of the remains and the period when mixing took place. In some cases, these records also helped to formulate reassociation hypotheses.

In some cases illustrated (Table 14-2), the variation in the number of individuals estimated using only anthropological analysis contrasted to the number after the incorporation of

Table 14-2: Examples of Commingled Cases Investigated by EAAF Showing the MNI Derived by Anthropological and Genetic Methods

Case	MNI (Preliminary)	MNI (Anthropological)	Integrated MNI (Anthropology + Genetics)
Forensic Service (Argentina)	>80	89 (85 adults by right tibia + 4 subadults)	97
Avellaneda A8 (Argentina)	---	8	8
General Lavalle (Argentina)	11 (documentary)	12 (right femur)	13
Rafael Calzada (Argentina)	14	14 (right femur)	15
Río Medina (Argentina)	---	4 (right femur)	11
San Andrés de Giles (Argentina)	5	5 (occipital)	5
San Martin (Argentina)	35 (buried in individual graves)	35 (right femur)	35
Tacanas (Argentina)	4 (testimonial)	4	4
Transradio (Argentina)	---	4 (right femur)	4
Ciudad Juárez (México)	---	---	18
Viejo Velazco (México)	2	2	2

genetics. This variation depended more on the degree of fragmentation, the absence of bone elements, and preservation conditions than on the degree of commingling itself. That is, in those cases of commingled remains (even without contextual information on the recovery) with good preservation conditions and where mostly complete bone elements are present, it is possible to estimate a number of individuals by anthropological analysis which does not differ substantially from that estimated by genetic analysis.

Genetic Testing

Regarding genetic analysis, EAAF experience was limited with taking samples from bone elements that were not those traditionally used for the identification of remains when a complete skeleton is available (e.g., teeth or femur/tibia diaphysis) until the moment we started to use forensic genetics broadly and systematically in the reassociation of commingled remains. Such methodology forced us to sample all kinds of bone elements and to evaluate not only which bone elements produced better genetic results, but also which sector within the bone element was more likely to provide better results. As illustrated here, it should be noted that for remains from cemeteries in Argentina, this posed a significant problem because, on average, from the traditional bone samples sent for STR profiling, over 40% needed complementary genetic analysis to reach acceptable STR profiling. This was due to degradation of genetic material. This fact, together with the magnitude and the incomplete condition of the commingled cases, motivated EAAF to undertake large samplings and to retest multiple bone elements both for reassociation and identification.

We provide here the results of the combined analysis of some commingled remains cases investigated by EAAF in recent years, regarding the reassociation and identification of the commingled remains belonging to 395 individuals (final MNI). Those remains were recovered from 23 Argentine cemeteries (provinces of Buenos Aires, Tucumán, Santa Fe, and Entre Ríos) in which the bodies were buried during the 1970s.

Because the aim is to analyze how different bone elements produce suitable genetic profiles, it is necessary to avoid other external factors and variables that could be affecting the quality of the profiles. For that reason, in the study, we included only those cases exhumed in Argentina, because this was a homogeneous sample in terms of time (1975–1979) and genetic analysis of the remains. Not only was the context of the remains similar, but the same DNA extraction and STR profiling protocols were used for all bone elements (Romanini et al. 2012).

In each case, the remains were analyzed in accordance with the methodology previously indicated and they were sampled by phases for genetic analysis aiming for identification and reassociation of remains. Regarding the genetic analysis, the bone samples were STR-profiled using primarily the commercial kits AmpFLSTR® Identifiler® Plus and MiniFiler® (Applied Biosystems). The samples showing degraded DNA characteristics yielding partial STR profiles were analyzed with noncommercial, non-CODIS, mini-STR genetic markers (Butler et al. 2003; Chung et al. 2004; Coble and Butler 2005). Although the results are not included here, many samples were also analyzed for mtDNA (HVR1 and HVR2 regions), autosomal SNPs, and Indels.

We analyzed the results for STR profiles, taking into account the maximum of 15 loci represented in the kit *AmpFLSTR® Identifiler® Plus.* Therefore, we have rated the quality of each STR profile as follows:

- FLAT: No loci reported
- POOR: 1 to 6 loci reported
- FAIR: 7 to 12 loci reported
- FULL: ≥ 13 loci reported

Table 14-3 and Figure 14-1 summarize the results of the analysis of 1,261 bone samples, grouped by categories based on the type of bone and the quality of the STR profile that was obtained.

To the naked eye, the quality of STR profiles is clearly different depending on the type of bone being sampled. However, it was necessary to systematize this first impression through statistical analysis, measuring the significance of the differences noted. When basic nonparametric statistics (Pearson Chi-square test and Fisher's exact test) are applied, significant differences in the quality of the STR profile based on bone element sampled are noted (Table 14-4).

The differences observed in more than half of the cases are statistically significant, systematically indicating a higher quality of STR profiles in certain bone elements (teeth, tibia, femur, fibula) compared to others with a high frequency of flat or partial profiles (humerus, ulna, radius). In an intermediate range, there are elements, such as the petrous portion of the temporal, with good results in nuclear DNA profiling, even more favorable than the long bones of the upper limbs and definitely better than the other sections of the skull (parietal, occipital) or the jaw, with the exception of teeth.

Surprisingly, after systematization, the tibia yields better results than the femur, although the latter is usually selected as more favorable for sampling, along with teeth. Similarly, it is noteworthy that elements like the vertebrae or ribs, even in *challenging cases* with aged DNA, produce significantly more complete STR profiles than the long bones of the upper limbs. Nevertheless, further analysis is required due to the small sample size (n).

Figure 14-2 reflects the quality of STR profiles based on specific bone elements after the information derived from statistical analysis is systematized. The objective of Figure 14-2 is to provide a visual prioritization regarding specific bone elements that produce more complete STR profiles (left side of the figure) compared with others of worse quality (gradually moving to the right side of the figure).

These results are also observed in complete skeletons, that is to say, between different bone elements within the same skeleton that were found articulated in an anatomical position in a grave.

Table 14-3: Quality of STR Profile According to the Bone Sample Type

Type of Bone		Profile				Total
		Flat	Poor	Fair	Full	
Femur	Count (N)	93	44	75	146	358
	%	26.0%	12.3%	20.9%	40.8%	100.0%
Fibula	Count (N)	12	6	2	16	36
	%	33.3%	16.7%	5.6%	44.4%	100.0%
Humerus	Count (N)	106	44	25	19	194
	%	54.6%	22.7%	12.9%	9.8%	100.0%
Ilium	Count (N)	50	15	9	5	79
	%	63.3%	19.0%	11.4%	6.3%	100.0%
Mandible	Count (N)	10	2	2	1	15
	%	66.7%	13.3%	13.3%	6.7%	100.0%
Occipital	Count (N)	13	3	3	1	20
	%	65.0%	15.0%	15.0%	5.0%	100.0%
Parietal	Count (N)	7	0	1	1	9
	%	77.8%	.0%	11.1%	11.1%	100.0%
Radius	Count (N)	27	8	3	3	41
	%	65.9%	19.5%	7.3%	7.3%	100.0%
Rib	Count (N)	3	2	1	1	7
	%	42.9%	28.6%	14.3%	14.3%	100.0%
Scapula	Count (N)	8	1	1	1	11
	%	72.7%	9.1%	9.1%	9.1%	100.0%
Temporal (petrous portion)	Count (N)	21	9	14	29	73
	%	28.8%	12.3%	19.2%	39.7%	100.0%
Tibia	Count (N)	22	8	24	44	98
	%	22.4%	8.2%	24.5%	44.9%	100.0%
Tooth	Count (N)	39	16	34	131	220
	%	17.7%	7.3%	15.5%	59.5%	100.0%
Ulna	Count (N)	43	9	9	6	67
	%	64.2%	13.4%	13.4%	9.0%	100.0%
Vertebra	Count (N)	2	1	4	3	10
	%	20.0%	10.0%	40.0%	30.0%	100.0%
Total	Count (N)	466	170	212	413	1,261
	%	37.0%	13.5%	16.8%	32.8%	100.0%

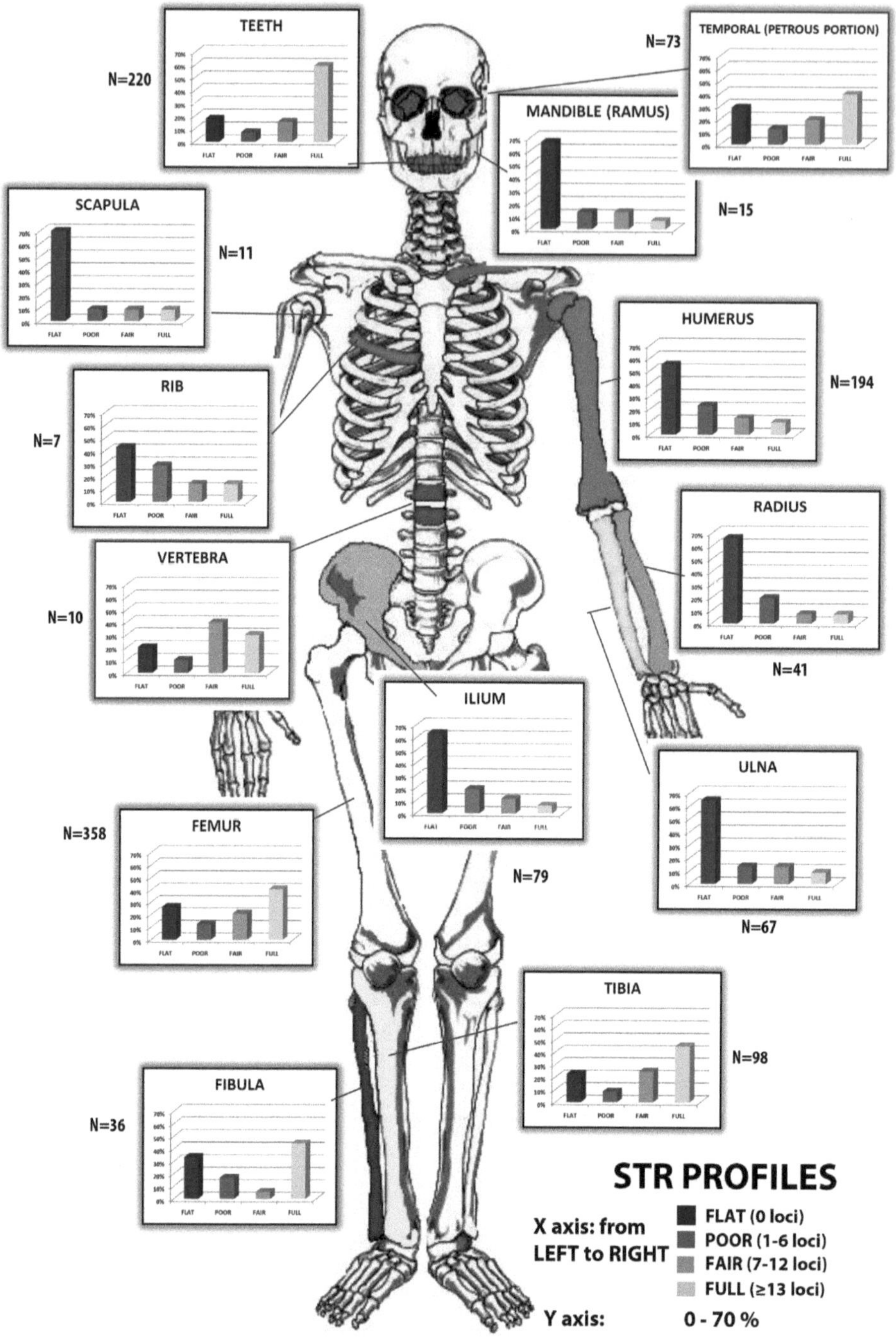

Figure 14-1
Representation of the STR profile quality depending on the type of bone sampled.

Table 14-4: Nonparametric Statistic Applied to the Quality of the STR Profiles vs. Type of Bone Sampled

Comparison		N Valid Cases	Pearson Chi-Square	Fisher's Exact Test	Exact Sig.	df	Statistical Significance	Recommended
Teeth	Temporal	293	9.311[a]		.025	3	Yes	Teeth
Teeth	Humerus	414	127.896[a]		.000	3	Yes	Teeth
Teeth	Radius	261	57.260[a]		.000	3	Yes	Teeth
Teeth	Ulna	287	68.701[a]		.000	3	Yes	Teeth
Teeth	Ilium	299	85.093[a]		.000	3	Yes	Teeth
Teeth	Femur	578	19.559[a]		.000	3	Yes	Teeth
Teeth	Tibia	318	6.537[a]		.088	3	No	Teeth[c]
Teeth	Fibula	256	10.343[a]		.016	3	Yes	Teeth
Parietal	Occipital	29[d]		1.869[b]	.745	3	No	Any
Temporal	Occipital	93		12.406[b]	.004	3	Yes	Temporal
Temporal	Parietal	82		6.852[b]	.031	3	Yes	Temporal
Humerus	Radius	235		1.653 [b]	.640	3	No	Any
Humerus	Ulna	261	2.939[a]		.401	3	No	Any
Humerus	Ilium	273	1.957[a]		.591	3	No	Any
Radius	Ulna	108		1.519[b]	.704	3	No	Any
Radius	Ilium	120		0.577 [b]	.947	3	No	Any
Femur	Temporal	431	0.287[a]		.962	3	No	Any
Femur	Humerus	552	82.125[a]		.000	3	Yes	Femur
Femur	Radius	399	35.451[a]		.000	3	Yes	Femur
Femur	Ulna	425	43.395[a]		.000	3	Yes	Femur
Femur	Ilium	437	54.994[a]		.000	3	Yes	Femur
Femur	Tibia	456	2.286[a]		.515	3	No	Any
Femur	Fibula	394	5.231[a]		.157	3	No	Femur[c]
Tibia	Temporal	171	2.188[a]		.534	3	No	Any
Tibia	Humerus	292	65.508[a]		.000	3	Yes	Tibia
Tibia	Radius	139	35.145[a]		.000	3	Yes	Tibia
Tibia	Ulna	165	38.061[a]		.000	3	Yes	Tibia
Tibia	Ilium	177	49.408[a]		.000	3	Yes	Tibia
Tibia	Fibula	134	7.917[a]		.046	3	Yes	Tibia
Fibula	Temporal	109	3.674[a]		.305	3	No	Any
Fibula	Humerus	230	28.540[a]		.000	3	Yes	Fibula
Fibula	Radius	77		15.221[b]	.001	3	Yes	Fibula
Fibula	Ulna	103	19.510[a]		.000	3	Yes	Fibula
Fibula	Ilium	115	24.745[a]		.000	3	Yes	Fibula

Continued

Table 14-4: Nonparametric Statistic Applied to the Quality of the STR Profiles vs. Type of Bone Sampled—cont'd

Comparison		N Valid Cases	Pearson Chi-Square	Fisher's Exact Test	Exact Sig.	df	Statistical Significance	Recommended
Vertebra	Rib	17[d]		2.827[b]	.537	3	No	Vertebra[c]
Vertebra	Scapula	21[d]		6.261[b]	.080	3	No	Vertebra[c]
Rib	Scapula	18[d]		2.359[b]	.701	3	No	Rib[c]

[a]< 20% cells have expected count less than 5.
[b]≥ 20% cells have expected count less than 5.
[c]Recommendation based on qualitative differences (not statistically significant).
[d]Further analysis required (small sample size).

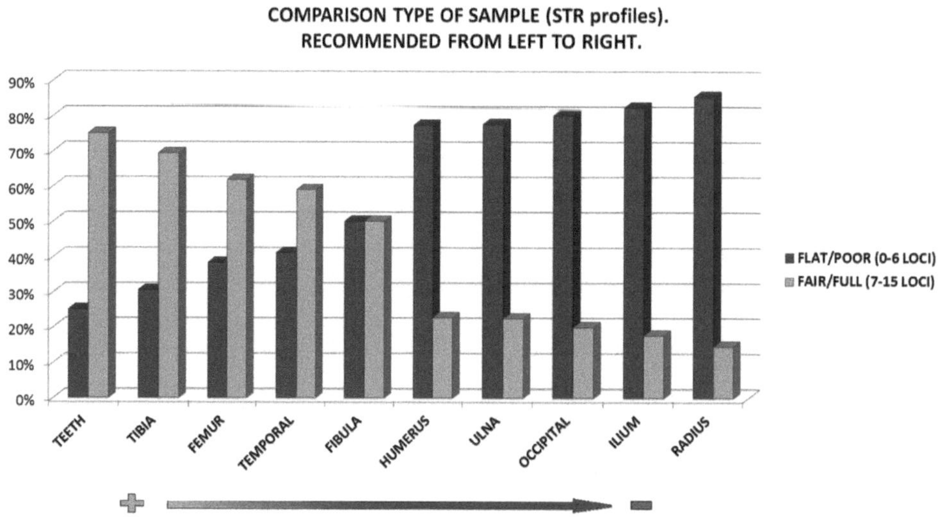

Figure 14-2
Bone elements recommended in sampling for genetic analysis (from left to right).

Thus, these results should not be attributed to taphonomic processes for commingled remains, but rather due to the structure of the specific bone. These suggested recommendations can thus be applied to bone sampling for genetic analysis in general, not only in cases of commingled remains. The reality with commingled remains, though, is that it is impossible to avoid sampling some elements where we know beforehand that it will be more complex to obtain a profile.

For some elements (flat bones of the skull, vertebrae, ribs, and scapula), we must increase the number of samples in this study to be able to confirm the results previously described because the current sample size (n) is small.

Analyzing statistically if the observed differences in bone type also apply to the laterality of the element (i.e., whether there are differences between the left or right side of the same bone

Table 14-5: Nonparametric Statistic Applied to the Quality of STR Profiles vs. Side of the Bone Sampled

Bone	N Valid Cases	Pearson Chi-Square	Fisher's Exact Test	Exact Sig.	df	Statistical Significance	Recommended
Femur (left/right)	350	8.585[a]		.035	3	Yes	Left
Fibula (left/right)	35		3.630[b]	.304	3	No	Any
Humerus (left/right)	192	2.317[a]		.509	3	No	Right[c]
Ilium (left/right)	79		4.163[b]	.251	3	No	Any
Radius (left/right)	41		5.668[b]	.129	3	No	Left[c]
Teeth (upper/lower)	220	3.310[a]		.346	3	No	Upper[c]
Tibia (left/right)	98		4.694[b]	.198	3	No	Left[c]
Ulna (left/right)	66		6.171[b]	.093	3	No	Left[c]

[a]< 20% cells have expected count less than 5.
[b]≥ 20% cells have expected count less than 5.
[c]Recommendation based on qualitative differences (not statistically significant).

or between upper and lower teeth), we note that only the femur shows significant differences, with the best quality profiles being found on the left side (Table 14-5 and Figure 14-3). It is not possible to explain the reason for this difference observed in the femur either by the sample number or by the anatomy of the bone. We recommend extending the analysis to other cases to confirm this result.

Intraskeletal Reassociation and Identification

By Anthropology

The scope and reliability of anthropological reassociations (morphological and osteometric) as well as the selection of samples for genetic analysis will primarily depend on two variables: the preservation of bone elements and the magnitude of the case (number of pieces and individuals). As previously stated, in cases with highly fragmented or incomplete elements, the selection of samples for genetic analysis will be higher and will include greater degree of isolated elements than body parts. In cases with well-preserved and complete bone elements, the homogeneity of the personal characteristics of the individuals represented in the skeletal remains can impair or reduce the reliability of anthropological reassociations. The higher the homogeneity, the greater the need to sample for genetic analysis.

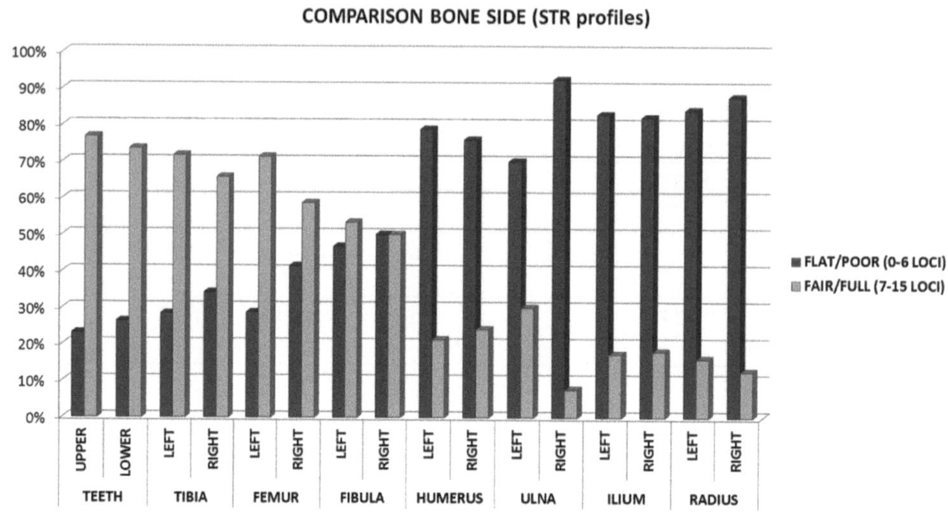

Figure 14-3
Nonparametric statistics applied to the quality of STR profiles depending on the side of the bone sampled.

Articulation and Pair Matching: Based on our experience, *in a homogeneous set* in terms of identifying features, we must be cautious about the reliability offered by the different joints in the anthropological reassociation (i.e., articulation and pair matching) of commingled remains, even in a good state of preservation. Our results regarding the reliability of articulations vary slightly from those described by other authors (Adams and Byrd 2006). Our results are quantified in the following manner according to the observed reliability (see Figures 14-4 and 14-5):

- *High reliability* (≥ 90% of correct classification): Pair matching and fixed joints of the axial plane (vertebrae, sacrum-pelvis).
- *Moderate reliability* (60%–90% of correct classification): Temporomandibular articulation, atlas–occipital condyles, humerus–ulna, radius–ulna, tibia–fibula, tibia–talus.
- *Low reliability* (≤ 60% of correct classification): Clavicle–scapula, clavicle–manubrium, sternum–ribs, ribs–vertebrae, humerus–scapula, radius–carpal, pelvis–femur, femur–tibia.

By Genetics

As explained in the preceding section, most of the missing persons in Argentina during the investigated period show homogeneity in reference to biological profile and personal characteristics, as well as insufficient antemortem physical data, thus complicating possibilities for combining genetics with other methods of identification. Such homogeneity hinders the possibility of intraskeletal reassociation without the support of genetic analysis, that is to say, relying on only the combination of various anthropological methods.

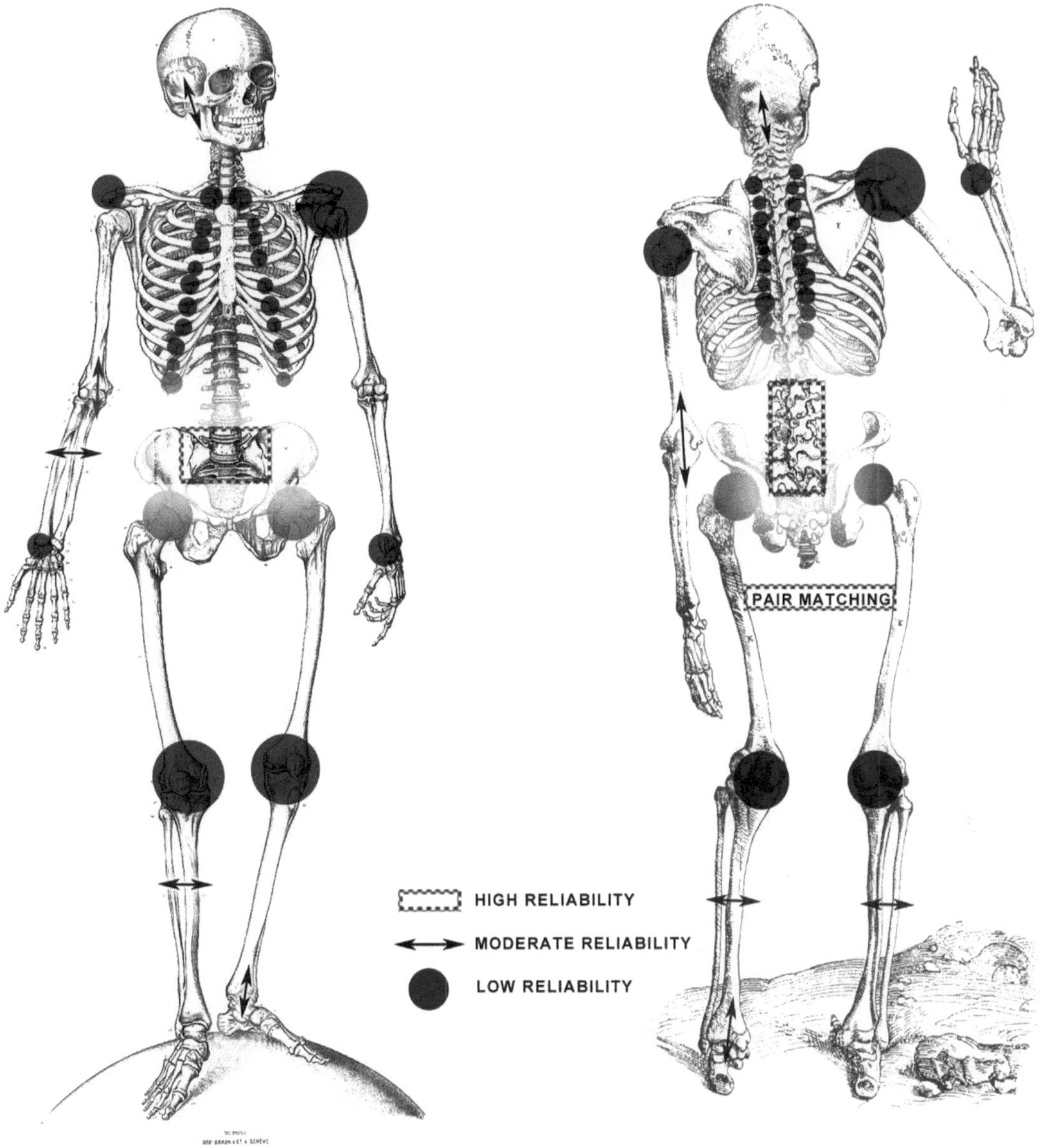

Figure 14-4
Reliability of articulation and pair matching in anthropological reassociation.

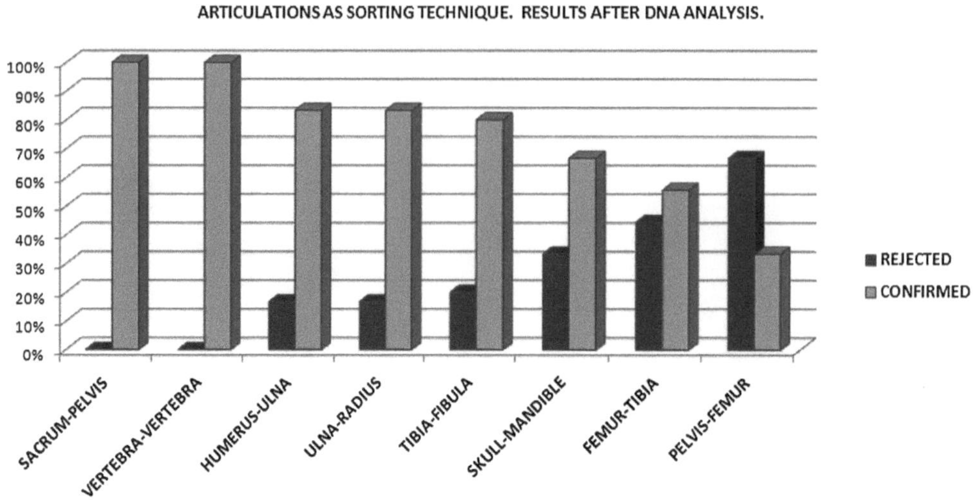

Figure 14-5
Reliability of articulation in anthropological reassociation. Results show confirmation or rejection of preliminary anthropological reassociation after genetic testing.

Two types of comparisons were realized with STR profiles obtained from commingled remains:

- *Direct matching:* Comparison of bone-to-bone profiles to corroborate that two bone elements belonged to the same individual, and regrouping isolated remains as greater bone sections or as partially complete skeletons.
- *Kinship analysis:* Comparison of STR profiles obtained from bone specimens with the STR profiles from reference samples provided by biological relatives.

In the earlier methodology section, we indicated the process of analysis followed to sort skeletal remains integrating anthropology, genetics, and background information. The most complete STR profile in each reassociated group was selected (without using a consensus profile drawn from profiles coming from different bone elements) and uploaded into the genetic software for comparison with the genetic database of reference profiles (kinship analysis). Each genetic match in kinship analysis with a likelihood ratio (LR) higher than 500 was evaluated using all the available anthropological and historical information. This meant a great amount of work that forced us to improve the database system and to create a structure for personnel in charge of reviewing cases. This decision was undertaken mainly due to the fact that few direct biological relatives are currently available, because of the long time that has passed since the disappearance events. These limitations in the availability of reference samples entailed analyzing an increasing number of genetic systems to compensate for the poor family pedigrees.

The result was a significant increase in the possibilities for identifications, which would have been impossible to detect mathematically if only taking into account the genetic analysis. However, cases reporting significantly high LRs were detected that, nevertheless, proved to be

Table 14-6: Adventitious Matches in Kinship Analysis. Argentinean Database (1,000 Bone Profiles; 9,000 Reference Samples).

Bone Sample	Reference Sample	Kinship	LR (Identifiler)	STR Loci Reported in Bone	Exclusion By
410552	901008	Sister	**251,181**	14	New reference samples (mother + two sons)
410718	903404	Daughter	**122,971**	15	Anthropology + case history (fundamental contradictions)
410032	901509	Brother	**49,010**	13	Anthropology + case history (fundamental contradictions)
410357	900680	Brother	**46,975**	15	Anthropology + case history (fundamental contradictions)
410677	901499	Mother	**33,453**	13	Anthropology + case history (fundamental contradictions)
410382	900177	Sister	**32,785**	14	Anthropology + case history (fundamental contradictions)
410161	902865	Brother	**30,000**	13	Mini-STRs non-CODIS

adventitious, or random, matches. The greater the size of the databases to be compared, the higher the probability of adventitious matches. In the case of Argentina, currently we are comparing a database of profiles of approximately 1,000 skeletal remains against 9,000 reference profiles from relatives ($\sim 10^7$ comparisons), together with the aforementioned fact of having few victims' relatives available for genetic comparison. Table 14-6 shows some examples of the highest LR values that became adventitious matches revealed by incorporating additional information such as typing more relatives, additional genetic testing, etc.

Although LR values shown in Table 14-6 may not be remarkable after combination with prior odds values, they stress the need to reconcile all the available information for a given case. When all the available information was considered (such as biological profile, as well as incompatibility between date of disappearance and date of death), it showed that genetic results were random matches. None of the donors listed in the table had other missing relatives or were biologically related to the families with which each of the cases described was finally identified by EAAF. The population of the disappeared in Argentina is primarily urban and with a low rate of inbreeding. It is therefore **random coincidence** (adventitious match), but it is essential to integrate the information and LR combination with *prior odds* to avoid incorrect conclusions (misidentifications).

Conversely, in some cases with a strong identity presumption, there were consistent profiles for the family group that were compared with the remains but yielded a low LR value. However, based on the integration of information, we added supplementary genetic analysis (mtDNA, Y-STR, SNPs, Indels, non-CODIS STR markers) or incorporated more relative donors (in many cases, deceased relatives were exhumed to take a bone sample, with the corresponding authorization of a family member and of the competent authority) to reach an identification.

Lessons Learned and Recommendations

We highlight and summarize here some of the findings, lessons learned, and recommendations that were cited throughout the chapter:

I. Methodology for analysis of commingled remains:
   - We recommend a systematic strategy for implementation and comprehensive analysis of the commingled remains which includes anthropological analysis, genetic analysis, and reconciliation with background information (or "case history"). A multidisciplinary approach means not only the participation of different disciplines in the same case, but also the integration of the results of each of them in the analysis, generating a comprehensive forensic report.
   - We also recommend recording and processing data in specific databases for anthropology and genetics that take into account the complexity of this type of investigation, protecting traceability (LIMS), and optimizing genetic profile comparison (matching). In general, for mass identifications (DVI, human rights violation investigations, etc.), it is necessary to deal with a large amount of antemortem and postmortem data. In addition to this, one must add the recording, control, and monitoring of samples for genetic analysis and the resulting profiles thereby generated. In sum, it is extremely necessary to deal with information in databases that not only allows one to store the information, but also provides traceability and comparison capability. In investigations involving commingled remains, this need is multiplied because the number of records (bone elements and samples for genetic analysis) and their mobility (initial inventory to the subsequent grouping as individuals) is much higher.
   - It is necessary to reinforce controls on traceability (of bone elements, samples, and genetic profiles) and to adapt the protocols and analysis procedures in cases involving commingled remains that consist of numerous elements, which throughout the sorting process will be removed/mobilized from their original group. In this respect, we recommend the selection of a coding system to avoid duplication, which is traceable and adequate in number and type of characters, to avoid transcription errors. We recommend the use of barcodes on genetic samples per bone element.

II. Sampling strategy by phases:
   - Sampling by phases implies a sequential strategy in which the next round of genetic analysis is determined based on the previous batch of results, always combining genetic and anthropological analyses.
   - Sequence: Anthropological analysis – anthropological reassociation – bone sampling – genetic analysis – anthropological reanalysis of remains – genetic resampling (if needed).
   - Genetic comparison strategy based on STR profiles. After one carries out an evaluation of nonrepetition of mtDNA sequences (and at the end of the sorting process), it is recommended to make reassociations by mtDNA for elements with degraded genetic material, but only in cases involving a small number of individuals and a closed context in terms of commingling.
   - Use of direct matching for intraskeletal reassociation, not by kinship analysis.

III. Intraskeletal reassociation:
   1. By anthropology:
      - Be cautious about the reliability offered by the different joints in the anthropological reassociation of commingled remains, even in a good state of preservation, especially in cases with a high homogeneity of the personal characteristics of the individuals represented in the skeletal remains.
      - In cases where bone elements are well preserved and after applying the usual reassociation criteria that define a major skeletal unit (body part), a crossed sampling strategy[4] is recommended.
   2. By genetics:
      - We recommend intraskeletal reassociation preferably through autosomal STR markers. In closed commingling contexts, the use of mtDNA is possible for the reassociation of some elements in which STR profiling failed. The nonrepetition of mtDNA sequences using skeletal elements that have shown a unique STR profile (different STR profiles indicate different individuals) must be evaluated.
      - We recommend reassociations by direct genetic matching and not by kinship analysis.
      - We recommend not generating consensus STR profiles by using different bone elements. After a group of elements is reassociated, the most complete STR profile may be used for kinship analysis.
      - Combine prior odds with LR (likelihood ratio) in the calculation of the *posterior probability* both for identification and for intraskeletal reassociation. If prior odds are not available because the number of missing individuals is not defined, inform results using LR.

---

[4] See "Phase II: Sampling for Genetic Analysis" earlier in this chapter.

- Decide on the posterior probability thresholds considered a reliable value to report an identification.
- Regarding a relatives' reference sample database, the low number of reference samples from direct blood relatives in many of the Argentinean families requires a compensation by increasing the number of genetic markers analyzed. In cases with multiple victims, it is necessary to implement specific strategies for donor searches, such as national collection campaigns, among others.
- In intraskeletal reassociation by genetic analysis, it is recommended to consider the case as an open context of commingling, although available background information may indicate otherwise. If the case is clearly a closed context of commingling, at the end of the reassociation process, consider combining all available information to lead to further reassociation of unassociated elements by *process of elimination.* This can be performed after the possibilities of sorting by anthropological and genetic methods are exhausted, and if there were no contradictions for the case.
- The possibility to assess the sex in isolated bone elements through genetics (Amelogenin) expands the possibilities of methodological validation on commingled remains. This validation is needed in most populations.

IV. When one is reconciling information, we recommend comprehensive consideration of a case, taking into account all available information (background information, anthropological, and genetic analyses). If there are fundamental contradictions (e.g., a genetic exclusion in a case with strong identity hypothesis, or inexplicable inconsistencies of *antemortem* and *postmortem* data in cases with high LR indicating a possible adventitious match), we recommend reviewing the process to discard errors by means of the traceability of the remains and the bone samples, as well as reviewing the results of the different anthropological and genetic analyses.

V. We also recommend use of identification committees to consider a case (identification and intraskeletal reassociation) in cooperation with those in charge of the various disciplines (anthropology, genetics, historical investigation) who took part in it.

VI. Report to authorities in charge and relatives clearly about the results, future possibilities, and the limitations in solving a case. If there are no legally restrictive regulations, allow the relatives involved to express their desire to receive the remains after they are identified or after the reassociation process is finished (which can take a long time and should be reported). Likewise, the disposition of the remains that cannot be associated and will remain mixed should be decided together with families and appropriate officials.

And Now What? Future Challenges

We have extensively considered the methodology of analysis and the need for multidisciplinary and systematic research when dealing with commingled remains, especially when the number of individuals is high. One issue that still has to be solved is how to deal with cases of such magnitude when there is no economic prospect of using genetic analysis, a situation that holds true for many of the countries that are trying to begin the recovery and identification of victims of mass disasters and human rights violations. To date, we can say that, despite the benefits of any technique (anthropological or genetic) the best approach integrates all available information and allows, without fundamental contradictions, a well-founded conclusion.

It is necessary to make progress in the scientific validation and proposal of anthropological methods that facilitate the reassociation of commingled remains, ascertain methodological guidelines, and systematize the reliability or the risk of certain steps. This is possible in investigations that, taking into account all the technical possibilities available, allow for the assessment of results and for measuring the reliability of certain methods.

This chapter is part of that effort.

Acknowledgments

We would like to thank Bradley Adams and John Byrd for their willingness to include us again in the discussion of this complex matter. To our EAAF colleagues (anthropologists and geneticists) for their efforts in recovering and identifying missing persons. And last but not least, to Ivana Wolff and Raymond Pettit for their assistance in the translation and their comments on this report.

References

Adams, B.J., Byrd, J.E., 2006. Resolution of small-scale commingling: a case report from the Vietnam War. Forensic Sci. Int. 156, 63–69.

Butler, J.M., Shen, Y., McCord, B.R., 2003. The development of reduced size STR amplicons as tools for the analysis of degraded DNA. J. Forensic Sci. 48 (5), 1054–1064.

Chung, D.T., Drabek, J., Opel, K.L., Butler, J.M., McCord, B.R., 2004. A study on the effects of degradation and template concentration on the amplification efficiency of the STR miniplex primer sets, J. Forensic Sci. 49, 733–743.

Coble, M.C., Butler, J.M., 2005. Characterization of new MiniSTR loci to aid analysis of degraded DNA. J. Forensic Sci. 50 (1), 43–53.

Doretti, M., Fondebrider, L., 2012. La Iniciativa Latinoamericana para la identificac6n de personas desaparecidas (ILID). Identificac6n científica de restos de personas desaparecidas. In: Penchaszadeh, V.B. (Ed.), Genética y Derechos Humanos. Encuentros y desencuentros. Tramas Sociales, Paidos, Argentina, p. 69.

Egaña, S., Turner, S., Doretti, M., Bernardi, P., Ginarte, A., 2008. Commingled skeletonized remains and human right investigations. Challenges from the field. In: Adams, B., Byrd, J. (Eds.), Recovery, Analysis and Identification of Commingled Human Remains. Humana Press, Totowa, NJ, pp. 57–79.

Romanini, C., Catelli, M.L., Borosky, A., Pereira, R., Romero, M., Salado Puerto, M., Phillips, C., Fondevila, M., Freire, A., Santos, C., Carracedo, A., Lareu, M.V., Gusmao, L., Vullo, C.M., 2012. Typing short amplicon binary polymorphisms: supplementary SNP and InDel genetic information in the analysis of highly degraded skeletal remains. Forensic Sci. Int. 6 (4), 469–476.

CHAPTER 15

Blast and Crash Incidents: Resolving Commingling at the Armed Forces Medical Examiner System

Laura A. Regan[1], Ladd A. Tremaine[2]

[1]*Headquarters United States Air Force Academy/Department of Biology, United States Air Force Academy, Colorado,* [2]*Armed Forces Medical Examiner System, Dover Air Force Base, Delaware*

Overview of the Armed Forces Medical Examiner System

The Armed Forces Medical Examiner System (AFMES) is a tri-service organization that supports the Department of Defense (DoD) and other governmental agencies and serves the American people by providing expertise in forensic pathology, forensic anthropology, DNA sciences, forensic toxicology, mortality surveillance, and forensic psychiatry. Through a DoD directive, the AFMES arose out of the Armed Forces Institute of Pathology's (AFIP's) Department of Forensic Sciences in 1988 (Stone 2011). The Armed Forces Medical Examiner (AFME) derives his or her authority from 10 USC §1471, *Forensic Pathology Investigations* (1999), which governs medicolegal investigations within exclusive federal jurisdiction and establishes specific secondary jurisdiction authority in order to support the interests of the United States. After the closure of the AFIP in 2011, the AFMES relocated to its current location at Dover Air Force Base (AFB), Delaware. In addition, the AFMES has regional medical examiners, operating under the authority of the AFME, stationed throughout the continental United States, and in Europe and Asia.

The AFMES is unique in that it is the only medical examiner function in the federal government and the only medical examiner system with jurisdiction in multiple locales throughout the country and overseas. As such, its purview extends beyond the boundaries of the Department of Defense to include support agreements with the Federal Bureau of Investigation (FBI), Department of State (DoS), National Transportation Safety Board (NTSB), National Aeronautics and Space Administration (NASA), Peace Corps, and other U.S. federal entities.

In addition to determining the cause and manner of death for all current combat fatalities and fatalities occurring within exclusive federal jurisdiction, the AFMES partners with multiple DoD agencies to help mitigate combat injuries and improve the survivability of combat troops. The AFMES provides full personnel accounting of all current combat and training

Commingled Human Remains. http://dx.doi.org/10.1016/B978-0-12-405889-7.00015-0

mishap fatalities, as well as all mass fatality incidents occurring within the jurisdiction of the AFME. Because of its unique position within the federal government, the AFMES has been exposed to a variety of commingling situations where current-day fatalities experience a high degree of fragmentation, primarily arising from air mishaps and explosive forces. The AFMES has developed standard operating procedures in which to separate, examine, analyze, and identify human remains resulting from these complex conditions.

Combat Considerations

Many blast events occur in open populations and can result in the remains of suicide bombers, civilian bystanders, nonhumans, or the traumatic amputations of surviving service members commingled with the remains of our fallen service members. While commingling resolution ideally begins in the field, the AFME is ultimately responsible for resolving commingling issues. Unfortunately, in a combat environment, the AFME and/or their designated representative(s) is/are usually far removed from the recovery process. Recoveries are quickly conducted, often under enemy fire, and usually by the units sustaining the loss themselves. For fragmented remains resulting from explosive events occurring in areas outside military control, specific provenience information is often lost. Aircraft mishaps typically have more complete documentation; however, recoveries occurring in a combat theater are very rapid to minimize exposure of recovery personnel to hostile forces and hopefully avoid secondary casualties. In these instances, the final resolution occurs at the AFMES facility at Dover AFB. With few exceptions, all remains and fragments thereof returned to family members must be scientifically identified via a minimum of one of three modalities: (1) antemortem/postmortem friction ridge (fingerprint/footprint) comparison; (2) antemortem/postmortem dental comparison; and/or (3) antemortem/postmortem or familial/postmortem DNA comparison.

AFMES Autopsy Protocols

The current Port Mortuary at Dover AFB opened in 2003 and was designed, in part, as a high-throughput autopsy facility in response to the events following September 11, 2001. All remains arriving at the Dover Port Mortuary follow the same work flow, whether they are complete remains or fragments thereof. Remains are transported from the combat theater or other locations where the AFMES has jurisdiction in a sealed human remains pouch (HRP), commonly referred to as a body bag. A sealed HRP and associated paperwork are placed in an aluminum transfer case outfitted with a radio frequency identification tag. The transfer case is tracked from point of embarkation to point of debarkation. Ice is placed outside the HRP to keep the remains cool and slow decomposition. Aircraft flying from the combat theater routinely stop over in Europe, where the HRPs are re-iced, and then proceed on to Dover AFB. The HRPs are sealed at the point of embarkation, and the seals remain unbroken until the medical examiner approves their removal.

Each set of remains arrives in its own HRP. Fragmented remains, referred to as dissociated remains, and aggregates of dissociated remains recovered from the same incident will be shipped in their own HRP. Dissociated remains are any remains not connected to the decedent by a tissue bridge. Transport paperwork goes through an initial review by a medicolegal death investigator, and then explosive ordinance disposal personnel run each HRP through a RAPID-SCAN®, similar to an airport luggage scanner, to screen for unexploded ordinance. Once cleared safe, the HRP is taken to the intake area where initial photographs of the exterior of the HRP are taken with the medical examiner number, if appropriate. Photodocumentation also includes the unbroken seal on the HRP and any associated tags attached to the zipper pulls.

The AFMES procedures for assigning accessioning numbers differ from many civilian medical examiner/coroner systems. This is due to the large volume of dissociated remains the AFMES examines. A medical examiner number (e.g., ME 14-XXXX) is the primary case number, and is assigned to a single decedent or torso at intake. The tags on the zipper pulls of the HRP are affixed at the mortuary evacuation points at embarkation and indicate "believed-to be" names of the decedent or whether the HRP contents represent an unknown decedent/torso, dissociated remains, or personal effects. In general, to qualify as a single decedent, the remains must possess the majority of the spinal column. Isolated crania or skulls are considered dissociated remains. This accessioning scheme prevents two medical examiner numbers being assigned to an individual decedent, minimizing confusion, simplifying case management, and eliminating deletion of redundant case numbers. Dissociated remains are accessioned under a separate Dover number (e.g., D14-XXXX) and are linked to a medical examiner number upon scientific identification of the individual dissociated remains. HRP content type can also usually be confirmed prior to breaking the seal on the pouch during the RAPIDSCAN® process, if in question. In cases of total fragmentation of the decedent (discussed later), the medical examiner will determine if a medical examiner number is appropriate after the dissociated remains identifications have been made, and will assign the medical examiner number after the fact to account for the individual and manage the overall case.

After the exterior photographs of the HRP are taken, the HRP is opened and overall photographs are taken of the contents as they are received. Prior to any manipulation of the remains, any evidence of forensic interest is removed by a medical examiner. After all evidentiary material has been safeguarded, the remains are examined to ensure no dissociated remains are located within the HRP. If dissociated remains are found in an HRP with a decedent, they are removed, photographed with documentation of the medical examiner number they were pulled from for provenience tracking, and assigned a separate Dover number or numbers, depending on the amount and condition of the dissociated remains present. Just because dissociated remains are found in an HRP, they cannot be assumed to belong to the decedent in the pouch. In incidents involving multiple, highly fragmented decedents, it is not uncommon for tissue from one individual to be adherent to another individual.

Sentimental personal effects such as rings, watches, and necklaces are photographed *in situ.* Decedents are frequently accompanied by a green personal effects bag that typically contains unit coins and pocket contents. Unit coins typically bear a military unit's patch and other insignia and/or verbiage that represent the mission and personnel of that unit. As a decedent passes through mortuary channels en route to the AFMES, coins are frequently bestowed upon the fallen to honor their sacrifice. All contents of this bag are laid out and photographed with the corresponding medical examiner number. The personal effects are turned over to personnel from the Joint Personal Effects Depot (JPED), who are present at intake, and who thoroughly inventory, clean, and return the effects (if appropriate) to the next of kin. The JPED is run by the U.S. Army and is also located at Dover AFB. All uniforms and personal protective gear, such as body armor, helmet, ballistic glasses, etc., stay on the decedent and are not removed until authorized by a medical examiner.

As stated earlier, any remains not attached via a tissue bridge to the decedent are removed, provenience annotated, and photographs taken. Once clear of all dissociated remains, the single decedent is then formally accessioned into the Mortuary Operations Management System (MOMS). The MOMS prints out bar-coded casework labels and paperwork that accompany the remains as they progress through the autopsy protocol. Remains are scanned to a remains handler's ID badge and then into a specific station as they proceed through identification stations, radiology, and eventually, the autopsy suite.

If applicable, remains pass next to the FBI station for fingerprinting. All service members have fingerprints on file with the Integrated Automated Fingerprint Identification System (IAFIS).The FBI conducts all antemortem/postmortem friction ridge comparisons for the AFMES. All Air Force aircrews have footprints on file; thus, footprints are also taken for Air Force aircraft mishaps.

Forensic odontology is the next station. The AFMES has no odontologists assigned to the unit; thus, primary forensic odontologist support comes from qualified individuals assigned to the Naval Postgraduate Dental School, Walter Reed National Military Medical Center, Bethesda, Maryland, who travel to Dover in a temporary duty status on an as-needed basis. In mass fatality incidents, the forensic odontologists are augmented by staff from the Dover AFB Dental Clinic. The majority of dental records are now digitally retrieved, but in instances where digital retrieval is not possible, the respective military service will arrange for overnight shipment of the dental records to Dover from the service member's home duty station, if the cases are to be autopsied in the Dover facility. Regardless of whether the dental staff has dental records in hand, a postmortem dental examination with digital bitewings will be performed. Odontologists supporting the AFMES prevent additional commingling issues due to secondary dissociation of remains resulting from complete resection of the hard palate by performing an alternate procedure to access the dentition in cases of extreme thermal insult and/or very rare cases of extreme rigor. They expose the jaw through facial dissection, which leaves all teeth associated with the decedent. A perioral facial incision is made, creating a tissue flap that exposes the mandibular ascending ramus and alveolar complex. The bone and associated musculature are then cut through, allowing manipulation of the dentition for radiography and examination. This procedure is performed only on remains that would not be

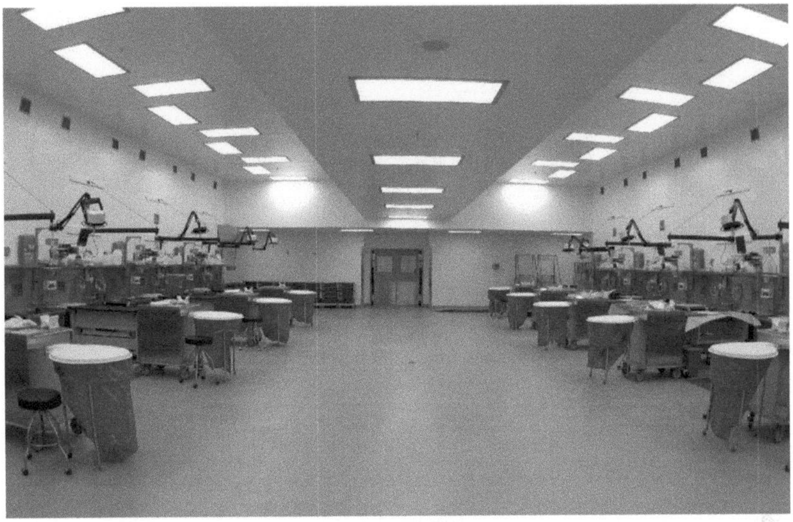

Figure 15-1
The Armed Forces Medical Examiner System autopsy suite.

considered viewable. Standard anterior and lateral head photographs are supervised by the medical examiner at intake, prior to any incisions being made.

After the dental exam, remains pass through to radiology, where they are imaged using both digital X-ray and computerized tomography (CT). Personal protective gear and uniform items remain on the decedent during this process. Radiographs are reviewed by forensic radiologists and are streamed to each bay in the autopsy suite. Forensic radiologists interact with the medical examiners at the tableside during the autopsy itself, assisting in locating and documenting pathology, trauma, and material of an evidentiary nature. In mass fatality incidents, the forensic radiologist will also review any associated medical records to assist in identification when unique implanted medical hardware is present.

This protocol is flexible enough that if bottlenecks develop at a specific station, the medical examiner can redirect remains to other stations to speed the process along. Remains then enter the autopsy suite (Figure 15-1) or, in the case of mass fatality events, will stay in a gurney hold area with an escort until space opens up in the autopsy suite. The autopsy suite contains ten bays, but additional space can be procured from adjacent mortuary areas for autopsy purposes, should the need arise.

AFMES Dissociated Remains Protocols

HRPs containing only dissociated remains follow the same protocol up through the photographs of the contents as they are received (Figure 15-2). At this point, a medical examiner or forensic anthropologist will remove all dissociated remains from the HRP for initial triage.

Figure 15-2
Overall photograph of dissociated remains.

Provenience information is often very limited, and most dissociated remains come in without a presumptive identification. Initial dissociated remains allocation is based on the potential for identification of the fragment. Dissociated remains containing dental or friction ridge material are segregated out and individually accessioned as well as all other remains meeting the AFMES standard operating procedure. Additional ancillary photographs are taken throughout this process. The dissociated remains are then assigned a unique Dover number and associated bar-code identifier through the MOMS. The MOMS generates casework labels and paperwork that accompany each individually accessioned dissociated remains through the autopsy protocol. Dissociated remains are again photographed with their accession numbers prior to being secured for storage. A gurney sheet containing bar-coded stickers for all dissociated remains on a respective gurney accompanies the gurney throughout the remainder of the autopsy protocol until dissociated remains are placed into secured refrigerated storage or turned over to Air Force Mortuary personnel for final disposition. All dissociated remains are scanned to a gurney handler's ID badge and then into a specific station. Each party involved in the process is responsible for ensuring all dissociated remains on a specific gurney are accounted for at each step. Anyone, at any time, has the authority to stop the line if he or she suspects there is an issue with the location of any remains. The line will cease operations until the situation has been rectified to the satisfaction of the medical examiner in charge. Dissociated remains containing friction ridge material are scanned into the FBI station for printing. Footprints are also taken for all dissociated foot elements from Air Force aircraft mishaps and have frequently been the primary scientific identification for these types of incidents. Dissociated remains containing dental material are scanned into the Forensic Odontology station for examination. Each individually accessioned dissociated remains is x-rayed, and all images are streamed to all workstations within the autopsy suite.

A medical examiner or forensic anthropologist will conduct the examination upon transfer of the dissociated remains to autopsy. All uniquely numbered dissociated remains are removed from their pouches and photographed with the accession number and a reference ruler. "Front and back" photos are taken. If the dissociated remains are clothed, "front and back" photos with the clothing on are taken, followed by "front and back" photos of the unclothed dissociated remains. Personal effects associated with the dissociated remains are given the same accession number, photographed, and stay with the dissociated remains. Radiographs are reviewed prior to examination. An "Autopsy/Specimen Description Sheet" is completed for each uniquely numbered dissociated remains. Information annotated on the sheet includes but is not limited to weight, dimensions, brief description, detailed remains summary, identification modality, and DNA analysis status. This same form is used for basic documentation of the decedent at autopsy. Ballistic and other evidence is collected as appropriate. Upon examination, the medical examiner or forensic anthropologist will determine whether the specimen is suitable for DNA testing based on condition of the tissue, scientific identification via another modality, and other criteria specified in the standard operating procedure. Cases involving a high degree of fragmentation are highly dependent on DNA for commingling resolution; thus, the AMFES medical examiner/forensic anthropologist is an expert at determining tissue samples that have the highest likelihood of producing a genetic profile. Turnaround times for the Armed Forces DNA Identification Laboratory (AFDIL) are as little as eight hours for a primary autosomal DNA identification based on a soft tissue sample. Routine dissociated remains DNA cases are usually completed in less than 30 days. In 2007, at the height of the wars in Iraq and Afghanistan, the Nuclear DNA Section of AFDIL processed 3,388 specimens and 1,327 DNA reference cards in support of AFMES casework.

In some circumstances, dissociated remains can be linked to one another or to a decedent via fracture matching, where two bony elements are fit together like the pieces of a puzzle. This identification technique becomes difficult to employ, however, when the number of decedents and number of dissociated remains are large. One aspect to keep in mind when examining large numbers of dissociated remains is that the process must be efficient and accurate. If DNA testing is available and a viable option, taking the time to create something such as a biological profile is not necessary and will only bog down the line (see also the Scientific Working Group on Disaster Victim Identification Forensic Anthropology subcommittee document, www.swgdvi.org).

Forensic anthropologists are well suited to examining dissociated remains because of their extensive knowledge of hard tissue morphology. This is of great benefit in determining what area of the decedent the dissociated remains originate from and in fracture matching two fragments of bone. Utilizing forensic anthropologists to assist the medical examiner in the examination of dissociated remains is a force multiplier during catastrophic events. Forensic anthropologists also take the lead on commingled skeletal cases. Protocols such as those espoused by the Scientific Working Group for Forensic Anthropology (www.swganth.org) are employed.

Total Fragmentation of the Decedent

One scenario that is frequently associated with cases from blast and/or crash trauma is that of total fragmentation of the decedent. In these situations, the accelerative forces are so extreme that a "body" no longer exists. This can occur when pressures greater than 300 psi (Armed Forces Institute of Pathology) are encountered or gravitational forces (G-forces) in excess of 350 times gravity (note: this G-force is a laboratory derived value; Society of USAF Flight Surgeons 2006; and The Naval Safety Center 2001). In cases of suspected total fragmentation of the decedent, the dissociated remains are examined and medical examiner numbers are assigned only after identifications of the dissociated remains have been made and the medical examiner is confident the individual is dead. The medical examiner bases this decision on identifiable tissue that can be linked to a fatal injury. Whereas a fingertip identified to the missing service member will prove representation of the individual, it will not necessarily indicate that the individual has died, because digit amputations are easily survivable.

Sometimes, the cases of total fragmentation are fairly straightforward. An example is a single-occupant fighter aircraft crash that occurred during training. Nine hundred thirty individual human dissociated remains were recovered from an approximately one square mile mishap scene. An additional 150 items of highly fragmented and damaged flight safety gear and personal items were recovered. All dissociated remains were carefully examined to ensure nonbiological material and nonhuman remains were not present in the assemblage and to rule out any potential ground losses. All remains were similar in taphonomy and morphology. Two dissociated remains were identified via antemortem/postmortem friction ridge (fingerprint) comparison. One dissociated remains was identified via antemortem/postmortem dental comparison, and four dissociated remains were sampled and identified to the manifested pilot via antemortem/postmortem autosomal DNA comparison. Based on the closed nature of the incident and no evidence contrary to a minimum number of individuals of one associated with this incident, all of the additional dissociated remains were presumptively identified to the pilot of the mishap aircraft and released to the next of kin.

A more complex incident would be one in which a dismounted (foot) patrol of several soldiers is subjected to an improvised explosive device (IED) blast. Stepping on the pressure plate of a buried IED can result in total fragmentation of the decedent due to the enormous forces generated from the primary blast wave. Additional fatalities and traumatic amputation casualties may also arise when the other individuals are located within the blast radius. The U.S. military takes its vow to return all service members home very seriously. If a service member cannot be accounted for after a blast, teams will put their lives on the line to search for the missing service member, even if they are believed to have died in the blast event. Often, when terrorist groups learn a service member is unaccounted for, they will falsely claim to have that individual in captivity. In these incidents, time is critical to ensure the missing service member is, in fact, not still alive and to prevent any others performing search and rescue/recovery operations from being injured or killed themselves. Normal operational timelines are accelerated and sampling protocols are adjusted in an attempt to find representation of the missing service member. In one case, only four dissociated remains of soft tissue with an aggregate weight of 121 grams (4.26 oz) were recovered and identified to a specific service member after his element was struck by an IED. The dissociated remains included a fragmented finger identified via antemortem/postmortem friction ridge (fingerprint) comparison and a fragment of intestine and two fragments of epidermis identified via antemortem/postmortem DNA comparison. Although the majority of the decedent was not recovered, the medical examiner determined the examined remains represented material that was not compatible with post-blast survival. The available investigative information and postmortem examination results were consistent with death due to blast injuries. The manner of death was ruled a homicide.

Subsequent Recovery of Remains and Final Disposition

Another way the AFMES differs from most civilian jurisdictions is at autopsy: the AFMES medical examiner makes the determination whether remains are intact or nonintact. If they are nonintact, there is the possibility that subsequent remains could be recovered and identified. After the remains have been scientifically identified and the autopsy has concluded, the medical examiner will notify the respective military service casualty office of the identification and condition of the remains. This will initiate a process whereby the family determines the course of action concerning the disposition of remains. If the remains are nonintact, the family also lets the military know what their preferences are in regard to notification of subsequently identified remains. Families choose whether they want to be told of any future identified subsequent remains. If they opt for notification, they will then make a separate disposition decision should any further remains be identified to their loved one. This is important because remains recovery in a combat zone can be separated in temporal space. Dissociated remains have been scientifically identified after being recovered over a year after the decedent died. Additionally, the AFMES strives to be as transparent with the families as possible. That is why family members legally entitled to the information can request copies of both the autopsy report and all autopsy photographs at no charge.

The AFMES is fortunate in that nearly all personnel serving in the military have a blood DNA reference card on file. As of November 2013, the Armed Forces Repository of Specimen Samples for the Identification of Remains (AFRSSIR) at Dover AFB housed over 6.7 million DNA blood reference cards of current and former service members, Coast Guard personnel, select DoD civilians, and others. DNA reference collection for identification of remains of service members began in 1992, and blood reference cards are stored for 50 years. Long-term retention of the cards makes AFRSSIR an important potential source of DNA references for outside jurisdictions, if they have the demographic information of a presumed decedent. In such an instance, the local jurisdiction would provide a copy of the unknown decedent postmortem profile to AFDIL to compare against the known profile. There is no all-encompassing genetic database of service member profiles. Only when a DNA profile is needed to assist in the identification of a decedent, or developing a profile is in the best interest of the service member, will it be run. An example of the latter is the case of a service member who is abducted by hostile forces in a combat zone. Inclusion of this profile in the decedent database will allow the AFMES to compare the missing service member's profile to those of all unknown remains examined by the AFMES. The DNA reference cards cannot be used for law enforcement purposes without a federal court order that meets certain stipulations, which has occurred only three times in the history of the AFRSSIR.

Disposition of remains is not the purview of the AFMES. If decedents are entitled to military mortuary rights and the autopsies are performed at the Dover AFB Port Mortuary, the AFMES will release the remains to the Air Force Mortuary Affairs Operations (AFMAO) located at Dover AFB, adjacent to the AFMES. AFMAO then works with the service casualty offices who liaise with the families to effect disposition, per the next of kin's wishes. For decedents not entitled to military mortuary rights, such as government contractors or personnel not affiliated with the DoD, the AFMES works directly with the contract company, investigating agency, and/or families and releases the remains to a local funeral home for final disposition.

It should be noted that not all military decedents will be transported to Dover AFB for autopsy. If a service member or someone else dies under the jurisdiction of the AFME, the AFME will determine where the autopsy is conducted. In many cases, autopsies can be conducted locally by AFMES staff or regional AFMES medical examiners if the military installation has an autopsy facility that will accommodate the number of decedents and condition of remains. In a case of a mass shooting on exclusively federal land, if the local supporting autopsy facility did not have the capacity to handle numerous fatalities, the decedents would be airlifted to a facility capable of managing the volume. The AFMES facility is ideal for this, because it was designed for high throughput and is located at a major Air Mobility Command transportation hub. In contrast, a flight training incident involving two helicopters and resulting in seven fatalities occurring near a major military medical treatment facility with a fully operational autopsy suite resulted in all fatalities and dissociated remains being transported to the local facility. The seven decedents were given medical examiner numbers issued through the AFMES at Dover AFB. The dissociated remains were given separate unique identifiers ascribed by the regional medical examiner. One hundred twenty-nine of 161 dissociated remains were identified to the seven decedents, primarily through DNA analyses. Only five dissociated remains were identified through antemortem/postmortem dental comparison. The degree of fragmentation ranged from one fragment for two decedents to 65 fragments for another decedent. Disposition of remains was effected from that location.

Examples of Commingling Resolution at the AFMES

The AFMES has responded to complex mishaps that included, in varying combinations depending on the scenario, multiple U.S. service members, DoD civilians, U.S. and foreign contractors, foreign military service members, local national civilians, and/or suicide bombers. Additionally, nonhuman remains are frequently recovered due to nonhuman skeletal elements being located in simple proximity to a fatal incident, animal involvement in an event itself (e.g., a donkey-based IED), or as a combat fatality (such as a military working dog). Often in air mishaps and blast incidents, significant post-crash fire and traumatic forces result in a high degree of fragmentation of remains, making scientific identification of non-American personnel and recognition of nonhuman remains virtually impossible in the field. All remains therefore are transported to the AFMES for scientific identification and examination. At triage, all grossly identifiable, nonhuman remains are segregated out and accessioned into the MOMS to maintain accountability of all tissue received by the AFMES.

In standard AFMES operations, the performance of an autopsy is not predicated upon first establishing a scientific identification of a decedent. The AFMES can and has waited for scientific identification prior to starting the autopsy in fatal, multinational incidents in response to requests by foreign governments to honor their cultural or religious practices or for diplomatic reasons. If decedents cannot be immediately identified through antemortem/postmortem friction ridge (fingerprint) or dental comparisons, then DNA sampling is conducted prior to autopsy. In these situations, decedents do not enter the autopsy suite until scientific identification or exclusion has occurred. When the decedent cannot be scientifically identified, the medical examiner must be confident, based on all investigative evidence, that all possible American fatalities have been excluded prior to examination and/or release for final disposition. When foreign government requests are contrary to the performance of an autopsy and the AFME concurs, then radiological and external examinations only are conducted by the medical examiner in the presence of an appropriate religious official after an identification or exclusion has been affected.

In one mass fatality event involving nearly 40 individuals, 84 human dissociated remains were accessioned into MOMS. Of these, 46 were eventually scientifically identified through a variety of modalities. Of the 37 dissociated remains sampled for DNA, only one did not yield a DNA profile. Thirty-eight dissociated remains were not identified, the majority of them being severely burned, and the bulk of the material being tooth fragments. See Table 15-1 for further details.

In another example, an armored bus carrying U.S. personnel and third-country national contractors was struck by a suicide bomber, vehicle-based IED. A post-blast fire ensued,

Table 15-1: Dissociated Remains Identification Modalities for Sample Incident

Fingerprint	0
Dental	10
DNA	34
Dental & DNA	1
Radiological & DNA	1
Unidentified dissociated remains	38
Nonhuman remains	4
Total	84 human/4 nonhuman

burning the rider manifest and making identification of the third-country nationals in the field impossible. All remains were therefore transported to Dover AFB for identification and autopsy. This investigation was further complicated by the multinational nature of the decedents. The FBI and Department of State worked with the foreign governments for identification media and in assisting with repatriation. In total, 13 victims died as a result of the blast. Twelve of the 13 were scientifically identified, including five U.S. service members, two DoD civilians, three U.S. contractors, and two foreign nationals. In addition, the remains of a 13- to 14-year-old male were recovered and were thought to be those of a local national who was alongside and exterior to the bus, prior to the explosion.

Throughout the conflict in Iraq, numerous convoys were targeted. In one such instance, a U.S. military convoy came under attack by rocket-propelled grenades and small arms fire. When the battle had concluded, a U.S. service member was missing and later confirmed abducted by hostile forces. Years later, after an extensive search and interviews with numerous informants, remains and U.S. military uniform remnants believed to belong to the service member were recovered by U.S. personnel and transported to the Dover Port Mortuary. The remains received consisted of 11 skeletal elements, all of which were incomplete and sun bleached, resulting in extensive periosteal and cortical delamination. The following elements were represented: mandible, fifth lumbar vertebra, right rib, right scapula, right and left humeri, right radius, right ulna, right tibia, left fibula, and a nonhuman femur. All human bone fragments were grossly morphologically consistent and appeared male, based on overall robusticity. While the only dentition remaining within the mandible were portions of the left first and second molar roots, a forensic odontologist was able to scientifically identify the mandible fragment with the missing service member, based on matching antemortem and postmortem morphological features including the root structure of the tooth remnants still present and a concordant radio-opacity in the mandibular body. The examining forensic anthropologists initially cut small windows of bone from three representative bones from the assemblage—the mandible, tibia, and right humerus—and submitted them for autosomal short tandem repeat (STR) DNA testing. Partial STR profiles were obtained only for the mandible and tibia, due to the extensive taphonomic degradation of the bones. No STR results were obtained from the right humerus. Only the DNA profile from the mandible was consistent with the missing service member's DNA profile. The original three bone fragments were resampled, and the remaining seven human bone fragments were subsequently sampled and submitted to AFDIL for mitochondrial DNA analysis. Mitochondrial DNA profiles were generated representing three different people. Six incomplete elements weighing 308 grams—the mandible, fifth lumbar vertebrae, right rib, right radius, right ulna, and left fibula—yielded a DNA sequence matching the blood reference card for the missing service member. The left humerus provided a second unique mitochondrial DNA profile. The other three elements—the right scapula, right humerus, and right tibia—yielded a third mitochondrial profile. Neither of these additional profiles was consistent with any missing U.S. personnel. The rigorous autopsy protocols employed by the AFMES detected additional commingling not grossly evident at examination, leading to the successful scientific identification of our missing service member and segregation of the unassociated skeletal remains of two further individuals.

The AFMES also deals with unconventional forms of commingling not often encountered in other medical examiner/coroner jurisdictions. In rare instances, the blast forces generated by an IED will cause fragmented remains from one individual to become embedded in another decedent. In one instance, an element was conducting a dismounted patrol in Afghanistan when an IED detonated, killing two soldiers and injuring several more. During the autopsy protocol, upon review of the radiographic imagery, the forensic radiologist noticed what appeared to be an anomalous bone fragment located in the left thigh of one of the decedents. The bone fragment was removed and identified by the forensic anthropologist as the head of a left talus. The decedent had both of his feet. The talar head was sampled for DNA, and the fragment matched the other soldier killed in the IED blast. This example demonstrates the importance of a full radiological survey and review when conducting medicolegal investigations of blast and aircraft mishap incidents.

Summary and Conclusions

In summary, the AFMES has had much experience with current-day events resulting in commingling of remains, especially explosions and aircraft mishaps. Their exposure through bombing cases such as the Khobar Towers, the U.S. embassies in Tanzania and Kenya, the USS Cole, the UN Canal Hotel attack in Iraq, and the response to the 9/11 Pentagon attack, the wars in Iraq and Afghanistan, and countless aircraft mishaps have provided a unique exposure and led to a distinctively AFMES approach to resolving commingling issues.

The opinions and assertions contained herein are solely those of the authors and are not to be construed as official or as views of the U.S. Department of Defense, its branches, the U.S. Army Medical Research and Material Command, the Armed Forces Medical Examiner System, or the U.S. Government.

References

Armed Forces Institute of Pathology, Blast Trauma. Unpublished.

The Naval Safety Center, Aeromedical Division, 2001. The Naval Flight Surgeon's Pocket Reference to Aircraft Mishap Investigation, fifth ed. Naval Safety Center, Norfolk, VA.

The Scientific Working Group for Forensic Anthropology. www.swganth.org.

Scientific Working Group on Disaster Victim Identification, In Press. Forensic Anthropology in Disaster Victim Identification Best Practices and Guidelines. www.swgdvi.org.

The Society of United States Air Force Flight Surgeons, 2006. Aircraft Mishap Investigation Handbook. Society of USAF Flight Surgeons, Brooks Air Force Base.

Stone, P., 2011. Legacy of Excellence: The Armed Forces Institute of Pathology, 1862–2011. Borden Institute, Fort Detrick, MD.

Title 10 USC §1471, Forensic Pathology Investigations, 1999.

CHAPTER 16

Forensic Investigation of Suicidal Bombings in Israel: Balancing Religious Considerations with Medicolegal Responsibilities

Tzipi Kahana

Disaster Victim Identification Unit, Division of Identification and Forensic Sciences, Israel Police

Introduction

Religion and cultural traditions play an important role in the practice of forensic medicine in most countries, regardless of whether there is separation between state and religion. The beliefs of the community as a whole, and of the relatives of the deceased in particular, influence all aspects of the medicolegal investigation of death, from the collection of the remains at the scene, to the investigation in the autopsy room, to their final disposition; in all instances, the victims' and survivors' religious and cultural concerns impact the process (Greenberger et al. 2012).

The controversy surrounding ethical and legal issues in the practice of forensic medicine in Israel is a good example of the effect of faith and of popular beliefs on the national approach to the investigation of death. Throughout the short history of the State of Israel, the religious makeup of the country has influenced crucial legal decisions regarding the management of victims of mass disaster, sudden unexpected death, and death under suspicious circumstances.

The treatment of commingled remains, being part of medicolegal investigations, is dictated by the laws and regulations of the community in which they are dealt with. The effect of religion and culture on forensic medicine in Israel is presented here.

Religious Beliefs Concerning Postmortem Examinations in Israel

Israel was established as a homeland for the Jewish people in 1948, based on the United Nations General Assembly Resolution 181, approved on November 29, 1947, which called for the partition of the British-ruled Palestine Mandate into a Jewish and an Arab state. The

Commingled Human Remains. http://dx.doi.org/10.1016/B978-0-12-405889-7.00016-2

declaration of Independence secured freedom of religion, taking into consideration that some of the holiest sites of the three main monotheistic religions are located in Israeli territory (The Holy Sepulcher, the Dome of the Rock, and the Wailing Wall). While the Basic Laws of Israel that serve in place of a constitution define the country as a "Jewish state," the Basic Laws and Common Law current in Israel protect free practice of religion following the pattern and practice of the Ottoman and British administrations in which members of the recognized and unrecognized religions are free to practice their religion.

In 2013, Israel's population was estimated as 8,002,300 individuals, of whom 75.7% are Jews and 20.6% are Arab citizens. Sunnite Muslims constitute 16% of the Arab population, about 2.5% of the population are Christian (mostly members of the Greek-Orthodox Church), and some 115,000 (1.5%) are Druze. Other religious groups, including Bahá'í, Buddhists, Hindus, and Samaritans, constitute the remaining 3.7% of the population. Over the last decade, about 200,000 workers, mostly illegal, from Romania, Thailand, China, Africa, and South America have settled in Israel (Israel in Figures, Central Bureau of Statistics 2013).

The modern-day laws and regulations regarding forensic investigation of fatalities, including the performance of autopsies, take into consideration the collective Jewish and Muslim beliefs, which object to any bodily intrusion.

Jewish laws and regulations stem from the Old Testament and from a collection of rabbinic teachings, the Talmud, known as "oral law." These central texts dictate current Jewish law, known as *halacha*.

The halacha is opposed to almost all forms of postmortem examinations because the dead body should be treated with respect. The Talmud (*Bava Basra* 154a) deals with the prohibition of dishonoring or defacing the human body. Maimonides, a medieval Jewish sage (1135–1204 A.D.), describes immediate burial as a sacred obligation incumbent upon all of Israel, at all times and in all places. Thus, an autopsy, which takes time and delays the preparation of the body for burial and desecrates the cadaver, is forbidden. In some cases, autopsies that would save the life of a currently ill person (i.e., help to diagnose an illness) are permitted (Rosner 1971).

Interpretations of the Talmudic laws by Rashi (1040–1105 A.D.) suggest that as long as no disrespect to the body is shown, delay of burial is permitted—for instance, to identify the remains, to elevate the dignity of the deceased, or to honor that person. Fulfilling the individual's expressed or assumed wishes regarding the disposition of his or her own remains should be honored and is therefore considered an acceptable reason for an autopsy when the procedure can help save a life (organ donation, research, or teaching) (Eisenberg 2007).

Similarly, in Islam, autopsies are considered abhorrent because their performance delays burial, causes harm to the body, and removes body parts. The Sharia, the book of Islamic law, states that the deceased should be buried as soon as possible, usually within 24 hours, and the burial should be as close to the site of death as possible.

Egyptian Rashid Rida's *fatwa* of 1910, titled "Postmortem Examinations and the Postponement of Burial," determined that there are reasons to postpone burial, and this has led to an expansion of his ideas to include medical examination for various reasons. The benefits cited include, among many others, that autopsies can lead to scientific advances or important medical diagnoses and enhance education. The Fatwa Committee at al-Azhar of 1982 also based their allowances on *maslaha*: autopsies should be permitted if medical students will learn from them, if justice prevails, and if contagious diseases are controlled. Still, the examination should take place only when necessary and include only relevant body cavities (Rispler-Chaim 1993).

It is generally agreed that an autopsy on an unidentified person following a severe accident is warranted and does not violate Islamic law. Additionally, when the law of the country in which the individual died requires that an autopsy be performed, this is permitted (Sheikh 1998).

Christian and Protestant societies in Israel have no religious or cultural opposition to postmortem examinations within the medicolegal or the civilian realms, because the performance of autopsy is considered useful for medical education, organ transplantation, and determination of diagnoses. It is considered an act of charity to perform an autopsy in order to help others (Pellegrino 2003).

The Druze tradition concerning death is deeply rooted in the belief that the soul does not cease to exist when a person dies but is reincarnated; in this context, defilement of a dead body is considered a negligible matter, and in many Druze villages, bodies are disposed of in mass graves. Nevertheless, the Druze look upon a delay in burial as disrespectful toward the deceased and prefer to avoid the practice of autopsies (Dana 2003).

As a rule, in Israel an autopsy can be performed if it is required by law, if the cause of death cannot be established otherwise, or if the results will be instrumental in saving a life.

History of Forensic Medicine in Israel

The decade of the 1940s, during the British Mandate over Palestine, saw the beginning of modern forensic medicine. Experienced local pathologists were engaged by British officials to perform autopsies, albeit there were the inherent conflicts of interest between various fractions of the population and the occupying authorities (Karplus 1969). After the establishment of the State of Israel, criminal law continued to be based on the legacy of British jurisprudence and incorporated some Ottoman rulings with Jewish and Muslim principles. Despite the fact that the Chief Rabbinate gave consent to conduct autopsies in select circumstances, the orthodox Jewish community continued to fiercely oppose the practice (Boglioli and Taff 1990).

The National Centre of Forensic Medicine in Tel Aviv is the main medicolegal facility in Israel. The Centre falls under the jurisdiction of the Ministry of Health and provides services to the Israel Police, medical centers, the military, and the private sector. Some 2,500 postmortem examinations, including autopsies, necro-identification, and external examinations are carried out annually. A second, smaller military facility was created following the Second Lebanon War in 2006, to expedite identification and burial preparation of military personnel.

The Anatomy and Pathology Act of 1953 provided the first legal framework for autopsy in the State of Israel. According to this legislation, an autopsy can be authorized by three physicians to establish the cause of death or for harvesting organs necessary for life-saving procedures. The 1981 Amendment to the Anatomy and Pathology Act, induced by orthodox lobbyists, requires the consent of next of kin for the performance of an autopsy, in addition to medical authorization.

Investigation of all violent, sudden, and unexpected deaths, as well as death in suspicious circumstances and due to alleged medical negligence, falls into the realm of the Israel Police. Autopsies in forensic cases may be ordered either by the police or by the court (Hiss et al. 1997).

When a criminal investigation or an issue of identification requires it, the court can order an exhumation, provided that the next of kin consent (Goodman et al. 2011).

Suicidal Bombing

The forensic investigation of suicidal bombing is conducted by the Israel Police in close collaboration with the National Centre of Forensic Medicine.

The first uprising (Intifada) of the Palestinian population against the Israeli occupation of Gaza and Judea and Samaria took place between the years 1987 and 1993 and ended with the signing of the Oslo Accords, providing for the creation of a Palestinian self-government authority—the Palestinian National Authority—and for the withdrawal of the Israel Defense Forces (IDF) from parts of the Gaza Strip and West Bank.

This uprising was characterized by a series of violent incidents including a few suicidal bombings. This type of attack was more common between the years 1994 and 1998, when 22 suicidal bombings took the lives of 141 victims and 23 perpetrators (Figure 16-1) (Kahana and Hiss 1998). The second wave of suicidal bombings, known as the "Al-Aqsa Intifada," took place between the years 2000 and 2006, in which 87 suicidal bombings resulted in the death of 581 victims and 91 perpetrators (Figure 16-2) (Hiss et al. 2002).

The medicolegal investigation of suicidal bombings has three main objectives: (1) ascertaining the identity of the victims and perpetrators, (2) clarifying the cause of their death, and (3) reconstructing the event. These tasks are carried out by diverse groups of forensic experts from various agencies and based on protocols devised to minimize the time in which

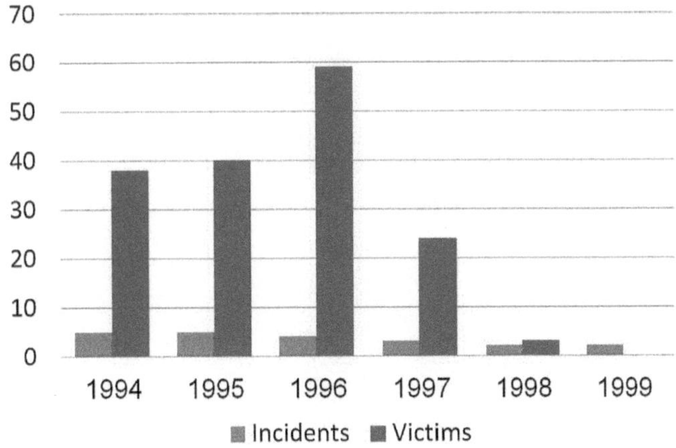

Figure 16-1
First wave of suicide bombing attacks in Israel; 164 victims and perpetrators perished in 22 attacks.

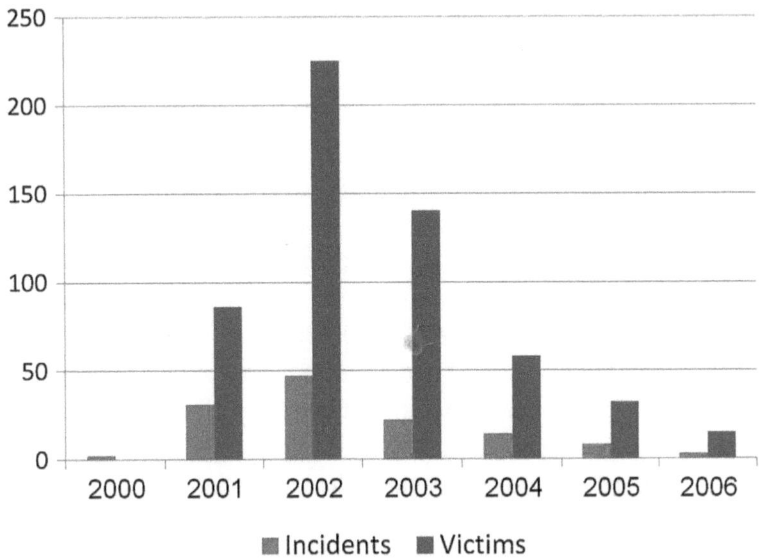

Figure 16-2
Second wave of suicidal bombing attacks in Israel; 672 victims and perpetrators died in 87 attacks.

the public can return to normal life, thus preserving the high resilience of the population without compromising standard forensic requirements.

The forensic investigation commences at the scene, following the clearing orders of bomb squad examiners who collect all relevant data on the explosive device and the medical emergency teams who have evacuated the wounded. The Scene of Crime Officers (SOCOS) collect and preserve evidence, photodocumenting the exact position of all bodies and body

Figure 16-3
Photodocumentation of fragmentary remains at the scene of a bombing in Burgas, Bulgaria, 2012.

parts and their spatial relation to personal effects scattered in the area (Figure 16-3). This is a pivotal clue for the ensuing identification of the cadavers and the reconstruction of the explosion. The remains are sequentially numbered, labeled, collected into body bags, and gathered in one central location in the vicinity of the explosion. From there, they are transported to the National Centre of Forensic Medicine for further examination. Since certain religions have legal requirements that are of concern to clergy in times of disaster, like the Jewish formalized requirements to collect and bury all parts of the dead, including blood, collection of all body fragments and blood-soaked objects is performed by orthodox Jewish volunteers, recruited and trained by the police since 1995 (Hiss et al. 2003). To ensure full cooperation between this civilian organization and the police, these volunteers undergo strict security scrutiny and are required to participate in all training exercises (Figure 16-4) (Karo 1565).

While the scene is being processed, a family information center (FIC) is activated in the vicinity of the forensic facility. The FIC not only serves as an assistance facility for relatives looking for victims of the bombing, but also to collect antemortem data. This center is staffed by police investigators, social workers, religious representatives of the affected community, and psychologists. The main objectives are to obtain information conducive to facilitating identification of the victims, collected in standard INTERPOL forms (DVI Reference Manual 2012), while at the same time providing psychological and religious assistance. DNA samples from relevant next of kin are taken and transferred to the DNA laboratory of the Israel Police to obtain profiles. Police

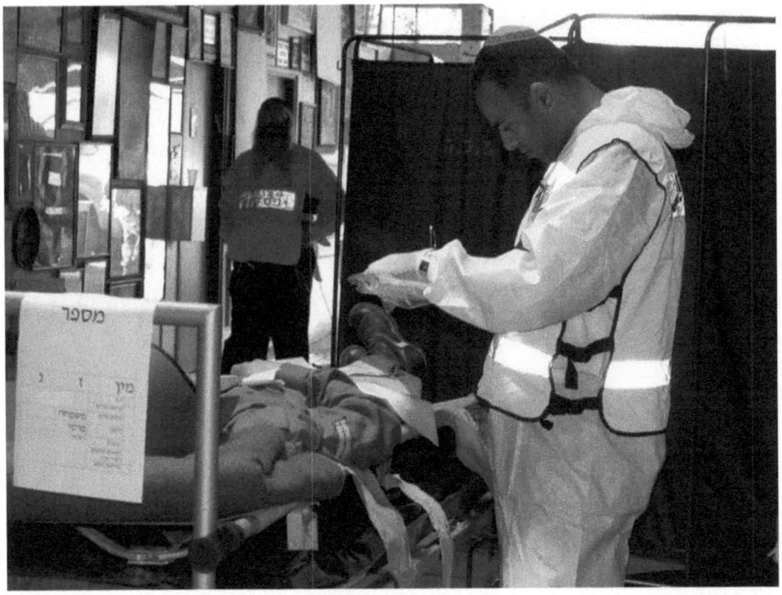

Figure 16-4

Orthodox volunteers and staff of the Israel Police participate in national DVI exercises alongside IDF personnel.

officers gather antemortem data of the potential victims from various repositories, e.g., the Automatic Fingerprint Identification System (AFIS) of the police, the military repository of fingerprints, dental and DNA data, medical centers, and insurance companies.

The aim of the thanatological examination is twofold: description of the cadavers to gather individualizing characteristics leading to positive identification, and evaluation of the injuries sustained.

Forensic pathologists conduct external examinations of the bodies and fill in postmortem forms that contain all relevant information to be contrasted with the antemortem data gathered at the FIC. Whole body photographs and detailed photographs of the significant characteristics are taken alongside radiographs and, in recent years, CT images as well. When possible, police disaster victim identification (DVI) experts take fingerprints from the cadavers. This is accomplished through a digital system that allows immediate transmission to the AFIS. Volunteer odontologists, recruited by the DVI Police Unit, conduct visual and radiographic examination of the oral structures, and teeth are extracted to create DNA profiles for identification (Hiss and Kahana 2000b).

After the complete bodies have been processed, the forensic teams then address the numerous body fragments typically encountered in bombings. The forensic pathologists classify all parts, describe and photograph them, and take tissue samples for DNA analysis. Anatomical reconstruction of the fragmented bodies is often achieved by physical matching of pieces, later confirmed by DNA analysis conducted at the Biology Laboratory of the National Centre of Forensic Medicine.

DNA technology is instrumental in the reassociation of body fragments required for the determination of the minimum number of individuals who died in the attack. The number of perpetrators of a specific attack is one of the most important criminal investigation issues (Hiss et al. 2003). Since this is a lengthy process that can cause the postponement of burial, the standard operating procedure (SOP) of the biology laboratories is slightly modified during the identification of mass casualties incidents, to allow for faster results.

The comparison of antemortem and postmortem data for positive identification is performed by the relevant experts and ratified by a forensic pathologist, followed by rabbinical assent. Identification is established through one of the primary modalities (DNA, fingerprints, or dental data) or two of the secondary modalities (medical data, tattoos, radiographic comparison, or other individualizing characteristics) (DVI Reference Manual 2012).

The second aim of the thanatological examination is clarification of the cause of death and reconstruction of the event. Six main physical phenomena result from explosions: (1) complete disruption of the body, (2) explosive injuries, (3) penetrating wounds from flying missiles, (4) internal lacerations and hemorrhages from the blast wave, (5) burns from thermal effects, and (6) blunt injuries from fallen masonry (Hiss and Kahana 2000a). The distribution and nature of the injuries indicate the victim's location in relation to the epicenter of the explosion (Figure 16-5). The ability to recognize the perpetrator and identify the explosive

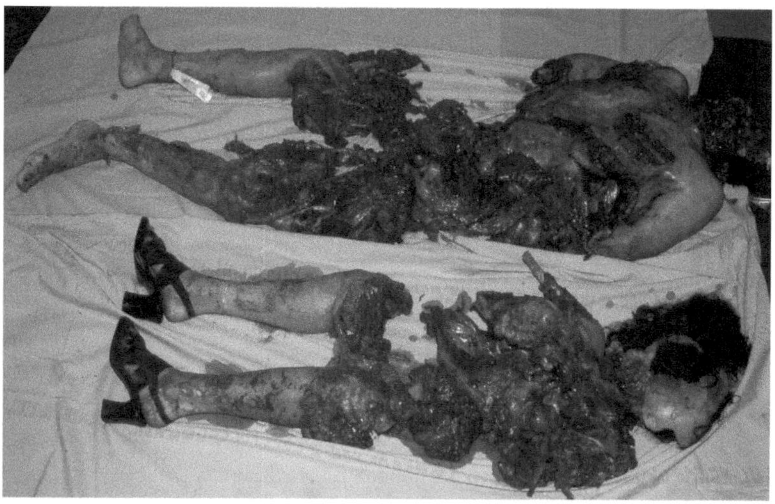

Figure 16-5
Anatomical reconstruction of cadavers to establish the position of the victim in relation to the explosive device.

device is crucial to the forensic investigation and based on the premise that proximity to the bomb directly corresponds to the severity of the injuries (Figure 16-6).

Based on the data collected from 109 suicidal bombings investigated by the Israel Police and the National Centre of Forensic Medicine, the modus operandi has been classified into four patterns. When the perpetrator carries the explosive device on his or her own body, i.e., Strapped Human Bomb (SHB), it can be detonated within an enclosed space (SHB1), resulting in great devastation and fragmentation of the cadavers due to the lack of dispersion of the expansion wave that results from the explosion (Figure 16-7); or in an open space (SHB2), resulting in greater dispersion of the cadavers, which are less fragmented (Figure 16-8). When the bomb is transported in a car, i.e., Vehicular Human Bomb (VHB) it can be detonated in the vicinity of an enclosed (VHB1) or an open (VHB2) space (Hiss et al. 2003) (Figure 16-9).

After the bodies and body parts have been identified, they are buried according to the specific religious requirements of the community. The reassociation of body parts is essential for the burial process. Although there is no explicit prohibition against commingling in any of the religions represented in the Israeli population, there is a deeply ingrained cultural aversion to this phenomenon, although it is understood by all the communities that the phenomenon is unavoidable. Nor is it required to bury the whole body within one grave. For the Jewish community, Rabbi Yitzchak Liebes ruled that burying a majority of the body fulfills the obligation of burial, claiming that a majority of something has the status of the whole thing,

Figure 16-6
Total disruption of a victim in close proximity to a bomb.

Figure 16-7
Scene of a strapped human bomb detonated within an enclosed space.

Figure 16-8
Scene of a strapped human bomb detonated in an open space.

Figure 16-9
Scene of a vehicular human bomb detonated in the vicinity of an open space.

and therefore, burying a majority of the body is considered to be burying the whole body (Eisenberg 2011). This ruling supersedes the necessity to identify all the fragments of a victim of suicidal bombing. The technological advances of DNA that would allow, in theory, to identify and bury together all the remains of one individual is a lengthy process that, if performed, would require storing the remains until they are identified, a notion considered repulsive to Muslim and Jewish traditions. The unidentified fragments of tissue are buried together in a separate plot of a cemetery that is not visited by the next of kin.

Nevertheless, the concern over the burial of commingled remains has been raised on various occasions in Israel by Jewish and Muslim communities, usually in cases of considerable fragmentation of the body such as in aircraft accidents or suicidal bombings. In instances in which the next of kin have raised a suspicion of commingled remains within the grave of their family member, an exhumation has been granted by the court of law, and significant compensation was granted to the families when DNA analysis proved their claim of commingling. The abhorrence to the possibility of commingling stems from the Jewish tradition of not burying "evil" alongside "righteous" (Bar-Gal and Azaryahu 1998).

Resilience

The ability of the individual to emerge as strong or stronger following a stressful or traumatic experience is known in psychology as resilience. Many factors account for higher or lower levels of resilience in an individual and in a population as a whole. Among the most important are the public's sense of comprehension of events, which moderates fear of the unknown, alongside the sense of control of events, which moderates feelings of dread. Other factors include strong social and family ties, coping strategies, optimism and sense of humor, and finally self-efficacy (Pollack and Wood 2010).

A unique element in the Israeli communal psyche is the high resilience of the population as a whole and on the individual level; this is probably best expressed in the flippancy of the old joke describing the traditional Jewish holidays: "They tried to kill us; they failed. Let's eat" (Pollock 2007). Some of the controversial lenient policies regarding forensic investigation of death, like the inclusion of religious volunteers at the scene of highly fragmented cadavers, the willingness of lawmakers to limit the practice of autopsies, and the involvement of orthodox volunteers at the scene of suicidal bombings, are but some of the key elements that maintain this high level of resilience. Investigations into the impact of religion on the resilience of various populations in Israel show that spiritual beliefs play a major role in the ability of the individual to readjust to the results of terror. On the one hand, Israelis are well known for their self-reliance, but on the other hand, they have a very high level of trust in official institutions when dealing with disaster, especially in all ritual aspects of death (Figure 16-10). Sociopsychological, socioreligious, and ideological factors possess buffering qualities in the face of stress (Kaplan et al. 2005).

Figure 16-10
Members of the DVI team of Israel Police and IDF personnel deployed to the scene of the suicidal bombing attack in Burgas, Bulgaria, in 2012. The military rabbinate of the IDF conducted morning prayers on arrival.

Maintaining the necessary forensic standards for effective investigation of death, while at the same time respecting the religious traditions concerning death and burial, is one of the most important balancing acts of the Israeli legislators geared toward preservation of the society's resilience.

References

Bar-Gal, Y., Azaryahu, M., 1998. Israeli cemeteries and Jewish tradition—Two cases. In: Brodsky, H. (Ed.), Visions of Land and Community. University of Maryland Press, College Park, MD, pp. 105–128.

Boglioli, L.R., Taff, M.L., 1990. Religious objections to autopsy: An ethical dilemma for medical examiners. Am. J. Forensic. Med. Pathol. 11, 1–8.

Dana, N., 2003. The Druze in the Middle East: Their Faith, Leadership, Identity and Status. Sussex University Press, UK, pp. 55–66.

DVI Reference Manual—Compendium to the INTERPOL DVI forms. 2012. http://dvi-training.info/HTML/index.html.

Eisenberg, D., 2007. How do we balance respecting the dead with the need to help the living? Aish.com. October 6, 2007. http://www.aish.com/ci/sam/48959971.html.

Eisenberg, D., 2011. Organ and tissue donation. Jewish Medical Ethics, Share Zedek Medical Centre News Letter. http://98.131.138.124/articles/JME/JMEM12/JMEM.12.1.asp.

Goodman, N.R., Goodman, J.L., Hoffman, W.I., 2011. Autopsy: Traditional Jewish laws and customs "Halacha." Am. J. Forensic. Med. Pathol. 32, 300–303.

Greenberger, M., Henson, T., Kates, S., Major, A., 2012. Legal issues in mass fatality events. In: Gursky, E.A., Fierro, M.F. (Eds.), Death in Large Numbers: The Science, Policy, and Management of Mass Fatality Events. American Medical Association, Atlanta, GA, pp. 239–262.

Hiss, J., Freund, M., Motro, U., Kahana, T., 2002. The medicolegal investigation of the El Aqsah Intifada. Isr. Med. Assoc. J. 4, 549–553.

Hiss, J., Freund, M., Motro, U., Kahana, T., 2003. The forensic pathology of terrorism in Israel—Two years of suicide bombing. In: Shemer, J., Shoenfeld, Y. (Eds.), Terror and Medicine: Medical Aspects of Biological, Chemical and Radiological Terrorism. Pabst Science Publishers, Lengerich, Germany, pp. 446–455.

Hiss, J., Kahana, T., 2000a. Modern war wounds. In: Mason, J.K., Purdue, B.N. (Eds.), The Pathology of Trauma, third ed. Arnold, London, pp. 89–102.

Hiss, J., Kahana, T., 2000b. Trauma and identification of victims of suicidal terrorism in Israel. Mil. Med. 165, 889–893.

Hiss, J., Kahana, T., Arensburg, B., 1997. Forensic medicine in Israel. Am. J. Forensic. Med. Pathol. 18, 154–157.

Israel in Figures. Statistical Abstract of Israel, 2013. N. 64. Central Bureau of Statistics, Israel.

Kahana, T., Hiss, J., 1998. Suicide bombers in Israel. Am. J. Forensic. Med. Pathol. 19, 63–66.

Kaplan, Z., Matar, M.A., Kamin, R., Sadan, T., Cohen, H., 2005. Stress-related responses after 3 years of exposure to terror in Israel: Are ideological-religious factors associated with resilience? J. Clin. Psych. 66, 1146–1154.

Karo, Rabbi Yosef, 1565. Sulchan Aruch, Even HaEzer. chapter 17.

Karplus, H., 1969. Present day forensic medicine services in Israel: Their development and legal background. In: Wecht, C.H., Karplus, H. (Eds.), Proceedings of the Fifth International Medico-legal Seminar. Pittsburgh Institute of Legal Medicine, pp. 17–22.

Pellegrino, E.D., 2003. Moral and religious concerns about the autopsy. In: Collins, K.A., Hutchins, G.M. (Eds.), Autopsy Performance and Reporting, second ed. College of American Pathologists, Northfield, IL, pp. 27–38.

Pollack, J.H., Wood, J.D., 2010. Enhancing Public Resilience to Mass-Casualty WMD Terrorism in the United States. Definitions, Challenges, and Recommendations. Sci. Appl. Inter. Corp. Defense Threat Reduction Agency, Advanced Systems and Concepts Office Report Number 2010 042.

Pollock, D.M., 2007. Therefore choose life: The Jewish perspective on coping with catastrophe. South. Med. J. 100, 948–949.

Rispler-Chaim, V., 1993. Islamic Medical Ethics in the Twentieth Century. E. J. Brill, Leiden, The Netherlands, pp. 72–83.

Rosner, F., 1971. Autopsy in Jewish law and the Israeli autopsy controversy. Traditio 11, 43–63.

Sheikh, A., 1998. Death and dying—A Muslim perspective. J. R. Soc. Med. 91, 138–140.

CHAPTER 17

Anthropologist-Directed Triage: Three Distinct Mass Fatality Events Involving Fragmentation and Commingling of Human Remains

Amy Z. Mundorff
Assistant Professor, Anthropology The University of Tennessee

Introduction

Identifying victims from mass fatality events requires the synchronization of several processes including, but not limited to, remains recovery, antemortem information collection, mortuary processes, death certification, family assistance, and finally, repatriation. Many different forensic disciplines are involved in recovering and identifying disaster victims. In particular, anthropologists have been increasingly involved with disaster victim identification in various roles from recovery and mortuary personnel to, more recently, management positions (Blau and Briggs 2011; Kahana and Hiss 2009; Mundorff 2012; Park et al. 2009; Sledzik et al. 2009). This chapter discusses one small aspect of the mortuary process, triage, and its interplay with other aspects of identifying highly fragmented and commingled human remains. Specifically, this chapter focuses on anthropologist-directed triage and how it differed during three distinct mass fatality incidents (MFIs): the World Trade Center (WTC) disaster, the crash of American Airlines Flight 587 (Flight 587), and the crash of the Staten Island Ferry. Each of these incidents involved significant variation in the number of victims, the number of recovered human remains, their degree of fragmentation, the site characteristics, and the recovery processes. Each of these considerations affected the triage teams' composition and duties.

Triage

The *Oxford English Dictionary* defines triage as "the actions of sorting according to quality," "to pick, cull, ... the assignment of degrees of urgency ... in order to decide the order or suitability of treatment..." (*Oxford English Dictionary* 1989). The term "triage" was commonly used in the early 1700s when describing the sorting of wool in degrees of fineness and quality. The military has also used "triage" to rank injured personnel in accordance to the

Commingled Human Remains. http://dx.doi.org/10.1016/B978-0-12-405889-7.00017-4

seriousness of their injuries, ensuring the most critically injured are treated first. As applied in this chapter, the term "triage" encompasses the first assessment human remains receive after they have been recovered from the scene of a disaster and transported to a mortuary or temporary mortuary facility. Actions performed during the triage examination can differ greatly depending on event characteristics, but the central feature in any mass disaster triage situation involves sorting material prior to processing through the disaster morgue.

The triage station is usually the first stage of the mortuary process in high-fragmentation mass fatality events (Mittleman et al. 2000). Traditionally, an anthropologist or pathologist directs triage, depending on the disaster type and the condition of the remains. The triage team is empowered to sort out commingling, identify and discard nonhuman remains, rearticulate or reassociate disparate pieces within a body bag, and anatomically identify fragments for later examination. Because an in-depth understanding of human skeletal anatomy drives all of these activities, triage of fragmentary human remains is most effective when directed by an anthropologist (Byrd and Adams 2003; Levinson and Granot 2002; MacKinnon and Mundorff 2006; Rodriguez 2005).

Every disaster is unique, and each incident's individual characteristics will determine triage team composition, how it functions, and where it is integrated into the identification process. Characteristics directly influencing the triage process include the number of deceased, the degree of fragmentation, and the taphonomy of recovered remains (Alonso et al. 2005; Leclair et al. 2004; Rodriguez 2005). It is well recognized that site characteristics, recovery-induced commingling, trauma inflicted by digging activities, and improper and unscientific recovery techniques complicate mortuary analysis (Egaña et al. 2008; Kontanis and Sledzik 2008; Tuller et al. 2008). These are some of the problems that are recognized and addressed during triage.

The Three Disasters

In each of the three disasters discussed here, human remains were first collected at the disaster scene and then transported to the New York City Office of Chief Medical Examiner's (OCME) mortuary in Manhattan for processing and identification. Upon reaching the ME's office, remains from all three incidents were examined at a triage station, which was directed by a forensic anthropologist. This was an important first step in the lengthy identification process. Significantly, the unique characteristics of each mass fatality required that the anthropologist's role at triage be tailored to that specific incident (Table 17-1).

World Trade Center

At 7:59 on the morning of September 11, 2001, American Airlines Flight 11 left Boston's Logan International Airport en route for Los Angeles, carrying 81 passengers, two pilots, and nine flight attendants. The aircraft was hijacked shortly after departure, diverted to New York City, and was

Table 17-1: Factors Influencing Triage Protocol for Each Disaster

World Trade Center	American Airlines Flight 587	Staten Island Ferry
Open population	Closed population	Open population
2,749 confirmed victims killed on 9/11/2001	265 victims	11 victims
~22,000 fragments recovered	~2,100 fragments recovered	~35 fragments recovered
8-month recovery duration	Several days' recovery duration	Recovery duration less than 24 hours
Recovery personnel untrained in forensic archaeology/anthropology	Recovery personnel mixed with OCME medicolegal staff	Recovery personnel directed by OCME medicolegal staff
Buried site, heavy machinery used	Surface recovery	Surface recovery
High Type 1 (recovery) commingling	Medium Type 1 commingling	Low Type 1 commingling
High Type 2 (disaster) commingling	Low Type 2 commingling	No Type 2 commingling

flown into the North Tower of the World Trade Center between the 94th and 98th floors at 8:46 a.m. Hundreds of people were killed immediately, and hundreds more remained trapped in the building. At 8:14, United Airlines Flight 175 also left Boston's Logan International Airport bound for Los Angeles with 56 passengers, two pilots, and seven flight attendants on board. This plane was also hijacked shortly after departure and diverted to New York City, and was flown into the South Tower of the World Trade Center between the 77th and 85th floors. Again hundreds of people were killed instantly, and hundreds more remained trapped in the building.

According to The 9/11 Commission Report, on September 11, 2001, New York City and the Port Authority of New York and New Jersey mobilized the largest rescue operation in the city's history (The 9/11 Commission Report 2004). At 9:58 a.m., less than one hour after impact, the South Tower collapsed in approximately 10 seconds, killing all remaining civilians, first responders, and emergency personnel who were still trapped inside. At 10:28, 102 minutes after impact, the North Tower also collapsed. Again, all remaining individuals in the building except for 12 firemen, one Port Authority police officer, and three civilians were killed.

Two thousand seven hundred and forty-nine victims lost their lives on September 11, 2001 in the World Trade Center disaster, and as of September 11, 2013, an additional four individuals have since died from medical complications related to the disaster. As of the 12-year anniversary of the WTC attack there have been 21,906 fragments of human remains recovered from the disaster site and the landfill operation, of which 13,723 have been identified (approximately 63%), leaving 8,183 fragments unidentified. Identification efforts have led to the accounting of 1,634 of the victims, or 59% of the missing. Because many remains were either completely pulverized in the towers' collapse or consumed in the fires that burned at the site, there are victims of whom nothing is likely to be recovered. However, as of this writing, the identification process continues and these numbers are likely to change.

After recovery and transport to the mortuary, the initial sort of human remains took place at the triage station. This sorting became increasingly complicated as the number of victims and their degree of fragmentation increased. The World Trade Center disaster is by far the most complicated of the three disasters to be discussed. As previously mentioned, there were 2,749 victims and nearly 22,000 fragments of human remains. This number does not include thousands of nonhuman remains that were recovered but discarded.

The World Trade Center site characteristics presented unprecedented challenges to recovery personnel. Because the remains were not scattered across the landscape, as often seen with aviation accidents, but were buried within the debris of seven destroyed buildings covering more than 16 acres, Ground Zero might best be analogized to a typical buried archaeological site. The debris mound, often referred to as "the pile," stood 70 feet above ground and was later excavated 70 feet below ground. And like an archaeological site, all of the excavated debris was sifted to recover artifacts, or in this case, human remains. Excavating Ground Zero took approximately eight months, and workers spent an additional month sifting through the debris sent to the Staten Island landfill. In 2006, a renewed search and recovery effort was initiated in response to unexpected discoveries of human remains around Ground Zero (Gill et al. 2011; Sledzik et al. 2009). However, in contrast to the original excavations at Ground Zero (2001–2002), the renewed efforts are within the jurisdiction of the New York City Office of Chief Medical Examiner. More specifically, forensic anthropologists are conducting the work, which has resulted in the removal and screening of more than 16,000 cubic yards of material; these efforts are still ongoing (Gill et al. 2011).

American Airlines Flight 587

On November 12, 2001, American Airlines Flight 587 crashed into a residential neighborhood in Queens, New York, approximately 90 seconds after takeoff from John F. Kennedy International Airport. The flight, en route to Santo Domingo, Dominican Republic, held 251 passengers, seven flight attendants, and two flight crewmembers. All were killed, as were an additional five people on the ground. According to the National Transportation Safety Board:

> *The probable cause of this accident was the in-flight separation of the vertical stabilizer as a result of the loads beyond ultimate design that were created by the first officer's unnecessary and excessive rudder pedal inputs. Contributing to these rudder pedal inputs were characteristics of the Airbus A300-600 rudder system design and elements of the American Airlines Advanced Aircraft Maneuvering Program (NTSB 2004).*

The crash of American Airlines Flight 587 occurred two months and one day after the World Trade Center disaster. Already on high alert for terrorism, the City of New York responded quickly with a wide variety of personnel from the Police Department, Fire Department, Port Authority, FBI, and the Medical Examiner's Office. Initially, investigators thought the crash might be related to terrorism, and law enforcement personnel were assigned to the recovery operation. The remains and airline wreckage were scattered over several blocks, destroying four homes and damaging six others. Due to the easy accessibility of the crash site, all of the approximately 2,100 fragments of human remains were recovered within several days.

Taphonomically, the remains recovered from the crash of American Airlines Flight 587 differed drastically from the WTC remains. American Airlines Flight 587, with 265 victims, involved approximately 2,100 fragments of human remains. Although the victim-to-remains ratios between Flight 587 and the World Trade Center disaster were very close—approximately 7.5 remains recovered for every victim—the disaster sites, recovery periods, and condition of the remains differed substantially (Brondolo 2004). In contrast to the remains at Ground Zero, Flight 587 remains were not buried, but scattered on the surface, destructive heavy machinery was not used in recovery, and, therefore, the remains suffered little secondary damage. Also, although the WTC excavations lasted months, this collection took a few days, and the fuel-induced fires at this crash site burned only for hours, as opposed to three months at Ground Zero. Finally, the short recovery period for the Flight 587 victims meant that decomposition was not as advanced as with the prolonged World Trade Center victim recovery. All of these factors directly affected triage protocols and identification success rates.

The Staten Island Ferry Crash

On October 15, 2003, the Staten Island ferry *Andrew J. Barberi* plowed into pier B-1, killing 11 passengers. Although this ferry carries up to 6,000 passengers, the accident occurred before evening rush hour, and only an estimated 1,500 passengers and 15 crewmembers were on board. With an annual ridership of 19 million, the Staten Island Ferry is second only to Seattle, Washington, as the largest U.S. urban ferry operation. That day, the ferry made its standard 5.2-mile trip from Manhattan to Staten Island, a trip that usually takes about 21 minutes traveling at approximately 15 knots (NTSB 2005).

The National Transportation Safety Board investigation concluded that the probable cause of this accident was "the assistant captain's unexplained incapacitation and the failure of the New York City Department of Transportation to implement and oversee safe, effective operating procedures for its ferries. Contributing to the cause of the accident was the failure of the captain to exercise his command responsibility over the vessel by ensuring the safety of its operations" (NTSB 2005).

The Staten Island Ferry crash will be the third mass fatality event discussed and contrasted. This incident involved 11 fatalities, approximately 35 fragments, and 10 near-complete bodies. These remains were recovered within a few hours, this time under the direct guidance of medicolegal staff from the NYC OCME. This was a quick recovery of predominantly surface-scattered remains. This incident involved substantially fewer victims and a lower victim-to-remains ratio (approximately 3.5 remains recovered for every victim) than the other two incidents profiled in this chapter. Reflecting this reality, the subsequent triage process was comparatively simple. Compared to WTC, the victim remains recovered from the Staten Island Ferry crash were not severely fragmented or commingled. They were not buried and they were not decomposed. Therefore, the human remains recovered from the Staten Island Ferry crash shared more taphonomic similarities with the Flight 587 remains than with those of WTC. However, unlike the victims from Flight 587, these individuals were not burned and were instead relatively recognizable.

The World Trade Center Disaster

Open vs. Closed Population and DNA Testing Decisions

Often, mass disasters are categorized as having either a closed population, in which the number and names of the victims involved are known, or an open population, in which this information is not available. The crash of American Airlines Flight 587, with a passenger list, was considered a closed population, while the Staten Island Ferry crash was considered an open population. The World Trade Center disaster was both. Although investigators were provided passenger manifests for the two planes that hit the buildings, as well as rosters of other probable victims who worked in the towers, the actual number and names of the victims in the towers remained unknown. The process of generating an accurate missing persons list with an open population is slow and complicated, and it took nearly three years to compile a final fatality list for the WTC disaster (Brondolo 2004). In light of the unknown number of victims and the degree of fragmentation, the Chief Medical Examiner, Dr. Charles Hirsch, along with Rudy Giuliani, the Mayor of New York City, decided to DNA test every piece of human remains no matter how small. Establishing this standard assured that no possible victim profile would be missed. Fulfilling this standard necessitated an exacting triage process, requiring the detection and dissection of small bone fragments that had become embedded in other fragmented remains.

The decision to DNA test every fragment was unprecedented. Investigators in mass fatality incidents generally do not DNA test every fragment, and the criteria for determining which pieces to test vary from incident to incident (Holland et al. 2003; Hsu et al. 1999; Meyer 2003; Mittleman et al. 2000; Mundorff et al. 2009; Olaisen et al. 1997). In a mass fatality event with an open population, such as the London Underground bombings of July 7, 2005, investigators considered both the remains' size and relative identifiability when deciding which fragments to sample. In that incident, fragments less than five square centimeters and unrecognizable were not sampled for DNA testing (Roberts, personal communication). As a result, approximately half of the recovered remains were sampled. Similarly, investigators of the September 11, 2001 crash of United Airlines Flight 93 in Shanksville, Pennsylvania, an incident with a closed population, also decided that about one-third of the recovered remains were suitable for DNA sampling. Factors that may mitigate against sampling include types of remains known to be unsuitable for testing, such as fat, or the condition of remains, such as those that are calcined or soaked in jet fuel. The criteria for determining which remains are suitable for DNA testing will change over time as the science of DNA technology evolves.

WTC Remains Recovery

Human remains were recovered daily from both Ground Zero and the Staten Island landfill operation. Barges transported material from Ground Zero to the landfill, where large pieces of building material were separated from the debris, which was spread out in open fields to be sorted. The dirt and other small bits were taken to sifters. In a process that is similar to screening the fill from an archaeological site, this material was shaken through industrial-size screens and sifters until the remaining material was carried onto a conveyor belt (Figure 17-1). Individuals, typically members of service such as police or federal agents, monitored the conveyor belt and collected each item of human tissue or bone fragment (Warren et al. 2003). Each of these items was bagged separately and transported to the OCME for processing and identification. This methodical sifting process allowed for individual remains collection, nearly eliminating incidents of recovery-induced commingling at the landfill. However, the process of excavation, transport, screening, and sifting, along with decomposition, caused articulated elements to become disarticulated from each other. As a result, disparate pieces later had to be reassociated by DNA. By contrast, the remains received from the disaster site were extremely commingled. Because Ground Zero accounted for most of the recovered remains, this extensive commingling greatly complicated the triage process (MacKinnon and Mundorff 2006).

Commingling from the WTC disaster can be reduced to two primary types. This chapter refers to Type 1 commingling as that involving remains collected together in one bag, but not

Figure 17-1
Service members monitoring the conveyor belt for human remains at the Staten Island landfill operation. *(Source: Rich Press, Copyright © 2001.)*

attached by hard or soft tissue. Therefore, the commingling is recovery-induced. The potential for this type of commingling has long been recognized, and most recovery operations are equipped to cope with it. An experienced practitioner can easily detect Type 1 commingling by examining the remains to see which pieces are actually attached to each other. When the remains are not attached, the triage team disassociates them. However, another more severe and difficult-to-recognize type of commingling was also common in the WTC site. Type 2 commingling, which is disaster-induced, was caused by the extreme destructive and explosive nature of the building collapses. The explosive force that blew over fire trucks and peeled stone façades from buildings also disintegrated human bodies, turning small pieces of bone into flying shrapnel, which became embedded in the soft tissue of other individuals. The tidal wave of debris that carried human remains blocks away, depositing them on top of buildings, also fused soft tissue to bone fragments from different individuals so completely that the remains appeared to be from the same individual. This type of commingling is difficult to recognize as compared to commingling commonly seen in other disaster scenarios. Additionally, the sheer number of fragmented pieces of human remains—nearly 22,000—complicated efforts to resolve both types of commingling.

Site formation processes primarily determined the condition of the remains. These processes include the forces that initially formed the site, manipulation for excavation, and transformations over time including decomposition (Schiffer 1987). In the World Trade Center disaster, these initial processes included both primary and secondary events. The primary events that created this "archaeological site" included the impact of the two planes, the collapse of the South Tower, the collapse of the North Tower *through* the debris of the South Tower, and the subsequent destruction of five additional commercial buildings. Additionally, subterranean fires burned for 12 weeks, water was applied to those fires, and remains decomposed over the 8-month excavation (Figure 17-2). Often, one or more of these factors are present at a disaster, but rarely, if ever, have they all occurred at one disaster site (Sledzik and Rodriguez 2002). These processes determined the shape and condition of the remains, in turn determining the methods used to process and identify them.

Secondary events also affected the composition of the remains and their condition upon arrival at the Medical Examiner's Office. The site consisted largely of 5,000-pound steel beams mixed with chunks of concrete, thus making a "by hand" deconstruction impossible. Large machinery, including grapplers and cranes, were brought in to assist (Figure 17-3). In order to place these cranes close enough to "the pile," workers first needed to create platforms for them, which involved bulldozing and compacting sections of the site. Additionally, as the site was excavated below ground level, a ramp was built to allow excavation equipment to move in and out of "the pit." The material bulldozed for these constructions came from the pile itself and undoubtedly contained human remains. When these platforms and roads were later excavated, human remains were indeed recovered from the fill. This manipulation of decomposing and already fragmented human remains caused further destruction and commingling.

Figure 17-2
Bucket of completely calcined remains recovered from one of the "hot spots" in Ground Zero that burned for 12 weeks. (Source: *Office of Chief Medical Examiner, New York City.*)

Figure 17-3
Complicated excavation of Ground Zero showing heavy machinery used.

The methods used to recover individual remains further complicated the identification process. It is well documented that excavations by untrained personnel and those performed in an unscientific manner may cause further commingling, subsequently affecting identifications (Egaña et al. 2008; Kontanis and Sledzik 2008; Tuller et al. 2008). The recovery and excavation of human remains from Ground Zero were performed predominantly by the Fire Department of the City of New York (FDNY) personnel. These individuals are not trained in techniques of forensic archaeology, excavation of human remains, identification or recognition of compromised human remains (especially calcined or fragmentary), or site formation processes. This lack of training complicated the recovery process and allowed for significant additional Type 1 (recovery-induced) commingling. Instead of consigning each piece of remains to a single bag, FDNY personnel filled body bags with potentially unrelated body parts before sending them on to the Medical Examiner's Office. FDNY also lacked knowledge and training on techniques for properly excavating a body found nearly intact yet buried within debris, especially those bodies in an advanced state of decomposition. Once the body is decomposed, the smallest amount of movement or disturbance easily disassociates body parts. These issues can be mitigated with deeper knowledge of human anatomy and the application of forensic archaeological techniques (Blau 2005; Skinner and Sterenberg 2005).

Intentional commingling at the site by the recovery personnel also complicated identifications. For instance, upon finding an empty monogrammed fire department bunker jacket during the excavations, FDNY personnel placed the nearest human remains inside the jacket before transporting it to the Medical Examiner's Office. It seems that in placing these pieces in the bunker gear, FDNY hoped identifications would be accomplished faster and that families would receive "more" of their loved ones because the remains were in a jacket with a name on it. Upon arrival at the triage table, however, anthropologists immediately detected these reconstructions. Often, these reconstructions were quite obvious, as in leg bones placed in jacket sleeves. In another instance, examination of what appeared to be the nearly complete body of a fireman fully clothed in bunker gear revealed two left feet, in boots neatly tucked into the bunker pants. The left foot tucked into the right pant leg was clearly not associated with this body yet had been grouped with it at the site during recovery. Although driven by understandable grief and the urge to identify their fallen, reconstruction activities at the site caused the triage team to more closely examine, and often separate into multiple cases, body parts found within clothing which ultimately slowed identifications.

WTC Triage

A temporary mortuary specifically for WTC was set up in the receiving bay of the Manhattan morgue, allowing regular autopsies to continue in the main autopsy suite. The WTC morgue was constructed to process a high-volume caseload. Two refrigerated tractor-trailer units were placed outside the mortuary, where the remains were held prior to triage, and eight tables were set up in the receiving bay. One table was designated for triage, one table held cases post-triage and awaiting examination, and six tables were staffed by medical examiners and their teams. The identification process flowed like an assembly line, from triage to medical examiner to other stations including fingerprint, X-ray, dental, personal effects, and final storage.

Initially, forensic pathologists staffed the triage station. However, within days of the disaster, the management team determined that an anthropologist should direct triage. Two main considerations motivated this change. First, only medical examiners were allowed to fill in death certification forms, and it was important to free them to work the exam tables. Second, the remains were highly fragmented, with soft tissue obscuring obvious anatomic landmarks. This meant it would be advantageous for individuals with a deeper knowledge of osteological detail to identify the elements recovered. Additional factors, such as the substantial amount of nonhuman remains recovered from the destroyed restaurants, also made it advantageous for an anthropologist to direct triage.

The triage team consisted of an anthropologist and up to five assistants. The assistants varied in skills and expertise from OCME employees and medical students to members of service from the Port Authority Police Department (PAPD), New York Police Department (NYPD), and Federal Bureau of Investigations (FBI) (Figure 17-4). These law enforcement agencies were incorporated into the identification process because of the criminal nature of the event, and their presence during triage allowed them to seize potential items of evidence collected along with the human remains.

Figure 17-4

View of the triage team in the OCME mortuary tent. *(Source: Rich Press, Copyright © 2001.)*

Protocols and standards employed in the triage process changed drastically over the 8-month recovery operation. Initially, the process was as follows: a body bag was taken from the refrigerated truck outside the mortuary and brought to the triage table where an anthropologist opened the bag and assessed the contents. Bags from Ground Zero contained a wide variety of material, ranging from a single whole body to dozens of small red biohazard bags each filled with numerous fragments of human remains. Additionally, building material, personal effects, and nonhuman remains were intermingled in these bags. Each bag was examined for unassociated and unattached parts within the body bag. Every piece of human remains that was not attached to another by hard or soft tissue was segregated. When such parts were found, they were removed individually, passed to an assistant, and placed in their own bag. Each of these bags became its own case. A case is a single set of human remains that is individually processed for identification and could be as small as a 1-inch bone fragment or as large as an entire body (Figure 17-5). These bags were then placed on another table to await medical examiner processing.

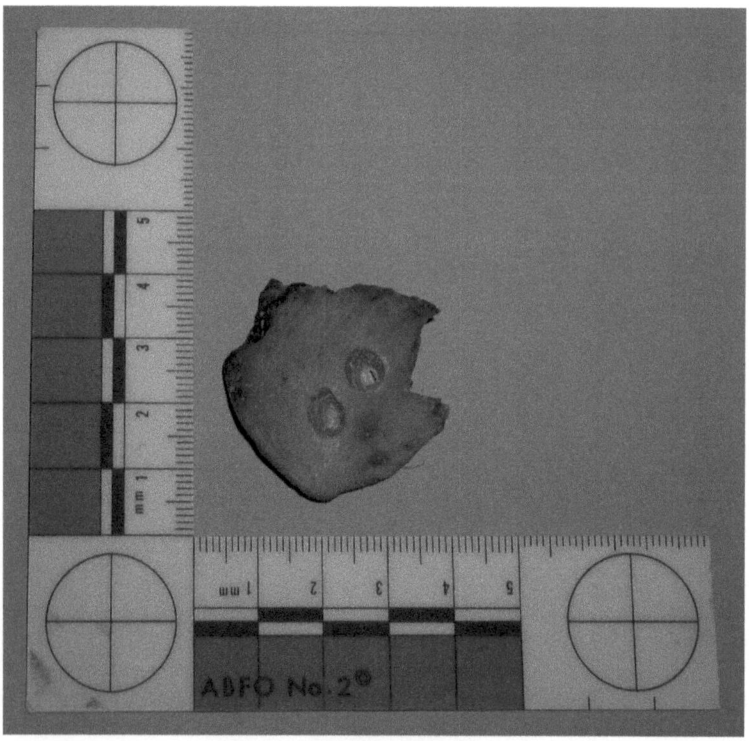

Figure 17-5
Fragment of distal scapula; one of more than 5,000 fragments from WTC that were approximately one inch or smaller. Note two drilled holes where DNA samples were removed. (Source: *Office of Chief Medical Examiner, New York City.*)

Within weeks, a coordination grid was established for Ground Zero, and recovery locations—usually written as a letter and number (e.g., K-10)—were recorded on tags attached to the body bags (Figura 2011). At this point, before opening a body bag, the triage team located the grid recovery tag if there was one. After the tag was located, that specific site designation followed all remains originally associated with that body bag. So the new cases, removed from the original body bag, were also labeled with the accompanying grid location. Although locator tags indicated from which 75-foot by 75-foot section of Ground Zero (which was about 16 acres in total) the human remains had been recovered, depth was not always accounted for. A fragment found on the ground surface of Grid K-12 as well as a fragment found at the bottom of the "pit" in Grid K-12 both received the same location designation, even though there may have been up to 140 feet of variance in depth between the two fragments. Additionally, bulldozing and road construction to assist excavations caused human remains to be moved and deposited outside their original grid location. On the other hand, the remains recovered from the Staten Island landfill operation were bagged individually directly from the conveyor belt and, therefore, did not require an in-depth triage examination, other than to discard nonhuman material.

Medical examiner personnel were initially caught off guard by the amount of destruction and fragmentation to the human remains. They simply possessed no theoretical schema to account for the injuries a human body endures in the collapse of a 110-story building. Compounding this, at the beginning of the disaster the sense of urgency was intense, and triage was sometimes bypassed altogether to speed bodies through identification. For example, larger body parts that initially bypassed triage in favor of quick identification generally possessed standard identifiers such as fingerprints or dentition. However, within weeks, medical examiner personnel came to appreciate the true force of the disaster and the extreme level of commingling. Because of this, investigators came to believe that small bone fragments were likely embedded in the tissue of body parts that had bypassed triage and that some cases of commingling might have gone undetected. The policy of testing each piece of remains made it imperative to retrieve these small fragments, and a secondary review of all of the remains was undertaken by a group of anthropologists. This process, known as the Anthropological Verification Project (AVP), detected and corrected instances of commingling that were missed in the initial examination (Budimlija et al. 2003; MacKinnon and Mundorff 2006). Of the nearly 17,000 cases re-examined, fewer than 100 were found to be commingled, and these were subsequently split into approximately 300 new cases. More significant was the lesson learned from having to reprocess thousands of cases, a costly endeavor both in time and money. As Byard and Winskog state, "One of the most important philosophies is to 'hasten slowly,' as the consequences of errors in identification due to rushed work could outlast the operation by many years, if not decades" (Byard and Winskog 2010:1).

In addition to implementing the AVP project, the triage process was strengthened to account for the extensive Type 2 (disaster-induced) commingling, which is impossible to accurately assess at a disaster site. Sorting out this type of commingling is much more complicated than looking for unattached pieces within a single body bag. Pieces of muscle and bone from different individuals can become fused together, mimicking the appearance of a contiguous piece. While extremely rare in the MFI literature, this phenomenon was also observed in Thailand following the 2004 Boxing Day tsunami (Zehner 2007). When remains reach the mortuary, fragments thought to comprise only one individual can reveal commingling with the use of radiography or tomography (Blau et al. 2008; Viner 2008). Therefore, the need to stringently triage all remains is imperative.

During WTC triage, it was not unusual to find skull fragments of one individual deep within another individual's thigh muscle, and rib fragments were frequently found embedded in other body parts. It became clear that bone fragments of multiple individuals could be commingled together into one large tissue mass. In fact, many cases that appeared to be independent body parts frequently had dozens of small bone fragments embedded throughout. This type of commingling has the potential to bias DNA analysis if the sample taken from the remains inadvertently includes a fragment from a different individual (Mundorff et al. 2008). For this reason, the anthropologist conducting the triage process began sorting out even the smallest fragments of bone.

Every piece of bone or tissue was removed and placed in its own bag for individual processing. It was not uncommon for anthropologists to reduce a body bag received from Ground Zero into as many as 100 new cases. When the anthropologist believed, based on morphological characteristics, that numerous unattached fragments within a body bag likely belonged to one individual, the new cases triaged out of that bag were grouped together for successive processing and cross-referencing. For example, a body bag might contain multiple ribs, all appearing to originate from the same individual—with no overlap in rib number or side—yet unattached by soft tissue because of decomposition. Even if it was thought these all belonged to the same individual, these ribs were not treated as one case because they were not actually attached together. Instead, each rib was bagged as an individual case. However, all of those cases were placed together into one bin so a single medical examiner could process them consecutively (Figure 17-6). Upon receiving a grouping of individually bagged remains thought to be from the same victim, the medical examiner cross-referenced the case numbers in the file of each potentially associated fragment. This notation indicated that, although these were separate cases, the anthropologist believed they might belong to the same individual. This information was useful later when some cross-referenced cases were identified to the same individual, but other cross-referenced fragments were not. Because there was additional documented evidence of possible association, these fragments could be further targeted for identification. Years later, it appears that many of the cases that were cross-referenced to a primary case have indeed been linked by DNA to that same primary case (Mundorff 2009).

Each of the World Trade Center disaster's individual characteristics contributed to the design of the triage protocols established in the mortuary. The number of victims, the number of recovered remains and their degree of fragmentation, and the condition of the remains were all influencing factors. Additionally, the duration of the recovery operation and the recovery

Figure 17-6
Separate bins of individually bagged remains that will be cross-referenced to each other as groups. *(Source: Rich Press, Copyright © 2001.)*

personnel's relative lack of expertise or training in archaeological techniques demanded a complicated and exacting triage.

The Crash of American Airlines Flight 587

The crash of Flight 587 is notable for the relative speed—only 28 days—with which the victims were identified. It is worth noting the factors leading to this rapid identification, especially as contrasted with the lengthy identification process of the World Trade Center disaster. First, this mass fatality incident involved a closed population, meaning a manifest existed documenting each victim's name. In addition, local residents provided information for those killed on the ground. This allowed the OCME to quickly begin collecting antemortem information, which facilitated rapid identifications. By comparison, it took years to even finalize the total number and names of missing persons for the World Trade Center disaster. Second, the remains' size and condition made them easier to identify. Although some remains were fragmented from impact and/or visually unrecognizable (as compared to a photograph of the individual's face) from extensive burning and charring caused by jet fuel-fed fires, many of the remains from Flight 587 were still large enough to autopsy. Often some part of the body with an identification modality, such as fingerprints or dentition, was present allowing for rapid identification. By comparison, the remains from WTC were fragmented into such small pieces (over 5,000 of which were no larger than an inch) that other means of identification were not available, forcing a lengthy DNA identification process. Third, the WTC disaster involved nearly 10 times as many fragments as Flight 587. Finally, because the crash followed closely on the heels of the WTC disaster, the OCME was already set up to process a major incident.

Because the cause of the crash was initially unknown, all of the Flight 587 bodies were autopsied in the presence of the FBI. This allowed FBI personnel, working alongside medical examiners in the autopsy room, to collect evidence to help determine if the crash was caused by terrorism. This also allowed for toxicological testing on the pilot, copilot, and passengers. Autopsies were performed when approximately half of the body was present; of the nearly 2,100 pieces of human remains recovered, 305 were large enough to warrant an autopsy. Therefore, identifications relied heavily on fingerprint, dental, and personal effects.

Victim remains began arriving at the mortuary by late afternoon the day of the crash, November 12, 2001. They were transported to the OCME and placed into a refrigerated truck outside the temporary morgue previously constructed to process the World Trade Center remains. The Flight 587 remains were recovered from the crash site in two types of bags. The large body parts—torsos and whole bodies—were collected in body bags, whereas the fragments were collected in smaller red plastic biohazard bags. Each bag was unloaded individually and brought to the triage station. The triage team consisted of an anthropologist and up to five assistants. Again, the assistants were personnel from the FBI, PAPD, and NYPD already present at the OCME working on the WTC remains. The anthropologist opened each bag to sort through the contents. Unlike WTC, with Flight 587 there were many relatively whole bodies or large body parts with little decomposition. The bodies were given priority over the fragments because they were to be autopsied and were likely to be identified quickly. Although the temporary WTC facility was used to triage and process the fragments from Flight 587, the bodies were autopsied in the main autopsy room.

Responding to the insight gained from processing the WTC disaster, the OCME had established a strict triage protocol by the time Flight 587 went down. However, this protocol was flexible, allowing modification according to a disaster's characteristics. The Flight 587 triage process was as follows: a single body bag was brought to the triage team and opened. An examination of the remains was performed to determine that everything within the body bag was indeed physically attached by hard or soft tissue. At the crash site, isolated pieces of human remains such as skull fragments, amputated hands and feet, and pieces of fat and soft tissue had been collected along with bodies and grouped into the same recovery body bag (Type 1 recovery-imposed commingling). These additional fragments were removed from the original body bag and placed in their own bags to await processing. If a body bag contained a body lacking a foot due to traumatic amputation and if a foot was also found in the bag, these two items did not automatically remain together. However, if tissue or skin held the remains together, or if the fractured bones conjoined with each other, then the two pieces were kept together. If this standard was not met, the smaller fragment was removed from the body bag, placed into its own bag, and processed with the other fragments after the autopsies were completed.

As compared with WTC, commingling in the Flight 587 remains was easier to recognize and generally resulted from lax recovery techniques versus the Type 2 explosive commingling previously discussed. As with WTC, recovery personnel at the Flight 587 crash site collected multiple unassociated body parts at the scene and placed them in the same bag. This form of commingling—Type 1 recovery-induced—is comparably easy to discern and mitigate during the triage process by separating out unattached and unarticulatable remains. Unlike WTC, at the Flight 587 crash site, very few nonhuman remains were recovered. Also unlike WTC, the Flight 587 body bags did not have locator tags because the site was not set up as a grid.

When it was determined at the triage station that only a single body or body part remained in a body bag, it was zipped shut, the word "triaged" was written on top (Figure 17-7), and a file containing a case number and all of the paperwork was assigned to the body. A red folder (to differentiate it from the neutral-colored ones used for WTC) in a plastic cover was attached to the top of the body bag, to accompany that body through all of the identification processing stations. As with the World Trade Center, the body part and its corresponding paperwork were then taken through all of the other stations by an escort, usually a member of service.

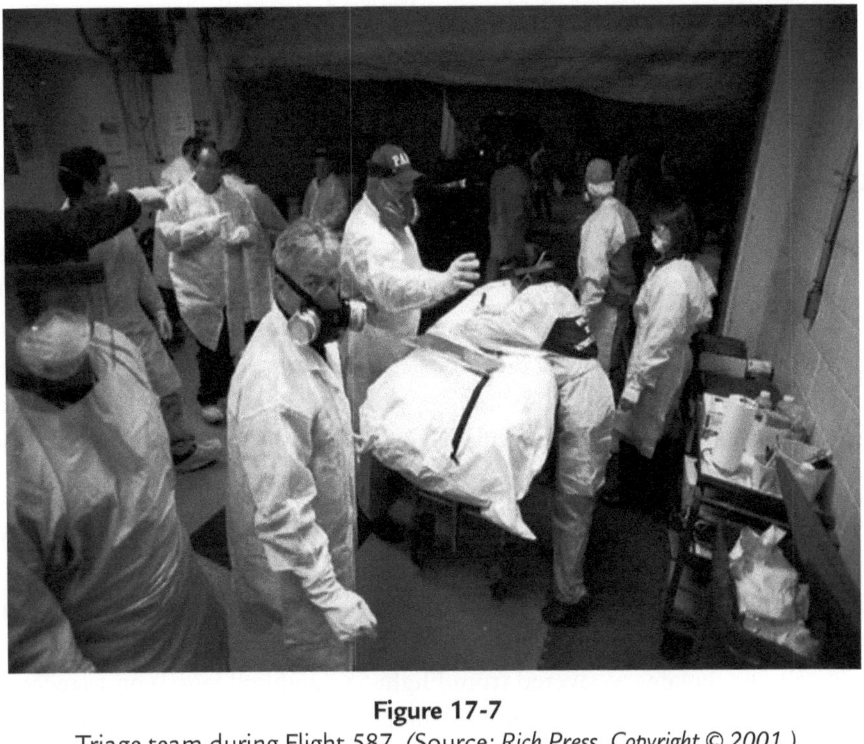

Figure 17-7
Triage team during Flight 587. *(Source: Rich Press, Copyright © 2001.)*

Depending on which part of the body was present, station stops might include X-ray, dental, and fingerprint, all followed by the autopsy.

After all of the large body bags had been triaged, allowing the autopsies to proceed, the small bags of fragments were triaged under the same protocols. Each bag was opened individually and examined by the anthropologist. Bags containing only a single fragment were closed and placed on the next table to await processing. If the bag contained multiple fragments, each piece was isolated and placed into its own bag, sealed, and then placed on the next table to await examination and further processing. The anthropologist was empowered to evaluate the fragments for possible reassociation with other fragments within the same recovery bag. However, reassociation of fragments from disparate recovery bags required verification by dental, fingerprint, DNA, or some other means. Since the fragments were processed after the bodies had been autopsied, no attempts were made to physically reassociate fragments to bodies. This would have been logistically impossible because many of the bodies were identified and released to funeral homes before the fragments were processed. Reassociation of fragmented remains from the Flight 587 and WTC disasters relied primarily on DNA. These reassociation methods differed significantly for the Staten Island Ferry Crash, which is discussed in the next section.

Following triage, each bag was assigned its own sequential case number and reopened for examination. All of the information relevant to that fragment was documented in the file, including injury patterns, personal effects, a detailed description of the remains, and information specifying which other stations the fragment visited. For instance, an amputated hand would go to the fingerprint station but not the dental station. The DNA sample was taken during the examination, which enabled the piece to be identified and reassociated to a body if other modalities of identification were lacking, such as dental or fingerprint.

The autopsies of the Flight 587 victims were completed in seven days, and the approximately 1,800 unassociated fragments were processed in 12 days (Vidoli and Mundorff 2012). Procedures for examination and documentation of these fragments followed protocols developed for WTC, and, as with the WTC disaster, every recovered fragment was sampled for DNA testing. This is unusual for a plane crash or any other type of incident with a closed population in which 100% *victim identification* can be achieved without testing every fragment. However, unlike WTC, after every DNA sample was tested and 100% victim identification was achieved, samples that did not yield full DNA profiles were not continually retested.

As with every mass disaster, recovery techniques affect how medical personnel process and identify victim remains. This is especially true with fragmented human remains because of the heightened potential for commingling or contamination. As seen with the WTC disaster, the techniques employed in recovering remains increased commingling, which in turn required a very strict triage process, even to the extent of separating remains found within clothing. Overall, the remains recovered from Flight 587 endured less Type 1 (recovery-induced) and significantly less Type 2 (disaster-induced) commingling than the remains from the World Trade Center disaster. Additionally, the number of victims and the site characteristics were drastically different between the two disasters, and therefore, the triage protocols for Flight 587 were adapted accordingly. Specifically, the nature of this disaster meant that measures such as cross-referencing and grid locators were not utilized. However, as illustrated with the next discussion featuring the Staten Island Ferry crash, well-coordinated recovery methods and fewer victims and fragments again necessitated modifications to the tasks performed during triage.

The Staten Island Ferry Crash

On the afternoon of October 15, 2003, the *Andrew J. Barberi* crashed into a concrete maintenance pier south of the docking point at the Staten Island Ferry terminal, which sliced through the front of the vessel (NTSB 2005). Ten people were killed instantly, and one more died later from medical complications. In addition, 70 passengers suffered severe injuries including amputated limbs (NTSB 2005). The vessel's primary impact area was the midship section on the main deck of the New Jersey side. However, as the allision continued, the concrete pier also passed through the passenger cabin. "All of the fatally injured passengers were found on the New Jersey side of the vessel's main deck" (NTSB 2005).

The Staten Island Ferry crash involved relatively few victims and normally would not stress an agency as large as the New York City OCME. However, several circumstances conspired to dictate that this should be designated as a mass fatality. First, the accident occurred in a public transit area, which meant there was no initial manifest of the victims, making this an open population. Second, the ensuing publicity resulted in thousands of inquiries from possible victim families, stressing OCME's internal systems. Third, because so many of the victims were reasonably identifiable, public and local officials expected speedy identification (Brondolo 2004; NTSB 2005). Finally, a significant number of amputated body parts and unassociated bone and tissue fragments were recovered from the boat and the water. Along with the 10 bodies, approximately 33 bags in total were removed from the site and transported to the Manhattan morgue. Taken together, these circumstances mitigated in favor of designating this incident as a mass fatality.

Emergency personnel were dispatched to the accident scene within minutes of the event. These included more than 300 personnel from the NYPD, 200 from the FDNY, 60 from the Emergency Medical Service, six Coast Guard vessels, the Army Corps of Engineers, and other rescue and support units. This response even included dive teams for individuals who might have fallen into the water (NTSB 2005). Along with this massive response, OCME medicolegal investigators arrived on scene to assess the casualties and participate in victim recovery. Following the 9/11 events, OCME MLIs had been working hand-in-hand with the FDNY and NYPD to streamline the response to mass fatality incidents, and this extensive multiagency training and communication helped ensure an efficient recovery and identification of the deceased victims.

Emergency personnel recovered several fatalities from the main deck, moving the bodies before the ME's team arrived. The rest of the victims and body parts were recovered over the next few hours by emergency personnel under the guidance of the OCME medicolegal investigators. MLI guidance helped limit the number of fragments placed into a single recovery bag (Type 1 commingling). This reduced commingling and contamination and ensured proper labeling of the recovery location for each individual remain. Even when found in close proximity, fragments that were not physically attached were placed in separate bags. However, this did not negate the need to stringently triage all remains when they reached the mortuary because it is impossible to accurately assess commingling at a disaster site.

The victims' bodies and recovered body parts began arriving at the Manhattan mortuary early in the evening on the day of the accident. Because the victims were mostly recognizable (nine of the 10 bodies), the Chief Medical Examiner decided to have the MEs perform a preliminary examination of the victims that evening for identification purposes only. The complete autopsies of the bodies and examination of the associated fragments took place the following morning.

The next day, the victims were laid out in the autopsy room, most with serious blunt force injuries, traumatically amputated limbs, eviscerated torsos, and significant head trauma. In addition to the 10 bodies receiving autopsies, bags of unassociated body parts including amputated limbs, organs, skull fragments, and pieces of fat and soft tissue were also brought into the autopsy room. Unlike WTC and Flight 587, at the Staten Island Ferry crash, there were no explosive forces involved with this disaster, minimizing fragmentation and its associated commingling. In fact, the minimal commingling was limited to Type 1. And, as mentioned previously, the MLIs' presence at the scene helped ensure that proper recovery techniques were utilized, significantly reducing this as well. As compared with Flight 587 and WTC, the triage process for the Staten Island Ferry crash was less concerned with sorting out commingled remains, instead focusing on reassociating fragments to nearly complete bodies.

In this incident, the triage team consisted of an anthropologist and an assistant with significant experience in mass fatality work and knowledge of human anatomy. As opposed to WTC and the crash of Flight 587, the triage and autopsy processes in this disaster were closely integrated, and the triage team worked directly with the medical examiners in a concerted effort to reassociate fragments with bodies during autopsy. The limited number of victims and fragments meant that quick reassociation to the bodies was often possible. As autopsies were being conducted, the triage team opened the recovered bags one by one, according to the OCME triage protocol. An initial sort was performed to isolate all of the individual fragments. As before, anything not attached to another fragment by hard or soft tissue was its own case. However, these cases were not rebagged as in the previous disasters discussed, but instead were laid out on a gurney. At this point, the anthropologist anatomically evaluated all of the displayed body parts and fragments.

Concurrently, the medical examiners conducting the autopsies evaluated the bodies for missing parts. With this information, attempts were made to reassociate isolated body parts with those bodies missing a correlative part. Many of these reassociations were simple. For instance, an isolated hand could be matched with a body that was missing a hand. For the association to be acceptable, the bones must conclusively conjoin at the fracture site. An exception to this rule would be when process of elimination is valid (Adams and Byrd 2006). When this standard was met, the isolated body part was not given its own case number, but instead was included with the body's autopsy case number and the separation/reassociation was noted along with the other injuries documented in the autopsy notes. In another case, a fragment of liver was reassociated to a body that suffered a partial liver avulsion. This is rare, but in some instances it is appropriate to rearticulate soft tissue.

Other cases were more complicated. For instance, multiple skull fragments were recovered from the accident scene. Many of these fragments articulated to each other and therefore were grouped together as a single case. However, because a few victims suffered head trauma, reassociating all of the skull fragments to any specific body was not always possible. Although some skull fragments were reassociated to a body, others could not be assigned to any particular individual. In these instances, each isolated fragment or group of associated fragments became their own case. A benefit of immediately reassociating fragments with bodies during autopsy is it reduced the number of parts being identified to that individual by DNA weeks or months later. In addition, reassociations during autopsy reduced the number of samples to be DNA tested, which ultimately accelerated the identification process for unassociated fragments.

The rest of the isolated fragments, including pieces of fat, muscle, and bone that could not be reassociated to any one individual, were assigned their own case number and processed individually following the same protocols as were used during the WTC and Flight 587 victim identification projects. This included a detailed anatomical description of the remains, information about which other fragments were found in association with that piece, the location of recovery (if documented) on the original recovery bag, and finally a DNA sample was removed. DNA testing allowed the unassociated fragments to eventually be reassociated to a specific body (all bodies had been sampled for DNA testing during autopsy).

As the preceding discussion demonstrates, because of little Type 1 (recovery-induced) commingling, and no Type 2 (disaster-induced) commingling, the triage process for the Staten Island Ferry crash differed significantly from WTC and Flight 587. Reassociations of disparate parts with bodies took place during the triage process for the Staten Island Ferry crash, which was simultaneous with conducting the autopsies. Incident characteristics such as a small victim-to-fragment ratio, little decomposition, and a controlled surface recovery dictated this process. In contrast, reassociations during WTC and Flight 587 triage were attempted only for fragments found within a single recovery bag. As compared to the other two disasters, triage for the Staten Island Ferry crash was still quite valuable but involved more reassociation of fragments to bodies than sorting out commingled remains.

Conclusion

Identifying victims from mass fatality events can be a long and complicated process. Many components including recovery, mortuary processes, death certification, and antemortem information collection affect the overall success rates. Other important factors affecting the identification process include the number of victims, the degree of fragmentation, the length of the recovery operation, and whether or not it is an open or closed population. This chapter discussed one aspect of the mortuary process, triage, and its interplay with the other aspects of the process of identifying fragmented remains from three distinct mass fatality events in New York City. Each event differed in the degree of fragmentation, recovery duration, and the number and population characteristics of victims, all of which was reflected in the triage process. Additionally, the methods used to recover the remains greatly varied between the different events, which also shaped triage protocols. Although the lengthy WTC recovery could not have been avoided, changing certain recovery practices could have helped in reducing needless commingling created at the site. This was demonstrated during the Staten Island Ferry crash recovery where OCME personnel were not only present at the disaster scene but were active participants organizing the recovery of human remains, greatly reducing commingling. Although this chapter illustrates the value of using personnel trained in recovering human remains, it must be noted that political, social, and cultural factors oftentimes place these decisions beyond the jurisdiction of medicolegal professionals, who must be able to adapt and contend with the condition of the remains as they are received.

References

Adams, B.J., Byrd, J.E., 2006. Resolution of small-scale commingling: A case report from the Vietnam War. Forensic. Sci. Int. 156 (1), 63–69.

Alonso, A., Martín, P., Albarrán, C., García, P., Fernández de Simón, L., Iturralde, M.J., Fernández-Rodríguez, A., Atienza, I., Capilla, J., García-Hirschfeld, J., Martínez, P., Vallejo, G., García, O., García, E., Real, P., Álvarez, D., León, A., Sancho, M., 2005. Challenges of DNA profiling in mass disaster investigations. Croat. Med. J. (46), 540–548.

Blau, S., 2005. One chance only: Advocating the use of archaeology in search, location and recovery at disaster scenes. Aust. J. Emerg. Manage. 20 (1), 19–24.

Blau, S., Robertson, S., Johnstone, M., 2008. Disaster victim identification: New applications for postmortem computed tomography. J. Forensic. Sci. 53 (4), 956–961.

Blau, S., Briggs, C.A., 2011. The role of forensic anthropology in disaster victim identification (DVI). Forensic. Sci. Int. 205, 29–35.

Brondolo, T.J., 2004. Resource requirements for medical examiner response to mass fatality incidents. Medico-Legal J. Ireland 10 (2), 91–102.

Budimlija, Z.M., Prinz, M.K., Zelson-Mundorff, A., Wiersema, J., Bartelink, E., MacKinnon, G., Nazzaruolo, B.L., Estacio, S.M., Hennessey, M.J., Shaler, R.C., 2003. World Trade Center human identification project: Experiences with individual body identification cases. Croat. Med. J. 44 (3), 259–263.

Byard, R.W., Winskog, C., 2010. Potential problems arising during international disaster victim identification (DVI) exercises. Forensic. Sci. Med. Pathol. 6, 1–2.

Byrd, J.E., Adams, B.J., 2003. Osteometric sorting of commingled human remains. J. Forensic. Sci. 48 (4), 717–724.

Egaña, S., Turner, S., Doretti, M., Bernardi, P., Ginarte, A., 2008. Commingled remains and human rights investigations. In: Adams, B., Byrd, J. (Eds.), Recovery, Analysis, and Identification of Commingled Human Remains. Humana Press, Totowa, NJ, pp. 57–79.

Figura, B., 2011. A Bayesian Approach to Disaster Victim Identification. Ph.D. dissertation. Binghamton University, Binghamton, NY.

Gill, J.R., Desire, M., Dickerson, T., Adams, B.J., 2011. The 9/11 attacks: The medicolegal investigation of the World Trade Center fatalities. In: Turk, E.E. (Ed.), Forensic Pathology Reviews, vol. 6.. Humana Press, New York, pp. 181–195.

Holland, M.M., Cave, C.A., Holland, C.A., Bille, T.W., 2003. Development of a quality, high throughput DNA analysis procedure for skeletal samples to assist with the identification of victims from the World Trade Center attacks. Croat. Med. J. (44), 264–272.

Hsu, C.M., Huang, N.E., Tsai, L.C., Kao, L.G., Chao, C.H., Linacre, A., Lee, J.C., 1999. Identification of victims of the 1998 Taoyuan Airbus crash accident using DNA analysis. Int. J. Legal Med. 113 (1), 43–46.

Kahana, T., Hiss, J., 2009. The role of forensic anthropology in mass fatality incidents management. Forensic. Sci. Policy Manag. 1, 144–149.

Kontanis, E.J., Sledzik, P., 2008. Resolving commingling issues during the medicolegal investigation of mass fatality incidents. In: Adams, B., Byrd, J. (Eds.), Recovery, Analysis, and Identification of Commingled Human Remains. Humana Press, Totowa, NJ, pp. 317–336.

Leclair, B., Fregeau, C.J., Bowen, K.L., Fourney, R.M., 2004. Enhanced kinship analysis and STR-based DNA typing for human identification in mass fatality incidents: The Swissair Flight 111 disaster. J. Forensic. Sci. 49 (5), 939–953.

Levinson, J., Granot, H., 2002. Transportation Disaster Response Handbook. Academic Press, San Diego, CA.

MacKinnon, G., Mundorff, A.Z., 2006. World Trade Center—September 11, 2001. In: Thompson, T.J.U., Black, S.M. (Eds.), Forensic Human Identification: An Introduction. CRC Press, Boca Raton, FL, pp. 485–499.

Meyer, H.J., 2003. The Kaprun cable car fire disaster—Aspects of forensic organisation following a mass fatality with 155 victims. Forensic. Sci. Int. 138 (1–3), 1–7.

Mittleman, R.E., Barnhart, J.S., Davis, J.H., Fernandez, R., Hyman, B.A., Lengel, R.D., Lew, E.O., Rao, V.J., 2000. The Crash of ValuJet Flight 592: A Forensic Approach to Severe Body Fragmentation. Miami-Dade County Medical Examiner Department, Miami, FL.

Mundorff, A.Z., Shaler, R.C., Bieschke, E., Mar-Cash, E., 2008. Marrying anthropology and DNA: essential for solving complex commingling problems in cases of extreme fragmentation. In: Adams, B., Byrd, J. (Eds.), Recovery, Analysis, and Identification of Commingled Human Remains. Humana Press, Totowa, NJ, pp. 285–300.

Mundorff, A.Z., 2009. Human Identification Following the World Trade Center Disaster: Assessing Management Practices for Highly Fragmented and Commingled Human Remains. Ph.D. dissertation. Simon Fraser University, British Columbia, Canada.

Mundorff, A.Z., Bartelink, E., Mar-Cash, E., 2009. DNA preservation in skeletal elements from the World Trade Center disaster: Recommendations for mass fatality management. J. Forensic. Sci. 54 (3), 739–745.

Mundorff, A.Z., 2012. Integrating forensic anthropology into disaster victim identification. Forensic. Sci. Med. Pathol. 8, 131–139.

National Transportation Safety Board, 2004. In-Flight Separation of Vertical Stabilizer, American Airlines Flight 587, Airbus Industrie A300-605R, N14053, Belle Harbor, New York, November 12, 2001: Aircraft Accident Report NTSB/AAR-04/04. National Transportation Safety Board, Washington, D.C.

National Transportation Safety Board, 2005. Allision of Staten Island Ferry Andrew J. Barberi, St. George, Staten Island, New York, October 15, 2003: Marine Accident Report NTSB/MAR-05/01. National Transportation Safety Board, Washington, D.C.

The 9/11 Commission Report: Final Report of the National Commission on Terrorist Attacks upon the United States. 2004 Government Printing Office, Washington, D.C.

Olaisen, B., Stenersen, M., Mevag, B., 1997. Identification by DNA analysis of the victims of the August 1996 Spitsbergen civil aircraft disaster. Nat. Genet. 15 (4), 402–405.

Oxford English Dictionary. 1989. Oxford University Press, Oxford, UK.

Park, D., Park, K., Ko, J., Kim, Y., Chung, N., Ahn, Y., Han, S., 2009. The role of forensic anthropology in the examination of the Daegu subway disaster (2003, Korea). J. Forensic. Sci. 54 (3), 513–518.

Rodriguez, W., 2005. Methods and Techniques for Sorting Commingled Remains: Anthropological and Physical Attributes. Paper presented at the American Academy of Forensic Sciences, New Orleans, LA.

Schiffer, M.B., 1987. Formation Processes of the Archaeological Record. University of New Mexico Press, Albuquerque, NM.

Skinner, M., Sterenberg, J., 2005. Turf wars: Authority and responsibility for the investigation of mass graves. Forensic. Sci. Int. 151 (2–3), 221–232.

Sledzik, P.S., Rodriguez, W.C., 2002. Damnum fatale: The taphonomic fate of human remains in mass disasters. In: Haglund, W.D., Sorg, M.H. (Eds.), Advances in Forensic Taphonomy: Method, Theory, and Archaeological Perspectives. CRC Press, Boca Raton, FL, pp. 321–330.

Sledzik, P., Dirkmaat, D., Mann, R., Holland, T., Mundorff, A.Z., Adams, B., Crowder, C., DePaolo, F., 2009. Disaster victim recovery and identification: forensic anthropology in the aftermath of September 11. In: Steadman, D.W. (Ed.), Hard Evidence: Case Studies in Forensic Anthropology. Prentice Hall, Upper Saddle River, NJ, pp. 289–302.

Tuller, H., Hofmeister, U., Daley, S., 2008. Spatial analysis of mass grave mapping data to assist in the reassociation of disarticulated and commingled human remains. In: Adams, B., Byrd, J. (Eds.), Recovery, Analysis, and Identification of Commingled Human Remains. Humana Press, Totowa, NJ, pp. 7–29.

Vidoli, G.M., Mundorff, A.Z., 2012. Victim fragmentation patterns and seat location supplements crash data: American Airlines flight 587. Aviat. Space Environ. Med. 83, 412–417.

Viner, M.D., 2008. The use of radiology in mass fatality events. In: Adams, B., Byrd, J. (Eds.), Recovery, Analysis, and Identification of Commingled Human Remains. Humana Press, Totowa, NJ, pp. 145–183.

Warren, M.W., Eisenberg, L.E., Walsh-Haney, H.A., Saul, J.M., 2003. Anthropology at Fresh Kills: Recovery and Identification of the World Trade Center Victims. In: Proceedings of the American Academy of Forensic Sciences, Chicago, IL, vol. 9, p. 278.

Zehner, R., 2007. "Foreign" DNA in tissue adherent to compact bone from tsunami victims. Forensic. Sci. Int. Genet. 1, 218–222.

CHAPTER 18

Recovery and Identification of Victims of the Colgan Air Flight 3407 Crash

Dawnie Wolfe Steadman[1], Dennis C. Dirkmaat[2], Mark M. LeVaughn[3], Raymond G. Miller[4], Laura A. Regan[5], Dianne Vertes[6]

[1]*Director, Forensic Anthropology Center, Department of Anthropology, University of Tennessee,* [2]*Mercyhurst University,* [3]*Chief Medical Examiner, Mississippi State Medical Examiner's Office, Department of Pathology, University of Mississippi,* [4]*Clinical Associate Professor, Department of Oral Diagnostic Sciences, University at Buffalo School of Dental Medicine,* [5]*Assistant Professor of Biology, HQ USAFA/DFB,* [6]*United Health Services, Wilson Hospital*

Introduction

The commingling of human remains is a common problem in mass fatality incidents (MFIs). The nature of the incident may result in extensive fragmentation and aggregation of bodies in a limited space, such as building collapses or structural fires, or dispersal of body parts across a large area, as in explosions or transportation accidents. Water from fire suppression efforts, human activity during the recovery effort, and rapid decomposition can also lead to commingling of human remains. Mitigation of a mass fatality event must include standard operating procedures (SOPs) designed to (1) systematically locate, document, and recover human remains from the incident site without incurring further alteration or commingling, (2) properly separate commingled remains of two or more individuals during triage, (3) ensure remains do not become (further) commingled during the identification processes, and (4) institute quality control (QC) procedures that systematically review the recovery, intake, identification, and body release processes during the incident to ensure released dissociated remains belong to a single individual. The goal of this chapter is to illustrate how early decisions in recovery and triage can significantly reduce commingling issues in a mass fatality incident by illustrating the forensic response to the Colgan Air Flight 3407 crash.

The Incident

Buffalo, New York, is known for cold winter nights and February 12, 2009, was no exception. Weather conditions included light snow, wind gusts to 22 knots (25 miles per hour), and temperatures approaching 0°F. Snow in the Northeastern United States had delayed flights that evening, and Colgan Air Flight 3407 (operating as Continental Airlines) took off from Newark Liberty Airport in New Jersey at 2118 (9:18 p.m.) after about a 2-hour delay. The aircraft was a

Commingled Human Remains. http://dx.doi.org/10.1016/B978-0-12-405889-7.00018-6

Bombardier de Havilland Canada DHC-8-402 Q400 with two turboprop engines and carried 45 passengers (including one off-duty Colgan Air pilot), two flight attendants, the captain, and first officer. The flight was scheduled for 53 minutes once airborne.

Upon approach to Buffalo–Niagara International Airport, the aircraft began to pitch (nose moving up and down) and roll (significant right-to-left motion) and rapidly lost altitude. The aircraft crashed on top of a house in a residential neighborhood of Clarence Center, New York, at 10:17 p.m., approximately five nautical miles from the airport.

The impact caused the jet fuel to ignite, and the fire was further fueled by a ruptured natural gas line at the home. The shut-off valve to the natural gas line was located under the impacted house, and the gas flowed for nearly 12 hours before termination (Figure 18-1). After the fire was extinguished, it became clear that the crash footprint was relatively small, consisting of a single residence and attached garage. The aircraft impacted the south side of the house with some debris traveling through the house. Two trees on the property had been sliced by the propellers as the plane crashed. Two residents of the home escaped with minor injuries, but a third was killed in the house, bringing the total number of fatalities to 50.

The Initial Response

Following a crash of a commercial airliner in the United States, the three principal agencies responsible for the investigation are the National Transportation and Safety Board (NTSB),

Figure 18-1
Fire suppression efforts at the crash site on February 12, 2009. *(Source: Photo courtesy of the Erie County Medical Examiner's Office.)*

Federal Bureau of Investigation (FBI), and the local coroner/medical examiner office (NTSB 2006). In noncriminal cases, the responsibility of scene management, including victim identification and recovery, falls to the local medicolegal authority. According to the National Institute of Justice (NIJ) Technical Working Group for Mass Fatality Incidents, local medicolegal authorities are "in charge of the documentation, disposition, and certification of all remains as well as morgue operations" (NIJ 2005:15). These directives were familiar to the Erie County Medical Examiner's Office (MEO) at the time of the Colgan Air Flight 3407 accident. Moreover, the MEO had established an SOP for mass fatality events and was able to respond quickly.

Medical Examiner Notification and Initial Actions

The NTSB, FBI, and the MEO in Buffalo were notified of the crash by 10:30 p.m. on the night of the mishap, and the NTSB and FBI immediately dispatched investigative teams to the crash site. The MEO began following disaster protocols and initiated a phone tree whereby all MEO staff were notified and told to report or await further directives. The initial staging site for responders was Clarence Town Hall, where the MEO Chief, Deputy Chief, Administrative Coordinator, and Chief Investigator met with those assembled from Emergency Services and the Department of Health; these same personnel then traveled to the crash site for an initial survey and assessment. The scene presented many challenges including fire, weather, and fragmentation of remains. It was decided that the morgue would be located at the MEO in downtown Buffalo. The infrastructure of the MEO includes an intake room, cooler, two autopsy suites, X-ray room, toxicology and histology laboratories, offices, and conference rooms. The initial intent was to follow the Erie County mass fatality plan, which included a Medical Examiner Response Team (MERT) and Continuity of Operations Plan (COOP). However, it was soon clear that additional resources were required for this incident.

Several resources were immediately contacted: local forensic anthropology and odontology consultants, the Armed Forces DNA Identification Laboratory (AFDIL), and the Specialized Medical Assistance Response Team (SMART). The MEO had pre-existing contracts with anthropologists at the Applied Forensic Sciences Department at Mercyhurst University in Erie, Pennsylvania, as well as a forensic dental consultant from the Buffalo School of Dental Medicine. The anthropologists were asked by the MEO to respond to the scene and assist with the recovery of the remains, and the forensic odontologist responded to the morgue. An AFDIL team was dispatched from Rockville, Maryland, where it was headquartered at that time. One mission of the AFDIL is to perform human identification DNA analyses of all deceased personnel under the jurisdiction of the Armed Forces Medical Examiner, and the laboratory is authorized to assist the NTSB and FBI with the identification of mass fatality victims. The Erie County Department of Health and local medical organizations sponsor the volunteer-led SMART to assist with medical emergencies within the county, including mass disasters. At the time of the incident, many SMART volunteers had previously interned at the MEO, so they easily integrated into the daily activities. In addition, DMORT was contacted by NTSB for activation of the family assistance center (FAC), though no decision had yet been made to activate the entire team.

Disaster Mortuary Operational Response Team (DMORT)

In 1992, the National Funeral Directors Association formalized a system of 10 regional teams that could help local jurisdictions manage mass fatality events. The Disaster Mortuary Operational Response Team (DMORT) organization was soon integrated into the National Disaster Medical System (NDMS) of the U.S. Department of Health and Human Services and became part of the federal task force for addressing emergency preparedness and response. Each DMORT can deploy forensic anthropologists, odontologists, pathologists, radiologists, radiology technicians, fingerprint experts, and funeral directors to provide body recovery and identification expertise as well as assist in the final disposition of the remains. DMORT has three disaster portable morgue units (DPMUs) stored on the east and west coasts that include the infrastructure required to establish and equip a full morgue. The materials are palletized and can ship via truck or airplane within 24 hours. Each regional DMORT also has personnel who operate the family assistance center, providing crucial information from the families to the identification teams (including demographic and medical information of the victims and DNA samples), as well as notifying families when identifications are finalized. DMORT teams have been formally deployed to more than 20 mass fatality incidents since 1993, most recently for the Haiti earthquake in 2010 and the Joplin, Missouri, tornadoes in 2011.

The DPMUs provide each discipline with a unique workspace and all of the equipment they require. For example, the anthropology station includes cleaning tools, reference materials (including age and sex casts), calipers, an osteometric board, and standardized data collection forms. The DPMU layout varies by the space provided but is typically U-shaped, with intake and triage at one end and DNA sampling at the other. The order of the stations in between typically depends on the nature of the incident to optimize workflow (see Steadman et al. 2008 and Sledzik and Willcox 2009). In most cases, the stations include intake, triage, photography, radiology, pathology, anthropology, dental, fingerprint, and DNA. After the remains are catalogued at intake, an escort (often local law enforcement officers or funeral directors) accompanies the remains to every station in the DPMU and then to the mortuary operations officer to be stored until release.

DMORT had been immediately contacted by NTSB for activation of the family assistance center, but the identification team had not been fully activated. As scene safety improved and activities on scene progressed, the decision was made to fully activate DMORT on February 14, and the advance team arrived that day. There were several advantages of activating DMORT in this incident, including providing the office with qualified personnel, portable X-ray units, digital radiography, computer hardware and software, and a dental identification program (WinID) specific to mass disasters. The digital and computer technology would also provide a more efficient workflow and more accessible record-keeping procedures. The DMORT digital radiology system is integrated with WinID, providing an efficient process for analyzing dental data.

The DPMU technicians and MEO Administrative Coordinator worked within the MEO building infrastructure to establish an incident workflow that would avoid congestion in corridors while ensuring that regular daily casework continued unimpeded. These adaptations were implemented, and the entire DMORT team began morgue operations at the MEO at 7:00 a.m. on February 16.

The following sections explain the procedures at the crash site and in the morgue for removing, transporting, storing, processing, and releasing human remains, with special attention given to mitigating commingling.

Recovery and Documentation of Human Remains at Crash Site

The MEO assumed responsibility for the recovery of all human remains on February 13 after the scene was deemed safe for processing. The NIJ Guidelines for Mass Fatality Incidents calls for the careful documentation of all evidence at the scene, including descriptions and diagrams of the spatial relationships of evidence and establishing a chain of custody on site. Thus, despite the scope of the incident, standard scene processing and evidence recovery protocols must be maintained. The MEO understood the capabilities of forensic archaeology with respect to documenting and recovering human remains at the crash site and tasked the Mercyhurst anthropologists with the recovery operation. The pressure to remove victims as quickly as possible with minimal or no documentation of context and provenience (i.e., detailed notation of item location) can lead to critical issues later. Hurried and unorganized recovery methods without regard to context can lead to an incomplete recovery of remains, further fragmentation, commingling, and disassociation of intact body parts in the field. These issues have significant consequences with respect to individual victim identification, duration of the victim identification efforts, subsequent associations of commingled remains, and the magnitude and cost of DNA analytical efforts (Kontanis and Sledzik 2008; Kontanis and Sledzik, this book, Chapter 21). The key goal of the excavation of victims at the Colgan Air crash site was to locate, uncover, document, and remove human remains without introducing further damage or commingling (Dirkmaat et al. 2010). Another goal was to complete these tasks within a reasonable time frame and to ensure no tissue was left behind in the rubble.

Recovery

The first morning assessment of the scene revealed that the crash debris containing human remains was essentially confined to a single residential lot and one house (Figure 18-2). The debris field consisted of a roughly linear mound of burned aircraft and house debris, approximately 4 feet in depth, encased in a relatively thick layer of ice as a result of the fire suppression efforts. Inside the debris field, the condition of the victims ranged from relatively intact and unburned to significantly burned and cremated.

The first step in the recovery involved the thorough search of houses and yards of the surrounding neighborhood block for crash debris. No human remains were recovered in this operation. Next, the street in front of the house was searched via a transect pedestrian search.

Figure 18-2
Daylight view of the crash site showing a portion of the debris field. *(Source: Photo courtesy of the Erie County Medical Examiner's Office.)*

A portion of a human limb was found adjacent to the street. A total station, operated through a joint effort with the New York State Police and the FBI, was used to document the provenience of this item and all other human remains throughout the recovery operation. In addition, all remains were photographed *in situ*.

After the periphery was cleared, the recovery operation focused on the debris field situated within the residential lot. The roughly linear mound of debris represented the remnants of the fuselage containing human remains, aircraft parts, and personal effects. A team of Mercyhurst University forensic anthropology faculty and students and FBI Evidence Response Team members began the excavation at the front of the plane (Figure 18-3). Simultaneously, firefighters began removing crash debris that did not contain human remains from the rear of the debris field at the back of the property.

Human remains were located within the crash debris field by clearing debris from the outer edge of the pile and working inward and toward the back of the aircraft. The larger pieces of aircraft or house debris were taken to large dumpsters on site for later analysis by the NTSB and/or FBI. Personal effects directly associated with the victims, such as clothing and jewelry, were left in place on the body. Unassociated personal effects were removed by excavators and released to law enforcement. Any remaining smaller burned matrix and ash were hand-screened on site by forensic anthropologists in ¼-inch mesh sifting screens to ensure small bone fragments were recovered.

When human remains were encountered *in situ*, debris was removed from above and around the remains until the entire body or body part was no longer entrapped in the debris pile.

Figure 18-3
Systematic excavation of the crash scene. *(Source: Photo courtesy of the Erie County Medical Examiner's Office.)*

Pulling and tugging to extract the limb or body part would result in unnecessary fragmentation. The remains were photographed, and the provenience was obtained by a total station before the remains were placed in body bags and removed from the site.

All discrete tissue found in the rubble received distinct field specimen numbers. In cases in which the cranial remains of a single individual were fragmented but still conjoined, heavy-duty plastic kitchen wrap was used to secure fragments. Damaged and fragmented hands were also wrapped in this manner. Without this procedure, fragments that separated in the body bag during transport to the morgue would be considered as separate morgue items, requiring individual numbers, analyses, and DNA samples, as discussed later (see also Kontanis and Sledzik 2008).

A different recovery strategy was required for the burned and cremated osseous remains found in the vicinity of the ruptured gas line that burned for nearly 12 hours. In this area of the debris field, all of the burned material (ash and cremated human remains) was removed *en masse* from the debris field and placed in containers. The provenience of the container contents was documented to identify the site recovery location. The containers were taken to the morgue where human odontogenic or osseous material could be removed by hand under better lighting conditions.

Because of the frigid weather, the first few days of the excavation required the debris field to be thawed first thing in the morning via portable heaters. Thereafter, tarps and conduits leading from heaters were used to keep the field thawed through the night. Excavations progressed rapidly and efficiently after the first day. The forensic archaeological team worked from the front to the back of the plane until they reached the back of the property in the house basement on the fifth day. Though the work days were relatively short due to extremely cold temperatures and limited daylight hours, the site was fully excavated, victims' remains carefully located, exposed, and removed, and all debris examined, screened, and removed in under 30 working hours. Further, the comprehensive forensic archaeological excavation of the scene resulted in the retrieval of nearly all recoverable human tissue.

Human remains identified by a temporary case number and total station provenience point were placed in body bags and carried to a staging area at the crash site. Each bag was logged and released by MEO staff to removal service personnel on contract with the MEO. A chain of custody log was completed for each trip between the crash site and the morgue. The New York State Police provided security escorts en route to the MEO.

Morgue Operations

The overall morgue flow system was organized and ran smoothly due to the well-trained DMORT personnel and good interagency communication. Daily DMORT briefings with different agencies were held to discuss progress, problems, and concerns. The goals were to register and process all human remains recovered from the field, document all incident-related injuries, and use as many scientific procedures as available to identify each individual.

Intake Procedures

The Erie County Medical Examiner's Office began examination of the human remains recovered from the aircraft crash site on February 14, 2009, prior to activation of DMORT. No triage was initially set up in the morgue. The MEO had implemented a numbering system whereby remains were given a human remains (HR) number at the crash site and a mass fatality (MF) number was assigned to each body bag transported to the morgue. Unfortunately, the remains of multiple individuals were found within some body bags. Seven MF numbers were examined by the MEO before DMORT support was requested. Morgue examinations were then temporarily suspended until DMORT was operational. In addition, a forensic anthropologist who had extensive experience with cases involving a high degree of fragmentation was brought in from the Armed Forces Medical Examiner System. This anthropologist served as the triage leader in the morgue.

When DMORT operations commenced on February 16, morgue accessioning procedures were modified to improve clarity and decrease potential for commingling. Because identification measures had already occurred with the first seven MF cases, this numbering system was maintained. As of February 16, 2009, however, it was repurposed to reflect only the number of "bodies" represented by the remains. The designation of a "body" was made to all remains that contained a majority of the spinal column. A separate body fragment, or "dissociated portion" (DP) number, was assigned to all human remains not associated via a tissue bridge to a "body." Such a numbering system gave any observer an easy way to account for how many bodies versus body fragments had been accessioned and allowed the MF number to serve as the primary case number, with subsequent DP numbers associated back to the MF number based on various positive identification modalities. This numbering system was appropriate for this MFI, but other case numbering schemes could be useful in other incidents, especially when fragmentation is more extreme, as in the World Trade Center (Mundorff 2009, this book, Chapter 17; Brondolo 2004), or when more complete bodies are recovered, as in the Tri-State Crematorium (Steadman et al. 2008).

All provenience information was maintained upon accessioning remains into the morgue. Photographs were taken of the body bags and their contents prior to examination or accessioning. The contents of each body bag were variable and might have contained a body, a body and dissociated portions, or just dissociated portions. While dissociated portions may have been transported to the morgue with a body, due to the nature of the incident and high potential for commingling, it could not be assumed that the body portion actually belonged to the body. As such, all remains not attached via a tissue bridge were removed from the body bag and given a separate DP number. Documentation was maintained as to field provenience if a dissociated portion was pulled from an MF case.

Due to the prolonged post-crash fire, many of the remains demonstrated advanced thermal damage, including calcination. A group of forensic anthropology graduate students from The State University of New York, University at Buffalo, assisted in the triage of calcined remains by sifting through material at triage to segregate dental material and remove any nonhuman/nonosseous materials. To facilitate downstream analyses, all dental and friction ridge material were identified on the outside of the remains bag/container. For instance, if remains were calcined, the fingerprint station did not need to open the container and examine the contents for friction ridge material, including fingerprints. This allowed cases to bypass these particular stations, which expedited processing and reduced the risk of DNA contamination by minimizing the amount of handling of remains.

Aggregates of unidentifiable remains, such as containers of many small, fragmented, calcined remains, were accessioned under one DP number. All materials that entered the morgue were catalogued for accountability purposes, even if they were not human. For instance, the charred remains of a cat that was thought to belong to the home owners of the impacted home were accessioned into the morgue. A total of 43 "bodies" and 432 dissociated portions were accessioned into the morgue from this event. SMART volunteers and MEO staff fulfilled DMORT's tracking protocol, working with DMORT to coordinate the movement of the remains through the various workstations.

Radiology

After remains were separated, photographed, and provided a case number in intake, the body bag/container was taken by an escort to the radiology station established in the MEO radiology room. Radiographs of each third of the unopened body bag were taken to document the location of any sharp or dangerous objects missed during triage and understand the orientation of the remains. This also allowed the forensic anthropologist to determine if more than one individual was present by examining the X-rays for redundant body parts (e.g., two left tibiae). Loose teeth could also be observed and recovered for the odontologists.

Fingerprints

Fingerprinting was accomplished by FBI investigators using standard techniques for fresh and decomposed remains. Fingerprint identification relied on comparisons of any available portion of the hands (fingers) and fingerprint records. These records can be obtained from government agencies if a victim has been fingerprinted for an employment position (e.g., federal position, law enforcement, teacher) or criminal proceedings.

Pathology

As per protocol in any commercial air carrier crash under the jurisdiction of the NTSB, the captain/pilot and first officer/copilot received complete autopsies, with the available fluid and whole tissue specimens recovered and sent to the Federal Aviation Administration (FAA) Civil Aerospace Medical Institute (CAMI) for toxicological evaluation. Otherwise, all human remains (HR) and dissociated portions (DP) were evaluated at the pathology stations located in the MEO main autopsy room. The pathologists also provided another evaluation of whether commingling of soft tissue had occurred. If commingling was found, the dissociated portion was returned to intake for renumbering.

The earliest remains recovered from the scene were the most complete and therefore most likely to be identified. Some of the major categories evaluated by pathology for narrowing down the identities of victims include sex, estimated age, estimated race, height and weight estimates, scars, marks, piercings, and tattoos. Orthopedic hardware and medical devices, such as pacemakers, aided in the identification of three of the victims of Flight 3407. Because there was extensive fragmentation and incineration of the passengers in this case, no visual identifications were possible, and the gross description of injuries became somewhat redundant. It was important to document the degree of injury and incineration as it related to the flight manifest, the intensity and duration of the fire, and other aspects of the crash site. Documenting (and photographing) clothing and personal effects is critical in the identification of any unknown person. Care was taken to remove all items from pockets, wallets, etc., and to describe clothes in detail, including information inscribed on labels.

Certain categories of information collected at the pathology station were less helpful toward achieving the goals of identification, injury documentation, or cause and manner of death determination. Lividity and rigidity, for example, though documented in every standard autopsy, achieved little toward any of these ends. Given the finite (though numerous) dead, details regarding head and facial hair (color, length, description), eyes (color, condition, visual aids), and finger and toenails (type, length, condition) added only time to the documentation process and contributed little toward achieving the ultimate goal of identification.

Anthropology

The anthropology station was located in the same autopsy suite as fingerprints and pathology. The anthropologists first viewed the radiographs of a case to confirm that only one set of remains was present, to help identify the body portion, evaluate whether any foreign objects were present, and assess the presence of any antemortem skeletal pathology, such as healed fractures, that could be useful for identification.

The next task of the anthropologists was to provide a formal inventory of the remains present and estimate age, sex, stature, and ancestry whenever possible. Given the availability of DNA and radiographs, significant time was not spent manually removing or dissecting soft tissue to reveal age or sex indicators. For instance, the anthropologists could discern the remains of a juvenile victim by the unfused epiphyses on the radiographs such that dissection of the epiphyses was unnecessary. In some cases, age estimations could be produced on bodies that underwent thermal alterations such that the pubic symphyses, ribs, and/or skull were exposed. The anthropologists also recognized nonmetallic prosthetics, such as plastic artificial patellae, that could be re-associated with knee replacement hardware that was given a different DP number.

One major role of the anthropologists was to take DNA samples in consultation with the AFDIL personnel stationed in the morgue. New, sterile scalpels and forceps were utilized to take deep red muscle samples, when available, because this tissue is rich in DNA. When muscle was unavailable, AFDIL then asked the anthropologist to take bone samples. In most cases, a rib was procured or a window of bone was cut from a long bone using an autopsy saw. In some cases, a whole bone was sampled (e.g., a phalanx).

Odontology

The goal of the dental analysis was to recognize displaced dental structures, maintain association whenever possible, and confirm potential commingling through structure inventory and recognition. Dental operations required an area for dental autopsy and radiology, record intake and storage, and a dental information technology center for data entry and comparisons. In consideration of the flow, the concept of "clean" and "contaminated" functions and sections needed to be determined. For the dental area, postmortem (PM) operations, such as dental autopsy and radiology, were considered contaminated and required appropriate personal protective equipment (PPE) and isolation. Antemortem (AM) dental record intake and data input was considered "clean," and no contaminated personnel, records, or PPE were allowed to cross an established barrier (Figure 18-4). Comparisons could be made in either section via a computer as AM and PM data were entered into the comprehensive dental

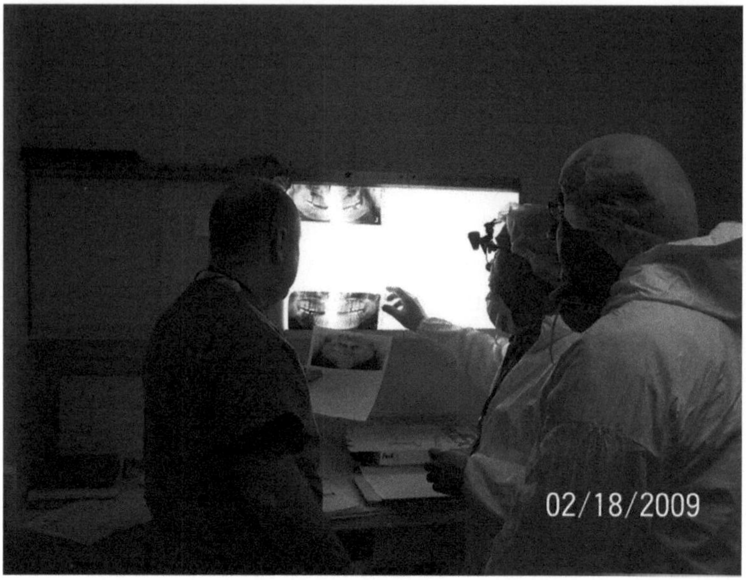

Figure 18-4
Part of the dental station at the MEO during morgue operations. *(Source: Photo courtesy of the Erie County Medical Examiner's Office.)*

identification program, WinID. Any established dental identification was approved by the dental section chief before being presented to the medical examiner for final confirmation.

Dental usually received specimens after they had been processed through the other stations. Radiography, specifically of the cranial, chest, and abdominal regions, was of significant value for the odontology section. The impact trauma to the victims caused occasional displacement of identifiable dental structures. Although primarily displaced into the head and neck region, dental structures can be found in the chest cavity and abdominal regions, even in an otherwise intact victim. When a dental structure was physically and anatomically displaced, there were no assumptions as to its source, and the specimen was designated as a dissociated portion.

Although fragmentation and disassociation of dental structures were common, commingling was not a significant issue with the victims presented to the dental section. This was verified by head, neck, and upper body radiography. The quality forensic archeological recovery at the scene was responsible for limiting commingling. Intact bodies were protected by wrapping of the head to prevent loss of associated but damaged dental structures. Fifty-two percent of those examined had a complete maxilla and mandible, and 64% had at least one complete dental arch.

The forensic dental autopsy included a complete set of postmortem radiographs and a comprehensive clinical exam that charted and documented the victim's dental profile. Based on the condition of the victim, resection (extraction) of the maxilla and/or mandible was sometimes required to adequately radiograph and visibly examine the dental structures. The

Table 18-1: DNA Sampling Scheme for Colgan Air Flight 3407

Phase	Receipt Date	Soft Tissue	Bone	Teeth	Hair	Total Samples
1	Feb. 17 & Feb. 23, 2009	42	90	0	0	132
2	Mar. 9, 2009	15	40	0	0	55
3	Apr. 1, 2009	6	7	1	0	14
4	Apr. 16, 2009	0	5	8	4	17
	Total	63	142	9	4	218

condition of the victims ranged from complete, intact bodies to small, segmented, maxillofacial structures. Isolated teeth and dental prostheses were also recovered.

As the recovery of the victims was nearing conclusion, many disassociated dental structures were excavated, and these were independently bagged and assigned DP numbers. There were 46 individual oral maxillofacial structures that were sent to the dental section for evaluation. Eighteen of these segments or structures were reassociated with victims. These were reassociated with 10 individuals, meaning several of the 18 DPs belonged to the same person.

DNA

Four AFDIL personnel were deployed to support the Erie County Medical Examiner's Office. One AFDIL responder was assigned to the family assistance center (FAC) to assist in collecting direct and familial DNA reference samples, answering family questions pertaining to the DNA identification process, and providing technical expertise to DMORT personnel who were conducting antemortem interviews. This initial collection effort resulted in the acquisition of buccal swabs from the families of 32 victims as well as personal effects (e.g., toothbrush) of four victims. Two of the victims had been in the military and had bloodstain cards on file with the Armed Forces Repository of Specimen Samples for the Identification of Remains (AFRSSIR). The AFRSSIR cards were made available to AFDIL as a known reference source for those two individuals. If known DNA references were unavailable for a decedent and the victim was identified by another modality, then a postmortem DNA sample was produced from the identified remains and served as the "self" reference standard for subsequent DNA identification efforts.

The other three AFDIL personnel were stationed in the morgue to answer questions by the other experts and guide the anthropologist in DNA sample selection. AFDIL personnel labeled, packaged, and transported the samples to the laboratory in Rockville, Maryland. There were a total of four phases of DNA testing. The samples collected during Phase 1 had the greatest potential of yielding positive results. Excessive burning is one of the primary factors negatively affecting a tissue's suitability for DNA testing as well as all other means of possible identification. In Phases 2–4, taking place from March 6 through April 14, *all* tissues

Table 18-2: Modalities Contributing to 49 Identifications. Some Individuals were Identified by Multiple Modalities

Modality	Number of Identifications
Dental	38
DNA	47
Fingerprint	12
Prostheses	3
Visual	0

were re-examined regarding their suitability for DNA testing (Table 18-1). As might be expected, through each phase, the yield of potential tissue and positive results diminished. DNA representation was never found for three individuals, although two were eventually identified via antemortem/postmortem dental comparison.

A total of 218 postmortem DNA samples were analyzed by AFDIL (Table 18-1). Full nuclear short tandem repeat (STR) profiles were obtained from 193 samples, and partial profiles were obtained from four samples. Forty-seven unique STR profiles were obtained for the decedents involved in this incident.

Identification Process

The medicolegal investigative process employed dental comparisons, fingerprinting, other unique identifying characteristics, such as prosthetics, and four separate phases of DNA testing to successfully identify the victims. Some of the victims were significantly heat-altered due to the prolonged fire affecting one area of the plane, so the recovery of small bone and tooth fragments in the field was important for identification. In one case, an isolated mandibular segment with two molar roots was examined and radiographed. Root canal filling materials were found and analyzed through microscopy, X-ray fluorescence, and scanning electron microscopy/energy dispersive spectrography (SEM/EDS). The filling material was traced to a well-documented antemortem record allowing for identification of this segment to a victim. This segment was the only structure to be identified of this individual. Without careful field recovery techniques and proper intake separation, this 7 × 3 cm mandibular segment could have been commingled with another individual, and the victim would not have been identified.

Table 18-2 illustrates the number of personal identifications provided by each modality. In some cases, a decedent was identified by multiple modalities. One person on the flight manifest could not be identified by any modality. It was suspected that the body of this individual was in the area of the ruptured gas line fire that burned for many hours. To test this hypothesis, examiners compared the list of seat assignments drawn from the plane's passenger manifest to the total station-generated map of the spatial distribution of the identified victim remains at the crash site.

Assuming none of the passengers changed seats during the flight, the missing victim's assigned seat was located in the middle of the burned area containing all of the cremated remains. The provenience data collected for every piece of human tissue, in combination with the careful recovery of the victims, screening efforts, removal of all debris from the site, and the multiple DNA submissions allowed the Medical Examiner's office to present to the family of the unrecovered victim a reasonable, scientific explanation for not finding any identifiable biological tissue of that individual (Dirkmaat 2012).

Early in the recovery process, the family members were informed by the MEO that it was unlikely all of the remains would be identified so as to avoid any unrealistic expectations regarding the extent to which their loved one's remains were whole and complete. Following all attempts to identify and reassociate fragmented human remains, the MEO decided to discontinue further efforts, and the remaining unidentifiable tissues were designated as "common remains." Further, in deference to the different customs and religious beliefs of surviving families, all common remains were entombed above ground. There was also a separate casket entombed above ground that contained many identified but unclaimed remains. These were reviewed for confirmation of identity, individually packaged, labeled, inventoried, and placed in a casket. An inventory map as to their location in the casket was generated and filed in the MEO in anticipation that someone at a later date may want to claim the remains.

Quality Control Prior to Release

It is a best practice to ensure redundant protocols are in place to mitigate and prevent commingling of human remains during a mass fatality incident. One last check involved a quality control procedure that reviewed the morgue procedures pertaining to each case (e.g., ensuring the remains were examined at all relevant stations), the documentation of inventory and injuries, and the scientific merit of the identification. Further, a forensic anthropologist and pathologist reviewed each set of human remains prior to their release to a family to ensure only identified portions were released.

While an anthropologist stayed a few additional days to assist with the quality control reviews, the DMORT operation ended on February 24, 12 days after the crash. This brief response time reflects the nature of the incident as well as efficient processing of the scene and human remains in the laboratory.

Findings of the NTSB Investigation

The NTSB deployed investigators to search for evidence concerning the cause of the crash. They successfully located the cockpit voice recorder and flight data recorders, which were intact. A special commission of the NTSB examined these recorders, reports of wreckage analysis, medical examiner reports on the captain and first officer, aircraft performance and maintenance reports, pilot training records, Colgan Air policies, and witness statements to compile a final report on its findings in 2010 (NTSB 2010). While significant ice on the aircraft's wings was an early theory regarding the probable cause of the crash, the NTSB found little evidence to suggest this was the primary contributor. The report cited multiple pilot failures in responding to a stall warning (stick shaker). Contributory factors included insufficient pilot training, pilot fatigue, and inadequate Colgan Air procedures for airspeed management.

Retrospective on Incident Response

Disasters will always bring out the best and worst of municipalities, teams, and responders. A jurisdiction's response plan and its teams will be tested. Weaknesses and strengths will be exposed, and lessons will be learned. These lessons may never benefit that jurisdiction again because mass fatality incidents are relatively rare, but they will be useful to others as they plan their response to the next mass fatality incident.

Mass fatality incidents involving a high degree of fragmentation cannot be approached in a similar fashion to routine medical examiner casework. The goals of the incident response and accessioning nomenclature should be decided on before remains recovery begins. Triage in these types of incidents is critical for minimizing commingling, yet is sometimes overlooked. Assigning a forensic anthropologist to morgue intake operations improved fragment identification and administrative processing of evidence. Moreover, the role of proper victim recovery methods at large-scale scenes such as a plane crash should not be overlooked. Search and recovery operations that focus on locating and removing bodies or body parts from the scene as quickly as possible run the risk of leaving remains behind in the rubble. In addition, disassociation and commingling of tissues are significantly enhanced. In the particular instance of Flight 3407, the systematic and thorough forensic archaeological recovery (and screening efforts) led to the recovery of nearly all tissues, the removal of all crash debris from the site, and the documented provenience of every portion of human tissue, large or small. These provenience data proved to be critical in the final determination of where one unidentified individual was likely located when the plane crashed and that the victim's DNA was destroyed in the ensuing gas pipeline fire.

Assigning an AFDIL responder to the FAC greatly facilitated the collection of family references and provided a technical expert to answer DMORT staff questions. AFDIL personnel involved in the early specimen collection process ensured high-quality evidence for DNA examination. Although no active military personnel were on board the Colgan Air flight, two individuals were identified by DNA comparison with pre-existing blood reference cards. DNA reference collection for identification of remains of service members began in 1992, and blood reference cards are stored for 50 years. At the time of printing, 6.7 million DNA reference cards were on file with AFRSSIR for current and former service members. Thus, the AFRSSIR is an important potential source of DNA references even when mass fatalities incidents involve civilians.

From a medical examiner perspective, the incident necessitated updates to the Erie County MEO mass fatality plan. For instance, the plan now includes a designated family assistance liaison from the MEO. For the sake of continuity, the victim's families should communicate with only one representative from the MEO. The bond between this designee and families is critical to establishing the trust necessary to ensure that families know that every attempt is being made to identify their loved ones, issue death certificates, and release their remains for burial. Changes were also made to the Medical Examiner Response Team (MERT) office division. Given the limited number of permanent staff, a more realistic plan was developed to assure that all aspects of scene recovery and morgue operations proceed smoothly and efficiently. Finally, the MEO added phases in the mass fatality plan to encompass additional stages of DNA reassociations. The quality control procedures were efficient and thorough and benefited from the teamwork of anthropology and pathology.

The questions regarding the mission goals need to be established at the outset so as to understand the process moving forward. Defining these goals will determine the response approach and minimize confusion. Most mass fatality incidents consider victim recovery, identification, and reassociation as primary to the mission. However, questions concerning to what extremes the recoveries, identifications, and reassociations will be taken are often difficult to answer. Should every possible specimen be tested for DNA identification? Should all attempts to identify dissociated parts and reassociate remains cease when at least one part of every victim has been identified? There is no definitive right or wrong answer, but there must be established goals as the process moves forward. Factors such as recovery team safety, condition of the remains, trauma, and even cost will be considered in the decision. Families and next of kin will also influence team decisions. The reasons for the decisions need to be clearly, logically, and truthfully presented to the families of the victims. Their input and their understanding that the recovery and identification rate of the remains will likely be less than 100% are integral. The success of the operation can be measured internally by the results and statistics of the recovery and identification process. There is, however, an external evaluation process. This is based on the perception of the victims' families that a reasonable effort was made to ensure a full accounting and that the final disposition of the remains was respectful and appropriate.

References

Brondolo, T.J., 2004. Resource requirements for medical examiner response to mass fatality incidents. Medico-Legal J. Ireland 10.2 (2), 91–102.

Dirkmaat, D.C., 2012. Forensic anthropology at the mass fatality incident (commercial airliner) crash site. In: Dirkmaat, D.C. (Ed.), A Companion to Forensic Anthropology. Wiley-Blackwell, West Sussex, UK, pp. 136–156.

Dirkmaat, D.C., Symes, S.A., Cabo, L.L., 2010. Forensic archaeological recovery of the victims of the Continental Connection Flight 3407 in Clarence Center, NY. [Abstract]. Proc. Am. Acad. Forensic. Sci. 16, 387.

Kontanis, E.J., Sledzik, P.S., 2008. Resolving commingling issues during the medicolegal investigation of mass fatality incidents. In: Adams, B.J., Byrd, J. (Eds.), Recovery, Analysis and Identification of Commingled Human Remains. Humana Press, Totawa, NJ, pp. 317–336.

Mundorff, A.Z., 2009. Human Identification Following the World Trade Center Disaster: Assessing Management Practices for Highly Fragmented and Commingled Human Remains. Ph.D. dissertation, pp. 106–107. Simon Fraser University, British Columbia, Canada.

National Institute of Justice, 2005. Mass Fatality Incidents: A Guide for Human Forensic Identification. NIJ Technical Working Group for Mass Fatality Forensic Identification, United States Department of Justice, Office of Justice Programs, Washington, D.C.

National Transportation Safety Board, 2006. Standard Operating Procedures for National Transportation Safety Board Activations. Disaster Mortuary Operational Response Team. Publication Reference NTSB/DMORT SOP.

National Transportation Safety Board, 2010. Aircraft Accident Report. Loss of Control on Approach. Colgan Air, Inc. Operating as Continental Connection Flight 3407 Bombardier DHC-8–400, N200WQ. Clarence Center, NY. February 12, 2009.

Sledzik, P.S., Willcox, A.W., 2009. Corpi aquaticus: The Hardin Cemetery flood of 1993. In: Steadman, D.W. (Ed.), Hard Evidence: Case Studies in Forensic Anthropology, second ed. Prentice Hall, Upper Saddle River, NJ, pp. 280–288.

Steadman, D.W., Sperry, K., Snow, F., Fulginiti, L., Craig, E., 2008. Forensic anthropological investigations of the Tri-State Crematorium incident. In: Adams, B.J., Byrd, J. (Eds.), Recovery, Analysis and Identification of Commingled Human Remains. Humana Press, Totawa, NJ, pp. 81–96.

CHAPTER 19

The Korea 208: A Large-Scale Commingling Case of American Remains from the Korean War

Jennie Jin, Ashley L. Burch, Carrie LeGarde, Elizabeth Okrutny
Joint POW/MIA Accounting Command Central Identification Laboratory (JPAC-CIL), Joint Base Pearl Harbor-Hickam, Hawaii

Introduction: JPAC and the CIL

The mission of the Joint POW/MIA Accounting Command (JPAC) is to conduct global search, recovery, and laboratory operations to identify unaccounted-for Americans from past conflicts in order to support the Department of Defense's personnel accounting efforts. These long-standing efforts by the government date back over 100 years, with the United States being the first country to enact such policy (Sledge 2005). The current command (JPAC), activated in 2003, is located on Joint Base Pearl Harbor–Hickam in Hawaii with three permanent overseas detachments in Thailand, Vietnam, and Laos.

JPAC recovery teams, led by a forensic anthropologist and a military team leader, deploy around the world in a search for the remains of more than 83,000 unaccounted-for U.S. service members lost between World War II through more recent conflicts. When recovery efforts at a site are complete, the JPAC teams return to Hawaii, where the remains and pertinent material evidence (e.g., dog tags, life support equipment, and personal items) are taken to the JPAC Central Identification Laboratory (CIL) for analysis. The CIL is the largest forensic skeletal identification laboratory in the world and currently has about 50 staff members including forensic anthropologists, odontologists, and war historians.

Currently, JPAC focuses mainly on World War II, the Korean War, and the Vietnam War. Of these major conflicts, the Korean War generates about half or more of JPAC's identifications each year. There are multiple ways JPAC gets access to the unaccounted-for American remains from the Korean War, such as exhumations of the Korean War unknown remains from the National Memorial Cemetery of the Pacific or recovery missions in North Korea. In this chapter, we focus on a large-scale commingled assemblage of missing Americans from the Korean War called "the Korea 208" (K208) that the United States government received from the North Korean government in the

Commingled Human Remains. http://dx.doi.org/10.1016/B978-0-12-405889-7.00019-8

early 1990s. The goal of this chapter is to present the analytical procedure of the K208 assemblage that originally contained as many as 600 commingled individuals.

Background: The Korean War and K208

The Korean War

The Korean War began on June 25, 1950, when the North Korean People's Army crossed the boundary of the 38th parallel and invaded the U.S.-allied Republic of Korea (ROK, or South Korea) to the south. U.S. troops entered the war in July 1950 as part of the United Nations (UN) forces fighting against the perceived threat of a global communist regime. Initially focused on the defensive goal of pushing communist forces out of South Korea, the war did not go well for the United States. The North Korean army overran ROK-UN positions within a month, pushing the ROK-UN forces down to the southeast corner of the Korean peninsula. However, a successful surprise counterattack by the U.S. Marines in September 1950 allowed ROK-UN forces to push the North Korean army back across the 38th parallel toward the Yalu River (also called the Amrok River in Korean), which serves as the North Korean–Chinese border.

Although the People's Republic of China warned they would intervene if the ROK-UN forces pushed too far north along to the Chinese border, the forces kept moving north under the wrong assumption that involvement by the Chinese was unlikely. Oblivious to the magnitude of Chinese involvement, ROK-UN troops were unexpectedly assaulted by hundreds of thousands of Chinese troops, resulting in two of the largest battles of the war (i.e., the Battle of Unsan and the Battle of Chosin Reservoir[1]), enormous casualties, and retreat back south of the 38th parallel. Peace talks began in the summer of 1951 as the fighting continued around the 38th parallel. Negotiations over the terms of the ceasefire continued for more than two additional years until the armistice was signed on July 27, 1953. This agreement designated a new boundary near the 38th parallel and created a 2-mile-wide demilitarized zone (DMZ) that still exists today. In the three years of the Korean War, approximately 36,500 American service members were killed. Of those, approximately 7,900 are still Missing In Action as of June 2013 (Defense Prisoner of War Missing Personnel Office statistics).

K208

One of the largest ongoing projects at the CIL is the K208 project. The K208 assemblage refers to the 208 boxes the Democratic People's Republic of Korea (DPRK, or North Korea) repatriated to the United Nations Command (UNC) in the early 1990s and subsequently turned over to the CIL for analysis and identification. As of December 2013, a total of 101 U.S. service members have been identified from the K208 project.

---

[1] "Chosin Reservoir" is a Japanese name for what Koreans refer to as the "Jangjin Reservoir." Today the reservoir is almost exclusively known as the "Jangjin Reservoir" in Korea. However, the name "Chosin" is used throughout this chapter because it is the name the U.S. military used during the Korean War.

The North Koreans claimed that each box represented a single U.S. service member lost during the Korean War. Despite the claim, it soon became obvious that most boxes contained more than one individual. The project now involves the task of analyzing a large commingled skeletal assemblage that contains the remains of hundreds of U.S. military personnel, along with ROK and possibly other UNC soldiers. The minimum number of individuals represented in the 208 boxes is currently estimated to be around 600.

The North Koreans provided a purported recovery location for each box, such as the name of the village where the remains were supposedly excavated. Most of the boxes (188 boxes) came from one of the following four regions: (1) Suan (97 boxes), the location of POW camps of the war in a region north of the DMZ; (2) East Chosin (48 boxes), the site of devastating U.S. losses during withdrawal from the area (Battle of Chosin Reservoir); (3) Unsan (23 boxes), the site of devastating U.S. losses from multiple heavy attacks by the enemy forces; and (4) Pyoktong[2] (20 boxes), the site associated with the POW Camp 5. The other 20 boxes were recovered near villages along the DMZ or along the coasts of North Korea (Figure 19-1).

At the time the CIL received the remains, there were few systematic anthropological methods to solve the commingling issue. One of the few publications on the topic was Snow (1948), which had been written after the author spent a year sorting commingled remains in the U.S. Army mortuary in Hawaii. It was not until the early 2000s when DNA testing became a more viable tool (in both the scientific and monetary sense) that K208 started to produce more identifications. Anthropologists at the CIL were able to begin using DNA comparison methods, primarily using mitochondrial DNA (mtDNA) coupled with anthropological analyses to segregate discrete individuals from the larger K208 assemblage for identification. It was during the early 2000s that the majority of the skeletal elements in the K208 were sampled for mtDNA testing.

Also, it is important to note that the increase of the number of family reference samples (FRSs) from the Korean War was crucial to making more identifications. Even if a bone yields a DNA sequence, it is less useful for identification if there are no DNA sequences from families for comparison. In 1999, only 15% of the Korean War FRSs were on file. The number has significantly increased in the past decade, and 89% of the FRSs (13,988 FRSs for 7,027 service members) are now on file for the Korean War missing.

A separate CIL laboratory space was renovated for use by the K208 project in 2008. In 2011, the K208 project team was formed to analyze the K208 assemblage in a more systematic and scientific manner. Case resolution and identifications have increased drastically with the combination of increased DNA testing/FRSs and the dedicated team. Although 61 individuals were identified between 1992 and 2011, 40 identifications were made between 2012 and 2013.

[2] There are various ways to spell Korean site names in English. Here we followed the spelling most commonly used by the U.S. military during the Korean War.

Figure 19-1
The purported origins of the K208 boxes. The numbers in parentheses represent the number of boxes from the area.

Adding to K208: Joint Recovery Operations

Between 1996 and 2005, JPAC took part in Joint Recovery Operations (JROs) with the DPRK in two main regions: Unsan/Kujang and East Chosin. During these recoveries, DPRK officials would accompany a JPAC recovery team to potential sites. Although the DPRK officials claimed that the sites were located based on witness testimony, it soon became evident that many of these sites were being staged by the North Koreans. JPAC anthropologists noticed that the sites were not undisturbed since the war, as the North Koreans claimed, but rather the remains had been recently buried after prior curation and storage (Pokines et al., 2002). The following statement from a CIL Search and Recovery Report written in 2000 summarizes the JRO excavation:

> *This site has multiple indications of major recent invasive disturbance, and some or all of the items in it were moved to this site from a different location. All evidence indicates that this site is a complete forgery, although it is likely composed of human remains and artifacts from the Korean conflict era. Any evidence obtained from this excavation for identification of the remains of unrecovered U.S. personnel should be treated with extreme suspicion.*

Both K208 and JRO elements have been extensively sampled for DNA testing, and interesting patterns started to emerge. The most notable pattern is the crossover of the elements between K208 and JRO accessions, i.e., the remains from a single individual were found both in K208 and JRO boxes. This issue has complicated the sorting of the commingled remains even further, because the remains from a specific K208 village could potentially go with remains from any of the JROs, even if the JRO recovery was in a geographically distant region from the purported origin of the K208 box. For example, most of the skeletal remains found during the JROs conducted in Kujang County (western North Korea) belonged to the individuals from Kaljon-ni (eastern North Korea) in K208. Interestingly, the individual's last known location almost always corresponded with the recovery location provided for the K208 boxes and not with the JROs. These patterns were clear evidence that the North Koreans did not repatriate all of the remains as part of K208, and planted the rest of the remains to different excavation sites later.

Due to the extensive commingling of K208 and JRO remains, K208 analysts needed to incorporate both assemblages during the anthropological and DNA analyses. This obviously increased the number of skeletal elements even more than what was initially present in the 208 boxes.

K208 Analysis: Segregation, Consolidation, and Identification

Segregation Analyses: How Bones are Segregated into Discrete Individuals

For a forensic laboratory dealing with highly commingled remains, it is crucial to ensure scientific accuracy and integrity without losing efficiency. In order to achieve this goal, K208 analysts created a standard operating procedure (SOP) for analyzing K208 remains and documenting casework. The SOP was developed in such a way that it can be applied to other large, commingled assemblages, not just to K208 specifically.

Due to physical space constraints, it is not feasible to simultaneously lay out all of the skeletal remains from 208 boxes. Therefore, K208 remains are analyzed village by village, i.e., pulling out the boxes from a single village at one time (typically 15–25 boxes). The remains in each box are laid out on a table for photography and inventory (Figure 19-2).

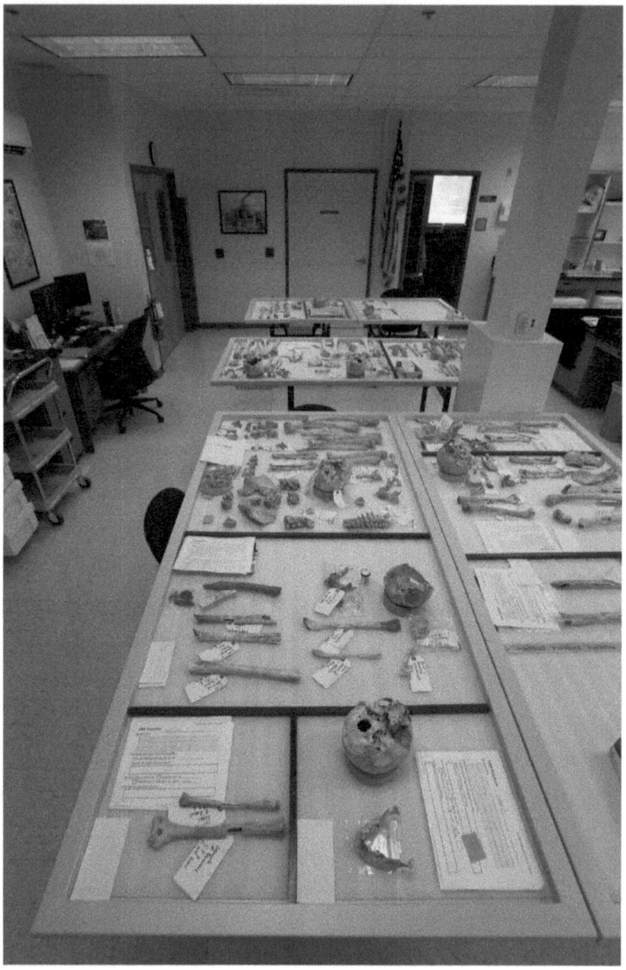

Figure 19-2
Overview of the K208 lab space. The remains are laid out by mtDNA sequences.

The analyst then uses the mtDNA sequence results to perform an initial sort of the bones. All of the DNA analyses are done by the Armed Forces DNA Identification Laboratory (AFDIL) in Delaware. The analysts at AFDIL send the K208 team a monthly updated mtDNA sequence chart that contains all of the mtDNA sequences obtained from the Korean War remains, including K208 and JRO. The chart is organized by mtDNA sequences. Under each mtDNA sequence, the following information is included: (1) a list of all the skeletal elements that yielded the same mtDNA sequence, and (2) a list of the missing military personnel whose FRS(s) is a match to the sequence.

It is important to understand that multiple individuals could share the same mtDNA sequence because mtDNA passes through the maternal line with no recombination and high copy number (Van Oven and Kayser 2008). Although this aspect of mtDNA is advantageous to track down maternally related individuals, it is the reason that mtDNA cannot be used as a sole method to segregate an individual. As of December 2013, a total of 587 mtDNA sequences had been reported from K208 and JRO assemblages. Given that there are duplicated elements with the same mtDNA sequences, the minimum number of individuals (MNI) for K208 is estimated to be around 600.

The analyst next places the bones sharing the same mtDNA sequences in the same analytical space. Most of the mtDNA sequences have bones from multiple boxes. The analyst then uses anthropological analyses to associate unsampled skeletal elements with those that have been sampled, thereby increasing the number of elements attributed to a sequence. Once all the elements for the mtDNA sequence have been pulled together (including the unsampled elements associated via anthropological analyses), the MNI is determined. If the MNI is more than one, the analyst attempts to further segregate subsets of remains into discrete individuals.

The anthropological methods most frequently used in this process are pair matching, articulation, taphonomy, and osteometric sorting. Of these methods, osteometric sorting is the most rigorous and least subjective method (see Byrd and Adams 2003; and Chapter 8 in this book). It is a metric analysis of bone size and shape that can supplement gross morphological assessments of pair matching and articulation. Skeletal measurements are taken within the same mtDNA sequence grouping following the measurement descriptions in Byrd (2008), Byrd and Adams (2003), and Moore-Jansen et al. (1994). The measurements are then compared with each other as well as with measurements from an osteometric database. The analyst chooses a statistical model most appropriate for the case data. For instance, Student's t-tests are appropriate for pair matching comparisons, and linear regression models are appropriate for comparing the overall sizes of elements from different regions of the body. Based on the resulting statistical probabilities, individual skeletal elements are accepted or rejected as being associated with remains sharing their mtDNA sequence. If necessary, additional sampling for mtDNA may be requested for bones that have not been sampled or that did not yield a sequence. Remains that are fractured should be refit (i.e., conjoined) prior to sampling for DNA.

A Report of Segregation (RoS) is produced documenting the preceding process. For quality assurance purposes, all comparisons, analyses, test results, or other case-related records are thoroughly documented in analytical notes in a systematic, organized, and standardized manner conducive to authentication and verification. The reports then go through internal peer review and quality assurance before they are filed in appropriate case folders.

Consolidation Analyses: How an Individual is Associated with a Name

When segregation analyses are complete, the next step is consolidation analysis to determine the identity of the individual. This begins with the list of FRS matches for each mtDNA sequence provided by AFDIL. Some mtDNA sequences are unique and have only one name association, whereas others may have hundreds of name associations to consider. Some mtDNA sequences do not match any of the FRS profiles in the Korean War database; therefore, no possible matches are listed. This could indicate that the remains belong to a U.S. loss with no FRS on file or that the remains are a non-U.S. loss. All possibilities are carefully considered. Name associations are deemed "consistent" or "inconsistent" with the remains based on the following analyses. All of these analyses are documented in the Report of Consolidation (RoC).

1) Loss Location

Previous identifications from the K208 assemblage indicate that the purported village from which the remains were recovered generally corresponds to an individual's reported loss location. Although there are some instances of crossover between villages, broad trends can be seen in the commingling pattern, allowing the analyst to create a short list of most likely name associations based on a comparison of loss location with recovery location. There is always a possibility of the remains not belonging to one of the names on the short list due to either lack of FRSs or the wrong purported origins provided by the North Koreans. However, a short list is still an important starting point for consolidation analyses. If there is no match from the short list, the analyst (1) re-examines the list of names and creates a second short list, or (2) requests an FRS if there is a reason to believe it is likely to be an individual with no FRS.

2) Biological Profile

There are not many cases where a biological profile can be used for exclusionary purposes because a majority of the Korean War missing share a similar profile, e.g., a young adult Caucasian male of average height. If the biological profile of a missing individual is not consistent with the profile of the remains, that individual is listed as "inconsistent."

3) Dental Analysis

If dental remains are present, the analyst requests that a CIL odontologist compares the dental remains to the antemortem dental records on file for the individuals on the short list. The odontologist provides a list of individuals that can be excluded based on the dental profile, or states whether or not a specific individual is a possible match to the dental remains. In some cases, if the dental profile is unique, the name associations can be narrowed to one. CIL odontologists are able to utilize a search engine that accesses a database of all available dental records for the Korean War missing. Searches are done when sufficient dental remains are presented and no other leads have narrowed the list of candidates.

4) Chest Radiograph Comparison

If clavicles are present in suitable condition, a chest radiograph comparison (CXR) may be requested. The CXR analyst compares postmortem radiographs of the clavicle(s) and C3–T3 vertebrae, if present, to antemortem chest radiographs of individuals on the short list.

Antemortem chest radiographs are available for approximately 70% of the U.S. service members missing from the Korean War, as a result of tuberculosis screening that was universally adopted across the U.S. Armed Forces in 1942 (Long and Lew 1945; Stephan et al. 2011). This method has been validated through a series of blind tests with 90% accuracy when performed by trained examiners (Stephan et al. 2011). Individuals on the short list are classified as a match, not a match, or cannot be excluded. The CIL is very close to engaging a new search engine capable of comparing a postmortem radiograph of the clavicles to the clavicles shown in the library of Korean antemortem radiographs. This search engine will work in a manner analogous to the dental search engine and search against the DNA FRS database.

5) Additional DNA Testing: Nuclear DNA (Y-STR and Autosomal-STR)

Despite all of the preceding analyses, some cases cannot be narrowed to a single name. If that is the case, the analyst may request an additional nuclear DNA testing for Y chromosome short tandem repeats (STRs) or autosomal-STRs. Although the majority of base pairs in a human DNA sequence are identical to those from another individual, there are also numerous regions in the DNA sequence that are highly variable between individuals (i.e., have a high degree of polymorphisms). STRs are one of these highly polymorphic regions in nuclear DNA with 2–6 base pairs of short sequences of DNA that are repeated numerous times (Schultes et al. 2000). The polymorphisms in STRs are due to the number of repeats of this short sequence and are commonly used in modern forensic cases (Stone 2008). Although nuclear DNA has a much higher discriminatory power than mtDNA, it is in lower abundance in cells than mtDNA making it more difficult to extract from degraded skeletal samples (Butler 2005).

Y-STR analysis uses the nonrecombining region of the Y chromosome that is inherited through paternally related males. Thus, Y-STR analysis is analogous to mtDNA analysis, which identifies related individuals across several generations (Schultes et al. 2000). If a missing service member has a pertinent FRS donor for Y-STR (e.g., brother or his son, paternal uncle or his son), additional Y-STR testing is requested if necessary.

Autosomal-STRs, however, are nearly unique to an individual because they are inherited half from the mother and the other half from the father. Because of this characteristic, various statistical models are used to calculate the probabilities of the remains and the FRSs to be related as full siblings, or parents, etc. (Butler 2005). A likelihood ratio is generated expressing how much more likely it is that the DNA from the skeletal remains came from a person with a specific kinship relationship to the unaccounted-for family members (i.e., FRSs) as opposed to from an apparently unrelated person (Butler 2005). If a missing service member has only a sister FRS, autosomal-STR testing is requested if necessary. Occasionally, both Y- and autosomal-STR testing are used to maximize the success rate of the analysis, especially when bone samples are not in good condition for DNA extractions. Combining the various DNA test results from a given specimen provides a very powerful tool for sorting commingled remains in addition to supporting the identification.

Identification of an Individual

When the RoS and RoC are completed, the K208 project manager recommends a case to upper management for identification. The case manager reviews the recommendation and assigns the case to a non-K208 analyst for Forensic Anthropology Report (FAR) to create a biological profile. This additional analysis is done in the blind, i.e., the analyst has no background information about the case. If there is concurrence, the case manager then recommends the case to the CIL Scientific Director for identification. If the Scientific Director agrees with the recommendation, the case will be identified and notification will be made to the family. If the Scientific Director does not agree with the recommendation, the case will be sent back to K208 analysts for further analysis, such as additional DNA testing. Figure 19-3 summarizes the K208 analytical procedure.

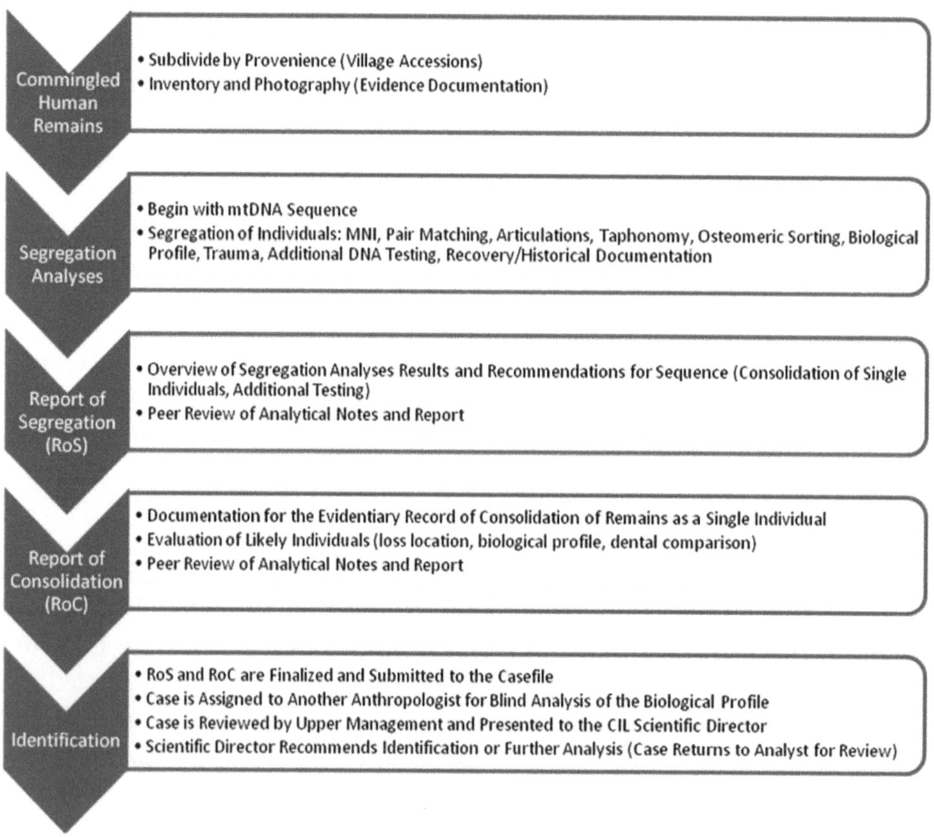

Figure 19-3
The summary of K208 analytical procedure.

K208 Case Studies

Case Study 1—Corporal "Turner": Intense Commingling

One of the K208 mtDNA sequences included remains from multiple recovery locations spread throughout North Korea. The remains came from the boxes with a purported origin of Kaljon-ni in East Chosin, Kundong-ni near DMZ, and Kujang County in the western part of North Korea (see Figure 19-1). Because these locations are over 100 km apart from each other, geographically speaking, it seemed unlikely that the elements from these three areas would belong to a single individual. To make matters worse, while the remains from Kaljon-ni and Kundong-ni were part of the 208 boxes unilaterally turned over by the North Koreans, the remains from Kujang County were from the staged burial sites recovered by the joint U.S./DPRK excavation teams (JRO) in the late 1990s and early 2000s.

However, anthropological assessment determined all of the elements sharing this particular mtDNA sequence to be associated with a single individual. The determination was based on a lack of duplicated elements, consistency in size, morphology, developmental stage, and taphonomy, as well as through pair matching, articulation, and osteometric sorting. Some of the unsampled cranial elements from the same box were also associated to this individual based on articulation and/or refitting.

Although the mtDNA sequence was rare within the AFDIL statistical population database (found only in about 0.05% of the total database; N = 5/10428), there were six U.S. servicemen unaccounted-for from the Korean War sharing this particular sequence. Of these six, two were lost in South Korea, and one was an air loss over the ocean, leaving three most likely candidates. Therefore, the hypothesis was that "Turner," "Hanes," and "Thompson" were the three most likely matches for these remains who were all lost near the vicinity of Kaljon-ni in East Chosin. Four independent analyses were done to narrow down the list to a single most likely name: biological profile, dental, chest radiograph, and additional DNA testing.

- Age-at-death estimation could not exclude any of the three individuals. Stature estimation, on the other hand, was helpful in this particular case. The point estimate for stature was 69.5 inches with a 95% prediction interval of 66.3 to 72.7 inches based on maximum length of a humerus. While "Turner" and "Hanes" fell within this range, "Thompson" was about an inch outside the prediction interval, making him a less likely match of the three.
- Dental analysis excluded "Hanes" due to an unexplainable difference in extraction pattern between the remains and his antemortem dental records. However, neither "Turner" nor "Thompson" were excluded.
- Chest radiograph comparison between the right clavicle and the antemortem radiographs of "Hanes" and "Thompson" was performed ("Turner" did not have an antemortem chest radiograph). Due to numerous discrepancies, both of them were excluded.

- At this point, "Turner" seemed to be the most likely candidate. However, additional DNA testing was deemed necessary to confirm the name association and the association of the remains to a single individual, not because there was any doubt to the anthropological assessment, but to be cautious given the high degree of commingling between villages. Both autosomal-STR and Y-STR testing were done because "Turner" had only sister FRSs, whereas "Hanes" and "Thompson" had brother FRSs. The nuclear-STR data from the humerus from Kaljon-ni was consistent with that of the mandible and femur recovered from Kujang County. These results confirmed the anthropological assessment of the remains being a single individual. Y-STR data excluded "Hanes" and "Thompson" as a possible match. A combined sibship index (i.e., likelihood ratio) calculated using autosomal-STR data showed that it was 168,000 times more likely that the remains belonged to "Turner's" sister's sibling than if they came from a random individual in the general population.

Multiple lines of evidence associated these remains to Corporal "Turner" to the exclusion of other reasonable possibilities, and he was officially identified.

Case Study 2—Corporal "Ellis": Minimal Commingling with Multiple Name Associations

One of the K208 mtDNA sequences included remains from only one village, Sinhung-ni, located in the area of East Chosin. However, these remains originated from nine different Sinhung-ni boxes. Anthropological analysis confirmed that the remains in this sequence represented a single individual based on a lack of duplicated elements, consistency in size, morphology, developmental stage, and taphonomy, as well as through pair matching, articulation, and osteometric sorting. In addition, previous assessment of the commingling patterns of Sinhung-ni remains established that elements purportedly from Sinhung-ni did not cross over with any other village. In other words, Sinhung-ni remains were commingled within Sinhung-ni boxes, but were not commingled across the entire K208 assemblage. This pattern was true for all identifications of Sinhung-ni remains.

Although it was fairly clear-cut to associate the remains as a single individual, the challenge in this particular case came with the possible name associations. While it was a relatively uncommon mtDNA sequence (found only in about 0.22% of the total AFDIL database; N = 23/10428), there were 35 service members missing from the Korean War with the exact same sequence. Of those 35 individuals, six had a loss location consistent with the purported recovery location of Sinhung-ni. Of those six, three individuals had been in the same military unit as individuals previously identified from Sinhung-ni boxes: Corporal "Ellis," Sergeant "Kent," and Private First Class "Sweeney." They were reported as Missing In Action in late November 1950 when their unit was engaged by vastly superior numbers of enemy forces. Given the historical documentation of their loss location and the purported origin of the remains, the hypothesis was that these three names were the most likely matches for the sequence. Three independent analyses were done to narrow down the list to a single most likely name: dental, chest radiograph, and additional DNA testing.

- Dental analysis excluded "Kent" as a match due to an unexplainable extraction pattern discrepancy, but could not exclude either "Ellis" or "Sweeney."
- Chest radiographs of the left and right clavicles were compared to the antemortem chest radiographs of "Ellis" and "Kent" because "Sweeney" did not have an antemortem radiograph. Numerous points of concordances were observed between the antemortem radiographs of "Ellis" and the postmortem clavicle radiographs. The superimposition of the postmortem radiograph on "Ellis's" antemortem radiograph demonstrated near exact correspondence. Thus, chest radiograph comparison concluded that the clavicles were those of "Ellis," not "Kent."
- At this point, it was clear that "Kent" was excluded, and the remains were most likely "Ellis." However, "Sweeney" was still a possible candidate. Consequently, additional Y-STR testing was requested. Four samples (left and right femora, right tibia, and right humerus) yielded verifiable Y-STR data that matched Y-STR data obtained from a known paternal-line relative (brother) of "Ellis" and excluded both "Sweeney" and "Kent."

Multiple lines of evidence associated these remains to Corporal "Ellis" to the exclusion of other reasonable possibilities, and he was officially identified.

Case Study 3—Two Individuals from a Single mtDNA Sequence

One of the K208 mtDNA sequences had skeletal elements from two distinct areas: Chongryang-ni in East Chosin and Namjung-gu in Suan POW Camp. Chongryang-ni was represented by only a left tibia, whereas the remains from Namjung-gu had almost complete sets of limb bones and cranium. Unlike the majority of the K208 cases where skeletal elements were from multiple boxes, the Namjung-gu remains were all from a single box. This did not necessarily mean that there was no commingling of the remains because previous analyses demonstrated that there were on average four individuals represented in each K208 box.

The MNI was two based on duplicated left tibia. Anthropological analysis determined that the Chongryang-ni element represented one individual (Individual 1), and the Namjung-gu elements represented a second individual (Individual 2). Some of the unsampled long bones from the same Namjung-gu box were associated to Individual 2 based on pair matching, articulation, osteometric sorting, and taphonomy.

Although the mtDNA sequence was uncommon within the AFDIL database (found only in about 0.02% of the total database; N = 2/10428), there were five U.S. servicemen unaccounted-for from the Korean War sharing this particular sequence. Two of these five individuals, "Lane" and "Saunders," were lost in East Chosin; thus, they initially were the most likely matches for Individual 1. Only one of these five individuals, "Graham," was captured in Suan POW Camp, making him the most likely match for Individual 2.

Individual 1

There were no methods other than additional DNA testing to confirm the name association for Individual 1 because it was a single tibia. The Y-STR data from this tibia was consistent with the Y-STR loci from "Lane's" brother's FRS. It also excluded "Saunders." Loss location and mtDNA/Y-STR data associated the tibia to Corporal "Lane" to the exclusion of other reasonable possibilities, and he was officially identified.

Individual 2

Despite the fact that there was a single most likely name for this individual, there was always a possibility of this individual being an unaccounted-for from the Korean War who had no FRS on file. Therefore, additional DNA testing was requested to confirm name association to "Graham." The Y-STR data from a femur and a tibia were consistent with that of "Graham's" brother's FRS. All of the evidence associated this individual to Sergeant "Graham," who died in captivity in Suan POW Camp at the age of 20.

Challenges

No Archaeological Context

One of the many challenges K208 analysts face on a daily basis is the lack of archaeological context. The majority of K208 remains are without a known provenience or context, with the exception of the remains from a few *in situ* JRO sites. There are no trustworthy site maps that can be used to associate remains based on their provenience or through the laws of superposition. The only available spatial information was provided by the North Koreans, which turned out to be not necessarily accurate. Even if the K208 team uses the purported origins of the remains to create a short list, there is always a possibility of the remains coming from a completely different area than claimed by the North Koreans (as shown in Case Study 1). This situation can be frustrating during the analysis and makes our reliance on DNA much higher than most other forensic anthropology cases where recovery provenience may play a bigger role.

Anthropology Is Not Enough? High Dependence on DNA

The high degree of commingling and the large number of elements involved make K208 an atypical forensic anthropological problem. Despite the rigorous anthropological segregation methods employed in K208, it is often challenging to segregate hundreds of remains into a single individual. It is fortunate that DNA analyses (mtDNA and nuclear DNA) are readily available for K208 which allow the analysts to segregate the remains into discrete individuals.

In addition, DNA testing often makes it possible to associate the remains to a specific individual if there is a match to the FRSs. Because of these advantages, DNA analysis has become a powerful and preferred tool in resolving commingling in K208. However, it is still crucial not to underestimate the importance of anthropological analysis. Unless every single element is sampled for DNA testing, which is realistically not feasible, it is the anthropological assessment which is used to associate and confirm that the remains belong to a discrete individual (see segregation analyses). If more than one individual shares the same mtDNA sequence, anthropological analysis is particularly useful in segregating individuals.

Commingling of Non-U.S. Personnel

Approximately 200 mtDNA sequences in the K208 do not have any matching FRSs as of this writing. This means the remains are either (1) from non-U.S. personnel; (2) from an unaccounted-for U.S. service member from the Korean War who does not have an FRS on file; or (3) from either 1 or 2 but the sequence is incorrectly reported, incorrectly entered into the database, or some other human error has occurred. Even if no names are associated with a particular sequence, the K208 analyst still conducts anthropological analyses to determine whether the remains could be associated to a single individual. When the remains are associated to an individual, albeit without a specific name, the remains are still consolidated. Of these, 12 sets of remains were confirmed to be Korean nationals based on mtDNA haplogroup, loss location, and material evidence (e.g., identification tags). These remains were repatriated to the South Korean government in 2012. The Ministry of National Defense Agency for Killed in Action Recovery and Identification (MAKRI), the Korean counterpart of JPAC, identified two of the 12 sets and returned them to their families. These 12 instances were the first times that ROK soldiers who went missing in North Korea during the Korean War were repatriated. This also confirmed that there are non-U.S. remains commingled in the K208 assemblage.

The issue gets more complicated due to the approximately 100 Asian American service members unaccounted-for from the Korean War. First, not all of the missing Asian Americans have FRSs on file. Because of this, the K208 team operates under the assumption that these remains could be Americans even if they have an Asian mtDNA haplogroup. Second, some of the missing Asian Americans with FRSs on file show up as a match to numerous mtDNA sequences with Asian haplogroups. This frequently happens with the unaccounted-for Korean and Japanese Americans. Despite the effort to identify them, additional DNA testing has yet to confirm the presence of missing Asian Americans in the K208 assemblage.

What If All the Methods Fail?

There are cases within the K208 that cannot move forward despite all the efforts put into identification. These cases fall into one of three categories: (1) no FRSs are associated with the remains; (2) all of the service members with matching mtDNA sequences are excluded via nuclear DNA testing; or (3) multiple names are associated that cannot be narrowed down to one. In a case with no matching FRSs, it is presumed that the remains could be from a non-U.S. national or a U.S. national with no FRSs on file. If no convincing non-U.S. material evidence is associated with the case, JPAC-CIL keeps the remains until a matching FRS is found. However, having multiple name matches to a mtDNA sequence does not always mean that the remains belong to one of those names. There were cases in which loss location and biological profile could not exclude any of those names. As a result, additional DNA testing was requested on these cases to narrow down the name to one individual. When nuclear DNA testing excluded all of the associated names, the case could not move forward any longer. Such cases are probably one of the service members with no FRS on file. In addition, in some cases we could not attempt nuclear DNA testing due to lack of a suitable FRS donor; e.g., maternal cousins cannot be used for Y-STR testing. If this is the case, we request additional relevant FRS donors through the service casualty office. All of these examples are clear evidence showing the importance of obtaining proper FRSs to achieve the fullest possible accounting of Americans missing during the Korean War.

Conclusions

The K208 assemblage is unique in the sense that it is highly commingled and large, with potentially 600 individuals represented. Contrary to what the North Koreans informed us in the early 1990s, the human remains in K208 contain considerably more than 208 individuals, including both U.S. and non-U.S. individuals. Due to the high degree of commingling, very little analysis was successful until rigorous mtDNA testing became available in the early 2000s. Since the mid-2000s, the K208 project started to contribute to an increase in the number of JPAC identifications with 101 U.S. service members identified as of December 2013. Although mtDNA testing is a crucial factor in solving the high degree of commingling in K208, employing more rigorous anthropological methods and having a systematic procedure in place also played important roles in increasing the number of identifications from K208.

Despite the technological advances at JPAC-CIL and AFDIL and the efforts by the K208 anthropologists, a number of cases in K208 still cannot be associated with any missing U.S. service members from the Korean War. Our ultimate goal is to be able to identify and return all of the American remains in K208 to their families. This would only be possible with (1) the continuous effort by the K208 anthropologists to segregate the highly commingled remains into discrete individuals and associate each set of remains with a specific name, (2) the increase of FRSs for both mtDNA and nuclear DNA testing, and (3) the continuous support by the U.S. government and the American people.

Acknowledgements

We thank Drs. John Byrd and Bradley Adams for inviting us to contribute a chapter to this book and for their comments on an earlier draft. We appreciate the comments from Dr. Pat Shipman. We also wish to acknowledge the great contributions and patience of AFDIL scientists who assist with the K208 project daily. This research was supported in part by an appointment to the Postgraduate Research Participation Program at the Joint POW/MIA Accounting Command administered by the Oak Ridge Institute for Science and Education through an interagency agreement between the U.S. Department of Energy and JPAC.

References

Butler, J.M., 2005. Forensic DNA Typing: Biology, Technology, and Genetics of STR Markers, second ed. Elsevier Academic Press, Burlington, MA.

Byrd, J.E., 2008. Models and methods for osteometric sorting. In: Adams, B.J., Byrd, J.E. (Eds.), Recovery, Analysis, and Identification of Commingled Human Remains. Humana Press, Totowa, NJ, pp. 199–220.

Byrd, J.E., Adams, B.J., 2003. Osteometric sorting of commingled human remains. J. Forensic Sci. 48, 717–724.

Long, E.R., Lew, E.A., 1945. Tuberculosis in the Armed Forces. Am. J. Public Health 35, 469–479.

Moore-Jansen, P.H., Ousley, S.D., Jantz, R.L., 1994. Data Collection Procedures for Forensic Skeletal Material, third ed. University of Tennessee Forensic Anthropology Series, Knoxville, TN.

Pokines, J.T., Berg, G.E., Adams, B.J., Bunch, A.W., Byrd, J.E., Holland, T.D., 2002. How not to stage a burial: Lessons from North Korea. Proc. Am. Acad. Forensic Sci. 8, 239–240.

Schultes, T., Hummel, S., Herrmann, B., 2000. Ancient DNA-typing approaches for the determination of kinship in a disturbed collective burial site. Anthropol. Anz. 58, 37–44.

Sledge, M., 2005. Soldier Dead: How We Recover, Identify, Bury, and Honor Our Military Fallen. Columbia University Press New York, NY.

Snow, C.E., 1948. The identification of the unknown war dead. Am. J. Phys. Anthropol. 6, 323–328.

Stephan, C.N., Winburn, A.P., Christensen, A.F., Tyrrell, A.J., 2011. Skeletal identification by radiographic comparison: Blind tests of a morphoscopic method using antemortem chest radiographs. J. Forensic Sci. 56 (2), 320–332.

Stone, A.C., 2008. DNA analysis of archaeological remains. In: Katzenberg, M.A., Saunders, S.R. (Eds.), Biological Anthropology of the Human Skeleton, second ed. Wiley-Liss, Hoboken, NJ, pp. 461–483.

Van Oven, M., Kayser, M., 2008. Updated comprehensive phylogenetic tree of global human mitochondrial DNA variation. Hum. Mutat. 29, E386–E394.

CHAPTER 20

Data Management and Commingled Remains

Michael Hennessey
Gene Codes Forensics

Introduction

Commingling occurs when the remains of more than one victim become intermixed. A thorough examination of remains during triage at the morgue should resolve most instances of commingling, but in some cases it may be detected only when other analyses yield contradictory results. For example, during the analysis of remains from the World Trade Center (WTC) attack of 2001, multiple DNA tests on the same set of remains sometimes yielded different profiles. In other cases, dental X-rays and DNA from the same set of remains were linked to different victims. Conflicting antemortem and postmortem data can also indicate commingling. In another case from WTC, the DNA from a victim's reference sample (a known personal effect) matched a set of remains, yet the jewelry on the remains was contrary to the description provided by the spouse. In each of these cases, visual examination in the morgue had not detected the presence of commingled remains.

A key lesson learned from mass fatality incidents (MFIs) is that one cannot rely on a single identification method to detect commingling. All postmortem results for a case need to be reviewed for consistency, and all of the postmortem data must be reconciled against all of the antemortem (AM) information associated with the identification. This administrative review process ("admin review") relies on being able to locate all of the case information in a timely fashion. Unfortunately, gathering such information is error-prone because missing data are not always obvious. For example, if there is a matching DNA result, one might not think to check if there is a *second* DNA test of the remains extant that may not match the reference sample.

The main point of this chapter is that even if great care is exercised in the recovery and analysis of remains, the identification process may be compromised if the data are not managed correctly and an investigator misses an inconsistency. This chapter examines the most common challenges in this regard and suggests several solutions. The framework presented here is that admin review is a data management process that spans the antemortem and postmortem information gathering systems and unites the various investigative methods

Commingled Human Remains. http://dx.doi.org/10.1016/B978-0-12-405889-7.00020-4

(anthropology, DNA, fingerprint, pathology, property, and X-ray). In this way, the detection and resolution of commingled remains is a multidisciplinary effort.

Unless otherwise noted, the examples in this chapter are real cases. The names and identifying numbers have been anonymized to protect the privacy of the families.

MFI Data

In response to an MFI, a family assistance center (FAC) is usually established to provide services to the families of the victims. In addition, interviewers at the FAC collect missing persons reports. Employers provide information about staff presumed lost at the scene, and other organizations (tour agencies, airlines, etc.) may also have data to contribute regarding the victims. Anyone filing a report is an informant, and this antemortem (AM) information can be divided into three categories:

1. Primary data for identification purposes: Fingerprints, X-rays (dental and others), and DNA are the principal methods of identification. Although other approaches can be used (such as tracing the serial number from a surgical implant), they are not applicable in most cases. While families do not typically bring X-rays or fingerprint cards to the FAC, they usually provide the contact information for the custodians of such data. DNA reference samples, on the other hand, are usually directly provided by the family.
2. Secondary data for identification purposes: Although not sufficient to make an identification on its own, descriptive information about the victim's jewelry, clothing, tattoos, surgical histories, or distinctive anatomical features can be used to generate investigational leads that can point to the correct primary data for an identification. Secondary data can also be used to return property to the families of the victims.
3. Administrative data for case management: A case number is usually established during the interview at the FAC and the victim's contact information (name, address, phone number, etc.) and demographic data (age, race/ancestry, gender, date of birth, etc.) are used to create and manage the case file. These data can also contribute to the creation of investigational leads as well as flag potential intake errors (e.g., the victim's age and date of birth are out of sync). Finally, data about the interview itself belong in this category: the informant's name and contact information, date and time of the intake, name of the interviewer, etc.

When remains are received in the morgue, they will generate postmortem (PM) data that are also primary, secondary, and administrative in nature. In many ways, the identification process at an MFI is a function of integrating the AM and PM information. This chapter reviews the principal challenges an investigator faces in reconciling such data.

Identification Errors at an MFI

The remains of victims at disasters are sometimes fragmented, so a victim's primary AM data will often match the primary PM data from multiple sets of partial remains. The reverse, however, is problematic: primary PM data from a set of remains linking to more than one AM case file (i.e., missing person) should undergo further review. Such cases are usually the result of commingling, investigative mistakes, or administrative error.

Commingling

MFIs are often associated with severe physical traumas (plane crashes, earthquakes, explosions, etc.) that can result in the fragmented remains of one victim becoming embedded in the tissue of another victim. Such cases are not always apparent to the naked eye and may not be recognized during triage in the morgue. For example, the tissue of Person A may become fused with the bone of Person B so that it appears to be articulated to it, open wounds can suffer DNA contamination from the blood of other victims, or recovery workers may place multiple sets of remains in one body bag. While it is standard practice to separate such remains into different cases during mortuary intake (i.e., triage), this is sometimes missed in the initial chaos of a disaster response.

Finally, commingling can occur during the autopsy process. For example, in Thailand after the 2004 Asian Tsunami (hereafter referred to as "Tsunami"), a few fingerprint teams severed fingers, made prints, and then set the fingers aside instead of returning them to the body bag (which by then had moved on to the next autopsy station). Rather than disposing of the fingers as medical waste at the end of their shift, they would place the severed fingers in the last body bag that they processed. This practice was eventually brought to the attention of senior management by pathologists who noted the absence of fingers on some bodies and the presence of extra fingers in other body bags.

Example: Commingled Remains

In one case at WTC, two separate remains with matching DNA profiles were linked to Ahmed Matar. The anthropology review showed that the first set of remains was an upper torso with a complete mandible and limbs, whereas the second set of remains was a complete mandible. The case file for the disarticulated mandible stated that it had been recovered from the chest cavity of the remains to which it was matched by DNA. The presence of two mandibles with the same DNA profile was a clear indication for the need for a complete admin review.

Odontologists matched the disarticulated mandible to the AM dental records of Walter Jones. They also confirmed that the mandible attached to the torso was consistent with the dental chart for Ahmed Matar. When the second mandible had been recovered from the chest cavity, a tissue sample was taken from it for DNA testing. Apparently, the force of the impact affixed tissue from the torso so firmly to the mandible that it appeared to be organic to it. As a result, the DNA profile for the loose mandible matched the torso and the personal effects of Ahmed Matar. At this point a tooth was taken from the disarticulated mandible, and DNA testing showed it was consistent with the reference samples for Walter Jones. The initial error was rectified, and both identifications were finalized.

Investigative Mistakes

Investigative mistakes can happen in one of three ways. First, errors may occur during the analysis of the remains or reference items, resulting in flawed primary data. Second, it may not be possible to generate a full fingerprint, dental chart, or DNA profile from remains that have suffered physical trauma, and such partial profiles of any kind are more prone to fortuitous matches. Third, the increased role of statistics in declaring a match introduces the potential for an analyst to overstate or understate the significance of a match if an error is made in calculating the match likelihood. In DNA, for example, manual data entry of equations in kinship software is vulnerable to typographical errors. A complicating factor in all three instances is that the analysis of the remains and reference items and the matching process of AM and PM data may be performed in different locations by different personnel.

Example: Investigative Mistakes

Investigative mistakes usually do not result in false matches because two victims would need to have nearly identical primary data, the analyst would have to make a mistake only at that single point of difference, and the error would have to be such that it transforms the primary data of the first victim to match the primary data of the second victim. Given the underlying frequency distributions of DNA, fingerprints, and dental profiles (which are all highly heterogeneous), it is more likely that an investigative error would result in a false exclusion than a fortuitous match. That said, there are two situations in which the potential for a false match increases: (1) DNA testing on degraded remains; and (2) DNA matching using partial profiles. These are related issues in that degraded remains often produce partial DNA profiles, but they lead to investigative mistakes in different ways (the same can be said for partial dental profiles, partial fingerprints, etc.)

Administrative Error

Administrative error occurs simply when the information is accurate but is in the wrong case file. This can happen with both AM and PM data, but AM records are more at risk because victims with similar names are more prone to having their case files confused. This potential increases if victims share other information such as an address or DNA donor (victims from the same family are especially vulnerable in this regard). But any two files can be erroneously combined if handled poorly. Administrative errors are mundane but ubiquitous.

Example: Administrative Error

In the spring of 2002, a whole body was recovered from WTC's Ground Zero with personal effects for Jason Arturo. An arm had already been identified as Arturo's by DNA in the fall of 2001. The whole body was tested for DNA, and it had a different profile than the arm. The laboratory file for Arturo showed that six separate DNA reference collections were received from the FAC in the fall of 2001. An audit of the collection logs at the FAC showed that only five DNA collection events had taken place for Arturo (this log had not been available to the laboratory when the arm was identified as that of Arturo).

At the FAC, victims were given case numbers while each DNA collection received a separate tracking number. The extra DNA reference item in Arturo's laboratory file had collection number 453. The log at the FAC listed collection 453 as belonging to Nathan Riley, victim number 227. One of Arturo's DNA collection numbers was also 227.

The author reviewed the errant DNA collection package and noted that numbers 453 and 227 were present, but with no label to indicate which was the victim number and which was the DNA collection number. Riley's name was also missing from the packing materials, a failure of the standard operating procedure at the FAC. The log showed that collections 453 for Riley and 227 for Arturo took place on the same day, so there was an overlap in their handling. It became apparent that Riley's victim number had been confused with Arturo's DNA collection number and that his reference samples had been stored in the wrong folder. Unfortunately, these were the reference items that were selected for testing from this case file.

After the error was recognized, Riley's samples were given their own case file, and all of Arturo's reference samples were tested. They matched the whole body recovered in the spring of 2002. The agency met with the Arturo family to explain the mistake and set about the task of disinterring the arm. The Riley family was notified, and the complete situation was explained to them. The arm previously released to Arturo was then released to the Riley family.

It has been pointed out to the author that if all the reference items had been tested in the first place, the conflicting profiles among the reference samples in Arturo's file would have alerted analysts to the problem. While this is correct, it ignores the fact that thousands of reference items were pouring into the laboratory, some of dubious quality. Testing everything would have delayed the identification process by months, without appreciably improving the chances of making identifications. In response, the lab chose to test the one reference sample from a case that had the highest potential to yield a DNA profile (usually a toothbrush).

This case illustrates one of the challenges posed by mass fatality identification projects: in order to spot conflicts within a case (or suspicious matches between unrelated cases), all of the AM testing would have to be completed first before any identifications could be made. But refusing to release *any* DNA matches until all reference items have been tested is not a viable policy given the urgency of making identifications and releasing remains as soon as possible. However, it *is* possible to compare the FAC collection logs to the case files in the DNA laboratory when a match is made. A simple audit of this kind would have flagged Arturo's case. Once the FAC collection log was available to the DNA laboratory at WTC, such audits became a routine part of the admin review, and discrepancies in other identifications were flagged as a result.

Likewise, while conflicting PM results from a single set of remains will eventually surface, this assumes that none of the remains will be released until all primary methods of analysis are completed. Again, pressure to release identifications in a timely manner may trump such a policy, and many fragmented remains are simply not amenable to multiple examination techniques. For these reasons, one cannot rely on conflicting primary data to flag all instances of commingling, investigative mistakes, or administrative errors. However, an investigator *can* review the secondary and administrative data for a match, because inconsistencies at this level would suggest that further review is needed.

For example, at WTC FAC, the husband of Donna Parker donated his wife's hairbrush as a source of DNA. The profile matched several sets of fragmented remains, including a hand wearing an engagement ring and wedding band with multiple diamond settings. A review of the property report filed by the husband listed only a single gold wedding band. An investigator called the husband and confirmed that Donna did not have a diamond ring and wore only the plain wedding band. Meanwhile, a search of the jewelry descriptions in the AM database found a match to both rings in the file of a different unidentified victim. The hand (and the other remains associated with the case) were removed from the Parker identification and placed under an anthropology review.

DNA Testing on Degraded Remains

DNA samples are often tested in batches, with liquid samples deposited into wells on a tray. Adjacent wells on the same tray can cross-contaminate each other, and tray-to-tray contamination can occur if robotic pipettes carry a trace sample from a well in one tray to the corresponding well in the following tray. The presence of two DNA profiles in the same well will be flagged during the technical review, but a well filled with a sample from remains too degraded to yield DNA will only show the profile from the contaminating well. In this way, the DNA profile of one set of remains can be incorrectly assigned to a second set of remains.

In one WTC case, DNA linked two remains to the same victim, but an anthropology review showed that the two sets of remains could not be from the same person. The anthropologist noted that one of the remains was badly burned, suggesting that its DNA was compromised. This remain was retested, and it failed to give a DNA result, confirming the anthropologist's hypothesis. A review of the laboratory process located the source of the contamination, and it was fixed.

This illustrates another benefit of the multidisciplinary approach: anthropology not only caught an errant identification but also alerted the DNA laboratory to an operational problem.

Partial DNA Profiles

A second scenario in which an investigative mistake can result in a false match is when working with partial DNA profiles. An error at a single point of comparison will usually not be enough to make the full profiles of two different people appear to be the same. But degraded remains may only yield a handful of genetic markers. When compared to the AM data, it is possible that the difference between a partial PM profile and a complete AM profile is so small that a single error of interpretation may be sufficient to lead an analyst to make a fortuitous match.

Summary of Identification Errors at an MFI

At an MFI, an investigator should not view a match between primary AM and PM data as an identification, but should treat it as the starting point of the investigation. The next step is to reconcile all of the AM and PM data (primary, secondary, and administrative). This admin review can catch commingling, investigative mistakes, and administrative errors that would otherwise go undetected. To audit a match, however, an investigator needs to review all of the information related to a case. As it turns out, locating all of the relevant data can be a challenge, especially with the AM files.

AM Information Intake Dynamics

At an MFI, numerous people will file missing persons reports for the same victim, but usually not as a single group. The spouse may file a report on the day of the disaster, a sibling may go to the FAC the next day, and the parents might fly into town later. It is unrealistic to expect that they will all go to the FAC together because some informants may have to travel a significant distance, whereas others are nearby and want to file a report immediately. People in different stages of grief may not be ready to visit the FAC at the same time, and some family members may be estranged and prefer to go to the FAC alone. This dynamic of staggered intakes was also quite pronounced after the Tsunami as survivors filed reports in Thailand, and friends and family in the home countries went to their local FACs to do the same, sometimes mistakenly reporting as missing individuals who had survived.

In addition to family informants, employers will provide AM data for staff that perish at an MFI, either as victims or responders. Because the World Trade Center was an office complex, most of the victims were at work when the attack took place, and their employers provided a great deal of AM information. Several employers played a liaison role, transferring DNA reference samples from families abroad to the FAC. The Fire Department of New York (FDNY) played a similar liaison role on behalf of the firefighters lost at WTC.

If an informant is unaware that a file already exists for a victim, the interviewer will create a duplicate file. And even when the informant knows that a case has already been opened, the interviewer may have to start a fresh intake if the existing file is not readily accessible. Or the interviewer may elect to use a fresh intake form, recognizing that informants sometimes provide conflicting information.

In addition to multiple informants, a single informant may initiate multiple intakes. In the time between a disaster and the establishment of the FAC, an informant may file a report with local police and then again with the police department in the jurisdiction of the disaster. These reports are usually forwarded to the FAC. The same informant may then call the FAC to open a report before visiting in person. Once there, the informant may not be able to complete the intake on the first visit because some of the questions can be a bit obscure (most people do not know their mother's shoe size or the phone number of their brother's dentist off the top of their heads, for example). Or they may need to gain access to a loved one's apartment to retrieve a toothbrush for DNA testing. Finally, they may be too grief-stricken to finish the interview in one sitting.

At WTC, it was not unusual for a case file to contain several intakes from the same informant. After the Tsunami, tourists filed missing persons reports in Thailand and then again in their home countries. After Hurricane Katrina, not only did officials collect AM data in the Gulf, but also some municipalities where survivors were relocated collected redundant missing persons reports.

All of the intakes for a victim need to be integrated at some point, but because most intake forms are quite long, they are rarely completed in full. When looking at files that might be for the same victim, a file manager is usually working with data that only partially overlap. This is especially true for updates from returning informants since the very purpose of a follow-up intake is to provide data that were not available during the previous interview. If different informants give conflicting answers (or if different interviewers record similar answers in a disparate manner), the file manager may separate the intakes until clarifying information can be gathered. On the other hand, just as comparing partial primary PM data to full AM data can lead to a fortuitous match, so can comparing two partial AM intakes lead to two files being wrongly combined.

Figure 20-1 represents the file from WTC for Chuck Monroe. It contained several intakes from the father, Vincent, and several from the spouse, Debbie. Not only did the intakes from Debbie and Vincent disagree on some basic demographic data, but the separate intakes from each informant were not consistent. Eventually, it was determined that there were *two* victims named Chuck Monroe and that their files had been mistakenly combined: one was unmarried and had a father named Vincent, whereas the other was married to Debbie.

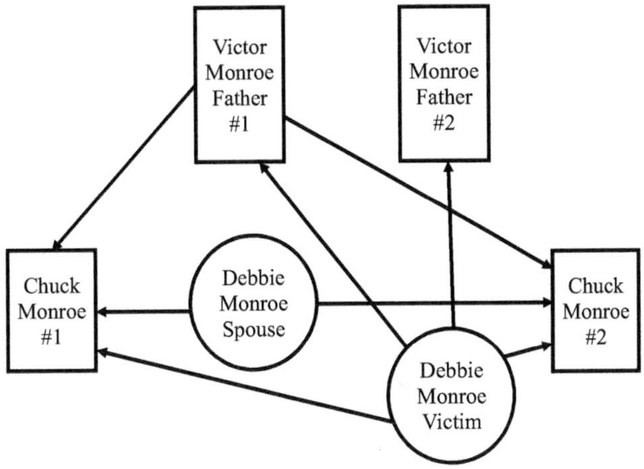

Figure 20-1
Chuck, Vincent, and Debbie Monroe: how many cases?

Complicating the matter was the discovery that there was also a victim named Debbie Monroe, and some of her information wound up in the file for Chuck Monroe because the informant and victim name were transposed during filing. As if that were not enough, the informant for Debbie Monroe was her father, a gentleman named Vincent Monroe. At this point, it appeared that Debbie and one of the two Chuck Monroes might be siblings. Their reference DNA was analyzed to establish that they were unrelated. The files for all three cases were reorganized.

Case Numbers

Issuing a Missing Person (MP) number for each victim can reduce many problems associated with victim names because it can be used like a case number to manage the files. When an informant returns to the FAC to provide more data for a case, the MP number can be used to link the update to the correct file. But this is not foolproof:

- An informant may be related to more than one victim and have several MP numbers. If the numbers are mixed up, then the data will be linked to the wrong case.
- Different agencies (FEMA, Red Cross, the police, etc.) will issue their own case numbers, which an informant may confuse with the MP number.
- The Missing Person number can be corrupted. At WTC, telephone intakes were given T Numbers (example: T-138) while personal interviews at the FAC got P Numbers (example: P-138). Managers at the FAC wanted to make this tracking number uniform, so they changed the "T" prefix to "P" in the master database so that T-138 became P-138. This meant that P-138 was in the system twice, linked to two different victims. As a result, some of the DNA reference samples and AM intakes were misfiled.

- Reading MP numbers is error-prone, as MP 1221 may be confused with MP 1212. If the victim list is alphabetized and assigned consecutive MP numbers, then victims with the same last names will have nearly identical case numbers: Lee (MP 133) and Lee (MP 134).
- Barcodes can help, but they cannot eliminate these problems. Their initial assignment may be incorrect, subsequent intervention in the tracking database can introduce errors, and incompatible barcode systems in a multi-agency response is likely. Even with barcodes, some file management will still be conducted manually.

Summary of AM Intake Dynamics

Multiple informants per victim and multiple intakes per informant can lead to AM files that are consolidated incorrectly. As a result, a victim's information may be spread out over several unlinked files, each lacking the data necessary to make an identification. If one file contains primary data that matches a PM case, an investigator may not realize that crucial information exists in another AM folder. Conversely, if data for Victim A are placed in the folder for Victim B, then a PM match to Victim A's reference items will be misidentified as Victim B. To better understand how these two outcomes occur and what an investigator can do in response, we need to examine the AM interview process in detail.

Challenges in the AM Interview Process

There are at least six possible points of failure in the AM interview process:

1. Incorrect information from the informant
2. Informant misunderstands the question
3. Lack of standardized answers
4. Typographical errors and transpositions
5. Handwriting
6. Data in the wrong field

Incorrect Information from the Informant

It is possible that the informant will provide incorrect information. In fraud cases, this is intentional. Once in the system, such information (and reference items) can become mixed with legitimate cases. For this reason, even fraudulent case files must be audited. At WTC, one fraud case had the same name as a real victim, and a personal effect from the legitimate case was accidentally filed in the fraudulent case folder. Even though no DNA testing was scheduled for the fraud case, its file was audited. The errant personal effect was discovered and used in the identification of the legitimate case.

Informants will also unintentionally provide incorrect information. Given the variety of people who go to the FAC (parents, spouse, children, coworkers, etc.) and the range of questions asked, it is to be expected that a given informant may be mistaken in some of his or her answers. This results in intakes with conflicting information that an investigator needs to reconcile. Because names and dates are often used to manage case files, they merit special consideration:

- Anglicized names: Foreign nationals often adopt Anglicized names while living in English-speaking countries. Friends, coworkers, and employers may refer to the adopted name, whereas parents and siblings use the birth name. For example, Won Park went by the name John Park at work, and his AM records at WTC included both names.
- Nicknames: An informant may provide the victim's nickname, such as Katie or Jack, while others provide the full name Catherine or John.
- Alias: Some people use an alias or go by their middle name. "Carl James Anderson" might be reported as such, whereas others refer to him as "Jim Anderson."
- Incomplete surnames: If a surname has multiple terms, one informant may give just the last term, whereas others provide the full surname. This happened regularly at WTC with Hispanic, Arabic, Asian, and African names. For instance, AM intakes for Hector Tirado Jimenz included both "Hector Tirado Jimenz" and "Hector Jimenz."
- Maiden names: A woman may retain her maiden name at work for business reasons. The employer, coworkers, and old friends may report her missing by her maiden name, whereas immediate family members will provide the married name.

Some of these examples may appear trivial at first. After all, anyone looking at the files for Catherine Bigsby and Katie Bigsby can see the likely connection. But this relies on some cultural familiarity. An American might know that Jack is a common nickname for John, but is that widely known abroad? The popular Southern nickname "Bubba" can substitute for any first name, a fact that may not be widely known outside the South. Conversely, how many Americans know that the Russian diminutive for Alexander is Sasha? Or that Jay can be short for Sanjay?

Spotting the similarities between the names in two case files also relies on their being in close proximity to each other. But when the victim list at WTC was sorted by surname, Carl James Anderson and Jim Anderson were separated by several entries (Clyde Anderson, Dave Anderson, etc.), diluting the apparent connection. And a search for "Tirado Jimenez" failed to retrieve the victim folder filed under "Jimenez." Only after the victim list was sorted by date of birth did the records cluster together.

As for dates, adult children don't always know the year of their parent's birth and may be too embarrassed to admit it, so they estimate the year. And couples can marry privately and have a public wedding later. In such cases, the wedding date provided by the parents will not match the date given by the spouse. This information is important when trying to link the date inscribed on a wedding ring to the wedding date reported in an AM intake file.

Informant Misunderstands the Question

"What is your relationship to the victim?" An informant at WTC answered "Father," but his DNA profile did not fit the family pedigree. A review of the intake showed that his date of birth was after the victim's, which meant that the victim was *his* father. The pedigree was revised, and it worked. This shows how administrative data (the donor's date of birth) can resolve problems.

Other questions can be misinterpreted by the informant: "Address?" (the informant's or the victim's?), "Parents of the victim?" (biological or legal?), and "Where did they work?" (location where they were working at the time of the disaster or the name of the employer?).

Lack of Standardized Answers

If interviewers use different terms to record the same answers, then a search of the AM database by one term will only find a portion of the relevant records. Additionally, if the AM and PM nomenclature is not consistent, then searching either database for investigational leads becomes problematic. Most forms use answer check boxes where possible, but some concepts require the interviewer to manually record the data, leading to more nonstandardized answers.

Jewelry descriptions in the Tsunami database included "YM," "yellow metal," and "gold." All are accurate, but a search with one term will fail to find records using the other terms. A mortuary report at WTC read "male, hair = none." A search of the AM database for men where hair was "none" failed to return the records for "bald" men. While all manually recorded data are subject to this problem, names, dates, and object descriptions are particularly vulnerable.

Names

There are three main issues with regard to standardizing name entries: generational identifiers, multi-termed names, and word order. Generational identifiers such as Junior and Jr. are accurate, but if interviewers use both, then separate intakes for the same victim will often lack matching names. A search for "Smith, Jr." will not find "Smith, Junior," and vice versa.

Multi-termed surnames present two challenges. The first is determining where the surname begins. The second is deciding how to handle hyphens. In a case from WTC, a woman named Alice Mayhew-Jones had separate AM intakes filed under:

- Alice Mayhew-Jones
- Alice Mayhew Jones
- Alice Jones
- Alice Mayhew (filed by the parents, who were estranged from their son-in-law)

Sorting the records by last name meant that Mayhew-Jones and Jones did not cluster together. Searching by "Jones" or "Mayhew" only retrieved half the records, and searches by "Mayhew Jones" failed to return Mayhew-Jones.

Regarding word order, in English it is typical to address someone by his or her forename but to list people alphabetically by surname. But some cultures do the opposite. If an American interviewer is told that the victim's name is "Kim Won Duk," he may reverse the terms to correspond to the "surname, forename" format, as in "Won Duk, Kim." But if the informant gave the name in the Korean style (surname first), then Kim is the surname, not Won Duk. Other informant–interviewer pairs may generate different combinations for the same victim.

Dates

The European format is day/month/year, whereas in the United States it is month/day/year. Because many disasters in the United States have an international dimension, both date formats will likely appear in the AM records, especially if foreign employers, embassies, or police agencies are involved in collecting information from the home countries. A wedding date on a foreign-sourced intake may read 7/3/75 while a report on a wedding band from a set of remains may be recorded as 3/7/75. Complicating the matter is that some software programs automatically format numbers as text. In this way, it is not immediately apparent that March 7, 1975, and July 3, 1975, could be the "same" date.

Objects

Certain objects associated with a victim can be useful to an investigator, such as jewelry, clothing, and tattoos. Unfortunately, it is very difficult to standardize their descriptions, as the "yellow metal vs. gold" jewelry example illustrates. For the Tsunami, AM reports came in from around the world, and there was a multinational presence in the morgue. As a result, AM and PM descriptions often reflected national variations in describing the same object. For example, swimwear was alternatively described as swimsuits, bathing suits, bathing costumes, bikinis, swim trunks, or Speedos.

This dynamic can extend beyond strictly physical objects to labels or associations. At WTC, searching the AM database for employees of "Cantor-Fitzgerald" would not retrieve records for "Cantor Fitzgerald" (no hyphen), "Cantor Fitz," or "Cantor." Each entry is accurate, but these variations made it challenging to find all of the cases related to the company.

Typographical Errors and Transpositions

All manual intake systems are prone to typographical errors, and MFI data are no exception. For example, in the clothing descriptions of the AM files at WTC, there were 26 variations on the spelling of "khaki." Transpositions can occur in phone numbers, addresses, and birth dates. Even names can be transposed, as an intake for "Andrew Clarke" was filed under "Clarke Andrew." In more than case, the informant and victim names were transposed. Not only did this make it harder to find the AM data for a victim, but it also put a living person on the missing list.

Handwriting

Many intake systems are handwritten. Not only is handwriting hard to read, but it encourages the use of abbreviations and acronyms, which may not be obvious to the reader. The forms often have limited space to record answers, forcing one to write smaller (reducing legibility) and use more abbreviations (reducing clarity). Entering handwritten text into a database later only increases the potential for transcription errors. A database at WTC had an entry for "AHOV," but no AM intake could be found for this person. Eventually, the file was found under the correct name, "Attov." The handwritten double lowercase letter "t" had been read as an uppercase "H."

Data in the Wrong Field

If an AM tattoo description is logged in the field for clothing descriptions, it is effectively hidden from an investigator searching for a match to a tattoo on a set of remains. A more common problem is that data can often be recorded in more than one place. For example, many forms have fields for describing a wallet and its contents. Most intakes also have a section for the driver's license. Because these are often found in the wallet, it is not unusual to see the driver's license documented in the wallet section of the form instead.

The generic instance of this dynamic is the intake question with check box answers where the last choice is "Other," accompanied by a blank text field. Although this design has obvious merit, it means that the answer may reside in the text field or the check box. As a result, a computer search of the answer check boxes for a question will often miss relevant records. In addition, most forms have a section on the last page for "Other Information." Data are often entered here despite the existence of a dedicated section for the information elsewhere on the form.

Error Rates in the AM Records

The Disaster Mortuary Operational Response Team (DMORT) is an agency of the U.S. government that assists local medical examiners at MFIs. The agency has an AM/PM data collection system called the Victim Identification Program (VIP). The AM portion is seven pages long with nearly 300 data fields for about 200 questions (there are more fields than questions because some questions ask for several pieces of information: address = street, city, state, and ZIP code). The author's experience is that an average initial intake for a case completes about 200 data fields.

If an AM interview is 99% accurate at each of the six possible points of failure, then an answer is estimated to be correct 94% of the time (0.99 ^ 6). The estimated error rate is 1 minus the estimated accuracy rate, or 1 – 0.94 = 0.06. With 200 data fields, a 6% error rate yields an estimated 12 errors per interview. But 99% accuracy is probably optimistic. Consider sitting in the comfort of your home making a purchase online. You are providing a small amount of personal information that is well known to yourself; there is no handwriting and no interviewer. It is just you entering data into a computer. Yet it is not uncommon to make simple data entry errors in this scenario, suggesting that the accuracy rate is less than 99% even under the best of circumstances.

Now imagine that you are at a FAC in a distant city being interviewed by a complete stranger regarding a loved one presumed dead in a disaster. The interviewer asks numerous personal questions, such as your wife's bra size or whether your brother was circumcised. Was he ever arrested? Was she on meds? The interviewer is polite but also fatigued from conducting multiple interviews in a row and hastily writes down your responses on a form that does not have enough space for your answers. Later this information will be entered into a computer by someone else who has already read through dozens of intakes that day alone.

In this context, 99% accuracy is unlikely. If we lower it to 95%, then the estimated accuracy of a data field is (0.95 ^ 6) = 75%, which is an error rate of 25%. Across 200 data fields, this is 50 problems per intake. A plane crash with 150 victims and three informants per victim would generate a data set with about 22,500 problems (150 × 3 × 200 × 0.25). If each informant has a follow-up interview during which he or she completes another 50 data fields (150 × 3 × 50 × 0.25), that is another 5,625 problems, for a total of about 28,000. It is worth stressing that this does not mean the data are wrong (although that is possible). In this context, it can mean that a correct answer is in the wrong field or was recorded in an irregular manner (Jr. vs. Junior, mixed date formats, etc.). As a result, the record will not be found by a search or sort of the files using those criteria. Furthermore, linking updates to the parent case file can also be challenged by such problem data.

Assume that there is one informant per victim and that they all make an initial visit to the FAC. Each informant then returns a few days later to provide a DNA sample. With 150 victims, that is 150 updates that have to be linked to the correct case. If this process is 95% accurate, then 5% of the follow-ups are at risk. That is about seven updates that are placed in the wrong folder, which impacts about 15 cases, or 10% of the total. One can see how this number increases with each successive round of updates or if more than one informant per victim is involved.

At WTC, there was a victim named Henry Niles and another named Henry Niles, Jr. They were unrelated. The son of Henry Niles made several trips to the FAC, as did many members of the family, resulting in numerous intakes and multiple tracking numbers for DNA samples. The son of Henry Niles was named Henry Niles, Jr., and on one visit to the FAC, his update was accidentally placed into the file for the *victim* named Henry Niles, Jr. because the person handling the file confused the informant name with the victim name. Unfortunately, this update contained his DNA reference samples, which were later used to erroneously identify a set of remains as Henry Niles, Jr. The error was only discovered during the admin review when the audit of the DNA intakes versus the case file inventory was shown to be out of sync.

Error Rates in the PM Records

PM records are vulnerable to (1) lack of standardization in the recording of data, (2) handwriting, (3) typographical errors, and (4) storing data in the wrong field. Assuming 99% accuracy at each possible point of failure means that a given data field is accurate 96% of the time (0.99 ^ 4). PM forms can run several pages with hundreds of data fields, but not every topic will be relevant for each set of remains, so assume that only 200 fields will be completed per intake. That means there are at least eight data problems per PM record.

Cases may be re-examined, and these updates need to be linked to the correct folder. If 25% of all autopsies are re-examined and 5% of these are incorrectly linked, then there will be about a dozen update errors per 1,000 cases. Since each error affects two cases, about 2.5% of all PM cases will have a filing error (1,000 × 0.25 × 0.05 × 2).

For example, assume there is an MFI with 200 victims and each body fragments into seven pieces on average. That is 1,400 PM cases. Eight mistakes per intake and a 2.5% updating error rate means a PM database with 11,235 problems. Again, this does not mean errors of fact only, but also correct data that are recorded in a manner that makes it difficult for an investigator to pursue a match or consolidate records. One can imagine how the potential for error increases as the number of victims and level of fragmentation increases. For example, at WTC there were more than 20,000 remains recovered from about 2,750 victims.

Addressing the Problems

While an ounce of prevention is certainly worth a pound of cure, the nature of disaster response seems to guarantee that there will always be problem data. The following sections look at prevention first and then address how to work with problem data.

Preventing Problems

There are several steps an agency can take to reduce data errors at an MFI. First, it should define the AM/PM intake forms it will use ahead of time. Because local authorities will likely receive assistance from DMORT, it is a good idea to preview VIP, available at www.dmort.org. Interpol also has a series of Disaster Victim Identification intake forms that may be helpful (www.interpol.org). An agency could use one of these systems and create supplemental forms to reflect local needs, or it could design its own MFI data collection system based on the missing persons forms already used in its jurisdiction.

After the intake system has been defined, the questions should be reviewed to standardize answers where possible, particularly for names and dates, as well as the abbreviations and acronyms for describing objects, concepts, and affiliations. It is critical that both the PM and AM systems use the same nomenclature. This is not a matter of finding the "correct" format so much as having a consistent approach.

Rather than limiting this process to those who will collect the data (mortuary staff and interviewers at the FAC), the planning process should also include the database managers who will administer the system as well as the investigators who will use it to make identifications: medical examiners, pathologists, odontologists, anthropologists, fingerprint examiners, and DNA analysts. Forensic biology is noteworthy here because DNA experts are not only often left out of disaster preparedness planning, but they are sometimes not even included in the immediate disaster response due to the perception that DNA testing takes too long. Because of this mindset, the protocol at many disasters is to initially perform only dental or fingerprint analysis in order to make as many identifications as quickly as possible and then turn to DNA for the remaining cases.

When finally deployed, DNA analysts often inherit policies and systems that do not reflect the needs of forensic biology, impeding their effectiveness. Concerns regarding the pace of DNA testing are often deflected by calling it the "method of last resort," and this is dutifully repeated by the media, perpetuating the notion that DNA testing is too slow to be incorporated from the outset. In many ways, it is a self-fulfilling prophecy. A notable exception to this mindset is the close coordination between the Armed Forces DNA Identification Laboratory (AFDIL) and DMORT. Not only are the protocols in place for DNA testing prior to a disaster, but DNA teams from AFDIL deploy with DMORT as part of the initial disaster response.

There are several benefits to including DNA in the initial identification effort. First, where there is any level of fragmentation, the DNA profile derived from a body part identified by fingerprints or dental can be used to identify other body parts of that victim that are not amenable to fingerprinting or odontology. Second, many disasters include families, and a DNA sample taken from remains identified by other modalities could then be used by geneticists in kinship analysis to identify the remains of biological relations. And finally, although fingerprints and dental are reliable, they are not perfect, especially in a disaster response where examiners from different agencies are suddenly thrown together and have to reconcile their different protocols and methods.

Computer resources should be secured to avoid handwritten intakes. Staffing rotations should be established for the morgue and the FAC. Liaisons at partner agencies should be included in the planning stages. Vendors that are expected to provide critical services, such as equipment and consumables, should likewise be included to ensure that they have the necessary surge capacity.

Conduct mock AM interviews. This training is not only valuable, but will test the efficiency of the intake system and may flag individuals who are not suited for handling grieving families.

Barcode systems should be established and checked for intra-agency compatibility. Tracking labels based on the barcode numbers should be readable by humans. A case name and number scheme should be developed to create a unique identifier for every *object* in the system. On the PM side, "objects" would include body bags, recovered property, and samples taken for fingerprinting, odontology, or DNA. On the AM side, "objects" include informants, victims, intake forms at the FAC, and reference materials submitted for fingerprints, X-rays, and DNA.

There are four general considerations in developing the label schema. First, it has to contain enough information to allow a human operator to handle it appropriately. For example, a file clerk should be able to tell at a glance whether he or she is holding an AM or PM folder.

Second, toe tags, file folder tabs, and test tubes can be quite small. This places a practical limit on the length of the label name. Using a tiny font to make a name fit does not support the first guideline. In these cases, it may be prudent to place small items in larger containers that can support larger labels.

Third, the label should not include any information that may be modified or updated. As has been shown, AM data can change with each intake, even for seemingly static concepts such as the name or date of birth. The problem is that corrections to a label are not backward-compatible. The old label already exists on boxes, on test tubes, and in printouts. It resides in spreadsheets and databases that may not be available for updating. An investigator working with an updated label will not be able to trace a reference sample backward through the system to its intake, voiding the chain of custody.

On the other hand, uncorrected label names are a source of confusion. At WTC, a reference sample for Jonas Clare had the prefix BM for Biological Mother. But it had a male profile. A review of the AM intakes for Jonas Clare showed that his wife brought their infant son to the FAC to provide DNA. Mrs. Clare signed a consent form for minors and under "relationship to donor," she wrote "mother." The interviewer entered this as the relationship *to the victim* in the database and a tracking label was created with the prefix "BM." This "mother" sample was flagged as a problem by every new analyst who saw it, consuming countless hours of staff time.

Changing the prefix to BS (Biological Son), however, would have created a different problem: the collection log for Clare at the FAC (maintained by a separate agency) still showed a single DNA donation from the "mother," and all of the transaction records for the case listed a BM sample. An investigator starting with the BS sample in the lab would not be able to work backward to find a DNA collection from the son of Jonas Clare, and someone auditing the case file starting at the FAC would see that a sample from the mother was collected but would be unable to find it in the DNA lab, triggering a search for the "lost" sample.

In the end, it was decided that being able to track the sample through the process was more important than a sample label with the correct relationship code, a decision the author supported. From a data management point of view, it is better to have a name that is flawed but consistent rather than one that is inconsistent. But the best approach is simply not to embed data about the sample in the sample name because this information can and will change.

The fourth guideline for creating a naming schema is that it be compatible with systems already in place. Collaborating agencies and vendors will have their own information management systems, complete with accessioning numbers, data fields, reporting tools, and standard operating procedures. It is often better to leverage those existing systems instead of imposing a new format. Simply put, changing one's standard operating procedure increases the potential for errors in the best of circumstances. Doing so during the chaos of responding to a disaster can only make this dynamic worse.

The situation becomes even more cumbersome when the label name attempts to capture information from the *internal* process at the supporting agency. For example, DNA testing is a complex undertaking with several process steps, and there is the potential for samples to repeat certain steps. Although the operating parameters of each step may be useful to the analyst interpreting the DNA results, there is no need to squeeze this information into the sample label. Such data are fully available in the laboratory's information management system (LIMS) and can be linked to the sample name as a supporting file.

Regardless, labels designed to display information regarding the handling of an object are easily compromised. After the Tsunami, body bag numbers were based on the nationality of the autopsy team. Unfortunately, countries rotated staff every few weeks, reducing the specificity of this number. Other autopsy teams were multinational in composition, rendering the number ambiguous. And as bodies were re-examined later, new autopsy teams added additional body bag numbers to reflect their nationality. This became a significant source of confusion because many body bags eventually had more than one tracking number.

Solving Problems

To audit a proposed identification or create an investigational lead, one must first assemble all of the potentially relevant AM records. First, conduct multiple searches that are broad enough to ensure that no relevant record is missed (this approach accepts that irrelevant files will also be retrieved). Second, compile the searches and cull unrelated cases by sorting the list through demographic details and removing the clusters of records that are disqualified. Manually review the remaining cases to consolidate or exclude. For example, search for Employer = Acme and Gender = Male. If the victim lived in New Jersey, sort the search results by State and omit all entries except those for NJ.

Some basic tips for conducting broad searches include:

- Use truncated surnames with wildcards to overcome typographical errors: Rama* will find Ramachandran and Ramashandran.
- Phonetic variations can find misspelled names: Lee vs. Li, Cane vs. Kane.
- Wildcards can find nonstandard uses of generational identifiers and hyphens: Hernan* will find Hernandez-Tirado, Hernandez Tirado, Sr., and Hernandez, Senior.

- Objects can be described in a variety of ways, so try synonyms such as gold & yellow, brown & brunette, or bikini & swimsuit. Consider acronyms and abbreviations, such as YM vs. yellow metal or FDNY vs. Fire Department New York City.
- Try reverse searches: if you are looking for files on Terry John, try putting Terry in the surname field. If a ring has a date inscription of 8/11/83, query the wedding date fields for 11/8/83 as well as 8/11/83.
- Look in related fields. Search the wallet and purse entries for driver's license information.
- Query the catch-all summary text fields in the intake form.
- Do not use AND with multiple field searches; instead, use "OR." Remember that many fields in an intake will be left blank, and records lacking data in a field will be excluded by searches that mandate data be present. A search for Gender = "Male" AND State of Residence = "New Jersey" will not return records where Gender = "Male" but the State of Residence field was left blank.

The key to finding all the relevant records is not to attempt a single, precise search that, one hopes, finds "the" record for a case. In fact, it could be argued that the only thing worse than a search that returns no matches is a search that returns some matches, creating a false sense of success. The search strategy has to exhaust all possible avenues of finding a relevant file.

The heuristic of conducting several broad searches and then excluding irrelevant records is a tactical approach for researching individual cases. There is also a need for a comprehensive, system-wide view of the data. First, one should map the AM and PM operations in order to identify the links in the chain where material and/or information is handed off between work stations and agencies. After the process has been mapped, then the inventory manifests between each link can be compared to reveal missing or surplus items. For example, remains will be recovered at the disaster site, moved to a local collection area, transported to the morgue's holding facility, pulled for autopsy, and then placed in storage. A different group will carry out each step, the performance of which will generate time and date stamps, employee names, and details specific to the function at hand: search teams will note the location where remains were found, evidence techs will list the property recovered, pathologists will provide autopsy findings, and mortuary attendants will note where the remains are stored. In addition to the body bag number and a master PM file that travels with the remains, each group may have its own record-keeping system complete with tracking numbers, barcodes, and databases.

If the morgue accessions a dozen remains from the disaster site in a single day and all are autopsied that day, then the mortuary storage log should also show the accessioning of a dozen remains that day. If not, that would be a cause for review. At WTC, the accession and inventory numbers did not always match because as anthropologists reviewed the remains in autopsy, they discovered cases of commingling. Those remains would be separated, creating a new case. In other instances, they determined that the remains were nonhuman and removed them from the system. Both were sound policies and explained for the disparate inventory numbers.

A critical component of mapping the system and reconciling inventories is defining the terminology used at each link in the chain. The FAC at WTC generated a P Number for each victim and a DNA Case Number for each DNA collection. This information, along with the DNA reference items, was sent to the New York State Police DNA laboratory. The NYSP database already had dedicated fields for tracking data, so the P Number was filed under its Incident Number and the DNA Case Number went in its Reference field. The Case field in the NYSP database was then populated with a tracking number called the WDI Number. When DNA samples were traced through the system, it was important to clarify which Case Number was being referred to, the one from the FAC or the one from the NYSP. It was also critical to know that the P Number at the FAC became the Incident Number at the NYSP and that the DNA Case Number became the Reference Number.

Generic terms such as "case," "file," "collection," "incident," "sample," "reference," and "item" were routinely used by agencies at WTC with different meanings, a phenomenon the author witnessed again in the Tsunami response. Although it may not be possible to standardize the usage of such terms across all links in the chain, defining their different meanings can reduce handling errors and facilitate tracing an item's chain of custody.

Conclusion

Preparing for the information management needs of a disaster ahead of time may not eliminate all of the data management problems that can arise when numerous agencies collaborate on a project, but it can reduce the scope of the problems that will emerge. A sound data management strategy after the disaster will allow for the effective integration of AM and PM records in support of the identification process. The critical dimension of this process is using the data to create investigational leads and then reconciling all of the information (primary, secondary, and administrative) when there is a match between AM and PM data.

CHAPTER 21

Resolving Commingling Issues During the Medicolegal Investigation of Mass Fatality Incidents

Elias J. Kontanis, Paul S. Sledzik

National Transportation Safety Board, Washington, D.C.

By definition, mass fatality incidents (MFIs) result in numerous deaths occurring over a relatively narrow time frame. These events produce complex multidisciplinary investigative challenges (Labovich et al. 2003; Lee et al. 2007; Ludes et al. 1994; Tidball-Binz 2007; van den Bos 1980). From a medicolegal perspective, investigators seek to recover and examine decedents in a dignified and respectful manner, accurately determine cause and manner of death, perform accurate and efficient identification of victims, provide for the rapid return of victims' remains to their legal next of kin, and exchange factual and timely information with families in a compassionate manner (Interpol 2009; Sledzik and Bryson 2010; Wagner and Froede 1993). Oftentimes, severe fragmentation and commingling of human remains are the byproducts of the causative forces and pose significant challenges to investigators (Sledzik and Rodriguez 2002). In a mass fatality context, the overarching tenet regarding commingling is that human remains with no anatomical/physical connection *must* be considered to be commingled (Mundorff 2008; Mundorff, this book, Chapter 17). This principle also applies to remains that are spatially associated but present no valid anatomical connection. From the perspective of the forensic investigator, resolving commingling, and ultimately decedent identification, requires careful management of both the human remains and the data generated during recovery and postmortem examination. This chapter examines effects of fragmentation and commingling on the identification process and discusses the role of triage during the postmortem data collection process as a means to facilitate recognition and reassociation of commingled remains.

Identification

Identifying human remains is a primary investigative objective for legal, cultural, and scientific reasons. Family members of the deceased require legal documentation associated with identification to manage the victim's estate and coordinate insurance benefits, wills/probate, and child guardianship (Pan American Health Organization 2004; Wagner and

Commingled Human Remains. http://dx.doi.org/10.1016/B978-0-12-405889-7.00021-6

Froede 1993). From an investigative perspective, identifying decedents can provide evidence to help determine the sequence of events resulting in the fatalities. For example, air crew identification and injury pattern analysis are often instrumental for determining and evaluating actions of the air crew at the time of the accident (Midda 1974; Read and Pillay 2000; Taneja and Wiegmann 2003). In addition, correlating passenger injuries with seating assignments may aid incident reconstruction and evaluation of safety equipment (Armstrong et al. 1955; Cullen and Turk 1980; Li and Baker 1997; National Transportation Safety Board 2007; Vosswinkel et al. 1999). More broadly, the humanitarian and moral obligations to identify the dead are nearly universal. State, national, and international humanitarian laws govern the status of decedents, the need to identify the dead, and the status of unidentified remains (International Committee of the Red Cross 1995; Pan American Health Organization 2004).

Mass fatality investigators often rely on a combination of positive and presumptive methods during the identification process. Ultimately, positive identification requires comparing the unique biological attributes that are a component of the decedent's antemortem record with those biological characteristics observed during postmortem analysis. Fingerprints, odontological evidence, DNA/molecular analysis, and the presence of surgical implants and anatomical anomalies are utilized for positive identification. Presumptive identifiers such as associated personal effects and the biological profile (i.e., sex, age, ancestry, stature, and characteristics of individuation) often provide an identification hypothesis that can be accepted or rejected based on a comparison of unique biological attributes (Steadman et al. 2006; Thompson and Black 2007). Presumptive attributes can also permit identification by exclusion in closed populations when all decedents in a definable category are accounted for.

Several factors influence the complexity of the fatality management and identification process and, ultimately, the success of the victim identification effort (Figure 21-1). The principal factors that will influence the complexity of the identification effort are the status of the victim population and the condition of remains. The victim population can be classified either as closed or open. Closed population mass fatality incidents are typified by commercial aircraft accidents, where relatively accurate passenger manifests are available soon after the accident. In a closed population event, the medicolegal objective is to account for all potentially identifiable remains for each decedent. Often, this approach does not require analysis of all remains, just those that have a potential to be identified. With open decedent populations, typified by natural disasters, neither the number of victims nor their names are known. Under these circumstances, best practice is to analyze and, if possible, identify every fragment recovered. This is the only way to provide an accurate accounting of decedents. Such an approach requires more time and cost, as DNA analysis is often the only way to provide this information.

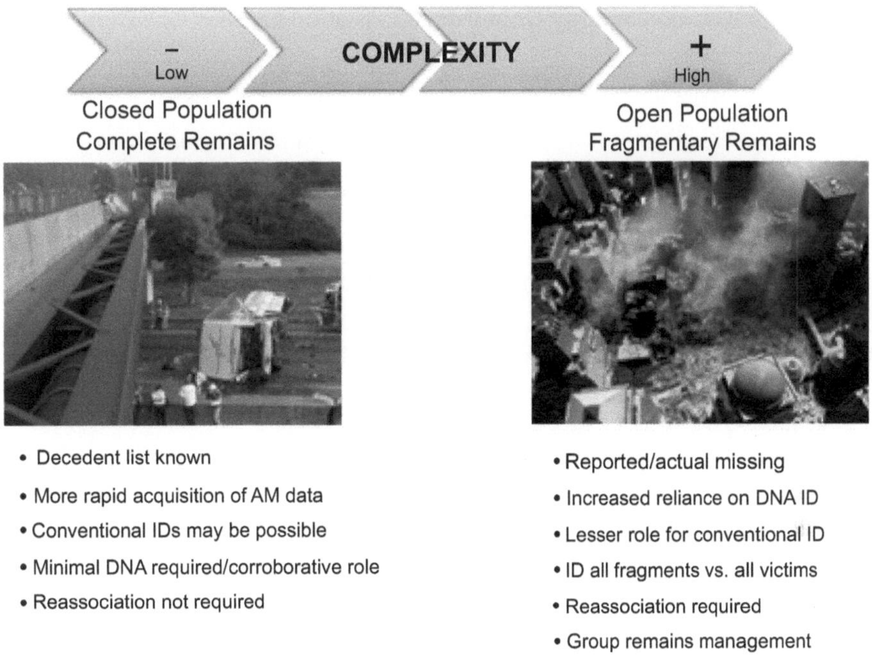

Figure 21-1
The principal factors influencing the complexity of a mass fatality medicolegal operation.

Fragmentation, Reassociation, and Identification: Influencing Parameters

The condition of human remains, particularly the fragmentation severity, will have a substantial effect on fatality management, decedent identification, and reassociation of commingled remains. In this chapter, fragmentation severity is described using the “fragmentation index,” which is simply the ratio of recovered remains to the number of decedents. Table 21-1 demonstrates the range of fragmentation severities observed during the investigation of several recent aviation crashes. Fragmentation severities range from a low of 1.0 remains per decedent (i.e., no fragmentation) resulting from the crash of the Bombardier CL-600-2B19 during an attempted take-off at a speed of approximately 231 feet per second, reaching an altitude less than 20 feet off the ground (National Transportation Safety Board 2007). The other end of the fragmentation severity spectrum is represented by the ValuJet Flight 592 DC-9 jet that impacted terrain at a 70–80 degree angle traveling approximately 675 feet per second (Mittleman et al. 2000). A total of 4,282 fragments were recovered, representing 38.9 remains per decedent. While the fragmentation index presents a coarse perspective on incident dynamics, it is broadly influenced by recovery strategies and postmortem data collection protocols. Recovery operations conducted by experienced personnel using systematic scene processing strategies will result in a realistic approximation of the fragmentation severity,

Table 21-1: Fragmentation Severity Data from 13 Aviation Crashes that Occurred between 1994 and 2009

Incident (Year)	Aircraft/Type	# of Decedents	# of Remains Recovered	Fragmentation Index	Months Dedicated to Identification
USAir 427 (1994)	B-737/Jet	132	1,771	13.4	2
ValuJet 592 (1996)	DC-9/Jet	110	4,282	38.9	3.5
Swissair 111 (1998)	MD-11/Jet	229	2,500	10.9	3.5
EgyptAir 990 (1999)	B-767/Jet	217	6,000	27.7	6
Alaska Air 261 (2000)	MD-83/Jet	88	950	10.8	4
Executive Air (2000)	BAE J-31/Prop	19	25	1.3	0.17
American 77/ Pentagon (2001)	B-757/Jet	188	2,000	10.6	3
United 93 (2001)	B-757/Jet	44	1,500	34.1	3
American 587 (2001)	A-300/Jet	265	2,077	7.8	1
US Airways 5481 (2002)	B-1900/Prop	21	43	2.1	0.23
Corporate Airlines 5596 (2004)	BAE J-32/Prop	13	30	2.3	0.5
Comair 5191 (2006)	CL-600-2B19	49	49	1.0	0.03
Colgan Air 3407 (2009)	DHC-8-400	50	447	8.94	3.5

whereas inexperienced personnel can introduce recovery biases that depress the fragmentation severity index (Dirkmaat 2012). Morgue protocols can also influence the fragmentation index. Managers responsible for postmortem data collection may decide that fragments classified as group remains will not be part of the tally, which will also depress the fragmentation index. Nevertheless, the fragmentation index is a useful concept for comparing the fragmentation severity between incidents with varying numbers of decedents.

As the number of decedents and the number of recovered human tissue fragments increase, forensic identification experts must make decisions about how best to use the limited resources of personnel, time, and funds. Data from 13 aviation mass fatality incidents suggest that there is no significant relationship between the number of decedents and the amount of time dedicated to the identification process when the effect of the number of recovered remains has been removed ($r = -0.101$, $p = 0.754$) (Figure 21-2, Table 21-1). The relationship with time becomes significant when the number of recovered remains per decedent (i.e., the fragmentation index), controlling for the number of decedents, is examined ($r = 0.659$, $p = 0.020$) (Figure 21-3, Table 21-1).

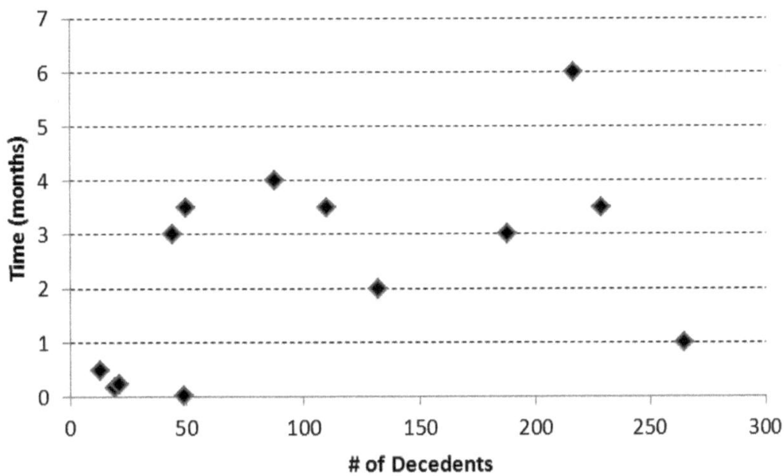

Figure 21-2
Data from 13 aviation incidents demonstrating the relationship between the number of decedents and the amount of time dedicated to the identification process.

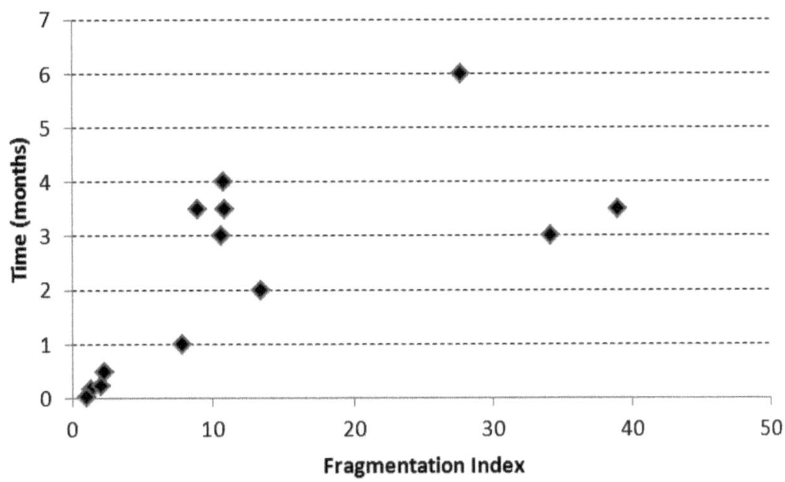

Figure 21-3
Data from 13 aviation incidents demonstrating the relationship between the fragmentation index (i.e., the ratio of recovered remains to the number of decedents) and the amount of time dedicated to the identification process.

While fragmentation severity appears to have a significant influence on investigative resources, the number of individuals cannot be neglected. For example, the investigative effort and consequently the amount of time required to obtain antemortem records will undoubtedly increase as the number of decedents increases. Even though the correlation between the fragmentation index and time is significant, the coefficient of determination (i.e., R^2 value) suggests that fragmentation severity is responsible for less than 50% of the change in the amount of time dedicated to the identification process. This finding emphasizes the confounding influence of additional variables on the identification process that have not been quantified, such as antemortem and postmortem data management practices (Kontanis et al. 2001; Tyrrell et al. 2006).

In addition to time, fragmentation severity will influence the utility of morphoscopic and molecular identification methods. Morphoscopic identification methods, such as fingerprint and odontological analysis, are based on physical examination of remains and do not rely on molecular identification strategies. Prior to the regular use of molecular methods for identification, biological tissue that could not lead to an identification based on a morphoscopic method was considered unidentifiable when fragmentation severity was high; however, with increased reliance on DNA, the majority of biological tissue is now considered identifiable. Figures 21-4 and 21-5 describe the relative contributions of molecular and morphoscopic identification modalities as a consequence of fragmentation severity. In these figures, the dependent variable is the number of identifications generated using either molecular or morphoscopic modalities expressed as a percentage of the total number of identifications. Figure 21-4 demonstrates that with increasing

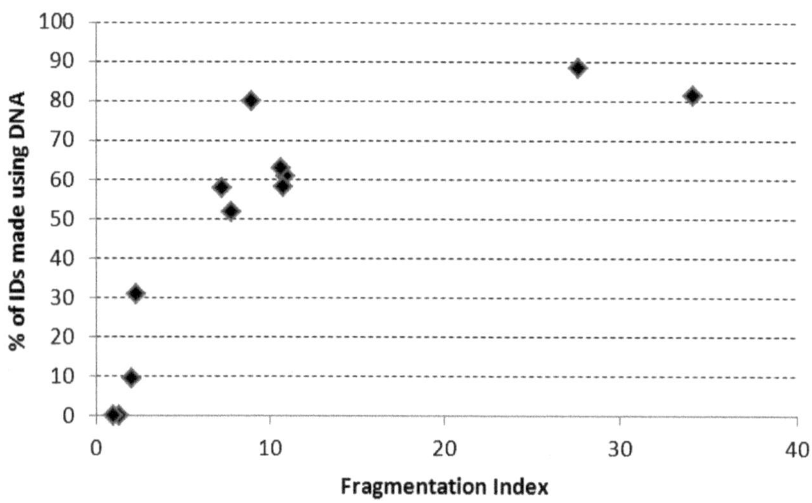

Figure 21-4
Data from 12 mass fatality incidents demonstrating the relationship between the percent of identifications made using DNA technologies and the fragmentation index (i.e., the ratio of recovered remains to the number of decedents).

fragmentation (controlling for the number of decedents) there is increasing reliance on DNA to produce identifications ($r = 0.795$, $p = 0.003$). Conversely, as the fragmentation severity increases, the utility of morphoscopic identification methods diminishes ($r = -0.795$, $p = 0.003$; Figure 21-5). In other words, relatively complete remains will have a greater chance of bearing the unique physical identifiers necessary for morphoscopic identifications. However, as fragmentation severity increases, the possibility of recovering fragments with friction ridge skin, dental remains, or other unique identifiers decreases. Consequently, the lack of unique morphoscopic features results in an increased reliance on DNA identification methods. These figures also demonstrate that the relationship between identification modality and fragmentation severity is asymptotic. Simply stated, even in cases of extreme fragmentation, morphoscopic identification will be possible for some of the remains. Furthermore, even with the liberal application of DNA technologies, a small percentage of the human remains may not be identified. Some remains may not be suitable for sampling, results may be inconclusive, or antemortem reference samples may not be available. Additionally, perimortem and postmortem factors such as thermal modification, contact with amplification inhibitors, and decomposition will destroy DNA or render it of low quality that is unsuitable for identification purposes (Prinz et al. 2007).

Managing the Identification Process: Applying Human Remains Triage Principles

An effective identification process largely depends on the application of appropriate morgue management principles. Incident morgue designs must allow for rapid yet thorough examination of decedent remains while meeting incident-specific investigative goals. This is

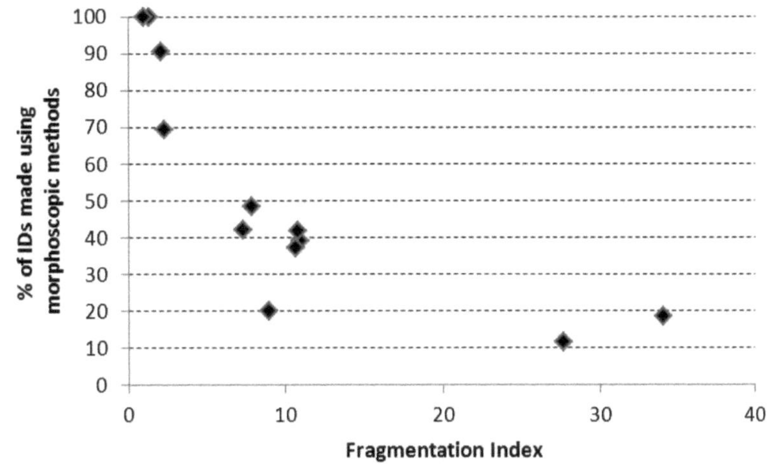

Figure 21-5
Data from 12 mass fatality incidents demonstrating the relationship between the percent of identifications made using morphoscopic methods (i.e., dental, fingerprint, medical comparisons) and the fragmentation index (i.e., the ratio of recovered remains to the number of decedents).

especially imperative when the fragmentation index is high. In disaster medicine, triage is used to successfully manage the initial care of mass casualty patients by sorting patients into predefined categories based on injury severity and treatment urgency (Auf Der Heide 1989; Bowen and Bellamy 1988; Nijman 1980). In order to perform this task, medical personnel are trained to rapidly and effectively assess and classify patients in a systematic fashion (Janousek and Jackson 1999; Kennedy et al. 1996; Robinson 2002). The concept of triage is readily applicable to the mass fatality morgue management system, where systematic decisions concerning the potential of fragmented remains to lead to an identification will facilitate postmortem data collection, and consequently, identification (DMORT 2001; Mittleman et al. 2000; Mundorff 2008).

Establishing Human Remains Triage Guidelines

Before postmortem examinations can begin, personnel responsible for data collection need to: (1) develop a human remains tracking system that takes fragmentation severity and commingling into consideration; (2) determine the need for and specifically define a group remains classification; (3) develop a triage probative indexing system; and (4) establish DNA sampling guidelines. Morgue personnel must also establish personal effects and evidence chain of custody stipulations with the appropriate controlling agencies. Personnel responsible for establishing human remains processing guidelines must understand that decisions made early in the process will have long-lasting and very significant consequences for the families of the decedents and for the agencies involved with the investigation.

Human Remains Tracking Systems

Designing and implementing an effective human remains tracking system are critical to ensuring the integrity of the chain of custody and to managing the massive amounts of data produced during the disaster victim identification process. An effective human remains tracking system should be intuitive and sequential, should not allow for record duplications, and should be designed to minimize audit complexity. The system should be scalable and applicable to varying conditions of remains encountered in a single incident and must account for the hypothesized fragmentation severity. The tracking system should not be revised after operations have begun. Modifications during an active operation will result in confusion and an increased risk of error. The human remains tracking system must not interfere with systems used for other incident operations such as tracking antemortem records or evidence, and it should not interfere with the tracking system utilized by the presiding medical examiner or coroner office to manage nonincident cases. Recovery tracking systems are applicable in the morgue only if they account for potentially commingled remains, a circumstance that is rare because most search and recovery numbering systems are designed to record provenience information for complete bodies or large fragments and do not always discriminate individual remains in severe fragmentation events. When extreme fragmentation and/or thermal damage (i.e., prevalence of calcined remains) is encountered, it may not be advisable for field personnel to sort and label individual fragments; however, it would be important to note if the material originates from an arbitrary unit or if it represents a distinct feature (e.g., assemblage represents contents of excavation unit 500E/500N or assemblage within confines of cockpit wreckage).

Group Remains Classification

Identifying fragmented and commingled human remains from mass disasters involves both scientific and ethical considerations. Before processing remains, investigators must decide whether the focus will be on identifying *all victims* or on identification of *all remains*. Advances in DNA technology provide forensic scientists with powerful tools to identify and reassociate remains that would have previously been considered unidentifiable. However, the existence of these tools does not argue for their exhaustive application. The term "group remains" is often used for remains that are not identified, or that are not examined further beyond the initial triage. Group remains are tissues that, under the highest scientific standards, are determined to be devoid of all potential identifiable characteristics attributable to a specific individual and/or yield no information useful to death investigation and the determination of incident causation. From a scientific perspective, the need for a group remains category is dictated by the condition of remains (i.e., fragmentation severity, degree of thermal modification, and decomposition severity), whether the decedent population is open or closed, and the availability of antemortem information. Additional considerations include family and public expectations and the availability of investigation resources. Even though a policy may dictate attempts to identify all fragments, this may not be possible, and thus the group remains category would still be necessary. Group remains classification guidelines must be clearly defined if remains are severely fragmented, and the presiding medical examiner/coroner should consider the capabilities of the DNA laboratory that will be processing tissue samples when establishing a DNA sampling threshold (i.e., limitations on sample type and minimum mass). Group remains guidelines are incident-dependent and, once established, should be changed only if the presiding jurisdiction is willing and able to reclassify tissue that has previously been designated as group remains.

The Probative Index System

Triage personnel should utilize an indexing system to systematically and objectively classify human remains according to their identification potential or investigative value. Table 21-2 provides a template for the development of such a system. The system relates the presence of positive and presumptive identifying features to the potential for a DNA, fingerprint, dental, or medical identification. Numeric values are assigned to each fragment based on the presence of attributes useful to the identification process. Remains with high probative scores

Table 21-2: A Template of the Triage Probative Index System

	Fingerprint	Dental	DNA	Morphology/Medical	Associated P.E.
HIGH (2)	High-quality prints attainable	Dental remains present with extensive restorations	Numerous high-quality samples that will yield a complete STR profile or mtDNA sequence	Unique morphological characteristics (e.g., biological profile, prosthesis, tattoo)	Personal effects possessing unique identifying information associated with remains (e.g., ring with inscription)
LOW (1)	Partial prints attainable	Dental remains with no restorations	Decomposed, thermally modified, and/or low mass sample that will most likely yield partial STR profile or mtDNA sequence	Fragment identifiable to anatomical region but no unique characteristics	Personal effects with no unique identification information associated with remains (e.g., shoe and sock associated with foot)
NONE (0)	No printable tissue (hands/feet missing)	No dental remains	Low mass sample or tissue with limited potential for extracting DNA (e.g., calcined bone, fibro-fatty tissue)	Fragment identifiable to broad anatomical category (e.g., skin, muscle, bone fragment)	No associated personal effects

are most likely to be identified or aid in the determination of incident causation, and thus are the highest priority for detailed examination.

The probative index must be designed as an incident-specific sorting tool, because factors such as the condition of remains, the availability of a victim list (i.e., open/closed population), and the availability and accuracy of antemortem information will impact the value of postmortem data. In principle, antemortem information drives the identification process, so investigators must take into consideration the availability and accuracy of antemortem data (Delattre and Stimson 1999; Kieser et al. 2006; Tyrrell et al. 2006). Investigative goals also need to be considered. For instance, if tissue samples for DNA analysis are collected from all remains, the indexing system can be modified to denote sampling priority. Systematic evaluation and prioritization ensures optimal use of available resources, which is an important consideration for high-volume morgue operations.

DNA Sampling Guidelines

Triage personnel must collaborate with DNA specialists to develop an appropriate sample nomination strategy, which is reflected in the probative index score. Important considerations include differential DNA preservation and the potential for sample contamination when evaluating the identification potential of fragmentary remains. The current state of forensic DNA science has proven very effective in resolving identifications and reassociating fragmentary remains in mass fatality contexts (Ballantyne 1997; Biesecker et al. 2005; Brenner and Weir 2003; Goodwin et al. 1999; Leclair 2004; Prinz et al. 2007). However, sample contamination still poses a substantial challenge, especially when degradation and commingling are apparent (Budimlija et al. 2003; Alonso et al. 2005). During the postmortem data collection process, the primary sources of contamination are other remains and investigators that have come in contact with the samples (Lygo et al. 1994). It is therefore essential to implement sample contamination mitigation procedures prior to field recovery and postmortem data collection operations. At the morgue, triage personnel must also consider whether tissue sampling will hinder subsequent morphological analysis. In such cases, the value of morphological analysis must be weighed against the potential for further DNA contamination or degradation. If the fragment is considered a good candidate for tissue sampling but of minor morphological value, sampling prior to invasive examination is recommended. Morphological analysis must, however, take priority if tissue sampling will compromise morphoscopic characteristics useful for individuation. Simply stated, there is seldom any good reason to destroy important morphological indicators prior to formal analysis.

Triage Station Staffing, Quality Assurance, and Control

Successful morgue operations are contingent upon collaboration with numerous agencies representing a vast range of investigative interests (Jensen 2000). Understanding their respective roles will mitigate improper handling or misrouting of personal effects and evidence during triage. Triage staff must also possess a detailed understanding of human anatomy and the multidisciplinary human identification process in order to accurately assess the probative value of each set of remains. Pathologists and anthropologists with prior mass fatality investigation experience are ideal triage station staffing candidates (Mundorff 2008; Mundorff, this book, Chapter 17). The triage station should also be staffed by evidence specialists to evaluate nonhuman material and photographers to document relevant aspects of the process, human remains, and evidence. Odontology, fingerprint, and DNA specialists should assess remains if the primary triage staff are unable to determine the identification potential of the remains according to pre-established guidelines.

Triage is a dynamic process, requiring constant re-evaluation during subsequent phases of examination. Analyses by the various forensic disciplines can reveal potential problems with initial commingling assessments and the probative index. Instituting formal quality assurance reviews will reveal any potential inconsistencies in these areas. Group remains must be re-examined at regular intervals to ensure that potentially identifiable tissue has not been improperly classified. Ideally, re-examination should include radiographic and visual assessment of group remains, which should reveal inconsistencies with the triage decision-making process.

Triage brings an additional benefit for understanding taphonomic processes related to the incident. Because it is the first morgue section that receives remains, triage personnel can observe patterns in the types of remains and evidence as they relate to search and recovery operations. Decisions made in the field can compromise the medicolegal investigation if recovery personnel fail to recognize human remains or draw the wrong conclusions regarding the spatial relationship of remains and other material (Dirkmaat 2012). Brannon and Morlang (2002) and Brannon and Kessler (1999) discuss how improper recognition and recovery of dental remains can negatively impact the identification process. Also, spatial relationships between human remains, personal effects, and evidence can be misinterpreted, leading to erroneous field decisions concerning unassociated personal effects and remains found in close proximity (Wolcott et al. 1980). Recognizing these patterns at triage could suggest improper recovery techniques and thus assist in guiding search and recovery efforts. Effective triage can serve as a communications link between field and morgue operations, one that can minimize the potential for recovery-induced commingling.

Mass Fatality Morgue Operations

Once morgue operations commence, investigators use the probative index to systematically examine, categorize, and route human remains and material evidence to the pertinent morgue sections and agencies (Figure 21-6). Decedent remains are brought from the scene to the morgue and placed in refrigerated storage until examined. Whenever possible, the examination process begins with radiographic screening of each container holding remains.

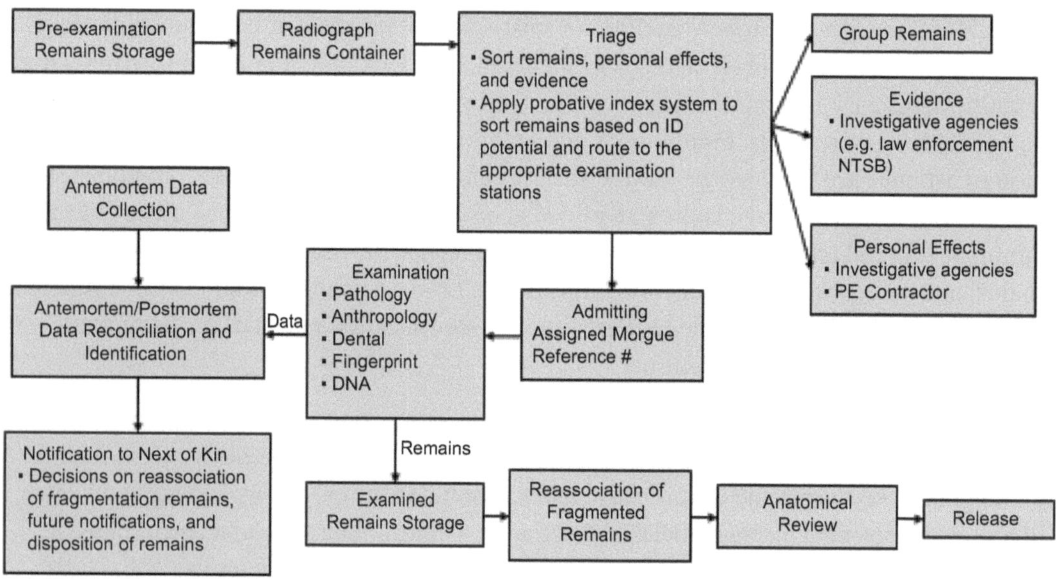

Figure 21-6
Flow of remains and data during a mass fatality morgue operation.

Radiographs provide triage personnel with an overview of the container contents and can be referenced to locate human remains and evidentiary material that would potentially be obscured during the external examination (Lichtenstein et al. 1980; Lichtenstein and Madewell 1982). Radiographic screening also has potential safety benefits, having been used to locate live ordnance prior to examination of the 1992 Persian Gulf War dead (Lichtenstein 1998), and during the 2001 Pentagon attack investigation (Rodriguez 2003).

The contents are then physically examined at the triage station, and items relevant to the investigation are identified. Material evidence and unassociated personal effects are documented and routed to the appropriate controlling agencies after the material has been photographed and described (McMeekin 1980). Personal effects that are physically associated with remains (e.g., jewelry on a finger) should not be separated at triage. Removal of such items should be conducted at the pathology station by personnel trained in documenting and describing personal effects associated with remains.

Forensic personnel at the triage station evaluate the remains to determine if any commingling is apparent. Remains with no anatomical connection or remains that cannot be easily reassociated are considered distinct and will be processed as individual fragments. Remains are then evaluated using the probative index system to assess their potential for identification. Remains that are classified as group remains are removed from the morgue flow based on previously established guidelines and are not assigned unique accession numbers. Remains meeting the criteria for potential identification or investigative value enter the morgue flow for documentation and postmortem analysis. If applicable, a triage form is completed to indicate specific routing of individual tissue fragments and decisions regarding DNA sampling priority are noted. Remains are directed to the admitting station where sequential accession numbers are assigned and are then routed to the applicable postmortem data collection stations. If commingling is noted during the course of subsequent examinations, the commingled remains will be routed back to triage, evaluated using the aforementioned protocol, and assigned a unique accession number. It is important to maintaining documentation to show a relationship between the original accession number and the accession numbers of remains that were commingled with the "primary" fragment. Upon completion of all examinations, identification, reassociation, and fulfillment of the other investigative objectives, remains are released from morgue custody for final disposition.

Essential to the success of the high throughput morgue operation is adherence to a quality assurance program that is designed to identify and mitigate errors and establish corrective actions to prevent recurrence. The quality assurance program should minimally ensure accountability of remains and other evidence in morgue custody with regular audits of storage units. Group remains should be examined at regular intervals to ensure that potentially identifiable tissue has not been improperly classified. Prior to release from morgue custody, personal effects and other categories of evidence should be examined to ensure that remains are not associated. Identified human remains should also undergo a final case review prior to release to ensure congruence between the physical remains and the information contained within the case file regarding biological attributes, identification methods, and reassociations (MacKinnon and Mundorff 2006). Finally, paperwork generated during the morgue operation should be audited at regular intervals to identify potential errors or missing information because it may be difficult to correct the discrepancies later in the process (Hennessey 2002; Hennessey, this book, Chapter 20).

Case Study: United Airlines Flight 93

The United Airlines Flight 93 investigation presents an example of how the triage concept was utilized to facilitate the identification process. Flight 93 crashed on September 11, 2001, in Shanksville, Pennsylvania, killing all 44 passengers and crew. Approximately 1,500 fragments were recovered, weighing approximately 600 pounds, which represents 8.5% of the estimated passenger and crew weight.[1] Fragmentation and commingling were significant issues that required personnel to develop a morgue operations plan that included a triage protocol (DMORT 2001; Sledzik et al. 2003). Prior to commencing morgue operations, triage personnel were briefed on the basic triage protocol and DNA tissue sampling guidelines to assure proper handling and routing of human remains.

Recovered material came to the incident morgue and went through a slightly modified version of the aforementioned postmortem data collection process. In this case, radiographs of the disaster pouches were unavailable prior to examination at triage. At times, ubiquitous soft tissue obscured embedded bone or evidentiary material, which made sorting remains based solely on visual inspection difficult. Investigators palpated tissue to determine the presence of bone or evidentiary material. Radiography would have allowed for more rapid and less intrusive examination. Selection criteria for remains that entered the postmortem data collection operation were based on individual specimen size and type. When commingling was discovered post-triage, remains were returned to the triage station for assessment, and if confirmed, one fragment would retain the original accession number and the other fragments would be assigned unique accession numbers. The newly segregated remains would go through the triage evaluation process independently and then proceed through the postmortem data collection process.

[1] The low percentage of the total estimated passenger weight recovered during the United 93 investigation is probably due to a variety of factors including impact forces and environment. A comparison of the United 93 and ValuJet 592 incidents illustrates the importance of recovery environment on the weight of recovered remains. The fragmentation indices are similar for the two crashes (United 93 = 34.09, ValuJet 592 = 38.93); however, United 93 crashed into a field, whereas ValuJet 592 crashed in a swamp. Approximately 4,000 pounds of human remains, representing 23% of the estimated passenger weight, were recovered from the ValuJet 592 crash site (Mittleman et al. 2000), compared with 600 pounds from the United 93 site. Passenger weight is largely composed of body fluids. Upon impact, particularly at high speed in a terrestrial environment, the majority of fluids will be dispersed into the surrounding environment. It is plausible that in an aqueous environment remains will maintain their weight; however, there is no empirical evidence that supports this hypothesis.

Processing remains took approximately 11 days. During this time, 12 individuals were identified using dental and fingerprint methods. In the following two months, DNA analysis resulted in the identification of the remaining 32 decedents and additional remains from those previously identified. Subsequent quality assurance, retesting, and remains reassociation was completed by six months after the event. On average, 12 specimens were identified per decedent (Figure 21-7). Of the approximately 1,500 fragments recovered, 1,000 (67%) yielded no information leading to identification. These remains, along with those not selected for analysis during triage, were therefore categorized as group remains at the conclusion of the investigation.

Family Assistance Considerations

In the past several years, the term "family assistance" (as it applies to mass fatality situations) has come to define a standard of care and services provided to the family members of decedents. In the United States of America, the Aviation Disaster Family Assistance Act of 1996 (U.S. Public Law 104-264, Title VII; 49 U.S.C. § 1136, 41113, 41313) and the Rail Passenger Disaster Family Assistance Act (U.S. Public Law 110-432, Title V; 49 U.S.C. § 1139, 24316) establish important rights for families of passengers who die or are injured in major aircraft or passenger rail accidents. These laws designate the National Transportation Safety Board (NTSB) as the lead federal agency to coordinate the resources of other federal agencies, the airline or rail operator, the American Red Cross, and local agencies in supporting family members (National Transportation Safety Board 2008, 2010). The legislation aims to address the fundamental concerns of family members, which include notification of involvement, victim accounting, access to resources, and disposition of personal effects (Figure 21-8). Family assistance operations may encompass travel to and from the accident site, lodging, informational briefings (including information on victim recovery and identification), disaster

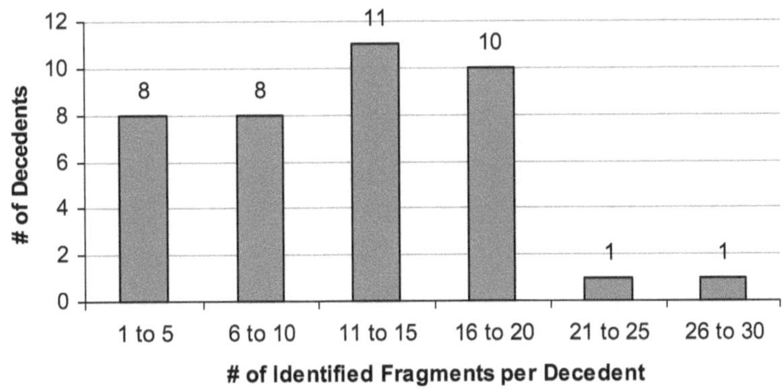

Figure 21-7
The number of identified fragments per decedent for United Airlines Flight 93. These are minimum estimates because approximately 1,000 fragments (67% of recovered remains) were not identified.

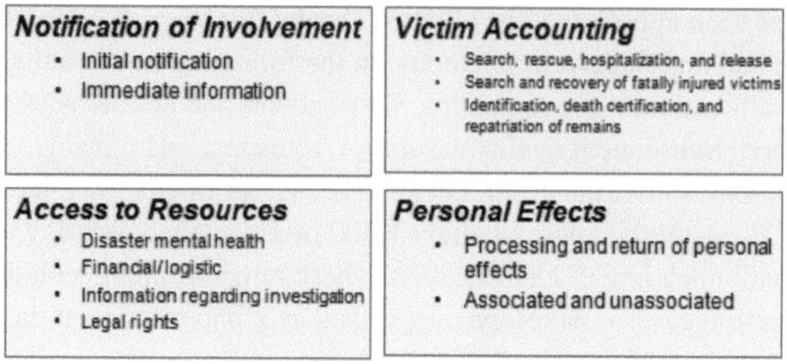

Figure 21-8
The fundamental concerns of victims and family members following a mass fatality incident.

mental health counseling, accident scene visits, memorial services, and long-term information sharing. The number of family members in attendance at family assistance functions varies greatly depending on the family dynamics of the passenger population, the accident location, and the ability of family members to travel to the accident site.

Victim identification is a critical aspect of the family assistance process (Department of Justice, Federal Bureau of Investigation, Office for Victim Assistance 2013; Levin 2004; Office for Victims of Crime 2000; Slater and Hall 1997; Sledzik and Bryson 2010). Families are involved in the identification process by providing antemortem information and, when appropriate, DNA reference samples. The medical examiner or coroner, as the primary authority responsible for the identification process, works closely with individual family members or in groups at family briefings to inform them about the various aspects of the victim recovery and identification operation (Robb 1999) and to reassure families that medicolegal personnel treat all remains with dignity and respect. During these meetings, families often ask for, and receive, specific information regarding the particulars of the recovery and identification operation, so it is essential for the presiding medicolegal authority to be prepared to actively engage with the families regarding these issues.

The issues associated with commingled remains also impact the family members of the decedents. Families often presume that the remains from disasters are complete and that they can be visually recognized. Families must be informed of the general condition of remains and the impact this will have on identifications, including the time needed to complete the process. It is necessary to explain that, even with the use of DNA technology, there is a chance that all remains will not be identified.

Families are also asked to make decisions about death notification, final disposition of remains, and other concerns. In cases of fragmentation, where multiple fragments from one individual are identified over a lengthy period, families choose when and how often they wish to be notified about identification (i.e., initially, each time an identification of the decedent is made, at the end of the process, or never). Families also choose if and when remains will be released to them: as they are identified or when they are reassociated at the end of the identification process. Family preference regarding the disposition of remains is optimally determined prior to the start of the identification process.

Because not all fragmented remains are identified, the medical examiner or coroner must decide, in conjunction with the families, about the final disposition of group remains. Families are informed of the potential for group remains, and preferably work as a group in close coordination with the presiding medicolegal jurisdiction to decide on the final disposition. If families cannot come to an agreement, the medicolegal authority takes action under the jurisdiction's statutes to address final disposition of the remains.

Additional Considerations: Policy, Ethics, and Family Expectations

The need to recover and identify disaster victims creates a set of unique considerations arising from the interplay of public policy, the capabilities and limitations of science, and the expectations of family members. The questions, asked by scientists, family members, and society, delve into concerns regarding the extent of resources allocated to conduct identifications, and expectations about what is returned to the family for final disposition. These questions are not unique to disaster work; forensic scientists involved in human rights investigations have raised similar concerns (Williams and Crews 2003).

Jurisdictions responsible for managing the medicolegal response to a mass fatality incident need to consider how resources should be allocated to conduct victim recovery, identification, and reassociation operations, and at what point these operations should terminate. Other issues that may need to be addressed include the ability to recover remains and the circumstances in which remains are no longer considered recoverable, due to either hazardous conditions or inaccessibility. Addressing these issues depends on the particulars of the disaster, desires of the family members (individually and as a disaster-specific group), cultural beliefs about death and final disposition of remains, societal expectations about what science can provide, and the availability of appropriate forensic tools and techniques (Pan American Health Organization 2004).

While scientists may endeavor to use all applicable techniques and technology in the identification and reassociation process, taphonomic factors may prevent expedient identification and return of remains. For intact remains, because the identifiable features (dental structures, fingerprints, etc.) are directly associated with the body itself, after the body has been identified, the individual has been identified. However, when fragmentation exists, there is no "body" to identify. Rather there are individual anatomical structures that may or may not contain identifiable features or reveal a probative DNA profile. When a specimen contains a unique physical feature that is identified as belonging to a decedent, the presumption is that that decedent is "identified," and multiple "identifications" can be made as additional specimens with individuating morphoscopic features and high-fidelity DNA profiles are reassociated to that decedent. However, not all fragments will be reassociated to an individual, which requires that these group remains be managed as an assemblage representing all decedents associated with the incident. Consequently, family members need to be informed of the presence of these remains and participate in the decision-making process governing their final disposition. When families expect that identifications will happen quickly and that whole bodies will be returned, scientists must readjust the families' expectations to make them more consistent with the taphonomic reality of the disaster. This difficult but necessary readjustment helps families better understand the reasons for the complexity of the identification and reassociation process.

One of the more complex decisions is whether to identify *all remains* or *all decedents* and the extent to which reassociations will be made. The decision is largely informed by the technological limitations of the DNA laboratory conducting the sample processing and analysis, but there is also a need to consider allocation of finite resources to such endeavors. In the case of an open population (where not all decedents are known) and fragmented remains, all viable remains should be analyzed for DNA so that profiles on all decedents can be obtained. Certainly, scientists are aware that not all DNA testing will lead to usable data, but the work must proceed so that all potentially useful information is available for identification. In a closed population where the decedent information is known, a focus can be placed on identifying the maximum number of remains for each decedent. In these cases, there is limited scientific value in testing very small fragments because the decedent population is known. However, the wishes of family members must be taken into consideration and balanced with the scientific merits of pursuing these analyses.

Agencies responsible for victim identification must have an understanding of these issues and must be able to articulate and clearly justify policies regarding the extent of the identification efforts. Family members of disaster victims want and deserve frank yet compassionate discourse regarding these issues. These discussions are difficult but critical for families to properly navigate the complex grief process wrought by a disaster. Transparency regarding mass fatality management policies also helps society appreciate that even in death their fellow citizens are considered and cared for. Forensic scientists must do this work for legal reasons, yet they choose to do it because it provides some solace to those in need. As Reyes Mate, Spanish philosopher and holocaust researcher, reflected (Memoria de Auschwitz, 2003): "For a civilization to deserve that name, all of life must be valued, including the absent life of the dead."

Conclusions

In order to develop a capable investigative strategy, personnel responsible for establishing mass fatality morgue operating guidelines must have a fundamental understanding of the effects of fragmentation and commingling, and their effects on the identification process.

Before the identification process begins, investigators should decide how best to manage fragmented and commingled remains and establish human remains and evidence processing guidelines. These guidelines must address human remains and evidence tracking procedures, group remains classifications, the probative index system, and DNA sampling issues. The aforementioned information is then synthesized, and a comprehensive triaging system is developed. Triage facilitates the investigative process by detecting and separating commingled remains and by directing human remains, personal effects, and evidence to the relevant morgue examination stations or agencies. Decedent identification success is not necessarily limited by the aforementioned variables, but the efficiency, effectiveness, and effort involved are affected. Keeping family members informed about the progress of identification, and the ways in which commingling and fragmentation impact the process, is a critical aspect of the medicolegal investigation of mass fatality events.

References

Alonso, A., Martín, P., Albarrán, C., García, P., Fernández de Simón, L., Iturralde, M.J., Fernández-Rodríguez, A., Atienza, I., Capilla, J., García-Hirschfeld, J., Martínez, P., Vallejo, G., García, O., García, E., Real, P., Álvarez, D., León, A., Sancho, M., 2005. Challenges of DNA profiling in mass disaster investigations. Croat. Med. J. 46, 540–548.

Armstrong, J.A., Fryer, D.I., Stewart, W.K., Whittingham, H.E., 1955. Interpretation of injuries in the Comet aircraft disasters. Lancet 265, 1135–1143.

Auf Der Heide, A., 1989. Disaster Response: Principles of Preparation and Coordination. CV Mosby, St. Louis, MO.

Ballantyne, J., 1997. Mass disaster genetics. Nat. Genet. 15, 329–331.

Biesecker, L.G., Bailey-Wilson, J.E., Ballantyne, J., Baum, H., Bieber, F.R., Budowle, B., Butler, J.M., Carmody, G., Conneally, P.M., Duceman, B., Eisenberg, A., Forman, L., Kidd, K.K., Leclair, B., Niezgoda, S., Parsons, T.J., Pugh, E., Shaler, R., Sherry, S.T., Sozer, A., Walsh, A., 2005. DNA identifications after the 9/11 World Trade Center attack. Science 310 (5751), 1122–1123.

Bowen, T.E., Bellamy, R.F. (Eds.), 1988. Emergency War Surgery, second ed. Department of Defense, Washington, D.C.

Brannon, R.B., Kessler, H.P., 1999. Problems in mass disaster dental identification: A retrospective review. J. Forensic Sci. 44, 123–127.

Brannon, R.B., Morlang, W.M., 2002. Jonestown tragedy revisited: The role of dentistry. J. Forensic Sci. 47, 3–7.

Brenner, C.H., Weir, B.S., 2003. Issues and strategies in the DNA identification of World Trade Center victims. Theor. Popul. Genet. 63, 173–178.

Budimlija, Z.M., Prinz, M.K., Zelson-Mundorff, A., Wiersema, J., Bartelink, E., MacKinnon, G., Nazzaruolo, B.L., Estacio, S.M., Hennessey, M.J., Shaler, R.C., 2003. World Trade Center Human Identification Project: Experiences with individual body identification cases. Croat. Med. J. 44, 259–263.

Cullen, S.A., Turk, E.P., 1980. The value of postmortem examination of passengers in fatal aviation accidents. Aviat. Space Environ. Med. 51, 1071–1073.

Delattre, V.F., Stimson, P.G., 1999. Self-assessment of the forensic value of dental records. J. Forensic Sci. 44 (5), 906–909.

Department of Justice, Federal Bureau of Investigation, Office for Victim Assistance, 2013. Mass Fatality Incident Family Assistance Operations: Recommended Strategies for Local and State Agencies. Electronic document, Washington, D.C. http://www.ntsb.gov/tda/doclib/Mass%20Fatality%20Incident%20Family%20Assistance%20Operations.pdf (accessed June 24, 2013).

Dirkmaat, D.C., 2012. Documenting context at the outdoor crime scene: Why bother? In: Dirkmaat, D.C. (Ed.), A Companion to Forensic Anthropology. Wiley-Blackwell, West Sussex, UK, pp. 48–65.

Disaster Mortuary Operational Response Team (DMORT), 2001. Flight 93 Morgue Protocols. Washington, D.C.
Goodwin, W., Linacre, A., Vanezis, P., 1999. The use of mitochondrial DNA and short tandem repeat typing in the identification of air crash victims. Electrophoresis 20, 1707–1711.
Hennessey, M., 2002. World Trade Center DNA identifications: The administrative review process. 13th International Symposium on Human Identification, Phoenix, AZ.
International Committee of the Red Cross, 1995. The Geneva Conventions of 12 August 1949 and Their Additional Protocols. Electronic document, Geneva, Switzerland. http://www.icrc.org/eng/war-and-law/treaties-customary-law/geneva-conventions/index.jsp (accessed June 24, 2013).
Interpol, 2009. Disaster Victim Identification Guide. Lyon, France.
Janousek, J.T., Jackson, D.E., 1999. Mass casualty triage knowledge of military medical personnel. Milit. Med. 164, 332–335.
Jensen, R.A., 2000. Mass Fatality and Casualty Incidents: A Field Guide. CRC Press, Boca Raton, FL.
Kennedy, K., Aghababian, R.V., Gans, L., Lewis, C.P., 1996. Triage: Techniques and applications in decision making. Ann. Emerg. Med. 28, 136–144.
Kieser, J.A., Laing, W., Herbison, P., 2006. Lessons learned from large-scale comparative dental analysis following the South Asian Tsunami of 2004. J. Forensic Sci. 51 (1), 109–112.
Kontanis, E.J., Ciaccio, F.A., Dirkmaat, D.C., Jumbelic, M.I., 2001. Variables Affecting the Success of Victim Identification in Mass Fatality Events. Paper presented at the 53rd Annual Meeting of the American Academy of Forensic Sciences, Seattle, WA.
Labovich, M.H., Duke, J.B., Ingwersen, K.M., Roath, D.B., 2003. Management of a multinational mass fatality incident in Kaprun, Austria: A forensic medical perspective. Milit. Med. 168, 19–23.
Leclair, B., Frégeau, C.J., Bowen, K.L., Fourney, R.M., 2004. Enhanced kinship analysis and STR-based DNA typing for human identification in mass fatality incidents. J. Forensic Sci. 49 (5), 939–953.
Lee, H.C., Palmbuck, T.M., Buturla, J.J., 2007. Scene investigation: The role of law enforcement and forensic scientists in bioterrorism and mass disasters. In: Okoye, M.I., Wecht, C.H. (Eds.), Forensic Investigation and Management of Mass Disasters. Lawyers and Judges Publishing Company, Inc., Tucson, AZ, pp. 1–22.
Levin, B.G.L., 2004. Coping with traumatic loss: An interview with the parents of TWA 800 crash victims and implications for disaster mental health professionals. Int. J. Emerg. Ment. Health 6, 25–31.
Li, G., Baker, S.P., 1997. Injury patterns in aviation-related fatalities. Am. J. Forensic Med. Pathol. 18, 265–270.
Lichtenstein, J.E., 1998. Radiology in mass casualty situations. In: Brogdon, B.G. (Ed.), Forensic Radiology. CRC Press, Boca Raton, FL, pp. 189–205.
Lichtenstein, J.E., Madewell, J.E., 1982. Role of radiology in the study and identification of casualty victims. Radiologe 22, 352–357.
Lichtenstein, J.E., Madewell, J.E., McMeekin, R.R., Feigin, D.S., Wolcott, J.H., 1980. Role of radiology in aviation accident investigation. Aviat. Space Environ. Med. 51, 1004–1014.
Ludes, B., Tracqui, A., Pfitzinger, H., Kintz, P., Levy, F., Disteldorf, M., Hutt, J.M., Kaess, B., Haag, R., Memheld, B., Kaemph, C., Friederich, F., Evenot, E., Mangin, P., 1994. Medico-legal investigations of the Airbus A320 crash upon Mount Ste-Odile, France. J. Forensic Sci. 39, 1147–1152.
Lygo, J.E., Johnson, P.E., Holdaway, D.J., Woodroffe, S., Kimpton, C.P., Gill, P., Whitaker, J.P., Clayton, T.M., 1994. The validation of short tandem repeat (STR) loci for use in forensic casework. Int. J. Legal Med. 107, 77–89.
MacKinnon, G., Mundorff, A.Z., 2006. The World Trade Center – September 11th 2001. In: Thompson, T.J.U., Black, S.M. (Eds.), Forensic Human Identification: An Introduction. CRC Press, Boca Raton, FL, pp. 485–499.
Mate, R., 2003. Memoria de Auschwitz: Actualidad Moral y Políca. Editorial Trotta, Madrid, pp.117–166.
McMeekin, R.R., 1980. An organizational concept for pathologic identification in mass disasters. Aviat. Space Environ. Med. 51, 999–1003.
Midda, M., 1974. The role of dental identification in mass disasters. J. Ir. Dent. Assoc. 20, 51–62.
Mittleman, R.E., Barnhart, J.S., Davis, J.H., Fernandez, R., Hyman, B.A., Lengel, R.D., Lew, E.O., Rao, V.J., 2000. The Crash of ValuJet Flight 592; A Forensic Approach to Severe Body Fragmentation. Miami-Dade County Medical Examiner Department, Miami, FL.

Mundorff, A.Z., 2008. Anthropologist-directed triage: Three distinct mass fatality events involving fragmentation of human remains. In: Adams, B.J., Byrd, J.E. (Eds.), Recovery, Analysis, and Identification of Commingled Human Remains. Humana Press, Totowa, NJ, pp. 123–144.

National Transportation Safety Board, 2007. Attempted Takeoff from Wrong Runway, Comair Flight 5191, Bombardier CL-600–2B19, N431CA, Lexington, Kentucky, August 27, 2006. Aircraft Accident Report NTSB/AAR-07/05, Washington, D.C.

National Transportation Safety Board, 2008. Federal Family Assistance Plan for Aviation Disasters. Electronic document, Washington, D.C. http://www.ntsb.gov/doclib/tda/Federal-Family-Plan-Aviation-Disasters-rev-12–2008.pdf (accessed June 24, 2013).

National Transportation Safety Board, 2010. Federal Family Assistance Plan for Rail Passenger Disasters. Electronic document, Washington, D.C. http://www.ntsb.gov/doclib/tda/NTSB%20Federal%20Family%20Assistance%20Plan%20for%20Rail%20Passenger%20Accident.pdf (accessed June 24, 2013).

Nijman, J., 1980. Triage: The evaluation of disaster casualties. In: Boer, J.D., Baillie, T.W. (Eds.), Disasters, Medical Organization. Pergamon Press, Oxford, UK, pp. 79–83.

Office for Victims of Crime, 2000. Responding to Terrorism Victims: Oklahoma City and Beyond. U.S. Department of Justice, Office of Justice Programs. Electronic document, Washington, D.C. http://www.ojp.usdoj.gov/ovc/pdftxt/NCJ183949.pdf (accessed June 24, 2013).

Pan American Health Organization, 2004. Management of Dead Bodies in Disaster Situations. Disaster Manuals and Guidelines Series, No. 5, Washington, D.C.

Prinz, M., Carracedo, A., Mayr, W.R., Morling, N., Parsons, T.J., Sajantila, A., Scheithauer, R., Schmitter, H., Schneider, P.M., 2007. DNA Commission of the International Society for Forensic Genetics (ISFG): Recommendations regarding the role of forensic genetics for disaster victim identification (DVI). Forensic Sci. Int. Genet. 1 (1), 3–12.

Public Law 104–264, Title VII, 1996. Aviation Disaster Family Assistance Act of 1996. October 9, 1996. Electronic document. http://frwebgate.access.gpo.gov/cgi-bin/getdoc.cgi?dbname=104_cong_public_laws&docid=f:publ264.104.pdf (accessed June 24, 2013).

Public Law 110-432, Title V, 2008. Rail Passenger Disaster Family Assistance Act. October 16, 2008. Electronic document. http://www.gpo.gov/fdsys/pkg/PLAW-110publ432/pdf/PLAW-110publ432.pdf (accessed June 24, 2013).

Read, C.A., Pillay, J., 2000. Injuries sustained by aircrew on ejecting from their aircraft. J. Accident Emerg. Med. 17, 371–373.

Robb, N., 1999. 229 People, 15,000 body parts: Pathologists help solve Swissair 111's grisly puzzles. Can. Med. Assoc. J. 160, 241–243.

Robinson, J.L., 2002. Army nurses' knowledge base for determining triage categories in a mass casualty. Milit. Med. 167, 812–816.

Rodriguez, W.C., 2003. Attack on the Pentagon: The Role of Forensic Anthropology in the Examination and Identification of Victims and Remains of the '9/11' Terrorist Attack. Paper presented at the 55th Annual Meeting of the American Academy of Forensic Sciences, Chicago, IL.

Slater, R.E., Hall, J.E., 1997. Final Report: Task Force on Assistance to Families of Aviation Disasters. Department of Transportation and National Transportation Safety Board, Washington, D.C.

Sledzik, P.S., Bryson, S.W., 2010. Mass fatality management. In: Koenig, K.L., Schultz, C.H. (Eds.), Disaster Medicine: Comprehensive Principles and Practices. Cambridge University Press, Cambridge, UK, pp. 312–325.

Sledzik, P.S., Miller, W., Dirkmaat, D.C., de Jong, J.L., Kauffman, P.J., Boyer, D.A., Hellman, F.N., 2003. Victim Identification Following the Crash of United Airlines Flight 93. Paper presented at the 55th Annual Meeting of the American Academy of Forensic Sciences, Chicago, IL.

Sledzik, P.S., Rodriguez, W.C., 2002. Damnum Fatale: The taphonomic fate of human remains in mass disasters. In: Haglund, W.D., Sorg, M.H. (Eds.), Advances in Forensic Taphonomy: Method, Theory, and Archaeological Perspectives. CRC Press, Boca Raton, FL, pp. 321–330.

Steadman, D.W., Adams, B.J., Konigsberg, L.W., 2006. Statistical basis for positive identification in forensic anthropology. Am. J. Phys. Anthropol. 131 (1), 15–26.
Taneja, N., Wiegmann, D.A., 2003. Analysis of injuries among pilots killed in fatal helicopter accidents. Aviat. Space Environ. Med. 74, 337–341.
Thompson, T., Black, S., 2007. Biological indicators and methods of determination. In: Thompson, T., Black, S. (Eds.), Forensic Human Identification: An Introduction. CRC Press, Boca Raton, FL, pp. 1–3.
Tidball-Binz, M., 2007. Managing the dead in catastrophes: Guiding principles and practical recommendations for first responders. Int. Rev. Red Cross 89 (866), 421–442.
Tyrrell, A.J., Kontanis, E.J., Simmons, T.L.I., Sledzik, P.S., 2006. Restructuring Data Collection Strategies and Investigation Priorities in the Resolution of Mass Fatality Incidents. Paper presented at the 58th Annual Meeting of the American Academy of Forensic Sciences, Seattle, WA.
van den Bos, A., 1980. Mass identification: A multidisciplinary operation. Am. J. Forensic Med. Pathol. 1, 265–270.
Vosswinkel, J.A., McCormack, J.E., Brathwaite, C.E.M., Geller, E.R., 1999. Critical analysis of injuries sustained in the TWA Flight 800 midair disaster. J. Trauma 47, 617–621.
Wagner, G.N., Froede, R.C., 1993. Medicolegal investigation of mass disasters. In: Spitz, W.U., Fisher, R.S. (Eds.), Medicolegal Investigation of Death: Guidelines for the Application of Pathology to Crime Investigation, third ed. Charles C. Thomas, Springfield, IL, pp. 567–584.
Williams, E.D., Crews, J.D., 2003. From dust to dust: Ethical and practical issues involved in the location, exhumation, and identification of bodies from mass graves. Croat. Med. J. 44, 251–258.
Wolcott, J.H., Menzies, R., Donahue, E., Hoffa, N., 1980. Use of personal effects in the Canary Island accident investigation. Aviat. Space Environ. Med. 51, 1019–1020.

CHAPTER 22

Mass Fatality Management and the Effects of Commingling

Elissia Conlon

Special Operations Division, City of New York Office of Chief Medical Examiner, New York

Introduction

Mass fatality incident (MFI) operations are complex and dynamic to manage. All too often a jurisdiction's introduction to the challenges of handling an MFI operation comes too late ... after one has occurred. This chapter discusses the components that drive a successful MFI operation and presents recommendations for mass fatality planning and preparedness. Specifically, this chapter identifies the criteria for characterizing an MFI, a crucial first step in establishing the necessary and appropriate operations that will ultimately result in the recovery and identification of those who perish. This chapter also speaks to the disparity between managing an MFI with intact bodies versus one with a high degree of body fragmentation and commingling. The realities of processing these two incidents, although potentially similar in general parameters (e.g., number of decedents), will yield significantly different operations in terms of length of operational time, cost, and resources required to make identifications. Finally, medical examiner/coroners (ME/C) need to recognize that MFI operations will be conducted under close public scrutiny and, as such, must be managed efficiently and openly. If the families of the decedents and the general public do not feel that the incident is being managed properly, this perception will define the overall success or failure of the entire operation. Although the "lessons learned" presented in this chapter do not address all the potential challenges that will be faced during an MFI, it is hoped they provide useful guidance to those unfamiliar with such events.

Defining a Mass Fatality Incident

"Mass fatality incident" (MFI) is an emergency management term that has been routinely used to identify an incident involving more remains than can be recovered, identified, and processed for final disposition by available resources. In colloquial terms, a mass fatality incident is an incident that will overwhelm local ME/C resources. This definition is ambiguous by design because it will vary by jurisdiction. For example, an incident that will overwhelm a small jurisdiction and be deemed an MFI may, in fact, result in routine

Commingled Human Remains. http://dx.doi.org/10.1016/B978-0-12-405889-7.00022-8

operations were it to occur in a larger jurisdiction and yet still be an MFI. However, owing to this ambiguity, there is sometimes hesitation to term an incident an MFI which may then result in a delayed activation of a jurisdiction's mass fatality plan. Some jurisdictions may wish to adopt more structured criteria for terming a mass fatality incident, such as defining a set number of individuals.

The New York City Office of Chief Medical Examiner (NYC OCME) has established the following criteria for defining an MFI within its jurisdiction, any one of which would trigger the designation of an MFI:

- Any incident having the potential to yield 10 or more fatalities.
- Any incident in which there are more human remains to be recovered and examined than can be handled routinely by NYC OCME resources.
- Any incident in which there are remains contaminated by chemical, biological, radiological, nuclear, or explosive (CBRNE) agents or materials.
- Any incident or other special circumstance requiring a multi-agency response to support mass fatality operations.
- Any incident involving a protracted or complex remains recovery operation.

Although these criteria are less ambiguous, they will allow any ME/C the necessary discretion to activate its MFI plan, expand, or, if necessary, cease an operational response based on incident updates.

Overview of Mass Fatality Incidents in the U.S. from 2000 to 2013

Immediately following an incident involving multiple fatalities, the public looks to its leadership for support and answers. "The responsibility for responding to natural and manmade incidents … begins at the local level with individuals and public officials in the county, parish, city, or town affected by the incident" (FEMA 2013:11). Leaders and emergency managers must prepare their communities to manage incidents locally. This is particularly true with incidents involving the loss of life. Therefore, it is incumbent upon every jurisdiction to plan for the unthinkable. But how does a jurisdiction plan for an undefined incident that may or may not happen?

In an effort to focus mass fatality planning efforts, a study was conducted within the Special Operations Division of the OCME in an effort to quantify mass fatality incidents within the United States between the years 2000 and 2013. The only MFI criterion utilized to warrant an incident's inclusion in this study was that there were 10 or more fatalities. Various means of collecting these data included requests for DMORT and NTSB deployments, rudimentary internet searches, and direct requests to medical examiner and coroner jurisdictions. Data collected represent incidents occurring between January 1, 2000, and December 31, 2013. The purpose for this data compilation was to encourage internal discourse surrounding the efficacy of disaster planning and to observe trends in MFIs in the United States.

Further efforts are underway to continue refinement of these data. One example of this ongoing work lies in qualifying reported fatalities as being either directly or indirectly related to an incident. Another area of refinement will address mass fatality incidents crossing multiple jurisdictions since, were the study to consider only the number of deaths in each jurisdiction separately, the MFI might not meet the threshold of 10 decedents considered for inclusion. Although these issues are not currently addressed, the data presented in this chapter will still establish for local fatality and emergency managers a framework for focusing local planning efforts to mitigate, respond, and recover from MFIs.

Numbers of Mass Fatality Incidents

It is immediately apparent from Table 22-1 that nationwide for the past 13 years the United States has endured a minimum of four MFIs with an average of seven MFIs per year. Additionally, the average number of fatalities per incident is 81. This average is significantly lower than the local responder or planner might anticipate, particularly when federal guidance such as the National Response Framework (2008), born out of incidents such as 9/11 and Hurricane Katrina, focuses planning efforts, and in large part funding for these planning efforts, on large-scale incident response. In fact, when the outliers from these data are removed, the average number of fatalities per incident drops to 52 (with 9/11 removed) or 33 (with both 9/11 and Hurricane Katrina removed). According to the data represented in Figure 22-1, the majority

Table 22-1: Mass Fatality Incidents from 2000 to 2013 in the U.S. Broken Down by Number of Fatalities Per Incident

Year	MFI	Deaths	Avg # of Deaths/MFI
2000	4	138	35
2001	10	3,356	336
2002	4	76	19
2003	9	258	29
2004	8	160	20
2005	10	2,090	209
2006	5	112	22
2007	8	137	17
2008	11	358	33
2009	5	98	20
2010	6	112	19
2011	7	638	91
2012	6	250	42
2013	4	71	18
Overall	**97**	**7,854**	**81**

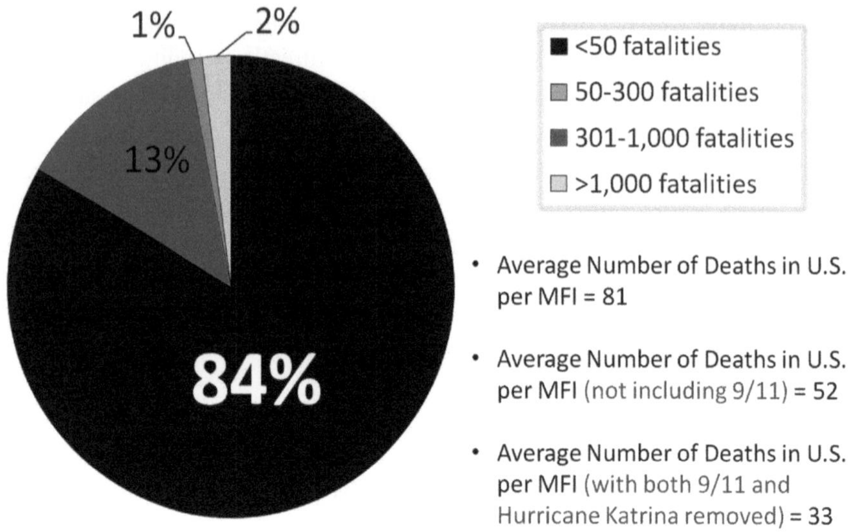

Figure 22-1
This pie chart represents the mass fatality incidents from 2000 to 2013 broken down by number of fatalities per incident.

of incidents (84%) involve fewer than 50 deaths with only 3% accounting for incidents resulting in 300 or greater fatalities. What we then learn from this analysis is that one's jurisdiction is better served planning for a smaller-scale incident response.

Categories of Mass Fatality Incidents

"The [U.S.] Federal interagency community has developed 15 all-hazards planning scenarios (the National Planning Scenarios) for use in national, Federal, State, and local homeland security preparedness activities" (White House Homeland Security Council 2006). These scenarios were designed to establish a comprehensive list of threats, man-made and natural, to the United States for which, as a nation, we should be prepared to mitigate, respond, and recover. The National Planning Scenarios include the following hazards:

Scenario 1: Nuclear Detonation—10-kiloton Improvised Nuclear Device
Scenario 2: Biological Attack—Aerosol Anthrax
Scenario 3: Biological Disease Outbreak—Pandemic Influenza
Scenario 4: Biological Attack—Plague
Scenario 5: Chemical Attack—Blister Agent
Scenario 6: Chemical Attack—Toxic Industrial Chemicals
Scenario 7: Chemical Attack—Nerve Agent
Scenario 8: Chemical Attack—Chlorine Tank Explosion
Scenario 9: Natural Disaster—Major Earthquake

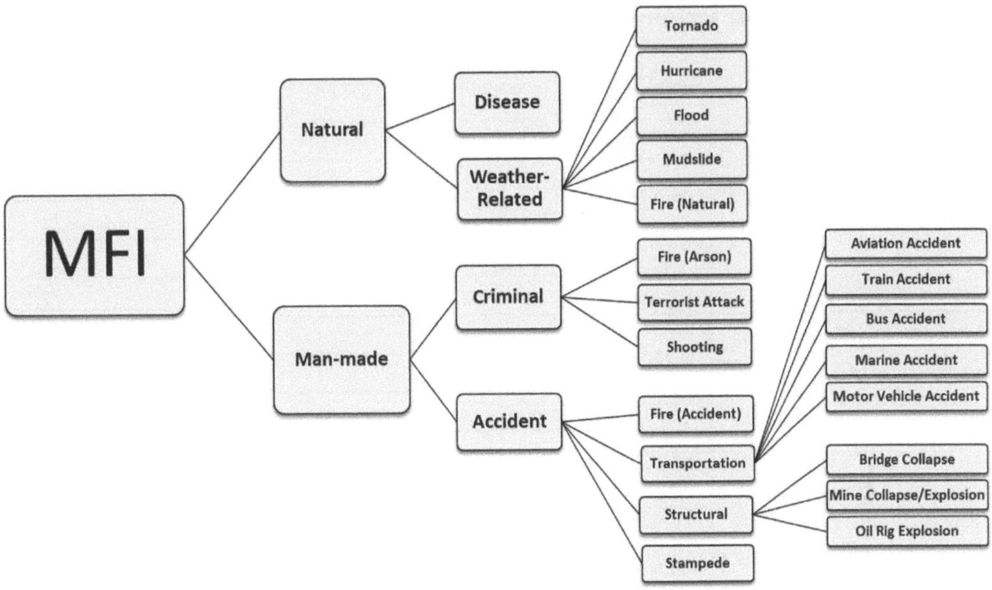

Figure 22-2
This depiction represents mass fatality incident categories.

Scenario 10: Natural Disaster—Major Hurricane
Scenario 11: Radiological Attack—Radiological Dispersal Devices
Scenario 12: Explosives Attack—Bombing Using Improvised Explosive Devices
Scenario 13: Biological Attack—Food Contamination
Scenario 14: Biological Attack—Foreign Animal Disease (Foot-and-Mouth Disease)
Scenario 15: Cyber Attack

Given the limited resources in most jurisdictions that are dedicated to mass fatality planning efforts, it was deemed prudent for this analysis to categorize the 97 incidents encountered in the United States since 2000 by type. This was initiated by defining whether an MFI was the result of natural or man-made forces. Federal homeland security experts identify only three of the 15 planning scenarios as deriving from nature: outbreak of biological disease, major earthquake, and major hurricane. However, the data in this analysis represent six incident types deriving from natural forces: disease, tornado, hurricane, flood, mudslide, and wildfire (see Figure 22-2).

The remaining 12 of 15 planning scenarios are not only derived from man-made forces but are specific to terrorist threats. In these data (see Table 22-2), it was discovered that terrorist threats represent only 3% of overall MFIs since the year 2000. It was also found that MFIs resulting from man-made forces were composed of seven categories, including fire (arson), terrorist attack, shooting, fire (accident), transportation, structural, and stampede (Figure 22-2). Although terrorism represents only 3% of overall MFIs since the year 2000 in the United States,

Table 22-2: Mass Fatality Incidents Broken Down by Number of Fatalities Per Incident Type

MFI Type	MFI Subtype	Category	MFIs (97 Total)	Deaths (7,854 Total)	Avg. # of Deaths/MFI
Natural	Weather-Related	Tornado	23	1026	45
		Hurricane	12	2471	206
		Flood	3	63	21
		Mudslide	2	24	12
		Wildfire	3	52	17
Man-made	Accident	Fire	1	100	100
		Explosion	7	108	15
		Bridge Collapse	2	27	14
		Marine	2	31	16
		Aviation	16	614	38
		Train	2	37	19
		Bus/Motorcoach	4	69	17
		Motor Vehicle	5	61	12
		Stampede	1	21	21
	Criminal	Fire	1	10	10
		Mass Shooting	10	154	15
		Terrorist Attack	3	2986	995

the resulting total number of fatalities is quite high at 38%, thereby warranting inclusion as a planning scenario; overall the number of incidents and subsequent fatalities resulting from either natural or man-made forces are almost even in numbers rather than the 5:1 ratio that the national Planning Scenarios suggest:

- 54 MFIs resulting from man-made forces caused 4,218 fatalities.
- 43 MFIs resulting from natural forces caused 3,636 fatalities.

Perhaps these data suggest that it is time for "…refinement and revision … to ensure the scenarios remain accurate … and embody the capabilities necessary to respond to domestic incidents" (White House Homeland Security Council 2006, Introduction, pg ii). This point is further confirmed by reviewing the top four mass fatality incident types (Figure 22-3):

1. 23 tornadoes resulted in an average of 45 deaths per incident.
2. 16 aviation incidents resulted in an average of 38 deaths per incident.
3. 12 hurricanes resulted in an average of 206 deaths per incident.
4. 10 mass shootings resulted in an average of 15 deaths per incident.

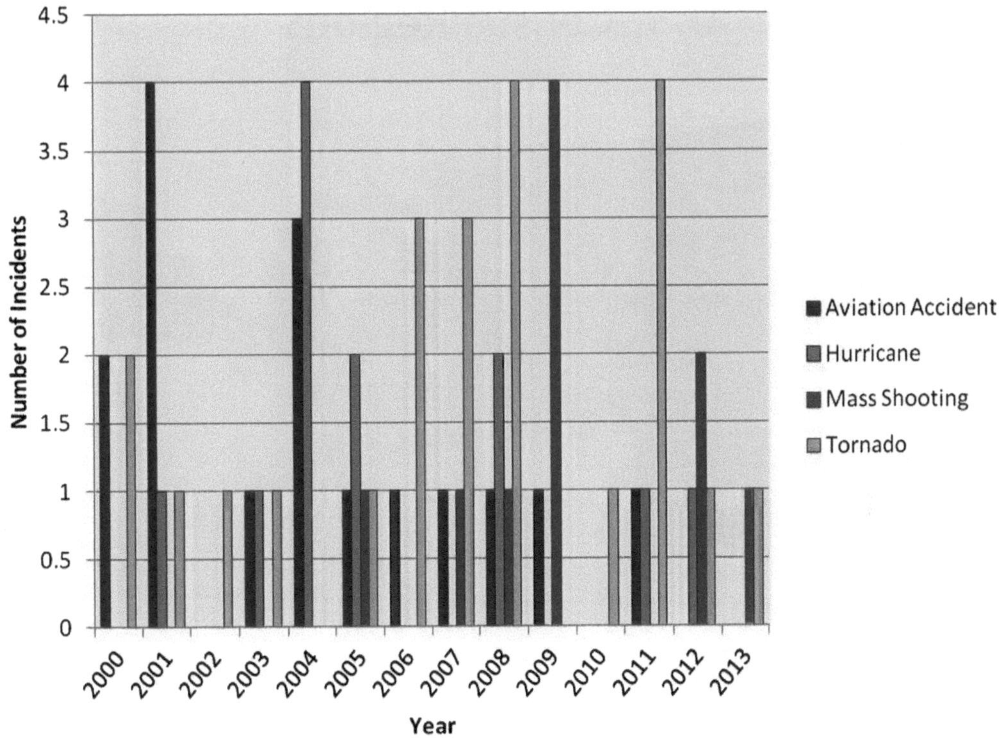

Figure 22-3
This chart represents the top four types of mass fatality incidents.

Geographical Locations of Mass Fatality Incidents

Finally, in defining the most effective and appropriate focus for a jurisdiction's planning efforts, we need to consider the hazards that are geographically proximal. Even allowing for some data overlap resulting from incidents that cross jurisdictional lines, it was possible to note the following geographic trends in the United States (see Figure 22-4):

- For jurisdictions that constitute the Northeast United States, there were a total of 17 MFIs, resulting in 3,583 fatalities. Of these MFIs, 93% resulted from man-made forces.
- For jurisdictions that constitute the South United States, there were a total of 61 MFIs, resulting in 3,963 fatalities. Of these MFIs, 85% resulted from natural forces.
- For jurisdictions that constitute the West and Midwest United States, there were a total of 31 MFIs, resulting in 967 fatalities. Of these MFIs, 72% resulted from natural forces and 28% resulted from man-made forces.

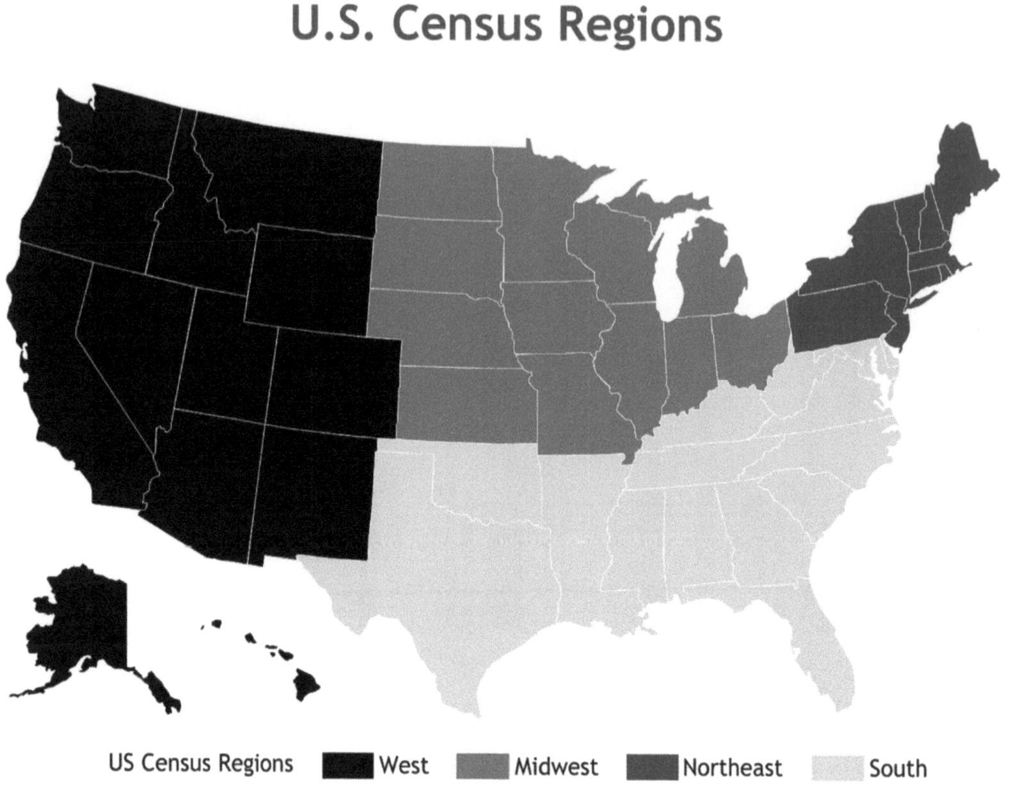

Figure 22-4
This map represents a regional delineation of the United States as defined by the U.S. Department of Commerce, Economics, and Statistics Administration, U.S. Census Bureau.

Note: The total exceeds 100% because locations overlap; there are 12 mass fatality incidents that cross multiple geographic locations.

Planning Considerations

> *To understand the breadth and scope of a disaster from the standpoint of a mass fatality management response, the [local ME/C] working in conjunction with other local and possibly state and federal partners, must initially assess the incident based on the quantitative and qualitative characteristics [referenced in Table 22-3], as each criterion influences the need to establish specific operation[s]. (OCME 2009)*

To effectively characterize a mass fatality incident, the local ME/C will need to establish an early presence on scene in an effort to ensure timely and accurate situational awareness. Particularly in the first hours following an incident, the only thing that one can be sure of is that there will be misinformation or exaggerated information. Therefore,

Table 22-3: The Criteria Required to Effectively Characterize a Mass Fatality Incident

Criteria	Qualification
Scale	Number of fatalities
Type of Incident	Is this a criminal incident, accident, or natural (e.g., outbreak of disease)?
Population	Is there an open or closed manifest? Is the population of victims known, or will a manifest of those involved in the incident need to be developed?
Condition of Remains	Are the remains compromised (e.g., visually unidentifiable, commingled, decomposed, charred, mutilated, fragmented, or whole)?
Rate of Recovery	A rapid recovery rate will require different resources than that of a protracted recovery operation. Consider that intact bodies may be amenable to a more rapid recovery than incidents resulting in extensive fragmentation and commingling. Such a recovery operation would be more complex and require different equipment and forensic personnel to conduct the recovery, in addition to requiring a longer time frame to complete.
ME/C & Infrastructure	How has this incident affected the agency's ability to respond? Consider an incident such as a hurricane where coastal flooding has compromised staff's ability to come to work, resulting in a diminished workforce. Similarly, perhaps the flooding has resulted in power outages to the facility. Sizing up the incident should include an assessment of the agency's ability to function and will drive operational decision making.
Contamination/ Infection	Could the remains have been exposed to chemical, biological, radiological, nuclear, or explosive materials? If so, the operation will likely be complex requiring significant resources to ensure the health and safety of workers.
Disaster Site Location Characteristics	Is this incident isolated to one fixed location/time, or is it distributive in nature? An incident occurring in multiple locations will stress resources. What types of topographic obstacles are present?

establishing an on-site presence, which can be as small as a two-person team, will allow the ME/C to: (1) establish jurisdiction over the decedent(s); (2) preserve the integrity of the victim identification process by incorporating the needs of the ME/C into the overall incident management operation; and (3) characterize the incident for the agency leadership so that decision making is informed and driven by actual facts on the ground. "An initial walk-through (scene assessment) of the incident site should occur prior to conducting the actual medicolegal investigation (Figure 22-5). This walk-through will allow the investigating agencies to coordinate activities and incorporate MFI objectives into the [incident action] plan [or IAP]" (DePaolo 2009, Module 25).

Magnitude

The local ME/C must quickly discern the magnitude of the incident (i.e., the number of decedents and the number of remains) with which their office will be faced. Similarly, the ME/C must be prepared to maintain the application of forensic best practices to ensure the highest confidence regarding the use of science to determine decedent identification, regardless of the magnitude. An incident that produces whole bodies will result in a very different

Figure 22-5
Conducting the initial walk through (scene assessment) at a training. *(Source: © NYC OCME, 2009.)*

operational response from one where there is a high degree of fragmentation and commingling. When a mass fatality incident results in fragmentation, a "small" incident will very quickly turn into a much larger incident. In a mass fatality context, the overarching tenet regarding commingling is that human remains with no anatomical/physical connection must be considered commingled (Kontanis and Sledzik 2008; Kontanis and Sledzik, this book, Chapter 21). On this basis, each unattached fragment must be initially considered to be a different victim until it can be scientifically reassociated.

An effective identification process hinges on the application of appropriate morgue management principles (Kontanis and Sledzik 2008; Kontanis and Sledzik, this book, Chapter 21). It is well recognized that site characteristics, recovery-induced commingling, trauma inflicted by digging activities, and improper and unscientific recovery techniques complicate mortuary analysis (Mundorff 2008; Mundorff, this book, Chapter 17). After remains are accessioned into the morgue, the identification process will begin with the morgue triage station. At triage, the ME/C is empowered to sort out commingling, identify and discard nonhuman remains, rearticulate or reassociate disparate pieces within a body bag, and anatomically identify fragments for later examination (Mundorff 2008; Mundorff, this book, Chapter 17). Therefore, the morgue triage station should be staffed by a multidisciplinary team composed of anthropologists or pathologists, photographers, and evidence and personal effects specialists. Because the triage station is the initial stage in the morgue identification process, the triage team is in a unique position to leverage their cumulative knowledge to observe patterns in the types of remains and evidence as they relate to search and recovery operations. Effective triage can serve as a communications link between field and morgue operations, one that can minimize the potential for recovery-induced commingling (Kontanis and Sledzik 2008; Kontanis and Sledzik, this book, Chapter 21).

Mundorff (2008; Mundorff, this book, Chapter 17) recounts three separate incidents, each involving varying degrees of fragmentation and the relative impact on the recovery and identification process: the Attack on the World Trade Center, American Airlines Flight 587, and the Staten Island Ferry Crash. The study demonstrates that with an increased degree of fragmentation, we will see a proportional increase in the time and resources necessary to recover and identify 100% of the victim population. Kontanis and Sledzik (2008; Kontanis and Sledzik, this book, Chapter 21) noted the same proportional relationship between the "fragmentation index" and critical resource requirements following investigation of numerous aviation accidents. The ME/C should be aware that a "small" MFI with extensive fragmentation and commingling will be much more complicated and require significantly different kinds and quantities of resources (personnel and equipment) than a comparably sized incident with intact bodies. Expectations will need to be managed when conducting this type of complex incident operation because this operation will require a greater amount of funding, time, and resources to successfully complete victim identification efforts.

Type of Incident

When planning for incident response, we need to consider the relevant impacts of each type of incident on the overall incident response. For example, following a natural weather-related incident, it is likely that several agencies within the impact zone of the weather system will be similarly impacted and focused simultaneously on ensuring continuity of their respective agency's operations in addition to their agency's role in the incident response. In situations such as these, there will be increased competition for the limited critical resources required to support overall incident management objectives, fatality management being one of many in this case.

Except in the case of an all fatal incident, fatality management objectives will always compete with other incident objectives, such as life safety. This is to be expected and may be appropriate. However, it does not mean that fatality management objectives should be delayed. Rather, it is the responsibility of the ME/C, when working with the incident command, to assert objectives when developing the incident action plan so that fatality management needs are addressed and placed with the appropriate weight in the overall response operation. To ensure that the comprehensive needs are addressed, the ME/C should predefine the critical resources that support MFI recovery and disaster victim identification operations and articulate these needs to the local emergency management office and the overall incident command at interagency briefings.

When considering a man-made MFI such as a criminal act, terrorist incident, or accident, we need to identify the various agencies that will be involved in each type of investigative response as well as each of their responsibilities and relevant jurisdictions. For example, on March 12, 2011, while traveling southbound on the New England Thruway, a World Tours Bus crashed. Although the initial point of impact occurred in Westchester County, the bus slid into the Bronx, NYC, and with it jurisdiction over the decedents fell to the NYC OCME (Figure 22-6). New York State Police maintained jurisdiction over the accident investigation owing to the location of this initial impact. Although NY State Police had jurisdiction over the accident investigation, the New York City Police Department (NYPD) worked in collaboration with both the NYC OCME and NY State Police to assist with the identification of the victims of this incident. This case demonstrates the importance of understanding the roles and responsibilities of our colleagues so that we can effectively work together to support the needs of families and friends of the deceased. With a few exceptions, the general rule of jurisdiction states that where a person dies is where the jurisdiction belongs except in those

Figure 22-6
Crash of the World Tours Bus on March 12, 2011. This picture demonstrates jurisdictional boundaries. *(Source: © NYC OCME, 2011.)*

that rely upon where the incident occurred to make that determination. This may become complicated when decedents are moved to an alternate jurisdiction for processing. Agreements should be established between jurisdictions, both geographic and governmental. This information can be obtained by working with local emergency management offices.

Open or Closed Population Incidents

Establishing an accurate victim manifest is a critical task for the ME/C to facilitate decedent identification following a mass fatality incident. An MFI will result in one of two situations with regard to the decedent manifest: either the population of those who perished is known (closed population), as is the case in most airliner crashes where there is a passenger manifest; or the population is unknown (open population). From the mass fatality incident data collected between January 2000 and December 2013, it is of note to mention that the majority of MFIs involve the latter, or open manifest, populations (see Figure 22-7).

Closed Population—When an MFI occurs where the population that is involved is known, such as an airliner or a sea vessel crash, it is critical for the ME/C to coordinate with law enforcement and related transportation agencies, will obtain the "passenger manifest," or list of names of those who are believed to have been on board the plane or sea vessel, and work with family members tó collect antemortem data to which postmortem data can be compared. In theory, identification efforts will be more rapid in a closed population scenario where the fragmentation index (Kontanis and Sledzik 2008; Kontanis and Sledzik, this book, Chapter 21), or the ratio of recovered remains to the number of decedents, is low.

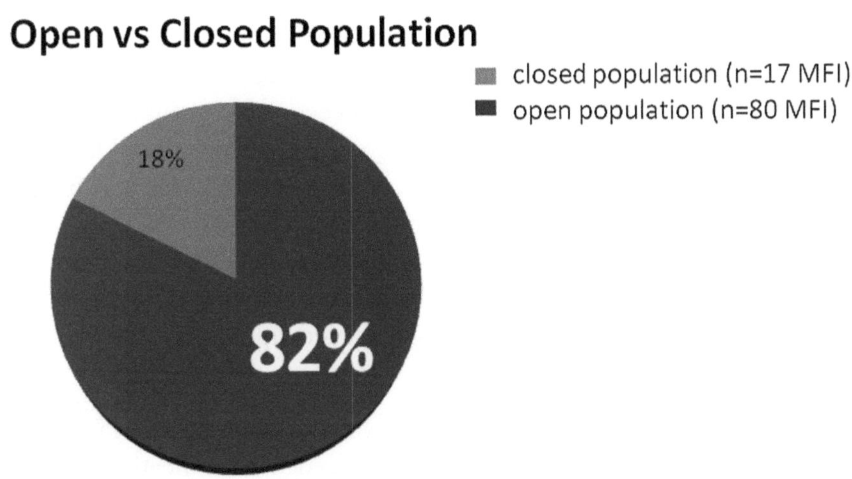

Figure 22-7
Pie chart representing the open versus closed population mass fatality incidents in the United States from 2000 to 2013.

Open Population—When an MFI occurs where the population that is involved is unknown both in terms of name and number, the ME/C must coordinate their activities with law enforcement and other investigative agencies to assemble a manifest of potential victims. It is recommended that a centralized system for the collection of missing person reports be established. Activation of a centralized missing persons reporting mechanism will enable officials to more quickly define the population of individuals actually involved in the incident. The ME/C uses this evolving victim manifest as a basis for identifying the potential next of kin (NOK) with whom they must coordinate the gathering of antemortem data. Typically, identification efforts will be more protracted in an open population scenario.

The limiting factor for effecting disaster victim identification is the ability to obtain antemortem data. Great care must be taken to develop an accurate victim manifest in collaboration with law enforcement. This is especially important when working to identify remains with a high degree of fragmentation and commingling because general practice is to analyze and, if possible, identify every fragment recovered. Only as the victim manifest is being developed and the NOK identified can the ME/C begin identification efforts. This includes a comparison of accessioned family DNA reference profiles as well as other medical and dental records against recovered fragmented human remains. Without the antemortem data collected from NOK, the ME/C will be limited to postmortem data collection without the benefit of analysis to yield identifications.

Condition of Remains

The condition of remains should also be considered for its addition to the complexity of disaster victim identification. It may take the ME/C some time to conduct the necessary forensic examinations to effect identification particularly when there are a large number of fatalities. An early assessment from field personnel should identify for the morgue leadership the condition of the remains. This information is necessary because it will support decision making with respect to preparing the morgue for the type of workflow that will be most conducive to decedent identification efforts. For example, if the report from the field indicates a high degree of fragmentation, then the morgue should prepare operations to support staffing and supplies necessary to potentially obtain a DNA sample from each fragment, as appropriate. If, however, this report indicates that the bodies are intact, then perhaps depending on the rate of recovery, morgue leadership may choose to utilize the routine operations workflow.

In an effort to ensure the accuracy of the disaster victim identification effort following an MFI, the ME/C should rely on forensic examination for all decedent identifications. Even when the decedent is visually identifiable, every effort should be made to conduct a scientific identification. Photographic documentation should be maintained and treated as contextual supporting evidence of identification. Instituting this protocol will reinforce the quality of the victim identification and reduce the possibility of errors. Errors, minor or not so minor, can cause additional distress to families, provide a foundation for questions of professional competence, and possibly lead to challenges during criminal proceedings or civil litigation (Jensen 2000).

When it is possible that a significant period of time may pass before the ME/C has the ability to process all cases, it would behoove the ME/C to collect identification data by obtaining a DNA swab/sample, taking fingerprints, taking a photograph of the face and any identifying features, and completing full-body X-rays of the decedent prior to placing the decedent in temporary storage. As long as these data are tracked and the chain of custody is maintained, this information can be used at any time during the victim identification process.

Health and Safety Plan

ME/C personnel operating at an MFI should not be placed at the same risk one might if they were engaged in life safety operations. MFI operations should be conducted in such a manner as to allow for more time to assess the hazards present at a mass fatality incident scene. Thus, planning should include the necessary efforts to identify and mitigate, where possible, any hazards present. For any incident involving potential contaminants, namely chemical, biological, radiological, nuclear, or explosive device or an unstable work site (e.g., building collapse), it is incumbent upon the ME/C to ensure that a Health and Safety Plan (HASP) is fully developed prior to initiating operations and observed during operations. A HASP is utilized to clearly identify training, medical support, type of personal protective equipment (PPE), and work-rest cycles for all MFI operations not being conducted in a facility (e.g., decedent recovery in the field).

Decedent Identification

It is important for trained ME/C personnel to conduct an incident characterization in Mass Fatality Management terms. Following this MFI characterization it is appropriate to brief agency leadership. This "boots on the ground" brief will afford the agency leadership the ability to make better informed decisions. One such decision will be the type of morgue processing that will be appropriate to the incident. Often, with an MFI, the cause and manner of death are known. Therefore, the morgue processes will be focused on the need to establish the identity of each decedent and the forensic examination to support any judicial process. In this case, the identification processes may supersede, or in some incident-specific cases outweigh, the need for an internal examination. The goal is to accurately identify all decedents involved in the incident so that they can be rapidly returned to their loved ones. However, there may be an ethical and/or religious dilemma in scenarios involving a high degree of fragmentation. Should the goal then be to identify every fragment, every individual, or both? A policy decision will need to be made early in the process as to the extent of the agency's identification efforts. As stated previously, incidents involving extensive commingling and body fragmentation will likely result in protracted identification efforts and, as such, expectations of families and the general public should be appropriately managed.

Lessons Learned

A Failure to Prepare for the Probability of an "All Fatal" Incident Will Result in a Complete Failure in Your Jurisdiction's Emergency Response Plan

Typically, emergency response plans focus on search and rescue operations and protection of life and property during the first hours of an incident. There is an inherent expectation in these plans that lives will be saved. What happens when there is no one to rescue or save? Response plans for a mass fatality incident are often overlooked. How do we recover, process, transport, and identify large numbers of decedents following a catastrophic loss of life? How do we speak with the families about sensitive information that will lead to their loved one being identified and ultimately returned to them? The majority of jurisdictions in the United States have no family assistance center plan. The time to develop a systematic process for the collection of antemortem data is long before the incident occurs. It is not a matter of "if" an MFI will occur—it is a matter of "when." And when it occurs, the ME/C will be responsible for knowing what is needed to support the operation and where to get it.

Mass Fatality Incidents are not Mass Casualty Incidents

When a mass casualty incident occurs, a perimeter is set, the scene is made stable, the injured are triaged and treated, and the investigation is conducted. Within a discrete period of time, generally a couple of hours to a couple of days or weeks, the operation will transition to demobilization, and operations will conclude.

This is not the case for a mass fatality incident. Owing to the complexities inherent in obtaining antemortem data, the process may continue for months or years. The impact of this interaction with families on forensic personnel should not be underestimated.

Strategies for minimizing physical and psychological stress on personnel should be incorporated into a jurisdiction's planning. They include:

- Strict control on schedules with forced days off. At the outset of an operation, identify the operational period or work schedule the agency will enforce. If the leadership plans to conduct prolonged 24/7 operations, shifts should be scheduled in 8- or 12-hour intervals. However, it should be stated that the ME/C community should exercise extreme caution regarding the decision to run 24/7 morgue operations. There may be great pressure from family and/or political groups demanding that operations run continuously until all victims have been identified and returned to their loved ones. However, given the limited forensic personnel that exist in most jurisdictions it is neither practical, nor appropriate to require these staff to work extended hours. It should be noted that the harder we push for results, as the limited work force grows weary, we will be more likely to see errors – an unacceptable result.

- Forced rest periods. Operations tend to unfold rather quickly, particularly in the immediate hours following an incident. It is up to senior leadership to make sure that their staff are taking the personal care required to ensure continuity of operations. There will always be the potential for an incident to become a long-term operation. Breaks must be taken so that staff have an opportunity to decompress, regroup thoughts, and refocus efforts.
- Peer-support coping strategies. Staff should be trained to look out for one another and report concerns to a direct supervisor. Similarly, supervisors should encourage open and direct dialogue with staff regarding questions or concerns with the incident operations.

Errors Will Occur—Expect them

The reality is that when humans are involved, we should expect mistakes. However, as forensic experts, we work in a zero-defect environment, and so our work is expected to be accurate 100% of the time. The alternative is possibly putting a family through the disinterment of remains because your office mistakenly signed off on an incorrect identification. Additionally, almost all mass fatality incidents result in criminal prosecution and/or civil litigation (Jensen 2000) thereby reinforcing the requirement for accuracy. So, how do we ensure mistakes do not occur?

Some examples of the types of errors typically found in handwritten forms are transcription errors, misspellings, juxtaposition of first name and last name, and unclear delineation of relationship between reporter and victim (Hennessey 2008; Hennessey, this book, Chapter 20). Each of these mistakes will thwart your office's ability to accurately and efficiently affect identification. As such, establishing a quality assurance and quality control (QA/QC) program will assist in minimizing errors and thereby support the primary objectives of your office. Some examples may include:

- Offer direct computer entry wherever possible to eliminate data transposition errors.
- Provide dual screens for both the interviewer and family when completing antemortem interview forms. In this way, the family can immediately see when an error is made and can direct the interviewer to make the correction.
- Establish both forensic and administrative review process to ensure that all paperwork and forensic exams have been completed.
- Establish a multidisciplinary forensic panel who must agree together on an identification prior to release of any decedent for final disposition.

Victim Identification Begins during Field Recovery

The victim identification process begins in the field. Following an MFI, any information that can point to the victim's identification should be left *in situ* so that the integrity of a victim's identification process can be preserved. ME/C personnel should manage the documentation, collection, and investigation of evidence supporting the identification process. All associated evidence, meaning evidence in direct association to the victim, should remain on the body, packaged in the body bag along with the victim for removal by the ME/C staff at the morgue. For example, one can research a cell phone in a pants pocket of the victim for potential family members who can be contacted to request information or provide DNA reference samples. Consider that the cell phone from the previous example was lying two feet away from the body and not in the pants pocket. This cell phone may still belong to this individual and therefore provide probative value toward this individual's identification.

Have a System for Managing an Enormous Amount of Data

Mass fatality management is a complex, data-intensive process. ME/Cs should consider that in the immediate hours following an incident between 10–100 calls will be made for every potential decedent involved in the incident. How will your jurisdiction manage this influx of calls reporting loved ones possibly missing? The absence of a dedicated missing persons reporting capability will likely result in a jurisdiction's 911 system being quickly overwhelmed and significantly delaying the ability of both law enforcement and the ME/C to create an accurate list of missing persons. Although many ME/Cs and local jurisdictions do not have a robust means of handling an enormous influx of calls, several jurisdictions plan to use existing information hotlines (e.g., 211 or 311) for missing persons call center operations.

To manage large amounts of ante and post mortem data, a system will be needed whereby the data collected from the field, in the morgue, and from families at the Family Assistance Center can be shared and reconciled effectively as a means to support victim identification. This system should have an audit trail so that changes can be tracked. Whenever possible, this system should reside in real time so that data can be shared by the relevant forensic specialties as it is gathered thereby resulting in efficient victim identification efforts.

DNA Is Still the Most Expensive, Most Complex, and Most Lengthy Identification Modality

Following an MFI yielding a high degree of fragmentation, DNA is the most accurate and effective modality for identifying remains and linking fragments to a missing person. However, whenever possible, other more efficient and cost-effective forensic identification modalities should be considered. For example, advances in fingerprint acquisition from deceased persons may result in the ability to obtain a "hit" from existing databases within minutes or hours. This methodology has proved both an accurate, timely, and cost-effective measure for effecting a scientifically-based identification. Dental comparison is a long-standing and efficient means of identification, often the best modality in fire deaths. The ME/C leadership should consider the incident characterization when deciding on the appropriate modalities that should be utilized to effect identifications. Keep in mind that DNA samples can always be taken early in the incident and run later if the case warrants. Morphological analysis must, however, take precedent if tissue sampling will compromise anthroposcopic characteristics useful for individuation (Kontanis and Sledzik 2008; Kontanis and Sledzik, this book, Chapter 21; Hines et al., this book, Chapter 13). For incidents involving extensive fragmentation and commingling, there will always be a high reliance on DNA for identification.

Rescue and Recovery Operations Must Occur Concurrently

The top lesson learned in almost every mass fatality incident in recent years, particularly in the aftermath of Hurricane Katrina, is that we must develop systems that allow for concurrent rescue and recovery operations. The ME/C community simply cannot wait for the priority of an incident response to shift from life safety and rescue to recovery and identification. To do so would do a disservice to the families of the victims and effectively compromise the ME/C's ability to effect disaster victim identification. Rather, the Incident Command should coordinate critical resources and incident objectives to ensure that recovery and identification operations are allowed to run concurrently with the rescue operation. When operations run parallel, rescue operations should leave decedents in place and report the location of decedents through the fatality management branch of the operation.

Have a System for Managing an "Open Population" Incident

To effectively manage an open population incident, the ME/C, the relevant law enforcement agency(ies), human services agencies, and local politicians must establish a partnership to develop an accurate decedent manifest of potential victims following a disaster. This is a resource-intensive, complex process and a critical first step in victim identification. The absence of such a system will result in the following:

- The public may have a limited ability to communicate with the government to report friends and loved ones potentially involved in the incident.
- Incident managers will sift through multiple ad hoc reports and lists of missing persons, resulting in an inefficient use of manpower at a time when this resource will be at a premium. For example, in the days following 9/11, as many as 40,000 persons were reported missing. The painstaking process that followed involved hundreds of investigators working for months tracking down leads from all over the United States and as many as 88 different countries. The actual number of fatalities was eventually determined to be 2,753.
- The public will lose faith in the leadership, and trust will be lost. When this occurs, the victim identification process will be negatively impacted.

It's about the Living / Manage Expectations

The noble work done to plan for and perform recovery and identification of the deceased serves to provide knowledge to their families. This work informs those families about what happened to their loved ones. In this way, the work of caring for the dead is actually done for the living. All efforts may not be successful, and there may be a subset of family members who will not be satisfied. Do not be discouraged or let this drive the process.

Ultimately, the way in which family interactions are managed will define the overall success or failure of the operation. Unrealistic or naïve expectations will only lead to an overall impression of failure even if the incident is handled "properly." Therefore, it is incumbent upon the ME/C to ensure that expectations are managed appropriately so that families, politicians, responders, forensic personnel, and even the general public have an accurate understanding of procedures, time, and resources required to facilitate disaster victim identification. When myths surrounding the forensic processes are dispelled and an environment of transparency is established, the trust of the public will be earned.

We do not Learn from Lessons of our Past

We repeat the same mistakes over and over again. Incident after incident our response operations become tunnel visioned and do not allow for concurrent investigation and recovery of remains. The result is unacceptable; our loved ones left lying in the street, in their homes, their dignity lost. With the advent of current social media outlets and the 24/7 news cycle, society now is faced with enduring horrifying images of these events in addition to dealing with their own personal resulting tragedies. These images will become the hallmark of the incident operations regardless of the successes of rescue efforts.

Furthermore, while we wait to conduct recovery and identification operations, families will begin searching for information about their loved ones on their own. This lack of information from the government will signal to society a lack of control over the incident and give way to further despair. It is therefore incumbent upon the ME/C community to ensure that the command element understands and accepts that fatality management operations should be run concurrently and can be done without interruption to rescue operations. The families of those impacted by a mass fatality incident must be provided every effort to accurately and efficiently identify their loved ones and have them returned to them without delay. In doing so society can begin to grieve and move forward with the process of healing.

Conclusion

One of the central tenets of plan writing is to plan for the desired state of preparedness. One should write how an agency should conduct operations. The gap analysis that will emerge will serve as a possible submission for your next grant application! The plan writing process itself will be similarly beneficial. This effort will establish relationships with neighboring jurisdictions or agencies whose agenda and authority perhaps overlap your agency's operational mission. Reviewing legal requirements and comparing how [y]our plan interfaces with other agencies will ensure [y]our expectations are accurate (Jensen 2000).

It is important to share in equipment technological advances and train together on this equipment. It is expensive and time consuming to continually stay abreast of research and then test and train on new technologies. However, if neighboring jurisdictions were to collaborate on research and training of operational response methodology and the procurement of related equipment, there would be an expanded opportunity for a more efficient use of limited preparedness funding.

Finally, review each operational response with lead stakeholders, identify the lessons learned from each incident, and draft improvement matrices. Most incidents will result in several actionable recommendations for how your agency can better respond to incidents in the future. These efforts together encompass a culture of preparedness that will alleviate some of the stress inherent to mass fatality operational response.

So why do we not learn from the lessons of our past? Limited resources in the form of staff, equipment, and funding result in perceived limited ability to leverage the aforementioned (planning, procuring, training, and reviewing). However, communicating with your ME/C colleagues is the key to synergy. Learn from each other's mistakes, and share equipment, training, and planning. Otherwise opportunities will continue to be lost, and the same mistakes will be repeated again and again.

Acknowledgements

I wish to acknowledge several NYC OCME subject matter experts for their contribution to this ongoing project; Ms. Emily Carroll and Ms. Maryann Mulawka for their tireless efforts in collecting and managing the mass fatality incident data represented in this writing. Special thanks should be given to Mr. Frank DePaolo for his conceptualizing the need for this study and professional guidance on this subject matter and to Dr. Bradley Adams for his scientific and constructive recommendations on this project.

References

DePaolo, F., 2009. Basic Medicolegal Death Investigations, Module 25—Mass Fatality Incident Response—Role of the MLI. Office of Chief Medical Examiner, New York, NY.

FEMA, 2013. National Response Framework, second ed. Federal Emergency Management Agency, U.S. Department of Homeland Security, Washington, D.C. http://www.fema.gov/NRF. NRF Resource Center.

Hennessey, M., 2008. Data management and commingled remains at mass fatality incidents. In: Adams, B.J., Byrd, J.E. (Eds.), Recovery, Analysis, and Identification of Commingled Human Remains. Humana Press, Totowa, NJ, pp. 337–356.

Jensen, R., 2000. Mass Fatality and Casualty Incidents: A Field Guide. CRC Press, Boca Raton, FL.

Kontanis, E.J., Sledzik, P.S., 2008. Resolving commingling issues during the medicolegal investigation of mass fatality incidents. In: Adams, B.J., Byrd, J.E. (Eds.), Recovery, Analysis, and Identification of Commingled Human Remains. Humana Press, Totowa, NJ, pp. 317–334.

Mundorff, A.Z., 2008. Anthropologist-directed triage: three distinct mass fatality events involving fragmentation. In: Adams, B.J., Byrd, J.E. (Eds.), Recovery, Analysis, and Identification of Commingled Human Remains. Humana Press, Totowa, NJ, pp. 123–144.

OCME, 2009. All Hazards Fatality Management Plan funded by the Office of Assistant Secretary for Preparedness and Response (ASPR), Grant 1 U3RHS0756-01-00. Office of Chief Medical Examiner, New York, NY.

White House Homeland Security Council, 2006. National Planning Scenarios, Version 21.3. White House Homeland Security Council, Washington, D.C.

CHAPTER 23

The Social Complexities of Commingled Remains

Sarah Wagner
George Washington University

Commingled remains present tremendous challenges to forensic scientists seeking to sort out and reassociate skeletal elements that have become mixed—whether purposefully aggregated during an episode of violent conflict or as a result of a catastrophic event such as a natural disaster or airplane crash. Those challenges extend well beyond the examination table. Often they are mirrored in the social and ethical dilemmas that arise when individual corporeal integrity is compromised in its posthumous state. What does it mean, "commingled remains," in a social sense? What are the consequences for those most intimately connected to the decedents whose remains undergo sorting, sampling, and reassociation at the hands of forensic scientists—that is, for the surviving relatives and the broader community of mourners?[1]

In seeking to answer these questions, this chapter explores the particular social complexities introduced by commingled remains into the experiences of grief and the rites that accompany caring for the dead. Despite their seemingly exceptional nature, commingled remains nevertheless expose the cultural specificity of values governing the obligations between the living and dead. They cast light on how a given community responds to violent rupture—what principles guide them; what resources are made available to them; and what patterns in practice emerge. Mixed-up bones need to be made sense of, requiring both literal and figurative reordering, and it is in that process of reordering that we perceive their social meaning.

At first glance, the argument seems counterintuitive: because of their aberrant state, commingled remains often prompt innovations in ritual acts to grapple with the extraordinary circumstances of death and postmortem conditions. Indeed, commingling frequently forces scientists, religious leaders, and surviving kin to deviate from accepted social practice surrounding proper funereal and burial ritual. Their resolution necessarily intersects with the

[1] In analyzing the kinds of violations against the dead buried in unmarked mass graves and the forms of redress attempted by forensic specialists, Adam Rosenblatt expands the realm of caretakers beyond surviving relatives to include what he terms the "community of mourners" (2010:949). This phrase is especially relevant in the case of Srebrenica, where "stakeholders" in the identification efforts include families of the missing as well as layers of postwar Bosnian society, both within the country and among the diaspora (Halilovich 2013:93–98; Wagner 2008).

Commingled Human Remains. http://dx.doi.org/10.1016/B978-0-12-405889-7.00023-X

demands of tradition and the exigencies of the physical remnants of the deceased, prompting negotiations especially among surviving relatives, as bonds of reciprocity are forged (or contested) when families seek the return of loved ones. But innovation and negotiation invariably reflect underlying expectations. In this sense, exceptions prove the rules in how societies respond to death, even in the most jarring and unconventional contexts.

Examining this tension between expected and improvised practice, this chapter approaches the social complexities of commingled remains through the lens of a particular example—that of the Srebrenica genocide.[2] Described as the worst atrocity to occur in Europe since World War II, the genocide took place toward the end of the three-and-a-half-year war, when Bosnian Serb forces, specifically the Army of Republika Srpska, overtook the United Nations-protected "safe area" of Srebrenica in July 1995, expelling its population of Bosniak (Bosnian Muslim) refugees[3] and, in the process, killing more than 8,000 men and boys. The majority of those victims were summarily executed and their bodies disposed of in primary and later secondary mass graves. Although extraordinary in the cause and conditions of the commingling that resulted, the Srebrenica genocide and its intricate web of mass graves provide a compelling example of the challenges inherent in scientific and social responses to such significantly disturbed remains.

The Scientific Quandaries of Commingled Remains: Intent and Uncertainty

The problems presented by the Srebrenica example derive not only from the partial and degraded conditions of skeletal remains deposited indiscriminately in illicit graves, but also from the commingled state in which the majority of them were recovered. Before one considers the specifics of those remains, however, it is important first to understand commingling in relation to intent—that is, as a purposeful act, at least in the case of violent conflict. In those circumstances, commingling demonstrates a fundamental lack of care: in times of war, bodies of the enemy dead are stripped of humanity, devoid of their sacredness—viewed literally as refuse to be disposed of or, as Sophocles warns, carrion left "unwept, unsepulchred, a welcome store for the birds ... to feast on at will."[4] Beyond unmarked graves, with commingling there is no attempt to bury the dead individually; on the contrary, the object of undifferentiated, common disposal often falls within the same design of destruction that subsumes individual identity within the targeted collectivity. It matters not the individual decedent's

[2] The International Criminal Tribunal for the former Yugoslavia has found that genocide was perpetrated in the UN "safe area" of Srebrenica, during the period of July 11 to July 19, 1995. See, for example: *Prosecutor* vs. *Radislav Krstić* (IT-98-33-T), Judgment, International Criminal Tribunal for the former Yugoslavia, August 2, 2001, <icty.org/x/cases/krstic/tjug/en/krs-tj010802e.pdf/> (accessed June 27, 2013).

[3] The term "refugees" is applied here not in the strict sense of international refugee law, but as it was used by Bosnians to refer to the forcibly displaced (*izbjeglice*) within the Podrinje region of Eastern Bosnia from 1992 to 1995.

[4] From R. C. Jebb's translation of Sophocles' *Antigone*.

identity, only that he or she belonged to the collective deemed threatening, polluting, or otherwise different.

The compromised boundaries between individual corporeal integrity and the aggregate group of victims extend into the identification process, complicating what is known and what can be known by the forensic specialists tasked with trying to disaggregate and reassociate individual sets of remains. In this sense, commingled remains are not just "mixed up" in the same way a single skeleton, haphazardly jumbled on an examination table with dirt and debris, can be regarded as "mixed up." What is lost is not merely the anatomical order and organization of the body, but also, critically and specifically, the wholeness and separateness of the individual. In resolving commingling in large assemblages of remains, forensic scientists are not simply "unmixing" the remains and restoring anatomical order—they are seeking to rebuild individuals, trying to address loss of life and identity, alongside loss of physical, corporeal integrity.[5]

With its purposeful aggregation, commingling introduces an element of uncertainty beyond that of a nameless set of complete or partial remains, which nevertheless are associated with one individual decedent. Where does one set of remains begin and the other end? How to distinguish and disassociate them? The work thus proceeds from a fundamental presumption: "In a mass fatality context, the overarching tenet regarding commingling is that human remains with no anatomical/physical connection must be considered to be commingled. This principle also applies to remains that are spatially associated but present no valid anatomical connection. From the perspective of the forensic investigator, resolving commingling, and ultimately decedent identification, requires careful management of both the human remains and the data generated during the recovery and postmortem examination" (Kontanis and Sledzik 2008:317). Provenience—the position of the artifact (here mortal remains) charted in time and space—informs the forensic anthropological examination in important ways, helping to parse out individual skeletal remains based on the "story" told by the grave (Tuller 2012:165).

Adhering to this tenet is especially critical in cases of mass graves where disarticulation and commingling are always real, pressing possibilities given the illicit nature of the sites and the criminal intent behind their creation: "Not only are bodies initially commingled, as they are deposited in the grave, but the conditions of the bodies prior to burial, decomposition processes, taphonomic conditions within the grave, and the intentional destruction and/or tampering of the bodies by those who buried them contribute to the eventual disarticulation and mixing of elements, more so when an initial (primary) mass grave is disturbed and bodies are moved to a (secondary) mass grave" (Tuller et al. 2008:7). Efforts to identify in good faith and according to standardized scientific protocol must nevertheless confront countervailing

[5] The author is grateful to Laurel Freas for these observations.

intent—criminal, malfeasant, or simply negligent. As we will see, the question of intent has played an important role in the legal reckoning of the Srebrenica genocide, including criminal intent evidenced by mass graves and, namely, secondary mass graves created to hide traces of the original crimes.

Srebrenica's Secondary Mass Graves

A flashpoint in the wars of secession that tore apart the territories and peoples of the former Yugoslavia, Srebrenica, Bosnia and Herzegovina, is known for its mass graves, in particular its secondary mass graves filled with commingled, partial sets of skeletal remains. Srebrenica had been a United Nations–protected "safe area," an enclave that housed at its height some 50,000 Bosniak refugees throughout much of the three-and-a-half-year war that ended with the signing of the Dayton Peace Agreement in November 1995. Four months earlier, in July 1995 the Army of Republika Srpska (Vojska Republike Srpske or VRS), led by Bosnian Serb general Ratko Mladić, overran the enclave, expelling 25,000 women, children, and elderly, and killing more than 8,000 men and boys.[6] In an effort to hide traces of the war crimes, several weeks later VRS forces and other local personnel returned to primary gravesites, and with heavy machinery, including backhoes and dump trucks, they dug up, transported, and reburied the victims' remains in secondary mass graves.

Forensic evidence provided at several of the Srebrenica-related trials at the International Criminal Tribunal for the former Yugoslavia (ICTY) has gradually sketched the network of associated graves. For example, the indictment of the Assistant Commander for Security of the Drina Corps (one of the six geographically based corps of the VRS), Vujadin Popović, outlined the temporal span and location of the secondary burial sites associated with the Srebrenica crimes:

> *From about 1 August 1995 through about 1 November 1995, VRS and MUP personnel participated in an organised and comprehensive effort to conceal the killings and executions in the Zvornik and Bratunac Brigade zones of responsibility by reburying bodies exhumed from initial mass graves at the following locations: Branjevo Military Farm; Kozluk; the "Dam" near Petkovci; Orahovac; and Glogova; and transferring them to secondary graves at: twelve sites along the Cancari Road (containing bodies from Branjevo Military Farm and Kozluk); four sites near Liplje (containing bodies from the "Dam" near Petkovci); seven sites near Hodzici (containing bodies from Orahovac); and seven sites near Zeleni Jadar (containing bodies from Glogova).*[7]

---

6 For a full account of the wartime enclave, its fall in July 1995, and the crimes that followed, see David Rohde (1997); Jan Willem Honig and Norbert Both (1997); Sylvie Matton (2005); and Wagner (2008:21–57).

7 The Prosecutor v. Popović, IT-02-57-I, Indictment, March 26, 2002, < http://www.icty.org/x/cases/popovic_old/ind/en/pop-ii020326e.htm> (accessed June 27, 2013).

The manner of disinterment caused severe skeletal disarticulation, and remains became highly commingled in the process with individual victims' skeletal remains scattered into two or more subsequent, secondary grave sites (Komar 2003; Stover and Peress 1998).

In the immediate postwar years, recovering and identifying missing persons, including the Srebrenica missing, were chief among the goals of repair and reconstruction (Wagner 2008). But the Srebrenica graves, with their trenches of commingled, partial bodies, presented a formidable obstacle, overcome only after significant political, financial, and technological intervention gave rise to a DNA-led identification system. Over the past two decades, the forensic efforts, assisted by the International Tribunal for the former Yugoslavia (ICTY), the International Commission on Missing Persons (ICMP) and its associated facility of the Podrinje Identification Project,[8] the local Federal Commission for Missing Persons, and later the Missing Persons Institute of Bosnia and Herzegovina, have contributed to the successful identification of over 6,877 Srebrenica missing.[9] The number, however, belies the complicated, necessarily piecemeal nature of this work. Many of those identified were individuals whose partial remains had been exhumed from multiple secondary mass graves;[10] piecing them back together has required significant resources and time. It has also necessitated improvisations of forensic work, religious ritual, and social practice, beyond and, in some instances, because of the success of the DNA technology.

As the case of Srebrenica's secondary mass graves has repeatedly underscored, recovering partial, commingled remains is at its core an incomplete process. From the very beginning, the VRS's intentional jumbling of bodies made identifying the missing a frustratingly disjointed endeavor. Scattered across Eastern Bosnia, the secondary mass graves were often linked to a common site of execution and primary burial location—what forensic specialists

---

[8] Since 1999, the Podrinje Identification Project (PIP) has existed as the primary facility dedicated specifically to the Srebrenica cases. Until 2010, it operated as part of the International Commission on Missing Persons, itself tasked with assisting the governments in the former Yugoslavia to account for 40,000 people missing as a result of the conflicts of the 1990s, including more than 8,000 men and boys missing from Srebrenica. In 2010, PIP was removed from ICMP and transferred to the local auspices, specifically the Tuzla Canton-run Commemorative Center (Komemorativni centar). See ICMP, Press Release, "Podrinje Identification Project: Successful Partnership between ICMP, MPI and Tuzla, " < http://www.ic-mp.org/press-releases/podrinje-identification-project-to-mpi/> (accessed June 27, 2013). Other international organizations integral to the recovery and identification process of the Srebrenica missing, especially in the immediate postwar years, include the Ludwig Boltzmann Institute of Human Rights, Physicians for Human Rights, and the International Committee of the Red Cross.

[9] On the creation of the Missing Persons Institute as a state-run entity, see Wagner (2010:35–41). The total number of identifications is as of July 2013, including those identified for burial at the Srebrenica-Potočari Memorial and Cemetery on July 11, 2013. For updated figures on reference samples collected and remains identified, see the International Commission on Missing Persons web page dedicated to its efforts in Southeast Europe: http://www.ic-mp.org/icmp-worldwide/southeast-europe/.

[10] Of the more than 6,000 identifications completed, approximately 2,000 are considered "partial remains," the majority of which were recovered from secondary mass graves.

working on the Srebrenica cases term an "event" (e.g., the executions that took place at the Petkovci Dam, where some 800 Bosniak captives were killed, are associated with five related secondary mass graves, Liplje 1, 2, 3, 4, and 7). Forensic archaeological evidence and, more recently, comparisons of DNA profiles for recovered remains have linked primary graves to secondary graves and secondary sites to one another (Congram and Tuller 2013; Vennemeyer 2012).[11] Furthermore, there is often significant overlap between primary and secondary graves sites, as the robbing was an incomplete act itself. Whether intentional or because of rushed or "sloppy" work on the part of the perpetrators, many complete bodies and body parts were left behind at the primary burial location[12] (Figure 23-1).

Commingling's Effect on Religious Ritual: Srebrenica's Collective Cemetery

Knowledge of these connections introduced troubling questions for the forensic specialists in the early years of the identification efforts: From a medico-legal perspective, how much of a body constituted enough to complete an identification and therefore resolve a case? How partial was partial, how complete was complete? The scientific dilemma had profound implications for social, especially religious, practice surrounding burial. Indeed, as the Srebrenica example makes clear, the forensic and social are mutually informing in the context of mass fatalities, not only in shaping the process of identification but also the ensuing decisions about how to care for the dead. Beyond assessing relative complete/incomplete remains, related questions arose surrounding communication with families of the missing—namely, the conundrum of how and when information pertaining to recovered remains was to be imparted: in 2002 and 2003, after comprehensive DNA sampling had began in earnest with the Srebrenica cases, local and international experts deliberated about when to present evidence of identification to families. Should they do so after all possibilities of recovery had been exhausted or as soon as any part of the skeleton was identified? By 2005, as the identification efforts increasingly turned to the hundreds of sets of partial remains recovered from secondary mass graves and stored in the Podrinje Identification Project mortuary facility, the issue of reburial arose. The nature of the ongoing excavation and exhumation activities meant that the fragmented bodies of the secondary mass graves would be recovered in stages, sometimes with years passing between instances of reassociation. Should those various elements also be returned piecemeal to the families, requiring multiple

---

[11] Matt Vennemeyer of the International Commission on Missing Persons has examined connections between execution sites and mass graves, using DNA to help map the five major "mass grave assemblages" (Branjevo Farm; Kozluk; Petkovci Dam; Lazete; and the Kravica Warehouse): "An Analysis of Linkages between Robbed Primary Graves and Secondary Graves Related to Srebrenica Missing" (2012). See also the report, "Bridging the Gap: Between the ICTY and Communities in Bosnia and Herzegovina," Conference Series, Srebrenica, May 21, 2005, available on the ICTY website: <www.icty.org/x/file/Outreach/Bridging_the_Gap/srebrenica_en.pdf> (accessed June 28, 2013).

[12] The author is grateful to Matt Vennemeyer for sharing this insight about the connections between primary and secondary burial sites.

Figure 23-1

Map of Srebrenica execution and mass grave sites. *(Source: "Bridging the Gap: Between the ICTY and Communities in Bosnia and Herzegovina," Conference Series, Srebrenica, May 21, 2005.)*

burials, or amassed over time to allow for as complete a single burial as possible? With already recovered and buried remains, would newly discovered, additional skeletal elements necessitate re-exhumation for osteological analysis?

For the Srebrenica families, the social reckoning of partial bodies and the inherently messy, complicated process of reconstituting individual identity have encompassed a careful negotiation of scientific practice, religious tradition, and cultural values. Nowhere is this more apparent than with the funeral and burial rituals that have accompanied the recovery of Srebrenica's missing. When the DNA-based program began to identify more and more partial sets of remains, the Islamic Community (*Islamska zajednica*) of Bosnia and Herzegovina was asked for its guidance. Its clerics crafted a theological response to the question of what merited enough—in terms of skeletal remains—for sanctified burial, drawing on Sharia law to argue that even one bone could be accorded the proper burial rites of the Muslim tradition, indeed that accorded to martyrs. Killed because of their perceived social membership as Bosnian Muslims, the Srebrenica victims were considered martyrs (*šehidi*) by the Islamic Community (Wagner 2008:216–219). Indeed, each of the slender white tombstones bears the same inscription, reminding the onlooker of this status: "I ne recite za one koji nisu na Allahovom putu poginuli: 'Mrtvi su.' Ne, oni su živi ali vi to ne osjećate" ("And do not say of those who are slain in the way of Allah that they are dead. Instead, they are living, but you perceive not").[13] Through these same theological deliberations, it was also determined that a permanent tombstone (*nišan*) could be placed in the collective cemetery of the Srebrenica-Potočari Memorial and Cemetery for each victim of the genocide, regardless of whether remains were in fact recovered (Figure 23-2).

This sense of communal reordering and remembering is a direct response on behalf of the Srebrenica survivors and the larger Bosniak community to the annihilating effects of the genocide, including the grisly conditions of the secondary mass graves (Nettelfield and Wagner 2014:41–45; Pollack 2003; Wagner 2008:182–85; 229–32). The overwhelming majority of families of the Srebrenica missing whose remains have been identified have therefore chosen to bury their loved ones in the collective cemetery in Potočari: as of July 11, 2013, 6,066 have been interred there, while only 226 individuals have been buried apart from the memorial center, for example, in family plots located on or near prewar residences. Notably, of that number, 113 individuals were identified and buried *before* the Srebrenica-Potočari Memorial and Cemetery held its first mass funeral and burial in March 2003—that is, before the possibility to bury one's relative in the collective space was made available to surviving kin.[14] A decade later, the nearly full cemetery attests to the families' and larger community's desire to recognize both individual and collective loss.

---

[13] The inscription is from the Surah Al-Baqara 154–157 in the Kur'an. See Bougarel (2007:179).

[14] The author thanks Nedim Duraković, Program Manager of the Podrinje Identification Project, for providing these data.

Figure 23-2
Tombstones (*nišani*) in the Srebrenica-Potočari Memorial and Cemetery. *(Photograph by the author.)*

Reassociation and Decisions to Bury

Despite the memorial center's imprimatur of the sacred, families nevertheless fretted about the possibilities of future excavations and additional recovered bones. Partial remains complicated the already fragmented process of ministering bodies that had been so violated in death and in posthumous disposition. Under normal conditions, funerary rituals work to contain and transform the contaminating presence of the corpse; they tend the spirits of the bereaved. Émile Durkheim notes that ceremonies of mourning have the effect of "bringing individuals together, putting them into closer contact, making them participate in the same state of the soul.... The group feels its strength gradually return; it begins to hope and to live again. Mourning is left behind, thanks to mourning itself" (2001:299). Just so is the atmosphere of the annual July 11 commemoration of the Srebrenica genocide: tens of thousands of people, the vast majority Bosniaks, convene in the open spaces of the Srebrenica-Potočari Memorial and Cemetery to witness the sanctified burial of victims whose remains have been identified over the previous year. Typically, there are 400 or 500 coffins being interred in individual plots within the collective cemetery. However, set against the interrupted and revived anguish of families for whom skeletal remains return in fragments over time, Durkheim's words underscore the aberration of ritual at hand. How many times should a family have to bury their loved one?

To be sure, the identification of partial remains does not always mean additional bones will be recovered. But the incomplete, interrupted nature of the process shades the ritual reckoning of death and forces upon the families and forensic specialists alike improvisations of practice. One of the primary and most burdensome improvisations relates to the passage of time. Contrary to social and religious prescriptions of how to care for the dead, many of the Srebrenica families have decided to hold off on burying partial remains with the hope that imminent excavations will unearth more bones. This is true for some 200 cases of the already identified.[15]

Such cases attest to a critical distinction within the overarching process of identification: notification of identification is often viewed and experienced by families as separate from their decisions regarding whether or when to bury their loved ones' remains, especially partial remains. One does not immediately trigger the other; rather, delay reflects larger social trends. Over the years, ICMP's Deputy Director of Forensic Science, Adnan Rizvić has noted a cyclical pattern to families' decisions regarding partial remains, one tied to the social practice of the annual July 11 mass burial. While a family receiving the news of identification in August will likely choose to delay burial—to wait and see if additional remains will be recovered over the next 11 months—a family notified in May or June, in the weeks preceding the annual commemoration, will often decide to inter the remains at the upcoming mass funeral held in Potočari.[16]

Still others decide to wait indefinitely, and this purposeful suspension of burial rites again reveals the intertwining spheres of social and scientific practice. While from year to year, the commemorative activities at the memorial center may have influenced families' decisions regarding burial, the broader momentum of secondary mass grave exhumations has played an equally important, if not more prominent, role in their deliberations. Srebrenica-related secondary graves sites were being located and exhumed nearly every year from 1998 to 2010. Extensive media coverage of the exhumations, especially of large graves excavated in the run-up to the July 11 anniversary, fueled families' hopes that additional remains might be recovered. The year 2011, however, ushered in a new era, with a significant drop in new identifications and reassociations than in previous years. Hundreds of family members were asked to consider burying the incomplete bodies of their missing relatives. Many of these partial bodies that had been "waiting"

[15] As of July 2013, 227 individual sets of remains had been identified but not yet buried; in 222 of those cases, families have chosen to wait for burial because the remains are incomplete—that is, they are awaiting the possible recovery and reassociation of additional remains with those already identified. In 5 of the 227 cases, families have decided to bury the identified remains in a location other than the Srebrenica-Potočari Memorial and Cemetery, but have not yet done so. Author interview, Nedim Duraković, Program Manager of the Podrinje Identification Project, June 27, 2013.

[16] Author interview, Adnan Rizvić, Deputy Director of Forensic Sciences, International Commission on Missing Persons, July 17, 2013.

or "lying" in mortuaries for years were in fact relatively complete, for example, missing the feet or an arm.[17]

Among such cases are remains recovered from one of the most challenging cluster of secondary mass graves associated with the crimes of July 1995: Liplje 1, 2, 3, 4, and 7. Located in the Zvornik municipality, some 40 kilometers from Srebrenica, the Liplje graves present forensic specialists and surviving relatives of the Srebrenica missing with enormous obstacles, stemming directly from commingling. Not a single set of complete remains has been exhumed from any of its graves. Instead, these are bodies so thoroughly decimated by the VRS efforts to hide the traces of the executions that took place at Petkovci Dam that the diagram depicting skeletal remains recovered and identified shown to the families is a sea of red—the color indicating what is still missing. Families contemplate whether to bury the scant collection of bones or wait for additional excavations. However, as the chief pathologist and director of the Podrinje Identification Project, Dr. Rifat Kešetović, explains to them, no new graves associated with Petkovci Dam, or with the existent Liplje sites, have been discovered since 2005, and there are no indications of future related excavations.[18] The sites are considered closed. Despite this information, some families still choose to wait. As one case manager who works closely with the Srebrenica families noted, theirs is a different sort of hope than in the years immediately following the genocide, when relatives of the missing held out for the possibility that their loved one might still be alive. Almost 20 years later, hope now circles around the possibility that more bones might be found, a fuller coffin interred, and a more complete reordering of the missing person and his remains achieved.

There are, however, competing clocks: relatives, especially parents, fear their own time will run out before subsequent recoveries, and they will not live to partake in the postponed burial.[19] Distance further frustrates the matter as many families left Bosnia in the wake of the genocide, their movement echoing the violent dispersal of victims' bodies. Material considerations constrain their ability to tend the dead, especially when remains are returned in stages. Families weigh costs of travel and time against the probability of future recoveries, the grim calculations born from the phenomenon of Srebrenica's mass graves. For the surviving relatives then, rather than being left behind, mourning lingers and resurges with the unsettling and complicating news of additional recoveries.

With the DNA technology's success in identifying partial remains exhumed from the secondary mass graves and, in rarer instances, revealing past errors of reassociation, the forensic

[17] Matt Vennemeyer, email to the author, July 10, 2013.

[18] Author fieldnotes, June 27, 2013.

[19] Hariz Halilovich writes about the parents of a missing boy from Srebrenica, whose partial remains, a femur and a piece of his skull, have been identified. The parents fear that "they might not live long enough to bury the complete body of their lost son" but nevertheless decide to wait for the possibility that additional remains will be recovered (2013:225).

specialists acknowledged the anxiety produced by the piecemeal recovery process. Designing a consent form that anticipated the unpredictable course of recovery and identification efforts, staff at the Podrinje Identification Project (formerly part of the International Commission on Missing Persons and now under the aegis of the Missing Persons Institute and the Tuzla Canton) began presenting families with options of what to do in the face of possible additional remains.[20] Among other required information, the form presents the following questions to the representative of the missing person (the primary contact among the surviving relatives):

- Do you wish to be notified about new DNA test results?
- If yes, do you wish to be notified (a) of every new DNA test result, or (b) when the mortal remains are relatively complete?
- Do you want the additional remains to be buried (a) along with those already buried remains, or (b) in the collective ossuary at the Srebrenica-Potočari Memorial and Cemetery?
- Do you wish to be present for the re-exhumation/reassociation/burial?
- Do you want the remains that have been found to date to be buried in the originally planned burial site?[21]

Guided by these options, families can choose to be notified each and every time a new bone is identified, to wait until a significant portion has been recovered, or not at all; they can choose to bury the newly recovered remains with those already interred, or to add them to the collective ossuary at the Srebrenica-Potočari Memorial and Cemetery. This final option is especially important because it signals the acknowledged limits of scientific intervention. It is known—and accepted—by the forensic specialists and Srebrenica families alike that not every bone will be reassociated and therefore identified. There will remain skeletal elements, whole and fragmented, either too small or too degraded to yield any conclusive DNA evidence of individual identity. Those unnamed fragments and tiny bones, often of the hands and feet, will be buried together in one central grave. In this manner, the communal ossuary offers relief to the distress arising from the lack of individual recognition. Located next to covered prayer space (*musala*) in the memorial center (Figure 23-3), it rests on hallowed ground, immediately adjacent to the place where the most formal acts of religious ritual are undertaken.

---

[20] On this transfer of control to local authorities, see: International Commission on Missing Persons, "Podrinje Identification Project: Successful Partnership between ICMP, MPI and Tuzla," Press Release, April 27, 2010, <http://www.ic-mp.org/press-releases/podrinje-identification-project-to-mpi/> (accessed February 5, 2013).

[21] JKP Komemorativni Centar Tuzla, "Saglasnost za ukop, odnosno reekshumaciju sahranjenih posmrtnih ostataka radi reasocijacije" (Agreement regarding burial, specifically the re-exhumation of buried mortal remains for the purpose of reassociation), on file with the author.

Figure 23-3
The covered prayer space (*musala*) at the Srebrenica-Potočari Memorial and Cemetery.
(Photograph by the author.)

Anticipating these dilemmas of circumstance and choice, the consent form structures future communication between the families and the forensic specialists, particularly the case managers at the Podrinje Identification Project, who are those responsible for relaying information to the families regarding identification. On one level, it sets the ethical parameters of decision making whereby expert and layperson agree to the terms under which information will flow and be acted upon. It becomes the roadmap for the discomfiting possibilities that lie ahead. On another, it negotiates the prickly terrain of authority over the dead, extending the possibility of collective rather than individual responsibility for future ceremonial mourning.

Re-exhumations at Potočari

Improvisation in forensic practice and social ritual converge on the occasion of re-exhumations, prompted by the recovery and identification of additional remains. These are carried out collectively: beginning in July 2006, on five separate occasions, forensic specialists working on the Srebrenica identifications have re-exhumed 212 cases.[22] Currently, there are several hundred additional cases for which re-exhumation will be necessary. While close family members may choose to attend, it is, first and foremost, a legal and scientific procedure with representatives of

[22] Re-exhumations took place in July 2006, May 2011, April 2012, May 2012, and December 2012.

the local court, the Podrinje Identification Project, the Missing Persons Institute, pathologists, anthropologists, and technical support workers all present to oversee and carry out the painstaking task of disinterring coffins to examine and reassociate newly recovered remains with the already buried bones. Notably, the re-exhumations are not religiously marked occasions—at least not in any formal manner. Unlike the July 11 mass funeral (*dženaza*), no clerics oversee the interrupted graves and disinterred remains; if prayers are recited, they are done so at the private, individual initiative of attending families. Rather, the acts of disenterring and reopening the coffins are laborious, and the forensic anthropological examinations, done on site, are time-consuming. As families have learned and shared with one another over the years, the process may take hours depending on how many other graves are subject to re-exhumation that same day. It is taxing to wait and disturbing to watch. Thus, fewer relatives have chosen to be present in recent years, opting instead to leave the macabre task to the forensic personnel.

Beyond reassociation, re-exhumations also index one of the most problematic developments within the Srebrenica identification efforts of recent years, as DNA testing has uncovered past mistakes—infrequent but painful ones nevertheless. Partial bodies returned to families and subsequently reburied have turned out to contain skeletal elements that do not belong to the same individual. Incomplete or erroneous forensic work, including osteological examinations, may have mistakenly reassociated elements with a set of remains identified primarily through DNA testing of samples cut from long bones.[23] A subsequent exhumation (at another secondary mass grave) reveals the error, when DNA testing provides evidence that recovered remains appear to be duplicative of skeletal material already buried. The finding requires that forensic staff re-exhume and re-examine the originally interred set of remains. The body—buried, dug up, ripped apart, and then reburied by the perpetrators—undergoes a different though connected series of disruptions, once again buried, dug up, and reburied by the forensic personnel. The first compels the second, but the intent behind each is entirely opposite: while the VRS sought to destroy identity, the forensic personnel strive to restore it. The effects of the indiscriminate violence, however, are profound, ensuring that even the most painstaking work to identify nameless remains is marred by the extent of commingling.

Though sanctioned and witnessed (both in a religious and scientific manner), the re-exhumations nevertheless underscore the imprint of violence on the lives of the Srebrenica survivors. In his essay on the collective representation of death, Robert Hertz concludes that "Mourning is in its origins the necessary participation of the survivors in the mortuary state of their relative; it lasts as long as the state itself" (Mauss 2009:145). For the families of the Srebrenica missing, in particular those who must care for bodies torn asunder and recovered in fragments, the disjointed, often suspended, mortuary state of their deceased protracts and intensifies their mourning. Grief is interrupted, and ritual extemporized. These improvisations help navigate the impasses of Srebrenica's partial bodies and partial knowledge, providing

[23] See Debra Komar (2003) on inaccuracies and errors generated in osteological analysis of Bosnian cases.

families with some source of comfort in the face of indefinite absence. At the same time, they testify to the unpredictable, uncertain work of forensic truth telling in a society where illicit graves still abound and bones still elude.

Conclusion: Commingling of the Dead and Living

The social complexities that arise as Srebrenica's commingled bones are sorted and sampled, and eventually identified, make manifest the highly orchestrated collective violence that produced the vast network of primary and secondary graves, as they do the communal grief that binds families of the missing to one another. Indeed, there is a striking connection between the living and dead in the instance of commingled remains: just as bones are mixed, so too are families conjoined, knowingly and unknowingly, in the process of identification, as the remains necessarily create implicit and explicit ties among the community of surviving relatives. The connection is forged through one of the very first steps in the identification efforts, when families are asked to provide blood samples to help identify their missing loved one. The act is an individual one, but families learn its collective worth as well. By providing their DNA reference sample, the surviving relatives help expand the pool of genetic profiles available, against which not only profiles from their loved one's skeletal remains might be compared, but also those of other missing. While their profile may not result in the identification of their loved one, through excluding a match, it will help strengthen the identification of another family's lost relative. Thus, providing a blood sample becomes as communal act, reinforcing the notion that the families of the missing are part of community, forged by the Srebrenica crimes and its grim legacy of mass graves, and thus have obligations not just to their own deceased but to the collective group of missing persons.

This sense of obligation and reciprocity resurfaces in the most problematic instances of re-exhumations, when it is determined that bones must be removed—not simply replaced—from already identified and buried remains. The disruption is understandably jarring and difficult to bear, and thus case managers underscore the collective once again: "You wouldn't want the bones of someone else's beloved in your son's (or brother's or husband's) grave." Set in this light, in the light of indefinitely delayed mourning that others might suffer, families accept the act of re-exhumation and removal as yet another (necessary) violation born from the initial crimes of July 1995.

As the Srebrenica cases reveal, significant lapses in time and the incomplete condition of the remains themselves introduce especially perplexing questions for the forensic personnel and families that redefine notions of scientific resolution and sanctified burial. The story of these partial, highly commingled remains remind us of the dynamic interplay between scientific knowledge and social meaning, defying facile claims of "closure" at the same time as they expose the necessarily improvisational side of caring for the dead whose bodies have undergone repeated dislocation and disruption.

Acknowledgements

I am grateful to staff at the Podrinje Identification Project, especially Enver Mujagić and Nedim Duraković, and Matt Vennemeyer and Tom Parsons at the International Commission on Missing Persons for their critical feedback at various stages of this work. Research for this study was supported by the National Institutes of Health (R01 HG0057020).

References

Bougarel, Xavier, Helms, Elissa, Duijzings, Gerlachlus, 2007. The New Bosnian Mosaic: Identities, Memories and Moral Claims in a Post-war Society. Ashgate, Aldershot, UK.

Congram, Derek, Tuller, Hugh, 2013. Spatial Analysis and Modeling of Missing Person Burial Locations in Multiple Armed Conflict Contexts. Presentation at the American Academy of Forensic Science annual meeting, February 18–23, 2013, Washington, D.C.

Durkheim, Émile, 2001. The Elementary Forms of Religious Life. Carol Cosman, tran. Oxford University Press, New York.

Halilovich, Hariz, 2013. Places of Pain: Forced Displacement, Popular Memory and Trans-local Identities in Bosnian War-torn Communities. Berghahn, New York.

Honig, Jan Willem, Both, Norbert, 1997. Srebrenica: Record of a War Crime. Penguin Books, New York.

Komar, Debra A., 2003. Lesson from Srebrenica: the contributions and limitations of physical anthropology in identifying victims of war crimes. J. Forensic Sci. 48 (04), 713–716.

Kontanis, Elias, Sledzik, Paul, 2008. Resolving commingling issues during the medicolegal investigations of mass fatality incidents. In: Byrd, John, Adams, Bradley J. (Eds.), Recovery, Analysis, and Identification of Commingled Human Remains. Humana, Totowa, NJ, pp. 317–336.

Matton, Sylvie, 2005. Srebrenica : un génocide annoncé. Flammarion, [Paris].

Mauss Marcel, Hubert Henri, Hertz Robert, 2009. Saints, Heroes, Myths, and Rites: Classical Durkheimian Studies of Religion and Society. (Edited and translated by Riley, Alexander, Daynes, Sarah, Isnart, Cyril) Paradigm Publishers, Boulder, CO.

Nettelfield, Lara J., Wagner, Sarah E., 2014. Srebrenica in the Aftermath of Genocide. Cambridge University Press, New York.

Pollack, Craig E., 2003. Intentions of burial: mourning, politics, and memorials following the massacre at Srebrenica. Death Stud. 27 (2), 125–142.

Rohde, David, 1997. Endgame: The Betrayal and Fall of Srebrenica, Europe's Worst Massacre since World War II. Farrar, Straus and Giroux, New York.

Rosenblatt, Adam, 2010. International forensic investigations and the human rights of the dead. Hum. Rights Q. 32 (4), 921–950.

Stover, Eric, Peress, Gilles, 1998. The Graves: Srebrenica and Vukovar. Scalo, Zurich.

Tuller, Hugh, 2012. Mass graves and human rights: Latest developments, methods, and lessons learned. In: Dirkmaat, Dennis (Ed.), A Companion to Forensic Anthropology. Wiley-Blackwell, Malden, MA, 157–174.

Tuller, Hugh, Hofmeister, Ute, Daley, Sharna, 2008. Spatial analysis of mass graves mapping data to assist in the reassociation of disarticulated and commingled remains. In: Adams, Bradley J., Byrd, John (Eds.), Recovery, Analysis, and Identification of Commingled Human Remains. Humana, Totowa, NJ, 7–29.

Vennemeyer, Matt, 2012. An Analysis of Linkages Between Robbed Primary Graves and Secondary Graves Related to Srebrenica Missing. Presentation at the Alpe-Adria-Pannonia International Meeting on Forensic Medicine, May 31-June 2, 2012, Sarajevo.

Wagner, Sarah, 2008. To Know Where He Lies: DNA Technology and the Search for Srebrenica's Missing. University of California Press, Berkeley, CA.

Wagner, Sarah, 2010. Tabulating loss, entombing memory: The Srebrenica-Potočari Memorial Centre. In: Anderson, Elizabeth, Maddrell, Avril, McLoughlin, Catherine Mary, Vincent, Alana (Eds.), Memory, Mourning, Landscape. Rodopi, Amsterdam, 61–78.

Index

Note: Page Numbers followed by f indicate figures; t, tables; b, boxes.

E

F

M

N

O

S

Kolibri 360 GmbH
Ferdinand-Jühlke-Straße 7
99095 Erfurt, Deutschland
produktsicherheit@kolibri360.de